W9-ACZ-945

Van Wyck Brooks
AN AUTOBIOGRAPHY

VAN WYCK BROOKS *has written:*

MAKERS AND FINDERS (A History of the Writer in America, 1800–1915: I. The World of Washington Irving, II. The Flowering of New England, III. The Times of Melville and Whitman, IV. New England: Indian Summer, V. The Confident Years: 1885–1915)

THE WINE OF THE PURITANS: A Study of Present Day America

THE MALADY OF THE IDEAL

JOHN ADDINGTON SYMONDS: A Biographical Study

THE WORLD OF H. G. WELLS

OPINIONS OF OLIVER ALLSTON

THE LIFE OF EMERSON

THE ORDEAL OF MARK TWAIN

THE PILGRIMAGE OF HENRY JAMES

EMERSON AND OTHERS

THREE ESSAYS ON AMERICA (America's Coming-of-Age, Letters and Leadership, The Literary Life in America)

SKETCHES IN CRITICISM

A CHILMARK MISCELLANY

THE WRITER IN AMERICA

SCENES AND PORTRAITS

JOHN SLOAN: A Painter's Life

HELEN KELLER: Sketch for a Portrait

DAYS OF THE PHOENIX

FROM A WRITER'S NOTEBOOK

THE DREAM OF ARCADIA

HOWELLS: His Life and World

FROM THE SHADOW OF THE MOUNTAIN

FENOLLOSA AND HIS CIRCLE

AN AUTOBIOGRAPHY (Scenes and Portraits, Days of the Phoenix, From the Shadow of the Mountain)

VAN WYCK BROOKS

Pastel Sketch, 1909
by John Butler Yeats

Van Wyck Brooks
AN AUTOBIOGRAPHY

Scenes and Portraits
MEMORIES OF CHILDHOOD AND YOUTH

Days of the Phoenix
THE NINETEEN-TWENTIES I REMEMBER

From the Shadow of the Mountain
MY POST-MERIDIAN YEARS

Foreword by John Hall Wheelock
Introduction by Malcolm Cowley

E. P. Dutton & Co., Inc.
New York: 1965

CONTENTS

Days of the Phoenix

From the Shadow of the Mountain

CONTENTS

FOREWORD

VAN WYCK BROOKS:
A MAN IN QUEST OF THE TRUTH

BY JOHN HALL WHEELOCK

IN 1904, during the fall of my freshman year, I attended one of the now legendary "punches" given by the old *Harvard Monthly*. The room was crowded. I knew no one and was beginning to feel rather lost, when I noticed standing near me a stranger, who seemed equally alone. He was of medium height and delicately made, with a face sensitive and youthful yet with a certain austerity and resolution in its expression that attracted me. The eyes, particularly, had a withdrawn concentration such as I did not remember having observed in any others. In a few moments we were talking. There was a gentleness, a geniality, about him that I had not expected, and he soon revealed, beneath a reserve that was only in part shyness, an almost mischievous sense of humor.

This was my first meeting with Van Wyck Brooks. My impression was one of extreme sensitivity, of something fastidious, even exquisite, holding severely in check an extraordinary vehemence of thought and feeling. The combination is an interesting one and gives to a personality something aloof and strange—an indefinable dignity that is in no way coldness or indifference. It is characteristic of the man that a long friendship—which so often replaces wonder and admiration with affectionate understanding—never, despite the affection and understanding between us, quite wore away this fascination of strangeness. My first impression remained and, to the last, Van Wyck Brooks had, for me, this element of mystery. He was, needless to say, unaware of this, and would have laughed at such a fantastic notion. He could laugh at many things, including himself. I have never forgotten his description of one of his occasionally required visits to the income tax expert at a great New York bank. The palatial quarters that house these top business executives, and the inscrutable aura surrounding them, filled Van Wyck with awe and misgiving as he was conducted over carpeted floors toward the inner sanctum, feeling, so he later told me, "Just like Little Red Riding Hood."

As a writer, a critic, and literary historian, Van Wyck Brooks again presents a rare combination in his equipment. He was, undeniably, one of the most learned of men—but not at all in the formal academic sense. His erudition, which was very real, was the by-product of long and passionate curiosity, the fruit of inclination and enthusiasm rather than of laborious intent. He wanted to get at the truth of things. His knowledge of literature and painting and history, and especially of American literature and painting and history, was detailed and inclusive, he had a phenomenal memory, and he took all these things for granted in his friends. How often, upon his mention of some to me absolutely unfamiliar name, I have had to confess my ignorance and listen, amused, to his incredulous rejoinder: "Why, Jack, what do you mean? Of course you know Katharine Wormeley's translation of Balzac!" On some of these occasions, I'm afraid I took refuge in a discreet silence, and came away a wiser but by no means a sadder man, for his talk was as individual and exciting as his writing. If, at times, under the stress of some deeply rooted animus, intensity of feeling got the better of his

natural reserve, and he went too far in expressing an exasperation, this intensity was part of his charm as, indeed, its projec-
tion in his writings is what gives them much of their color and
force. He did have, at one time, I remember, a certain animus
against the Old South. The people there, in his opinion, were
too much occupied with riding, hunting, and dancing, with
statesmanship and administration. They didn't, Van Wyck
thought, spend enough time writing memoirs and books—a
situation that has since, we can all agree, been more than abun-
dantly remedied. One felt that he cared more than most men
are capable of caring, about books, about ideas, about the rightness or wrongness of things, about getting at the truth. One
felt that, for him, the lives and movements of other days were
as real, as immediate, as if they were going on just around the
corner, and his sensitiveness to the mood and spiritual temper
of a writer, his ability to think himself into another life and
time, were reinforced by a gift for imaginative re-creation that
is often irresistible. These talents are already evident in such
early books as those on John Addington Symonds, on H. G.
Wells. They are further developed in *The Ordeal of Mark
Twain, The Pilgrimage of Henry James, The Life of Emerson,* three psychological biographies that form a significant
portrait of the American mind and its background.

It is interesting to observe how soon Van Wyck Brooks
found himself, how early the insights and impulses that informed his writing took shape. It was during his sophomore
year, I think, that he planned a series of articles under the
general title, "Viewpoints." They were to be written by repre-
sentative undergraduates of every type, in the hope of pre-
cipitating a body of opinion that might lead to some sort of
intellectual rapport or uncover some unifying and characteristic point of focus. These articles appeared in the *Harvard*

Advocate, and were significant in their purpose, even if they failed to fulfill the expectations of their originator. He also, shortly after he had graduated, issued privately a small pamphlet titled *The Soul.* This affords us, under the subtitle, "An Essay Towards a Point of View," many indications of the road he was to travel in later years. I remember, too, during undergraduate days, our numerous talks in the little room on Charles Street—with its death mask of Keats on the wall, its chaos of books, papers, and clothes strewn about—and his vehemence, that so often amazed me, on matters about which I was either too lazy or too immature to care very much. Poetry was, at that time, our chief intellectual bond, for Van Wyck had begun as a poet, though he soon laid his verse aside in favor of the work that made stronger claims on him. But during our freshman year we had published anonymously, in collaboration, a booklet, *Verses by Two Undergraduates,* containing some dozen poems by each of us. Van Wyck's were good, and fastened themselves immediately upon my memory—to this day I know most of them by heart. This became a deadly weapon. In the later years, I could always reduce Van Wyck to a state of extreme anguish by reciting to him, from memory, at some inappropriate moment, one or more of his longer pieces. He could not retaliate, for he did not remember anything of mine from this youthful collaboration of ours.

It has become the fashion today to regard the earlier work of Van Wyck Brooks as his main achievement. It is as the author of *America's Coming-of-Age, Letters and Leadership,* and the studies of Mark Twain, Henry James and Emerson, books of protest and of criticism, that he makes his chief appeal to the younger generation. And it is true that these are the books that cleared the air for a more wholesome creative life in America and tilled the ground in which many vigorous talents were able to take root. In his emphasis on our native note, as opposed to the then prevalent literary provincialism, his courageous holding up of the mirror to our spiritual life, his insistence upon the cultural communion out of which great literature arises, and his early discernment of the deep cleft, in the American soul, between idea and practice, Van Wyck Brooks was a forerunner, a voice crying in the wilderness. But this was only one part of his achievement. He had been a pioneer. Now he saw his vision coming true, and turned to the other and essential task that lay ahead: to bring to life for us our entire literary heritage, to exhibit the pageant of genius in our country, and give us, in his own phrase, "a usable past." *Makers and Finders*, his five-volume history of the writer in America, "effected," to quote Malcolm Cowley, "a revolutionary change in our judgment of the American past. . . . It rediscovered—one might almost say that it created—a historical background for the new American writers . . . endowing them with a collective memory and conscience, besides a sense of their own traditions." This was the second and greater part of the achievement of Van Wyck Brooks, a man in quest of the truth; truly, a man driven by the furies. Throughout a lifetime of the most intensive labor, six o'clock every morning found him at his desk, summoned by some inner voice to the task for which he was born. He could not rest until that task had been fulfilled.

The work of Van Wyck Brooks is the work of a literary historian who is a critic in the larger sense, an artist, a creator, whose judgments are arrived at by indirection and are implicit, as in a work of art, rather than formulated. His is, indeed, a memorable achievement. Yet all his work as a writer, his monumental creations as a historian of literature, do not, to my mind, constitute the sum total of the achievement of Van Wyck Brooks. He has said that "great literature is a great man writing," and he revealed, in his own personality, the greatness of spirit that makes these words applicable to himself. His quest for the truth embraced a larger field than that of literature alone. In an age of cynicism and the belittlement of the human condition, he was one who believed that the situation of man, however tragic, is meaningful and the opposite of the absurd.

Van Wyck Brooks believed in the possibilities of life, its dignity and worth, here and now. He is one of those who give us courage to face the future. Was there ever a human being more patient, more modest, more ready to understand and to foster the groping talent, the writer who had not yet found himself! His interest in the younger generation remained alert and unflagging. At the beautiful home in Bridgewater, that he and Gladys Brooks made so hospitable, young writers of promise, later to become famous perhaps but as yet unknown, always found welcome and inspiration. Van Wyck Brooks approached with an almost reverent eagerness every manifestation of the honest creative impulse, however humble, however frustrated. He had an equally lively hatred of all that was false or pretentious. He kept undiminished to the end his extreme responsiveness and sensitivity, his capacity for caring tremendously, about literature, about life. The universal affection his warmth, his integrity, and innocence of heart aroused in all who knew him, either in person or through his books, this is perhaps his greatest achievement. His reputation will grow with the years. His influence will be implicit in the work of writers yet to come.

On the occasion of Van Wyck's seventy-fifth birthday, at a dinner given in his honor by The American Academy of Arts and Letters in 1961, I read a poem of mine addressed to Van Wyck some sixty years ago, while we were both freshmen at college. I should like to close this tribute with a poem, written quite recently, which I inscribed "In Memory of Van Wyck Brooks," and have called "Dear Men and Women":

In the quiet before cockcrow when the cricket's
Mandolin falters, when the light of the past
Falling from the high stars yet haunts the earth
And the east quickens, I think of those I love—
Dear men and women no longer with us.

And not in grief or regret merely but rather
With a love that is almost joy I think of them,
Of whom I am part, as they of me, and through whom
I am made more wholly one with the pain and the glory,
The heartbreak at the heart of things.

I have learned it from them at last, who am now grown old
A happy man, that the nature of things is tragic
And meaningful beyond words, that to have lived
Even if once only, once and no more,
Will have been—oh, how truly—worth it.

The years go by: March flows into April,
The sycamore's delicate tracery puts on
Its tender green; April is August soon;
Autumn, and the raving of insect choirs,
The thud of apples in moonlit orchards;

Till winter brings the slant, windy light again
On shining Manhattan, her towering stone and glass;
And age deepens—oh, much is taken, but one
Dearer than all remains, and life is sweet
Still to the now enlightened spirit.

Doors are opened that never before were opened,
New ways stand open, but quietly one door
Closes, the door to the future; there it is written,
"Thus far and no farther"—there, as at Eden's gate,
The angel with the fiery sword.

The Eden we dream of, the Eden that lies before us,
The unattainable dream, soon lies behind.
Eden is always yesterday or tomorrow,
There is no way now but back, back to the past—
The past has become paradise.

And there they dwell, those ineffable presences,
Safe beyond time, rescued from death and change.
Though all be taken, they only shall not be taken—
Immortal, unaging, unaltered, faithful yet
To that lost dream world they inhabit.

Truly, to me they now may come no more,
But I to them in reverie and remembrance
Still may return, in me they still live on;
In me they shall have their being, till we together
Darken in the great memory.

Dear eyes of delight, dear youthful tresses, foreheads
Furrowed with age, dear hands of love and care—
Lying awake at dawn, I remember them,
With a love that is almost joy I remember them:
Lost, and all mine, all mine, forever.

INTRODUCTION

BY MALCOLM COWLEY

A FTER Van Wyck Brooks finished the last volume of *Makers and Finders,* the most important work of his later years was his three books of memoirs. The first of these was *Scenes and Portraits* (1954), the second and liveliest was *Days of the Phoenix* (1957), and the third, more discursive, was *From the Shadow of the Mountain,* which appeared in 1961 when Brooks was seventy-five. Not one of them has received the attention that each deserves. We owe a debt to his friend and publisher, Elliott B. Macrae of Dutton, for reprinting all three in this one volume.

I think of them together as Brooks's memoirs rather than his autobiography in the strict sense. Of course the work is autobiographical too; it tells us candidly what we need to know about the author's family, education, career, and guiding purposes. Still, it is less concerned with these or with his inner world—except in one moving chapter of *Days of the Phoenix*—than it is with the outer world, which for him consisted mostly of writers and painters. He looked at them all with an observant and hopeful eye. *Scenes and Portraits,* the title of the first book, might be applied to the work as a whole.

In rereading it we note again what we might have forgotten, that Brooks was a painterly writer, with a gift for rendering character by costume or gesture and atmosphere by his choice of images. One of the best of his many interiors painted in the

Dutch style is Petitpas' restaurant in the Chelsea district of Manhattan, where old J. B. Yeats, the poet's father, used to preside over a tableful of writers without publishers and artists without a gallery. Among the occasional guests was Blaikie Murdoch, a Scotsman of wide and curious learning, who "followed his own personal notions of style," Brooks says, "sprinkling commas over his writing as a Parsee sprinkles red pepper over meat . . . Bald as a tonsured monk, with a mind as ripe as old Roquefort cheese, Blaikie Murdoch was living in a basement somewhere, cooking his meals on a gas-jet, not far away; and, as he talked, he would stealthily manœuvre stray crusts of bread on the table into the yawning pockets of his old brown jacket."

We remember Murdoch by those crusts of bread, as we remember old Yeats by his impractical wisdom and his delight in fine words, including the name of the disease from which he was to die. When he heard that he was an "antique cardiac arterio-sclerotic," he said to Brooks, "I would rather be called that than the King of the South of Egypt." Among the other guests at Petitpas', we recognize Alan Seeger by "the long black Paris student's cape" that he borrowed one winter when he had no overcoat, and Brooks himself, then in his early twenties, by his splendid waistcoats and the holes in the bottoms of his shoes. Every detail helps to re-create the atmosphere of a time when young writers were poor by choice as well as necessity and when many of them wore poverty as a uniform, but with a flower in the buttonhole.

Old Yeats, poor as the youngsters who surrounded him, was a portrait painter without commissions, and he was also Brooks's tutelary spirit. Once he said that the genius of his art was "largely a genius for friendship." The best portraits are painted, he explained, when friendship governs the relation of the sitter to the painter. Brooks took the principle to heart, and perhaps that is why he has devoted less space in this volume to himself than to his friends. He gives us heroic portraits of Max Perkins, Ned Sheldon, that brilliant playwright crippled and blinded by arthritis, Waldo Frank, Sherwood Anderson, and many others, including most of the rebels who surrounded him when he was writing the early essays that announced a second American renaissance. Meanwhile the author himself is revealed not so much directly as by reflection, with his friendships serving as mirrors of his own shy, loyal, dogged, scrupulous, idealistic, but not unworldly spirit. As for his career, we see again that it had logical consistency and, almost to the end, continued growth of a sort not often found in the lives of American writers.

For himself Brooks had only one ambition from the days when he went to high school in Plainfield, New Jersey. He wanted to be a writer, and he knew almost from the beginning what kind of writer: not a novelist, not a poet—though he wrote some early verses—but a critic. At first he thought of becoming an art critic on the model of Ruskin, but soon he began writing about books. "I was convinced," he says, "that criticism in some form was the most delightful activity one could dream of in this world. I even felt that everything might be expressed in criticism, as others have felt about music or fiction or sculpture." Gradually this private ambition developed into a public and largely unselfish one. That was for two good reasons: because he couldn't hope to become a critic of stature unless he had new, important, preferably native works to criticize, and because he couldn't succeed in his personal aim unless he helped to create an atmosphere in which other young writers might succeed. Thus, his career would depend in two ways on the general fate of American letters.

That fate seemed dubious in the years from 1904 to 1907, when Brooks was an undergraduate at Harvard. It was a time when the Eastern universities regarded themselves as trading posts beleaguered on the edge of Indian country, where they offered a stock of cultural goods to the younger natives. Almost all the goods had been freighted in from Europe. Students received the impression that there had once been an American literature of sorts, but that it lay "a generation or more behind us," as the poet George E. Woodberry told his Columbia classes. He expressed only a tempered admiration for that older literature, which had produced, he said, not one poet who was even of the rank of Thomas Gray. His judgment was echoed at other universities. When Barrett Wendell of Harvard wrote a book about American literature, he made his readers feel—so Howells said—that the subject was "not worth the attention of people meaning to be critical." Our past was thus abolished as a field of study, and hardly a course was offered at Harvard or elsewhere that dealt at length with American writers. As for the present, Woodberry disposed of its claims to attention in the article on American literature that he wrote for the eleventh edition (1910) of the *Encyclopædia Britannica*. He concluded the article by saying that the social tradition and culture of the American people

> . . . make them impenetrable to the present ideas of Europe as they are current in literary forms. Nor has anything been developed from within that is fertile in literature. . . . The intellectual life is now rather to be found in social, political and natural science than elsewhere, the imaginative life is feeble, and when felt is crude; the poetic pulse is imperceptible.

Yet Harvard in those days was full of aspiring writers, some of whom would become Brooks's lifelong friends. They all wanted to produce enduring works, but they saw little hope of producing them in their native land where all the fruits seemed blighted. One of the aspirants, who looked forward to being an art critic, told Brooks in a letter that American criticism was virtually all "broken meat from the European table." The moral he drew was that one should "Sit at the first table, not the second," and he hurried off to Italy, where he planned to emulate Bernard Berenson. Other Harvard friends went to Paris or London or a German university; any city in Europe seemed to have a better climate for writing than New York. In those days Brooks himself believed "that the only chance an American had to succeed as a writer was to betake himself [to Europe] with all possible speed." He raced through college in three years, then traveled by steerage to England, where he nearly starved as a free-lance journalist and published his first book at the age of twenty-three.

As soon as the book appeared he went back to New York, in obedience to another and opposite belief that he held at the same time. "I was convinced as well," he says, "that a man without a country could do nothing of importance, that writers must draw sustenance from their own common flesh and blood and that therefore deracination also meant ruin. For me, at that time, the American writer could neither successfully stay *nor* go—he had only two alternatives, the frying-pan and the fire; and the question was therefore how to change the whole texture of life at home so that writers and artists might develop there."

His early ambition, without changing in essence, had found a new goal that would be retained for the rest of his life— though at different times he would follow different paths toward the same destination. Happily the question he tried to answer was not so broad and futile as it sounds. As a critic, a single dissenting voice, he realized that he couldn't do much "to change the whole texture of life at home." He might, however, do something to change our conception of the writer in America, and the writer's conception of his own task, always with the aim of encouraging himself and others to do better work, the best that was in them. To this aim he devoted himself with admirable consistency and—let it be recorded—with an amazing degree of success.

There is one field in which the success can be measured. When we think of the contempt for American authors, mixed with ignorance about them, that prevailed in universities during the reign of Barrett Wendell; when we contrast it with the reverence for many of the same authors that is now being proclaimed in hundreds of scholarly monographs each year, as well as being revealed statistically by the multiplication of courses in American literature—while living writers share in the glory reflected from the past by being invited to the campus as novelists or poets in residence—we might also remember that Brooks had more to do with creating the new attitude than anyone else in the country. Not a few of the academic critics who attacked him in later years were men whose careers would have been impossible if Brooks had not found them a subject and broken a path they could follow.

I said that he tried different methods of approaching what always remained the same goal. In reality there were only two of the methods, and each of them belonged to a different stage of his career. In the earlier stage, which lasted from 1909 to 1926, he was the prophet of a new literature, and his method was a combination of exhortation, admonition, and holding up to scorn. America in 1915, he said, was "like a vast Sargasso Sea—a prodigious welter of unconscious life, swept by ground-

swells of half-conscious emotions." Ideally the country might
have looked for direction to its poets and novelists and critics,
who serve as "the pathfinders of society; to them belong the
vision without which the people perish." But the writers themselves were lost. "What immediately strikes one, as one surveys
the history of our literature during the last half century, is the
singular impotence of its creative spirit. That we have always
had an abundance of talent is, I think, no less evident: what I
mean is that so little of this talent really finds its way. . . . The
chronic state of our literature is that of a youthful promise
which is never redeemed."

I am quoting from three of Brooks's early essays: *America's
Coming-of-Age* (1915), *Letters and Leadership* (1918), and
The Literary Life in America (1921). Together they composed
a manifesto for the new generation of writers, one that has been
compared in its effects with Emerson's address "The American
Scholar," delivered at Harvard in 1837. Emerson did more than
anyone else to produce what was afterward known as the
American renaissance. There was something Emersonian in
Brooks's tone, and writing in the early days of a second renais-
sance, he found as many eager listeners.

He did not merely offer lamentations, which were justified
at the time; he also diagnosed the weakness of American writing and offered a prescription for making it stronger. As compared with the writing "of almost any European country"—and
the comparison with France and England was never far from
Brooks's mind—its principal weakness was that "Our writers all
but universally lack the power of growth, the endurance that
enables one to continue personal work after the freshness of
youth has gone." Instead of developing into great men of letters, they had surrendered easily to commercialism and convention, largely—Brooks told us in italics—because they had lacked

"the sense that one is *working in a great line.*" His prescription followed from the diagnosis: we should develop a tradition in American literature and, by studying its history, we should try to discover what he was the first to call a "usable past."

The two famous biographies that he wrote during this period were part of the search for that past, but they were also cautionary tales; they showed the consequences resulting from two different answers to his old question, whether American writers should live abroad or stay at home. *The Ordeal of Mark Twain* (1920) presented the example of a great American author who stayed at home and crippled his talent by yielding to native conventions. In later years Brooks revised the book to incorporate new facts, but he never changed his central judgment of Mark Twain's career. *The Pilgrimage of Henry James* (1925) told the story of another great author, one who live abroad and who suffered equally—so Brooks insisted—through losing touch with his own people. About James he was never sure of having been completely fair. "I was to realize, looking back," he says, "that I had been quarreling with myself when I appeared to be quarreling with Henry James. For, like many of my friends, I too had been enchanted with Europe, and I had vaguely hoped to continue to live there. It struck me that if I was always 'straining to read the face of America,'—Paul Rosenfeld's phrase for my obsession—it was because of an over-determination, and perhaps the question of expatriation had so possessed my mind because this mind itself had been divided."

There was a time when "I was pursued especially," Brooks also says, "with nightmares in which Henry James turned great luminous menacing eyes upon me." That was during the prolonged nervous breakdown that he suffered after 1926, when his life became a succession of doctors, nursing homes with barred windows, and dreams of self-annihilation. "I could no longer sleep," he says, "I scarcely sat down for a year, I lived in a Plutonian psychical twilight." When he emerged from this "season in hell," as he calls it in that moving chapter of *Days of the Phoenix,* he was ready at the age of forty-five to start a new career.

Its goal would be the same as in his earlier career, that is, to give us a new picture of the American writer, of what he had done in the past and of what he might achieve. But Brooks had changed during his season in hell, and he was now temperamentally unable to follow his earlier method of combining exhortation with admonishment like a prophet in Israel. As for holding up to scorn or writing cautionary tales, both seemed alien to his new character, for the wound in himself had made him loath to expose the wounds in others. He looked eagerly now for things he could praise, especially in the lives of earlier American writers who had been long neglected. At the same time his experience in sanitariums had given him—or helped to give—more patience, a stronger sense of discipline, and a new habit of rising early in the morning, never later than six, and going straight to work. He was ready now to move toward his goal by a second method based on patient scholarship.

The five volumes of *Makers and Finders* took him nineteen years to write, or about four years for each volume. During that time he worked ten or twelve hours a day and read five thousand American books, some of which had not been opened by anyone else for more than half a century. What seems remarkable in this age of collective undertakings is that he did the work unaided by collaborators, research assistants, or even a secretary. He copied out all the quotations, and "I have not found one error in transcription," he said in a letter to a Harvard classmate, Samuel Eliot Morison, who had questioned some statements in *The Flowering of New England*. Besides Brooks's passion for the sort of accuracy that one couldn't demand of a hired assistant, he had another reason for being his own copyist. "It's the only way to get the feel of an author," he explained. "Passages copied by someone else don't have the same meaning." The manuscript of each volume was written in his small, nervous, angular, hard-to-decipher hand at the rate of never more than a page of three hundred and fifty words each day. It was the sort of purely individual project on a grand scale that has seldom been carried out since the days of Prescott, Parkman, and the other great New England historians.

The work as it progressed had an interesting critical reception. For *The Flowering of New England,* which was the first volume to appear, in 1936, though it came second in Brooks's plan for the series, there was something close to universal praise. Almost the only discordant voices were some of those on the political left, where one heard complaints that Brooks was no longer a leader and prophet, but had turned to "scholarly storytelling." The stories of course had a purpose, but the left-wing critics were slow to grasp it. Among the academic reviewers, Morison was the only one who thought that Brooks had been reckless with his facts. Brooks was disturbed by the charge and wrote his classmate a seven-page letter, not for publication, a copy of which was found among his own papers marked *"Important—*to keep."

> So far [one page of it reads], in going over my book, and the various criticisms of it, I have detected 14 mistakes. This includes two mistakes (the same mistake repeated) regarding the Franconia Notch, also the error about the sloop Harvard, and about H. G. Otis, who was not a merchant. . . . Some of these errors are exceedingly slight, and even on the ragged

edge of truth. Observe, I am not defending this ragged edge.
I did not say that Otis's punch-bowl held ten gallons. I had,
and thought I conveyed, a different visual image in saying
that "ten gallons of punch evaporated out of it," i.e., that the
punch-bowl was refilled. Again, regarding the sloop Harvard,
I did not specifically say that it was moored at the port, and I
certainly thought it was, and I gladly accept the blame for my
misstatement. (On looking through my notes, I find that I got
this impression from Lowell's *Cambridge Thirty Years Ago:*
"Cambridge has long had its port, but the greatest part of its
maritime trade was, thirty years ago, entrusted to a single
Argo, the sloop Harvard," etc.) The error was not in the transcription, but in a faulty inference from it. It seems to me, in
the case in question, the inference was not unnatural, but I
freely confess my error in 14 cases.

Now why do I dwell on this? To show you that I am not
disinclined to be careful about "pesky facts" and to ask you
how you justify the charge that I "throw my facts about." . . .

In truth the charge, though made in good faith, could not be
justified except by adducing some inconsequential errors that
Brooks was glad to correct, and it was seldom repeated in reviews of later volumes. The first of these, *New England: Indian Summer* (1940), had an autumnal rather than a springlike
charm as compared with *The Flowering,* but this other quality
was equally appreciated by its reviewers, some of whom bab-
bled in a delirium of praise. There were attacks, however, in
three or four scholarly journals, and there were more of these
after *The World of Washington Irving* (1944), which Brooks
regarded as the best of his books. Dealing as it did with the
early writers of the Republic, many of whom had been forgotten even by scholars, it conveyed a happy feeling of exploration
and rediscovery; but academic critics complained about Brooks's
method. They said that he was wasting his time on minor
figures, that he wasn't truly critical, and that in fact he wasn't
writing a history of American literature of the sort that could

be assigned to their students. The complaints were louder after *The Times of Melville and Whitman* (1947), and loudest after the series was completed with *The Confident Years* in 1952. By that time, moreover, the attacks on Brooks's method were being accompanied by others on his conception of American literature as a whole.

It has always seemed to me that the critics had reason, not for rushing into battle against Brooks, but for discussion and disagreement with him about that last grand question. At the end of *The Confident Years* he tries to define the American tradition that he has been presenting in narrative form all through the five volumes. It is, he tells us, a belief in the inherent goodness of men and in their capacity to govern themselves; it is "the tradition of Jefferson, Paine and Crèvecoeur and the roundhead side in the English civil war,—with all the typical American institutions . . . and it was this that Europeans had in mind when they complained that American writers had never been 'American enough.' "

> From this [he continues] had sprung the great body of writers from Benjamin Franklin down to a regiment of poets, romancers, historians and thinkers who had given the country, in literature, a character of its own, and to deny this was to deny that America had a character, that it was anything but a congeries of exiles from Europe. This was the core of America, in fact,—to the world America meant this or nothing,—it was what the "Latin genius" was to France; and where else could one find the American "uniqueness" to fit the prescription of Eliot himself that "the culture of each country should be unique"?

But is Brooks defining the only American tradition in literature? One notes in this final chapter of *Makers and Finders* that he seems obsessed with T. S. Eliot, whom he accuses, in effect, of having betrayed the essential spirit of the nation.

Might it not be more accurate to say that Eliot has followed
one American tradition in preference to another? Brooks himself has earlier made it clear that Eliot had many American
predecessors, both in choosing to live abroad and in his attitude
toward the art of letters. Other critics have traced his lineage
as a writer through Henry James back to Hawthorne or, more
circuitously, back to Poe by way of the French symbolists, who
were proud of having adopted many of Poe's ideals. I am not
the first to suggest that there are at least two traditions in
American literature; perhaps there are several. If we prefer to
have only two, there is the tradition that Brooks extols as being
essentially American, the tradition of the sunny, expansive
writers who believed in human improvability, and beside it
another tradition that is dark, intensive, pessimistic about
human nature, and preoccupied with form rather than message.
Both have been long established in this country. If Brooks's tradition goes back to Franklin and Emerson, the other might be
traced to Charles Brockden Brown, at the end of the eighteenth
century, or even to Jonathan Edwards.

It was Brown who said in a letter: "An accurate history of
the thoughts and feelings of any man, for one hour, is more
valuable for some minds than a system of geography; and you,
you tell me, are one of those who would rather travel into the
mind of a ploughman than into the interior of Africa. I confess
myself of your way of thinking." That suggests another way of
distinguishing the two traditions: there are the writers in
breadth and the writers in depth; there are the morning writers
and—thinking of Brown and his successors—the twilight or noc-
turnal writers. In Philip Rahv's famous distinction, somewhat
different from the one I have been suggesting, the literary
Redskins are at war with the Palefaces. Most but not all of the
writers whom Brooks praises for being essentially American

are Redskins. The great men in his tradition are Emerson, Thoreau, Whitman, and after them Mark Twain (in *Huckleberry Finn,* but not later), William James, Parkman, Howells, Dreiser, and, among the generation of the 1920's, Thomas Wolfe. In the other tradition the great names are Hawthorne, Melville, Henry James, Henry Adams, and Faulkner.

And must we choose one side or the other? If there *are* two sides, that is, and only two—a questionable proposition—must we vote that only one of them is truly American, thus abandoning the writers on the other side to Europe or the feudal past or simple neglect? I have to confess that by temperament and training I feel more drawn to the writers in depth than to the expansive morning writers in the Emersonian line. But our literature is not so rich that it can afford to surrender any of its great men, Emerson *or* Hawthorne, Whitman or Melville, Parkman or Henry Adams, Brooks or Eliot; we need them all. By defining the American tradition restrictively, Brooks makes it seem poorer than it was in fact—and also poorer than he has made it seem in his five volumes of narrative. The academic critics had reason to argue with him on this point. Most of them, however, made the same sort of mistake as Brooks by rejecting another group of authors, exactly the ones that Brooks admires in his final chapter.

I have said too much about that one chapter and thus have neglected his real achievement in *Makers and Finders.* It was not to define the American tradition, but rather to present it as a Tolstoyan novelist might do, in a grand historical pageant that flows on author by author, scene by scene, and volume after volume. For the first time he proved by narration, description, and quotation, rather than argument, that this country has had a continuous life and character in literature.

I have never been impressed by the academic complaints about Brooks's method, most of which were based on various misconceptions of his purpose as a historian. Academic critics like to feel that a work on American literature can be assigned to some familiar type; that its orientation is social or political or biographical or psychological, or that it is a history of ideas, or that it chooses the major authors and studies their work in depth. *Makers and Finders* belongs to none of these types, and in fact there is no real parallel in American or European scholarship for Brooks's attempt to recover a literary tradition where none had been thought to exist. Since the goal was new, he had to find a new method of reaching it, and this is what most of the critics have failed to understand.

Part of his method was to suggest, as a landscape painter might do, the special atmosphere of cities and sections where literary movements started or flourished or declined. One remembers particularly his pictures of Boston after the Civil War, in *New England: Indian Summer,* and of Philadelphia at the end of the eighteenth century, in *The World of Washington Irving,* but there are dozens of these effectively painted literary landscapes. A more important part of the method was to emphasize the interconnections among writers, the points at which they came together to form a field of radiating forces that was almost like a magnetic field. For an example of such emphasis, one might turn to *The Times of Melville and Whitman* and consider his treatment of Bayard Taylor, the flimsy poet and entertaining traveler who was long regarded as a rival of the great New Englanders. Brooks devotes eight pages to his literary career, about the same space that would be assigned to him by an old-fashioned literary historian. The new-fashioned historians, in their preoccupation with major writers, would give him no space whatever; perhaps they wouldn't mention his name. But men like Taylor are essential to Brooks's purpose, for, as he tells us in his memoirs, "It is the minor books or writers that body forth a culture, creating the living chain that we call tradition."

The facts to be mentioned about this minor but once famous writer are chosen with the "living chain" in mind. Brooks doesn't tell us the date of Taylor's birth (1825) or give us the titles of his principal works in verse or prose. What we learn about him is chiefly:

1. That he belonged to the staff of the New York *Tribune,* like many other talented authors of his time (and elsewhere in the book Brooks lists them by name).
2. That he made his reputation by walking through Europe and sending back letters to the American press. On his return he was invited to dine with Bancroft, Cooper, and Melville, while N. P. Willis wrote an introduction to his book of travels.
3. That he had grown up in southeastern Pennsylvania, which in some ways resembled rural New England as described in the novels of Harriet Beecher Stowe—"which the novels of Bayard Taylor in turn resembled,—though the people were less keen and their interests were narrower and simpler, as Taylor's novels were dimmer than Mrs. Stowe's." (One notes that Brooks's critical comments on his authors are often expressed as comparisons with other American authors of the same period.)
4. That Taylor was first inspired to travel by reading Washington Irving, N. P. Willis, and Longfellow's *Outre Mer,* and that later it was Irving who advised him to visit the Orient.
5. That he lectured on American literature in Weimar, Goethe's city, and introduced a distinguished audience to the works of Emerson, Longfellow, and Bryant.

There is no need to cite other facts of the same nature from the eight-page passage on Taylor, or to list the forty-two pages on which his name is mentioned elsewhere in the book, always in connection with other names, for I think that by now the nature of Brooks's emphasis is clear. What interests him in Taylor, as in many authors of second or third rank, is not their books primarily or their private lives, but chiefly their points of contact with fellow authors. I think it was Bernard De Voto who complained that Brooks's subjects never fall in love and never have children unless the children are authors too. The omission of family matters weakens some of his portraits, but families are inessential to his purpose. He is trying to show that American writers, besides existing in the social world, also moved in a closed system of their own. By revealing their points of contact he creates, as it were, a medium in which the writers existed and in which they transmitted energy by collision, like so many planets or atoms. Many critics, including Eliot and his followers, have talked about the value of a literary tradition, but they have left its nature a little vague. Brooks was the first author in any language to make a tradition real and almost palpable by presenting it as a rich texture of meetings, readings, and ideas passed from one writer to another.

For all the critical attacks it had to withstand, *Makers and Finders* effected a deep change in our judgment of the American past and hence, I think, in our vision of the future. It will remain for a long time our greatest sustained work of literary scholarship. But Brooks's story doesn't end with the completion of the last volume a few days after his sixty-fifth birthday in February, 1951. During the next twelve years he wrote ten other books, all conceived in the same spirit as *Makers and Finders,* though not, of course, on the same grand scale. He was continuing to revive our memories of neglected heroes. Except for the memoirs, my favorite among his later books is the one about that peppery, corncob-pipe-smoking Scotch-Irishman, his old friend the painter John Sloan, who, in his good early work, was a novelist in color, just as Brooks himself is here again a landscape painter and portraitist in words. The landscapes are chiefly those of the New York art world in the pioneering days of the Armory Show.

After *John Sloan* I should place Brooks's defense and appreciation of William Dean Howells, a book that complements his earlier biographies of Mark Twain and Henry James in a way that *The Life of Emerson* had failed to do. Howells was a lifelong friend and rival of James, as well as the closest friend of Twain, and his career reveals still another approach to the provincial narrowness and iron conventions that had ruined so many American writers. Instead of fleeing to Europe with James, or letting himself be partly crippled by the conventions as Twain had been—or rising serenely above them with Emerson—Howells had flourished within the conventions while somehow preserving an integrity of purpose. He had also done more for his fellow writers, including the rebels of the 1890's, than anyone else of his time.

Brooks felt instinctively drawn to Howells and, in his later years, even came to resemble him. They were both short, solid men (though Brooks never let himself develop the paunch that Howells carried with dignity); they both had quiet good manners and dressed quietly well (Brooks with a half-inch of white cuff showing at the end of his sleeves); they both had very high foreheads and white soup-strainer mustaches (though Brooks's features were less old-Roman than Howells' and gave an impression of shy benignity). Both men were utterly devoted to the art and profession of writing books, and both suffered at the end from neglect. "I am comparatively a dead cult," Howells said in a letter, "with my statues cut down and the grass growing over them in the pale moonlight." Brooks for his part complained more than once of being "an infra-red type" surviving in an ultraviolet era of pessimism. Remembering the Chinese proverb, "A man is more the child of the age he lives in than he is of his own father and mother," he sometimes felt that the changing times had made him an orphan.

But the neglect was less harsh in Brooks's case than in that of Howells. It was softened by many public honors and, in a more gratifying fashion, by a stream of visits and letters from young writers who had been heartened by his work. One of them wrote, "I feel less like a nomad whenever I finish one of your books. Even at my loneliest, I feel sustained by the record of men before me who have struggled toward consciousness.' A novelist said, "My work grows out of what went before. I feel I'm in the line." Another added, "One gains a real feeling of participation. . . . Our struggles of today fall into a new perspective." Brooks listened to these new voices as old J. B. Yeats had listened to Brooks, in the years when they sat together at the long table in Petitpas' garden.

Old Yeats's confident spirit pervades this volume of memoirs. Because of his wisdom, Brooks says, "J. B. Yeats was to leave behind him a great and abiding memory in many minds, for, whatever the virtues of Americans may be, wisdom is not one of them and most of his friends had never seen a wise man. . . . Who had ever heard of an American sage since the days of Emerson and Thoreau?" It becomes clear in retrospect that Brooks was trying to lead a sage's life. The story indirectly told but vividly suggested in his memoirs is that of an author who has followed a single line of development with complete integrity. It was in 1921 that Brooks asked a famous question: "Of how many of our modern writers can it be said that their work reveals a continuous growth, or indeed any growth, that they hold their ground tenaciously and preserve their sap from one decade to another?" Clearly there were no such American writers at the time, since Howells had died the year before and the new men were still too young for their careers to be judged. If there were a few such writers by 1960—Brooks himself among them—the change was partly owed to the work he had done for the literary profession in this country, by restoring its traditions and giving its members a past on which to build.

Scenes and Portraits

MEMORIES OF CHILDHOOD AND YOUTH

For
GLADYS,
CHARLES, KENYON
and
PETER BOUDINOT BROOKS

CHAPTER I

A WALL STREET SUBURB

M Y EARLIEST friend Maxwell Perkins, my lifelong friend, used to say that every man has a novel in him. The idea was not originally his,—it was, in fact, a commonplace,— but, being a man of character, he made it his; and I always felt that he might have written a first-rate novel himself if he had ranged over his own life. He was in his way a novelist born, but instead of developing this bent in himself he devoted his intuitive powers to the development of others, leaving his mark, as everyone knows, on the fiction of his time and the work of some of its best writers. As for myself, I have never wished to write a novel. But the scenes and characters of my younger days have come to seem to me like a novel that I read long ago, and I have often thought of reviving that novel.

I was born in February, 1886, in the unloved state of New Jersey. That, like all other states, this had its lovers, I only became aware in later days; for the "old Jersey element," as I heard it called when I was a boy, was remote from the little world in which I grew up. Our families were in it but not of it,—they were inveterate New Yorkers whose local affections and pride were invested elsewhere and who lived for genera- tions there without becoming naturalized, any more than the inveterate Philadelphians across the state. The old Jersey element had fixed immemorial ways of its own that were thought of as generally narrow, provincial and dull, while the new-comers had brought with them not only a current of world life but a mind that was more complex and more aggressive. The suburbs were all theirs and the fullness thereof; and, as their interests and loyalties were otherwise engaged, the state had become a prey to all manner of abuses. Yet its history had been honourable in the days of the Boudinots and Captain Law-rence, the young man who said, "Don't give up the ship." There lived John Woolman and Philip Freneau, there Feni-more Cooper was born, like Stephen Crane and Randolph Bourne still later; and various eighteenth-century New Yorkers had sent their sons to school there to learn to speak pure Eng-lish undefiled. Alexander Hamilton and Aaron Burr had studied as boys in Elizabeth, and the poet Shelley's grand-father had been a merchant in Newark where Sir Bysshe Shel-ley, the merchant's son, was born. But the two great cities that flanked the state on east and west had as it were depolarized the New Jersey mind.

My native town was Plainfield, a name that used to mortify me in my hyperæsthetic youth, for it struck me as naive; and I was greatly relieved when I found that the name of Tolstoy's place, Yasnaya Polyana, meant the same thing in Russian. My grandfather Ames had gone out there in 1869, to be near his office in New York, building the brown stucco house with spreading verandahs and a mansard roof in which I spent the first years of my childhood. For my father and mother soon abandoned the smaller house with the mansard roof in which they had set up housekeeping after their marriage and lived with my mother's parents from that time forward, moving after my grandfather died into a new house on the edge of the town that was not without some slight architectural pretensions.

This was the largish yellow brick house in which my formative years were passed and which was later characterized as "colonial outside, baronial inside" by one of the friends of our circle who passed for a wit. For the house fell at last into more affluent hands, and the new owners doubled its size and plastered it with the panels and doors of an ancient English manorhouse they had bought from the Duveens. By that time too the old picket fences had been stripped away on all the streets, with the beds of canna lilies and the cast-iron fountains, the monumental urns and painted deer-hounds, and the quiet Quaker village where Woolman had preached in the meeting-house had become a full-blown Wall Street suburb. Even the name of Peace Street had vanished forever.

I little realized as a child the dramatic events that were taking place in the outwardly tranquil dwellings of our friends and neighbours so many of whom were involved in the operations of that savage and lawless epoch of American finance. The trusts were in those days being formed, oil was spouting from Western lands and the country seemed to be drunk with a passion for riches, but, as money was never spoken of, it could scarcely have occurred to us that some of these neighbours were financial buccaneers and brigands. Nor did we ever think to ask why their wives, our mothers' friends, spent so much of their time in darkened rooms, seated in Bath chairs, attended by nurses, the victims of "nervous prostration," the secrets of which the Freudians had not yet exposed. I was always instructed to walk on tiptoe through the dim corridors of one such house with which my mother was often in communication, delivering my messages to the nurse without whom this friend of our household never thought of stirring out of doors. That this was a kind of strategic protest against her husband's double life I did not become aware for many years,

and I even doubt if the lady in question knew quite *how*
double this life was, though she certainly knew it was far from
straight or simple. Everyone was aware in time that he had
escaped a prison term only because his brother had become a
bondsman for him, while he had an unauthorized family somewhere else; but this was after his big steam-yacht had been
swept away, as he had swept away the savings of his coachman
and his servants. For years a professional "capitalist," as he
called himself in *Who's Who,* he had sat in the seats of the
mighty, with a whole floor at the Waldorf, and when my
mother went with his family to Cuba they were received at
Havana like travelling princes. For the capitalist had financed
the new water-works there, and the cardinal in person showed
them the ashes of Columbus, which had not yet been trans-
ferred to Santo Domingo. But when the blow fell one could
only admire the code of sporting ethics with which both he
and his wife played the game, reduced as they were to living
in three or four rented rooms with a few remnants of silver and
one good old portrait. *He* found a small clerical job in the
town,—the *ne plus ultra* of humiliation,—and walked home at
the day's end with a leg of mutton under his arm and a fresh
carnation still in his buttonhole. *She,* moreover, after spending
years fanned, like the Pope, in her invalid's chair, rose with
zest and cooked the leg of mutton. Both had an air of happiness and confidence at last.

One could tell many another tale of what a French writer
might have described as the grandeurs and miseries of Wall
Street in this age of buccaneering, the story of another friend,
for instance, a much more famous financier who had been
known as one of the "Big Four." Ruined by underestimating
the cost of a great municipal enterprise which he had financed
in New York, he was finally obliged to retire to a Harlem

hall-bedroom, but, with a small pension from Pierpont Morgan and a membership in his college club, he cheerfully played the game in reminiscence. He liked to recall his old battles on the Exchange in Broad Street and how, on a certain afternoon, between two and four o'clock, he had conjured out of E. H. Harriman three quarters of a million. At another time he had put together all the locomotive plants and organized the Locomotive Trust. It was his office in which my father had a small post towards the end of his life, after vainly endeavouring to survive as an independent broker, a work for which he was as ill-equipped as I would be myself, for he had no competitive instinct whatsoever. How many other ups and downs, not to say scandals, we heard of, muffled as they were in the reports that reached our ears,—for one, the descent, like an empire falling, of a certain conspicuous family we knew when the head of the house was convicted as an embezzler and absconder. Then there was the neighbour with the cherry orchard, a lover of children,—and we all loved him,—who vanished, as we gathered, into prison; and another family that blossomed out with governess-carts, tandems, grooms, liveried footmen and a tally-ho that also vanished—whither? Vast red sandstone houses rose, like so many Kenilworth castles, with turrets, verandahs, balconies and porte-cochères, with arches, fountains, coach-houses, kennels and stables and with sons who had an air of owning all creation and whose thoughts and talk were entirely about yachting and coaching. Pathetic these boys were destined to be, how often, when they grew up, for almost invariably their worlds collapsed about them. Some of their fathers ended like George Francis Train, who sat on a park bench in New York, feeding the squirrels, and who, after owning steamship lines and building street railways in England, lived in a charitable retreat for down-and-outs.

But beside the "wildcat speculators," as people used to call them, there were the quiet solid men of money, unobtrusive often to the point of being mousy, whose dwellings lined the streets in our corner of the town. No one would have supposed that they were presidents of New York banks, or perhaps of the Cotton Exchange or Western railroads, heads of large mining companies and corporations, for, millionaires almost to a man,—the town had more than a hundred of these,— they seemed to be governed by motives of protective coloration. When, later, I read the American novelists, of whom I knew nothing as a boy, I found that in the case of every character who was a big business man I could replace the original with a name from Plainfield. There was not one type whom I had not somehow known, from Howells's Silas Lapham to Tarkington's Tinker, the "plutocrat," and from Sinclair Lewis's Dodsworth to the Cowperwood of Dreiser. But, looking back, I am still convinced that Henry Adams was quite right when he said that Americans really cared little for money,—less, at least, than various other peoples,—that they pursued it only for want of other interests; for money-getting, with these neighbours of ours, while often a pursuit of power, was even more what it seemed to be, a game. It was the great sport of that epoch, as hunting grizzlies might have been, a sport not always lovely but dangerous and amusing; and the manner in which these friends accepted their losses was sometimes in the best tradition and spirit of sport. I remember the force of utter disgust with which my mother exclaimed "What's *money!*" at a certain juncture in our own family life, as if, in fact, money were too contemptible even to be thought of in comparison with some menaced human value. Yet we, at least, never had money, as our neighbours understood the word; we were sup-

posed to be poor, more or less. I believe this feeling underlay
our whole small world.

In any case, with its ups and downs, it seemed to be a stable
world, permanently supported by cast-iron customs, by a ritual of
living that was immemorial, or assumed to be, and that extended
into every corner of existence. There was even a ritual of smoking, as I remember, looking back at the complex paraphernalia
in my father's den, the only room in which he was encouraged,
behind the plush curtains that veiled his door, to perform the
elaborate mysteries of this masculine rite. Those were the days
of smoking jackets and smoking caps with buttons on top, and
my father's den was a small museum of implements for smoking, candles for lighting cigars, brass trays and pipe-racks. It
was a fixed note of my father's life that I should pick in the
garden for him a flower to stick in his buttonhole at the breakfast-table, while he had a maxim for every occasion, such as
"doing as the Romans do" or never being "the first by whom
the new is tried." When, later, he saw me wearing my trousers,
like Prufrock, with the bottoms rolled, he always said, "I see
it's raining in London"; and a code for everything accompanied
the maxims, how you should tip your soup-plate and what sort
of hat was right for an ocean voyage. He uttered his maxims
humorously and lightly but never with any real doubt that life
was based on laws and there they were, another of them being
that one might wear threadbare clothes, if need were, so long
as one's linen was utterly and immaculately fresh. Those were
the days when young men, job-hunting, wore frock coats and
top hats to make an impression even in a newspaper office; and,
while my father could never have rivalled the sartorial mag-
nificence of some of his friends, he dressed in the ceremonial
manner of the time. His idea of undress was a blue reefer or
a black pea-jacket; but he commonly wore a broadcloth coat, a

cutaway with short tails, a flat-topped derby hat and striped worsted trousers. With these went the usual assortment of seal-rings, scarf-pins, watch-charms and massive sleeve-buttons that paralleled the brooches and bangles of the feminine sex. His shirts, starched like steel breastplates, were made for him with collars that gradually turned into saws about his neck, and his straw-yellow silk handkerchiefs, exhaling a perpetual eau-de-Cologne, spread from his pocket as voluminously as flags or sails. They were like the enormous handkerchiefs from which we saw parlour magicians extract a brace of rabbits or a basket of eggs.

My mother was not behind my father in feeling that she was always right, if only because her feet were on the Rock of Ages, and her usual reply was "We won't discuss it" if anyone questioned the laws on which our little world seemed to be built. Any dissent was "very provoking," and this evolved into "aggravating" if the dissent was repeated or even prolonged; and yet she was always ready to laugh if one cornered her and teased her until one broke down her by no means fortress-like defences. Years later one of her younger friends told me how, in church, when both were listening to a rather pompous sermon, my mother whispered, "Marian, what *are* the eternal verities?" —referring to some generalization which the clergyman had uttered. Easily amused as she really was, she had to support the official views,—or felt that she had to support them,—on all levels of life; and her way of defending any of these was to say it was "so considered," though the question never arose, considered by whom? It was not cricket to ask this question, which might have resulted in a wholesale retreat, nor was it fair to challenge her statement, regarding churchly matters, that "all the best minds" agreed about them. We knew, or I knew, that "all the best minds" meant Phillips Brooks, for my

father and mother were Episcopalians, as all my four grandparents were, and never supposed that they could have been
anything else. To be anything else, from their point of view,
was somewhat quaint or queer, slightly droll in the case of
Methodists or Baptists, and what, save a Presbyterian, could
one otherwise be? I gathered that the Presbyterians, among
whom we had many intimate friends, were prone to a somewhat excessive evangelical zeal, while Roman Catholicism was
a picturesque foreign religion that only one person we knew
visibly practised. This was an old French lady whom everybody knew and who lived in a gambrel-roofed house too near
the railroad. In her house George Washington had spent one
of the nights of his eight migratory years as an old campaigner.

It strikes me that Napoleon's phrase for history, "a fable
agreed upon," applies to the state of mind of the world we
lived in, and of every other society too, for are not all cultures
based on rules of a game that people half-consciously agree to
play? They well know these are "vital lies," or lies at least in
part, shifts that can be defended only in a measure, like the
summary simplifications regarding religions and races. that
characterize the tribal point of view. These latter really mean
no more than Benvenuto Cellini meant when he said that the
people of Ferrara were "very avaricious," that "all" of them were
the same in this respect; and the fictions in question are only
maintained because they are felt to be safeguards of security
and tribal order. The young people who discarded them,—
who were constrained to do so, reading *The Way of All Flesh*
and the Freudian writings,—condemned themselves to playing
lone hands against the universe, with no underlying sense of
security whatever. And how safe, with all its fictions, this world
seemed. For us all Democrats were Ferrarese, not avaricious
but somehow base, and I remember my brother and me, at

election time, when I was six, burning a stuffed pillow that we called "Grover Cleveland." Our automatic Republicanism made for the sense of security that sprang from the regularity of everything around us, the winding of the clocks on Sunday mornings, the universal parade to church and the ceremony of "lying down" in the middle of the day. Did not everyone's mother, presumably, go upstairs for this? The grinding sound of the coffee-mill that rose early from the kitchen mingled with the other summer sounds, the mowing of the lawn and the far-away beating of carpets, the whirring of the water-sprinklers, the rocking of hammocks, bespeaking not only security but endless time for everything, long hours for reading and dreaming of other sorts of worlds.

One really lost oneself in these, whether Thackeray's world or Vasari's, or the mediæval scene of *The Cloister and the Hearth,* and no one felt the need of relating these worlds to one's personal "problems," the universal need of a later epoch. I remember my mother as always embroidering table-cloths, napkins and doilies, which she covered with forget-me-nots, pansies and sprays of wild roses,—in the end I inherited a trunkful of this work of her hands,—or reading with a friend the French that she often spoke with my father at table or playing Mozart, Beethoven, Schumann or Chopin. She had been a pupil of Richard Hoffman, Malvina Hoffman's father, and played, I am quite sure, exceptionally well, and her piano had been used by Paderewski, who had taken it on one of his tours and whose name often greeted my infant ears. Chopin was always her favourite, and if, as Tennessee Williams says, "in memory everything seems to happen to music," I would say that with me it happened especially to Chopin. "Every-thing" seems to have happened to the notes of the nocturnes and études that I remember as accompanying my earliest childhood, floating through open windows on summer afternoons, accompanied in turn by the buzzing of an occasional fly. To this day I always associate Chopin with ladies in white organdie dresses and the gentle flapping of curtains in a languid breeze.

My mother, for the rest, was conscientious, however it bored her so to be, for, like my father's in earlier days when youth and pleasure met, her natural taste was all for the frivolous and gay. I still have a handbook about cotillions with my father's name in it, a relic of his blazer-wearing tennis-playing twenties before ill-health and misfortune crippled him. But he was conscientious too, and he invariably spent his holiday afternoons reading out loud at the hospital to the men in the wards. He usually read Dickens or Mr. Dooley, whom he really revelled in, partly because he had himself a quarter-infusion of Irish blood and liked the flavour of the brogue when he was in good spirits. My mother took my brother and me on "nature walks" on Sundays, although I am sure she felt far from at home in the woods, with the pungent skunk-cabbages and the salamanders under the rocks; nor can I believe that she greatly enjoyed some of the books she read to us, even the *Pilgrim's Progress*, one that I remember. For no more than my grandmother could she go too far along the attenuated path of the supposedly improving. My grandmother tried to read aloud *Rollo at Work* on one occasion, but she was so overcome with laughing over its priggish absurdities that she stopped somewhere in the second chapter. But both took seriously, especially my mother, the rights and wrongs of the spoken word, enunciation, inflection, good usage and so on, together with the superiority of Worcester's Dictionary, in all these delicate matters, over Webster.

Meanwhile, the domestic arts had been virtually forgotten,

mainly, no doubt, because servants were so cheap and abun-
dant, when households like ours, without any pretensions,
could have seven maids with seven mops for less than the wages
of one fifty years later. It was supposed that my mother knew
how to make a blueberry pie because, in some legendary past,
she had really made one, but the only visible demonstration of
anything approaching this was my grandmother's annual battle with currant jelly. For two or three days the rear quarters
of the house were turned upside down while this tumultuous
ceremony was played out to the end, a whole-souled survival
of the days of my grandmother's childhood in Plattsburg that
suggested the emblematic ploughing of the emperor of China.
The great red cheesecloth jelly-teats dripped all over the laun-
dry-tubs, over buckets, pails, caldrons, bowls and soap tureens,
while Christine the chambermaid, Ingrid the cook and my
nurse Rosie, who ruled us all, were called into constant requi-
sition. Even the gardener was pressed into service, the tender
of the currant patch, the earthy odorous Alsatian Floret
Wormser, a name that my grandmother felt was too improb-
able to be entertained, so she said that for us "Floret" meant
"Lawrence." From that day forward Lawrence he remained.

I dimly remember the simpler time, the horse-and-buggy
age, when Jerry, the baggage-master, was busy at the station
and one saw the liveryman Albert Heddon jogging through
the streets in the phæton with the tasselled canopy and the
buffalo-skin blanket. I can still hear my grandmother saying,
"Now, Jerry, be sure the checks are all on the right trunks."
The Civil War was still quite close and there were three generals in the town, one of them General Fitz John Porter, the
ultimate hero of a *cause célèbre*, whose elder daughter had
been one of my mother's bridesmaids. There were colonels and
majors on all sides, and even the dentist, Dr. Wells, had been

a captain at Bull Run and liked nothing better than to talk about it. Pinning one down and shutting one up with what he called a rubber dam, he discoursed about the fight at the old stone bridge. During the Civil War itself Hawthorne had prophesied that after the war "every country neighbourhood will have its general or two, its three or four colonels, half a dozen majors and captains without end." Our town was in this respect like all the others.

How many odd characters, for the rest, how many queer folk there seemed to be, as many as one found in Russian novels, —even the novels of Tolstoy, which we had in the house,— types that vanished in later days into sanitariums or were smoothed out by psychoanalysts. There were, for instance, the Von Ohls, reputedly well-born Germans who had fallen upon evil days and drove into town, to market, in a ramshackle gypsy trap and who lived in a rotting old house on the edge of a swamp in the woods that always evoked the story of *No Haid Pawn*. For there was a pond near by this breeding-place for ghosts and a gigantic bloodhound that rushed out once at Max Perkins and me when we were searching in the swamp for turtles. We stood back to back, half expecting a horrible death, only to discover that the old hound was toothless. But odder than these were the "old New York" people,—or some of them, at least,—with whom we were more or less connected, Miss Spencer, for one, who lived by herself with a Great Dane called Nero and an orange-tree that spread through the floor of her parlour. Miss Spencer still wore the bonnets and mantles and tippets of the days when she and my grandmother were both young, almost the days of the red-coated portrait of her English grandfather who had settled in New York and married the young French lady in pale yellow satin. A perfect pair of oddities were our cousins Richard and Lottie Brown, the deaf old bachelor and spinster brother and sister whom I somehow associated with Charles and Mary Lamb. Their father had been the partner of Philip Hone, the mayor of New York who kept the Pepysian diary that has often been reprinted, and I still have a set of Coleridge that Cousin Lottie gave me, along with her father's letters of travel. For many years he had been president of the Mercantile Library in New York and his peregrinations as an old-time merchant had led him all over the South and the West, and Europe as well, in the eighteen-twenties and thirties. He had fallen in with Daniel Webster at St. Louis in 1837 and had raced in a packet-ship against the "Great Western," finding himself on one occasion, travelling from London to Paris, in the company of the poet laureate Robert Southey.

One other character who comes back to me, and whom I saw constantly as a child, bore the delightful name of Cecilia de Medina, an impersonation of the tragic muse, as she always seemed to me, with her black lace, her fans and her mantilla. I felt that only Goya could have done justice to her, while, in fact, this great friend of my grandmother was neither Spanish nor of the stage, although she was the daughter of a once-famous actor. She had married, however, in Morro Castle, in Havana, the son of the Duke of Medina who was governor of Cuba, and she always wore a ring, an intaglio surrounded by diamonds, that Napoleon had given to one of her husband's forbears. Her father, long dead, like her husband, had been William E. Burton, the proprietor of *Burton's Gentleman's Magazine*, which Edgar Allan Poe had edited for a while in Philadelphia, publishing in it *The Fall of the House of Usher*. Burton's Theatre in New York had been the most popular of its time, but the actor himself, an Englishman, convinced that he was vulgar, had never permitted his daughter to see him on the stage, and the dark air of grandeur that she retained for me was merely the natural expression of a histrionic epoch. She was tall and marked in every line of her spare pale face with a high distinction. With her sister, Mrs. Massett, she was always "going back," to Dresden or, more often, Vevey,—in any case, Europe,—after two or three years in America that invariably aroused for the European scene the longing that Europe aroused for America soon after.

There were various literary people in the town, among them Julian Hawthorne, who lived in a little pinkish house with tall pointed windows, like a miniature Venetian palace forlornly astray. A daughter of Julia Ward Howe,—Florence Howe Hall,—lived near the Hawthornes on the Scotch Plains road; and, while Edmund Clarence Stedman had spent part of his youth in one old house, Bret Harte's wife and daughters still lived in another. They had been virtually abandoned by the almost-great writer of whom Mark Twain said that his heart was "merely a pump without any other function." But, if the spirit of any author was active in the town, one might perhaps have said it was Washington Irving's, for half the population had old Dutch names that were all to be found in Knickerbocker's history of New York. There were Beekmans, Van Burens, Bogarduses, Van Zandts and Van Boskercks, Van Rensselaers, Laurenses, Brockholsts, Schuylers and Suydams, a fact that apparently interested nobody, for it was very well known that New Yorkers knew nothing and cared nothing about their forbears. It was because they knew nothing about them that Washington Irving had written his book, for which they abused him roundly after he had done so; and Edith Wharton testified that even in her later day "the New Yorker was singularly, inexplicably indifferent to his descent." The history of New York had been a succession of names that were known for a time and vanished to give place to another set, for the city was "permanently in transition," as Henry James put it, and in this way very unlike Boston where the same names remained at the top and even gathered prestige with the generations. Whatever the reasons for this may have been, —and one of them was that Bostonians were cannier investors than New Yorkers and kept their fortunes,—the Knickerbocker families that had once been known were all represented by survivors in the town along with relations of families that were not yet snowed under. For me Washington Irving was still alive, or he came alive, as I should say, when later I was told that my grandmother had met him. This was at a party in her uncle's house where she had spent her vacations as a school-girl in New York. "A very pretty compliment from a very pretty girl," he had said in reply to one of her remarks.

CHAPTER II

MAXWELL PERKINS

THE NOTE of Washington Irving survived in the name of the Knickerbocker ranch, a household word during all my boyhood years,—the Texas ranch of our friends the Tweedys, the closest of my family's friends, some of whom, in fact, were our next-door neighbours. Two Tweedy boys with two nephews of Washington Irving had opened this ranch just after the Civil War, and there my brother, who went through Princeton with the older sons of our time, spent several rapturous summers as an amateur cowboy. They all came north for school and college, and José, the younger son, so called by his Mexican nurse, was equally my special friend and the friend of Max Perkins. He was the perfect type of the engaging ranchman, deeply tanned, manly, frank, with the winning smile and drawl of what Owen Wister called the world's greatest playground for young men. With his atmosphere of round-ups and barbecues and pack-trains in the mountains, José was the "Virginian" to the life, the embodiment of the romantic code, as we saw it, of the plains, and I always thought of him when I read of Kit Carson's grave reserve, his distaste for noise and boastfulness and his loyalty and courage. These traits, openly mentioned then, went underground in after days when it became the fashion not to use "words."

I have often wondered how far this friendship with José

prepared Max Perkins to understand Hemingway later. The
"aunts," meanwhile, the Tweedy "girls," one of whom lived to
be ninety-nine, remained our friends even to the fourth generation. For half a century before she died, "Miss Belle" always
suggested to me the somehow electrified mummy of Rameses
the Great, as if he had escaped from his funeral wrappings
and leaped out of his painted box in a wild wish to know what
was happening in the world. For, wrinkled, with her eyes
sealed tight and tiny as she was, she all but ran down the
stairs like a twelve-year-old child, and, perching on the edge
of her chair, alive with intelligence, fresh feeling and wit, she
threw herself into the minds of the oldest and the youngest.
She had prophesied that her elder nephew, aged ten, would
be the banker that he became, in England, later, and she said
to my little son, whom I sometimes took to see her, "Charlie,
don't miss *anything!*"—she was then ninety-seven. *His* comment was, "Why, Miss Tweedy's a genius!" as I always
thought she was, if genius can be defined as the quintessence
of concentrated life, and if uncommon mnemonic powers are
also a part of this, for her memories went back almost a hundred years. When I became interested in American history,
somewhat late in life, she described for me the funeral of
John Quincy Adams, which she had actually witnessed in
1848, and she showed me a picture of the checked gingham
dress in which, in 1855, she heard Thackeray lecture in New
York on the Four Georges. To test the memory of Dexter
Tiffany, her old beau of a nephew, who was eighty-four himself, I believe, at the time, she asked him if he could remember
the day when Major Anderson lunched with them after the
guns had gone off at Fort Sumter. "Deck," as my mother
called him, was annoyed by this, for he too was proud of his
memory, and, when I was writing about New England, he told

me about his grandfather, the old gossip Bela Tiffany, who had
lived in Boston. This grandfather, he averred, sitting in taverns
on Washington Street, had told Hawthorne several of his own
"twice-told" tales.

At no age at all,—thirteen, in fact,—I had become, as I shall
explain, both interested in the history of art and informed
about it, and since then I have often thought of some of the
pictures in the Tweedy house that were unlike the pictures on
other walls. In most of our houses there were dusky copies of
Raphael madonnas or Ribera monks, Murillo beggar-boys or
Caravaggio gamblers, brought back from abroad perhaps by
some travelling uncle,—there was often a "Beatrice Cenci"
somewhere in a corner,—but, besides the huge golden Thomas
Cole in the shadowy hallway of the Tweedy house, there was
a supposed Canaletto and a supposed Bronzino. I say "supposed," for no actual claims were made for them; and who, in
those almost pre-expertizing and altogether pre-Berenson days,
was really sure of the provenance of anyone's "old masters"?
I mean, of course, in provincial collections, though these had
all come from the Newport house of "Uncle Edmund"
Tweedy, of whom Henry James wrote in *A Small Boy and
Others*; and, for that matter, at Hampton Court in 1899 the
pictures were still attributed virtually at random. One by an
unknown Flemish painter had been labelled in the dim past
a portrait of Raphael by himself and was still so labelled. But,
authentic or not, the Tweedy pictures were as magical for me
as one or two under the skylights of the town museum, the
"Job Male Art Gallery" that never quite lost its terrors for
me because of an early encounter with the donor in person.
When I was three or four, Job Male had lived opposite
my grandfather's house, behind a fence with pickets that
bulged at the sides, and I somehow took it into my head that

these bulges ought to be removed and crept across the street, with a hatchet, to remove them. How I found the hatchet I cannot guess, nor can I remember how I evaded my nurse's vigilant eye; but it comes back to me vividly enough that I chopped off two of the bulges before relentless fate caught up with me. The door suddenly opened and there on the threshold stood Job Male himself, like an angry God with eyes fixed on the sinner. I had been seized red-handed, for there was the hatchet, and I did not have a chance to tell a lie.

The "art gallery" in question was meagre enough, though ample as to numbers, academy pictures of the fourth rank, battle-scenes and what not, like the little girl in a field of black-eyed Susans. But there was one Italian picture, "Cleopatra and the Asp," that might have been the real thing, though of course it was not, for one never knew where, in those casual days, in any odd corner, one might happen upon something interesting and even quite good. One picture there, for instance, though certainly not a masterpiece, was unmistakably better than any of the others, a picture with a history too, as I discovered later, John Vanderlyn's "Marius Among the Ruins of Carthage." I do not know whether it was this or the other version,—in San Francisco,—that Napoleon medalled at the Salon in 1805, but, quite different from the other, it was almost as good, and Vanderlyn, while far from great, was an early American painter who knew his trade. How had it strayed there and whither did it vanish when all these pictures were later auctioned off, victims of a local birth of taste, regarding the gallery generally, that also carried the Vanderlyn away? It was the great *revolution* in taste that had scattered elsewhere,—everywhere,—the remnants of the "gentlemen's galleries" of fifty years before when the Lewis Raycies of whom Edith Wharton wrote in *False Dawn* came into their own with pictures that Ruskin approved of. But not even these were above suspicion in the most instructed quarters, in the households of the Perkinses and their grandmother Perkins at Newport, the widow of the old Boston critic and historian of art. "Bruen Villa," which I knew later when I was at Harvard with Max, was virtually a museum not only of paintings but of objets d'art of every sort that sometimes turned out to be genuine and sometimes not. Assembled in the easy-going days when Charles C. Perkins had lived in Florence,—where Max's father was born,—a friend of the Brownings and a member of W. W. Story's circle, many of these objects were challenged later, even the superb Michelangelo drawing, a sketch for the "Last Judgment," that hung in the Plainfield house.

Max Perkins himself had a marked talent for drawing. I have lately found sketches of his in my college notebooks, and I remember that he sometimes carried a sketch-book in his pocket and constantly drew figures and especially heads. They were sometimes heads of Napoleon or his favourite Shelley or his later idol Mark Twain, with a corncob pipe; and they were often heads of a pure Greek type quite like his own, for he was a beautiful boy, Praxitelean. Had this gift descended from his grandfather Perkins, who had studied painting with Ary Scheffer?—studying music in Germany as well, for he had been a composer too, and his whole life had been passed in an atmosphere of art. Charles C. Perkins had been for a while the conductor of the Handel and Haydn Society, and he had given to the city of Boston Crawford's statue of Beethoven, the first statue of any sort of artist that was erected in the country. It was one of this grandfather's uncles who had discovered William Rimmer, the interesting sculptor of the statue of Hamilton in Boston; and I had read his own *Tuscan Sculptors,* as I was to read in time the book on Ghiberti and his school that he wrote in French. When Max and I were in college, his grandmother gave us, to hang in our literary club, a number of letters from various old friends of theirs in Italy and Boston, among them Browning, Longfellow, Lowell and Motley; and at Newport, in her atmosphere of early Victorian elegance, she talked about her old Italian days. She suggested to me the pictures of Salvator Rosa, for she recalled banditti in wild passes of the mountains and travellers robbed on the road in the middle of the night, along with musical *soirées* in Rome in the days of Pio Nono, Walter Savage Landor and *The Marble Faun*. The names of "Harry" and "Willie" James recurred in Mrs. Perkins's talk, together with the family of Charles Eliot Norton,—immemorial Newport friends,—one of whose daughters I remember as present in the house.

As for the Perkins clan whom I knew so well at home, I think of them as a raft of Boston culture,—one of those rafts that were to be found in many another American town, serenely riding the wild waters of the world around them. Not that our world was very wild or that they were the only Bostonians,—there were many New Englanders, at least, among our friends; but they somehow threw into the boldest relief the New York character of our own life, which seemed to me so different from the character of New England. I never ceased to wonder at the strength of the local atmospheres, the flavours that persisted so pungently for two centuries or more and kept the old provinces and colonies so distinct; for although my own grandfathers had been Vermonters they had both been absorbed in New York and I always felt like a foreigner when I entered New England. As it happened, I was taken every summer for two or three months to Kennebunkport, or to Saunderstown, Quisset, Magnolia or Maplewood, New Hampshire, usually travelling on the Fall River boat that might have been crossing the ocean so alien to me was the world in which we arrived. Exciting enough was the shuffling sound of the porter's feet in the corridor on the heavy red carpet outside the stateroom door, the tinkle of the ice-water pitcher and the knock that followed, the clanking of the loose brass key in the stateroom lock. And to what new sights and sounds and scents one wakened in the morning in that world of clambakes and lobsters and salt-water taffy, of Salem Gibraltars and briny smells, whiffs of hemlock, spruce and fir and the odour of fresh pine as one opened the wardrobe doors. Then there were the Indians who camped near the summer hotels and sold sweetgrass baskets, arrows and birch-bark canoes, and the buckboard excursions to some spot in the woods where the ladies gathered autumn leaves and read nature books aloud, sitting on the rocks. And the harvest fêtes at the mountain resorts, the flag-draped arches and the coaching parades, the huge floats decked with goldenrod and asters! Far away seem those young girls swathed in flowers as the "spirit of autumn" and those evanescent structures of cheesecloth and bunting, emblems of a summer scene that vanished fifty years ago and survive now only in Howells's novels.

Even years later when, at forty-five, I was writing about New England, I felt as alien there as I had felt as a boy, as an English boy might feel on his first visit to Scotland, for the Yankee dialect was as palpable as the language of Burns. Especially in Maine I felt this in those dying seaports that never died, in the rough-shingled fish-houses on the dilapidated wharves,—which were always falling down but never fell,—where the old sea-captains, basking among the lobster-pots, seemed to have been fixed for all time in their stage of decay. They liked to sleep in hammocks, though their houses were full of good beds and their wives made every effort to keep them indoors; but, as

soon as their wives were asleep, back they went to their hammocks again, for they lived, as one saw in their dwellings, in a
dream of the sea. Like ships, these dwellings were covered with
hatch-ways and companion-ways, ladders and piazzas that were
built like bridges and decks, climbing as it were all over their
fronts and sides, with captain's walks to survey the ocean and
masts for the flags that waved from them,—every house, in fact,
a Yankee vessel. All this, of course, delighted me, but it could
scarcely have seemed more foreign; and, for the rest, I had
been brought up on the usual pleasantries about New England
that in those days filled the pages of the comic magazines. I
had heard virtually at birth "Mr." Choate's toast to the Pilgrim mothers who endured all the troubles of the Pilgrim fathers and had had to put up with the Pilgrim fathers too, the
climax of the New York jokes about baked beans and the
"Boston look" and little boys with goggles and bulging foreheads. *My* only immediate scholarly forbear,—oddly enough, as
it seemed to me, inasmuch as both my grandfathers had come
from New England,—was my father's Irish grandsire, whose
nose was always in a book, as an uncle who remembered him
told me later. He had read not only Latin and Greek but Hebrew, by no means to his advantage as an importer of woollens;
while "thoughtful" New England was generally regarded by
the little world I knew as in some way cold and dry, pedantic
and forbidding.

I only dwell upon this now because these distinctions of atmosphere seemed to count so much in the small world in question, in which at the same time "the West" was a kind of wild
Siberia that swallowed up unsuccessful uncles and cousins. I
somehow identified Boston with too many books, and my
grandmother, who was well aware of the world but totally detached from scholarly circles, regarded my liking for these with

a faint touch of scorn. She had a story about one of her brothers
who had gone to a New England country college,—Dartmouth,
I think,—and come back for his winter vacation with Gibbon's
Decline and Fall for "light" reading, which was not the kind
of lightness that our New Yorkers understood with what Howells called "the levity of their old Dutch blood." For while the
English element in them generally predominated over any
other infusion of whatever other strains, their racial intermix-
ture,—as I was happy, later, to know,—was precisely that of the
two greatest New York writers. Like Melville and Whitman,
they were equally English and Dutch. Because of all the influences that played over my childhood, I felt that I was myself
an ingrained New Yorker, and I had the sense of coming home
when, writing my literary history later, I turned from New
England to the world of Washington Irving. But when I think
of New England now in relation to this other scene, I remember Fenimore Cooper's attitude towards it, for Cooper, although born in New Jersey, had spent his whole life in New
York state and knew, none better, what he called "New York
feelings." He scouted the "Blarney Rock of Plymouth" and said
"Nothing Yankee agrees with me," while most of his New
England characters were either mean, like Ithuel Bolt, or, like
Remarkable Pettibone, figures of fun. But he was obliged to
praise whole-heartedly the intelligence of the New England
folk and recognize their "high and honourable distinctions."
Could anyone have quarrelled with him for that?

Now the Perkinses were not only New Englanders, they
were even doubly so, for they united the two great lines of
Boston and New Haven,—Harvard and Yale,—the twin immemorial schools of the mind of New England. Max, descended
on one side from the old East India magnates,—some of whom
had been Loyalists in the Revolution in Boston,—was, on the

other, through his grandfather Evarts, the Senator and Secretary of State, descended from John Davenport and Roger Sherman. I mention this merely because I have known few other Americans in whom so much history was palpably and visibly embodied, so that one saw it working in him, sometimes not too happily, for his mind was always in a state of civil war. And this was the old *English* civil war that he never quite fought through, the war between Roundhead and Cavalier one or the other side of which constantly came to the front at crises in his life. How often Max talked King Charles to me to make me talk Oliver Cromwell, beaming when I did so because I was putting into words what he,—or the other side of him,— really felt. One side was the romantic adventurous boy, indolent, graceful and frank, all gaiety, sweetness, good spirits and animal charm, drawn to the John Reeds of his time and the heroes of Richard Harding Davis, soldiers of fortune who lived a knight-errant's life. This was the Max who arrayed himself in splendour, whose appetite for pleasure was unending and keen, and who liked to remember that one of his forbears had ridden against Paul Revere and beaten him in a horse-race once in Boston. This side drew him to Scott Fitzgerald, while the other was the side that rose in rebellion in London when he met three young swells in Parliament Square. I remember his picture of them swaggering towards him, and I saw that his fantasy clothed them in the plumes and ruffles of King Charles's men while all his Cromwellian blood rose up against them. This other side of Max believed in living against the grain and doing the "hard way" whatever he had to do, and he might well have said what his grandfather Evarts really said, as Henry Adams reported in the *Education*. "I pride myself on my success in doing not the things I like to do but the things I do not like to do" was the motto of the old Roman statesman

whom I saw sitting at the window once in his house on Second Avenue below Stuyvesant Square. For one day when I was
in town with Max we visited this house, then lost in the slums,
with the wide tessellated pavement in the entrance-hall, so
large a house that when it was demolished two apartment-
houses, the "U.S. Senate" and the "Evarts," were built on the
site. *This* Max was always scolding me for following the line
of least resistance, setting out in cold blood to do what I wished
and liked instead of what, so obviously, I *ought* to do. Here
was the descendant of Jeremiah Evarts who had preached abolition even in the South and in consequence spent a year in a
Georgia gaol, the foil of the child of the art-loving grandfather,
along with the uncle who discovered Rimmer as Max himself
discovered so many writers. One side appreciated the writers,
the other side helped them, an ambivalence that explained why
Max never became a writer himself and why he became the rock
on which others leaned. He was himself a character in some
of their stories; and sixty-eight books were dedicated to him.

When the novelist Galsworthy visited this country he told a
common friend that Max was the most interesting American
whom he had ever known, and not the least interesting thing
about him was this perpetual war with himself that made him
in the end a "prey to sadness." For it seemed to me that he fulfilled Kierkegaard's phrase for accidie, that malady of so many
monks in the Middle Ages, the "despairing refusal to be oneself" which really means that a man "does not give the consent
of his will to his own being." It struck me as symbolic that, in
his office in the publishing house, two pictures always faced
him on the wall behind the desk, a photograph of an old schoolmaster, an austere New Englander, and one of the Saint-
Gaudens monument for Mrs. Henry Adams. For me the old
Yankee head, which I too had known in life, evoked Dr.

Arnold of Rugby's well-known phrase, "the silent pleasure, so dear to every Englishman, of enduring, resisting, and struggling with something, and not giving way." Alien as the sentiment was to me, I always admired it in Englishmen, in the classic type of the civil servant working with selfless devotion, in jungles, in deserts,—wherever,—for the "natives" and the Empire. For Max the Empire was the publishing house and the natives were the authors, the authors who kept the Empire going and whom he served devotedly but also with respect and frequently affection. So he served Thomas Wolfe with and for whom he spent hundreds of hours labouring through jungle-like nights in the middle of summer. He even told Wolfe that he regretted not having kept a diary "about the work that both of us were doing . . . the triumphs and surrenders that went into the making of a book,"—as a nurse might keep a diary about the progress of a fever-patient or a consul in the tropics about some local insurrection. But heaven knows how many repressions this involved for the other Max, one, for instance, that recalled to me Dr. Johnson's saying, "Every man thinks meanly of himself for not having been a soldier." For I know there was an anxious time when Max would have been a soldier, and would have thought better of himself, *except* for the Empire.

It was this kind of resignation that produced the "sadness," the fatalistic sadness of the veiled figure designed for Henry Adams, the old friend of his grandfather's family in Washington whom Max's mother had known so well and who in a way had been part of his own life. So Saint-Gaudens had also been, across the Connecticut river from Windsor, where he made the bust of the Senator in his summer White House and where Max had met General Sherman and Benjamin Harrison when he was a boy and learned to take presidents and generals almost

for granted. There, in old houses beside the lake, the clan gathered in the vacation months, the Thackerayan uncles and the
aunts and older cousins who might all have stepped out of
Punch in Du Maurier's time. Many weeks I spent there with
Perkinses and Evartses and the stream of little girls in pigtails,
faintly suggesting the *Peterkin Papers,* that flowed on, un-
changing, from decade to decade. It seems to me that, even
now, if I were to drive past, on the long road from Canada that
runs through Vermont, I should still see them there, in white
dimity and sashes, an endless succession of Alices in Wonder-
land, playing croquet on the lawn, all in the golden afternoon.

No one could have known Max who did not understand
what Windsor, or Vermont in general, meant for him, the deep
stake in the old rural America from which the foreground of
his life was in many of its elements so far removed. One of his
visions was to own and edit a country newspaper, such as
Bowles's *Springfield Republican* once had been, and in Windsor he had been the boy who knew guns, hunting and fishing
and the "wonderful river trips" that he remembered in a letter.
All this drew him to *The Yearling* of Marjorie Rawlings, as to
Hemingway, Thomas Wolfe and *Huckleberry Finn,* for which
he shared the passion that, more than any other of a literary
kind, bound the American novelists of the new time together.
"The best part of a man is a boy," he wrote in a letter to one of
his authors, some of whom were boys themselves and who
found in him a father, just as he sometimes found in them a
son. It is with "young authors . . . that our great hopes lie," he
said, for old authors "never surprise" while "young ones *can*,"
and he seemed to be naturally inclined away from the old and
the traditional and towards the experimental, the native and
the new. It was not surprising that he should have felt, as he
wrote to Wolfe, "There could be nothing so important as a

book can be,"—what *might* have seemed remarkable was that
he should have recognized at sight such un-Thackerayan talents as Ring Lardner's, for instance. It was still more remarkable that he was the first to recognize them and that he led the
movement away from British standards in novel-writing in the
most conservative publishing house in New York. There for
years W. C. Brownell had vainly struggled with his own belief that America was merely a "literary dependency" of England, and Max's family atmosphere had perfectly borne out
Emerson's phrase that we had our "culture" from one continent and our "duties" from another. His eyes had scarcely
rested on anything more American than Arundel prints, Elze-
vir Ciceros and Horaces, Méryon etchings and seventeenth
century Italian bookcases and chests, brought back from the
city of Dante and Ghirlandajo, and his father had a way of astonishing the natives with remarks about art that left small
room for anything likely to appear on their own scene. One of
his father's dicta was that "bad art" was not "art" at all, and he
applied this to E. A. Abbey's Boston frescoes, the praises of
which at the time were in everyone's mouth. One might have
expected that Max's taste, when it developed, would be severe;
but who could have guessed it would be so direct, so uninflu-
enced by prejudice, so unclouded by secondary feelings, so immediate, so fresh? Had not Windsor and all it stood for done
this for him?

There were many of us later whose "culture" was originally
European and who found ourselves "turning homeward," as
Emerson put it, because of elements, deep in ourselves, that we
were unaware of but of which we became aware as time went
on. For the rest, Max's epistolary style was distinctly eighteenth
century, and so it remained, as one saw when his letters were
published,—the result of a taste I shared with him for the

world of Swift, Addison, Defoe and Pope that especially included the circle of Dr. Johnson. How well we seemed to know
these men, as characters and writers, just as we knew the poets
and critics of a later generation of whom Max's favourite was
Shelley and De Quincey was mine. The legends of these English authors were all as vividly real to us as the lives of any of
our friends. But it interested me, when his letters appeared,
that what Max remembered from the life of Swift was not the
romance of Vanessa, which everyone talked of, but something
a novelist would have observed, that Swift liked to sit in taverns on greens listening to the talk of teamsters and coachmen.
Just so Stephen Crane had sat by the hour in Bowery saloons,
fascinated by the rhythm and tempo of living speech, and this
went far to explain to me Max's intuitive understanding of the
writers of his own time in his own country. He knew, knowing
the eighteenth century, that the most enlightened ages had
been, as he said, the most free-spoken,—which opened him still
further to the young mind of his time,—as he knew that good
writers "always feel anxious" and "ought to have trouble," as
he put it, "getting under way" with a fine book. No one was
more aware that, with their "subconscious confidence," good
writers have vastly less confidence in beginning a book than
men who merely follow the trade of writing; and he always
found it a good symptom when a true writer felt greatly dis-
couraged and even, at moments, desperate in writing a book.
He knew that books, like people, should be "sized up in their
own terms" and in terms of the particular writer's capacities
and interests, and he was always on the side of the author not
only against the public but against the publisher as well. Less
than a handful could understand the writer's point of view, he
said, while "the true artist has always insisted upon making his
book what he wanted it" and should never be censored by edi-

tors or any outsider. This understanding enabled him to out-
line whole novels more than once that subsequently his authors executed or to suggest that in writing their books they
should follow certain forms that proved to be entirely responsible for their ultimate success. Meanwhile, he affirmed that
"the only important things" were "loyalty, fortitude and honour," and he felt that to be "born knowing this" meant going
at least a part of the way towards being "a great writer in
more than the technical sense."

What, after his death, came back to me as chiefly character-
izing Max was a certain unwavering nobility,—an elevation
that many who did not possess it revered in him,—with the
kind of "high gentlemanlike bearing" that Thackeray ascribed
to Pendennis, whom in various ways Max followed as a model.
This in turn recalls to me the influence, in our time and place,
that novels seemed to possess over manners and behaviour, especially Thackeray's, written "in the gentlemanly interest," although Dickens's characters were the best known of all. But
the names of the people of Dickens were commonly used as
epithets, Micawber, Pecksniff, Murdstone, Uriah Heep, and no
one thought of acting out these characters in real life, as they
acted out Thackeray characters and the women of Jane Austen.
The only exception that I remember was Sydney Carton in
A Tale of Two Cities, the young lawyer whose labours we had
in mind when, grinding for college examinations, we wrapped
wet towels around our heads at night. But at home I felt
sure that Colonel Newcome was always in General Sterling's
thoughts as he passed our house with stately tread, appearing
in mid-afternoon, bent slightly forward, with long drooping
moustaches and his pearl-grey gloves draped over his walking-stick. He was on his way down-town for a chat with
the bookseller Mr. Estil, and it was on one of these afternoons

that, in the post-office, he observed Mrs. Perkins licking a postage stamp. Approaching her boldly, he exclaimed, "Mrs. Perkins, that is something I never expected to see a lady do in public." Had Thackeray ever aspired to that altitude of manners?

But our whole scene comes back to me as a pageant of Anglo-American fiction, beginning with the rector of Grace Church, benign, with his shovel hat, who was surely the walking image of the Vicar of Wakefield. We had not yet reached the time when the Vassar girls all went Botticelli, with Primavera draperies and languishing postures, still less the bar-fly days of nymphomaniacs and alcoholics that followed the publication of *The Sun Also Rises*. Nor were young boys given to emulating Huckleberry Finn as their great-grandfathers had emulated the heroes of Plutarch, though I knew more than one whose later life was crippled by the Little Lord Fauntleroy fever that possessed their mothers. They were kept, with hair in curls, in black velvet and lace until they were ripe for analysts and sometimes asylums. There were also not only Gibson girls but Trilbys and Isabel Archers, studied from Henry James's *Portrait of a Lady,* and dozens of Miss Poles and Miss Matildas, in grey or black mousseline-de-laine, who might have been characters in *Cranford*. They too had sometimes persuaded themselves that to be a "man" was virtually, by definition, to be "vulgar." But in general these characters owed nothing to a book. In America and England alike they had grown that way.

CHAPTER III

AT THE SEMINARY

THERE WAS scarcely more than a touch of *Cranford* in the nunlike circle of the Seminary, the big brown school for girls with the cupola on top, and only when some widower, who had perhaps a daughter there, laid siege to one of the younger and prettier teachers. Standing in a grove of chestnut trees, with winding walks and flowering shrubs, and with rustic arbours and a playhouse near the garden, this was Miss Kenyon's peculiar domain where the abbess and her flock instructed three generations of the daughters of the town. There lived, moreover, for a winter, a year, or even for two or three years, while they were building new houses or abandoning old ones, a handful of families who were more or less congenial but who kept to themselves for the most part in their own sets of rooms. Among these for a while were the Perkinses and my own family, too, and Rockwell Kent with his lawyer father and mother. There was an extension, with wings, at the rear, and three large verandahs over which the wistaria vines climbed up to the roof, and, within, two staircases curved upward from the entrance hall, with Boydell prints lining the walls under the high ceiling. At one side was the library of which the lady from Pittsburgh said that "culture stuck out all over it"; and there, on Saturday evenings in winter, one of the gentlemen read aloud to a circle, grouped round the samovar, drinking

38

tea. For gentlemen were never referred to merely as men. I remember hearing, as I passed the door, phrases of Kipling and
Lafcadio Hearn, the favourite authors of the moment.

In summer, in the shade of the vines, on one of the verandahs, Miss Kenyon seemed always to be reading Browning or
Faust; for she not only personified culture, in the nineteenth
century sense of the term, but she was a missionary of culture
to the town as well. It was she who had founded the women's
club in the parlour of the Seminary,—"to pursue all the means
of culture within reach, whether by study or writing or listening to others"—in the days when lecturers began by saying "as
Emerson says" or "as Lowell says" and ended by discussing
Agassiz, botany and what not. This was in the strenuous earlier time when there was a Plato Society too, led by an Irishman from Trinity College in Dublin, an eccentric schoolmaster, an Episcopal clergyman,—Dr. Johnstone was his name,—
who had long since entered the fold of Tammany Hall. As I
heard of the Plato Society, its meetings always suggested to me
the austere Athenian raptures of a still earlier Concord and I
pictured them as taking place in the light of white lamps and
gas-jets that exploded, at the touch of a match, with a loud report. They expressed, meanwhile, states of mind, remote indeed from the Wall Street world, that now persisted only in
the Seminary, whither Miss Kenyon had brought back her
own recollections of Concord which she had visited in the seventies on more than one occasion. She had witnessed, at the
School of Philosophy, the assemblage of the sages, the venerable Alcott, Elizabeth Peabody and Emerson, in his slat-
bottomed chair, listening with pleased attention, though he
seldom spoke. Since then she had drawn to the Seminary, sometimes to address her girls, a number of writers and scholars who
were famous in those days and some of whom came for annual

visits and even stayed for a week or two because they enjoyed Miss Kenyon and felt at home there. Marion Crawford came, for one, and Julia Ward Howe, his aunt, who lectured,—with the daughter who lived in the town—on the art of conversation and on Dr. Howe's adventures in the Greek Revolution. (Arriving on the very day when Byron died at Missolonghi, he had become, as everyone was supposed to know, the surgeon-general of the navy of the rebellious Greeks.) Others who came were Mrs. Custer, the widow of the general, who talked about garrison life on the northern plains, and Thomas Nelson Page, who read *Marse Chan*. A constant visitor was John Fiske, who sometimes brought his music with him, for he liked to play in the evening and occasionally sang.

What did Miss Kenyon think herself about these unusual guests of hers, and what was her own life during all these years?—questions I never thought of asking and never would have asked if I had not come into possession of her journals and letters. I had later married her grand-niece who had lived as a child in the Seminary and who was permitted to come to the table with John Fiske, when she was four or five, on condition that she was to remain absolutely silent. For Fiske was by then grotesquely fat in a manner that excites a child, and the situation was not improved when the child in question whispered, "Would he mind if I said something *nice* about him?" Miss Kenyon herself was devoted to Fiske and the something large about all his views that was very reassuring after the pettiness of others, and she delighted in his series of lectures on American political ideas, for one, and his talk about Huxley, the generous, his friend in England. But she felt the lack of a certain something in Julia Ward Howe that would have made her a really great woman, something, as she said, that slips over the boundary of selfishness or prudence and creates the complete devotion which runs all risks. And why did she lament, in her poem "To the Brownings" their indifference to her poetry when she had done so much to interpret *them?*—which struck Miss Kenyon as rather weak, especially in one who had followed so well her own unique vocation, which was not the poet's.

Miss Kenyon could scarcely have expressed her feeling for the Brownings. She had shelves of early editions of both these poets, and she was given to reading them religiously with the "Browning Encyclopædia" sometimes at her elbow. One day, with a special friend, she spent an afternoon in honour of Mrs. Browning's birthday, setting out pictures of husband and wife on a table in her room, with their books and vases of violets placed among them. Then the two read together the Portuguese sonnets alternately, with passages from Mrs. Orr's biography of Browning. "O for Browning's courage!" she exclaimed in her journal at the end of a day when her life seemed to be a failure and she asked, "In which direction shall I look for the light?" Browning for her was "Shakespeare's equal in versatility," and she felt that, writing for an age to come, he could easily afford to be so little understood during his lifetime.

But Browning was only one ray of the great sun of culture that was represented for her, as for so many, by Goethe, one of whose apostles, another of her friends, was also a frequent visitor at the Seminary. This was Thomas Davidson, the peripatetic Scottish philosopher whom William James called "a knight-errant of the intellectual life," and who had established in London the "Fellowship of the New Life" of which the Fabian Society was presently an offshoot. The "most intensely alive man whom I had ever met," as Havelock Ellis was to call him a few years later, Davidson conducted schools of philosophy in the Adirondack mountains, at Farmington and at Saint

Cloud, near Orange, New Jersey. He lectured at the Seminary on the "four great religious poems," Job, the *Oresteia*, the *Divine Comedy* and *Faust*, while he talked, as he wrote, on the frieze of the Parthenon also. His great theme was the course of European thought,—"with regard to the highest things,"—together with the "heroes of spiritual thought" and the problems which the nineteenth century was leaving for the twentieth century to solve. He asked Miss Kenyon to accompany him, with a party of friends, on a walking tour through the Black Forest, through Switzerland and over the Alps.

As a local apostle of culture herself, Miss Kenyon read Dante with a class of her own, while she started another to awaken an interest in Homer, and one day two ladies waited on her to suggest a class for the study of *Faust*, the book to which all roads led in the world of culture. To herself she read Aristophanes, *Obermann*, the *Iliad*, Fanny Burney's journal, the life of Landor, while she conducted an inner life of which she recorded day by day the discouragements, the efforts, the resolutions. She dreamed that she was "smothered under the rubbish of circumstances" over which she seemed to have little control, feeling that there was a power within with which to free herself if only she could discover how to use it. She was oppressed with a sense of hurry,—"I think in a jerky fragmentary way. I move with nervous haste, head, feet and tongue"; and, endeavouring to correct this, she looked into William James again and copied out parts of his lecture on Habit. Then, consciously moving and speaking more slowly, she wrote with deliberate motions of the hand to overcome this "hurried and spasmodic action." Another problem was what to do with girls whose "want of delicacy" betrayed them into foolish escapades and whom she would gladly have given up if this had

not been to confess that she lacked the wisdom and the strength
to convince and conquer.

Among the many questions that Miss Kenyon asked herself
was how to achieve real solitude for meditation,—and was she
not making too great an effort to live up to an ideal when possibly the real that she had was better? She wondered what
would have been the result if she had been encouraged to live
a writer's life rather than a teacher's, and she wrote in praise
of silence,—"Let me learn to voice only what I wish to continue resounding in the atmosphere." One whole rainy afternoon she spent walking on the southside verandah, thinking of
Thoreau and listening to the rain, and, looking through the
rain, she seemed to feel a soft veil fall suddenly over the hard
practicality of life. She often had these moments of illumina-
tion. It was all she could do to control herself and continue a
conversation when she looked at some dry oak-leaves, on another occasion, through an upper-storey window, against a
background of pine; and she was carried away by the charm of
the coming and going of vehicles, depositing the girls at the
door, on a winter morning. How picturesque this bustle of
omnibus, carriage, hack and sleigh amidst the whirling snow
and biting wind. She responded to the first note of the wood-
thrush in spring as well as to the woodbine leaves, the white
orchis and sumac that she brought home from walks in the
woods in October. Sometimes William Hamilton Gibson came
out for a Sunday at the Seminary, talking about fungi, spiders,
flowers and birds, and then everything that had life crept or
flew for her or expanded along the horizon of his conversation.
An occasional moment seemed to her "wholly divine," when
she stepped to the window, for instance, while her classes were
changing, and looked at the phenomena of nature out of doors.
The dry rustling of the brown leaves reminded her of her rela-

tion to it, or the silent slow falling flakes against the evergreen hedge; and a golden branch, struck by the sun, opened the portals of an unseen world for her as well as for Æneas. Then the sudden clashing of the school-bell brought her mind fluttering down again to scratch among the gravel for grains to nourish her brood.

Once, in her sitting-room, while she was reading Lowell aloud, she felt a sudden thrill as if her "friend" were near, and she was so affected that her face flushed and her attention wandered from the reading. The thought flashed through her that he might have left the body simply in order to share in her pleasant employment, and she made no effort to repel the influence when her companion asked for the time,—it was five minutes before ten o'clock in the evening. Was this the result of their recent discussions of the Psychical Society, or her reading of Balzac's *Ursula* or what not? Or was it one of Wordsworth's "strange fits of passion I have known"? Minutes became hours before she felt "wholly withdrawn from the influence." It happened that her circle had been for a while concerned with planchette, which sent messages from an unknown cousin in Constantinople, while, saying that its own name was "At No Man's Disposal," it talked about "Nefter, the place where undeveloped souls go." The circle, however, did not long encourage these peeps into the spirit world when Miss Kenyon's niece from Radcliffe began to hear raps, and, meanwhile, her "friend" made bodily appearances every year,—he was a regular visitor at the Seminary.

Who was this "Mr. B." to whom Miss Kenyon referred so often? He was Harrison Gray Otis Blake, Thoreau's most intimate friend, perhaps, to whom at least he had written most constantly and fully. The two had camped out on Monadnock together, and Thoreau had used in *Walden* long passages from

AT THE SEMINARY 45

his own letters to Mr. Blake, who had been appointed executor
of his literary papers and had published a series of volumes selected from the journals. One of those Unitarian ministers who
had withdrawn from the pulpit because the least weight of
theology was too heavy for them, twice married and twice be-
reaved, he had retired with an income to a life of literary leisure in his birthplace, Worcester. There he discussed with a
friend, on Sunday afternoons, the theory of evolution and
metaphysics. He had been one of the seven members of the
Harvard class at the Divinity School whom Emerson had addressed in 1838, shocking the old guard in that "refulgent
summer," and he found, as he wrote to Miss Kenyon, that for
him at sixty-five life had a profounder beauty than when he
had been young. With all his fluctuating moods, he still agreed
with Emerson that "the night was made for the day, not the
day for the night," and, telling Miss Kenyon the story of his
life, he asked for hers in turn,—what had been her history,
what had been her experiences? "I felt hardly worthy," he then
replied, "to be the correspondent of one who has struggled so
nobly and conquered so bravely . . . somewhat as Thoreau may
have felt after receiving a certain letter from Mrs. Emerson."
He quoted Thoreau again as "expecting the visitor who never
came," meaning that no one living could approach his ideal,
but for seventeen years before he died he wrote to Miss Kenyon
constantly and almost as constantly came to see her. It pleased
him, as he drew near the town, to leave the train at some station near by and approach his friend on foot, walking into
Plainfield.

When and where had they first met? At Concord in 1879,
at the sessions of the School of Philosophy and the house of the
Alcotts, where Louisa Alcott had remarked to them that men
were "not practical" and that she was "not philosophical," nei-

ther were her sisters. At the school, Miss Kenyon wrote, "Mr. Blake's silence was the finest thing said," and they walked together to Thoreau's grave and rowed on Walden pond, which was desecrated already by human innovation. For there were boat-houses on the beach and boats full of noisy girls profaned the spot where Thoreau had once embarked. They picnicked on the river, botanizing, even discovering arrow-heads of white quartz, and, sitting on the bridge that arched the flood, Mr. Blake read aloud some of the letters that Emerson had written to him. They read *The Ring and the Book* together in a grove of hemlocks beside the stream, for Browning was his favourite poet as well as hers, and he was happy that there was "another so grand realm in which we may meet," as he presently wrote in one of his letters from Worcester. They looked forward to many such readings, talking freely as they read, prepared for disagreements on other matters, permitting the widest differences so that their intercourse might rest on a basis that could not readily be shaken. He gave her fragments of Thoreau's handwriting and first editions of all his books, and she suggested that he should make the pocket edition of "Thoreau's Thoughts" that was to find more readers than any of them.

Meanwhile, they discussed in their letters all manner of questions, hoping, as Mr. Blake wrote, that "we may seek in the right way and help each other by our experience and insight." He was devoted to Fénelon, who seemed to condemn him for being "too eager and anxious for celestial moods," defeating his own aim thereby, but, although he enjoyed the long walks that made one content with life and the world, he still believed in "the attitude of expectation." He had found in certain late experiences "hints of eternal life," as if "time and the world might be dropped without any real loss." She, on her side, compared Carlyle and Emerson. With what noise and how much smoke Carlyle drilled and blew up the rocks in his way while Emerson remained quietly and serenely the master, putting down into the crevices the delicate rootlets that silently grew so that the rocks were broken without noise or smoke. When the correspondents were unable to meet they wondered if this, in itself, might not in some way enhance their relation because it would increase the "other treasure"; and they reciprocally thought of themselves as prisms that "sift the sunbeams," unlike the sort of people who "intercept the light." Rejoicing in his "calm exalted nature," Miss Kenyon wrote poems "To H.G.O.B.," and once she blamed herself because he had not come. "Had I set myself to the music which he hears," she wrote in her journal, "he would have drawn near to listen; but I have deliberately filled my hours with the worldly activity and bustle which he abhors. How could he approach? He will scarcely come until I call him, strongly, irresistibly. Shall I? Can I? Let me not tempt an adverse destiny by anxiety or haste."

Elsewhere she spoke of Michelangelo and his relation to Vittoria Colonna as "more beautiful to me than ever"; and did she not perhaps feel that her relation to Mr. Blake had somewhat the same character as theirs? Michelangelo had been sixty-three and the austere Marchioness forty-six,—virtually their own ages,—when the relation began; but there came a moment in Miss Kenyon's case when she must have been aware that her own feeling was not entirely Platonic. One day she found on the table downstairs a letter from her friend which she slipped at once into her black silk bag, planning to read it when the tumult of the day was over,—conscious that his summer visit had not been what it should have been, she had urged him to repeat it in October. Then, at last opening the letter, what did she find?—that he had gone off to Mount

Mansfield and another lady had written to him, asking him to visit her in New Hampshire. This lady had sent him a mere postal card, yet he had spent a day with her, and she had joined him for another day's trip in the mountains. What two or three earnest letters of her own had asked for and not received, a simple postcard from another had gained,—his presence; and, well as Miss Kenyon knew that she herself lacked beauty and charm, she felt nevertheless stung to the core. Thoughts, many of them no doubt unjust, surged through her and kept her awake all night, and she rose thinking of what he had said, that every friendship ends in tragedy, to which she had replied that *theirs could not.* For, she had said, "We only wait for what is given, demanding nothing." And could she say this now?—could she think it any longer? "Here," she felt obliged to think, "here is the fitting and final end," for "I see I have expectations, demands even." Yet this was not the end, by any means. His visits increased, on the contrary,—his letters now came every week,—and she wrote, "We are both older and calmer every year," though she noted that his birthday, April 10th, was usually cold and snowy and the buds of the cherry tree seemed always late. On his return from the World's Fair in Chicago in 1893, they still read Browning together,—*The Ring and the Book,*—and on the verandah after dinner they talked about the "angel guest, seeking the angel in every human being." Even after his first stroke and against the judgment of his friends he insisted on coming to see her and stayed for a week. She met him in the city and took him back for a last good-bye, for they both knew they would never meet again.

Years before this, on a tour of Europe with George P. Bradford, the old Brook Farmer, Mr. Blake had gone out of his way to stop at Turin to meet Miss Kenyon's other great friend, to whom she had given him a letter, the "Martha Washington of Hungary," Louisa Ruttkay. "I know well what you say," he wrote, "that to meet a true and noble person is better than seeing Europe," and he was not disappointed, nor was Madame Ruttkay, who was living with her brother, the "Liberator," Louis Kossuth. In glowing terms she wrote to Miss Kenyon about him. At that time, in 1881, he had seen Miss Kenyon only once, although they had since exchanged photographs and letters, and he was bursting with curiosity,—"Tell me *all* about Miss Kenyon!" he had exclaimed at the outset of this meeting in Turin. "I will not repeat what I said," Madame Ruttkay then wrote. "You know so well what my heart, overflowing in love to you, can dictate. His face (that noble face!) was beaming with joy and he said, 'That is just how her letters have impressed me'. The clear ringing laugh which burst from his lips every time I touched upon your individuality sounded to me like the fresh irrepressible joy of one who had found a treasure for which he was searching a long time. How well I recognized the young soul in that eye arched by a time-bleached brow. Your tact will tell you what use to make of the description of the short but very pleasant call. Only do not let prejudices enter into your decision. Those are only fit food for the crowd, and its mediocrity, but not for your developed soul."

What were these prejudices that Madame Ruttkay had in mind as she fostered this little romance through the middle eighties? Mainly, of course, the question of age, for "it is hard to be ridiculed when time," as she wrote, "has bleached our hair." She knew this well herself, for she was as old as Mr. Blake, and "only when you have attained our age will you understand the trials of a pure aspiring soul imprisoned in a withered frame . . . Do not condemn him, my dearest." As a widow, she too had known all this, "in contact with a gifted person of unusual intellect, a kind heart and attractive manners and appearance." Was this conceivably Colonel T., her brother's younger comrade-in-arms who had lived with them so long in the country near Turin, in the villa with the terrace that faced the Alps? Mr. Blake's demeanour was contradictory, but her friend should not be surprised by that, for the more contradiction there was in it the more affection he had for her and the battle he was fighting against prejudice so much the harder. Let her friend be careful not to break over misunderstandings in letters, "for I should be very much mistaken if there is not *real* congeniality in your characters . . . He who through his soul to triumph over feverish excitements continues to love goes to the grave fresh and young, if he has lived a proper life. But because the majority of humanity does not live the proper life the world looks on love in advanced life with ridicule . . . You do not know how often I am looking at you, in the abundance of my love, praying for you and fearing for you that the battle will be hard because, according to the light, the shadows must fall!"

As the years continued and the battle went against them both,—for Mr. Blake was, as he said, an "undecided person,"— this question dropped out of a correspondence that was prolonged for twenty years, from 1875 to 1894. In that year Louis Kossuth died,—"my brother, protector and loving companion," as Madame Ruttkay wrote to her "darling friend," and she herself, at seventy-eight, returned to die in Budapest, from which she had been exiled for forty-five years. Her friendship with Miss Kenyon had begun just after the Civil War, in which two of her sons had fought, the boys she had brought to the United States who had joined the Northern army, one becoming a major, another a colonel. She had followed Kossuth

when he came over in 1851 and toured the country in triumph like another Lafayette, the "guest of the nation," the
romantic hero that Garibaldi also was and virtually as much in
England and France as well. His family had been banished
from Austria with him, and Madame Ruttkay had fled with
him to Turkey,—in 1849,—where he had been imprisoned for a
while. She had lived in Plainfield off and on, where one of her
sons continued to live,—although she was to survive all three
by many years,—and where she had found with Miss Kenyon
"a home in days when I needed it most," she wrote, "suffering
from loneliness, crying for companionship." For the last fifteen years of her brother's life she had lived with him in Italy,
returning for brief occasional visits to this country,—to "my
only friend," as she called Miss Kenyon, "to whom I can open
the recesses of my heart," for "you are to me *what none* of my
friends are." She visited the Concord School of Philosophy
with this "precious daughter of my love," sending her regards
later to Mr. Alcott, and she too read Browning aloud with
Miss Kenyon, delighting also in "Thoreau's Thoughts," which
she read fifteen minutes every day. On her bookcase in Turin
stood likenesses of Ruskin and Herbert Spencer, and she asked
Miss Kenyon for a photograph of John Fiske, together with
one of Emerson, to place beside them.

Her earlier letters had been written from the villa, with the
fish-pond and the terrace, which they had been obliged to
abandon, outside Turin, after Louis Kossuth had brought back
from his botanical excursions no less than four thousand Alpine
plants. Fourteen years older than herself, he was still able at
eighty-seven to walk, without stopping, more than three hours
a day, and every year he had gone for a while to one of the
Swiss valleys,—"full of the spirit of excursions,"—or perhaps
Lake Como. Once he had spent two months in Naples, visit-

ing his son, who was the director of all the railroads there, watching an eruption of Mount Vesuvius that interested him greatly, for he was deep in the study of natural science. But he preferred the mountains, loving those "high locations" that did not agree with Madame Ruttkay,—so that she preferred to stay at home,—always returning with fresh plants to replace some of the older ones that had been "contaminated by civilization." Madame Ruttkay loved what she described as "the charming little tribe of crocuses, primroses and lingering snowbelles" that tried to "lift their little heads above the snowy ice-cover" in March, "facing the chilling blasts of the wind." There stood the touching snowbelle, as she called it, with dark clouds overhead, while it gave gladness and joy to the human eye, bearing up against adversity with courage and submission. It was "easy enough for the rose to be bright and beautiful in the sun." But the snowbelle!—no other flower taught her so much as "this little pilgrim solitary." With all her disappointment and sorrow over the indifference and the death of her sons, with whom her relations had been clouded, she said, by distrust, she had to keep up her courage in the presence of her brother, for he was "easily influenced by sadness."

When the weather had forbidden her taking part in Louis Kossuth's long daily walks, she had walked herself in the greenhouse, with the flowers for companions, joining him when he returned in the study, for he went out in all kinds of weather, even when he was obliged to carry an umbrella. But his brain was busy with astronomy now, with cipher-filled papers spread out before him, and they scarcely exchanged a word before sitting down to dinner. Her brother had a favourite dog, an immense white Newfoundland, that had his own plate by the table and a portion of each dish,—be it the finest dessert, he must have his share,—and, not to be without dainties, as he did not eat pears or grapes, he had his portion of the cheese. Then Madame Ruttkay was obliged to peel chestnuts for him, after which the cat Minnie had to be fed, and all this took an hour before they went into the billiard-room, where her brother made the balls fly for an hour or so. At eight they took their seats at the whist table. Her brother was kind and affectionate,—even as she was writing he came into the room to show her some rosebuds plucked in January; but they had no neighbours there and, as Madame Ruttkay said, "Seclusion is uncongenial to me . . . I chafe under the separation from the great imperfect human family, and my soul cannot expand without human sympathy and contact." Her brother himself had been in frequent intercourse with Mazzini until his death in 1872, but he had become so accustomed to solitude that the effort of conventionalities had now become almost unbearable to him. Mr. Blake had also had this "obstinate love of seclusion" that so many superior men shared with him, and this was the only fault she had found in Thoreau, who was "one of Nature's high priests." How much deeper in the human heart he would have planted his beautiful thoughts if he had lived closer to humankind. Her brother also turned his back on sympathetic gestures that would have influenced humanity, as it seemed to her. But, lonely as she was, and remained in Turin, she had drawn lessons of endurance and calm from the view on their terrace of the range of snow-covered peaks. How the Alps proclaimed the power of God with their shining granite faces! The setting sun tinted them every minute with a different luminosity, from the soberest purple to the brightest yellow and red, raising and expanding her heart with that glorious sight.

But they had been driven into Turin by an untoward incident that made it impossible for them to continue in the village. They were Unitarians, and when their friend Colonel T.

died the villagers rose against their Protestantism. While the
Vaudois minister was reading the burial service, they shouted
insulting remarks into his ears, hooting and laughing at them
all, in a demonstration managed by the priests, so that they almost expected to be assailed with stones. "My poor old brother
said, 'Such an insult was never done to me in my life!' You may
well imagine our indignation," Madame Ruttkay wrote; and
Louis Kossuth and his sons decided that the coffin could not be
left, exposed to some further outrage, in the village. So they at
once arranged for a proper funeral in Turin, "with all the military pomp due to their old friend's station." The burial took
place in the Protestant cemetery there, and then, for two weeks,
for a change of scene, they had all gone to San Remo. But
Louis Kossuth had been deeply moved, he had wept like a
child at his friend's death, and the emotion had been prolonged, as Madame Ruttkay said, by the inhuman action of
these soi-disant Christians. Inasmuch as, besides, they were remote from medical assistance, the sons were unwilling for them
to remain in the village, so, selling the villa, they had settled in
the city, laboriously moving her brother's collections and his
library of more than three thousand books. The solitude of the
winter would have been almost unbearable without the society
of their dear old friend, and Turin had so many public gardens
that one did not miss the country there as much as one might
have missed it in other cities. They had taken an apartment
with windows opening on one of these beautiful parks with
flowers and a great fountain facing their parlour, "shooting
high its lively drops that chase one another like so many flying
diamonds," as Madame Ruttkay put it. "When I step on the
balcony I feel I am in a garden. But I miss my beautiful Alps
with their snowy caps and their shifting shadows and clouds
gilded by the rays of the sinking sun."

There, as before, she had few social pleasures,—in any case, difficult for "one of my age and my past,"—partly because she hesitated to accept invitations when she was so seldom able to return them. Her brother never went anywhere and he was disturbed by the least social interruption, and she rarely went out in the evening because she did not "like to come home with the valet." She met a few French people of the Vaudois society, a few Italian countesses and the English in Turin,—she visited on Lake Como the wife of the English consul; but she had found society very limited in this town, where almost everything "overstepped the boundaries of womanhood." It was restricted to tea and whist, a little mediocre piano-playing and a few admiring remarks about pretty toilettes; while, as for her own toilette, she was not shabby, and that was really all one could say about it. However, if her family life had not been so frigid, it would all have been quite pleasant; but her brother had no time for demonstrations of affection. He was very good to her,—he had just left the breakfast-table provoked with himself because he had eaten a peach which he was afraid was the best in the dish,—but he was absorbed in his books and manuscripts, writing his memoirs, volume by volume, and working regularly nine or ten hours a day. This harrowed up the past for him, he came to his meals "with a flushed face as if he were in a fever," and "emotion," as Madame Ruttkay said, "is dangerous for aged people,"—she knew that her presence and care were essential for him. His only diversion was to go to his billiard-room with two Italians who came to play with him; but, approaching ninety, he was without any other relation to help in a foreign land in time of need. It was hard to be old, weak and alone in exile! To be sure, his son, Francis Kossuth, the statesman of later years, already famous in Italy, was there at times, but he was a busy civil engineer, director of the sulphur mines and building steel bridges in Egypt over the Nile. Even their good friend Dr. Basso had become unpunctual, fighting with filial devotion against an infirmity that made him a "most pitiable spectacle," Madame Ruttkay said. For he was infatuated with a red-haired Irishwoman in Turin and in consequence he was as negligent as he was distracted. For the rest, "By what trivial means are we often enslaved in our life!" Madame Ruttkay exclaimed in her solitude, as she worked on her memoirs. The servants,—two men, Italians both,—did not understand the Hungarian ways to which her brother was so partial, for, with all his wanderings through the world, he had never changed his habits or his love for "our Hungarian mode of cooking." Changes of diet were impossible at his time of life, so she had to assist in the kitchen, which she found distasteful, "inseparable from bad odours and grease spots on my dress." This kept her, besides, in a nervous condition that was disadvantageous for all mental work.

In her secluded monotonous life, she therefore turned more and more to the "darling friend" who, "though a daughter in years, so thoroughly understood" her "thoughts and foibles," knowing that when the old lame postman brought her one of Miss Kenyon's letters "many a wave" would be "lulled to rest in my tired head." For "you are always the first," she wrote "to whom I send my message of love . . . Your letters are the water of life to me." She only regretted that prolonged separation, while it did not eradicate the love from one's heart, took away some of the "eloquence" of letter-writing, and she craved "the trifling details of daily life to chain our thoughts together . . . You see how persons of Mr. Fiske's mind are attached to you. What attracts people to your house? The intellectual atmosphere which your individuality has diffused there." Had she not known this herself? She had never since found anyone with whom reading, for instance, was such a delight, and there was nothing in Turin to compare with her friend's society, "nothing above kindly everyday chattering." She mentioned a French weekly paper, *La Nature,* which her brother took, suggesting that if her friend subscribed to this review of the sciences it might further their interchange of thought. Then she continued with a word of counsel about managing the school and "your noble and religious work, the education of young children." It was true that in 1874 she had urged Miss Kenyon to give up the school because "systematic occupation fetters high natures,"—why not devote herself to literature?—and Madame Ruttkay had suggested that they might take a house together in which she could spend half the year. She would have to spend the other half with her brother in Europe, but they could support themselves by raising silkworms. Meanwhile, she discussed the authors she was reading, Amiel, who had just died in Geneva, Edgar Quinet's histories and Emerson, whom she enjoyed "beyond expression." How had her friend felt about Emerson's lectures? And was not the true greatness of Herbert Spencer that he put "sympathy" as the regenerating power foremost to lead humanity to final perfection? Miss Kenyon, in turn, sent Madame Ruttkay reports of the Dante lectures she had just heard in Concord, together with some of the American poets whom her friend was eager to know and especially John Fiske's philosophical writings. It was Louis Kossuth who had begged for the photograph of Fiske, for he had been delighted with *The Idea of God,* and he cherished other connections with Miss Kenyon's country. Madame Ruttkay had bought for him *Picturesque America,* which he enjoyed, as she said, "beyond my expectation," and his son Francis, who was pleased with the book, said he would make some oil paintings after a few of the charming woodcuts in it.

How many other questions rose in this lively correspondence, in the seventy-nine long letters of Madame Ruttkay that I was to find years later in a bundle in a trunk,—among them the question of the education of women beyond the role of being wives and mothers. Sad was their state in Europe, or in Italy at least. There were in Turin only three married ladies who did not have lovers,—so her Italian friends told her,—and, alas, for the unmarried. What was to be done for the elevation of women? Then there was Fénelon, Mr. Blake's favourite, whom she had read in the dark hours when her own sorrow had seemed too great to bear. His theme was self-crucifixion, but she herself could only believe in the kind that promoted self-respect. He saw human nature too much as depraved and debased, while she felt that instead of frightening people with overdrawn pictures of corruption and vice one should show the heights it can attain by self-discipline and love. She quoted against Fénelon other French writers who said that his pictures of depravity were unreal and false, existing only in the writer's mind and swallowed by the reader only because he was unwilling to confess that he had less experience of life. Then, regarding the love of God, which meant for her simply the love of virtue, she disagreed again with Fénelon, for, while he taught that to do God's will we must renounce ourselves, for her the divine will was in harmony with our own nature. Why, if we lived rightly, should there be any antagonism between our nature and God's will? Then Madame Ruttkay discussed Rousseau's *Confessions*. Miss Kenyon was reading this, and she was impatient for her friend's opinion, for so many turned away in horror from the book. "I could not find in it this abomination." At one time when she herself had thought of opening a school, a friend had warned her not to leave it on the table, not that she herself had read the book!—O no!— whereupon Madame Ruttkay had given her a lesson. She had felt obliged to say, "You know we can become virtuous only after knowing good *and* evil and *choosing* the good. Otherwise we can only be ignorant."

Madame Ruttkay went on to praise the thirst for knowledge that linked one with the teachers of humanity in a brotherly circle. How much more precious it was than worldly posses- sions! Then she exclaimed in 1889, "I am sure our spirits have met at the grave of Browning. A shining star has set in the intellectual world." Ten years before this she had opened her arms to Miss Kenyon's niece who, as a young art-student, spent a year with her. When this niece became my mother-in-law, I marvelled over the variety of games, each more ingenious than the last, that she knew how to play, games of solitaire that she had learned from Louis Kossuth, who had contrived them to while away the time in prison. Under surveillance in his cell, he had found a place behind the door where the guard could not observe him, and he felt he had saved his mind by inventing these games. My mother-in-law well re- membered the noble-looking old man, with the black velvet smoking cap and the white beard, in the library, with his herbarium, the bust of himself in military dress and two or three good pictures, among his books.

There came a time when Madame Ruttkay wrote to her friend in America, "You must fix me in your memory as hav- ing grown very old." She added that she took comfort in the promise, "According to your days will your strength be"; but she heard the warning, "The evening is at hand, fill your lamp." Those moments of enthusiasm that had once carried her soul above persecution, penury and sorrow appeared now only like so many falling stars, making the darkness more visible after they vanished. "My soul," she said, "is like a harp, the broken cords of which show what it was, not what it is." For a number of years her mind had been turning back to Hungary. To her great joy a Hungarian family had become neighbours in Turin,—the father had shared in the rising in 1848,—and she listened, bowed with emotion, when the daughter and the niece played Hungarian airs on the piano. In fact, she said, "I burst out crying." She noted the excitement over the discovery near Budapest of a great Roman amphitheatre, and, regretting that "our language is not spoken in any other country," she mentioned some of the new Hungarian writers. There was, for instance, a great new work, *The Tragedy of Man,* which her brother considered superior to *Faust* and which was less burdened with the metaphysics that had made Goethe's poem so difficult for her. Then, knowing how poor her country was, without any guide-book to speak of it, she compiled an article to draw the attention of travellers to it, as they were drawn to Italy, Switzerland and France. She meant to show the advantages and the practicability of a trip from Vienna,—so much frequented,—through Budapest to Constantinople; and, touched by the attention and the praises of "our people . . . showered on me by their letters and papers," she longed to go back to her own country.

Perhaps, Madame Ruttkay said, where there was so much to be done,—in Hungary, especially for women,—she might "drop the seed of future harvests." Touching were the manifestations of love and admiration that came to her brother on his birthdays, sheaves of telegrams, hundreds of banquets held at home and albums signed by more than thirty thousand people. In 1889 a delegation of eight hundred and fifty Hungarians came to Turin to protest their loyalty to Kossuth, sending a deposit to the bank of forty thousand lire in order to guarantee their expenses. They were all of the educated class, judges of the supreme court, deputies, professors, lawyers, journalists and artists, and, together with a poet who read an ode, they had brought with them a large iron caisson filled with Hungarian soil. On her brother's ninetieth birthday another delegation wished to come, but a public dispute had arisen about the date. Was it September 19th or was it April 19th? Alas, they could not remember themselves precisely, and the Bible in which their parents had written down their birthdays had been lost when misfortune had scattered them all. Had the Austrians thrown this away, or had it been sold along with her brother's furniture at the public auction? They had been able to remember only the year; and, strange to say, the parish church in which her brother was baptised had been burned with all its records.

Already, when her brother was away at Lake Como, "to still the craving of my heart to live in my native land" she had gone back for a visit, receiving "ovations of an astonishing grandeur," beginning at their father's grave where she found hundreds of people waiting for her. Crowds met the train at every town, with veterans of 1848, deputations, choruses, banquets, torchlight processions, and she was escorted everywhere with banners and throngs of peasants in their native costume. Whole villages had turned out to meet her, and from dawn to dusk she had had to wear her best dress!—and her friend knew that her wardrobe was very slender. But how ironical her life seemed, "a farce of the first order," after those "months of ovation befitting only the most illustrious people," when she returned to Turin. She found her poor brother, at eighty-eight, bent, as usual, over his desk, toiling from seven to eight hours a day to earn his daily bread, finishing the fourth volume of his memoirs. For he had refused pensions from Victor Emmanuel and Napoleon III and would not accept alms from anyone. Besides, she had found the visit very disappointing. The people seemed to have lost all their principles and courage, and her old friends disgusted her by their hyper-loyalty to the present regime to which, in order to hold office, one had to belong. "I saw their eyes looking round to ascertain if there was anyone near to see their hearty welcome to a sister of Kossuth . . . I am willing now to stay and die away."

Nevertheless, when her brother died in 1894, Madame Ruttkay returned to Budapest, and there she remained to the end with her nephew Francis, who devoted the rest of his life to the welfare of their country. Great was the excitement when a crowd of a hundred thousand people met them at the station for the funeral procession, with a specially constructed hearse and six black horses and with nineteen funeral cars and two thousand wreaths. There were black flags and drapery everywhere, for the whole population was in mourning, and Maurus Jókai delivered the funeral oration. But what did this mean for the future of Kossuth's son Francis? Honoured and happy in Italy, he had left that life behind in order to maintain the principles of his father at home, and, as leader of the party of independence, he found himself thwarted at every turn, for the ministers were all sycophants and toadies of the imperial regime. For the happiness of their people how little her dear nephew could do! To the last Louisa Ruttkay was constant to the spirit of 1848,—she remained a child of the year of Revolutions,—faithful as well to her friend in America, that "accomplice of Prometheus," as she called Miss Kenyon, "in stealing the heavenly spark."

CHAPTER IV

MY FORBEARS

IT WAS in the nature of our suburban world that everybody had come from somewhere else, from Philadelphia, New York or Boston or the pre-urban countryside that for me meant Lake Champlain and the valley of the Hudson. At that time attics were domestic museums that evoked a family's past, with spinning-wheels and broken old portraits in corners, and one I knew contained an ark that was packed from the bottom and overflowed with straw-coloured paper money of the continental congress. In ours there were piles of Plutarch's lives, Burns and *Godey's Lady's Book*, Griswold's *Female Poets*, the *Sparrowgrass Papers* and a red morocco music-album including the "Battle of Prague" that my great-grandmother had used at Emma Willard's school. I looked with horror on these mouldy old books, among them the *Travels of Mungo Park*, in "Harper's Family Library," stacked near by, published in the days of Andrew Jackson for whose prodigious hirsute head on certain old stamps we plundered trunks of letters. There was a portable writing-case containing grisly souvenirs, the locks and curls of ancestral hair that literary circles a century ago passed from hand to hand and memorialized in poems, among them curls of the same great-grandmother who had died when she was very young, a friend of the "poetesses of Plattsburg," the Davidson sisters. Her papier-mâché sewing-table, inlaid with mother-of-pearl and lined with old-rose satin, stood there too, suggesting scenes as remote from our Wall Street suburb as any scene, still American, could well be.

Outside there were pink and white peonies brought down from Plattsburg. There they had grown for generations in the legendary garden, the paradisaical garden of which I gathered as a child that people had driven from Albany in flocks to see it. There my great-grandfather had raised figs by some miraculous method of his own, outwitting Nature ten miles from the Canadian border, inventing the apples and the grapes that sometimes bore his name and for which he received the medals that are still in my possession. His grandfather Platt and his three great-uncles had founded the town in 1784, and it was generally assumed by us that the fruit-clusters in the trees there were more splendidly ripe than the fruit in other gardens. Along with my mother's Eastlake furniture and the relics of the blue china craze that had raged at the time of her marriage and were scattered through the house, we were surrounded with Plattsburg spoils, old Canton china, Duncan Phyfe chairs and engravings of Trumbull and West in walnut frames. These scenes from history recalled the part the engravers played in naturalizing an American mind that had broken away from England.

Plattsburg was always to remain for me an emblem of the old agrarian world that seemed more normal for Americans than the world of trade, a European interest, comparatively speaking, when ours was a nation of farmers almost to a man. Had we not lost much in serenity and depth when "business" triumphed over agriculture? I wondered if this older life would not have suited my family better than the life which they had known for two generations since my two grandfathers, "Green Mountain Boys" both, had come to try their fortunes in the city. They had arrived at about the same time as Horace Greeley, who had also come down from Vermont, for the Yankees of this inland state drifted as naturally to New York as the Yankees of the eastern seaboard drifted to Boston. Both had prospered in business there and both had married New York wives,—my Plattsburg grandmother was one of these,— and they had in time become so absorbed in the metropolitan atmosphere that they had lost most of the traces of their original New England. As a child, at least, I heard little of this, while I heard much of "old New York," for even my Plattsburg grandmother had gone to school there, at "the late celebrated Madame Chagaray's," as Henry James called it in one of his stories, where she had acquired her wondrous "Chagaray French." This was a joke with all of us, for my father, who had spent five years in France, had learned *not* to speak the French of Stratford-atte-Bowe, in which, as I later read in a novel of Constance Fenimore Woolson, the girls were taught to "grimace" at my grandmother's school. Miss Woolson, who was also a pupil there,—Fenimore Cooper's grand-niece,—described the school in *Anne* as Madame Moreau's, where "the extreme of everything called accomplishment" was taught, with a "vast deal of nonsense in the latest style." With grimacing in French this included "squalling" in Italian,—as an ill-natured parent said in the novel,—actually taught by Lorenzo da Ponte, who had written the libretto of *Don Giovanni* and of Mozart's *Figaro* and *Così fan tutte* as well. Julia Ward Howe had been his pupil at Madame Chagaray's, that good-hearted little old Frenchwoman whom everyone called Tante, with a plain black satin dress and a shrewd face. A special friend of my grandmother there had been one of the granddaughters of Fenimore Cooper, whom she visited at Cooperstown in Otsego Hall.

During these years, off and on, my grandmother had lived with her "Uncle Nat," the universal family benefactor, whose villa at Fordham was to house in time the priests of the Catholic Orphan Asylum that stood in his old grounds overlooking the Harlem valley. His venerable relict Aunt Eliza was one to whom my brother and I were obliged to pay an annual visit of obeisance in the upstairs cabinet in which she sat, in lavender satin and lace, looking out at the Stanford White tower of Madison Square Garden. I recall this daughter of Jacob Lorillard as like some ancient bonze, enthroned, presumably forever, in a Buddhist shrine, one to whom only words of ceremony were ever addressed by anyone, to thank her, in our case, for the goldpieces that she sent us at Christmas. Then there was Cousin Walter Jones upon whom we had to call because he also gave us goldpieces at Christmas and whose middle initials, "R.T.," signified "Returned Twice," whereby hung a tale that had once been told me. But how many dim cavernous New York abodes, crammed with bric-a-brac, draped with plush, with tasselled sofas and whatnots, knickknacks and easels, filled with vague awe my suburban eyes, accustomed to the bright openness and the unencumbered windows of our semi-rural dwellings. These dusky domestic interiors put me in mind of Egyptian tombs, each more Cimmerian than any of the others, dark indeed yet not too dark to be filled for a child with colossal shadows that sometimes materialized as the widows of old-fashioned merchants. Nebulous pier-glasses mounted upward until they were lost in cloudy ceilings, and there were massive doors that were never opened or that, being open, were never shut. There were pictures, spoils of the old world and redolent of grand tours that had culminated in Rome and Raphael, or sometimes native products of old New York, relieved by portraits of gazelle-eyed young women with naked drooping shoulders and with lyrebirds or parrots perched on their uplifted hands. How often in later years I wonderingly passed those brownstone fronts now plastered with the gilded letters of retail trade. I scarcely knew how I was related to the multitude of cousins with whom my parents cherished their connection, even as I gathered, to the third and the fourth generation, and with whom they talked about Dr. Dix or Mr. Dodsworth, the dancing-master, or the organist of Grace Church, Mr. Helfenstein. Or about Miss Comstock's school where my mother had gone in West Fortieth Street and where, as one of her old beaux told me when he and she were both eighty-six, she had let down little notes on a string from her window.

Of my Brooks grandparents I knew little, for both had vanished before I was born, but they too savoured in their fashion of old New York, where my grandfather had been a cotton-broker, buying his cotton in the South, storing it in his warehouse and shipping it to England. An old law-clerk of one of my uncles told me that his first house had stood on Broadway near the corner of Rector Street, where his family had lived on the lower floors while the third floor was the loft where the cotton was kept till the ships were ready to receive it. Sometime in the eighteen-forties he had moved to "modest" Macdougal Street,—as an old New York story-teller called it,—where my father was born, rising as his fortunes rose to the house that he built on Lexington Avenue, 279, just above 36th Street. But his fortunes fell when the Civil War destroyed the Cotton Kingdom and ended his own connection, as a merchant, with England, so that he was obliged to declare himself a bankrupt, though he subsequently repaid his creditors dollar for dollar when he had become the manager of a department-store. I assume from this that he was not only what Ruskin called his father, an "entirely honest merchant," but able as well, though beyond this I know little about him except what I find in the portrait of him that Charles Loring Elliott painted in the eighteen-fifties. In its Washington Irving pose this typifies the moment.

As for my grandmother Brooks, she was half of Dutch descent, while her father was the Irishman of whom I delighted in hearing as a child because, as I was told, he had come over in a barrel. Had he *lived* in the barrel for weeks and weeks, and, in that case, how had he been fed? Or had he been merely *rolled* on to the ship in a barrel, after which he had emerged on deck like a robin from its shell? No one could answer these questions that simmered in my mind. My great-grandfather was one of those rebels who had fled from Ireland with a price on their heads,—in Emmet's rebellion, I think, though of this I am not sure,—escaping as Hugo Grotius had escaped from prison in a chest that was carried out supposedly filled with soiled linen for the laundry. During his last illness, my father told me, the doctor had purloined his books, two or three of these each time he came,—the more valuable Greek and Latin books,—depositing them in the library of the New York Historical Society, which was then down-town. I tried to find them there years later, but could not trace them in the multitude of books,—I might have been looking for minnows in the open ocean. On her other side, my grandmother was a great-granddaughter of Henry Wisner, the well-known powder-maker of the Revolution who brought the great chain down from Poughkeepsie with his friend Gilbert Livingston and stretched it across the Hudson to stop the British ships. Greatly affected, as he wrote, by Thomas Paine's *Common Sense* and possessing a "strong predilection for republican institutions," he was the only New York member of the first Continental

Congress who voted,—against instructions,—for independence.

Not only had my father's father and mother died some years before I was born but my father was a semi-invalid in the years when I knew him, so that his youth and his family connection were more or less veiled for me and came to me rather like scenes from some old novel. I remember the office in Nassau Street in which he carried on a business that every day grew more fictitious as the "National Nickel Company," whose name was blazoned on the door, along with my father's name, faded out. With the big seal and the letter-press, a hogshead of ore stood near the desk to show the quality of the nickel that existed in the mine, but I was told that the nickel was too far down to be readily worked and the mine itself was too far from the Nevada railroad. How to finance it all, how to get down far enough and how then to transport the precious metal, this was the problem that wore my father to the shadow he became, he who had once been so gay and who remained so witty. The mine was like Colonel Sellers's Tennessee land or Colonel Carter of Cartersville's visionary railroad, and almost every family we knew followed some such mirage in the West, oil in the Indian Territory, copper in Montana. For years my father had lived like Tantalus plunged in water up to the chin with unreachable fruit-laden branches over his head, and the worst of the irony of it was that he had once owned a world-famous mine and traded it for this chimera in the Nevada mountains. I still have an indenture showing that he had bought in San Francisco, for fifteen thousand dollars, in 1880, the Arizona copper-mine from which a Boston company later drew sixty-eight millions supplying the United States mint.

Had my father been miscast in life? Had he chosen the wrong role to play or had he been assigned this role by "Mr.

Leighton," the partner, seventeen years older than himself, who had snatched him at the college gate and thrust him, like the devil himself, into the Wall Street inferno? For so I read the story, filled as my own fancy was with scenes from four-teenth-century Italian painters. It was Mr. Leighton who, tak-ing my father as a junior partner in his early twenties, had sent him to Europe for ten years to represent the firm, but, sure as I felt that my father should never have been a business man, I was melodramatic, no doubt, in my view of the case. I feared and hated business and saw it as the Moloch that devoured whatever was best in the American mind,—which prepared me to become a socialist a few years later,—but in all probability Mr. Leighton was in no special way to blame and really got less out of life even than my father. For, caring much for money, he lost his great place on Long Island, where he had had a stud of racing-horses, and, condemned to living obscurely uptown, he could not pay the German "boy" who continued, without wages, to care devotedly for him. I remember the old man,—Stutz beside him,—in his small office near Printing-house Square, with the glittering eye of a Quintin Matsys miser, hovering over the ticker-tape as if at any moment some number might mean millions again for him.

But, thinking of my father's youth, I can imagine that he felt like Mark Twain's young man in *The Gilded Age* for whom there was nothing but success in all his wide horizon and to whom the paths to fortune seemed innumerable and open. It had never appeared so easy to "go into something," Mark Twain said, as it seemed on Broadway then on a spring morning when one was walking cityward past the long line of "palace shops," listening to the hum and roar of the multi-tudinous traffic. It was Philip Sterling who felt this way as he too thought of the mine in the West that ultimately made him a "person of consideration," in those days when the newspapers were full of mining news, the jargon of mining-camps and mining-stock quotations. What glamour Bret Harte's stories and Mark Twain's books threw over the mines in that epoch of great mining fortunes and the romance of the West, the glamour that haloed the paintings of Albert Bierstadt and Thomas Moran that were everywhere to be seen in public buildings. In the intervals of his life abroad, my father had known all of this when he too had gone to San Francisco, crossing Arizona in a Deadwood coach, surrounded, as I pictured the scene, with howling Apaches. I saw him later in Bret Harte's tales as one of the young men who appeared from New York representing "Eastern capitalists" investigating mines; and after his death I always carried the lucky silver dollar that he had picked up in San Francisco. It was a Mexican dollar with the Emperor Maximilian's head that had jingled in his pocket for thirty years and that I lost ten years later, after it had travelled over half the world, on the day when I arrived in the city where my father had found it. Wherever I went, in whatever I read, I seemed to find my father then, in Menlo Park, in far Wyoming, where one of his friends was a ranchman, in the Garden of the Gods in Colorado. Especially I thought of him in the dead mining towns with chimney-stacks standing forlorn amid broken walls and with furnaces built by New York companies to smelt ore that was never found and that lay now half buried in sand and sagebrush. One saw coyotes wandering through streets, once lined with churches and saloons, where lizards basked now on heaps of wreckage, ruins so time-worn, silent and grey that they might have been as old as the ruins of which Volney had written a century before.

My father had never gone West again after those first exciting years when he had already faced the other way, when "going to Paris," as people said, was almost the only alternative to going into an office or a store. How lucky my father must have felt that he was going to Paris, where he lived in the rue Gluck behind the opera-house, when he was not in London, or in Brussels, or The Hague, cities in which he also spent five years. I felt as if I had lived myself, in some previous incarnation, in all these enchanting places I heard so much of, places that in a sense I saw in the souvenirs of all of them that filled, with the Plattsburg relics, every corner of the house. There hung the big painting by Van Heemskerck van Beest that my father had bought in Amsterdam, where the artist, so amusingly named, had actually lived,—indeed, there were two of them, father and son, whose pictures were in the museum there, as a Dutch professor told me many years later. Wonderful to me, this name,—too good, or too Dutch, to be true,—endowing with humour and mystery alike the sea-scape in which I saw a survival, a last weak remnant, of the great Dutch school. This was the artist whom Thoreau encountered, strange to relate, at Fairhaven, near the Yankee port of New Bedford, as he wrote in his journal—"the well-known Dutch painter of marine pieces" by name "Van Beest," who "talked and looked particularly Dutchman like." The entry in Thoreau's journal was dated 1855; but was it the father or the son with whom Thoreau had fallen in and whom my father encountered twenty years later?

With how many other mementos of my father's life in Europe my infant eyes were familiar,—the red sandstone column, a copy of Hadrian's column, brought from Rome, the prancing Richard Cœur de Lion, the dancing figures, also in bronze, that turned into candlesticks when one removed their hats. There were albums of lithographic "views" of Paris and

Touraine, the châteaux of Seine et Oise in soft light colours, carved Swiss figures redolent for me of edelweiss and alpenstocks, bottle-stoppers also carved grotesquely. There were rows of French yellowback novels and a painting of Chillon, where the so much poetized prisoner languished in the dark, another of the falls of Schaffhausen and a chest brimming over with European scenes that one scarcely had to open one's eyes to see. There was the fountain at Brussels, so dear to Americans, the Mannikin, and pictures from the Musée Wiertz, the mad rich Belgian painter whose vision was a singular mixture of Rubens and Poe. How well I knew that chamber of horrors with the headless corpse on the guillotine, the suicide, the man buried alive, Napoleon in hell and the lunatic mother in the act of dismembering her child, which I was not forbidden to see as I was forbidden to *read*,—precisely because of its horrors,—the novel *Quo Vadis?* Then there were double photographs that one slipped into the stereoscope, still more thrilling so miraculously round were the objects and people one saw in this, so that one seemed to be *in* the panorama.

I never even began to guess how my father had spent these years abroad from which he had brought back certain ceremonious ways, removing his hat, for instance, not only when funeral processions passed but when he encountered men as well as women. Once he had had occasion to take his hat off to Napoleon III when he was crossing the park at Chislehurst in England and the exiled emperor, walking alone, approached on a diagonal path and gravely took off his hat and bowed to him. My father had bought at the Tuileries, at the auction of 1873, a set of Napoleon dinner-plates which we had in the house, together with a sable cloak that the Empress Eugénie had supposedly worn and that was kept in a box in a closet upstairs. What a part this imperial pair played in the American imagination, still played, indeed, when I was growing up and when we had neighbours who were second cousins of the Empress Eugénie, after whom my mother as a girl had named her doll. These neighbours were also grandchildren of the empress's American grandfather, the old consul at Malaga in Spain, and I remember hearing that the empress, who never wore anything twice, sent boxes of finery to these cousins in far-off New Jersey.

Nothing could have been more romantic than European royalty in American eyes,—the Bonnie Prince Charlie, for instance, after whom my father had been named Charles Edward, as others bore the ducal names of Clarence and Percy. But my father's old life was a mystery to me, his life at the Langham, for instance, in London, the vast hotel in Portland Place that stood through the second world war, bombed and gutted. There, where he had lived so long, where he took my mother on their honeymoon later, had he not often seen Mark Twain, who was living there at the same time, and Ouida, who had her salon in the same hotel? Its one discomfort, my grandmother wrote, when she had stayed at the Langham, was that she had only sperm candles in her bedroom, though she added, "I am told that the English like the gloom." My father had been quite accustomed to living without gas-jets. For the rest, to rebuke my lack of interest in something,—I do not remember what,—he told me of an incurious man he had met in London whom he had asked in the city one day, as he was passing the Monument, what this flame-topped tower represented. "Young man," the Englishman replied, "I have passed that tower every day for twenty-eight years and never thought to ask." One moment of my father's life deeply impressed me. He had arranged to sail home on the "Ville de Paris" in 1874, and he was on his way to the train that would have taken him to Le Havre when something in him warned him not to sail. This premonition was so strong that he went at once to the steamship office, cancelled his passage and cabled to his mother in New York that he was coming home on the following steamer. That was the voyage on which the "Ville de Paris" vanished. No trace was ever found of it again.

Earlier still, my father had belonged to one of the volunteer fire companies that raced to fires with gorgeous fire-engines, almost as gay as Sicilian carts, with scarlet ladders and vignettes that were painted by John Quidor and other good artists. He had witnessed the burning of Barnum's Museum,—he had a picture of the scene, the ruined building covered with icicles and snow,—in the days when he had learned by heart, as I supposed in my childhood, all the operas of all the Italian composers. For which opera did he *not* know by Verdi, Donizetti, Bellini, Rossini,—whom his mother described in her diary as "our favourite composer,"—from *Lucia* to *La Sonnambula* and *The Daughter of the Regiment*, from *Norma, Traviata* and *Aïda* to *The Barber of Seville*. They were the operas whose arias and recitatives had passed into the rhythms of Whitman's *Leaves of Grass*,—for Whitman wrote some of his poems while listening to them,—and for me this taste was always a part of old New York, where Lorenzo da Ponte had first introduced it.

Many a time my other grandmother had seen this old man at Madame Chagaray's,—the grandmother who brought me up or to whom I felt closer than I felt to my mother, for I was bound to her with special ties. She had married a son of Fisher Ames, the namesake of his kinsman, the Boston orator of the post-Revolutionary epoch. But, fond as I was of my grandfather, it was her forbears who interested me, for they seemed so vital and so picturesque, the admiral-uncle who had captured New Orleans as Farragut's second-in-command and others whose portraits hung on the dining-room walls. Near by hung a painting of my grandmother's great-grandfather "raising the first liberty-pole in the Revolution," the farmer-colonel who had lived in Poughkeepsie where the Baileys and Platts intermingled and whence they spread to Plattsburg and New York. My grandmother's great-uncle Chancellor Kent had been living when she was a child in New York, where another great-uncle was postmaster for twenty-six years and where her brother, the lieutenant in the navy who died in Charleston harbour, was a young lawyer before the Civil War. There lived that other uncle, too, whose drawing-room Robert Weir pictured in the semblance of Scott's house, "Abbotsford," with the family and their dogs gathered round the fire, a picture that worked, with others I saw, on a child's imagination like certain stories I heard of long-dead cousins. To one of these a "British officer," uncommemorated otherwise, had presented the "British Poets" in their greenish box, the fifty small volumes over which I used to pore,—"one of the greatest belles of the last generation," as Philip Hone wrote in his diary in 1839. This was the year in which she died, "a girl of seventy-nine years . . . lightsome and gay," as Philip Hone put it, whose Wall Street house had been the "resort of all the fashionable gallants of the day" and remained, he said, "the standard of elegance and taste." In her last illness she re-fused to receive any visitors, leaving orders that no one was to see her after death, unwilling as she was that those who had known her when she was beautiful and young should witness the progress of decay.

Although the links were growing thin that bound her to the Plattsburg past, my grandmother kept up her connection with it, and I dimly remember my great-grandfather, that Luther

Burbank of the north, with a Paisley shawl wrapped round
him, sitting by the fire. In his youth he had been for a while
a planter near New Orleans,—where my grandmother had
been to a school that still exists,—at a time when so many men
from New York and New England were settling in Louisiana
and Mississippi. But, unable to endure the climate there, he
had returned to spend his life in the old Plattsburg house
with the long driveway that was lined with locust trees and
a buckthorn hedge, the house that my grandmother sold after
his death, destroying the barrels of papers that she found in
the attic. She had these brought down and dumped in the
garden, where they were burned like leaves, though a few of
the papers blew off in the wind, and someone noticed that one
of these was a letter that George Washington had written to
my grandmother's great-grandfather in Poughkeepsie. When
I saw this later in an uncle's house, I wondered what else had
rekindled the flames of this all too final holocaust in the ancestral garden.

As for my own great-grandfather, I was five when I saw
him, as he had been seven when the Battle of Plattsburg occurred, and I recently discovered an old interview with him in
which he related his memories of it. He had picked up on the
family grounds, after the battle, the cannon-balls that were
piled in a pyramid in the circle of the driveway, although he
must have had some help, for there were more than fifty of
these and a few of them were 32-pounders. They were missiles
of the American troops who had bombarded the old stone
house because they knew the British had commandeered it.
That was in 1814 when his father had taken the family away,
seven or eight miles, to a neighbouring farm, for safety, while
his grandfather, Captain Nathaniel Platt, refused to leave the
place and stayed there with the British general and his staff.

During the Revolution, before he had gone to Poughkeepsie, he had raised the first company of soldiers on Long Island, and he said he had never turned his back on a redcoat yet and did not propose to do it then. When one of the younger officers insolently asked him who he was, he replied, "Captain Platt of the Revolution, and be damned to you, young man," and, when the Yankee ships won the fight, he said to the officers, "Wait till tomorrow and you will be 'Burgoyned,' every soul of you." They broke camp and left that night, burning the fences behind them. Yet after the war the British general sent the old man a dinner-service of which two plates remained when I was a boy. How little attention historians have paid to the indignation of the country squires as one of the main causes of the wars with England, the local notabilities who had ceased to feel they were subjects of the king and regarded the British simply as impudent invaders. Like all dependent people who have reached a certain stage of growth, they resented their own position as colonials or "natives," though sometimes, far from democratic, they thought of themselves as predestined to rule, while expecting other folk to vote as they were told. What led the Ogdens of Ogdensburg, the Gansevoorts of Gansevoort, the Coopers of Cooperstown and the Platts of Plattsburg to settle in these northern wildernesses? Partly the hope of perpetuating the landed aristocracy that was already dying even in New York state. The magniloquence of the inscriptions on some of their tombs matched the proud faces that one saw in the portraits of Trumbull and S. F. B. Morse, Sharples and William Dunlap who came up to paint them.

One could easily trace in the records of any of these families the inner struggle that marked the Revolutionary time, or the years after the Revolution when the old English element was at war with the American element of the new-born nation. How the new native point of view was evolving from the British I saw, for instance, in the record of the Baileys and the Platts before they went north as pioneers and when Poughkeepsie, where they lived, was for a while the capital of the republic of New York. There Governor Clinton also lived and Washington, Hamilton, Burr and Jay were present at the Poughkeepsie convention of 1788 that ratified, for New York, the Constitution; and the struggle between the old and the new divided the household of the farmer-colonel who had raised the liberty-pole in the Revolution. One of his sons was Theodorus Bailey, the United States senator who had joined Jefferson's party with the Livingstons and Clinton, while James Kent, later the Chancellor, who had married his sister Elizabeth, was his defeated rival in the same election. Kent, living in the Bailey house, had studied law in the library of this Jeffersonian rival, the brother of his wife, whose views he hated, calling them the "vulgar sophistries of the Revolution," for he was a passionate adherent of Hamilton himself. He had welcomed with rapture as they appeared the *Federalist* papers that upheld the "English party's" philosophy of property-rights against the "French party" of Jefferson that signified for him bad manners, low morals and rude dress. Riding circuits in Western New York, on horseback, following dim forest trails, he was disgusted with the backwoods democrats and with the liberty-poles they raised, no longer in protest against the king but against the taxation of the Federalists who were in power at the moment. Meanwhile, his closest friend was William Bailey, the brother-in-law who shared the views that formed the basis later of Chancellor Kent's *Commentaries on American Law,* views that owed little to the rebel "Enlightenment" from which was to descend in time the most distinctive and interesting thought of the country. It was with William Bailey that he went to Montreal, on a pleasure jaunt, in 1795, travelling from Plattsburg where the Platts, the Baileys and the Kents had bought four thousand acres, and more, of land. By the intermarriage of brothers and sisters these families formed a numerous clan, and, like Fenimore Cooper the novelist's father, their friend in the west of the state, they had thrown themselves into the land-speculation of the time.

To me as a child how picturesque was the tale of the founding of Plattsburg, when these forbears sailed up the Hudson and the waterways northward, ascending Lake Champlain in what they called their batteaux, the low flat boats that contained their possessions and their slaves. They manumitted these in time,—the last slave "Pete" in 1808,—while they brought seasoned Poughkeepsie timber to use, with the stone, in their dwellings and seeds of the Poughkeepsie poplars to plant by the lake. From these were to spring all the poplars of Plattsburg, Port Jackson and Cumberland Head. Only an occasional clearing broke the deer-haunted forests of upper New York where they built their blockhouses to protect them from Indian raids, with a forge, an ashery, a paper-mill, a grist-mill, a market-house and the first academy between Troy and Montreal. Nathaniel Platt was commissioner of roads and Charles Platt acted as a doctor whose fee for bleeding an Indian was a beaver-skin, for there were Iroquois all about, as numerous as the catamounts and sometimes no less fearsome to the lonely settler. To me the story suggested the legends that recounted the founding of cities in earliest England, in Greece, from the beginning of time when pioneers trekked up waterways, felled the timber and built their forts to secure them against hostile tribes or aboriginal marauders. As regularly as birds build their nests men had followed this pattern for thousands of years, the farmers succeeding the hunters in the waterside village.

Later it struck me that Fenimore Cooper had pictured the founding of Plattsburg in his tale of the founding of Cooperstown at just the same moment when his own father, the judge, had arrived in 1785 with the daughter who had had "advantages offered only by the city." His Templeton might have been Plattsburg in all respects, it seemed to me, from the dark forest of mighty pines to the French traders and Indian John, the emigrés, the sugar-maple boilers and the potash-makers. Among the Plattsburg settlers were the Saillys and the Fouquets, fellow-countrymen of Cooper's Monsieur Le Quoi, and there the supposed "Dauphin," Eleazer Williams, published in 1813 his spelling-book in the language of the Iroquois nations. I seemed to see in Plattsburg another Leather-Stocking's hut and a tavern like the "Bold Dragoon" of *The Pioneers,* as I saw the same pedlar there with jack-knives and jew's-harps, calicos, tobacco, mirrors and potash-kettles. There were the sleighs and the skaters too, with the cutter on the ice that Currier and Ives were to picture in so many of their prints of similar bustling settlements in the northern forest; and I saw in the furniture of the Cooper "mansion" the clumsy mahogany tables and beds that I had known so well from the house at Plattsburg. Even in their politics Cooper's judge and my great-grandfather's father,— who was a judge as well, like Chancellor Kent,—would have agreed as heartily as I would have disagreed with both, sharing myself the views of the Jeffersonian brother. It was this judge with the opinionated choleric face whose bewigged portrait looked down upon me as a child and who, on a panel on his tomb,—in the name of the Maccabees,—asked us all to grant him "great honour and everlasting fame." I could see, moreover, in the Plattsburg decanters the brandy, rum and gin that were served, in *The Pioneers,* with the cider and flip at those rustic feasts,—ending in custards and sweetmeats and four kinds of pie,—of bear's meat and venison, turkeys and fricasseed squirrels.

What a pity, it seemed to me, that we had no old novelists to evoke this patriarchal life of the pre-urban past, no one better than John W. De Forest in *The Wetherel Affair,* so feeble beside Aksakov's *A Russian Childhood.* Fenimore Cooper alone had recalled it faintly, and he had done little to body forth a chronicler's remark about Plattsburg that it had "all the luxuries of a seaport" in 1792. At that time, and later, what might have been the "tune on the harpsichord," and what the "philosophical conversation" that travellers were said to have found there in "polite circles"?—circles that, to my fancy, consisted of young ladies dying of consumption, with ringlets that shone "black as the raven's wing." They were all symbolized for me by the flower-paintings and the music-books and the youthful "female" poems of Emily Thurber, my grandmother's mother who had died so young, like the Davidson sisters whom she knew and whose poems were extolled by Poe and by Washington Irving. Had not the painter-inventor Morse edited the poems of one of these, as Robert Southey had written a memoir of her, comparing her to Chatterton, while Mrs. Southey, the poet's wife, had composed a sonnet addressed to their Plattsburg mother? The historian Prescott had called Lucretia a "little flower of paradise" that had lived, like Malherbe's rose, "for the space of a morning," this damsel whose "bursts of poetic fire," in the manner of Ossian and Thomas Moore, Poe had described as "wonderful" and "thrilling."

Nor were these the only Plattsburg poets, or poets con-

nected with the town in death; for what should I have discovered later, among the family gravestones there, but the
name of the once famous and precocious John Blair Linn?
This brother-in-law of Charles Brockden Brown, who wrote
a memoir of him, had known that he too was "doomed to an
early grave," and in fact he had died in 1804 after marrying
another of the sprightly daughters of the old farmer-colonel
of Poughkeepsie. A Philadelphian, like Brown, who had gone
to New York with a passion for the stage and had had a success with a play when he was eighteen, he had become a minister who challenged Dr. Priestley for his Socinian attacks on
the divinity of Christ. He had published several books of
poems, the last of them *Valerian,* hoping "to promote the literature of his country," the pious wish of so many writers who
flourished in the decades when the literature of their country
was about to begin.

But how many names, with his, survive in letters that I
have discovered in which oxen and apples and cattle-fairs are
mingled with comments on "Pioneer Balls" at which other
forgotten kinsfolk were evidently present. As my great-grandfather wrote of one, there were also "2500 others who are not
particularly related to us," though I was to encounter descendants of many who were more or less related wherever, in years
to come, I went in the world. For my grandmother's cousins,
so called,—among them step-cousins and cousins-in-law,—were
as numberless as the sands, it seemed to me, and I was to find
them not only in New York but in London and in Dresden,
in Washington, in Charleston and in San Francisco. Even at
sixty-five, in Paris, I was to meet a family of them who had
so far drifted away from their Anglo-Saxon base that they
were half Dutch and half French. I had grown up knowing
all their names, knowing that I was to visit them and always

finding that they expected me, and they always seemed to me real cousins because my grandmother had brought them so vividly together. But, as I grew older, they grew more and more remote, until, for the most part, these shadowy connections were lost to me like phantoms that melt in the air.

CHAPTER V

"EUROPE"

IT WAS understood in the world I knew that a voyage to Europe was the panacea for every known illness and discontent, and I supposed that my father, who had crossed the ocean so many times, was versed in all the laws that governed travel. While, at a pinch, in foreign lands, one might go third-class on trains, only first class was thinkable on any kind of ship; and it usually took a day or two for one to get one's sea-legs and feel at home with the captain and the passenger-list. The French boats had the best cuisine, the White Star boats were excellent and made good time,—for men a desideratum, —the Cunarders especially were safe but not so attentive to the sick, and the North German Lloyd had its particular virtue. My father had a special cap for use at sea alone, with a little book in which he recorded the names of the ships on which he sailed and kept the log on all his ocean voyages. The "Bourgoyne" and the "Bretagne" were legendary names for me, with the name of the old and the new "Britannic" on which my parents had gone abroad on their honeymoon in 1882. If the most frequent illness we knew was the European fever, the Baedekers, more than thirty of them, that filled shelves with old Tauchnitz books, suggested an unfailing cure for this.

Was it merely a child's idea or did not Americans in general

feel that Europe was a realm of magic, permanently fixed, secure and solid as the Alps, regrettable in some ways perhaps,
but inviolate and sempiternal as a scene or a playground? It
was questionable morally and still more so politically from the
point of view of republicans who were children of the Pilgrims, but it was incontestably a paradise of culture that had
scarcely known a beginning and would never know an end.
Did it occur to our elders, or would it have occurred to us if
we had been in their shoes, in their generation, that even
cathedrals might crumble away or that history, for them and
the world they knew, was not, in Toynbee's phrase, "com-
fortably over"? Whatever their circumstances were, or their
own personal ups and downs, for them the social order was
immovably safe and all the important wars had been fought
and finished long ago, for mankind had passed beyond the
cut-throat stage. How few realized that the underprivileged
who outnumbered them by a thousand to one were bent on
continuing history to their own advantage, for what reason had
they to be satisfied with it, or the subject peoples of Africa and
Asia who were no longer willing to be humble dependents?
This was the time when H. G. Wells, as I later discovered,
already felt that he was the one-eyed man in the country of
the blind, filled with a sense of the helplessness of flabby muscles and soft brains in the face of the general catastrophe that
he saw as impending. But no such feeling disturbed for Americans the iridescent fabric that was interchangeably thought of
as "culture" and "Europe," the continent every corner of which
stirred in their breasts an emotion evoked by some novelist or
artist, some composer or poet. The misery they saw on every
side, the cancerous mothers exposing their breasts in the
porches of churches in Italy, the cripples and the beggars were
preordained elements of the picturesqueness the painters had

memorialized. They were *tableaux vivants* that paralleled the pictures in museums.

To the child that I was myself when, at twelve, I was taken abroad for a year's frisk in these celestial pastures, there was no such thing as the cant of culture of which one later heard so much or what others called "unreal appreciation." It was all a bedazzlement, magical, simply, from the first rapture of approach, with the long black point of the Lizard running toward the ship, and, a day later, the ascent of the Scheldt, the red-tiled roofs of Flushing and at last the verdurous court-yard of the Antwerp hotel. My father, who had come over with us, knew Brussels, as he knew Antwerp, well, and, know-ing what pleased his imagination, whether it was good or bad, he took my brother and myself to the Musée Wiertz. He was a little amused, for the rest, by the fervour I displayed at my first encounter with "old masters," assembled in numbers, a fervour that mounted week by week and reached full flood in Dresden long after my father had left us to travel without him. For it was in Dresden that my mind first came to life, at the Zwinger, moreover, in the gallery that I learned by heart, so that for years I could close my eyes and see all the pictures on half the walls, or all except the cabinets of the little Dutch masters. From that day forward through the rest of the year, when I was approaching fourteen, wherever I happened to be, for a week or a month, in Vienna, Rome, Florence, Naples, Paris or London, I spent every morning in a picture gallery, roaming about from room to room, with a neophyte's zeal for the religion of the history of art.

Reading again, not long ago, the *Præterita* of Ruskin, I dis-covered that this idol of my childhood had been also thirteen when he was awakened mentally, as I was, by a book,—in his case, by Samuel Rogers's *Italy*, with vignettes by Turner, in my

case by Mrs. Jameson's *Italian Painters*. For this book confirmed the feeling that I had derived from the pictures themselves, starting me on a course of reading that,—to quote Ruskin's phrase,—"determined the main tenor of my life." It was
one of those popular handbooks, so characteristic of the nineteenth century when tens of thousands of people in the English-speaking countries were interesting themselves in a measure in affairs of the mind, another of which,—Mrs. Radcliffe's,
—ended with a descriptive list of the "twelve great masterpieces of painting." Why twelve, and why just these,—among
them Paul Potter's "Bull"? Even a child could see the absurdity of it, as one could see the absurdity of all the flat assertions
in which the guide-books revelled in those days. One was expected to believe that a certain statue in the Lateran museum
was "the finest statue in the world," as one picture was "the
second finest altar-piece"; yet the list of the "twelve masterpieces" was, in fact, no more absurd than Somerset Maugham's
enumeration of the "ten greatest novels." The mere specificity
of it focussed the mind on this object or that, like the stars
and double stars of the Baedeker guides. But Mrs. Jameson's
book, no other, was my open-sesame, and I might not have
read Berenson if I had not read this. I might not even have
discovered Ruskin, the favourite author of my whole adolescence, who illumined economics as well as art for me; for
Munera Pulveris and *Unto This Last* were to affect me later
as much as the Italian studies affected me at first. To what
fortuitous or trivial events, as they may seem, when one looks
back, one owes perhaps this first awakening, a view, a book,
a face in the street that strikes a prepared sensibility with the
force of a mystical message kindling the mind. It may be a
square of yellow light, on a dusty floor, on a morning in spring,
seen for the first time in the year, exciting the eye, that sud-

denly turns a boy into a landscape-painter, opening a new world of desire for him. Up to that time, for my part, I had collected birds' nests merely, pestering the birds themselves by stealing their eggs, and I scarcely remember reading anything but *Uncle Remus* and *Cudjo's Cave*, Frank R. Stockton and Edward Lear's *Book of Nonsense*. It was my brother who had been the reader and who had been found at three or four reading Macaulay's history upside down.

As for Ruskin, I even unknowingly followed him in attempting to make pencil drawings of pictures in museums. One of these was Fra Angelico's "Crucifixion" in the Louvre, where Ruskin, on his first visit to the continent, had made his first sketch. He had drawn Rembrandt's "Supper at Emmaus," obtaining a permit so to do, while I was stopped by one of the guards and told that the lowest age-limit for this, whatever the case may have been, was now fifteen. Ruskin had become an admirable artist, as one saw in the drawings he made for his books, while I had no luck at all with my few efforts, sketching Roman ruins, street-scenes and what not; and moreover I outgrew the wish to write the art-criticism that I loved and turned to another branch of this kind of writing. Not only was I never an art-critic but I had an almost morbid dread of so much as attempting to write about painting and painters, although I have known more painters even than writers, and although from the first I was convinced that criticism in some form was the most delightful activity one could dream of in this world. I even felt that everything might be expressed in criticism, as others have felt about music or fiction or sculpture, —in the last case, Michelangelo, as everyone knows; and certainly Ruskin, for one at least, expressed in criticism a good half dozen sides of life. Years were to pass before I knew how many Americans of my time shared, mostly on the economic side, my feeling for this writer, for I never heard of the Ruskin clubs that flourished in the West and included among their members Jack London and Carl Sandburg. Nor could I have known that Charles A. Beard was founding Ruskin College at Oxford almost at the moment when I was discovering him in Dresden. Ruskin stood for the Utopian impulse that was deeply planted in the American mind and that awoke in me also in time; and it was this common impulse, fostered by Ruskin in both of us, that was to lead me to Lewis Mumford.

Meanwhile, Ruskin drew me to shelves of art-historians, who drew me into the study of history as well, and presently theology, from the Flanders of Thomas à Kempis to Cardinal Newman and even Jonathan Edwards. For years, when I was at home again, two engravings of Newman hung on my walls, and I even translated passages of Newman into Latin, while I also erected an altar in my room with a seventeenth-century Italian crucifix above it. Under the influence, in part, of a high-church clergyman whom I served for two or three years as an altar-boy, I vaguely intended myself to enter the Church, and I lived in a dream of the Middle Ages and of Italy and Catholicism, which somehow seemed to me one and the same. I shared the reveries of Marius the Epicurean when, as Walter Pater said, he "played at priests," playing "in many another day-dream" also, "replacing the outer world of other people by an inward world as he himself cared to have it." During those years, in New York or wherever, I haunted this Catholic church or that in order to recover the feeling of Italy again in the colour of the embroidered copes and stoles, the odour of the incense and all the intoxicating overtones of the liturgical words. I even carried in my pocket boxes of wax-matches because of their incense-like perfume when I blew them out, and I noted the feast-days of saints and involved myself in my pre-college years in long theological discussions with two or three friends. For the rest, I was engulfed in that "old world" feeling which so many Americans used to share, a feeling that was induced by their new-world living and that invested the commonest objects, every fan-light or door, abroad, with its own special exotic mystery and charm. How many books I read as a boy, from *Romola* to *The Marble Faun,* from Byron's *Childe Harold* to *Mornings in Florence,* bring back that feeling now at the turn of a page, as they bring back a time when, in Leo Stein's phrase, I was "only concerned to know and not to understand." I felt that nothing was expected of me which I could not carry out some day and life seemed to consist of moments that were never to end.

But, returning to Dresden, one moment there might well have broken the spell for me, suggesting a twentieth century that none of us dreamed of, when my brother and I were stoned in the street by a gang of little German boys who, with this angry gesture, signalized our country. We did not know what was in their minds until Frau Schörke, who was teaching us German, explained that many of the Germans were in sympathy with Spain and resented our victory, that year, in the Spanish-American war, over one of the European countries. Centuries had passed since any outsiders had challenged the power or the cultural supremacy of Europe, and these Germans expressed what countless Europeans were feeling. I might, but did not, realize then that Fra Angelico, whom I so loved, had not uttered the last word on life or art and that the comity of nations was not yet achieved, though I made in Dresden one small discovery that everyone made in that generation, expressing it in the phrase, How small the world is. For one day Colonel Ricardo, a British officer, and his wife arrived at our Schnorr-Strasse pension with a Mr. Herdman, all fresh from India and, like others in half the towns of Europe, seeking the kind of "economy" that we sought ourselves. Was it not on the very first day that Mr. Herdman, observing me, on my way out to the Zwinger, as I recall it, asking me to post a letter for him, held it up before my eyes so that I could not avoid reading the address? And what did I see there but "Sion Mills, County Tyrone," words evoking the Emerald Isle that I had written a score of times, assisting my nurse Rosie who was writing to her mother. And who was Rosie? Rosie Morris, whom Mr. Herdman had "always" known,—the Morrises had been "our tenants for generations"! There was Rosie, even then, holding the fort for us at home, while her name rang in the German air at this encounter of East and West, this meeting of India and America in far-away Dresden.

What ineffaceable other impressions Dresden was to leave in me before we turned southward in the spring to Vienna and to Venice, beginning with Christmas, more glamorous than ever in this land of lebkuchen and marzipan, of gingerbread mannikins, music and Hänsel and Gretel. All the old Northern mythology seemed to come to life then in the winter afternoons that darkened early, filling the glittering streets with mysteries and shadows, while the great flares illumined the snow that covered the booths of the Yahrmarkt with all their enchanting wares brought in from the country. What miles there were of pitchers and cups, wood-carvings, trinkets and porcelain pipes, grotesqueries of every sort, with peasant designs, delightfully irregular, often crude, poetic to the unaccustomed eye and savouring of Grimm's fairy-tales and Heine. There was the old king of Saxony, too, whom one saw sometimes in Prager-Strasse and always at high mass in the Dom on Sundays and who looked like Santa Claus himself with his long white whiskers and the air of grandfatherly benevolence that radiated from him. I could not have realized how fortunate I was to have seen the Zwinger, the Schloss, the Dom and the lovely Brühl Terrace before they were demolished; and how often at the opera, to which I was taken three or four times every week, I heard Frau Malten, still singing, the original Brunhilde. Scheidemantel, too, in full voice also in 1898, was one of the old group of Wagner's singers. Among the operas that I heard, thirty or forty of these at least, there must have been a dozen that have long since ceased to be performed.

I can scarcely think of Italy now, or of my first visit there, without at the same time thinking of Arthur Ryder, later the great Sanskritist of whom I recently read in *Life* as the teacher of the atomic scientist Oppenheimer. He was at that time a student at Leipsig whom we encountered in Venice, where he too happened to be staying at Danieli's, then at Bologna, then in Florence and finally in Rome, after meetings in railway carriages and the same hotels. Before we parted I looked upon him as a youthful uncle or older brother, so much of my own time I had spent with him, at Fiesole, in the Boboli gardens, at San Miniato in Florence, at the Palazzo Vecchio and Santa Croce. Together we saw Michelangelo's house and presently in Rome we walked together, visiting the Mammertine prison and the Palatine hill,—on a rainy morning in this case of which he later wrote as "one of my best memories of Rome." We drove together on the Appian Way and together we sketched in the Forum, where I used the sketch-book my mother had given me in Florence; and he afterwards referred in a letter to "those days in Rome" as "good beyond anything I ever experienced before." He recalls to me now the young Americans in the early novels of Howells and James,—writer-friends who for years were thought of together,—those cultivated young New England men who roamed through Italy taking notes, discussing Lombardic architecture and Tuscan sculpture. Ryder was certainly one of those types that still exist in life, no doubt, but have vanished from the *dramatis personae* of the American novel. My mother attracted him greatly, "more," he wrote later, "than I could tell her," adding in his letter that he did not "distinguish her very clearly from the other madonnas." He must have had in mind certain late madonnas who were decidedly mischievous and distinctly pretty, for so she was, I think, at the time when he knew her. When later he wrote this to me I was reading the journals of Gamaliel Bradford, who had made me the executor of his literary papers, and I discovered there that Bradford had pictured my mother in the heroine of one of his unpublished novels. Fifty-three years after he had first known her in the Adirondacks he still remembered her frocks and their pinkness and blueness.

Just as in that Italian spring, wherever I went in later years, I was always rediscovering Arthur Ryder, first at Harvard, where he was teaching when I was a freshman there, and later in California when he was at Berkeley. While one caught in his Sanskrit translations the savour of femininity, he had come to live the life of a guru or a sage, the gaunt lonely scholar's life, wholly devoted to things of the mind, with its monkish altitudos and renunciations. I saw in him a late survivor of the New England Renaissance and the old Concord Orientalism, a solitary like Thoreau and equally full of disdainful pride, contemptuous of the machinery of scholarship and academic living. As in the case of so many ascetics, his perpetual self-discipline had blunted his human sensibilities: he had largely lost the capacity to sympathize with others and he had small respect for his fellow professors. He described the head of the history department, an Oxford historian, and his underlings as "a sham giant surrounded by real pygmies," the height of an academic wit that is touched with malice; and, following the wisdom of the East, he thought Western philosophy "frivolous" because of its unconcern with the problem of salvation. Ten years might go by before one knocked on the door of his room,—a plain room like a Hindu hermit's cell,— and the same voice answered from the same desk-chair in which, when one opened the door, one saw him still sitting, twisting the very same forelock. Meanwhile, indifferent to renown, he carried on his real life-work, as one of those creative scholars, lost in this country, who might have been famous in the England of Edward FitzGerald, for he was an artist as a translator who, as it were, soliloquized through the medium of the Indian poets and the Indian wits. All his translations were flavoured with his own original personality,—*The Little Clay Cart* and the *Shakuntala,* so often performed, in Ryder's versions, at Harvard, in Berkeley, in New York, and the Bhagavad-Gita, the Panchatantra and the versions in "Everyman's Library" that introduced thousands of readers to these writings of the East. I wondered in the nineteen-twenties why they did not share the vogue which the Chinese and Japanese poets had at that time, when Lin Yutang became almost as popular as Mencken, dispensing the "cynically contented" worldly wisdom of the earth-bound realistic Chinese mind. But this, with its note of the art of living, was closer to an American mind that had drifted far from Concord and the Transcendental and that was Epicurean and also humanistic. Confucius was congenial alike to Jefferson and Mencken.

Arthur Ryder remained for me a type of the Indian scholar-sage, a sort of American version of the Oriental wise man; and there were other characters of whom, as a child, I had glimpses in Europe less fleeting than everyone's glimpses of the pageantry of kings. As for this, at any hour, in Berlin, Vienna, Rome, a hush would fall over the street as the Kaiser flashed by, or perhaps the mustachioed King Humbert, with mounted guardsmen; and in this way I saw Queen Victoria twice, half covered with her parasol, on afternoons in spring on the Riviera. But were not Larkin G. Mead, the American sculptor in Florence, and the Greek widow of the old critic W. J. Stillman as remote from the twentieth century scene as the Widow of Windsor who had given her name to the epoch in which these two ancients had appeared and flourished? Both were connected with cousins at home in whose house I had often seen the Pre-Raphaelite paintings of one and the sculpture of the other,—a relief of their uncle William Dean Howells by his brother-in-law who was also their uncle, the last survivor of the circle of W. W. Story. This Roderick Hudson of an earlier time,—Larkin G. Mead of Vermont,—who had settled in Italy in 1862, had astonished the natives in Brattleboro with a colossal figure in snow that Lowell memorialized in his essay *A Good Word for Winter*. Since then he had sculptured the Lincoln monument for Springfield, Illinois, the original of which was still in his studio in Florence, where the old man, whose work seemed already archaic, was still the professor of sculpture in the Florentine academy in which Michelangelo had taught. Well I remember Larkin Mead, with his skull-cap and long white beard, surrounded by the Renaissance paintings that filled his house,—at least in appearance not unlike George Frederic Watts, whom I was to see in his studio on a certain afternoon. There, in London, I was taken to meet the astonishing Marie Spartali, who was only in her sixties then but whom I saw later, at eighty, erect and still young, with a red rose in her hair. It was easy enough to understand how Swinburne, seeing her in her youth, advancing across the lawn on a summer afternoon, could only murmur feebly, "She is so beautiful that I want to sit down and cry." She had outlived by decades the romantic Stillman who had founded the first American art-journal, *The Crayon,* though this perfect type of Pre-Raphaelite beauty who had posed for Rossetti's "Dante's Dream" still painted the pictures that could scarcely be distinguished from the master's.

Meanwhile, to return to Arthur Ryder, it was in Italy that I fell in with another sort of mentor,—six years later,—who scorned for quite different reasons the machinery of life. I was in college by that time and returned with my father and mother for a beatific summer by the Bay of Naples, a visit of which my impressions are now so entangled with those of the first that I am scarcely able to distinguish between them. My father was taken seriously ill, as it happened, in Sorrento, so that he and my mother were virtually prisoners there, and, roaming along the coast alone, I encountered at Capri an Englishman, a professional tutor in Italy who was taking a vacation. He was attached to a family, famous in Naples, who lived in a town called Penne in the Abruzzi, a mountainous wilderness, I gathered from him, horrid in the ancient Roman sense, a kind of Siberia to the Neapolitan eye. I pictured it as like Recanati, the dreary birthplace of Leopardi that evoked all those eloquent longings to escape to Rome, and G. E. Marshall had come to Capri, eschewing impedimenta, although not in Arthur Ryder's way. Nor did he share the guru-like scruples of Ryder regarding the acceptance of money for the teaching of wisdom, for he was an Epicurean merely with a "constitutional disinclination to work between meals," as I remember he put it. He wished only to be assured of enough to eat, an easy-chair, a bed, a fire in cold weather and a handful of books, and all his possessions were in one valise that he opened whenever we stopped for a night, removing his white linen trousers with his socks and his shirts. For I travelled about with him to Ischia and a number of towns on the islands or in the neighbourhood of Naples. Whatever he had worn he set soaking in a wash-bowl, hanging it out of the window to dry in the night, so that, sans any underclothes, garters, belt or necktie, he was always not only unencumbered but impeccably fresh. For me the simplicity of it was a philosophic lesson. He wore nothing else but a striped blue blazer and a straw hat with the arms of Caius College, Cambridge, embroidered on the hat-band. This emblem being a cardinal's hat, various villagers with whom we fell in supposed that he was some sort of ecclesiastic. They stooped and kissed the hem of Marshall's sleeve.

He was, in fact, a Catholic, albeit an easy-going one who used the Index, he said, as a guide to good reading and who spoke of the priest at Penne, his friend, as the spiritual father of the whole town and the natural father of at least half of it. The prince and the princess there were by no means on good terms because of their goings-on with servants and the young men of Penne, and the princess, recently returning from Rome, had found that her lover had been spending his time in bed with an itinerant prima donna. Nor was their heir to be outdone, Marshall's sixteen-year-old charge, who was to be a titular archbishop when he came of age, as I understood that one son was in every generation, or ever since the family had produced a pope. But for a few weeks every spring they all mended their ways to prepare for the annual visit of their great Roman cousins, who had preserved, in appearance at least, the austerity, the stately style, and even the puritan morals of their antique forbears. Great was the awe they inspired in the C.'s, as Marshall represented them, minding their

P's and Q's, scrubbing up their manners, rehearsing their general behaviour like refractory children before the impending visit of some Aunt Henrietta. Had I not seen them, or supposed I had,—the Neapolitan upper crust,—in the dining-room at Sorrento where I was left alone when my parents were upstairs at the hour of dinner and when the great hall was full of guests the like of whom I had never met and who seemed to be a family party on some gala occasion? Who were all these little bejewelled men and these swarthy ladies in evening dress who were playing verbal tennis between the tables and who, to my crude adolescent American eye, suggested a lively chaos of bedizened monkeys? I presently discovered that half the *marcheses* and *principessas,* the great world of Naples, in short, spent every August,—and spends it still, perhaps,—in this Sorrentine hotel, the world of which, through Marshall, I had had a glimpse behind the scenes and in which I saw a species of *commedia dell' arte.* How easily one fancied these nimble shapes in masks and wigs and plum-coloured coats, or as figures in Guardi's paintings or the operas of Mozart or Casanova's eighteenth-century setting.

For I was at an age when one looks for types, for living illustrations of the books that one has read and the paintings one sees, finding them too easily, as I found in Marshall a Yellow Book type, a sort of Max Beerbohm character, which of course he was not. But why did he impress me? Because, in my second Harvard year, he confirmed my distaste for "efficiency" and the "strenuous life," for many of the ideas and ways that prevailed at home, living himself on nothing a year, and wholly "inefficient," yet making at the same time so much of life. He was a many-sided man, delightful on all sides. For several years we wrote to each other while he drifted from Capri to Devonshire, to Algiers, the Canaries, Teneriffe, Rome

and where not, to me recalling always my summer on the bay
that supposedly inspired the wish to see it and perish. With
him, at Dombré's Grand Hotel Piccola Sentinella,—of which
who could ever forget the reverberant name?—I saw the sun
rise over Casamicciola and the hollow of the town like an
upturned seashell emptying on the beach. Behind rose the
rambling mountain of Epomeo, surveying the ruins left by the
recent earthquake; and I remember the grapevines of Ischia
heaped one upon another with bulging clusters of fruit overhanging the road. From every hillside along the coast ancient
columns and mosaic floors protruded like so many plums from
a ragged fruitcake, whether at Cumae or Baia or Posilipo,
over the vine-clad stands of the lemonade-vendors with dilapidated wicker chairs assembled before them. How still were
the hot afternoons, broken by the humming of insects alone
and the quick darting of lizards on the white-washed walls,
hung with purple morning-glories, over which the oleanders
spread their spear-like leaves and bright pink flowers. Among
the great oaks and the olive-trees in the cloisters of old monasteries tattered frescoes clung to the broken walls and massive
doors led into courts where the Middle Ages had not awakened
to the nineteenth century or even to the sixteenth.

After that summer for several years I was obsessed with
Italy, where I had filled my diary with Ruskinian pages about
ambones and mediæval pulpits covered with mosaics and where,
near Amalfi, I had read Rossetti all day long, looking out
at the Isles of the Sirens. But I felt the oppression of so much
that was beautiful and that overwhelmed one's own power to
respond, and I could understand why artists, from motives of
self-preservation, reacted towards the bitter and the squalid. I
felt the danger of what Melville described as "falling into
Plato's honey head" and, as he added, sweetly perishing there.

CHAPTER VI

HARVARD: 1904–1907

W HAT DREW me to Harvard, a stranger in a strange land with which I had few associations? I went to Harvard just as students in the twelfth century went to Paris because, for me also, Abélard was there; for I knew I was a writer born, —I seemed always to have known this,—and I supposed that Harvard was the college for writers. It was intensely literary, as it had been for three hundred years,—it was even more literary in my time than ever,—attracting many like John A. Lomax, whose work was ignored by the Texas professors and who came to study ballads with the far-famed Kittredge. While I did not know what I wanted to write, I knew that write I must and even the kind of writing that I was fit for; and for my purpose Harvard was the greenest of pastures.

On the evening of my first day I was taken to a punch at Holworthy Hall where a tumbler of unwatered whiskey was placed in my hand, and, hearing the cry "Bottoms up!" I poured it down my throat, swooning as I did so on the floor. I was conducted homeward by a sophomore who later became a famous Unitarian divine. On my second evening, at another punch in the sanctum of the *Harvard Monthly*, I met the poet John Hall Wheelock and various other literary men with whom I soon found my natural level. But my loyal friend Max Perkins, who had arrived the year before and wished to give me a chance to know the "right" people, arranged to have me join at lunch the boys from the famous New England school where he had been himself for two or three years. What misery was that for me, tongue-tied and thin-skinned, not knowing how to escape from this purgatory, while the young barbarians at play threw crusts at one another and sometimes threw butter on the ceiling. Nor was I very much happier when I found myself launched into a "final" club where I was surrounded by oarsmen and football players. I was the "mollycoddle" among the "red-bloods,"—Theodore Roosevelt's words, much quoted at the time,—but, floating in a dream that was sometimes a nightmare, I learned at last where I belonged and what to frequent and avoid in the way of circles. I was glad, from that time on, to be an outsider everywhere except in the world that by nature I was *inside* of; and I always liked Ruskin's phrase for writers, that they should be "fit for the best society" and, being fit, should then "keep out of it." I agree that to be fit for it is not the easiest thing in the world, but to keep out of it was natural and simple for me.

The circle in which I felt at home gathered at the Stylus Club, the straw-yellow wooden house, 41 Winthrop Street, where I spent my last year in college living with Max. Downstairs, late in the afternoon, our literary friends met for tea, produced by Mrs. Amy, the Australian housekeeper who was used to boys and brought in piles of crumpets and other goodies. The walls were lined with the framed autograph letters that Max's grandmother had given us, while in my room upstairs hung my death-masks of Pascal, Canova, Thackeray and one or two others. There hung also the old engraving of John Quincy Adams, always my favourite president, that had come from Plattsburg. For a time, at least, Max and I rose every morning at six o'clock to read aloud together some book or other,—Herbert Spencer's *First Principles,* for one, though why just this I cannot say, unless it was for masochistic reasons. For Max was by no means a lover of early rising, and he had written for the *Advocate* an essay "On Getting Up in the Morning" that humorously expressed his detestation of it. But the Cromwell in him was uppermost then, and, sometimes wearing a Norfolk jacket, like Professor William James, he usually dressed severely in black and grey. He had given up gay neckties and corduroy waistcoats, and, while planning a novel, I think, like Pendennis, about his "griefs, passions and follies,"—another "Leaves from the Life-Book of Walter Lorraine,"—he had reformed like Pendennis when he had spent all his money. He saw little of his old Fencing Club friends, while he was kind in a hundred ways to various other students who offended his taste, teaching at the Social Union, where I also had a class, and going in for the study of economics. This was partly, it seemed to me, because he did *not* like to know about railway rates and fire-insurance statistics. One of our friends wrote to me, "If Max wants heavy thought without water or ice in the glass, why not mathematics?"—and again, "Tell Max to glance lightly over the faces of the star students in philosophy courses and ask himself if they are a race of thinkers." But vain were all such ironies and admonitions. Max slept in a tiny attic, with a table and a cot, that needed only a candle stuck in a bottle to reproduce the first act of *A Gentleman of France,* for at that time he idolized the "real soldiers of fortune" of Richard Harding Davis like the old Confederate officer General MacIver. Max too would have liked to fight under eighteen flags, living betweenwhiles in some casual room in a hotel with a trunk, a blanket and a sword for all his possessions. But he was indignant when anyone remarked that he also had a sense of the picturesque.

Meanwhile,—to continue for a moment with Max before I go back to the Stylus Club,—we spent dozens of evenings together roaming over Boston, dining perhaps at Marliave's or at one of a score of old-fashioned hotels of a kind that was rapidly vanishing in volatile New York. They were sometimes disreputable in a more or less amusing way like the burlesque theatres that flourished near Scollay Square or like the "Bell in Hand" where the sawdust that lay on the floor might have been there since the days of Samuel Adams. Having long since become a drinking-place for workingmen, the "Bell in Hand" enforced, to keep students away, the Massachusetts law against drinking for minors, and Max and I circumvented this by wearing large blond false moustaches. The barman could not challenge these without the risk of retaliation in the possible form of a suit for personal assault. We went to the Italian puppet-theatre where, night after night, for weeks on end, one could watch the *Gerusalemme Liberata* and listen for another thirty evenings to the *Orlando Furioso*. But I at least was not interested then in the old Boston culture that was to stir my mind in later years. Nor did I know that modern architecture had, in a sense, begun with Richardson in Boston,—the creator of Sever Hall, where I passed so many hours,—and with Louis Sullivan, the Boston boy who had settled in Chicago and developed the ideas of the old Boston sculptor Greenough. For the rest, for breakfast Max and I often went to the "Holly Tree," the coffee-house that so many of the celebrities frequented, among them "Copey" who uttered there an oft-repeated epigram comparing, in the matter of their freshness, poems and eggs. There too one saw Pierre La Rose, Santayana's friend who was also our general friend in the circle of the Stylus, although he was older than the rest of us and had once been an instructor,—he was a decorator now and a designer of

books. He was redecorating the Boston Art Museum. Pierre
La Rose personified the Pre-Raphaelite aestheticism and the
dilettantish Catholicism that flourished at Harvard.

When I think now of the Stylus Club I remember J. M.
Barrie's remark, "People who drink tea are really just as interesting as people who drink whiskey, only Mr. Kipling has
never discovered it." Whiskey flowed in all circles I knew
and there was a potent Stylus punch that also flowed on occasion; but what a good custom was the drinking of tea, then
prevalent at Harvard, to enliven conversation and bring minds
together. It brought together, on our afternoons, Max, Jack
Wheelock and George Foote, Edward Sheldon, George and
Francis Biddle, Hermann Hagedorn, Alfred Kidder, the an-
thropologist of later years, B. A. G. Fuller, already writing on
Plotinus. Among a dozen others was the member who thought
Kipling was the only true successor of Milton and Shakespeare,
and he has recalled to me Barrie's remark, though I do not
remember whether he drank only whiskey. What I do remember is that his uttered observation had at the moment an effect
as of the shattering of glass; for, literary as we all were, the
"Harvard aesthete" was the type to which a majority of the
members were more or less related. Harold Bell represented
this type in its extremest form, a New Yorker, born "with a
gold spoon in his mouth" like an Edgar Saltus character, a
lover of luxury and cats, a gastronome and gourmet. Another
Tancred Ennever, he also dressed with extreme distinction,
travelling as well, on occasion, with a courier and a servant;
and later, invariably true to type, an amateur archæologist, he
joined an expedition to excavate Sardis. He had a rather cruel
face, dead white, with full red lips, that suggested the protrait
of a Borgia, boldly painted, and, aspiring to create "perfect
prose," he wrote sonnets in the manner of Oscar Wilde that

were printed in a splendid quarto bound in white vellum. He liked to quote Baudelaire and Huysmans, Mallarmé and the Marquis de Sade, and he persuaded Bruce Rogers, in those days at the Riverside Press, to design the menu for his twenty-first birthday dinner. What a Neronian feast was that, in a great room at the Somerset Club, with place-cards in the manner of Louis XVI, set in eighteenth-century type, dishes from four or five countries and musicians from New York.

It could not be truly said that this *esprit précieux* was dominant anywhere at Harvard or even at the Stylus; but, except in Copey's circle, the literary note was very far removed from the journalistic. I personally came in the end to share Jacques Maritain's aversion to "the shameless ascendency of the god Æsthetics taken as the ultimate end of human life," as I preferred dogs to cats or the canine to the feline which seemed to me summed up in Santayana. But this did not attract me to Kipling's personality or the school-followers of Kipling in the magazine world. Who could have escaped the charm of Santayana's *style,* which I discovered, like so many, in the library of the Signet, where I was the librarian and where I can still see *The Sense of Beauty* in a shadowy corner of the shelves. It was only later that I found so much that was unsympathetic in the "cynic and Tory in philosophy," his phrase for himself. This was after I had come to feel the magnanimity of William James, at whom Santayana always looked down his nose, as if in the nature of things the post-Catholic reactionary was better than the post-Protestant believer in mankind. Everything Santayana wrote contained an assumption of superiority when he was merely different, in point of fact, thrown on the defensive because he had been hatched from a Spanish duck's egg in a Yankee barn-fowl's nest. So I came almost to feel what the grand old Gaetano Salvemini felt when I asked him years later, on shipboard, if he liked Santayana. "No," he said, *"with enthusiasm!"* throwing up his hands; though I could not deny that, wandering alone, a stranger and exile everywhere, Santayana lived the true life of the sage.

But disliking the feline aestheticism that Santayana stood for did not make Kipling's masculinity more winning for me, his glorification of the "men who do things" and his cult of the efficient of which we had heard too much in our native air. Aestheticism in some form or other really did rule our minds, and if there was any one writer to be found in every bookcase, in my time at Harvard, it was Walter Pater. Edward Sheldon asked his mother, in a letter that I later saw, to send him copies of *Marius* and *The Renaissance* because "the copies at the Library are always out"; and the same taste extended to Yeats, whose vogue was just beginning and whose poems we scribbled all over our lecture notebooks. The Celtic revival was at its height, the Abbey Theatre was on everyone's tongue, with Lady Gregory and Synge's *Riders to the Sea,* and there was a general feeling in literary circles that the best English poetry was Irish now. The Irish seemed to have escaped the hurly-burly of the nineteenth century, the industrial century in which writers were supposed to have made too many concessions to the Philistine taste. I remember with what excitement Ned Sheldon and I heard Florence Farr and called upon her at her hotel in Boston. This was the lady who finally retired to a Buddhist convent in Ceylon and who recited Yeats's poems, to a psaltery that Dolmetsch made for her, and sometimes acted in his plays.

According to Coleridge, the possession in youth of anything like perfect taste is a virtual proof of the absence of genuine talent, and the cultivation of taste at Harvard was not only occasionally mistaken for talent but sometimes went far to stultify it. The atmosphere of Cambridge proved often to be sterilizing, but this was perhaps the necessary price it paid for being literary as no other atmosphere has ever been in this country. No outsider could have failed to observe that in any street-car thereabouts half the passengers were reading magazines or books, a fact that Audubon must have remarked in the early nineteenth century when he called Massachusetts "the reading state." The days of the New England Renaissance were, in 1905, not too remote and living survivors, or epigoni, were still to be seen, Thomas Wentworth Higginson, for one, the frail old man with the legendary past who lectured with a quavering voice now and then. Charles Eliot Norton, the confidant of Emerson, Carlyle, Ruskin and Lowell, still opened his house to students for readings of Dante, and, what was most striking, all the professors, whatever their specialties might be, seemed to be in addition men of letters. That William James was a born writer everybody knew, but Josiah Royce had written a novel as George Herbert Palmer translated the *Odyssey* and produced the definitive edition of George Herbert, the poet. Santayana was a poet himself, and Shaler, the geologist, was the author of an epic poem in no less than five volumes,— *Elizabeth of England* this was called,—while Bliss Perry was a well-known essayist and Barrett Wendell wrote novels and plays and talked as if writing books was a common occupation. I remember Barrett Wendell saying that when you wrote a book you must be sure it opened and ended well, that the parts between did not matter so much, which,—silly as this seemed in a lecture,—comes back to me as a note of the place and the time. For it implied that writing books was something everybody did and that most of us, in turn, would probably do. Just so, in quite elementary classes, it seemed to be assumed that we would naturally wish to look up for ourselves some history of the university of Padua or the Collège de France, that we were instinctively scholars as well as writers; and, when the professors talked with students about their careers and the future, they spoke,—if these were literary,—as men who knew. How true this was I am reminded by another letter of Edward Sheldon who discussed his plans with Dean Briggs, and with Baker and Wendell, all of whom agreed that one could not both write and teach or that, if one taught, one could write anything but textbooks. "If you want to write anything else, don't teach at all!" (For I suppose that their own books had been written mostly in their younger days and that they had since felt in some way thwarted.) Ned Sheldon continues, "They all say, 'Have the pluck and courage to face everyone and say, "I am going to write, even at the risk of complete failure and humiliation."' "

Nothing could have been more Emersonian, and in this sense the spirit of Emerson was still alive in his old college. I dare say even that in literary students the sense of the vocation was at that time in Harvard stronger than elsewhere. The poet Edwin Arlington Robinson was the kind of Harvard man of whom I knew numbers then or later, who followed their bent at any cost, committed up to the hilt, whatever the risks might be or the consequences. But Emerson, in another sense, seemed scarcely to be there at all, though the hall of philosophy, just opened, had been named for him,—I mean the Emerson who said, "Make much of your own place," not hankering after the "gilded toy" of Europe. William James kept up this line with what Santayana called his "American way of being just born into a world to be rediscovered," and James had countless followers of whom I ought to have been one and would have been if I had been maturer. How deeply I came to admire and love this enemy of all despair, of authority, dogma, fatalism, inhu-

manity, stagnation; but the Harvard that I was prepared to
know was much more the college of Charles Eliot Norton
whose mind looked backward in time and across the sea. This
was the Norton who never set foot in England without feeling
that he was at last at home, he said; and when, for the word
"England" one substituted "Europe," with the Middle Ages
and the history of art, one had the Harvard temper that I knew
well. It was the temper of Henry Adams who had lost all hope
for the modern world and saw nothing in the American scene
but "degradation," while, like Norton, he also preached the
gospel of mediævalism as an escape from the vulgarity of the
American present. That the world had been steadily going to
the dogs since the time of Dante was the complaint also of
Barrett Wendell, who deplored the American Revolution that
had sundered us from England and the guidance of the British ruling class. Irving Babbitt was all for authority and for-
malistic discipline as against the Jeffersonian vision he connected with Rousseau, the traditionally American belief that
men, freed from unjust social conditions, were sufficiently good
to be trusted to rule themselves. Then there was Santayana
who described himself as an "American writer," or said he
could not be described as anything else, but whom Lee Simonson remembered as always "gazing over our heads as if looking for the sail that was to bear him home." He was repelled
by everything that characterized American life, preferring a
world "run by cardinals and engineers," rejecting as "all a harvest of leaves" the New England Renaissance and its best essayists, historians, romancers and poets. His smiling contempt
for the efforts of men to better the world and humanity was
reflected in a host of Harvard minds that were reversing the
whole tendency of the great New England epoch, dismissing
its faith in progress as "the babble of dreamers." One and all

tended to revert, temperamentally, if not in fact, to the old European rigidities of the mediæval order, to the cause of "the altar and the throne," hierarchy and clericalism, against the fluidities that were bred by American living.

All these influences, brought together, created a special frame of mind that made "the Harvard graduate," as Henry Adams put it, "neither American nor European"; and there were other elements that went to form this anomalous brew in the twentieth-century decade that I remember. Adams's own theory that the universe was running down was merely an extreme form of the general feeling that we lived in a uniquely unlovely and degenerate age in which it would have been far better not to have been born at all, as Charles Eliot Norton constantly told his classes. It was no time, in any case, for the romantic "expansiveness" that Irving Babbitt attacked with every breath; and the hatred of modern civilization that one heard expressed on every side predisposed one in favour of anything that was not modern. In reaction against the Puritanism of the New England forbears an Anglo-Catholic movement throve in Boston, and there was a semi-serious cult of royalism also, with a branch of the Jacobite Order of the White Rose. The members offered expiation on the annual feast of St. Charles the Martyr, led by Ralph Adams Cram, the prior of the chapter, the architect-disciple of Henry Adams; though this could not rival the cult of Dante, which Mrs. Jack Gardner also embraced and which had been established at Harvard for two generations. It had given birth, with the Dante Society, to Longfellow's and Norton's translations and to Lowell's and Santayana's important essays; and Dante was an omnipresent interest like the dramatists of Shakespeare's time, who were constantly studied and performed as well. Another Harvard note of the moment was the Sanskrit that Babbitt had studied with Lanman and that spread the renunciatory attitude which had something in common with Santayana's wisdom of submission, while the urban point of view and the classical stress on order and form had long since supplanted the romantically rural. For the rest, Remy de Gourmont and the French Symbolist poets, steeped in mediæval reverie, were a new mode of the young, some of whom discovered these poets in the library of the Union in *The Symbolist Movement in Literature* of Arthur Symons. There others happened on Flaubert, with his "green ooze of the Norman cathedrals," the Flaubert who said that he laughed when he found the corruption in anything that was supposed to be pure, when, in its fairest parts, he discovered the gangrene. Flaubert contributed his touch to the weary, all-knowing, sophisticated tone, the mocking tone that was sometimes assumed at Harvard, and John Donne provided another note that was to reverberate through the "new criticism" that followed the first world war. John Donne, neglected in England, was an old New England favourite of whom Emerson and Thoreau had written in earlier times,—even Bronson Alcott had written of him,—while James Russell Lowell and Charles Eliot Norton had both brought out in the eighteen-nineties new editions of his poems. Dean Briggs was only one professor who talked of Donne familiarly as a poet about whom everyone went to extremes, whom people inordinately hated or loved and whom he personally cherished as one who preëminently "made the far-fetched worth fetching."

When one added these tastes together, the royalism and the classicism, the Anglo-Catholicism, the cults of Donne and Dante, the Sanskrit, the Elizabethan dramatists and the French Symbolist poets, one arrived at T. S. Eliot, the quintessence of Harvard. Together they shaped his opposition to the "cheerfulness, optimism and hopefulness" that stood for the point of view of the great days of the past, as they shaped also his inevitable vogue in an age prepared to feel with him that poetry can be found in suffering and through suffering only. They shaped the course that led him, quite logically, to England, to which others were drawn temporarily, or only in part, to be drawn back later by powerful elements in their own minds of which at the time perhaps they were unaware. For the "European virus," as Henry James had called it, attacked its American victims in varying degrees, but in some degree or other it attacked most literary minds at Harvard because America there seemed nugatory. What Henry Adams had said of Boston, that it was "up in all things European" but that it was "no place for Americanism" was all the truer at Harvard now where "Americanism" meant Philistinism and by no means what, originally, it had meant for Adams. The special new-world character that all the Adamses had held so dear, seeing it as something elevated and something noble, had become with time there, and elsewhere too for literary minds, associated with William James's "bitch-goddess Success." That New England had a special dispensation was sometimes understood, but what Barrett Wendell called "the wilds of Ohio" were generally identified in these matters with the rest of the country. Henry Adams had somewhere spoken of the "vague look of wondering bewilderment" one always saw on the face of the Boston man who had "discovered America" for the first time; but few at the Harvard I remember wished to discover America or questioned Matthew Arnold's verdict on it. "He who cares," Arnold said, "for the interesting in civilization" will feel that the American sky is "of brass and iron," and many shared the feeling of the most famous of all the expatriates that to live under this meant "brooding exile."

At that time one could discern few signs of the new America that was to dawn, for literary minds, about 1910, when a new culture was being formed, even a new language, the voice of a new spiritual continent and climate. Everyone knew that there had been an American literature of sorts that lay "a generation or more behind us," as the poet Woodberry at Columbia told his classes, but this seemed remote and unrelated to what Woodberry also described as our own "period of dubious fame." But even of that older literature Woodberry was not too proud,—it had produced, he said, not one poet who was even of the rank of Thomas Gray; while the leading critic of the time, Brownell, had obviously found little joy in the writers whom he described in his *American Prose Masters*. For Harvard ears these writers were "of little lasting potence," Barrett Wendell's phrase for all of them, and, as Howells put it, Wendell gave his readers the impression that American literature was "not worth the attention of people meaning to be critical." Henry Adams, who was unaware of Emily Dickinson and Stephen Crane, as of Winslow Homer and Albert Ryder,—though he prided himself on his alertness and his feeling for art,—was typical of the cultivated American public in his belief that in literature and art the country produced nothing "any longer." This recalled the feeling in Germany in Goethe's youth that the literary products of the country were beneath contempt, the conviction that German literature was barbarous which did not change till Lessing established a new epoch for the German mind.

Within four years of leaving college I was to find myself, briefly, teaching American literature on the Western coast, getting up my lectures under a live-oak tree there, on a circular bench on that very Californian campus. Those were the days when English departments were casual and listless and young instructors lectured at their ease, keeping one day ahead of the class and speaking as I spoke with a mind that was full of everything except my subject. What I really cared for then was Italian painting and the mediæval Church, together with the eighteenth century and the European writers round whom Georg Brandes, the Dane, had woven his enchantments, and I had scarcely read "Our Poets" of whom I was to write, in *America's Coming-of-Age,* so cavalierly. In what I both said and wrote I reflected the impressions I had gathered at Harvard,—for, even then, I was still in my early twenties,—where English authors were always cited in preference to Americans, even when these could also be called classics. Invariably one heard of Thackeray, rarely of Hawthorne,—Carlyle, not Emerson,—Charles Lamb rather than Thoreau; and merely to have mentioned this would have been thought chauvinistic, a word that was applied to me when later I did so. I was never tempted to "find salvation" in Longfellow or Whittier, as various unwise critics had a way of saying when I had merely come to feel the relative importance of writers whom I had damned with the faintest of praise. For I had been all too convinced that our literature was wholly "narrow gauge" and that an excess of patriotism was the fault of our critics, as I can see in the reviews which I wrote in college, at a time when, as Santayana said, "We poets at Harvard never read anything written in America except our own compositions." What was there, we might have asked, in America to read? For the Harvard imagination the country was a void, and Joe Husband reflected the general feeling when George Moore asked him in London why he had "hewn coal of his own free will." Joe Husband was one of my classmates who had written a book called *A Year in a Coal-Mine,* relating his experiences there when he left college, and he had replied to George Moore as follows: "If I had been in Europe I might have gone to live in Montmartre as you did, but being in America there was nothing for me to do but go down into a coal-mine."

It was natural that, with this frame of mind, so many then and later went either to George Moore's Montmartre or to George Moore's London, with a feeling like Henry James's Theobald in *The Madonna of the Future* that they were the "disinherited of art." Were they not "excluded from the magic circle . . . condemned to be superficial," since the soil of American perception was so poor and thin, so that they had "ten times as much to learn as a European" and could only "come into their own" as suppliants in Europe? There was Henry James himself to show what they might achieve by this, the James who, in 1905, reappeared in Cambridge and delivered in Sanders Theatre his lecture on Balzac. The return of Halley's comet was a minor sensation beside this prodigious event at Harvard, when the orotund voice of the great panjandrum rolled like an organ through a hall that could scarcely contain the aura of his presence. I always marvelled when later critics supposed that they had "discovered" James and that he had been ignored like the writers in his own stories, the figure in whose carpet no one saw, for *The Golden Bowl* had gone through four editions in its first year and *The Ambassadors* was serialized in a New York monthly. Gertrude Atherton related in a novel how, when he visited San Francisco, society was torn between James and anti-James factions, and innumerable novelists from Edith Wharton to Willa Cather imitated him, while he was the darling of almost all the critics. He was "our one great writer" to Percival Pollard, who liked to connect himself with "the Jacobites drinking to the king over the water," and Huneker remarked that Henry James might be "the discoverer of the fiction of the future." Brownell ruined his own style by following James's, and Edgar Saltus and Edgar Fawcett dedicated novels to James, whose prestige grew more imposing every day. He was the greatest of all the Americans to whom distance lends enchantment, who seem to grow larger than life when they are invisible in Europe, like spectres of the Brocken, those magnified shadows that are cast by observers, when the sun is low,—gigantic misty images,—upon a bank of cloud.

One of my friends spent a summer reading Henry James to prepare for the composition of his own Jamesian novel, while for another, a professional novelist in later years, Henry James was a model in all respects. For, as he wrote, he dwelt himself "in a world of delicately shaded, not too strong emotions and sensations." The old letters of this friend remind me that "all Harvard," all we knew, was in those years "marching on Paris" or marching on London, while a letter from another friend remarks that the American critical world was virtually all "broken meat from the European table." What was the obvious moral then?—"Sit at the first table, not the second." He quotes a saying of George Foot Moore, whom he had heard in the chapel, "Sin is not doing what you are able to do, the best you are able to do, in life," an Emersonian sentiment, surely, but one that, for my friend, plainly meant going to do it in Europe. One had to be careful not to "run off the track at the point of Patriotism," that "open switch to the American train of thought"! This friend had gone in for art-criticism, or the kind of art-historical study that was to flourish presently at the Fogg Museum, an interest that I shared with him and that suggested the mode of life for which Bernard Berenson especially stood at Harvard. Berenson, already a half-mythical figure, seemed to embody in our time a type that Pater described in *The Renaissance,* in the essay on Winckelmann, who had lived in Rome and of whom Hegel said that he had "opened a new sense for

the study of art." Berenson, with his all-curious mind, had
wandered over Europe with vague hopes of becoming another
Goethe, developing himself on many sides before, as he felt
later, he had been betrayed into expertizing. In Italy he had
explored minutely the Marches and the region of Siena, searching monasteries and churches for works of art, returning again
and again to the enchanting adventure.

Long after I had lost the wish for this manner of living, I
continued to admire Berenson's philosophy of art, his feeling
that its function was to build a house for humanity to live in,
to serve civilization by humanizing life. He called this life-
enhancement, a notion that was far beyond the kind of aesthe-
ticians whom Maritain censured. It was the true humanism
that was travestied by others, and Berenson's liberality matched
the Goethean breadth of mind that kept him fresh, eager and
alert when he was approaching ninety. He was never to lose
his confidence in life as well worth while, or, despite its devilish propensities, in humanity either, his faith that liberalism
was sure to reawaken, cast as it was, like Brunhild, under a
spell of sleep. Meanwhile, the interest in Italian art throve in
the Harvard air, and Mrs. Jack Gardner's collection, which
Berenson had so largely formed, seemed rather an expression of
this than a creator of it. It filled the Harvard mind with images
that cropped out in scores of novels and poems,—in Eliot's
phrase about Umbrian painters, for instance, and the trumpets
and eagles that evoked Mantegna. The characters of the long-
dead novelist friend of whom I have just spoken suggested
Florentine ladies in brocaded dresses, or ladies of Titian, trans-
posed into modern terms; and in how many other novels Boston girls wore nets of pearls and were pictured as resembling
girls by Lombard painters. Occasionally, they had oval Sienese
faces. As often as not, when the young men spoke of lives they

might have chosen they thought of drifting down Venetian canals in gilt and vermilion barges at carnival time, or floating through Limbo like Paolo with Francesca, or riding into Florence in the time of lilies. They thought of a palazzo exquisitely hung with faded silk brocades and bedrooms with upholstery in old rose and gold, or a villa at Fiesole, smothered in flowers and overlooking russet roofs and Brunelleschi's dome not far away.

To recall this Harvard frame of mind one has only to glance at the novels that John Dos Passos wrote a few years later, *One Man's Initiation* and especially *Streets of Night,* with their constant evocation of the Renaissance and "distant splendid things." The names of Fra Angelico, Lorenzo Monaco, Gozzoli "stream through" the young man Fanshaw's mind, and he says to himself, "Pico della Mirandola would not have been afraid of such an impulse." He thinks how wonderful it would be to have yellow curls like Dürer's in the portrait of himself at twenty-eight, and he remembers the scalloped wavelets, the blown hair and the curves like grey rose petals of Botticelli's wave-born Venus. He tells himself that he will never be able to look Donatello, or the Ghiberti doors, in the face again, and his mind drifts once more to Orvieto and the great Signorelli frescoes in the cathedral there. In *One Man's Initiation,* the ambulancier Martin Howe spends afternoons in France, during the first world war, looking at the Gothic windows of the lantern of the abbey, thinking that if this were the age of monasteries he would, without a moment's hesitation, enter one. He sees himself working in the fields, illuminating manuscripts, calming his feverish desires and drowsing them in the deep-throated passionate chanting of the offices of the Church,—visions that possessed as well many another young Harvard man who wished to escape from the banalities of modern living. Like Dos Passos, in the end, many of these, in reaction, turned towards whatever was "salt in the mouth" and "rough to the hand," to the crass actualities one found in the poems of E. E. Cummings and Conrad Aiken, evoking the slums, the gutter and the "sore of morning." They confronted the world they knew in a drastically questioning frame of mind, whether in fiction, or in poetry, or in criticism.

Meanwhile, at Shady Hill, still dwelt the tutelary sage or saint of these absorbing Harvard prepossessions, Berenson's teacher, Ruskin's friend, the rarely distinguished little old man, the incarnation of "culture," Charles Eliot Norton. Twice I was taken by a friend who had grown up under Norton's wing to Sunday "Dante evenings" in the golden brown study in which Henry James felt he had received his "first consecration to letters" forty years earlier in 1864. There, in the presence of "Dante Meeting Beatrice," the picture that Rossetti had painted for Norton, half a dozen young men, interested, curious or devout, listened with copies of the *Paradiso* open in their hands. They followed the text while Norton read aloud, like a learned, elegant and venerable priest dispensing sacred mysteries to a circle of heretics, perhaps, who were unworthy of them. One felt there was something sacramental even in the sherry and the caraway cakes that a maidservant placed in our hands as we were about to depart.

No doubt these impressions of Harvard are rather too special and personal to convey any adequate sense of the scene as a whole, but in those days the "elective system" permitted a student to follow his bent unconcerned virtually with anything that did not amuse him. So one saw only what one wished to see there. I often wondered if I had learned anything at Harvard that I could not have learned equally well at home, reading, listening to music and looking at pictures, and I think

I was chiefly impressed by the goodness of some of the professors, Dean Briggs, for instance, Bliss Perry and Edward Kennard Rand. It seemed to me later that I had never been
touched by anyone's intellect until in 1909 I met J. B. Yeats,—
the old Irish artist in whom I found a master,—no doubt because I was too immature to appreciate the philosophy of
Münsterberg and Royce or the history for which I listened
to Professor Haskins. I learned from Mr. Lowell, in "Government,"—a "science known only to Harvard," as one of my
friends said in a letter of the time,—that our President governs
but does not reign, that the English king reigns but does not
govern and the President of France neither governs nor reigns.
Then, having read in connection with this, Bryce's *American
Commonwealth*, I saw and heard the beguiling James Bryce
in person, the member of Parliament for Aberdeen with his
humorous air of a moulting cock bantam, whom Mr. Lowell
brought to the class one day. From another lecturer I learned
why the poets of Italy, as Dante said, ceasing to write in Latin,
wrote in Italian,—so that the girls could understand their
love-songs; for one otherwise lost these electric sympathies,
quick flashes of response and eyes that changed from line to
line. But little remains in my mind to recall the Harvard of
that time aside from a few phrases that characterize various
professors, or characterize them at least for me,—like Professor
Baker's "after all" or Münsterberg's "wiz uzzer worts" or Mr.
Lowell's "Now what actually happens is this." While my literary interest was counterbalanced by little else, however, there
were many mansions in the house of literature at Harvard, and
Kittredge, Briggs, Baker and Mr. Copeland, Bliss Perry and
Irving Babbitt inhabited not mansions merely but worlds of
their own. If anything brought some of these together it might
have been a feeling for Thackeray in the English novel and

Tennyson as a poet. So great was the stress laid on these that one could already have foretold an anti-Tennysonian and anti-Thackerayan reaction.

Years later, it seemed to me that of all my Harvard teachers I had probably learned most from Irving Babbitt, much as he repelled me and little as I liked his curiously inhuman brand of humanism. With everyone else who aspired to write I had my course with "Copey" but somehow never hit it off with him, unlike Max Perkins, his publisher later and his favourite at the time who was to bring him a wide audience with *The Copeland Reader*. I was "wilful and stubborn," Copey said, and the reason for this was that I did not wish to write in the manner that pleased him, although I could not have said just why, and possibly did not learn why, until I fell in with J. B. Yeats. This true-bred artist and man of letters scarcely saw a line I wrote, but he constantly talked of the writers of the so-called Irish Renaissance so many of whom had grown up in his studio and presence. He had educated some of these in his informal fashion, and he liked least the traits that Copey praised. Not emphasis, or the striking phrase, or Kipling's kind of vividness but the opposite of these, for him, betokened good writing,—Anatole France's *pas d'emphase*, vividness without effect and the phrase that is not striking but that haunts the mind. With these went the virtue of staying at home in one's imagination instead of going out and "seeing life," for he cared for the inner eye as he despised reporting; while Copey, who was an old newspaperman and Boston theatre critic, prepared his pupils for journalism by admiring just this. "I would never have seen what I did see had it not been for your teach-ing me," said John Reed, dedicating *Insurgent Mexico* to him, and one saw in *The Copeland Reader*, by his omissions and choices alike, what most appealed to Copey in American writ-

ing. He included selections from Heywood Broun, Richard
Harding Davis, Alexander Woollcott, O. Henry and R. C.
Benchley,—entirely omitting Emerson, as he omitted Howells,
—and his idols were the great journalist writers, especially
Defoe. A lover of histrionic effects as well as good reporting,
he had written a life of Edwin Booth, and, an actor himself
as a public reader, he liked young men who were actors too,
particularly when they were also very good-looking. Copey,
in fact, loved every kind of gallantry, the kind above all that
is visible in the figure and the face, the most understandable
of all tastes but one that tends to create a bond with the extro-
vert rather than the introvert mind of the writer.

There were two or three Copeys in the "uncut" state in
every seaport down in Maine, in Calais, for instance, where
he was born and where the old pharmacist said to me once,
"Did I know Mr. Copeland?—I went to school with Charles."
He showed me a photograph of their graduating class with
Copey standing five paces apart from the others, and the old
man said, "Charles was like that always." Having escaped what
he described as the "Ph.D. death rattle," Copey abounded in
his own sense at Harvard, where "Every man in his humour"
was the motto for professors who were actors often and characters all the time. What an actor Kittredge was when, falling
from his dais, he exclaimed, "At last I find myself on the level
of my audience"; and Irving Babbitt, tossing and goring the
writers he disliked, seemed to be acting the part of Boswell's
hero. Babbitt was another Dr. Johnson in his grunts, blowings
and gurgitations, roaring his opponents down, harsh and abrupt
in manner and voice, repeating "There are tastes that deserve
the cudgel." He recalled the tournaments of abuse that flourished in the Renaissance when the *odium theologicum* turned
into an odium of scholars and learned squabblers covered with

insults the "monsters" and "rogues" who said them nay over some question perhaps of the dative case. Did not the elder Scaliger call Erasmus, for opposing the worship of Cicero, a "drunkard" and a "scoundrel," as he called Étienne Dolet the "ulcer of the muses"?—and did not Schoppius in turn prove that the name Scaliger was identical with "jackass" in the Vulgate? He or some other also proved that among Scaliger's forbears there were no less than four hundred and fifty-nine liars. It was from Babbitt, no one else, that I first learned these facts, which in certain ways suggested his own personal temper, for he talked at times like the literary bully-boys who, in the eighteenth century, waylaid Voltaire.

What was the reason for the exasperation that characterized his manner? In part that he was miscast as a professor of French, a "cheap and nasty substitute for Latin," as he called it once, when he had wished to teach the classics. Convinced that French literature lacked, as he put it, "inwardness," he studied it "chiefly to annihilate" it, said Paul Elmer More; while Babbitt, who had some of the masculine virtues, had none of the feminine virtues that he despised in critics and their work. All zeal himself, all partisanship, and without elasticity, he was quite unaware of the irony,—for others,—in his praise of what he called "poised and proportionate living"; and, indifferent to novelists and novel-writing as to painting and to music, he yet laid down the law for artists and art. He challenged, in *The New Laokoön,* comparison with Lessing, who had lived a full artist's life as a playwright and poet, as, at least vicariously, Dr. Johnson also had, surrounded by poets, musicians, painters and actors. In Babbitt's life there had never been a Reynolds or a Garrick, a Goldsmith, a Burney, or a Gibbon, and painful to read were the pages in which he apologized for his own lack of experience in the world of art. He was negative in this realm of thinking and gauche when he adopted the Erasmian name of Humanism for his sect of thought, for he was a born sect-founder whose bias betrayed him when he virtually competed with Dowie for the attention of New York. What a sorry sight was that when, like a baited bear, this scholar contended with the profane New Yorkers, many of whom would not have known the difference if, instead of a Babbitt, he had been a Lessing.

What Dickens's Mr. Jellyby said, "Never have a mission," Babbitt should have said to himself long years before; but, aside from his doctrines, he was a teacher of passionate intensity and a positive personality at a time of indecision. His doctrines, repugnant to me then, grew still more repugnant the more I became aware of my own thought and as I grew in sympathy with "the great wave of radicalism" that was "sweeping over the world," as Babbitt put it. It never seemed to occur to him that this universal movement had sprung from the actualities of modern living, the need of twentieth-century men to shape their society and plan their world, together with the desire of the masses for their place in the sun. And why should there be any opposition between the humanitarian and anything that could rightly be called humanistic?—a question that only arose for me when later I *read* Babbitt to whom, at the moment, as a teacher, I was so indebted. For I owed to him my first initiation into the history and problems of the art I was to practise, and especially into the writings of Renan, Taine and, above all, Sainte-Beuve, who had almost all the qualities I admired so greatly. Sainte-Beuve's wish to "particularize," his love of the specific,—so far from the generalizing tendencies of Brunetière and Taine,—was one I soon identified with the passion for the "concrete" that J. B. Yeats was always praising. How enlightening were Sainte-Beuve's phrases about the master faculty,—the ruling trait in characters, —and families of minds, with his "group" method in criticism and his unfailing literary tact, his erudition subdued by the imagination. How wonderfully he maintained his poise between the romantic and the classic!—and I sympathized deeply with the Sainte-Beuve who wrote the life of Proudhon and believed in the relief of the depressed and the progress of the world. In many ways Sainte-Beuve influenced me,—even perhaps his weakness in making all his characters "six feet tall," the minor ones too nearly on the level of the major,—and I owe this, and much else, to Babbitt, along with his faith in the permanent in man and his praise of the *honnête homme qui ne se pique de rien.* Feeling that I might have been another kind of man myself and that I might have done a dozen other things, I was never tempted to pique myself on any special knowledge of my own or to pass for anything but a "damned literary person."

CHAPTER VII

DIASPORA

I HAD scarcely been out of college a month when I found
myself in England. I had crossed in the steerage, sharing a
room with a Frenchman, the chef of a Soho restaurant in
London who spoke little English as I spoke little French,
though we talked about the stars as we roamed the deck. For
those nights in July were calm and bright, and at least I could
say "étoile" and he "Cassiopeia." During the day, for want of
a chair, I sat on a coil of rope, reading *Tom Jones,* full as I
was of England. Other college friends of mine, equally full of
Germany or France, were hastening to Berlin or Paris at the
same moment, for my college experience and my earlier years
had turned me towards the old world as similar prepossessions
also turned them. Like a mysterious music heard from behind
the scenes, "Europe" had always been present in our associations, in our pictures and our memories and in what we
read, and we felt it was the predestined scene of our real
beginnings. We had to "fight out the duel between what was
given to us and what we were driven to prefer," a phrase I
found later in a book by Francis Hackett who, to fight out his
duel, had turned the other way.

As Francis Hackett, who became my friend, was one of the
European literary men who were to be drawn to my country
in accelerating numbers, I was one of the host of Americans

who, in the pre-world war years, were drawn, for both positive and negative reasons, to Europe. But why in the steerage?—why did this strike me as so romantic, though I was to find it dull and flat, a rather tame adventure, for all the smiling good will of my comrades of the voyage? I was possessed by the *nostalgie de la boue* of so many writers in those days, and the steerage for me was related to the slums which Stephen Crane signalized in his remark that the Bowery was "the only interesting street in New York."

One of the unfathomable mysteries to me has always been the *zeitgeist* that causes young men of an epoch to act in the same fashion, to follow the same way of life without knowing one another or even discussing their tastes or their hopes or their plans. With a subterranean understanding between contemporaries who have never compared notes, who have never met, they seem to behave as instinctively as birds in a flock, and many of the young of my time and even the decades that followed had a "sentimental reverence for sordid things." I found this phrase later in a study of the time, which said that they "rejected most of the ways of life of the middle class,"—if they were artistic or literary, it goes without saying; and one can see how true this is when one thinks of the "Ash-can" school in New York, the painters whom presently I was to know so well. How full the poems of that time were of dingy furnished rooms, cocktail smells in bars, "putrid windows," sawdust on floors and disintegrating cigar-stubs in gutters, expressing the feeling I shared so fully of the attraction of "mean streets" that Arthur Morrison, for one, described in London. I did not know Eugene O'Neill when he haunted the New York waterfront and shipped as an ordinary seaman on a British tramp, nor did I know Wenny in John Dos Passos's *Streets of Night* who was looking for a job on a railroad section-gang. But, just

as Joe Husband worked in a coal-mine, another of my friends
"rode the rails" to see "how the other half lives," a motto of the
moment. This was all part of the fascination that outcasts
and the so-called lost possessed for the imagination of my
moment,—whether for social, spiritual or aesthetic reasons,—
and it never surprised me that, as he put it, Stephen Crane had
got his "artistic education" on the East Side of New York. The
slums were never to lose their charm for me.

For several years, in London first and later in New York, I
was to live among the scenes of the "Ash-can" painters, and
so did Max Perkins, in Boston, for a while, my only intimate
college friend who did not instantly sail away to Europe.
Max spent a summer at a settlement-house, "district visiting,"
more or less, while teaching, reading economics and learning
to typewrite, before he decided to go to New York like the
Richard Harding Davis young man who took the first train
from Yale to become a reporter. Copey, no doubt, the old
newspaperman, had worked on Max's imagination; and had
not Pendennis been a literary journalist before he became a
novelist in London? It had not escaped *me* that Pendennis
was a patron of the pawnshops with which at least I was
familiar for a number of years, while Max, I am sure, was
influenced greatly by Barrie's *When a Man's Single* at the
time when he was living at the "Palmetto" in New York.
How magnetic was this tale of the "blue-blooded" but "hard
up" young man who, on the "Silchester Mirror," hungers for
Fleet Street and finally goes to London, becomes a reporter
and wins the beautiful girl, of course, in the end. How engaging were those scenes of the young newspapermen at home, in
armchairs, with their feet on the hearth and the gas blazing
in their lodgings, or in the reporting-room where, being on
the press, they could "patronize the Tennysons" if they wrote

reviews. It was understood that young reporters were subsequently destined to "take a high place in literature," as Barrie expressed it; and certainly, in Max's case, before he went into the publishing house, reporting resulted in several capital stories. The buried novelist in his mind had full scope, for instance, in his much talked of report of the Vanderbilt cup race.

I know that in going to London I too was partly influenced by Barrie's picture of Fleet Street journalism, visibly embodied, for Max and for me, in a common friend at Harvard, the seasoned correspondent Frederick Moore. Eight years older than either of us, the author of *The Balkan Trail*, a well-known book in current-historical circles, Fred Moore had come to Cambridge to spend a year working with Copey, feeling that in English composition he had much to learn. Originally a New Orleans man, quixotically honourable, with an irresistible masculine simplicity and charm, he had proposed that I should go to London with him, or meet him there, certain that I could not sink and would learn to swim. Himself a "true soldier of fortune," a Davis character in actual life, a staff-correspondent of the *Morning Post* and *Times*, he was admired and really loved, as I discovered in London soon, by every editor to whom he introduced me. On his lips the phrase "free lance" was an incantation and he made "London journalism" seem pure romance, while the London of writers, in a deeper sense, meant much to one who had been trained to think that his own country was a "literary dependency" of England. For me Boston was not interesting nor was New York magnetic yet,—or to anything like the degree it soon became,—and the girl who later became my wife had gone to Paris to spend three years with her mother and her brother, who was studying architecture at the Beaux-Arts. At home both my father and my grandmother had died during my college years and my mother was happy to forward my interests and plans, while I had made half-hearted efforts to establish myself in New York, especially on the *Evening Post,* my El Dorado. For the weekly essays of Paul Elmer More had some of the magic for me that Sainte-Beuve's *causeries* once had for young writers in Paris, and More himself had given me a book to review in a paragraph, a gesture that led to nothing further. I had even laid siege to William Dean Howells, asking him to solve for me the unanswerable question, how to begin as a writer, and no one could have been more sympathetic than this little round-shouldered bunch of a man who seemed not so much to walk as to roll about the floor. With his crepe-like wrinkled wise old face, he was as kind as a man could be; but what could he say to a neophyte who wished to write "editorials" except that one did not begin at the top of the ladder?

Within a few months, or a year at least, my friends had scattered all over Europe, whether because they were more drawn there or repelled by their own country or whether they shared these feelings in equal measure. A few of them felt that America was uniquely repellent, but these had never heard the song of Artero de Quental, "What a sad fate, my boys, to have been born in *Portugal.*" One of my friends complained, "Liberty in America is like the liberty of a man packed in a crowd. There is no policeman, but he can't move"; and again, "Every true thought in my mind is repugnant to everyone at home. To be myself is to be impossible there." Another wrote, "The thing that hangs over me like a gallows at home is the set and rigid form you are required to force yourself into." There were some who would always have chosen dead cities before living wildernesses, and others for whom America was "detestable . . . barren and sordid," while others again, prepared to go home and embrace the "money shuffle," seized a few months of grace in Sicily or Capri. Resigned to joining their fathers in business until the time came to retire, they basked in Taormina, on balconies, writing sonnets.

One friend, of German origin, returned to spend a year or two in the old house of his family in a village on the Rhine; another went to Lyon to study at the university in what he called that "laborious bourgeois city." A third visited cousins in Ireland "beside the Blackwater," the locale of certain poems that he presently published, while my Henry Jamesian novelist friend settled soon in Florence, not far from another who was writing on Florentine woodcuts. One classmate, who knew Berenson and was deep in the study of Duccio, worked in Italian archives to prepare for his book, and one who was composing literary portraits had gone to stay on the Breton coast at an inn that had once been a château of the Rohans. Then he moved to a sort of peasant hotel, on a beach, beside the ocean, where the chickens and occasionally a pig strolled in at the windows and where he paid eighteen francs a week, less than four dollars in those days, for his room and his meals, together with his washing and his wine. Three musical friends had gone to Berlin, whence one of them wrote from a queer tall building where the odours of chloroform and cabbage mingled on the stairway,—for some of the tenants were dressmakers and the rest were dentists; but he had a huge study with a grand piano that made up for all the reek and a knowledgeable old Pomeranian music-master. With his friends near by he had there "the most delightful part of college . . . in this peculiarly characterless city of Berlin," which resembled London, Paris and New York and every other great city, in fact, in all those qualities that in each were "not distinctive."

Berlin, as he put it, was "metropolitan but characterless" and therefore "the exact reverse of Boston."

Nor, in choosing for a while to live abroad, were these the only friends of mine who were forerunners of the so-called Expatriates later in days before changes in the spiritual climate both in America and abroad sent literary minds in general home to stay. My closest friends,—with Max,—Jack Wheelock (John Hall Wheelock) and Edward Sheldon set out for Europe almost as quickly as I did, although Ned Sheldon was already a success in the theatre in New York with *Salvation Nell*, produced when he was still in college. He was busy following up this "divine comedy of the slums," as Mrs. Fiske called it, working in Italy and France, at Fontainebleau, in Normandy, on Lake Como, "dizzy with labour and drinking nothing but coffee and whiskey," he wrote, "with a copy of Congreve in one hand, Wycherley in the other." Jack Wheelock had gone to Göttingen, where his uncle was a professor, planning to deal in his doctoral thesis with folksongs that had never been collected for which he travelled through Hungary and Montenegro. He wandered as well over Germany, avoiding the fashionable resorts and sights, frequenting beer-gardens, cheap theatres, merry-go-rounds and the river-boats that plied between old red-roofed cities, enchanted by girls with "old-world eyes and Gioconda half-smiles," he wrote, and "a hungry wonder under the high cheek arch." He felt at rather a disadvantage beside the German students who spoke four languages almost as mother-tongues,—and for whom other Americans were often "fish-blooded,"—but he engaged in a duel that left him with gashes eighteen inches long and made him for all time, for me, the prodigy of beaches. Besides Max, almost the only friend who stayed at home was Harold Bell, who had for several years his Europe in Cambridge, where he bought a house built in the Italian style with a tower, a *piano nobile* and a loggia that was already paved with stone. Harold Bell erected a high wall about this villa, which Pierre La Rose redecorated in pink and grey, and, living together in "Grey House," the two friends planned Renaissance banquets with Pico della Mirandolas gathered round the fountain in the garden. I was not there to see how far they were able to carry out these dreams that Walter Pater perhaps had kindled in their minds, but one of their first guests was the Cardinal-Archbishop of Boston.

I did not know, when I went to London, how many aspiring writers had much the same idea at about the same moment, Ezra Pound, Eliot, John Gould Fletcher, Conrad Aiken, "H. D.," and others like John Cournos, all within a lustrum or a decade. Numbers of these, like Elinor Wylie and Robert Frost in 1915, were to publish their first books in England, as I published mine, and most of them arrived with a little of the feeling of the young man Walter Anthon in Robert Herrick's novel *The Gospel of Freedom*. It had been in the air they breathed, in college or at home, that one should not "write for the provinces" but should go to London, in order to begin one's career at the "centre," perhaps to "get in" and get to be known and discussed by the world that counted there. I was too naive myself for this particular shade of thought,—a feeling that was to vanish totally within fifteen years,—and romantic motives governed me, notions of Grub Street and "living in an attic" or, like George Gissing, lodging in cellars. I had delighted in all the stories of penniless assaults on literary fame, the story of Crabbe who sold his clothes to pay for a last meal and of Goldsmith who was caught at home with his breeches at the pawnshop. For I lived in a dream of literature and everything amused me if it brought back the experience of some great writer,—De Quincey, for instance, in a garret with rats, sharing his crust in Soho Square with the waif whom he had picked up in Oxford Street. How eagerly I walked into 4 York Street where De Quincey had written *The Opium Eater* and infected the clerk whom I found there with my infatuation, for, previously unaware that the house had a history, he took me into the upper rooms where the tattered wall-paper hung loose in the damp half-darkness. Like Barrie's hero, I was "pleased with poverty" in and for itself, a taste that J. B. Yeats was to confirm in me,—and a good taste it is, I am convinced, for writers,—one that led me into some odd adventures during the eighteen months that I spent in London. I lived in a little street off the Strand, in King's Road, Chelsea, where I rented an empty studio and slept on the floor, in Pimlico for a few months and at 16 Old Compton Street, where I had a room at Beguinot's,—at that time Roche's. A dingy old copy of a Correggio in a heavy gold frame hung over the bed, and a mirror flanked the gas-jet in this ten-shilling chamber.

Meanwhile, I had set about entering "London journalism" with the letters that Frederick Moore had given me to various editors who invited me to lunch and tried to discourage me at first but only succeeded in filling me with great expectations. I was presently at work in Curtis Brown's agency in the newspaper and magazine department, placed in the charge of Mr. Snell, who asked my age and if I drank and why the devil I wanted to go into this business. The benign old growler Mr. Snell, with his air of an English Mark Twain, had once been a reporter on the New York *Herald*, and he told me that all American reporters were cads, thieves and crooks while the English were all scrupulous, generous and easy-going. After this we lighted cigarettes and went out to lunch.

My task was to clip stories from English newspapers to be sent back to America and rewrite European articles in American style,—on pain of "not getting there" I must make them "breezy"; and Mr. Snell told me that I must also write articles outside the office and bring in as many as I could write. He sent me on assignments for an article on the London parks and another on the trained dogs at the railway stations that collected contributions for the widows of employees, a third on the cinema and a fourth on Lord Fairfax, the Virginian who had returned to England to enter the peerage. I interviewed a tattooer who professed to have plied his trade not only on the backs of the Czar and the Prince of Wales but also on the arms of Lady Randolph Churchill, and I was sent to Canonbury Tower where Oliver Cromwell, who had visited there, had left behind a boot that had just been discovered. This boot had been sold for a hundred and fifty pounds. Then one day an earl fell into a lake and this little timely incident afforded a reason for an article on the forbears of the earl, for earls were supposed to interest Americans, like anything involving the "haunts" of Burns, or of Wordsworth or Sir Walter Scott or Dickens. For instance, some slight alteration in the Bull Inn at Rochester, the memorable scene of the ball in *The Pickwick Papers*. I was asked to return to the railway stations and characterize their "psychology," or describe them in terms of persons in history or fiction, and, in fact, at Euston, Major Pendennis came naturally into my mind as at Fenchurch Street I thought of Fagin.

But it did not take me many months to realize that "journalism," whether in London or New York, was not for me, that I had not the slightest knack for "stories" or "adventure" or for articles, indeed, in any form. I was possessed with ideas for books, which I planned at the rate of a dozen a year, a new

book every night before going to sleep, predestined as I was,
however, to do my share of hack-work, at intervals, for many
years to come. I was to have a hand in thirty-one translations,
while reviewing, rewriting other men's books, editing a volume
of Houdini's tricks, ghost-writing the memoirs of Iliodor, the
"mad monk" of Russia. How much literary drudgery I was
fated to perform, beginning in London where I abridged for
the *Wide World Magazine* the autobiography of Geronimo,
the Apache chief. I wrote columns for a Manchester paper on
American railroads and Tammany Hall, the "Religion of
Theodore Roosevelt," Bryan and what not, with an article on
"Harvard and American Life" for the *Contemporary Review*
and a series of articles on the lives of famous correspondents.
I described the outstanding exploits in each man's career,
Edward O'Donovan's adventure at Merv, Blowitz's coup with
the Berlin treaty, the journey of W. B. Harris to Tafilet. There
were others on Sir Donald Mackenzie Wallace, George W.
Steevens, Archibald Forbes and the "thousand mile walk across
China" of Morrison of the *Times*.

Frederick Moore commissioned these,—for he soon joined
me in London,—and showed me how to bring out the drama
in the stories, all of which I wrote in the Reading Room of
the British Museum, the scene of so many tragedies and
comedies of Grub Street. There I was surrounded by earnest
students and American genealogists, like the primrose-haired
girl in Harold Frederic's novel, and I saw Bertram Dobell there
with his battered top hat and grizzled old men in threadbare
morning coats. Some of these dozed behind piles of ponderous
books and stealthily drew from their pockets papers full of
crumbs, and many gave point to the sad implications of the
well-known sign in the lavatory, "For casual ablutions only,"
which I found still there. A few were diving for pearls in the

deep waters of learning. They were all Henry Ryecrofts for me, Gissings of a later day who had also perhaps breakfasted on dry bread, carrying with them a crust to serve for dinner, and who settled themselves every morning at their desks with books which "by no possibility could be a source of immediate profit."

In the meantime, Fred Moore came and went, at first to report for three London papers the Casablanca massacres in the fall of 1907; and presently I saw him off for Constantinople. He was the personification of the "nose for news," with an extra sense for events that were about to happen, events that nothing in the papers suggested to others; and, having foreseen that the Sultan was to be deposed on Sunday, he reached Constantinople on Saturday afternoon. Other friends joined me,—half the Harvard I had known turned up sooner or later in Piccadilly Circus; and who should appear at the British Museum but Irving Babbitt, tamed and kind, who walked with me four times round Russell Square. In this neutral atmosphere I saw that I had misapprehended certain Harvard characters who had seemed forbidding, among them the terrible dean with the octagonal glasses who had found so many reasons for upbraiding me in college. Seeing him from afar one day in the Brompton Oratory, I darted behind a pillar to evade his eye, when, caught and cornered, I perceived that his eye was all benevolence and that he actually rejoiced in my immunity in London. Joe Breck arrived, still preaching Berenson, whom he had just seen, and full of the "occult balance" of Duccio's pictures and the "intellectual centre" he discovered in them; and Tinckom-Fernandez, the half-Hindu friend who was to live with me in New York, also spent two or three days with me in Chelsea. Then he sent me a rondeau of his own composition. Lee Simonson followed and another

friend with whom I heard Bernard Shaw prove that the world
and women could get on very well if men were abolished
altogether; and T. H. Thomas later came and stayed two
months with me in lodgings in a French house in Pimlico.
Our meals were brought up to a large airy sitting-room that
was hung with sentimental coloured prints which the landlady said she had put up especially for us and which we could
only remove by slow degrees.

Tommy Thomas was at work on European "letters" for some
paper at home, and he had just finished his book on eighteenth-
century French portrait-engravers, which made him at once
an authority in a fairly large field. I was to see, in connection
with this,—and marvel over it all my days,—how swift and sure
is the response to authority in England; for Tommy took me
to the National Gallery where he told the director,—Sir Charles
Holroyd, I think,—that a certain Dutch portrait was attributed
to the wrong painter. It was a portrait of Descartes, as I seem
to remember, though I do not recall the name of the other
artist, but Holroyd was all ears at once and said we must go
upstairs and look the portrait over and discuss this question.
He listened while Tommy made his case, then, finally convinced, he tore off the label and put it in his pocket; and the
name of the other painter soon afterward appeared there.
I pictured to myself the pompous protests a provincial director
at home would have made if a young stranger from abroad had
suddenly appeared and questioned one of his official attribu-
tions. Holroyd, candid and direct, recognizing a mind that
knew, fell without a moment's hesitation into conformity with
it.

Much I liked the English,—and, while there were certain
English types that I always found detestable, there are certain
American types I have found still more so. I liked their his-

trionism too, their pleasure in bearing and dress, the pageantry
that suggested to me a perpetual ballet, as when, for instance,
responding to a knock at my grimy Soho door one day, I confronted a footman in livery on the landing outside. He was
an emissary from one of my mother's three families of cousins
who lived in England in a splendour I had seldom seen at
home, but, for my imagination, he might have stepped out of
a Sheridan comedy or a Hogarth picture of the contrast of
high life and low life. Amusing to observe, however, this
was the world that Goethe described as "suitable only for
women and people of rank,"—it was a kind of play that I
found rewarding only when I saw it across the footlights; and
at twenty-one, meanwhile, and shy, I was an outsider in my
own world, unlike various friends who made themselves at
home there. Some of these friends were lunching with Shaw
and playing tennis with H. G. Wells, or, like Joe Husband,
spending hours with the "elderly old blackguard" in Ebury
Street,—J. B. Yeats's phrase for George Moore. For Joe's handwriting had seemed to Moore "as beautiful as Mallarmé's," he
wrote, and it had occurred to Moore that Joe might be persuaded to make a transcription on vellum of *The Brook Kerith*.
But I saw these great men also across the footlights,—Shaw,
for one, who reminded me of the Etruscan warrior in the
museum in New York, for he had, with his grey beard, the
muscles of a boy. Many times I heard him speak, an aging
man springing from his chair with youth in every gesture and
sally of the voice. I often saw Chesterton's bushy head, and
one day in St. Martin's Lane I encountered J. M. Barrie, pipe
in mouth, with his deep black eyes and bright red necktie. He
was turning down an alley to the stage-door of the theatre
where *What Every Woman Knows* was about to open. Then
at the British Museum I stood beside a familiar face that said

to the young man at the desk, "Any books for Ellis?"—and I was surprised when the young man asked "What initial?" and the man with the beard was obliged to answer "H." For I had instantly recognized Havelock Ellis.

Many years later AE wrote to me that one should never try to meet celebrated persons, that in the end one inevitably met the persons whom one was intended to meet, the persons whom one had truly a reason for knowing. He said that, for instance, in Donegal, on the shore of a lake, he had observed a man standing as lonely as a seagull and that, falling into conversation with him, this man quoted the Upanishads, the book that he himself was constantly reading. It had always been that way with him,—destiny brought one face to face with those whom it was good for one to know; and I had vaguely felt this too, as I have experienced the truth of it, for in time a writer meets everybody and what does it matter? What is good is that he meets his real comrades of the spirit. But I was fearful in earlier days that my diffidence might be cowardice and that "seeing Shelley plain" was a young writer's duty, as Boswell had sought out Voltaire, Rousseau and Hume before he set his cap at Dr. Johnson. I felt that in failing to follow the example of Boswell I might be missing something of real value, as J. B. Yeats felt when he missed the chance to meet Rossetti, who had seen and liked one of his early pictures. All the young artists of Yeats's time who aspired to a kind of poetic art had been agog about Rossetti, who sent three messengers to him with invitations, and "I did not come," Yeats later wrote. "I think I was afraid of the great man, diffident about myself and my work." Yeats added, in *Early Memories*, "To be afraid of anything is to listen to the counsels of your evil angel," and I dare say it was so with me, for I stood in awe of all the men who were eminent in my craft.

I felt about far lesser men what Flaubert felt about Shake-speare,—that he would have died of awe if he had met him; and I was frightened by the mere sight of Swinburne, whom anyone might have seen on Putney Hill. For every morning at eleven o'clock he passed through the gate of "The Pines" for his walk up the hill over Wimbledon Common. I had felt a slight shiver of awe whenever a bus marked "Putney" passed me anywhere in the London streets, and I could not have expressed the mysterious excitement with which I observed that quiet dwelling. The old bookseller on the corner had often been in the house, he said, where books were piled in thousands on chairs and sofas, and sometimes the poet, for whom he bound books, sent word asking to borrow one which he had somewhere in the house but could not find. I had to light a cigarette to give me an excuse to glance at the little turbaned figure whom I saw emerging.

Diffident as I was, however, I was not unfriended during the numberless hours that I roamed about London, sometimes with "Uncle Nick," who had spent years in New Zealand, the old retired barrister who lived at Roche's over me. There he had known Samuel Butler, who had later lived in Clifford's Inn in the days when he had a "little needlewoman"; and, in fact, the old circle of Butler, or the remnants of it, gathered for dinner at Roche's now and then. Uncle Nick and R. A. Streatfeild, the editor of Butler,—the music critic,—despised the rival circle of Yellow Book survivors, the "rank crowd" that Ernest Dowson had formerly brought there, as much as they despised the placard religion of the tabernacles and almost as much as they loved the music of Handel. Uncle Nick, who had seen the soldiers marching off to the Crimean War, remembered hearing Disraeli in the House of Commons dis-missing as "mere coffee-house babble" the thunders of Gladstone who denounced the "Bulgarian atrocities" of 1875: he had dropped his monocle with a click against one of the buttons on his coat in the silence that accompanied his smooth-faced defence of the Turks. The old-fashioned rationalist Uncle Nick, who strolled through the streets with his arms behind him, was a great concert-goer in his afternoons, and he spent mornings in auction-rooms and rummaging the book-stalls where he made extraordinary finds in the penny boxes. In one of these later I saw a copy of my own first book which had been exposed for a while in the sixpenny box, where I had observed it many times with the rain bespattering it so that the gilt on the cover grew dimmer and dimmer. When it sank to this penny box I rescued the book.

Uncle Nick's favourites were seventeenth-century authors, Fuller of the *Worthies,* for one, Sir Thomas Browne and the Jeremy Taylor of the exquisite essay on Marriage, while, an epicure as well as a bibliophile, he was devotedly attached to all the French people in the house where he had lived so long. He told me about the little dressmaker whose room was on the top floor and who had at last despaired of making a living. Unable to pay her bill, she had confided to Uncle Nick that she had to go on the streets "like everybody else," and that evening the chef knocked on her door, asked how large her bill was and said, "Here's the money. Don't be a bad girl." The next morning the cellerer came up and gave her ten pounds more, and before evening every man in the house had offered her money "to be good on." So much for the French,— "and in Soho," Uncle Nick added.

Among others who were kind to me was Mrs. John Richard Green, the widow of "Short History" Green whom I had read as a boy (and thought of as an early Victorian with his white neckcloth),—and there was Mrs. Green, still young, the witty

red-haired senator of the still far from conceived of Irish Free
State. When later I told J. B. Yeats that I had met Alice Stop-
ford Green he said that her father had wished to marry his
mother long before either he or she was born,—if they had
married there would never have been a poet Yeats,—and I
could tell him of the evenings when Mrs. Green kept open
house and her Irish officer-nephew held the floor there. His
way of keeping the conversation in his own hands was to say,
"You're right, you're right, you're per-r-r-fectly right,—there
was never a truer word spoken," a device that struck me as
worthy of Benjamin Franklin. For, paying full tribute to the
value of others' ideas, he was able in this way to continue
expressing his own. Kind, too, to me was Spencer Wilkinson,
not yet an Oxford professor, though he had the white beard
of Father Time, who put me through my Harvard Greek,
reciting the passage from Homer that I sometimes spout even
today to the ocean waves. He blew me up for not spending a
guinea on the twenty volumes of Lessing in German which I
had just seen, as I told him, on a neighbouring book-stall, for
perhaps he had never encountered an American who had not
a guinea to spare for books that in any case he could scarcely
read. I would have liked to spend the guinea on the little
portrait of Carlyle that stood for months in the window of a
Chelsea junk-shop, a portrait for which I was told the sage
had sat for the painter,—"W. Greaves,"—an old man who was
still living in a street near by. A year later, when I was in
New York, I read one day that Roger Fry and various other
critics had "discovered" Walter Greaves and said he was almost
the equal of his teacher Whistler, and that his pictures
were selling for two or three hundred pounds and even his
drawings now brought forty or fifty. But the critics soon
changed their minds; and, returning to London in 1913, I

saw some of his drawings in a print-seller's window that were priced at five or ten shillings just as before. His vogue had risen, his vogue had passed, all within a year or two, and the old man was a nobody again, still living.

One friend whom I made at the British Museum was an Anglo-Polish painter who was reading Pater and certain Latin poets,—he was thrilled by Propertius, who suggested to him subjects for pictures,—and with whom I stayed for a week or two in Paris, where I had urgent reasons for spending Christmas. Carol F.-W. was at work on drawings for a Polish translation of the Rubáiyát, and he had exhibited at the autumn Salon that year and was having some success selling his pictures. Lee Simonson was with us there,—he was in the circle of Gertrude Stein, intending at that time to become a painter,—though presently Carol F.-W. wrote to me from Warsaw, in exile for a time from both Paris and London. His family were all away,—it was summer in the empty house, with the housekeeper "safe under lock and key" and everything done up in muslin and brown paper wrappers, and he had nothing to do in Warsaw but gossip with his aunt, walk through the charming parks and read Kipling and Ouida. The acacia trees were loaded with blossoms whose scent came up into the window and gave him romantic thoughts as he lay in bed, and it struck him that I would enjoy this "little Paris," as he said the Varsovians somewhat imprudently termed it. For the whole town might have been packed into the Place de la Concorde. And yet its career was the most tragic in Europe; it was even more tragic than the career of Paris,—and who could have guessed in 1907 how tragic the career of Warsaw was still destined to be?

In that direction my mind never roamed, though I thought often of Italy, of Naples and Florence and the Campo Santo at Pisa with the long wild grass and the buttercups that looked up at "The Triumph of Death." Closing my eyes, moreover, I also saw Gibbon's old house at Lausanne where at that time his library was still reposing. I could see the garden and the southward view overlooking the slope to the lake and the mountains of Savoy rising beyond. But the London streets filled my imagination as I measured the cracks in the pavement, feeling that if I stepped on a certain crack I might expect to succeed in my next undertaking, for my mind was very far away from the journalistic work I did and fixed upon what I thought of as my personal writing. Still the Harvard aesthete, I caught myself writing about Tammany and Bryan in the style of Arthur Symons or Yeats's prose.

How little time meant as, at twenty-one, thinking of all I was to do, I walked hour after hour on Hampstead Heath, stopping perhaps for tea at Jack Straw's Castle. Sometimes I sat like Poe's "man of the crowd" in the bay-window of a coffee-house and, catching sight of someone who interested me on the street outside, I put on my hat and followed him until it was dark. The coffee-house was usually a Lyons or an ABC where sardines on toast cost fourpence with a penny for tea, and occasionally I walked at night under the acetylene flares of the stalls when the Soho streets were a nightmarish phantasmagory. I felt myself hallucinated and moving through illusions. Once, in the East End, it struck me that every man I saw was legless or armless or wanting a nose or an eye, as in some Beggars' Opera or Hogarthian hell; and meanwhile at Roche's I read Leopardi, Pascal and *Wilhelm Meister* and planned especially a study of Vernon Lee. I read this sympathetic writer day after day at the British Museum, though my book dwindled into an essay for a magazine at home, while I dreamed of another on the English art-critics from Reynolds to Pater and John Addington Symonds, of which at least I wrote one long chapter on Hazlitt. For I was still thinking of the art-criticism that I had begun in a juvenile way with a paper, at fourteen, on Paolo Uccello, the first composition that I remember writing except for an infantile story called "Mary the Cook." But I was a slow and laborious worker, as I have remained, in fact, for I never write more than a page in the fullest morning, and I envied writers like Hilaire Belloc whose secretary I knew,—it was she who typewrote my first book. He would send Miss B. a wire telling her to go to his country-house for the period of a recess in Parliament, and there, in a fortnight of mornings, prowling in his study, he would dictate the whole of a long novel. It was all impromptu, for he was active politically and had little time to think of writing, although sometimes, reviewing for the *Morning Post,* he would leave a taxi ticking below while he bounded up the stairs with an armful of books. He would take the first book off the pile, run his eye through it and begin to talk, dictating ten reviews in fifty minutes, which seemed to me astonishing because Belloc was almost a great writer at times and could never have been called a common hack. But his review of Frederick Moore's *The Passing of Morocco* set me wondering about this sort of mind, for, in his hasty way, he made only one point about the book and on that small point he was mistaken. As I remember it, he said that the Foreign Legionaries did not wear little red caps in Morocco, and Moore, who was fresh from that country, had seen the red caps. What made it all the stranger was that the half-French Belloc had had as a young man his military training in France and the French army was one of his great subjects.

At the approach of spring, in February, 1908, Fred Moore came to my rescue once again, for my mind had turned back

to America, which seemed to be my theme, and I was eager
to write a book about it. Full of questions about the country,
I felt I might answer some of these if I could find the place
to work them out, and Fred suggested a village in Sussex,
West Chiltington, near Pulborough, where one of his friends
was living, a black and white artist. At that time J. L. C. Booth
was on the staff of *Punch*, in which every week he had a
drawing,—usually some hunting scene, with horses and
hounds,—and he found me a room with casement windows in
a farmhouse called "The Friars" where once Queen Anne was
supposed to have spent a night. It was also supposed that a
monk lay buried in the cellar, for the house was a fragment
of an old monastery; and there I was to spend four months
writing *The Wine of the Puritans,* which was published in
London in the autumn of that year. There was a rambling old
attic and my walls were papered over ancient beams and hung
with gilded mottos I was glad to put up with, for I was fond of
Mrs. Adams who woke me up tinkering at the fire and depositing my breakfast by the bed. I thrashed about in my tin tub,
boiled my shaving water, dressed half out of the window
watching the starlings, drew my table up to the hearth, glanced
at the newspaper and lighted my pipe, a corncob that was
called a "Missouri meerchaum." Mark Twain had popularized
this even in England. Then, reading my letters first, I set to
work. I took my midday meals with Farmer Adams and his
wife downstairs in the tinselled dining-room, where we had
mutton, hot or cold, seven days in every week, invariably
topped off with suet pudding.

In the afternoon, sometimes alone, at other times with
Moore or Booth, I went for a ten-mile walk over the Downs,
or to Storrington or Arundel, still further away, and occasionally the parson, Mr. Caldecott, who had time on his hands

to kill, sent me a little note suggesting a stroll. He addressed me as "U. S. A. Brooks" in the first of these. We passed gypsies camping by the roads and a Tree of Justice that was hung with stoats and with weasels, owls and moles dangling from the branches, as a Christmas tree is hung with coloured balls, while the buds came out on the other trees and the primroses and daffodils blazed in clearings in the woods and over the fields. They filled at Easter the little church with the twelfth-century frescoes so that it looked like a jewel-case lined with yellow velvet,—not an inch of stone showed through the primroses that blanketed the walls; and there Mr. Caldecott preached with his riding boots visible under his cassock and the choir consisted mainly of our friend Booth. It was only a year later that Booth and Moore, returning to Constantinople, were shot, and all but fatally, in a cross-fire in the streets when Booth, shot first, dropped his camera and Moore, stooping to pick it up, felt a ball passing through his shoulder and his neck. He fell like a log and could not twitch a finger,—he was paralyzed for a year from neck to heels; but he recovered to spend a long life of adventure in the Near East, in China and in Washington at last. Booth was not so fortunate. Giving up his work on *Punch*, he farmed for a while in Australia and then he was killed at Gallipoli in the first world war.

I, meanwhile, had been thinking much of Americans and America, which I seemed to see better in perspective, living abroad, and which, for some reason, possessed my mind, supplanting as an interest more and more my interest in the Middle Ages and the history of art. I did not realize at all how much the *zeitgeist* controlled me here, just as it controlled my feeling for living in the slums, or how many other American minds were moving on lines that were like my own with similar dislikes and hopes regarding our country. The authors of

Babbitt and *Marco Millions,* like Waldo Frank and many another, felt as I felt about the predominance of business, together with the nervous tension of life at home and its provincial immaturity. It seemed to me later, looking back, that all the young writers of my time had been asking, What is wrong with American living?—not realizing that anyone else had been asking the same question,—seeking for answers in one form or another and whether they wrote poems or plays or novels or short stories or criticism. Some shared the typical Harvard feeling that Americans were born Philistines and could only become anything else through contact with Europe, and I actually supposed that the only chance an American had to succeed as a writer was to betake himself there with all possible speed. But could that solve the problem? I was convinced as well that a man without a country could do nothing of importance, that writers must draw sustenance from their own common flesh and blood and that therefore deracination also meant ruin. For me, at that time, the American writer could neither successfully stay *nor* go,—he had only two alternatives, the frying-pan and the fire; and the question was therefore how to change the whole texture of life at home so that writers and artists might develop there. For writers and artists were the centre of the universe for me,— the oyster existed solely to produce the pearl. With whatever degree of absurdity or sense, these ideas were to fill my mind, with certain related ideas, for a long time to come, leading eventually to my studies of Mark Twain and Henry James, neither of which ever quite satisfied me. The fault of both, especially the latter, was that in order to make my case,—which had some truth at least on the plane of types,—I was obliged to force individuals into general categories, to fit complex persons into beds of Procrustes. And yet, to a large degree in both cases, I think, the individual tallied with the type.

One influence that had brought to a head my feeling about America, shaping as well the first form in which I expressed it, was the English writer G. Lowes Dickinson,—an amateur sage, I would call him now, not to disparage him but to mark a distinction. His book *A Modern Symposium* had greatly impressed me, and my friends and I must have had it in mind when, in college, we formed a group to discuss various questions once a fortnight. Each member was supposed to represent some particular point of view, as the poet, the painter, the musician, the economist and so on. Dickinson became the rage on his second visit to the United States,—he was almost a national idol for a few years,—and the reason seemed to be that he so disliked the country, in which he was able to find nothing that was good. One might have found in all this a masochistic element, as if Americans liked whips and scorpions, and at any rate it showed our appetite for criticism, for the movement of national self-scrutiny on which we were embarked. We seemed to be hungry for punishment, in the phrase of the moment, as if the impulse of the "muckrakers" had spread beyond the political sphere and invaded every corner of American living and thinking. To Dickinson, America was a barbarous country where no life of the spirit could survive and from which the artist was inevitably driven to Europe, inasmuch as only there could he exist and create, a land without leisure, religion or beauty whose ideal was an activity for its own sake that repelled all thought of disinterested contemplation.

This chimed well with my juvenile fantasy and the questions I was disposed to ask, Where so many were prosperous, why were so few happy?—Where there was so much humour, why was life so joyless?—Where there was so much intelligence, why was there so little writing that was good?—and why was I abroad when I believed in living at home? All these questions boiled up and over in the unripe little book that I wrote, in the form of a dialogue, in the Sussex farmhouse,— writing it first as a series of letters and then as a long essay before I followed Dickinson in his conversations. I had in mind a French phrase that I had picked up somewhere, "It is not night but only the absence of day," for, seeing the actual America merely, and not too much of that, I saw nothing of the potential that counted for me later. The book was published before I went back to New York.

CHAPTER VIII

NEW YORK

FIVE YEARS later I returned to England to spend another eighteen months writing and teaching a class of working people. But now for three years I lived in New York. "Why waste the best years of your life in a new country?" my Soho friend, Uncle Nick, had written to me, and in fact my reasons were mainly practical, for America to me was negative still, as it was to so many of Henry James's people. I still saw chiefly what it lacked, beside the older civilizations, instead of what they lacked and America possessed, the virgin soil Turgenev saw in his own "great fresh country" where each could feel that he had a role to play. For that I was still far too immature.

I found a room in a lodging-house on West Twenty-third Street in New York, in the old block that was known as London Terrace, built three generations before on the family farm of the bishop who wrote the poem that begins " 'Twas the night before Christmas." There were three big trees in the front yard, with a cast-iron fountain and a bench, and, within, the kind of furnished rooms that O. Henry so often described with half-broken chairs and the odour of mildewed woodwork. It was kept by a brawny Scotswoman with a drunken husband, and there was an ancient libidinous chambermaid, always dressed in rusty black, who might have stepped out of an eighteenth century novel.

There I found already established another Scot, a gentle soul whose foot was also on the first rung of the literary ladder. R. W. Sneddon was a humorist from Glasgow who had had some sort of connection with the theatre there and who longed to live in Paris but feared he was destined to remain under the Stars and Stripes,—"more stripes than stars." He dreamed of the *vie de Bohème* that appeared in his unpretentious tales and the plays that he wrote or adapted from certain French authors, sitting ten or twelve hours a day, concocting jokes for *Judge* and *Puck* or toiling for *The Smart Set* and *Harper's Weekly*. Serenely laborious, pipe in mouth, with his little Parisian coffee-machine, he wore a brown robe that was like a Franciscan habit, and, making each year a hundred dollars more than he had made the year before, he aspired to be out of debt in some measurable future. He was approaching this by a sort of arithmetical progression, outdistancing one or two housemates who had no such hope or even any such ambition. For the house soon became a Grub Street dormitory. Tinckom-Fernandez settled there, joined for a summer by Conrad Aiken, whom I saw briefly then and never knew well, and, among others, two English actors, one of them an ex-naval commander whom I was to meet again in later years. Charles,— to omit his other name,—had two large theatre trunks filled with gaudy clothes that he wore on the stage, including a white flannel suit with purple braiding, and sad was the day when Mrs. Lloyd locked him out with the clothes inside because he had not been able to keep up with the rent. Then Violet,—to omit her other name,—bailed out the theatre trunks and carried Charles himself away to Egypt.

It was a discouraging household, especially in winter, when

the trains on "Death Avenue," at the corner, ploughed through
the snow and one had to resort to the free-lunch counter at
the saloon across the street that was one of Edwin Arlington
Robinson's haunts. For Robinson had lived eight years before
in a brownstone house a hundred yards away. But there was
much brewing of rum-punch and tea in my big room at the
front, with the death-mask of Thackeray and the crucifix over
the mantel, and with J. B. Yeats's drawing of himself hailing
Sneddon and me on the street only to be left behind in the
weary distance. For I had met Yeats soon after my return to
New York. I was still at the infantile stage, moreover, when
misery seemed to me picturesque, even the groans of poor
devils regretting their existence, and I was full of my own
histrionics, dramatizing everything I did, sometimes in the
manner of Sentimental Tommy. I delighted in holes in my
trousers and the bottoms of my shoes, wearing at the same time
a flower in my buttonhole or dressing as far as I could in the
opposite extreme. I felt I acquired a secret strength by reacting
in this way against the popular pattern of the young business
man, a type that seemed to me as insipid and banal as the
rows of young maple trees on suburban streets. I supposed that
by so doing I somehow connected myself with the venerable
race of unworldly or vagabond writers who had shared this
cult of shabbiness, poverty and failure. Occasionally, wishing
to appear old-fashioned, I wore my grandfather's round sleeve-
buttons, and, longing for an excuse to wear tortoise-shell glasses,
I had my eyes examined, finding that they were all too tire-
somely normal. I passed through the mimetic phases that young
writers usually undergo, imitating this man's gestures and
that man's walk, while, at the same time, I was inept on the
actual stage, with neither the talent nor the presence of mind
of an actor. In college I had been obliged to act in a German

play, in which I appeared as a young baroness with a blonde wig, though I understood so little German that I scarcely knew what the play was about and felt like a shanghaied sailor waking up at sea. Then Sarah Bernhardt appeared in Boston depending on supers from Harvard to fill up the cast when she played in *Fedora,* and Edward Sheldon and I were chosen to act as gendarmes and arrest her and conduct her off the stage to her throne in the wings. Fortunately, on that occasion, I did not have to utter a word, but I could hardly have felt more relieved to escape from the boards and the footlights if I had been arrested myself to be discharged soon after.

Meanwhile, I continued to relish the slums, their colour and variety, the stir in the streets, the craftsmen plying their trades in little shops, and often I spent the whole of a Sunday at a café in East Houston Street, reading and writing at one of the marble-topped tables. I was surrounded there by the real mysteries of the ghetto and by Yiddish actors and newspapermen playing chess and drinking tea like figures from the Russian novels I was greedily absorbing. Among these were some of the East Side characters whom Hutchins Hapgood was writing about, types that had interested Stephen Crane who had lived on Twenty-third Street too, across the way from me, a dozen years before. His housemate Edward Marshall, the crippled correspondent, lived there still, nursing his recollections of the mercurial Crane, a name to me almost as vague then as Edwin Arlington Robinson's name or the name of Theodore Dreiser, who was also in New York. In time these names were to make the town magnetic to an imagination that saw itself in 1909 as lost and astray there. I scarcely knew even the name of Frank Norris, who had read the manuscript of Dreiser's first book in the office in which I presently found myself working.

For, loyal as ever, Max Perkins, already at Scribner's, had discovered a place for me with Doubleday and Page, assisting Walter Hines Page on *The World's Work* magazine, with which for most of a year I was to be connected. Harry Steger, the editor there, shepherded O. Henry, locking him up with a case of whiskey in the hotel bedroom where he had to turn out the stories that Doubleday published. These stories fascinated J. B. Yeats who found them, like Kipling's, all tinsel but quite without Kipling's vulgarity and elaboration, and Yeats said that O. Henry wrote such queer English and was yet so delicious that perhaps one ought to forget Addison and Swift. Meanwhile, Harry Steger introduced me to Francis Hackett, who enabled me to write, for the Chicago *Evening Post*, anything that came into my head, in my own way; and what a relief was that to me, out of my element as I was on Mr. Page's strenuous magazine. It was true I was encouraged to publish in this an interview with Howells, who had been so kind to me two years before and who was living now in West Fifty-seventh Street with a small workroom adjoining a big studio with skylights. The room contained only his table and chair with another chair for me and a bookcase entirely filled with his own publications, four or five shelves, at least, of Howells's books; and this hero of the young realistic novelists was naturally annoyed that I had not read more of his own novels. I doubt if I had read more than one, though I was to read them all in time, drawn almost as deeply to him as to William James, for, in spite of his conventional entanglements, Howells had a beautiful feeling for life and a spacious and generous understanding of it. When the interview was over, he asked me to ride down-town with him on one of the new Fifth Avenue motor-buses, and I remember the alert curiosity with which, from our seat on the top, this old story-teller stud-

ied the crowds on the sidewalks. It was at about this time that
I also saw Mark Twain,—whom I had never seen alive,—lying
in his coffin; for, observing the crowd on Fifth Avenue in front
of a church, I had climbed up to the gallery and looked down
upon him. The funeral was over but the lid of the coffin was
open, and there lay the author of *Huckleberry Finn,* with his
white hair spread loose, dressed for the last time in his white
flannels.

But this chance of a literary interview with Howells was
rare at the Doubleday office, where, among other miscellaneous
tasks, I arranged and edited the humdrum campaign speeches
of President Taft. In this air of advertising schemes and "hitting the women of the country hard," I fostered a little plan
that came to nothing, although one of my friends and I discussed it on a walking trip down the Connecticut valley, starting in the shadow of Ascutney from the Perkins house at
Windsor. This was to set up a small printing-press like Miss
Yeats's Cuala Press to bring out essays and translations of
writers whom we liked, one of the day-dreams that possessed
my mind as I wandered about the New York streets or over
Brooklyn Bridge on a starry night. Or lunched at the Lafayette or at Scheffel Hall, the big dim German beer-cave with
the frescoes under the Gothic roof that was the scene of one of
O. Henry's stories. For, as it comes back to me, there was no
escaping this story-teller whose trail was all over the New
York scene of those days. My Doubleday career, as I ought to
regret, was like Wilkie Collins's business career, characterized
by its "full, vivid, instructive hours of truancy," and even now
I sometimes feel that I should apologize to Mr. Page whom,
in his way, I thought magnificent. I often stretched the lunch
hour to two hours or more reading Balzac's novels at the Lafayette, where one all but lived these novels in the coffee-room at

the front of the house, surrounded by French merchants playing dominoes and chess. The setting recalled the old Francophile New York of the days when ex-President Monroe still lived in the Egyptian dwelling on the opposite corner.

In Mr. Page's company I found one or two other friends, Edwin Björkman, for instance, and Tom Mackenzie, the rapscallion son of a South African judge,—I am not repeating his actual name,—who was yet so open-handed and so engaging. Disowned by his father, he had come to America as a table-steward on a White Star liner, rolled barrels for a few months in a Standard Oil yard, tended the door at the Mills Hotel, driven a taxi and consorted with thieves, while preserving his innocent air of a well brought up schoolboy. How round and big were his brown eyes, how charmingly eager his face, how fresh the flower in his buttonhole, how delightful his voice, and he lied, took laudanum, stole everything in sight,—his American grandmother's diamonds at last,—and bragged about his hair-raising criminal adventures. He had joined our asylum for incurables on West Twenty-third Street, and there he received a convenient cable summoning him home, along with his small boy's vanity and a large camera from the office. Seeing him off at the steamer, I also foresaw for him a life-term, at best, in some foreign prison; and what was my astonishment, fifteen years later, when I heard from him again,—he was editor of the principal newspaper in a great dominion. He had seemed merely an over-ripe fruit that had fallen from the tree of the dying world which Edwin Björkman's philosophy had left behind, concerned as this was with the *élan vital* of the new world that was coming to birth not only in Björkman's mind but in all our minds also. For which of us did not believe that we were on the verge of the "wonderful era" of which Jack Wheelock, in Germany, had written to me? Jack was carried away by *Jörn Uhl*, Gustav Frenssen's novel, as others, then or presently, were carried away by *Jean-Christophe* or *Pelle the Conqueror* or the notion of "creative evolution." That the world had been preparing to take a new step in social advance most of the men I knew agreed in feeling, and Jack Wheelock expressed the general mind when he went on to say, "What a triumphant era we face! The great movement is upon us and the 'muckrakers' in America and the troubles in Russia,—with the upheaval through all the rest of the labouring classes in Europe,—are but signs of the coming day. The labouring men are beginning to realize that it is unnecessary for a hundred men to live a life of agony that one may live a life of unhappy wealth . . . Revolution in Russia is imminent and when it takes place its effect will be as stupendous as that of the French Revolution and followed by as glorious an outburst of song."

This was the general feeling of the pre-world war years, the dawn of the "century of the child," as Ellen Key called it, a child that was going to be fed on H. G. Wells's "food of the gods," as many thought in that expansive time. Edwin Björkman thought so, busy as he was on *The World's Work* reporting projects of social advancement and reform, while he also wrote essays on Francis Grierson, Robert Herrick, William James and various other voices of the "new spirit." He popularized especially the Scandinavian literature that flowered in the American mind so briefly but so fully and, throwing so intense a light on the vital problems of the time, stirred the will that was bent on solving them. I had caught my first glimpse of the socialist movement at Harvard when Jack London, still in his twenties, lectured at the Union, with his open shirt and the shining face of a sailor boy fresh from the sea, vibrant with expectancy, vitality, hope and promise. Even Max

Perkins, the sceptical Yankee, was touched by socialist ideas
and he wrote me a thirty-one page letter from a hospital, after
an operation, deploring the regime of competition. He was
convinced that, freed from the profit motive, man would become an entirely different creature and that a negligible part
of his time would have to be given to material work when
machinery replaced slavery for the masses.

While I cast my first vote for the socialist ticket, I was a
chameleon, mentally, still, turning in any direction that caught
my fancy, with never an average moment or a confident moment as I went through my metamorphoses. Socialism seemed
to me "fairly insipid with veracity," to use Henry James the
elder's phrase, but otherwise I had not found my East and
I was only certain that write I must and wholly on my own
terms. All manner of hopes were held out to me if I would
wait for another ten years and make teaching or office-work
my principal interest, putting my whole heart into this for a
time, but something in me that seemed to me quite as organic
as my lungs obstinately refused to agree to do this. Obliged to
earn my living, I was bent on avoiding at any price the kind
of official entanglements that mortgage one's conscience, and
I clung to mechanical half-menial jobs that I could fulfil con-
scientiously without involving my imagination in them. It cost
me nothing, then or later, to refuse invitations to editorships
and other supposedly important and lucrative positions, of
which, in the end, numbers came my way, as when, for instance, Alfred Harcourt asked me if I would like to be "the
W. C. Brownell of Harcourt, Brace and Co." I was not obliged
to put into words my failure to respond to this, for Harcourt,
the brilliant publisher, was an appreciative reader and always
extremely kind to me, and I did not need to tell him how
often I had seen Brownell himself wandering, during the mid-

day recess, in the neighbourhood of Scribner's. I thought of Brownell, the personification of his own "democratic distinction," as the finest critical intelligence of his time in New York; but how little of this had left its deposit in the few small books he wrote, which seemed to me increasingly anæmic and sterile. Mistakenly or otherwise, I felt that his vitality had been drained off in the publishing office; and how fully I seemed to understand the dying Tolstoy's flight from home and the kind of responsibilities that I so dreaded. Day after day, in 1910, I followed in a state of enchanted suspense the newspaper stories of "Tolstoy wandering on," escaping from Yasnaya Polyana in his peasant blouse and boots, hoping perhaps to join the Dukhobors. In his last desperate pilgrimage this greatest of novelists seemed to me an emblem of some deep necessity of artists and writers.

Meanwhile, my college friends were turning homeward, one by one, reappearing from Europe and settling in New York, Joe Breck, for example, who was now at the Metropolitan Museum and with whom I discussed vague plans for a collaboration. I looked on the history of art as a sort of possession of my own, jealous that anyone else knew anything about it,—a well-known adolescent feeling,—while at the same time I was not unwilling to share it with someone who knew ten times as much as I. Another day-dream begotten by Ruskin was a plan for a history of the Utopian idea which Lewis Mumford later carried out,—for he was a disciple of Ruskin also in those days,—striking with this book the keynote of a high career that I was to follow with the utmost of respect and wonder. Mitchell Kennerley had brought out an American edition of the small book of which I had paid half the costs in England, and he was to publish within two or three years two other books of mine, studies of H. G. Wells and John Addington Symonds.

I came to regard these rather coldly, feeling, as Havelock Ellis felt, that publishing books of criticism too early is an error,— unless a writer is prepared to eat his words; but when years later Mitchell Kennerley took his own life in New York I wondered that there had been so few to praise him. What did it matter in the end that he sometimes played a double game? He made little or nothing out of his exasperated authors, and who else would have printed them, who else would have looked at their first little books, which Kennerley delightedly acclaimed and so charmingly published? Like John Lane in England, whose agent he had been, he backed books often at a loss, with a feeling for talents that no one but he distin- guished; and he should be remembered as the friend of a whole generation of writers whom, in surprising numbers, he first brought out.

Edward Sheldon was living in New York, though only in- termittently, for he was already too popular to do his work there, with half the most famous women of the stage waiting in his anteroom to talk over plays that he was to write for them. He seemed to breathe telegrams and his suitcases bulged with unopened letters, while he remained unspoilable with his high good spirits, passing from triumph to triumph in a world that I knew nothing of but always ready for adventures in any other world. Occasionally at rehearsals he would ask me to take out to lunch some actress who struck me as a formidable creature,—for I always spelled the word Actress with a large A at that time,—thrusting into my hand a purse that was filled with golden ducats, well knowing that in all probability my pockets were empty. But I observed that the more dangerous the ladies looked the surer they were to ask for milk toast and rice pudding. Ned's plays were coming out virtually at the rate of two a year,—the most popular of all, *Romance,* in 1911,—

mingling the glamorously erotic that he so loved in Byron with the bawdy, the macabre and the clownishly funny. Nothing amused him more than a barker expounding the merits of a side-show freak,—"*Is* she fat? Is she *fat?* Oh, my, my, *my!*"— which presently appeared in his play about Coney Island.

This was one of the notes he struck in the showers of postcards that came from him when he broke away in order to do his work. He was perhaps in England near J. M. Barrie and Arnold Bennett or staying with the Norman Hapgoods in some quiet village, in a rectory all roses without and dimity within, playing tennis in the afternoon with William Faversham, across the green, in the court of an Elizabethan manor-house. He would write about Tetrazzini's singing or Mrs. Campbell's Hedda, or he would quote something that Annie Russell had said to him, or possibly Viola Allen or Margaret Anglin. He was travelling with John Barrymore in Italy again, rewriting scenes and even whole plays for him, "unbinding" this "Prometheus," as Gene Fowler later said, "awakening him to his mission." Or he was on Lake Como, in a big old frescoed farmhouse, surrounded with tuberoses and heliotrope as he worked on a play. He wrote from Urbino, Ravenna, Tivoli, Parma, a town all seventeenth century with a perfumed brocaded cathedral, Correggios, great candelabra and altar-cloths of gold. He sent me two or three photographs of the theatre in the Farnese palace, a ruinous old barn of a place with seats out of plumb, with battered equestrian statues in it, wooden cupids with broken heads and a vast worm-eaten dusty abandoned stage. The sunlight that came through chinks in the roof threw spotlights on the floor of this, and, standing in one of these, he looked out at the empty tiers and imagined that he was a Scapin or a Scaramouche. He saw himself with high heels and a small black mask. Then he wandered on to the

picture gallery with the portraits of the old duchesses and
dukes, together with their dwarfs and lapdogs, all alike. They
were very pink and white, with slanting eyes and small full
mouths, secretive and suggestive as the closed shutters of a
house at noon.

Once in England Ned Sheldon went to see Eric Bell, in the
shining new sanitarium with the quiet trained nurses to which
Eric, another of my Doubleday friends, whom Ned, whom
everybody loved, had been condemned for tuberculosis. J. B.
Yeats was especially fond of this nephew of the publisher
George Bell who had come to New York for adventure and
broken down there,—for he "wouldn't follow rules," Yeats said
sadly,—and he had been shipped home again, doomed to spend
his remaining days among minds like "tubercular cabbages," as
he put it in a letter. One of the patients was a medical student
who had just reached the Rider Haggard stage, one was a
rubber planter who quoted Kipling and one was the sort of
Englishman who stares at you for an hour and says, "That's
rather a decent tie you have on." Eric was as much in revolt
against England as I was against America: he laughed at his
unimaginative countrymen who were always seizing colonies
and climbing mountains. Why their mania for "aiguilles" and
"cols," their singular wish in Switzerland "to get to the top of
everything and sit on it"? He had been himself in Switzerland,
at another sanitarium, where he thought the scenery was too
theatrical, with its picture-postcard villages and clear-cut peaks;
and, as for the English, he could not see them as idealistic
altruists whose one real dream was "improving the condition
of the natives." He had fallen in love with what he called my
"genial and to me congenial country" where he had begun to
write articles and impressions of people, free-lancing and even
attempting Casanovian memoirs, while, tall and well-made,

witty and gay, with a wonderful sense of the absurd, he had wildly indulged a natural taste for mischief. At home again, dying at twenty-seven, obliged to eschew the "great indoors," he was, he said, getting to be like one of Hardy's minor characters, "developing into one of those chaps who can tell the hour by looking at the sun and tell the time of year by watching the birds."

Ned Sheldon was always quoting Eric who spoke of the kind of party, for instance, after which all the guests, on the following morning, felt obliged to write notes of apology to everyone else. He said that the only trouble with living at home was that you were treated as one of the family. Struggling to keep alive while he seemed to be bent on destroying himself, Eric had escaped for one winter, at least, in New Hampshire, living as a hired man on the place of the painter Abbott Thayer, labouring as he had learned to do in Switzerland. He felt like Michael Fairless in *The Roadmender*, as he said, in his little hut covered with snow there, sallying forth at seven in the morning to work in the woods or fields, winning his bread again with two dollars a day. He found the real happiness in manual toil that Tolstoy had discovered, with the white old snow-capped Monadnock looking on as he cleared away fallen timber with his axe, listening in the evening while Abbott Thayer discussed his researches in protective coloration and living with the family, who were all for the simple life. They started going to bed, in relays, at seven.

No one guessed that Ned Sheldon, at almost the same age, was beginning to die, like Eric, on the physical plane, though, the more he was disabled, the more his spirit came to life as in one of the great souls one found in the lives of the saints. The time was not far off when he was to write, "I can walk a little. I go from bed to couch,"—he had walked eight steps with each foot in less than six minutes,—and when he said that he was unable to move his legs at all,—"or I should take to-night's train and burst in on you." It was after this that he became the "father-confessor of the theatre" in New York and what Thornton Wilder called the "dispenser of wisdom, courage and gaiety" when he dedicated to Edward Sheldon *The Ides of March*. Living vicariously in the careers of his friends, a counsellor and guide for each of them, uncannily perceptive as well as heroic, he was, in a time when everything overshadowed wisdom, the only wise man whom many knew. Confronting day after day the abyss of non-being, he submitted to find bread in stones and life in the blank mind, and all without self-pity, objective towards himself and, full of pity for others, always laughing. Blind and unable to turn his head, he could not see the model of the galleon in full sail on the shelf behind him, but whoever placed it there perceived the symbolism that no one who ever saw him could have missed.

I had left Doubleday's, meanwhile, feeling that I was out of place attempting the kind of magazine writing one did there, and, explaining my case to Mr. Page, I said good-bye to him, happy enough to escape from a false position. J. B. Yeats called me the most impulsive man he knew, but I never regretted that I was impulsive then, for I reasoned that if I acted promptly something would turn up in line with my real interests, as I saw them. And, as it happened, the Standard Dictionary had lost a definer of words that day and I was engaged at once to take his place, thus beginning a two-year stretch as one of an army of professional hacks, working on a dictionary and presently on an encyclopædia. Twenty-five dollars a week was the usual reward for taking all knowledge as one's province, for writing articles on Chinese literature, Arabian poetry and Italian art or re-phrasing definitions from the rival Webster. At five cents a definition, I could earn this amount in five hours a day, and, finding that if I did more, the rate was reduced proportionately, I kept a margin of time for my own writing. For the encyclopædia I took notes at the Astor Library, the architectural fantasy on Lafayette Street, undergoing what Frank Moore Colby called the "trials of an encyclopædist" when he was himself the editor of a similar work. But I learned something about words and about arranging facts and discriminating among authorities,—most important of all,—and, for the rest, I could not see that the witty Colby, whom I met, had been "badly damaged" by his calling. He described this as "twenty years among the barebones of all subjects and seeing the full rotundity of none." One of the encyclopædias that Colby worked on collapsed at the completion of the letter A. Mine did not collapse until it went through D.

Many times since those days I have wondered about my comrades there, the regiment of "writers for the booksellers" with whom I laboured, a remnant of Grub Street, astray from the eighteenth century, that included R. W. Sneddon along with me. Even Jack Wheelock worked with me on the dictionary of proper names, side by side with an elderly colleague who turned on the gas in his room one night because he could not face his sixty-fifth birthday. "What a pity," the editor said, "when he had got our style so well!"—when, triumphantly fulfilling the law of adaptation to environment, he had been a success, if he had only known it. There were possibly fifty others in this legion of hacks who drifted with the literary tides like a mass of seaweed, settling for a few weeks or months wherever there was work for them to do, then shuffling on their coats and moving on. It might be another encyclopædia or a set of business manuals or a popular world history in a dozen volumes, but when a project had been carried through there was always another to be taken up and they turned on one tap as easily as they turned off another.

It was a foreign legion, mainly, made up of threadbare soldiers of fortune, decayed scholars, illusionists, renegades, misfits, Englishmen who had lost caste and unfrocked Irish priests, together with a handful of young aspirants for the literary life. Most of them were veterans who had been jostled and broken by our metallic American world and who were truly nomads of a twilight of letters, O'Shea, for one, who might have been a scholar-hermit in the Ireland of the saints and Donnelly with Barry Lyndon airs. Another was Morgan, if that was his name, who could relate in seven tongues the exploits of his fifteen years as a soldier in Morocco. I think of them all as generalized in a type that might have been William Maginn, the original of Thackeray's Captain Shandon, the founder of *Fraser's Magazine,* who spent most of his life in debtors' prisons, inerrant as he was, "barring drink and the girls." If not always "bright," like Maginn, they were always "broken."

Among all these comrades there was only one whose secret I ever learned. This was the Nabob, as the others called him, who was different indeed, in appearance at least, from the shaggy-chinned derelicts about him, with his hawk's nose and eye and the grey drooping moustache that fell with such admirable curves from his well-shaven cheeks. His coat had been cut with distinction, his apple-green scarf was of exquisite silk, his spats were never dishonoured by a fleck of mud, and, looking more ducal every day than he had seemed the day before, he inspired a kind of awe in the breasts of the others. For, humbled as they had been by life, they saw him as a creature of the upper air, toiling in their limbo, presumably, for some reason of amusement, in charge of the division of "art" on the encyclopædia with which for a number of months I was connected. It happened that, having completed the articles on Avicenna, Buddhism, the Chinooks and finally Denmark (Literature),—rising in the alphabet from A to our terminal letter,—I found that I was expected to deal with Bernini, Bramante and Brunelleschi, and thus the Nabob's eye fell upon me. "By the way," he added, when we had discussed the preliminaries, "I have a new cap here. If you are going out of town on Sunday, will you take it and break it in for me?" It was a new idea to me that caps were broken in, and this was a cap of many colours that scarcely fitted into my philosophy of costume. But I took it, feeling vaguely that the cap would prove to be a clue, for the Nabob had begun to interest me.

Not long after this I went to see him. It was an icy night, just before Christmas, and I imagined the cosy evening we might have before the fire, chatting about Bernini and Brunelleschi. Expecting to see a well-stocked library, an elderly bachelor's haven, perhaps with an old master or two and a Roman bust, I stopped at No. 13, one of those brick houses in Stuyvesant Square that sometimes already sheltered birds of passage. But I was rather surprised when the Nabob, coming to the door himself, led me up four flights of stairs, and I found myself in a hall bedroom, a servants' room in former days, with an iron bedstead, a bureau, a huge wardrobe and two chairs. There was not a book in the room, or even a picture, save for one photograph representing the well-known face of an elderly eccentric, the garrulous son of a celebrated diplomat father. This man had made a few stabs at fame by writing reminiscences of certain crowned European heads he had encountered as a boy and, oddly enough, there was something in the face that closely resembled the Nabob's hawk-like distinction. A gas-jet, high on the wall, threw a merciless glare

over the room. The Nabob opened one of the drawers, drew
out a stub of a candle, lighted it and set it on the bureau,
though its flame was drowned in the oily flood of the gas.
Then he said abruptly, "Why not call me Jack?"

Our efforts to launch a conversation were not very successful. We tried Brunelleschi, but I could see that the Nabob
had something much on his mind, and it came over me that
I was the first person with whom for years he had had a
chance to talk. I felt that, whatever his secret was, I was about
to hear it when he went over to the bureau and, opening the
drawer again, drew forth an armful of magazines and books.
Turning page after page, he showed me this illustration and
that, and there he was in every one of them. There were the
hawk's nose and eye, the grey moustache with its admirable
curves, there was the Nabob in all his sartorial splendour, as
an old Virginian colonel or a Scottish duke. He was perhaps
descending a palatial stairway or leading down the aisle a
bride divinely fair, holding a levee at some garden fête or be-
nignly saluting his daughter at her moment of betrothal.
Now thirty years old, now seventy or eighty, he was always
the perfect cavalier, for the Nabob's fortune had literally been
his face. Providence had given him the mask and bearing that
dukes should have, and he had shown his gratitude for years
by sitting for the illustrators as a model.

Then he unlocked his wardrobe, and there were the coats
that had so dazzled our dingy Grub Street limbo. There were
the waistcoats, the walking-sticks, the hats on the shelf, the
spats on the floor in a dozen piles exposed to the glare of the
gaslight. One by one he took them out and tried on this cap
or that, turning about the little room,—shabbier still by contrast,—showing me all the trophies of his ruling passion. It was
for this that the Nabob toiled every day as an unexposed au-

thority on the history of art. This was the glory for which he saved and schemed, to which he came home at night and awoke in the morning, his profession, his story, his secret, his destiny, his existence.

As for myself, it seemed to me that I was marking time in these miscellaneous drudgeries of the literary tyro, but time meant little to me then,—there was so much to spend or waste in the long vague stretch that lay before me. Later I found in Chateaubriand's *Mémoires d'Outre-Tombe* a phrase that expressed the feeling of so many in those days: "Let the young generations wait in hope,—there is a long time coming yet before we reach the end." That, at least, was my feeling about myself and about the world; and how sad it was to seem to me forty years later that young people could no longer feel that way.

CHAPTER IX

YEATS AT PETITPAS'

For a good part of a year John Butler Yeats had been living in New York before Edward Sheldon and I fell in with him in a little room in an old hotel where he sketched portraits of both of us in the pastels that he had just taken up. He had come over in 1908 with his elder daughter Lily, who was exhibiting embroideries in Madison Square Garden, and he had refused to go home again, although he was seventy at the time, saying, "To leave New York is to leave a huge fair ... In Dublin nothing happens except an occasional insolvency," whereas "here anything may happen" and "a sort of gambling excitement keeps me here." A lady who was cunning about the future had said to him many years before that he would not win success until he was old, but that then his success would be universal; and he had found Dublin, where he had painted everybody's portrait, not too sympathetic for an artist. He remarked in a lecture that "malignant criticism" would have been the fate of Watts if this English painter had been obliged to live there, and that if he had been "born in Dublin Watts would have read for the 'Indian Civil' and perhaps—passed," bidding farewell to art. The only thing the Dubliners admired was "mundane success," he said, a preference we others had found also in New York, but Yeats was uncommitted here, with the world all before him and a sense that life for him was "just beginning." Like Swedenborg's angels he felt he was advancing toward the springtime of his youth, putting forth every day new shoots of talent.

So he seemed to his New York friends, the artists and writers who gathered about him when he had settled at Petitpas' in West Twenty-ninth Street, the boarding-house kept by three sisters from Brittany with the restaurant in the back yard where Yeats sat at the head of one of the long tables. If some of these artists and writers were young and not invariably discerning or wise, they gave him all the sympathy he could have wished for, with the companionship that he said artists hungered and thirsted for, proud and solitary as they might affect to be. For, he said, "The artist gives that he may receive," and all these companions understood how rare were his own powers of growth,—he seemed to develop new faculties under their eyes. It was true that his portrait-painting was not as good as it had been in the fine pictures that I was to see in Dublin, pictures that seemed "to come to us," as Yeats observed of his favourite Watts, "out of the mists of memory and romance." From Watts he had first learned the true meaning of painting; and what profundity there was in his treatment of Standish O'Grady and John O'Leary, of George Russell,—AE,—and Katherine Tynan Hinkson, making all the surrounding portraits seem brittle and shallow.

That he was a "born portrait-painter imprisoned in an imperfect technique," Yeats was to write later to his elder son; and this had become more apparent as his life went on. But, at seventy, taking up pastels, he also wrote his first play, and these were only two of his new ventures, for, finding himself "quite an orator," he wrote the essays many of which I carried away for *The Seven Arts* and *The Freeman* later. "I was afraid to return to Dublin, afraid as a child dreads the fire," he remarked in one of the letters that were afterwards published,

"and I may add that New York saved my life . . . a dark saying which I could elucidate"; and there he was like the growing boy that he said an artist should always be,—"who is
never and never will be a grown-up." He continued, "An old
man should think of the past, but I am still interested in the
future,"—except when the death of some old friend brought
back "that long-vanished dream of my youth and marriage";
and saying, "We are happy when we are growing," he was
always looking for "improvement in my work" and what he
called "an immense change in my fortunes." No wonder he
attracted other artists and writers.

This old man eloquent, so "eagerly communicative,"—a
phrase in his *Early Memories* that was self-descriptive,—found
himself therefore surrounded by Robert Henri, John Sloan
and other bright souls, both men and women. They dined
with him at Petitpas', where George Bellows also appeared,
with Glackens, the brothers Prendergast, a number of young
writers,—among these Alan Seeger and Eric Bell,—and our
Twenty-third Street actor friend who spoke of the "perpetual
look of surprise" of Fred King of the *Literary Digest,* another
who was there. Yeats shook his head over Eric Bell's adventures of the flesh, almost condoning the sins, wholly loving
the sinner, admiring also, as poet and man,

> the eager
> Keats-Shelley-Swinburne mediæval Seeger,

whom, in *The Day in Bohemia*, John Reed described.

> Poe's raven bang above Byronic brow
> And Dante's beak,—you have his picture now;

and all he required, to complete the picture, was the long
black Paris student's cape that my brother-in-law-to-be had
worn at the Beaux-Arts. It was like the black military cape that
Poe took with him when he left West Point and that he

wrapped round Virginia when she died on her mattress of straw, hugging the tortoise-shell cat to keep herself warm. I lent Alan Seeger this cape for a winter. Meanwhile his "remote and dignified courtesy" greatly appealed to J. B. Yeats, with the eyebrows and long eyelashes that Yeats liked to sketch, his red lips against the dead white face, and his habit of looking downwards, chin on hand,—"a man to me infinitely more interesting than Rupert Brooke," as Yeats wrote to the son whom he always called "Willie." Occasionally W. G. Blaikie Murdoch also appeared at Petitpas', the Scottish nationalist who had written a book on the "greenery-yallery" Nineties and was full of strange learning especially about Japan. Blaikie Murdoch followed his own personal notions of style, sprinkling commas over his writing as a Parsee sprinkles red pepper over meat so that the substance is invisible under the coating. His writing was packed so tight with commas that it could neither move nor breathe, and I once had to spend half a day removing from one of his articles enough at least to let in light and air. Bald as a tonsured monk, with a mind as ripe as an old Roquefort cheese, Blaikie Murdoch was living in a basement somewhere, cooking his meals on a gas-jet, not far away; and, as he talked, he would stealthily manœuvre stray crusts of bread on the table into the yawning pocket of his old brown jacket. How similarly helpless in the brazen world were many friends of mine who were only at home in the golden world of art.

For me, as for most of us, Yeats himself was invested with the glamour of the literary revival in Ireland, so renowned at the time, and his talk abounded in recollections not only of "Willie" but of AE and Synge, Lady Gregory, the Abbey Theatre, George Moore, Dunsany. We had special reasons for our interest in this, for we felt we were on the verge of a not dissimilar movement of our own, the first phase of another revival that expressed an American coming-of-age, an escape from our old colonial dependence on England. Yeats himself said, "The fiddles are tuning all over America," as in Ireland they had been playing for a decade or more, and various figures of the Irish movement were living in New York and also appeared at Petitpas'. By far the best known were the Colums, Padraic and Mollie, and there was also Frederick Gregg who had once been regarded as Ireland's hope in poetry by AE and others. Gregg was a writer on the New York *Evening Sun*. Another of the friends of "Willie's" youth,—indeed, his most intimate school friend in Dublin,—who had settled in New York with his Russian wife was a tall black-bearded Orangeman, the son of a member of Parliament and the founder of the Hermetic Society that gave rise to the movement. For that coming together of a group of young people who were interested in the wisdom of the East and met to discuss the Upanishads and the Vedas had led in turn to an awakening of literary minds, just as their study of the Indian mythology and traditions had stirred their feeling for the Irish mythology and past. From the Hindu gods it was only a step to the gods of ancient Ireland. Charles Johnston had lived in India as a civil servant, translating the Bhagavad-Gita and other scriptures; and in Dublin, where he had been a leader of the Theosophists, he had married Madame Blavatsky's niece. This "splendid placid woman, like a summer sea,"—J. B. Yeats's phrase that perfectly described her,—virtually ran the Russian cathedral in East Ninety-seventh Street, for she was an ardent member of the Orthodox church. Her Presbyterian-Buddhist husband had become a staff-writer on the *New York Times,* a learned, austere and humourless man who wrote a book called *Why We Laugh* and who liked to dine with the father of his old Dublin friend. In their up-town apartment the Johnstons kept open house, and Charles Johnston, as I remember, had a passion for ice cream and used to send out for this at all hours of the night. Like AE and "John Eglinton," who was called the "Irish Emerson," he delighted not only in Emerson but in Whitman and Thoreau, the American sages who were devoted to the wisdom of the East and whom J. B. Yeats admired also. At least, Yeats had been one of the first to acclaim Whitman in earlier days and he had read *Walden* to "Willie" at the breakfast table. The poet Yeats later recorded that this occasioned the writing of his poem *The Lake Isle of Innisfree.*

The younger Yeats came to Petitpas', too, when I was in California, so that I failed to meet this extraordinary man,— although some years before I had heard him lecture,—and I think J. B. Yeats was somewhat afraid of the formidable son who seemed not to overflow with human affection. In every way humane himself, he was at ease with other people who abounded with the milk of human kindness, and a passage in a story of Willa Cather put me later in mind of him and what I supposed was his feeling about William Butler Yeats. "When kindness has left people, even for a few moments, we become afraid of them," Willa Cather says, "as if their reason had left them,"—leaving "a place where we have always found it"; and this notion was confirmed for me when I read J. B. Yeats's *Letters to His Son* whom he chides more than once for being "inhuman." He could not refrain from reproaching the poet for being "laconic and cold" in a letter to his "old and good friend Charlie Johnston"; and he asked, "As you have dropped affection from the circle of your needs, have you also dropped love between man and woman?" Writing again to his son as "a man who has cast away his humanity," he feels that "Willie" is tending toward the Nietzschean line, which belongs to "the clumsy and brutal side of things," proud as he was of this man of genius who had "given a tongue to the sea-cliffs," the first-born of his four gifted children. The two profoundly respected each other,—there was never any doubt of that,—and the son knew how much he owed his father; but the father would have understood Dolly Sloan and made allowances for John Sloan's wife when the son could not understand and could not forgive her. Mrs. Sloan mistakenly supposed that W. B. Yeats had money to spare when, visiting New York, he stayed at a great hotel,—at Lady Gregory's expense,—with the Irish Players; and, feeling that perhaps he did not know how sadly poor his father was, she went and appealed to him to assist his father. It was a blunder, but human, as J. B. Yeats would have seen at once, for all the fierce pride of the gentleman that he shared with his son,—aware as he was that Dolly Sloan, who had "no bravery at all," he said (meaning no bravado, no parade), had "the courage of the devil." For the sake of what lay behind it, he would have pardoned the blunder; he would not have felt merely the cold contempt with which his son bowed Dolly to the door, uttering one phrase only, "Good day, Madam."

No doubt the poet had reasons enough for turning against the human, seeing this perhaps as "all too human," like so many other writers of the post-war years; but the father's humanity bore, nevertheless, the same relation to this frame of mind that the sun bears to the moon as we see them from our planet. It was the fruit of an expansive age, and the culture that reflected this,—a diastole as compared with the systole of the age that followed,—and it had behind it a universality that everybody recognized and that many, like Yeats himself, have found in Shakespeare. If not the fruit of security too, insecure as the person might be, it sprang from a whole-hearted feeling about men and about life; and what strength lay behind the remark in the *Early Memories* of J. B. Yeats, "I am a cheerful and perennially hopeful man." It mortified him, he went on, to be so cheerful, convinced that he "shared this gift with all the villains . . . for it is their unsinkable buoyancy that enables these unfortunates to go on from disaster to disaster and remain impenitent." But, loving the sinner, as Yeats did, he saw the goodness in the sinner too, finding "man's inconsistency always a charm"; so that, worshipping human nature, as he said Shakespeare did, he found himself in a really impregnable position. One could not be too human; one could scarcely, in fact, be human enough; and for Yeats, who had "suddenly amazed" himself, "by coming to the conclusion that revealed religion was a myth and fable," this was all that was left for the law and the prophets. He had been reading Butler's *Analogy* as a student at Trinity College in Dublin when this counter-revelation suddenly surprised him; and it had settled for him the question of becoming what his father was, "a respectable Episcopalian clergyman."

This was the keynote of Yeats's thinking and of his portrait painting too, an art whose genius was "largely a genius for friendship," regarding which he further said that the best portraits were painted when friendship governed the relation of the sitter to the painter. He added that even its technique was "mainly a technique of interpretation," and in order to secure in his work the relation of friendship he seemed positively to shun lucrative commissions. Choosing to be fond of me and having trouble painting me, he would not listen to me, as he worked on my portrait, when I begged him to spend his time on more profitable sitters, although he was in arrears with the rent of his studio in Dublin and kept dreaming of people fishing and catching nothing. No, he knew my face now,—he had got another canvas and was bent on doing me again,—he was determined to do me to his own satisfaction, with a little bust of Goethe in the picture, resting on a volume of Bernard Shaw and W. B. Yeats's *Ideas of Good and Evil*. For he was convinced that his first portrait of me was a failure. He had come to my office in the rain in despair, so depressed that he could not sleep; and he sent me sketches of himself facing the canvas in hope, in exultation, in dejection and at last in triumph. This was all because I had had the joy of establishing with him a human relation and because we could talk congenially while he painted, as he had encouraged his models to talk in Dublin and in London, especially when the girls talked about "nothing." For he said he was not so much interested in any "interesting things" they told as in their "natural gift as truthful tellers,"—in short, in themselves, in the human nature that pleased him as it pleased Charles Lamb, whose note, he said, was a certain "capricious wildness."

It was by this criterion that he divided the goats from the sheep, the people of Belfast, for instance, from the other Irish in a country where "we solved all our doubts in matters of conduct," he said, "by thinking well of our fellow creatures . . . We prided ourselves upon it," he added in *Early Memories;* "we considered it a gentlemanly trait," unlike "the puritans who cling to their creed of the badness of human nature because it helps them in their unnatural war of commercial selfishness." I cannot guess what Yeats would have thought if he had lived into a later time when "original sin" was the rage with the literary young and when this had ceased to be identified with "puritanism" and became the mark of a High Church Anglican line. For him it was the special mark of the "dull people of Belfast" who were always talking of their commercial triumphs and a large part of whose religion might be stated in the phrase, "The man who sells his cow too cheap goes to

hell." Yeats's clergyman father had said, "Nothing can exceed
the vulgar assumption of a Belfast man,"—who liked to think,
Yeats went on, "My sons and my daughters and the men I employ are bad and naturally faithless, therefore let me coerce
them." Had not Bunyan talked the same way with his "Mr.
Carnality," his "Mr. Facing-Both-Ways" and so on, finding
epithets and names to belittle and degrade the temple of human nature and all its altars? I remember the distaste with
which Yeats repeated a phrase of Kate Douglas Wiggin, the
popular novelist whom he met one afternoon, "Whenever I
hear of human nature, I want to use a whip."

For himself, he would rather have listened to a Mayo man
whistling a tune, or telling a fairy-tale or a ghost story, than to
the greatest man in Liverpool or Belfast, and the Irish were
natural writers of plays, for they were like people sitting at a
play, watching the game of life, enjoying their neighbours. It
was in the nature of things that Ireland had produced in
Farquhar, Congreve and Goldsmith, in Sheridan, Oscar Wilde,
Shaw and Synge, all the ablest dramatists of latter-day England; for the Irish, with their inborn love of dialogue, were
"surrounded by a dialogue," said Yeats, "as lively, gallant and
passionate as in the times of the great Eliza." Would not
Shakespeare have liked to sit "with the courteous peasants
round their turf fires, listening to their musical sentences and
their musical names"? Inevitably plays like Synge's rose out of
their folk-tales and wild philosophy, rich in poetry and humour. They knew no distinction between the natural and the
supernatural, and in this Yeats himself was sometimes like
them.

For, with his love of whatever was human, he lived at moments on the border-line where it passed into the subhuman
or the superhuman, and I remember the perfect good faith

with which he received and passed on the news that the banshee had been heard crying round his brother-in-law's house. George Pollexfen, the astrologer, a solid man of Sligo, had died, wrote Yeats's daughter, just before dawn, and one of the nurses had awakened her when the crying first began because the other nurse was so alarmed. All three women had heard the crying, which they supposed was a cat before they fully realized it was the banshee,—it sounded like an old woman in distress; and, often as I saw Yeats repel the usual gush about fairies, there were no doubts in his mind on that occasion. His voice was all gravity and awe as he read me the letter. It put me in mind of the stories about AE, for instance, who would suddenly say, in the woods, in the Dublin mountains, "There is a figure over by that tree," and, taking out his pastels and sketch-book, would begin to draw it; and of his Blake-like visions of ancient gods in forest glades and the spectral maidens and children whom he had seen. Then there was Mrs. William Sharp who told me in London once how, in Provence, on the road, on a blazing day in August, she had felt something twitching at her dress and, looking down, saw it was a faun, complete with furry flanks and a boy's face. She and her husband,—"Fiona Macleod,"—had plainly seen this faun, which scurried across the road into the brush beside it. Once, when her husband and the poet Yeats were frying eggs on their kitchen fire and the two were talking about the fairies, Yeats, seeing the pan was suddenly empty and unaware that he had spilled the eggs, exclaimed to Sharp, "You see what's happened now!" Was he only half convinced that the fairies had purloined the eggs,—because fairies do not like to be talked about? Who knows what goes on in certain imaginative minds? In the case of J. B. Yeats, I am sure only of one thing, that he believed in dreams as omens. He was always dreaming and telling his dreams in one of which his own father appeared and asked "How long I expected him to support me," a sign of the lifelong distress, no doubt, of the man with a family on his hands who has never quite been able to make ends meet. Yeats often consulted Mrs. Beattie, a professional palmist whom he knew in New York, and he always followed her advice if it agreed with his wishes.

All this confirmed his own belief that the Irish were mediæval still, while it showed that he was himself quintessentially Irish, one of a race with "time to enjoy themselves and for the sake of enjoyment to be courteous and witty and pleasant." They were mediæval again, he said, in thinking that "how to live is more important than how to get a living," although, as for himself, he had honestly followed "the chimera of success," and no one with imagination could ever have reproached him. If he liked America in many ways, it was because he found so human the American ideal of "happiness for oneself and others," while he disliked at the same time its doctrine of getting on and its nervous energy and efficiency, both damnable to him. For they killed good manners, conversation, literature and art. His own politics were akin, he said, to those of "American hopefulness," and he liked the "buoyant American full of courage with the key of the future in his pocket," much as he disliked the American habits of emphasis and dogmatism, partly because he felt they were his own faults. He also disliked the "sour-faced socialists" for whom artists and poets were egoists and who dragged down and trampled on the aesthetic sense, saying that he was himself a socialist, meaning that he was for socialism when, and only when, this too was human. Why did he turn against Walt Whitman, drawing mischievous caricatures of the "emotional man" in letters to me, remarking that his poems were not works of art and that he was not a poet but a bard, a judgment that Whitman himself would gladly have accepted? Yeats had, as ever, a very good reason, that Whitman stood for the effort to turn into poetry "the collective mind," but this was another way of saying that Whitman too was imperfectly human, to recall the standard by which Yeats judged all things. He was largely indifferent to AE for a similar reason, saying that he was at once a mystic and a materialist who valued "liberation" only as a "mystical doctrine." England for him was inhuman too,—"your villainous old country," as he described it in a letter to an English friend,—the country "where everyone hates and distrusts his neighbour,"—though his general Irish resentment was always tempered by a special delight in particular English men. And how rapidly his feeling about England changed when the country was menaced in 1914 by those whom he saw as the still more inhuman Germans. "I am enjoying the unexpected in finding myself in agreement with England," he wrote at the outset of the first world war, and he could not say too often that "Ireland must help England" in the lean years he foresaw as following the war.

Human as Yeats was, however, and, above all, companionable, he was in no sense a gregarious man: he was, rather, one of the solitary men who live "in the hermitage of their own minds" and "follow the untrodden way that leads to the surprising." He abounded in these phrases describing the type from which he felt all poetry sprang,—just as prose was the language of the socially-minded,—much as he loved conversation, the forte of the Irish and, from his point of view, their greatest possession. "Whenever any Irish reform is proposed," Yeats said in one of his essays, "I always ask, How will it affect our conversation? France has her art and literature, England her House of Lords, America her initiative. We have our conversation." But he combined with this the solitary spirit that had always sustained itself by reverie and dream, and, going off every afternoon for long walks alone, he occasionally took a ticket for some unknown station in New Jersey. Did he hear there "the bird of poetry singing to itself in the heart of the wood, coaxing and admonishing its own soul, thinking nothing of others"? Ever since he had left school he had "lived under cloudy skies," he wrote, "leaving happiness behind me," acquainted with the solitude that Americans never knew, he said, for they knew, he added, nothing but movement. They should have adopted the three legs that represent the Isle of Man, for these would have suited them better than the eagle,—given as they were to modes of motion and making war on solitude, frequenting the highways and the main roads. It was "implicitly and even explicitly an offense for them to steal away," as he put it, "into by-ways and thickets," and what a price the Americans paid in the "frantic brand-new egotism" that marked, for one example, the American woman. For she was no longer a mystery. Behold her pacing Fifth Avenue with her business-like air, thin-lipped, with eyes bright and hard as jewels, the embodiment of commanding decision with her young athlete's figure but as easy to read as an old almanac. What had become of the lines of allurement? She no longer undulated with slow grace; she was neither feline nor was she deerlike. She no longer possessed the three-fold charm of mystery, subtlety and concealment.

Here, as in everything else indeed, Yeats was paradoxical, perpetually veering between incompatible positions, but always in the spirit of his own remark that what was important to preserve was not mental consistency but integrity of soul. "A poet should feel himself quite free to say in the morning that he believes in marriage and in the evening that he no

longer believes in it," and in this sense—I quote one of his letters,—he was a poet, while his integrity could never have been
open to question. He liked diversity for its own sake, and one
might add mischief too,—"I tried several times to roll in the
apple of discord, but they all looked as if they did not see it,"
he said, for instance, regarding a certain conversation; and he
constantly posed antitheses, contrasting views or types of mind,
all of which corresponded with facets of himself. He would
compare the "solitary" with the "companionable" man or the
"man of temperament" with the "man of soul," or he would explain the difference between "conviction" and "opinion" or
between the "emotion" he distrusted and the "feeling" he admired. He deplored once "this entangling web of grey theory
in which I have spent my life,"—though, in fact, its greyness
was seldom apparent to others,—and it troubled him exceedingly and even drove him to desperation when he was pressed
to define the terms he used. For example, he often praised
"character," and then he would praise "personality," of which
it turned out that "character" was the enemy or the "ash"; but
what did this matter when, in the end, one knew he was
praising something real about which he had important things
to say? When he dispraised character he meant merely that he
disliked petrifaction, when he praised it he meant that he
liked singularity and strength, and because they favoured these
he praised the old-fashioned home and school, brutal as they
had been in many respects. For, along with unhappiness, they
tended to produce the individual differences which followed
from the solitary life they also bred, so that, like trees in a wood
that differ in each case from their fellows, every boy evolved on
a different plan. "Talent is the commonest thing in the world,"
he said on one occasion. "The rare thing is character. It is
character that gives one a point of view,"—a truth that became

apparent to all his friends as they advanced in life and saw scores of brilliant talents wither away.

Because of this wisdom J. B. Yeats was to leave behind him a great and abiding memory in many minds, for, whatever the virtues of Americans may be, wisdom is not one of them and most of his friends had never seen a wise man. So all-pervasive was the cult of youth at the time when he was living in New York that wisdom indeed was all but unrecognized there; and one might say that in America the wise man was an obsolete type,—the species was extinct, the mould was broken. Who had ever heard of an American sage since the days of Emerson and Thoreau?—and I doubt if Yeats would have been recognized either if he had not been so happily endowed with articulate talent, warmth of heart and wit. His sayings delighted artists because of his plastic imagination, because the gates of wisdom for him were the eyes and he knew shapes and surfaces, forms and colours and how the light fell on chairs and walls; and he delighted writers whether he was wise or not, for there was something like wisdom even in his folly. He was not irresponsible when he said that Napoleon and Cromwell and Theodore Roosevelt belonged, as compared with artists, to the "servile class"; and when he remarked, "An indulged facility is the clever man's curse in painting and writing," he won the minds of all his listeners. How frequent these perceptions were!—as when he observed, "The tangible is valuable only for the sake of the intangible"; and he pleased writers as much by what he said of words as by what he said in disparagement of phrases. Dostoievsky avoided these because, as Yeats put it, "he avoided half-thoughts and self-deception,"—and "in avoiding phrases he escaped being literary,"—while words, unlike phrases, were Yeats's delight. In *Early Memories* he recalled that his father had loved strange words: "A new word was to him, as to me, a pearl of discovery, fished up out of some strange book he had been reading, and we would enjoy it together"; and his son, the poet, shared this pleasure. Did not W. B. Yeats so delight in the name of the disease from which he died that the pleasure almost consoled him for having the disease? When he heard that he was an "antique cardiac arterio-sclerotic," he said, "I would rather be called that than the King of the South of Egypt." With what relish, in his turn, J. B. Yeats repeated an expression of his father's dearest friend Isaac Butt, the founder of the first Irish Home Rule party for whom Yeats himself had devilled as a young law student. The words were "mimetic, kittenish, ferocious." Yeats loved to quote the servant girl who was happy when the priest, her employer, returned because there had been "the colour of loneliness in the air," and he almost approved of Swinburne because his gift of language was "like the sea for strength and copiousness."

There were many who delighted in Yeats's reminiscences, his talk of Samuel Butler and Heatherley's art school, where the two had been fellow-students in London in the sixties, of York Powell, the Oxford professor, and the Fenian leader John O'Leary who had spent nine years in an English prison. Sometimes he talked of his wife and his children when they had lived in London and he tried to make his way as an illustrator, and I felt as if I myself had known their faithful old servant Rose and Mrs. Yeats, tending her window-box, homesick for Sligo. There still comes back to me a phrase from a letter of one of his daughters, "There has to be one person in every house to find lost things and feed the cat," for he constantly read his letters aloud, drifting off into remarks about painters and painting, poetry and what not. Once, for instance, at a midday meal, he expounded Æschylus to me, and once he observed that the northern races are all for big women who are like plough-horses while the Mediterranean races prefer humming-bird women. On another occasion he talked for an hour about John Stuart Mill's housemaid, who burned up Carlyle's manuscript of the *French Revolution*, deducing her ancestry from this fact and relating how three generations later her great-grandson ended his life on the gallows.

Then I remember an evening at Petitpas' when Robert Henri, outraged, said that he had sent three pictures to an Academy show and that two of the pictures had been sent back while the third, a portrait, had been hung in the worst possible position. Yeats's reply to this was, "Hanging committees are always right," while he glanced round the table defiantly for signs of disagreement. He continued, "If they hang a good picture in a good place, everyone says, What a good picture and how appropriately hung. If in an indifferent place, they say, What an indifferent picture and how appropriately hung. Then, if the picture is hung in a bad place, they say, What a bad picture! However it may be, the committee is always right." One day Yeats related to me a story that was told him by R. A. M. Stevenson,—the art-critic who was a cousin of Robert Louis. The two Stevenson cousins with two other Scotsmen, one a grandson of Christopher North and one who drank a bottle of whiskey a day, were out for a walk in Edinburgh, when they were all quite young, for the sole purpose of breaking the Sabbath. On the outskirts of the town they met four clerks who were evidently also bent on breaking the Sabbath and, after they had agreed together to set about converting the clerks, Bob Stevenson got down on his knees and prayed for them. The four clerks, greatly moved, promised that they would go back to town and never attempt again to break the Sabbath, whereupon Stevenson rose to his feet and, bursting out laughing, said, "Why, men, we're making fools of you. We were out to break the Sabbath ourselves." But by this time the four clerks were seriously back in religion again, and they set out in good earnest to convert these pagans.

What did I learn myself from Yeats? He taught me to cherish the concrete, eschewing the abstract and the speculative wherever one could,—for this word concrete was always on his lips, savouring for him of the green bough of life beside which, as he felt, all theories were grey. I had found this preference in Sainte-Beuve already and later I found it expressed again in Blake's phrase "Art and science cannot exist but in minutely organized particulars," words that I was to recall when the time came for me to write my history of the literary life in the United States. Meanwhile, in reaction as most of us were against a commercial world and the puritanism that we somehow identified with it, we were especially happy in all that he said of material success and the waste of life involved in the pursuit of dollars. We had already been attracted to Dublin by Douglas Hyde's characterization of the business world there as the "antique furniture department," an expression that might have been Thoreau's as a philosophy like Thoreau's lay behind Yeats's own remarks about poverty and idleness. When he spoke of the "sacred duty of idleness," he meant "that idleness which is so diligent, idleness, the teeming mother of the arts," the diligent idleness of birds that sing as they build their nests and of old country parsons like White of Selborne. "Only a great and varied culture can instruct us how to traverse the wide expanses of idleness," as he once put it, expanses that will grow wider and wider as the eight, six and four-hour day involve the majority more and more in leisure. Yeats's way of achieving idleness was the way of poverty, freely embraced, a hard way that had always been the way of the wise, like Thoreau, when they were not endowed with this world's riches. Yeats had not sought this deliberately and he saw the disadvantages of it. "A man shackled in impecuniosity," he said once, "is like a bird tied by a string. The bird flies up to tumble back distractedly." Yet he also said that the "angel of impecuniosity" had always given him his freedom; and who could wonder that he did not wish, or only half wished, to jeopardize the protection of this sensitive angel?

When, many years later, in Dublin, I met the painter Jack B. Yeats and spoke of his father's courage in crossing the ocean to start life anew at threescore years and ten, he said, "As you mention courage, how about this? Once my father's eyes gave out momentarily and he believed that he was going blind. But, saying nothing about this, he called for my sister Lily and began dictating a novel to her. If he was no longer to be able to see to paint, he would turn himself into a writer and the sooner the better." In fact, without ceasing to paint, he became a writer, and all in the natural course of things; but what force of life the story represented, the force that kept him in his adventurous exile so buoyant and so bountiful and, as he said, so cheerful and full of hope. This was the man whose last words, addressed to a friend, in the middle of the night, were,—as he lay dying in his room in New York,—"Remember, you have promised me a sitting in the morning."

CHAPTER X

CALIFORNIA

O NE DAY in August, 1910, walking along Twenty-third Street, I noticed that the door was open in the dingy building where John Sloan had his studio on the top floor, so I ran all the way up to tell John and Dolly that I was going to be married. There I found J. B. Yeats, who admired Sloan greatly, even to the point of writing to "Willie" that England and America had "produced only two serious painters, Hogarth and Sloan (not including Blake who was more poet than painter and not including landscape painters"). Sloan at that moment was painting a picture of the long table at Petitpas', with Yeats at the head, myself at his right and Alan Seeger at his left, chin on hand, and, having me there as a model, he seized the occasion to work for two hours painting me. He had already painted Yeats in the act of sketching one of the group, with Celestine Petitpas bending over the table.

They were all sympathetic when I gave them my news, although Yeats presently sent me a note to tell my wife-to-be that Darwin called marriage a great waste of time. Nevertheless, it was for this I went to California a few months later, early in 1911, feeling for the West a chilly fear as of something far away, though I could not have answered the question, far from what? I was thinking perhaps of what Ruskin wrote about a scene in Switzerland which he compared with a corner

193

of the Rocky Mountains, some hypothetical spot that was un-
speakably grand, asking why this latter stirred him but did not
move him deeply, as in the case of the former, with tragic
emotions. For me too, obsessed with history, the West was a
void, though I had only to see California to fall under the
spell of it, beginning with the sunlight over the live-oak trees.
It was February and at first I was puzzled by this light: why
did it seem so magical, why so strange? Then I saw it was a
winter sun shining over a summer scene, an entirely new
combination to unaccustomed eyes. For I was used to so much
greenery only under a summer sky; and, besides, how strange
was this vegetation, the flowering mimosas, the manganita, the
tangles of cactus, the palms, the eucalyptus. The fuchsias grew
like shrubs in the gardens of Berkeley, where there were
streets called "ways" on one of which lived Arthur Ryder, the
friend of my childhood in Italy, now professor of Sanskrit.
Carmel was a wildwood with an operatic setting where life itself also seemed half operatic and where curious dramas were
taking place in the bungalows and cabins, smothered in blossoming vines, on the sylvan slope. There were sandy trails for
streets, wandering through canyons carpeted with moss and
with great white pines that caught the wind and shreds of the
grey fog that swept in from the sea. There I was married in
April, and I was to return there, three or four times at least,
for many years.

In Carmel I spent several months before the college term
began and I undertook to teach at Leland Stanford, living in the
alfresco fashion that everybody practised on this quite romantic
peninsula of Monterey. The wild past was still present there
with even the remains of an outlaw's camp, the hut of Joaquin
Murieta in the San José canyon, where Easter lilies grew as
daisies grow elsewhere; and there was the forest scenery that

Robert Louis Stevenson, after his visit, pictured in *Treasure Island*. There were the white-washed Mexican shanties of John Steinbeck's *Tortilla Flat* and the old adobe house where John Steinbeck himself was living when I returned to the peninsula later, one of those dwellings with Castilian roses covering the red-tiled roofs that survived from the old Spanish Mexican colonial times. If, moreover, one no longer saw the caballeros of the eighteen-forties with strings of bells on their embroidered pantaloons, Jaime de Angulo, with his Arab horse and his red sash and El Greco beard, had all the look of a revenant from that earlier time. This was the Spanish ethnologist-doctor who had lived with the Indians in the Southwest, where he collected the Indian tales that he was to put into final form as a dying man forty years later on his mountain-top ranch. There was never a figure more fantastic than Jaime de Angulo came to be in those days when, living alone, looking out at the Pacific, a decayed Don Quixote, ragged and mad, he boxed with a pet stallion and carved his meat with a great knife that hung from his middle. But Carmel at all times abounded in every sort of anomalous type,—for one, the old newspaper-correspondent who conversed every night with the people of Mars and had twelve typewritten volumes of these conversations. George Sterling, the poet, who had precisely the aspect of Dante in hell, a suicide later, like his wife, haunted Point Lobos where the poetess Nora French had leaped from the cliff; while others who had come from the East to write novels in this paradise found themselves there becalmed and supine. They gave themselves over to day-dreams while their minds ran down like clocks, as if they had lost the keys to wind them up with, and they turned into beachcombers, listlessly reading books they had read ten times before and searching the rocks for abalones. For this Arcadia lay, one felt, outside the world in which thought evolves and which came to seem insubstantial in the bland sunny air.

I often felt in Carmel that I was immobilized, living as if in a fresco of Puvis de Chavannes, for there was something Theocritean, something Sicilian or Greek, in this afternoon land of olive trees, honey-bees and shepherds. There was also, down by the Big Sur, or, rather, beyond on the coastal trail, a no man's country as far as San Luis Obispo, a wilderness, sinister and dark, where, supposedly, robbers dwelt, another "Rogues' Harbour" like that of old Kentucky. One heard all manner of ominous tales of mysterious people hiding there, murderers who had escaped there, renegade whites and outcast Indians living in huts and caves, and the evil that seemed to brood over the region was all the stranger and more marked because of the splendid beauty of the mountainous coast. Even the lonely upland ranches that straggled by the road, north-ward from the Big Sur, overhanging the ocean, seemed some-how accursed or sad as one passed them on foot, as I did that first year on a three days' ramble, stopping at one ranch, for instance, where a tragic-looking woman was living quite alone with her steers and her sheep. At another ranch a burly bruiser with the look of a Mexican Brigham Young was riding with a troop of women, lashing his cattle. Long before Robinson Jeffers had published his poems about that coast one felt there a lurking possibility of monstrous things.

At that time I did not know Robinson Jeffers, nor do I remember on which of my visits to Carmel I began to see him, always at the same time on the ridge between Carmel and Monterey where the old trail through the pines joined the road. At four o'clock in the afternoon, invariably, if one happened to follow this trail, emerging from the woods on the brow of the hill,—where the gulf of Monterey appeared, sud-

denly, below,—there, overlooking the long slope with live-oaks
scattered over it, Jeffers drove by in his old Ford. One could set
one's watch by this coming of the poet in his brown tweed
coat with his collar thrown back in the manner of Audubon or
Byron, driving to Pacific Grove by way of Monterey. Then a
few years later I used to see him on my walks around the
Carmel point when he was building Tor House on the bluff
above the dunes. He seemed to be always toiling up the cliff
trail as I passed, with a boulder from the beach on his back,
like Sisyphus; for, with only the occasional help of a mason, he
set up this massive house himself with the tower that looked
like a primitive Norman keep. Later he surrounded it with
wild sweet alyssum, and a path of abalone shells led up from
the gate. White pigeons circled round the tower, suggested
perhaps by the white pigeons over the pueblo near Taos that
had for him, no doubt, a special meaning.

For Jeffers, who looked like an Aztec with his slate-grey
heavy-lidded eyes that reminded one of the eyes of an old
tortoise, lived in the Stone Age, mentally, in a sort of historical
vacuum, and seemed to be naturally drawn to the prehistoric.
He surrounded himself with mementos of this like the rock-
pile resembling a cromlech that he built behind the house. In
one of his poems he saw all history as a "rotted floor" sagging
under man's foot, and for him humanity was simply "the
mould to break away from," while, with no concern for the
living world, his mind harked back to primordial times before
men were obsessed with the illusions of philanthropy and progress. I remember the pleasure with which he pointed out to
me that the stones in the walls of a big house near by were
laid as they were in King Arthur's castle of Tintagel. But even
that period was late for him; and, wholly removed as his mind
was from the modern human world, he would have felt more

at home in the circle at Stonehenge. America did not exist for him, its towns or people, its literary life, even the best poets of his own time, and he and his wife on their travels always went to the British Isles, or, rather, the small islands surrounding Ireland and Scotland. They knew all of these, the Arran isles, the Orkneys and the Shetlands, where they found ruins and where they loved the fog, for they were "angry with the sun" that overpowered them at home,—to quote another phrase from Jeffers's poems. There they found old whalebones too, bleached driftwood and the fossils that took them back before the time of man, feeding the poet's fantasy of the pre-historic. No humanistic mind could sympathize with Jeffers's nihilistic point of view, but, for all its bleakness, there was no doubt of the real grandeur of feeling or of the elevation that marked his poems.

As a matter of fact, antipathetic as the burden of his work might be, this poet was destined to survive many changes of fashion. Pointedly ignored in years to come in the dominant critical circles, he possessed an integrity that weathered both attacks and silence, an unmistakable indivisible unity and wholeness of belief and mood that one finds in very few writers in any generation. Yet how deadly to the human sense was this belief in violence, which had been, as he said, "the sire of all the world's values" and which led him to choose for an emblem the hawk,—he named his "Hawk Tower" after it,— that one saw constantly poised over Point Lobos. Accepting Spengler's eternal recurrence of otherwise meaningless culture-cycles, he defended primitive barbarity as the fate of mankind, seeing it as quite good enough for the species he despised with his own active neo-Calvinism. For he was the true child of his father, the theological professor who had taught him to read Greek when he was five, so that Æschylus and Sophocles were also in his blood along with the predestinationism of Jonathan Edwards. While his people were "all compelled, all unhappy, all helpless," a phrase that one found in *Thurso's Landing*, they were also, on the whole, "vipers" and justly damned; and this drew Jeffers temperamentally to the leaders of the Fascists for whom men were inferior animals to be driven with whips. But I often wondered why he took the Spanish civil war so hard that after it he seldom wrote again. He was evidently confused by this, and it struck me that perhaps, admiring the hawk for so many years, he had never previously watched the hawk really in action. For this defender of the bird of prey was the most humane of men who had never himself killed either bird or beast.

What was it in the Carmel atmosphere that so conduced to violence?—for Jeffers's themes had usually a basis in fact there. I almost witnessed a murder, for instance, that reappeared in a poem of his. It was committed at night in a shack in a eucalyptus grove where a Mexican woman with a Cuban husband stabbed her lover, a Filipino, and thrust the body into an oven outside. The crime was clumsily gruesome enough and brutally careless as well, for a passer-by saw the body in the early morning while the murderers were found, asleep and indifferent, within; and although I had not seen the crime, I saw the child who witnessed it, the daughter of the Mexican woman who was present in the shack. With eyes that seemed permanently frightened, she kept the gate for a number of years at the lodge of a wild park not far away. But nihilism too was endemic in Carmel, like suicide and murder and along with the Mediterranean beauty of the scene; and it seemed the right place for Henry Miller to say that "it doesn't matter a damn whether the world is going to the dogs or not." For Henry Miller was to live in time on the ridge near Jaime de Angulo, adding that it does not matter either "whether the world is right or wrong" or whether it is "good or bad." Who was there to say him nay in the world that Mary Austin called "culturally and spiritually the most impotent society that has yet got itself together in any quarter of the United States"?

The world that Mary Austin meant was the world of the *rentiers*, rich and poor, who had swarmed all over California, not the real California people whom one seldom saw and who had much of the character of the first pioneers. I remember a fruit-raising family whom I encountered at San José and who might have been one of the great clans of a primitive race, and everybody must have been struck by the independence of the San Franciscans, who had none of the provinciality of Middle Western people. They had chosen, for instance, a few decades before, to make a pet of William Keith, the painter of the Barbizon school that was dominant then, who had first painted the high Sierras in the manner of Bierstadt and Thomas Moran when this newly discovered grand scenery had astonished the public. But Keith had presently taken to heart Whistler's remark about Switzerland, saying it had produced no landscape painters because the scenery there was on too vast a scale, while he also pointed out that the great landscape painters had come from countries where the scenery was mild and tame. Of course that was not true, for the Chinese had painted high mountain scenes and the only question was how one saw and did them, but Whistler put an end to the American ten-acre pictures; and Keith went to France, saw the Barbizon painters and began to paint clumps of trees himself, hillsides and pastoral glades on the Berkeley campus. No old drawing-room about the bay would have been complete without a Keith, for the San Franciscans were sure they had a good painter, and it did not interest them that nobody else was aware of this, or ever, so far as I know, discovered it later.

One found this independence elsewhere only among the Bostonians, who cared nothing about others' opinions regarding their pets. As for Carmel, meanwhile, everybody painted there, the new abstractionists along with William M. Chase, who opened a school there before he died and whom I had often seen in New York, with his beard, his high hat and the long black ribbon of his *pince-nez*. Then one day Thomas Moran appeared, bringing back the seventies, the days when my father had known the old Far West. This lifelong friend of my parents-in-law, active as ever at eighty-three,—whom Ruskin had once guaranteed a living if he would return to England where he was born,—still talked about Whistler and the pot of paint he had flung in the face of the public as if he were a bad boy living round the corner. Moran defended the "honest painting" that Ruskin had praised him for, representing the leaves on a tree as a naturalist sees them, and he spoke of the Grand Canyon as he had known it and painted it when the old geologist Agassiz was living. Honest painting meant for him painting this in such a way that one knew the sandstone from the limestone and the limestone from the slate.

Meanwhile, at Leland Stanford, where I had begun to teach, Hans Zinsser, the bacteriologist, was my next-door neighbour, a young man delightful to look upon and as picturesque on his half-bred horse, a mixture of Arab and broncho, as Jaime de Angulo. He was a real caballero, or I should say a Teutonic knight, mettlesome as a racehorse, both fiery and winning, and really a knight-errant too, for his friends were constantly in distress and he seemed to be always riding to somebody's rescue. I never knew anyone in whom the protective instinct was so strong, who, young as he seemed to the end, was so paternal, while, with his masculine physical charm, he had an opalescent mind and a nature that struck everyone with its variety and fullness. "Reacting," as he wrote, "like an Æolian harp to every wind that blew," he was in active revolt against specialization, for Goethe was always in his Rhineland German mind and his desire was also to live in the "whole." One might have thought it was a matter of chance that he happened to be a scientist instead of an all-round mind of the Renaissance type, for, playing his fiddle, he kept up with three or four other arts while he maintained a great laboratory with a dozen assistants. Turning out sonnets and other poems that were unpretentious but often good, along with his bacteriological books and papers, he upbraided me for the literary narrowness through which I failed to resemble some Frenchman or other. Meanwhile, how expansive and what a companion Hans Zinsser was on an all-day tramp over the hills at Palo Alto with a pouch that was full of gargantuan sandwiches and the bottle of wine that he brought along for lunch in the shade of a moulting eucalyptus.

Hans Zinsser's first wish had been to write before he discovered in biology too the sort of romantic appeal he had found in the arts, and eventually, in his *Rats, Lice and History*, he made the life of a disease more moving than most biographers are able to make men. He cared for his writing, he said to me, intrinsically more than for anything else, and, as he showed in the case of Hart Crane later, he entered the minds of writers by a deep inner line. He told me about his relations with Crane, whom he had met on shipboard when both were on their way to Mexico, and Crane, as I gathered from meeting him once, was a difficult man to approach or touch,—at least I found him thorny on a first encounter. But Hans, talking poetry with him, had bridged the gulf at once, and, seeing

how mentally ill he was, gave him the fatherly counsel that
Crane himself commemorated in one of his poems. He recorded
his "humble fond remembrances of the great bacteriologist"
who had besought him to follow the pattern of living in which
he might have found a happy fulfilment, and this was emblematic of Hans's relation to writers, to whom he was drawn
as one of them. I remember one of my friends, a writer, who,
after meeting him casually, said, "Your Dr. Zinsser strikes me
as a genius"; and so he was if, as Coleridge remarked, it is a
mark of genius to carry into mature life the feelings of a boy.
For he lived as a boy lives who is always setting out for adventure; and for him there was no waste of life to be exchanged for a crowded hour, for all his hours were crowded
with productive excitement.

Hans Zinsser recorded his first glimpse of David Starr
Jordan, the president of Stanford University, in a hotel bedroom, sitting on the bed and trying to pull the largest boot he
had ever seen over a still larger refractory white-socked foot.
More than once I later witnessed the same scene in hotel rooms
when, as Dr. Jordan's secretary, I travelled in England,—after
I had left Stanford and was teaching there,—and when he
was lecturing at Oxford and Cambridge and dictated letters to
me, labouring, while he talked, with his huge congress gaiters.
In all respects Dr. Jordan was big, awkward and benign, and
the real magnanimity that went with his elephantine bulk
evoked a kind of reverence as it evoked affection. It was true
that he had a bad name for dismissing professors with un-
popular views, Thorstein Veblen, for instance, and Edward
Alsworth Ross, for like various others in similar positions he
was at the mercy of the donors of the time for whom, as they
said at Stanford, professors were "cheap."

As a college president, Dr. Jordan was probably out of his

element, for he was by nature a dreamer and too easily coerced, and I remember the puzzled look with which he said of Veblen, "What can you do with such a man?" For Veblen had had a way of asking his girl students to spend week-ends with him in a cabin in the woods. I had scarcely heard of Veblen then, though I was to read him delightedly soon, marvelling when I met him a few years later that he had played such havoc with the other sex,—for no troll in the forests of Norway could have been more ill-favoured; but in Carmel I often saw Mrs. Veblen and hired her weary old horse for picnics with the children down the coast. Once, moreover, on a moonlight night, a buxom damsel called on me and said, "I was the girl who caused all the trouble," thinking perhaps that since I was at Stanford I might pull wires to get Veblen back, although I was the least important of young instructors. But, to return to Dr. Jordan and the lectures on peace that he delivered abroad when I travelled with him as his secretary, he was one of the many good minds of the time who could not believe how much of the brute, how much that was pre-reasonable survived in civilized man. Nor could Bernard Shaw or Lowes Dickinson believe this either. But I could not understand why later this naivety was so despised, as if it was intrinsically contemptible as well as stupid, considering Swedenborg's belief that the most celestial angels have scarcely any perception of the existence of evil.

That teaching was not my vocation I discovered at Stanford soon, for neither in fact nor by choice was I a scholar, and I was too full of my own thoughts to enter as a teacher should into the minds of students. I had seen great teachers like Gayley at Berkeley,—Professor Gayley of the "Classic Myths," —who, for the sake of their students, threw time to the winds, writing an occasional book as a secondary matter, while, for me, not to be writing a book was not to be alive at all and I wrote parts of three while I was at Stanford. One was the life of John Addington Symonds that Mitchell Kennerley soon brought out, another was *The World of H. G. Wells*, which I was to finish in Brittany a year or two later, and the third was a book on French pensée-writers, *The Malady of the Ideal,* a phrase of my favourite Amiel, who figured in it. Later I worked over a new translation of Amiel's *Journal* that my son made and that was more comprehensive than Mrs. Humphry Ward's, twice as long, in fact, and far more faithful; while the small book in question was beautifully published in London by the idealistic Tolstoyan A. C. Fifield. A tale hung thereby for me, for Fifield, the publisher of Samuel Butler whose lodgings had been near his office in Clifford's Inn, was one of those high-minded souls whom one found in the radical circles that abounded on all sides before the first world war. Fifield, a countryman and a true lover of humankind, was solely concerned as a publisher to produce fine books finely, while he lived, I was told, on the proceeds of his small farm, one of a host of imaginative men who were organizing Fairhopes and Waldens in almost every corner of America and Europe. They were bent on leading men out of the morass of materialism, hoping to save the world from poverty and war and trying to rescue the resources of life from greedy speculators and place them under control for the use of all.

I met at Stanford a few of these types not only among the professors but among the students, occasionally ex-miners and ex-cowboys, some of them at the socialist "local" that flourished in the town, an institution one found all over the West. These locals, as a rule, were led by immigrant "intellectuals,"—a word I heard then, I think, for the first time,—Germans, Jews and Russians with minds that were full of Karl Marx and Freud,

Krafft-Ebing, Nietzsche, Bakunin, Kropotkin. I did not by any means realize then the part which these socialist locals were playing all over the country in the pre-war decade when there was a feeling of revolt in the air that went with what Max Eastman called the "just-before-dawn of a new day." The revolt was largely against the Spoon Rivers, the Gopher Prairies and Tilbury Towns, the Zeniths and Winesburgs that were appearing, or were soon to appear, in the novels and poems of a new generation of writers, but also against the social conditions which the muckrakers had revealed along with the Lawrence strike of 1912. These socialist locals were centres of light for the young people who were growing up with an interest in ideas where ideas were few, in certain cases preparing them for descents on Greenwich Village and for resonant later careers as movers and shakers. There one felt more than anywhere else that this was a renascent time, opening, as one young writer said, a "golden twentieth century" that was going to be very different from the "dark" nineteenth.

A number of motives soon drew me into this circle, or the fringes of it, where Big Bill Haywood appeared on one occasion,—for the I. W. W. had come to the fore at this time,— with a son of the "Chicago anarchist" Schwab and a picturesque Irishman who had belonged to the Hermetic Society in Dublin. Still a theosophist, Varian, as I think his name was, corresponded with AE and knew Charles Johnston in New York, and in general it seems to me, looking back, that all the liveliest minds I knew were involved in one way or another in radical movements. They attracted sensitive generous young people, the most imaginative, the most humane and those who most enjoyed using their minds, appealing not only to their sense of fair play but to their feeling for adventure and the joy of living. To me at that time the most winning of all types, historically and actually, were the rebels and revolutionaries from Mazzini and Kossuth,—and the "romantic exiles" of Herzen's generation,—to the socialist saints of the present like "Babuschka" and Tchaikowsky, whom I had met in Copey's rooms when he visited Harvard in 1906, the hero of the Russian revolution of the previous year. Tchaikowsky, with his patriarchal beard, was a vivid example for me of those "wanderers of the Russian land" of whom I had read, prophets of a world that had not yet come into being and that might well have no room for them. One of my friends was a district leader of the Revolution of 1905 who had been arrested for reading aloud to peasants the American Declaration of Independence,— they had met in crowds, by torchlight, in the Russian woods,— and who had been sent to Siberia and escaped to Stanford, where he was teaching economics. Merely to affirm that there were any "unalienable rights" was as much of a crime in Russia as it later became to differ in belief or opinion from the communist czar, and my friend Max Lippitt, who called himself Larkin in those days, was a type of the old Social Democrat. He stood for the intelligentsia who had joined the ranks of the working class to become their strategists and their tacticians,—"going to the people," as they said in Russia,—a type that vanished in Europe and America in the age of reaction of the world war years only to re-emerge in Africa and Asia. There was never a man more carelessly brilliant or more generous towards others, cynical as he was in regard to himself, than this Oblomov that he had become, all but engulfed in inertia, as if revolutionary activity had broken his mainspring. Max Lippitt was always an emblem for me of the mutual attraction that naturally exists between Russians and Americans whose minds are permitted to meet.

In this circle I encountered another type that was new to

me, the Hindu revolutionist Har Dayal, who was teaching Indian philosophy at Stanford but mainly in order to conceal his real life-work as an organizer of Indian rebellion. He carried this mystification so far as to stage at my house a colloquy with an Indian professor who had come from the Punjab and who proclaimed his nationalism while Har Dayal boldly affirmed that the international social revolution was his only interest. The Punjabi was masquerading as a taxidermist in San Francisco while Har Dayal, as I discovered later, was conducting a school for terrorists in Berkeley, living like a saint or a fakir in a small room near the railroad, with only a single chair for an occasional guest. He slept on the bare floor, for he had no bed, disdaining even a rug to cushion him, as I found when he spent a night sometimes at my house, living on milk and unbuttered bread with one old brown tweed suit, detached as he was from the vanities of the world and the flesh. "I am a revolutionist first and everything else afterwards," Har Dayal remarked in a letter to me, and he perfectly exemplified the point of view that I presently found in the *Revolutionist's Catechism* of Bakunin. In this the revolutionist "has no interests, no affairs, no feelings, no attachments of his own, no property, not even a name"; for he has broken with the codes and conventions that govern other people and has only "one thought, one passion: revolution." Whatever promotes the triumph of this is moral, Bakunin says, whatever hinders this triumph is immoral, and friendship, love, gratitude, honour itself must all be sacrificed to "the cold passion for the revolutionary cause." Everywhere the revolutionist must insinuate himself, turning everything and everyone to his purpose, a character one found in some degree in Turgenev's Bazarov and in Dostoievsky's Verhovensky in *The Possessed*. That, as I knew him, to the life, was Har Dayal.

For, whether as an Indian nationalist or an anarchist inter-
nationalist, he was a revolutionist at every moment with a
shrewd psychological knowledge of the value of the martyr's
role for attracting and retaining disciples to carry out his work.
I think he was entirely sincere in saying that he would gladly
have been burned alive in front of the post-office at Palo Alto
because this would have raised up a host of ardent apostles,
and he knew the utility of self-mortification in its effect on
others as well as in fanning his own flame. He had studied
the life of Ignatius Loyola, trying to discover the secret of
Loyola's influence over his adherents, and he had the *Spiritual
Exercises* and the history of the Jesuits in mind when he
planned his own "Fraternity of the Red Flag." Novices in this
were obliged for a year to submit to the guidance of one of the
members, accepting the "eight principles of radicalism" that
were listed in the programme and taking the vows of Poverty
and Homelessness, Humility and Purity and the final vows of
Service and Propaganda. The members were to renounce all
wealth, pledge themselves not to earn money or to become
parents at any time, while they were to repudiate every other
social tie and dedicate themselves to "simplicity and hardship."
The object of the order was to establish universal brotherhood
by abolishing private property, patriotism, religion and marriage.

How many disciples Har Dayal won for this cause I do not
know,—he said I would "never make a good propagandist of
the Emma Goldman type"; but I knew he had established
somewhere a "Bakunin Institute," which he called the first
"monastery of anarchism." He hoped to gather recruits for his
order in Italy and France, where he had lived, and open another monastery in Switzerland; and meanwhile India was
always in his mind, which seemed to combine in a curious way

the opposite types of the "yogi" and the "commissar." Nationalism was his ruling passion and had been since the time when
he was so notorious as a student at Oxford, planning with
other Indian students an order of Hindu ascetics to boycott
British institutions in their own country. He was convinced
that the British were undermining the Indian character and
that the Raj was quite as absurd and unjust as a growing body
of Englishmen agreed in feeling, while nothing could stop
the insurrections that were always breaking out there in spite
of all the espionage and all the seizures. They were the result
of what Wells called "the resentment of men held back from
life, with their mouths gagged and their hands bound behind
them," fighting an Empire that George Orwell described as
"simply a device for giving trade monopolies to the English."
As Orwell went on to say, you hated your own people when
you heard your Oriental friends called "greasy little babus,"
and you longed for a rising that would "drown their Empire in
blood," a feeling that Americans like myself seemed to have been
born with. But, while one understood it, Har Dayal's nationalist
propaganda,—which he soon ceased to conceal after I knew
him,—was rather a strain when one perceived that every breath
he drew and every hand-shake had an ulterior purpose. He
sent propaganda chocolates to the children of his friends, be-
stowing on them propaganda kisses, because he thought the
friends might serve his cause, while he regarded lectures as
"a kind of drum to get people together," the "real work" of
"interpenetration" beginning later. I was happy, none the less,
teaching in England the following year, to forward letters and
packages of "literature" for him, though, warning me against
expressing any sympathy for India there, he said, "Never tell
anyone anything about me." I must be "on my guard" against

this one or that one, for Har Dayal was sure that his own friends were shadowed. But he also wrote, "The British government sends spies all the time, which affords a revolutionist much amusement and relaxation in an otherwise intense and strenuous life."

At last Har Dayal was arrested in Berkeley and vanished for a time,—he had left California, forfeiting his bail,—reappearing at Lausanne and presently in Holland, whence he continued to write under various names. One of these was "Würsten," another was "F. Sulzer," a third, more frequent, was "Israel Aaronson." The war was imminent or breaking out, it was a most disheartening time, the intellectuals were cutting a sorry figure and there was no longer any true philosophical class in Europe, he said, to take large views and interpret human interests. Where were the Erasmuses and the Goethes who had once transcended "national cultures"? Even Kropotkin had gone the way of all the rest, the learned and the wise, submerged in partisan blindness. Har Dayal felt personally "cramped and choked in this atmosphere," and he said, "I think that the next half century will be marked by great reaction all round." Finally, when the war was well advanced and I had returned to New York, a letter came from him at Scheveningen, containing mysterious references to journeys to Constantinople, which I was not to mention in writing to *him*. But he wrote mainly to ask me if I would like to go to India as a "lecturer on religion and philosophy" or as a "correspondent," saying that ample financial arrangements would be made for me and for my family in the United States. If so, would I cable to Israel Aaronson in Scheveningen. He ended, "Very busy and sad. Please come without delay." Well knowing that only the Germans could be making these "arrangements," I replied that I was strongly in sympathy with the Western allies.

It was not till 1918 that I heard from Har Dayal again. This time he wrote under his own name from Sweden, where he was lecturing all over the country on India, earning his living so, at the same time studying philosophy and learning Greek. He had been stationed at Constantinople for three years during the war in charge of the German propaganda to detach India from England, and, thrown with influential Germans, he had been disillusioned with them and had come to detest their "absurd country." He had got to the bottom of their junkerdom, seeing them in Turkey, and found them far worse than the English had been, and he was convinced that their greedy ambition and their confidence in force were a menace alike to Europe and to Asia. There must be no Germans east of the Suez Canal! In short, he now believed in "Home Rule within the Empire," the dissolution of which could only result in a change of masters for all the weaker peoples; and this conversion of Har Dayal was presently greeted in the London *Times* as one of the important results of the first world war. It was a conversion that later led to his return to England where he founded a "Modern Culture Institute" and, writing books on Buddhism and rationalism, took up the study of science, zoology, botany and physics. Years later, in 1938, he returned to this country to lecture and came out to Connecticut to spend a day, sitting upright in his chair with a bunch of red roses in his hand for my wife and with the white teeth still gleaming in his dusky face. That week the British government had given him permission to go home again and he murmured, half incredulously, over and over, "The road to India is open." Ten days later, however, he was dead. At that moment he was only fifty-four years old, but his heart stopped in Philadelphia.

Thenceforward, whenever I met an Indian, I was always introduced as "The man who knew Har Dayal"; and his name occurred to me again ten years later, more or less, when I was presented to Jawaharlal Nehru. What could I possibly say that might interest this great man? Casting about for something, I heard myself uttering the phrase, "Do you remember Har Dayal?" and, with a wan smile, the great man said, "We *all* remember Har Dayal," though just how he was remembered I forebore to ask. The overtones of Nehru's reply seemed to speak volumes, and I reflected that some of these volumes I had read in California when Har Dayal and I were still in our twenties.

CHAPTER XI

IN ENGLAND AGAIN

IT WAS Alfred Zimmern, at that time, or lately, a fellow of
New College, Oxford, who drew me back to England in
1913, arranging for me to teach in the Workers' Educational
Association of which he was one of the two government in-
spectors. The other was Dover Wilson, the Shakespeare
scholar, of whom I saw something during the summer when
the association met for a sort of congress or parley of lecturers
and students. Sir Alfred Zimmern, as he later became, had
fallen in with J. B. Yeats and joined his circle in New York at
Petitpas', where he had made friends with Eric Bell who gave
him a letter to me, and he had come to see me at Leland Stanford. He had published *The Greek Commonwealth* and had
just returned from a visit to Greece; and the green rolling
treeless hills about San Francisco bay had instantly struck him
as resembling the landscape he had known there. I could
never have guessed that forty years later, when he had come
back to this country to stay, we were to meet again as old
friends and neighbours. "It is the dedicated people," he wrote,
"who make the wheels of the world go around"; and he was
an illustration of his own remark.

Thus it happened that once again I lived in England for
eighteen months, this time with my wife and one small son, at
Richmond for six weeks, on the Isle of Wight during the

summer and for a year in Kent, in the suburb of Eltham. My teaching took up little time, for I had only one class,—at South Norwood, near Croydon; and if any students could have softened my stubborn egoism, they would have been these working men and women. Milkmen, shoemakers like old Mr. Baird, who read Greek and came from Lynn, where he had been a district political leader and had once talked with Disraeli fifty years before, carpenters who quoted Horace's odes, they put me on my mettle and made me feel that I was an un-educated man. For they assumed that one could not be edu-cated unless one read Greek and Latin as easily as English. My course was nominally on the English essayists, and it struck me that the class included rudimentary specimens of all the types of mind that came up for discussion. There were embryo Lambs, Carlyles and Macaulays among them, with one actual survivor of pre-Darwinian times. This ancient boatmaker of ninety-six came not so much to listen as to drowse in a friendly atmosphere; and he rose to speak to me at the end of an eve-ning when the theory of evolution had been the subject of debate. He asked me if I had read Dr. Adam Clarke's *Com-mentary on the Holy Scriptures,* the book which I was to hear of again as Bryan's great authority at the time of the Dayton trial in Tennessee. When I told the old boatmaker that I had not read it, he said, "Ah, but you should read it. For Dr. Clarke proves that the serpent could not have tempted Eve because the serpent has no vocal organs."

With what zest, on the other hand, a young mechanic told me that he was studying Aristotle because "You can't read Aristotle without being a good man," while a young potter named Emery who for six years had attended classes talked about his pottery like a mystical poet. These men cared for literature in and for itself without regard to economic questions, and, while I was expected to relate my subject to their background and experience, they studied for the sole purpose of enriching their minds. They did not seem to be concerned with altering their status in the world, they were interested in Bernard Berenson's "life-enhancement," with all the devoted enthusiasm that characterized many New Englanders in the days of Elihu Burritt, the "learned blacksmith." Har Dayal, who urged me to go and see Kropotkin,—something I failed to do, and much I regret it,—also told me that I must study the "class-psychology" of my worker students and tell him about the new types that I encountered. For "I am always interested," he said, "in variations from the normal. They always indicate new social forces." But one note of this class-psychology that would have disappointed him was a passive acceptance of the caste-system that prevailed in England, the "most class-ridden country under the sun" as George Orwell called it,—or so it struck one outsider who was equally impressed by the personal ardour of so many of these seekers of learning.

That a truly apostolic feeling lay behind this movement I saw at the congress in Oxford, where I spent a week in a huge seventeenth-century study with a cubicle for sleeping in and windows looking over lawns and gardens. New College was locked away from the streets and in these summer vacation days one heard no sound but an occasional tangle of chimes. Zimmern himself personified this apostolic feeling, up to his neck as he was in the cause of education and visiting other congresses in Bangor and Cambridge. Yet not only did he find time to be good to me but he was a master of the art of dealing with people. It was perhaps not easy to reconcile some of the older dons to this irruption of Scythians in their quiet college, swarming about the gardens and lawns at tea-time, or to reconcile the old colonel, for instance, also visiting the college, who was mildly curious about the working class. For him it called up associations of "these little messenger boys one sees running about one's club," regarding whose probable fate he asked various questions. The librarian of the House of Commons and two members of Parliament were there as well, and the conversation recalled to me Lowes Dickinson's *Modern Symposium,* so varied were the points of view, so articulate the speakers. One saw in the evening at dinner, moreover, the pleasure that Englishmen take in ceremony and social histrionics when the company left the table and adjourned to the end of the room where desserts had been set out with decanters of port. The old colonel whose remarks were so inept amused himself all evening long with a little game he played quite by himself, finding occupation of the most engrossing sort in the way he examined his watch and adjusted his glasses. Obviously, what he said meant less to him than the highly distinguished manner in which he said it. For the rest, the company were seated in a semicircle with the two end men about ten feet apart, and the decanters were placed in cups on a small wooden railway, sloping downward and running between these ends. The decanters were supposed to make their way unaided, but they invariably stuck in the middle of the course, whereupon the two men at the ends rose to help them on their way, as they had been doing supposedly for hundreds of years. It would have been far simpler to hand or shove the decanters about; but who would have dispensed with this charming little game? It seemed all the more charming to the players no doubt because Addison or Gibbon had perhaps played it a century or two before.

The talk I heard at Oxford, sometimes adding a word myself, tended to break up any fixed ideas one had, as it broke down in one's mind pet phrases and clichés. Alfred Zimmern took me to see Bishop Gore, who lived as a saint might live in a corner of his palace, the white-bearded patriarch who seemed as wise as J. B. Yeats and who grieved from the bottom of his heart over the trials of the workers. He was especially concerned, I remember, with the horrors of lead poisoning, a risk of the pottery workers who had come there with us. It pleased me to be told that the bishop was a socialist, but I saw in Oxford that one had to know just what one meant by this when so many members of the peerage were socialists also, when others who seemed equally advanced called themselves Tories and even Wells's "new Machiavelli" passed backward through the parties and ended as a conservative rejuvenescent. All this led me to think of the differences between America and England, as it led me to see the good in various conditions of English life that, in one way or another, were different from our own. Its cultural centralization was one of these conditions, the focussing of the general mind so that every English feeling and thought had its instantaneous effect on every other. With statesmen coming down from London to debate in the Union, students could be in close touch with the centre of affairs, and, because society was a coherent organism, new books could have an immediate effect upon it. I asked Walter Lippmann, whom I met in London, if he could imagine a book of his influencing legislation in the United States, if he could conceive of members of Congress reading *A Preface to Politics* and introducing measures that were based upon it. Yet Zimmern told me of a friend of his who had advocated certain acts in a book he had recently published and who saw these acts presently passed through the aid of a friend in the cabinet,—within two years his dreams had become laws. An inner circle ruled, for ill and for good, as I saw when Dr. William Temple became the Archbishop of

Canterbury, fifteen years after I had heard he was going to become so. A devoted schoolmaster with socialist leanings, he too had been at Oxford at this congress of workers in 1913, and I had been locked out with him one evening at New College where his future was already prearranged.

As I recall it, the word "discussion" was the keyword of the moment, in England as in literary circles also in New York; for the general feeling was that all problems could be solved and that the way to solve them was to talk them over. It was supposed that, on the whole, reason governed the general mind and that a fund of good will lay behind it, for few people realized how vast and dark were the irrational forces in men before the first world war so suddenly evoked them. Countless others like myself were full of H. G. Wells's faith that we were "in the dawn of the great age of mankind," and although, like Shaw, as he went on, Wells grew more cautious in his hopes, he felt that the human mind was indefinitely plastic. He did not cease to believe that "education" would win in the race with "catastrophe," and reasonably soon; for he shared William James's faith in the godlike power of the intelligent will to control heredity, instinct and its own planetary setting. He looked with amazement at the confusion and waste of the world, the chaotic indiscipline of men and their ill-adjusted effort, their planlessness and their spasmodic aims, convinced that it was in their power to build another sort of world and a human race that was orderly, happier and finer. He wanted men, he said, to be "intensely alive and awake," with "thought like an edge of steel and desire like a flame," and he believed that all this could be brought about, at least in large measure, by discussion. For this the "new Machiavelli" started the "Blue Weekly," a "centre of force," as he put it, to leaven the press, to get at the universities, to clarify the public mind, to organize research and to foster literature and art. In the novel this weekly was a huge success: it was read by all the people who formed public opinion, maintaining "a stream of suggestion against crude thinking."

Later, the teaching of H. G. Wells lent itself to the saturnine jeers of an age that had lost all belief in the will and in progress, an age for which these ideas were in some way trumpery and in no sense even "great illusions." The mere survival of mankind, of men and the state to which they belong, had become the primary concern of public thinking, and it had always been understood that under these conditions all questions of the "good life" must be deferred. This had been affirmed by Aristotle. For only when survival can be taken for granted can men spend time or thought on organizing what he regarded as the true life for mankind, so that what is impracticable comes to seem futile and, being futile, also inane, a fate that befalls in war-time much that is noble. Wells's vision was essentially noble,—it was totally misconceived when it was called merely a dream of material progress; for are the material and the spiritual unconnected? Countless young men and women felt that mankind was on the march, "entering on a world movement," a "vitalizing epoch," greater than "the Renaissance and the Reformation," as Arnold Bennett remarked in one of his essays, to be fulfilled by coöperation, by knowing how the other half lives, by propagating fresh ideas and by discussion. Alike on both sides of the ocean one constantly encountered groups like the Pentagon circle of Wells or Lowes Dickinson's "Seekers."

Everywhere in London one heard discussions of this question or that, of the "Mental Deficiency Bill," for one example, at a great meeting in Essex Hall at which, as I remember it, every phase of opinion was represented. The question was the compulsory segregation of the so-called feeble-minded, and, with Cecil Chesterton in the chair, the speakers included a syndicalist, an Irish orator and an old-time democrat. There were two or three Liberal speakers, and a typical Fabian stood out, using all the Fabian phrases, with his back to the wall, for everyone else was against him, as I picture the scene, and especially the chairman's brother, who came lumbering in. With his whale's bulk, with his three chins and a high dull roaring squeal of scornful disagreement, G. K. Chesterton laughed at all the others. One felt as if the whole of England was audibly involved in this debate, something that one could scarcely feel in the vast National Liberal Club, though the air in this seemed fairly to quiver with discussion. It was there in the long hazy smoking-room, with its crowded little tables and its pillars and bays and groups of men sitting in armchairs eagerly talking,—with faces and accents that set the mind adrift across the British Empire from Rangoon to Jamaica,—there I met H. G. Wells himself, introduced by Lippmann, with whom I had been lunching elsewhere in the club. I was almost too excited to speak in the presence of this red-faced man with his shrill asthmatic voice, a half-cockney squeak, pouring forth words like a freshet in spring and looking as if he was on the point of a fatal stroke of apoplexy even as he stood there. I said I was writing a book about him, which evoked from him a benevolent glance, but not till thirty years later did I hear that he had read it. When I then met him in New York he recognized my name. "Yes," he said, "you wrote a book about me when you were young and unwise," and I was ready by that time to accept his verdict.

Although in those later years I saw Walter Lippmann rarely and we had followed paths that were far apart, I had several meetings with him in this pre-war London. Then, early in

1914, he wrote to me from New York. We had found that, in our thoughts of America, we had much in common, and he hoped to establish communication with others who were "working on the same puzzles and trying to see into the same fog." He knew a few young men, scattered through the country, who seemed to be arriving at a common understanding, and he told me about a plan for a new "weekly of ideas" that he and a group of his friends were about to start. He felt sure that *The New Republic* was something America needed badly, and it struck me at once as an actualization of Wells's "Blue Weekly" adapted to American conditions and the American mind. It was "to put a critical clinch," as Lippmann said, "into discussion and infuse American emotions with American thought," having "no party axe to grind" and, although "in direction socialistic," not so either in allegiance or in method or phrase. It was to be humanistic, but not in Irving Babbitt's sense; it was to relate the "noble dream" to the "actual limitations of existence"; and Lippmann hoped that in every part the paper would be "vivid with the humours and sights and sounds of American life . . . and yet," he added, "imaginative enough to point through them to a more finely disciplined and what Wells calls a more spacious order of living." (Phrases that bring back Wells himself and the way in which his view of life pervaded the thinking and writing of the young men of that moment.) Herbert Croly was to edit the paper, with Francis Hackett as literary editor and S. K. Ratcliffe as an English correspondent, and with Alfred Zimmern in the picture too and Graham Wallas, who had appeared in a somewhat equivocal light in one of Wells's novels. I had met Ratcliffe at this time, henceforth another lifelong friend who knew every state in America as if he had lived there and who has lived in twenty or thirty states, and Graham Wallas who examined me orally to see if I was qualified to teach in Alfred Zimmern's W.E.A. Later he discussed in his *Art of Thought* my book *The Ordeal of Mark Twain*, regarding which he kindly wrote to me, "I know of no book more fitted than this of yours to reveal to an original-minded young student the obscure and difficult process by which, for those who have courage and patience, the will-to-create becomes the art of creation." This pleased me as much as to hear from a friend who had talked with Freud in Vienna that he too had read and approved of my book.

I might have had later a closer connection with Lippmann and Hackett's *New Republic* if I had been more at ease in magazine writing, but it sometimes cost me a week of laborious effort to turn out a simple book-review. The thought of a dead-line paralyzed me; I entirely lacked the presence of mind that an article-writer must have, like an after-dinner speaker, and my later attempts to earn a living on *The Seven Arts* and *The Freeman* were accompanied by a chronic sense of disaster and defeat. What misery to spend five nights sitting up till three o'clock to find oneself represented in print by a wretched composition that seemed to be still half-baked and wholly inexpressive. But, to return to Walter Lippmann, his words bring back to me some of the excitement of that hour of the literary life, the feeling of intellectual adventure and philosophy in action that filled, before the first world war, so many minds. The mental aura of Randolph Bourne, whom I was to know so well, was altogether composed of this expectant feeling; and *The New Republic,* as one first heard of it, seemed already the symbol of a great coming epoch.

I had first met Lippmann at D. J. Rider's bookshop in a little court just off St. Martin's Lane, the den of a second-hand bookseller who had two small rooms, the shop at the front and an office at the rear. Dan Rider himself, the most lovable of men, with a stubby pipe and a cockney voice, always laughing or chuckling, sold next to nothing,—he seemed to prefer giving his books and pictures away; and he would sigh with annoyance when he heard the little bell announcing that some outsider had opened the door. For him these interruptions were like Gothic invasions, for he seemed to live for conversation, mysteriously active as he also was, with a hand in all manner of pies as an editor and publisher as well as a literary agent. He had bought up at sixpence a copy the whole stock of remainders of Samuel Butler's novel *The Way of All Flesh* before Bernard Shaw had made its author known, and he arranged for the English publication of Mitchell Kennerley's authors in New York. It was this that brought Lippmann and myself together in his office, where he sat surrounded with piles of books, with lithographs and etchings and with various writers and oddities whom he befriended. When I was in the country he wrote to me, "Lippmann is a great boy. He gets more into a day than the whole population of England. His time-table is worked through with the regularity of a railroad." Of course Walter Lippmann's mind was of a rather special type, but he was mature at twenty-three or so when most of us were floundering about in a prolonged adolescence.

It was at Dan Rider's that I also met Jo Davidson, who became from that time forward a part of my life, although twenty-five years were to pass when I scarcely saw him; and several survivors of the Yellow Book circle drifted in and out there with remnants of the circle of William Morris. Rider lived at Hammersmith, where Morris had had his Kelmscott Press, and the aesthetic and the socialistic met in his shop on equal terms as they met in Morris's mind or in the mind of Shaw. Rider had been an active worker in the socialist organizations at which Shaw himself had often spoken, debating on a famous occasion with H. M. Hyndman, the grand old man of English socialism. I spent an afternoon with Hyndman in the Hampstead garden of Rider's friend, the American "millionaire socialist" Gaylord Wilshire, who had made in Los Angeles a fortune in billboard advertising and edited *Wilshire's Magazine*. It was he who had given in New York the notorious party for Maxim Gorky to which Mark Twain refused to go, and, impelled to undo the conditions that had made his fortune, he was directing *The Syndicalist* in England. Hyndman, in appearance Rodin's double with his massive shoulders and chestnut beard, flat-crowned, stocky in build, in all ways robust, still dreamed of waking up some morning to find himself prime minister of the sort of reorganized England for which Morris had longed. The most winning of men, deferential, benign,—calm, rational and keen-witted too,—he burst into furious flood like Old Faithful, the geyser, if someone uttered a remark that struck him as inane.

Another frequenter of Dan Rider's shop was Holbrook Jackson, the historian of the nineties when yellow was the colour of the day, the outrageously modern, and Robert Ross appeared there too, Oscar Wilde's champion and dedicated friend, with a small group that met at the Café Royal. But whom did one not see on the plush-covered sofas or reflected in the mirrors of this long since transfigured rendezvous near Piccadilly Circus, from Lord Alfred Douglas with his rakish air and the old satyr Crosland to the sculptor Jacob Epstein and his wife. These latter, sitting side by side, ample in girth, swarthy in hue, looked like a pair of Bedouins just out of their tent. For the rest, who could forget, at Dan's, the latter-day Costigan,—Miss Emily Fotheringay's father in Thackeray's novel,—who also fell downstairs, thanks to a loose carpet, he said, but in all probability propelled by a foot that he had libelled. A well-connected Dub-

liner, the aging nephew of an earl, Captain Stephens made a
furtive living as a gossip-monger writing for a scandal-sheet,
while he served also as a spy for the French embassy in London keeping an eye and ear cocked for the Germans there. He
was always pulling out of his pocket soiled scraps of paper
with shady tales about his cousins and their friends picked up
from servants, and with his air of dilapidated elegance he lived
on the razor-edge of the British law that punishes defamatory
statements. So did Frank Harris who published him in *Modern Society*, as I think it was called, and presently had to leave
England to escape from this law, pulling down Dan Rider,
financially, with him. For Dan had printed his *Oscar Wilde*,
or arranged to have it printed, on the understanding that they
were to divide the subscriptions, and all the subscriptions were
sent to Frank Harris in France, leaving Dan to pay the bills
unaided. The printers turned to him and, unable to pay them,
Dan Rider, ruined, was obliged to close the shop.

There I had often seen Frank Harris, who looked like a
race-track tout or an old-time stage villain with his handlebar
moustaches,—he might have been a Mississippi steamboat gam-
bler,—the legendary Harris who had once been a cowboy and
had written stories of the Western plains after he began his
career as an editor in England. There too I had seen Strindberg's wife, the second or perhaps the third, the "Scandinavian
Duse" who was running a night-club and whose constant motto
"Je suis au bout des forces" came into play that very afternoon.
For suddenly, at Rider's door, appeared another woman, a mil-
liner with an unpaid bill who had tracked her through the
streets and who had cornered her at last, saying, "I've got you
this time," while malicious animal magnetism shook the room.
There, on how many other occasions, currents of another kind
spread from Jo Davidson's presence, all animal glow, for Jo

Davidson had a "special gift for loving" like Willa Cather's old Nebraska farmer's. He was one of those irresistible people, stimulating as the winds of spring, who, as J. B. Yeats said, "go out into the streets, along the roads and gather in their friends by armfuls." But, loving many, he loved a few with a tireless life-long affection; and this man who was sometimes accused of head-hunting was loyal above all to friends who were humble and obscure.

With these first days of my friendship with Jo I associate Georg Brandes, the great Danish critic who had appeared in London and whom I had heard at Essex Hall lecturing on Nietzsche, the "aristocratic radical," his famous correspondent. I had read Brandes with rapture at Stanford, beginning with *Main Currents,*—in which in a vast panorama one saw all Europe evolving from one epoch into another,—carried away by the picturesqueness of this literary portrait-painter whose supple mind was almost as broad as Goethe's. He had related in his autobiography how Kierkegaard's religious thought had first aroused him when he was a student in Denmark and how he had turned against Kierkegaard because he could not believe that that which was contrary to all reason was the highest truth. It seemed to him, moreover, that his own defects were weaknesses which ought to be combatted and might be cured, not irremediable sins requiring forgiveness; and, meanwhile, feeling in himself, as he said, "the strength of a whole generation," he had ranged from country to country, studying their cultures. He had found in Taine especially a master and deliverer who had freed him from the pedantry of his Dano-German training; and, able to embrace minds as various as Hans Christian Andersen and John Stuart Mill, he had become the model of a good European. I was all the more drawn to him because he loved painters and painting too and because of his watchword, "As flexible as possible when it is a question of understanding, as inflexible as possible when it is a question of speaking."

I had told Jo Davidson about this first lecture at Essex Hall, at which Bernard Shaw had introduced Georg Brandes, taking command of the audience and, with his usual fiery wit, running away with the occasion, speaking for an hour. The little old goat-bearded critic might well have been vexed by this, but he seemed to be as smilingly pleased as the Cheshire cat whose whiskers, like his, stuck out at random; and Jo, who was determined to make a bust of Brandes, went with me to the second lecture at Caxton Hall. The subject was Shakespeare and the lecture was elementary, for Brandes took no pains to say anything new; but at the end Henry James climbed up to the platform from the front row and the chairman, Edmund Gosse, introduced him to the speaker. Just then I became aware that Jo had vanished. Making his way to the platform, he persuaded Brandes to stop for a moment, on the following morning, at his studio, near Brandes's hotel; and, when Brandes arrived, Jo met him with modelling clay in his hand and quickly sketched his head as he was looking at the sculpture. At the end of five minutes, when Brandes was leaving, Jo showed him the little sketch which pleased the great man so much that he gave him a sitting. The head that followed was one of Jo Davidson's best.

Looking back later, it seemed to me that Brandes and Davidson had something in common as creators of what came to be called the planetary mind, for Brandes, with his art of cross-fertilization, interpreted one to another the notes of at least half a dozen nations. Meeting some of the greatest men of England, France and Germany, he had been struck by their ignorance of the merits of their compeers even in countries that were closely akin to their own; and he had been equally at home himself not only in France, Germany, Italy and England but in Denmark, Norway, Sweden, Poland and Russia. Jo Davidson had a similar protean gift for penetrating minds of all races and types, so that, as a "plastic historian," he became in the end a United Nations in himself, representing the generation in which appeared the "global" sense, the sense that Whitman, his favourite poet, called "orbic." If Davidson's busts were assembled from the four corners of the earth one would find half of modern history in them, and no other record of the sort can duplicate this record of a world that is both one and pluralistic. Jo Davidson loved its diversity as well as its oneness.

I had never met, and was never to meet, so naturally happy a temperament, with malice toward none,—quite literally,—with charity for all, so buoyant and so free as Jo's, a man who had taken to the world as he said he took to London, "like a duck to water." For him it was always a World's Fair, like the old fair at St. Louis at which, as a boy, he drew portraits and did sculpture in sand; and, with none of the prejudices or fears that govern the lives of most people, he passed through life like a ship under full sail. His was the kind of lordly freedom, rare in our unhappy time, that characterized so many artists in more genial ages, and he was an illustration of Franz Kafka's saying, "I like the Americans because they are healthy and optimistic." Born before people were conditioned to see mainly the stupidities and the sins in men, he saw the heroic in high life as he saw it in low life, drawn as he was especially to those who have made history in our time, whether they were saints or poets, soldiers or statesmen. Unmindful, even unaware of the conventional overtones that reputations have for other people, he approached his subjects with the innocence of an artist

or a child, finding the great irresistible, as he also found door-
men and garage mechanics, helplessly charmed by the human
nature in them. In a way he became the person while doing
the portrait, and his forms more real than living men sprang
from an interest in character that was lost in a later comparatively dehumanized time.

Jo Davidson had all the traits that came to be regarded with
a certain hostility and suspicion when they appeared in artists,
exuberance, fertility, productivity and the inborn vitality
that in certain quarters was even considered vulgar. It was not
till many years after the war that I fell in once more with him
after seeing so much of him for a few months in London, the
"Gomorrah-on-Thames" of Ezra Pound, who had settled there
in 1909 and whom I met for a moment with his friend John
Cournos. I found some of my own impressions in Pound's later
published letters, in his remark, for instance, at about that moment, "You can no more interest London in the state of the
American mind than you could interest Boston in the culture
of Dawson or Butte, Montana." That seemed to me natural
enough in 1914. For we Americans at that time had few literary claims to press and were better employed in quietly learning from others, true as it was that within a few years two
Americans, Eliot and Pound, established themselves in a way
as teachers of the English. I remembered the story about Sainte-
Beuve when he was reproached in an interview for knowing
and saying so little of the interviewer's country,—one of the
Scandinavian countries, I think it was,—"Well, *do* something.
Then we'll talk about you," which struck me as good for Americans to apply to themselves. For one could not have reproached
the English for lacking curiosity,—there too they were our superiors on the literary plane; and they have continued to be so
if by curiosity one means an eager interest in the affairs of

culture. So at least one would suppose comparing the primitivism of many of our writers with the traces of an active culture one finds, for example, in Aldous Huxley's novels and the poems of Auden,—the "conversational parsley" that Hemingway dismisses and that seldom garnishes the American literary dish. Dean Inge symbolized for me the kind of curiosity one found so general in England and so rare at home, for as often as not, wherever I went in London, there with his apron and gaiters was the gloomy dean. Three times at public lectures he sat in the chair in front of me,—one was a lecture on Tibet by Sir Francis Younghusband,—and whenever I entered a picture-show there he was wandering about, bent on seeing whatever there was to be seen. It struck me that Dean Inge must be the most curious man in the world, for I reflected that if I encountered him eight or nine times in three months I must have missed him on scores of other occasions. The sight of this ubiquitous man embarrassed me: it made me feel like a detective shadowing him.

One friend I met in London, or, rather, one who became my friend, was the poet from Little Rock, John Gould Fletcher, whose first remark, as he sat down at the Soho restaurant table, was that he had published in one month five books of poems. It was true, moreover, small as these were, each with a different imprint, and he had paid to have them published. I remembered at once that I had seen his queer white skull-like face peering out through the crimson curtains of the Harvard Union, a face to which in college I had never attached a name, and here it was, a poet's face, in London. Fletcher was an old man's son, and he seemed to have been born old himself, stiff-jointed, with big angular bones and stooping shoulders; and, as a stranger from the South, he had been, as he wrote, the "most forlorn and hopeless individual" at Harvard. He had felt

as lonely and depressed as Maxim Gorky appeared to be when
Fletcher saw him, with his Russian boots, there, looking at Major Higginson's portrait by Sargent, a picture that hung in the
Union where Fletcher himself had spent most of his time and
where, in the library, at nineteen, he had begun to write
verses. Following the lead of Arthur Symons, he had found in
the Union the French Symbolist poets whom later he had introduced to Ezra Pound, for, with means of his own, he had left
Harvard and gone abroad to study, falling in with this other
American poet in London. Pound borrowed armfuls of his
books and presently published the essays that popularized
these French poets in literary circles as part of his campaign to
dislodge the English mind, violently, from its Georgian and
academic rut. This was all again part of the more general
movement of the "new poetry," so called, that put to rout the
established poetic forms. Amy Lowell, arriving in London, was
astonished to find two young Americans there who seemed to
care more for the new poetry than anyone at home.

    When I met Fletcher he had passed already out of his Walt
Whitman phase, although he had actually discovered Whitman in London, as a socialist surveying the crowds in Cheap-
side and the Strand, and he was absorbed in imagism, in Rim-
baud's theory of the *alchimie du verbe* and the recently much
talked of Chinese and Japanese forms. Excited by the Russian
ballet, he wrote tributes to Nijinsky, glorifications of colour,
pæans to dancing. It was much later that I knew him well
when he had returned to America and found that essentially
he was a Southern poet, charmed by the old romantic regions
of the South and the Southwest, the heroic saga-lands, as he
called them, of the American past. He went back to the country he had visited earlier with our classmate Alfred Kidder on
an archæological expedition to the New Mexico desert, the

world of the Apaches, the Navajos, the Penitentes and the legendary Seven Cities of Cibola; and he became deeply involved
in the regionalist movement of the South against the spiritual
inroads of the industrial system. But this was just before the
cause of Southern regionalism was abandoned by the rising
generation of Southern poets. After his twenty years abroad,
Fletcher was perhaps too late to have shared fully in the renaissance of American writers, as he was too late to share in the
development of the South,—while he had forfeited meanwhile
his connections in England,—so that with all his stubborn honesty and his great gifts as a poet and critic, he was somehow
lost in the chaos and rush of the time. Amy Lowell too had
been all but forgotten when Fletcher came to his unhappy end,
eclipsed by new writers who are destined in turn for the same
sort of oblivion unless they can endow with a memory their
negligent country. Yet even the English sometimes forget their
good writers. Who speaks any longer of J. D. Beresford, the
author of the trilogy of Jacob Stahl which everyone read with
zest in the first world war years, a lame frail grave man with a
lined ascetic face whom I met in the company of the poet
Walter de la Mare?

How many strange fish, for the rest, one found inhabiting
the depths of the ocean of London, living in clefts of the rocks,
seldom visiting the surface. One was the old essayist Francis
Grierson about whom I had heard so much,—Edwin Björkman
had written a paper on him. He was said to live over a grocer's
shop somewhere in Twickenham, although no one saw him
there or knew his address; but he would emerge in response to
a letter at the Bridge House in Richmond, where he received
admirers and correspondents. These meetings were promptly
written up in the local newspaper, the *Twickenham Times,* the
readers of which were led to suppose that Grierson was a liter-

ary potentate to whom all the great of the earth made pilgrimages. For, humble as the guest might be, he was described as a
world-famous professor or some other sort of lion or cock of the
walk, the secret of it being that Grierson had a Sancho Panza
who not only served as a press-agent but supported him as
well. He worked for a small wage, I think, as a tailor's assistant. When Grierson dined with my wife and me and I took
him to the door to say good-night, there was a strange man sitting on the steps,—it was Waldemar Tonner, the Polish-
American whom Grierson announced as his secretary and who
had been waiting there all the evening through. For thirty
years already Tonner had spent his time and strength maintaining the romance of Grierson's greatness, a practical soul
who worshipped his master and struggled with the world on
his behalf, for the high-minded Grierson was as helpless as the
hero of Cervantes.

Scotsman that he was by birth, Grierson had grown up in
the American West, to which he had been brought when he
was six months old, in a log-cabin in the Sangamon country,
surrounded by the strange frontier types whom he described in
his book *The Valley of Shadows*. He had heard the last Lin-
coln-Douglas debate and served General Frémont as a page
before he had made his way, at nineteen, to Paris where he had
become the musical prodigy of whom Mallarmé remarked that
he was "the first real poet of the piano." He had lived with the
elder Dumas there, playing in the salons that he described in
his *Parisian Portraits*, presently starting a second career with a
little book written in French of which Maeterlinck said that it
influenced him more than any other. Within the last few years
he had collected from Orage's weekly the essays that appeared
in the small green volumes *The Celtic Temperament* and
Modern Mysticism, along with the beautiful memoirs of his

Mississippi boyhood, while he gave occasional piano recitals at which he professed to think that ancient Lydian airs flowed through his fingers. There was a touch of the charlatan in him, but there was a curious innocence too in this tall man with his worn old tweeds, his drooping moustache, pink cheeks and crimson necktie. The moustache was evidently dyed and he rouged his cheeks, and that he wore a wig was also apparent from the white hairs that straggled out over his ears; and later when he was caught by the rain and obliged to stay in my house I was sorry that I could not help him in the matter of cosmetics. How without rouge would he be able to appear in the morning, not to speak of wax for his moustache? But only his wig was askew when he came down blithely. In appearance he was evidently living up to an early portrait of himself painted at the court of the czar when he had played there, a portrait that was reproduced in one of his books and showed him as a romantic of the time of Dumas. Still dwelling, with his courtier's air, in this old royalist Europe, he was equally full of the frontier West and Lincoln,—of whom he drew wonderful portraits in his writing and his talk,—and he was to die in America at last, "calm and serene" as he had lived, or so said Waldemar Tonner a few years later. He had settled in Los Angeles, where all the retired prophets go, possessed by dreams of the "invincible alliance" of England and America, between which for so long his own mind had wandered.

CHAPTER XII

TURNING HOMEWARD

W HEN THE first world war began in August, 1914, I was
in Brittany for the summer at St. Jean du Doigt, living
in a douanier's house facing the inn and the square, finishing
a book I had begun on the shore of the Pacific. Every foreigner
knew at once that only two courses were open to him, either to
get out of the way or to share in the struggle, but, turning
homeward soon myself, I never supposed it would be thirty-five
years, or virtually that, before I again saw Europe. For I do not
count one dark season that I was to spend there. I had always
felt that one lived abroad far more intensely than one lived at
home, that years there were better than cycles in our own
Cathay,—our "Anglo-Saxon China," as Melville had called it;
and this was a common feeling not only with Americans but
with countless South Americans, Africans, Australians, Asi-
atics. For in cultural matters Europe was the sun from which
all the continents drew light and heat; and all from that moment were thrown back on themselves. Things fell apart: the
centre could not hold.

I had known in England a Cingalese, a young art-critic of
ample means, who returned to Ceylon as I was returning to
New York and who, in letters that he wrote to me,—"whistles
from the other side of the wood,"—described his feeling of
exile and desolation in Colombo. He quoted Henry James's

remark, "For those who have been happy in Europe, even Cambridge the brilliant is not an easy place to live in," adding, "Ceylon is not even brilliant" and "the East is not meant for anyone to live in but merely to look at and admire from a safe distance. . . . When you have lived in the West you have irremediably taken the poison of thought into your system and the East is ever after impossible," although he was planning himself to translate *Gil Blas* and Plato into Cingalese and to paint because a painter must stand up at his work. "If one sits down in Ceylon one goes to sleep." In how many other far-away lands one might have heard similar cries, evoked from young aspirants who had feasted at the table of Europe and feared that they were destined, at home, to starve, just as one heard them in Boston, in New York, in every corner of our own world, culturally colonial still for all the Walt Whitmans. But because the European centre could no longer hold,—whether or not Europe was "dead and stinking," as D. H. Lawrence said, shaking his beard,—a new Ceylon was eventually to rise and a new India and China, compelled to make the most of their own resources. A new America too was to rise, in the literary sense, centered no longer on the East but mainly on the West, and within a short time the American writer found all he required in order to exist, in atmosphere and material alike, within his own country. For these were the years in which America came of age.

Of this I had had premonitions, especially in England, where I had written a book that summed them up in a rented house in the suburb of Eltham that belonged to two old ladies who were descendants of the voyager Captain Cook. In the little room in which I worked stood Captain Cook's sea-chest, an old trunk bound in battered red morocco, and I sometimes used this as a seat while writing *America's Coming-of-Age* with a feeling that I too was engaged in adventurous voyages. It happened not only then but earlier and later that my mind turned back to America when I was abroad; for, just as I had written my first book *The Wine of the Puritans* in Europe, so I was to plan *The Writer in America* there. I had gone to Ireland at sixty-five hoping to write a book about it, with notes that I had collected and with questions to ask, feeling that here was my chance to realize a wish of many years by hatching at least one book of travels. But after three weeks I seemed to know less about Ireland than I knew at the start while I was full of thoughts about my own country,—with which I seemed to be locked up mentally for life,—and this was the way it had been in England so many years before when the first world war was on the point of breaking out. To me it seemed clear in 1913 that we were to have a renaissance, that extraordinary forces at home were at work in the silence and that what we required was a critical movement to release these forces, to harrow the ground for the "seed beneath the snow." For there was no doubt about the snow, the cold complacency, the self-satisfaction that accompanied the provincial isolation of the American mind, paralyzing the creative powers which were depressed already by the "cultural humility" that Randolph Bourne deplored. At Petitpas', W. G. Blaikie Murdoch had spoken of the "servile deference" which the European critic met in the United States, saying, "The American people are largely convinced that his verdict is perforce of greater moment than theirs." One had somehow to rectify this feeling of inferiority and the false sense of superiority that coëxisted with it, uniting the notes of censure and hope and obliging young writers to question their world while they were finding a world in their natural setting.

These premonitions were sound enough, as the new poetry

presently showed, with Robert Frost, Ezra Pound and Amy
Lowell, with the flowering of the novel in the twenties and the
plays of O'Neill, not to mention American architecture and
American painting. *The New Republic* had come in with the
tide at a moment when, in Europe, the most symptomatic book
was *The Decline of the West,* which scarcely included the
American West that Whitman had called the predestined home
of this country's distinctive realities and ideas. Europe was
Spengler's declining land, and to many Americans, turning
homeward, the shade of Virgil seemed to say what it said to the
young man in *The Cabala* of Thornton Wilder, "Seek out
some city that is young. The secret is to make a city, not to
rest in it." They were prepared to agree at last with Santayana's
observation, "All nationalities are better at home. . . . When
you transplant the species it suffers constraint and becomes
sickly or intrusive or both at once," partly because they had
seen for themselves how true this was or had been in the case
of Americans they knew or of whom they had heard. As time
went on they felt less and less the tension that had been so
marked between their American "duties" and their European
"culture," especially on the Eastern coast and, above all, in the
Harvard men who were "neither American nor European," as
Henry Adams put it. These men had felt overwhelmingly the
beauty of the old world and the charm of life and manners that
went with it, and, born, like myself, with Baedeker as it were
in the cradle, their minds had been Europeanized almost at
the outset. But they were inclined now to see the importance
of solving this tension by cleaving finally either to America or
Europe, attaching themselves to some country that could serve
them as a homeland, for was not the poet Yeats right when he
said, "One can only reach out to the universe with a gloved
hand,—that glove is one's nation"? A few continued to main-

tain the tension, whether they suffered in consequence or not, as it seemed to me that John Gould Fletcher suffered, for he was too old at forty-five, after so many years in England, to remake his life successfully on American terms. The case was less clear with Conrad Aiken and his lifelong liaison with "Ariel's island," for the "instability, restlessness and dissatisfaction" he ascribed to himself may perhaps have resulted in much that was good in his work. But when Eliot embraced, as a nation, England, forswearing the country of his birth, with the social and political philosophy that characterized it, he illustrated the truth of Yeats's remark. I was myself a convert in the other direction, and I was to be accused in time of the convert's zeal.

But I foresaw none of this when I returned in 1914 at a time of arctic loneliness for American writers when no one felt the common purpose that later writers, looking back, attributed to these years of the tuning of the fiddles. It is always the other time that is the time of "purpose." I only felt, as I remember, that my own curtain was about to rise, that my real life as a writer was about to begin, while I was scarcely aware how naturally most of the writers who were soon to appear took and retained the Americanism they had been born with. Oak Park, Illinois, gave Hemingway, as it gave Frank Lloyd Wright, something that New Jersey, New York and Harvard had failed to give many of my friends along with me, the instinctive feeling about their country that enabled them to live anywhere without even a momentary second thought about it. This was the frame of mind which the world-war epoch established on all sides within a decade or two, while, for good and ill,—for much of both,—the word "European" virtually ceased to ring bells in the American breast. The rise of Mussolini, of Hitler, of Stalin alienated many who had loved the old liberal

Europe and felt at home there, and the decline of romantic feeling and the feeling for classical culture destroyed in others the tie between the new world and the old. On the other hand, the rapid growth of American biography and history created a general interest in the American scene, by so much no doubt reducing the interest in Europe. Did not the Europeans, moreover, wish Americans to be "American," and had they not always wished this in literary matters since Goethe regretted that Washington Irving wrote on European themes instead of the themes that made Cooper so excitingly new? No American poet had ever been the nine days' wonder in England that Vachel Lindsay was in 1920 when he was described as the only American who "mattered" in poetry because he was "totally and exclusively" transatlantic. The great reproach had always been that our writers were "not American enough," that America, as Shaw said, returned to Europe its exports at second hand instead of "at last producing an art of its own."

I returned with my wife for a winter to our native Wall Street suburb,—our Yasnaya Polyana in New Jersey,—where we had lived at the Seminary, off and on, in earlier days, under the sign of Miss Kenyon, in the aura of the Brownings. My mother and my brother were still living in the town, and Max Perkins also lived there still, while J. B. Yeats often came out from New York for portrait-painting visits and to lecture in the houses of our friends. Thrown back upon myself there, I thought of my own childhood and the state of introversion into which I had passed, silently withdrawing myself, at about fourteen, a state that was unconsciously designed perhaps to guard me against influences with which I already felt at war. I had never been at home there or anywhere but in my own mind where I lived in a fantasy-world remote from "business," —the business that was never talked about but that somehow pervaded this native scene where I wondered if even my father had ever been at home. It struck me that my father's friends had been bankers and stock-brokers by default, for I saw them in retirement apparently happier as amateur photographers and what not than they had seemed in their feverish gambling years. One was an almost first-rate classical scholar, another carved walnut chests that were beautifully wrought. Had my father's practical failure in life over-affected my own mind, as his European associations had affected it also, so that perhaps his inability to adjust himself to existence at home had started my own European-American conflict? Undoubtedly in certain ways I identified myself with him, while I belonged to a generation that had turned away from the business life, like Windy McPherson's son in Sherwood Anderson's novel. I realized, for the rest, in my native town the truth of the Chinese proverb, "A man is more the child of the age he lives in than he is of his own father and mother."

In any case, I had broken away effectively from this childhood world, following a line that had its inner logic, erratic as it seemed to others,—or so I felt,—the sort of line my brother could not establish for himself, so that indecision and doubt were to rule his existence. Unwillingly a lawyer, by nature a scholar,—more than I was or wished to be,—with a passion for historical studies and for languages and travel, he should have been, it seemed to me, a professor of history at Princeton, where he had been the poet of his day. The university press there published his verses with the Tahitian title *Mauna Roa*, for Tahiti, the "Land of Let-It-Alone," was one of the many ports of call that he visited in his restless haunted life. His panacea, as he wrote once, was "packing up and leaving in the morning" for Normandy, Newfoundland, the West Indies, Italy or Oxford, or "going back to Princeton" where he might

revive perhaps his "old buried life of the poet and dreamer."
He had run down to Georgia, when General Longstreet was
still living on his farm, to interrogate this ancient about
Chickamauga, and he camped out in the Rockies where so
many lost their minds, he said, from the "mountain gloom of
Ruskin's *Modern Painters.*" Buying a horse and an outfit, he
visited deserted mines that recalled to him our father's mining
ventures, and he was struck by the "sad far-away look" in the
eyes of our father's old friend in Wyoming,—in the eyes of all
the veteran ranchmen there. Translating Greek, German and
Anglo-Saxon poems, he wrote a novel that was more or less
modelled on Pater, and he had known hours of fulfilment as
an ambulancier in France and as head of a Negro industrial
school in Alabama. But more and more he came to resemble
those Hamlets of the French Symbolist poets who turn away
from their loves, preferring their dreams; and at last, when his
life was an afternoon without any mornings, he was prepared
to "embrace the doom assigned."

How had I escaped, if escape I did and only partially at best,
from so much of the sadness and wreckage that surround a
life? The earliest dream I remember was a dream of flight, and
as this recurred in my childhood constantly, and even in my
later years, I invested it with a complex meaning as time went
on. I must have been very small when I experienced this
dream first, one evening, as it comes back to me, after my
mother, still young and gay, leaving for a dinner-party, had
kissed me good-night. I presently fancied I was on the lawn
when a Hindu, suddenly appearing, in a coat of many colours,
chased me with a knife,—a glittering knife that he held in his
outstretched hand,—and, just as he approached me, running, I
soared into the air and floated away, free, aloft and safe. On
other occasions the fiend was not an Oriental, he was merely

a nondescript minatory figure that pursued me, and I was not even anxious when I saw him approaching, for I knew I possessed the power to float away. The Freudian idea of this dream I revised with my own. It is an old notion that writing provides for the writer a vicarious existence in which he can take refuge from the menace of life, its miseries and mishaps and often insoluble problems, together with his own ineptitudes, his disabilities as a man, his weaknesses, fatuities, inadequacies, gaucheries and blunders. It was always to be so with me, my sanctuary, my retreat in a world in which, without it, I would have foundered, and I was seldom to lose my trust in the power that quite obviously saved me, on two or three critical occasions, from the Hindu with the knife.

What struck me, finally, in my native town, which I had left after my college years and was to leave for good at the end of one winter,—when my wife and I settled in Connecticut, near many of our friends,—was the almost pure "Anglo-Saxonism" of the world I had grown up in as contrasted with the world I had come to know. The first title of *America's Coming-of-Age* had been *A Fable for Yankees,* for out of sheer habit I had felt that our countrypeople were "old American," in the anthropologists' phrase,—and my publisher pointed out to me what I knew perfectly well, that Americans were no longer Yankees, even of the South. They were as multi-racial as the crew of the "Pequod" in *Moby-Dick,* and only "society," in the narrower sense, maintained the old American base, whether in my birthplace or in the country at large. It is true, in that ancestral world there was something reassuring, a cosy homogeneity that one lost with regret, as there was a charm in the literary world that accompanied the social world and that I sometimes saw during these years. Occasionally on Sunday afternoons I went to the Century Club in New York where one of my un-

cles by marriage was the oldest living member and where, as
we mounted the stairs and entered the great gloomy upper
rooms, Rip van Winkles rose from all the sofas. They were ancient New York editors, architects and authors who had acted
in some cases as diplomats and consuls abroad and who, at the
sound of our footsteps, roused themselves from their afternoon
naps, plucking their beards, like the old men of Homer.
Then, presently gathering in a circle, they began to talk, ex-
changing recollections of the acting of Macready and Walter
Savage Landor's style and the days when they had served as
attachés with Lowell and Motley. My venerable uncle by marriage remembered hearing a speech that Lamartine delivered in
the Paris of Louis Philippe. To me it was delightful, but
Homer himself was scarcely more remote from the Greenwich
Village I knew and my friends who were writers, Russians,
East Indians, Japanese and as often Italians and Swedes as
men of my own nationality from Iowa and Kansas. I had always assumed that one had to be outside society, in the narrower sense, in order to be inside the world I cared for; and
this was no longer an "old American" world.

I realized that I had grown up in a crowded little corner of
the country, with windows opening towards Europe and closed
towards the West—of which, as my writing showed, I knew
next to nothing; but, presently repatriated, I was a convert to
a state of mind, not in any important sense to a mere visible
country. As an actual nation the United States was nothing
greatly to boast about, for its virtue was largely the result of
fortunate conditions; and for this I felt only the affection that
people usually feel,—whether Welshmen or Indo-Chinese,—
for the lands of their birth. I detested the giant Business and
its more and more veiled will-to-power, and what I came to
cherish was a certain philosophy or point of view that one

found expressed, quite clearly, in the American scriptures, the great books of the eighteen-fifties, by Melville and Whitman especially, that had much in common with Lincoln and with Jefferson and Paine. These books conveyed the uniqueness of the American tradition, a line that was paralleled by other lines that ran through other American writers but that ran also through writers of other countries, while *this* line had no parallel in Europe or elsewhere, for it sprang from the nature of the republic, its essence and aim. It expressed a country that was settled "by the people of all nations," as Melville said, and that "all nations" might therefore "claim for their own,"— in short, the cradle or the germ of the world state of the future in which all men were "children of an equal brood."

That to foster this germ was the mission of the country the greatest American writers had thought, and Whitman went on to say that America, the "inheritor of the past," was in consequence the "custodian of the future" of mankind. Melville's deduction from this larger premise was that American writers should forthwith take "the practical lead in the world," although neither Melville nor Whitman foresaw the world wars that were coming or the cultural retreat and decline that were inevitably to follow. They could not have foreseen the reactionary notions that American critics were to adopt, while the most influential literary circles denounced as outmoded and vulgar the great beliefs that were basic in the history of the country. But if they had foreseen all this, would not these writers have said with Blake that "without contraries is no progression" and that without periodical returns to the irrational forces of myth and sleep humanity cannot maintain its intelligence and will? That, for the rest, their ideas were not of their own time alone but had a long future before them, and a long past behind, these writers would have been more convinced than ever. They spoke for a democratic socialized world with a humanist philosophy based on the positive elements of all religions; and this was the world that I too hoped to see.

Days of the Phoenix

THE NINETEEN-TWENTIES I REMEMBER

NOTE

THE PAGES THAT FOLLOW are a continuation of my *Scenes and Portraits: Memories of Childhood and Youth*. They take up the story of my life, work and friendships from the year when I settled in Connecticut. Of the six years since I had returned from Europe at the beginning of the first world war, I had spent three in New York, two in California and one in the Wall Street suburb of my childhood.

In gathering together my memories of the nineteen-hundreds, I have had in mind a remark of W. B. Yeats. Urging his father, J. B. Yeats, to tell the story of his life, the poet said, "It would tell people about those things that are not old enough to be in the histories or new enough to be in the reader's mind, and those things are always the things that are least known."

CHAPTER I

CONNECTICUT: 1920

I N THE years that followed the first world war the quiet Connecticut countryside attracted many of the New York writers
and artists, for the low rolling hills there seemed to favour
those who cared more for the state of their minds than the
state of their fortunes. They were drawn to the pretty villages
and the old farmhouses that were built by faithful craftsmen
a century before,—two centuries in many cases, or nearly three,
—master-carpenters working in a fine tradition, following Palladian manuals of the colonial time. In the woodland clearings, on the slopes, there were natural pictures on every side
that brought back Giorgione or perhaps Cézanne, and the antique dealers from the city raided the region for the lowboys
they found on lonely roads. The villagers, who had often been
swindled, occasionally cherished as antiques even the stuffed
owls that also abounded in their houses,—they thought any old
book might be a rare first edition; but one still found in 1920
serviceable tables and settees that had been made there in the
sixteen-hundreds. These, with chests of oak and pine, were
emblems of a country that could no longer be called new or
young, for they had been shaped and put together in the
winding lanes there when Molière was living in France and
Milton in England.

This note of the native Connecticut air meant much to the newcomers who were settling in abandoned farmhouses and remodelling barns, aside from the tranquillity one found there in a war-torn world and the charm of old hand-hewn beams and drooping elms. For in many cases the artists and writers had grown up in a still raw West or had returned from Paris in search of "roots," that shy and impalpable quiddity the lack of which, they felt, had made them frequently shallow and generally restless. No word was more constantly on their lips unless it was the native "soil" or "earth," and this obsession lay deep in the minds of urban cosmopolitans whom one saw toiling now with spade and pick. Some of them flew back and forth between their farms and Hollywood, alternating weeks in the studio with weeks in the field, and one found fashion-designers digging rocks out of streams and laboriously piling them up for a dam and a pool. They lovingly pointed out to friends the iron H-hinges on their doors, the twelve-inch planks on their floors and their cavern-like cellars, and they measured the immense cut stones in border walls along which three men could walk abreast. They seemed to draw a secret strength from the old Yankee farmers who had occupied and tilled the land before them, and one met occasionally a survivor on the road who could still speak of the customs and laws of the past. He might answer off-hand, if one asked him what was wrong with some pseudo-colonial house that had just been erected, "The ridge-pole's too high by fourteen inches." In this paradoxical decade, equally full of despair and hope, there were many who flouted tradition and many who sought it, and it was reassuring for these to live in a long settled region. They found at least a rill of tradition there.

No European could understand this constant American talk of roots, or why it was that expatriates discussed expatriation,

—a word that scarcely existed in any other country,—wondering about their "responsibilities" when they were abroad and how long they could safely stay in Europe. Sinclair Lewis told me later that he had read one of my books to find his roots in Connecticut before he moved there, for he had been racketing round the world for the last half-century and felt he had to belong somewhere at last. He had returned to Minnesota, but the world he had known as a child had gone and he could not live with the new people; then he remembered that all his forbears had come from Connecticut and he had returned to this old home of the Yankees. It was true that he did not stay there long, but the question of expatriation was never out of Sinclair Lewis's mind; and it was against the dangers of this that the painter Robert Henri had warned the young dancer Angna Enters. "So many artists go abroad," he had said to her, "and something happens to their work. You must never let that happen to you." But this was natural, surely, if there was any truth in certain comments of other Europeans, that America was "not a blood-homeland," as D. H. Lawrence said, or that Americans were "not yet at home in their unconscious." (This was Dr. Carl Jung's diagnosis.) For me this question was still acute when, in 1920, my wife and I bought a village house in Westport, for I was colonially minded then and was perhaps to remain so, owing to certain elements of my youth and education. It took me twenty years or more to live down what I felt then, a frequently acute homesickness for the European scene, for I had experienced all too fully the widely shared consciousness of a drop in one's emotional thermometer on returning from Europe. It was like the change, for a swimmer, from salt water to fresh. I understood why it was that Thoreau had refused to go abroad, fearing to lose the feeling of his "native woods and pastures," for Americans were so often overborne in Europe. A long immersion in American life was to cure me completely of any lingering fears of expatriation; but this ambivalence characterized my outlook in the twenties, as I was to realize later, looking back.

Westport still had a rustic air, with a wooden hotel on the post-road; and often, on one of the rocking-chairs that lined the long piazza, one saw Bill Hart surrounded with his cronies. The famous and opulent cowboy, the hero of the Westerns, had scarcely emerged from the chrysalis of the old-time actor, but, still a tiro at mounting a horse, he dazzled all the little boys with his trick of lighting a match by flicking a thumbnail. William S. Hart, with his feet on the rail and a ten-gallon hat on the back of his head, recalled a simpler world in the so-called jazz age, while in some of the plain little houses that lined the village streets one found surprising variations of Yankee types. There might have been the scholar I was to know in after years who came "south" for the winter from his village in Vermont, just as the Orkney islanders, to warm their bones in January, descend for a touch of the tropics to Edinburgh. This was the philosophic soul who learned Chinese at seventy-five and who was studying Sanskrit when I knew him at eighty. Our own introduction to the town had been a drive with a friend who took us out to dinner at his solitary farmhouse, showing us, as we sped past, a house where .a woman had hanged herself and another where a Swedish officer had murdered his wife. Then, at a turn of the road, a woman in black was bending over, gathering dandelions, and my friend said she was old Kate who had killed her father with a bread-knife and had just been released from the asylum. I had only begun to take it in that all towns were Spoon Rivers and that Edgar Lee Masters had shocked the country merely by showing what one should have known; but

I had found and was to find too many other sorts of life ever to believe in the general depravity of men.

The cottage in which my wife and I were to live for twenty years stood on the old post-road that was called King's Highway. It was perched on a high, rocky, woodsy corner, and the poetess who had lived there and built a tree-house overhead had painted the rooms in the new Greenwich Village fashion. One was canary yellow, another pale apple-green; others were Chinese blue and terracotta. In front a row of Lombardy poplars dropped their golden leaves over the stone wall that shut us in, and we constructed a terrace on the slope over the garden with a table under the shade of an old apple-tree. It was a true *Künstlerheim,* as one of our friends called it, one of the many in whose talk, as we sat under the branches, I felt the time-spirit prompting me.

No one can ever be fully aware of what a given decade means, or whether it is a "period" or an "epoch," as Charles Péguy put it, he who found himself in a tame and pallid 1898 when he longed for a fierce and heroic 1793. But thirty years later, in literary circles, the decade of the twenties was to look rather like an epoch in the minds of the young, at least when they compared it with the decades that followed; and indeed, in those days that were thought of as a little Renaissance, there was much afoot in the world of writers. American writing itself had come to seem important, although it was still ignored in academic circles, where Thackeray and Tennyson were treated as twin kings of our literature and all the American writers as poor relations. It was regarded as "a pale and obedient provincial cousin about which the less said the better," in the phrase of Ernest Boyd, and Christian Gauss at Princeton, as Edmund Wilson soon pointed out, chimed in with Woodberry at Columbia and Wendell at Harvard. He too looked down his nose at American studies. But the idea that America was a dependency of England had vanished, with the world war, from the minds of writers, who were now inclined to agree with Melville that the time had come for America "to set, not follow precedents." They were acutely aware of the country, its promise and its weaknesses, and the problems of the writer living in it, and they were concerned especially with the art of writing.

These questions interested all our friends as we sat under the apple-tree, and it was largely true that American writing had come of age, along with other aspects of the life of the country. This was a time of transition between the colonial or provincial past and the world-minded America of later decades, a time when, in spite of the war that destroyed in Europe so many hopes, this country seemed to be starting, artistically, afresh. A friend of mine in London wrote that England was "a mere standing pool" whereas our American criticism was "living," because in England critics felt that nothing remained to be done while we had "an end for America" and were "working towards it." So, too, at about this time an English traveller noted that literature in England was "in a blind alley" and that we had "the growing end of English literature today" because we had "a new hope with a new impulse." Of this, in fact, there were many examples in the sudden appearance of new good writers and of little theatres and little magazines, with *The Dial, The Masses, The Freeman, The Seven Arts* and *The New Republic,* the New School for Social Research and the Whitney Museum. Most of these institutions rose within a dozen years, following *The Smart Set* of Mencken and the emergence of the "Eight," which marked, with the Armory Show, a new moment in painting, and one might add the Theatre Guild and the discovery of American folk art as notes in this American Risorgimento. (To use the word that Ezra Pound preferred to the commoner American Renaissance.) People were talking *ad libitum* about the "American experience," the "American language," the "American rhythm" and what not, and Vachel Lindsay had announced a great "flowering of art and song," a "spiritual harvest" appearing in the Middle West. There Masters and Sandburg, Eliot and Pound, Sherwood Anderson and Sinclair Lewis were soon to be followed by Hemingway, Dos Passos and Fitzgerald, and Willa Cather was to show in her novels and stories the general aesthetic resources of that multiracial region. In her work one saw the dawning talents of the new immigrant strains that blossomed in prairie villages and bleak ranch-houses, singers like Cressida Garnett, Hungarian violinists and German pianists from Western mining towns. These were among the characters one met in Greenwich Village.

Sooner or later, as an outpost of New York, Westport was to witness many of the types of this time of discovery and youth; for there came Sherwood Anderson and Scott Fitzgerald, along with the New England poet Robert Frost. There, too, lived Paul Rosenfeld, of all our Westport circle of friends the most aware, I think, of the promise of the country, alive as he was to music and painting as well as to literature and an absolute worshipper of art. "To have artists about one is wonderful," he wrote in a letter, "and to be loved by them almost divine," and no one recognized and hailed so many of the new talents from Georgia O'Keeffe, the painter, to Marianne Moore. When he built a cottage not far from ours, he employed to paint it not two house-painters but two "art-artists,"—in the phrase of a politician much quoted at the time,—members of the circle of Alfred Stieglitz, who was Paul's elder cousin and to whom he looked up as a prophet and almost a father. As I passed the house on afternoon walks I saw the two sitting on the roof, in the sunny May weather, discussing art, and they were there for many weeks, occasionally taking a moment off to fill their brushes for a few strokes of paint. But Paul, who had ample means, never thought of hastening them, for helping impecunious artists was one of his chief pleasures: it was, in fact, his way of offering thanks to the artist-clan who made the world luminous and habitable for himself and others. "I wish I might do something to make your life and everybody's life in the U.S.A. more fruitful," Paul wrote to one of our friends. "I should like to be able to fight for you and all the rest who are doing good work, and create some sort of atmosphere in which it is easier for such as you to exist." He had mourned over the young musicians who were killed or wounded in the war and the painters who were starving to death in Russia, and he was beloved in turn as a true-born citizen of the fatherland of art who scarcely admitted any other allegiance.

Art for Paul could be only "pure." It had no connection with history, economics, society or any alloy, and artists for him were sacrosanct, moreover. He thought of it as treason if, in any fashion, one challenged their claims; and, generous as he was to me, he looked at me askance when I published *The Ordeal of Mark Twain*. There, from his point of view, I had committed two sins, "attacking" a writer, in the first place, and, secondly, regarding him from the social, not the aesthetic, point of view. He felt I was handing a writer over to the secular arm of the Philistines and, in so doing, betraying my own caste; and he excommunicated Carl Sandburg a little later after praising him also highly in *Port of New York*. He had rejoiced in the "wonder and song" that Carl Sandburg had found in his Western towns, in the Mississippi valley that he

saw as the top of the globe, saying that Sandburg had virtually done for the Western townspeople what Synge had
done for the language of the Irish peasants. I had first met
Sandburg in Paul's own rooms in town, but, for him, this
poet had committed an act of treason that was even graver
than my own, for he had written a book in praise of Edward
Steichen, his brother-in-law and an old associate of Stieglitz.
The trouble was that Steichen had broken the unwritten code
of artists by using his photographs in advertising; and how
could one pardon anyone for defending such a man? This was
a sin that Paul could see only as mortal. Nor could he endure
bleak thinking in criticism. He referred to the "sad disgruntled beings" who wrote *Civilization in the United States* and
who complained that the American soil was unfriendly to the
growth of art when there was John Marin, for one, blooming
and singing. Did not Marin, all ebullience and high spirit,
suggest a fruit-tree rooted in good ground?

Like Huneker, who said he had always rejoiced when he
caught the first glow of a rising sun, Paul too was a yea-sayer
who had much in common with this earlier star-finder of the
various arts. But while Huneker had discovered, for America,
European talents, Paul found these talents at home, and few
of his swans turned out to be geese, for he saw in his own
time what others were to see twenty years later. There had
been a day for him when any German village, or any garden
in Holland or balcony in France, had stirred him as New
York had never done, but another day came when the port,
as the steamer approached it, had filled him with a sense of
confidence and strength. He had found himself entering a
country where, as he said, it was "good to be," where a new
spirit was obviously dawning, and, if "every generation," as

John Sloan said, "is *the* generation to an artist," no one was more aware than Paul of this one.

It was true that in painting Paul scarcely strayed beyond the borders of Stieglitz's group,—he could not in his heart believe in a painter who did not have the Stieglitz *imprimatur*; but in literature and music,—his special field in criticism, —he was adventurous and prophetic at the same time. In his musical chronicle in *The Dial* he saluted Carl Ruggles and Ernest Bloch and said "Roger Sessions goes to a great career," for he found in American music, at last, the robustness and the vibrancy that had been generally lacking in the older composers. In literature too he was one of the first to acclaim the new novelists and poets who were beginning to appear in the early twenties, among them E. E. Cummings and Wallace Stevens. A true apostle of all art, Paul would appear from time to time with a picture of Marsden Hartley's under his arm, or one by our fellow-Westporter Arthur Dove which he called "a sort of *Leaves of Grass* through pigment," covering our dining-room walls with them for a few weeks or months so that the new sun would also dawn for us. He was all for what he called "the dream growing out of reality," which he welcomed in Marin, Dove and Hartley, while he turned away from the bloodless dream of Arthur B. Davies, for instance, that left reality itself wingless and shoddy.

Nothing could have been more remote than Paul's impressionistic style from the stripped prose that soon became the vogue, one all romantic luxuriance and sometimes rhapsodic, the other analytic, spare and cold. Paul, as a man of feeling, was to find himself less and less at home in a world of cerebration and specialization, while he brought his readers what later critics scarcely wished to bring them, the glamour of a literary life that seemed all enjoyment. Some of the essays in his *Musical Portraits* were among the finest of their time, those, for example, on César Franck, on Berlioz, on Moussorgsky and on Wagner as a symbol of his epoch and Debussy of ours (or, one should say, of the period when this essay was written). For the rest, it was Paul's misfortune that he wrote occasionally as if English was not his native language. He had grown up in a music-loving German-Jewish family with early associations that were Central European, and his writing abounded in preciosities, neologisms and archaisms that one seldom found in the work of born writers of English. Paul's exceptional gift of style made it all the plainer that he was not quite at home in the language he wrote in, and all this told against him in the minds of later writers who had none of his cultivation and little of his talent. But there were many of all schools who felt they were indebted to him, as critic, editor or friend, for their public existence, and no one deserved more the epithet of Emerson,—he was a consistent "patriot of the muses' country."

Paul had been our first Westport guest, in 1920, in the garden. He had joined us at a nursery lunch with rice pudding and the children. Meanwhile, either at his house or at Karl Anderson's near the beach, Sherwood Anderson appeared for an occasional visit, and, although these were his roaming years in the mid-America that he called "my land," he even thought for a while of living near us. I had first known him earlier, and he sometimes wrote to me from the strange places where he liked to be alone, wandering with what he described as "mystic vague impulses," but with a clear eye also, from town to town. He would disappear for months, no one knew where he was, or he would set out on a walking trip across Illinois in ploughing time; and he wrote once from Reno that he felt "people by thousands" somehow "drifting in and out of me."

His actual physical feeling of being completely in rapport with every man, woman and child along the street had become so intense one afternoon that he felt obliged to "hide" himself to rest. From the time when, as a little boy, he had tagged at the heels of older men, listening to their talk, observing their quirks, working himself in the fields with them or tending horses at county fairs, he had been aware of all sorts and conditions of men. But he was especially drawn to the human grotesques and the obscure of whom he wrote, "It is they who have given me life." For he shared the preference of the "little people" over the "big" so generally shown in novels of the two world wars, in which the officers are never as good as the men; and I remember that at Westport once he burst out about Robert E. Lee, against whom he seemed to have a special grudge. He said he was going to write a book about the Civil War that would put these stuffed shirts in their places. To this degree Sherwood carried the cult of the rank and file, the magnet of the American imagination.

Aside from his people, Sherwood's mind was alive with images of the West. He wrote to me, for instance, about *Poor White,* the story of a "Lincolnian type from Missouri," that the book was "about laid by, as we say out here of the corn crop in early October. It is in shocks and stood up in the field. The husking is yet to do." But he kept repeating, "It's lonely out here" and "We are all struggling in a vacuum . . . One gets this queer sense of carving a stone that will be cast into a stagnant sea, into the Sargasso sea, as you suggest" (in my book *America's Coming-of-Age*). This loneliness, which we all felt, drew him into the Stieglitz circle, and there, and still more later, in the circle of Gertrude Stein, he began to worry about "sophistication." In Stieglitz, loving his tools and materials, Sherwood saw the craftsman whom he admired above all other types, a symbol of the old wagon-builders, organ-builders and harness-makers who had been swept away by the factory system. But in the Stieglitz atmosphere there was another element that spoiled his natural simplicity a little, for it made him feel that he should follow what he called "European moods" instead of the "old mood" of his early stories. Luckily, he could return at times to this old mood that belonged to him, and how good it was to hear him talk about "Buck Fever" and "Hannah Stoots" in his newspaper days in Virginia later. But in much of his work he became artificially simple, with a naivety that seemed both forced and knowing. It was this that Hemingway took for affectation when he travestied Sherwood Anderson in *The Torrents of Spring*.

Sherwood's two brothers in Westport were troubled by this trait of his, or, I should say, the mendacity it sometimes led to, the conscious use of fantasy in dealing with fact. Of these two, Karl, the painter, was altogether without guile, and Ray was all too genuinely simple. This maverick, a much younger man, could not stomach Sherwood's "lies," insisting that their grandmother was Italian, for example, when everybody knew that she was German; and in fact Sherwood's non-fictional writing would have been far more interesting if he had not strayed over the fictional border. But in all this drawing of the long bow he was following the father whom he described in the character of Windy McPherson and from whom he had inherited the gift of story-telling that seemed in all three brothers exactly the same. When Ray stopped me on the street to tell me how, when he was a boy, he had caught mud-turtles in Ohio, I could not believe it was not Sherwood speaking, and when I read a novel once that Karl took it into his head to write I felt that Sherwood must have written this novel.

The voices of all three brothers were as much alike as the themes and the style of their stories.

With John Held, who created it partly in his drawings and his stories, the note of the jazz age also resounded in Westport, where Scott Fitzgerald, who presently spent a summer there, summoned the fire department during one wild party. He was ready when the firemen came with an explanation that not his house but he and his friends were "lit." After another party a young man whom we all knew laid himself down on the post-road to be run over by a truck. This was the day of the bootlegger and the "liberated love-making" of Edmund Wilson's *Memoirs of Hecate County*, tales of the princess with golden hair and the shooter of snapping-turtles who lived, if not in Westport, certainly near us. As one of a younger generation,—we had a new generation every five years, Stieglitz said,—Wilson visited Paul in the early twenties, and later I wondered if Paul had not suggested to him the art-critic who appeared as the fictional narrator in this book of stories. Near us lived Guy Pène du Bois, and Everett Shinn, one of the "Eight," bought a big house on the post-road surrounded by a wall where he was writing novels and plays to work off some of the energy that his painting seemed unable to exhaust. One night at our house he acted out a whole play for us, and the fiery wiry little man sprang about our living-room, now speaking in the voice of one character, now of another. A few doors from us was the novelist William McFee, the retired ship's engineer who had grown up in England. He had sailed with coal from Cardiff to the Canary Islands, with kerosene to Yokohama, with cotton from Charleston, to Singapore, Surabaya and Rio de Janeiro, and, after writing *Casuals of the Sea* during a brief visit home, he was at work on *Harbours of Memory* in Westport. There, off and on, were the Prendergasts, Maurice and the younger Charles, who lived there always after his brother's death,—the master-craftsman who knew so well the superlative wood-carving of Italy and Spain and who framed so many of Mrs. Jack Gardner's pictures. It was during these years that he developed, in his gilded images and gesso panels, an art of happy visions, all his own, with flashing fountains, windblown girls and the fairy-tale animals and ships of a personal Yankee golden age and world.

In Westport lived the grocer who struck a key-note of the time, as it comes back to me in a very different epoch,—a picturesque man who had once been a trader in the jungle of South Africa and who let his accounts with artists run for years. One day he showed me a postal order he had just received from Bali settling the bill of a painter that was ten years old, and his comment was that in all his experience he had never had a bad debt that concerned a man of the brush or a man of the pen. I was all the more impressed by this because two Westport tradesmen could not be induced to send me bills at all and I had to wait three years, in one case, in the other nine, before I knew what I had spent over their counters. They looked on outstanding bills as money in the bank, one of them said, and it was evident that long experience had justified this virtually instinctive faith in men. I wondered at the time if New England was peculiarly honest. But I think Sherwood Anderson's trust in man's essential decency was generally characteristic of the mind of the country. It was certainly characteristic of most of the writers, who still saw man as basically good, indefinitely plastic and capable of introducing a new order in the world. If, thirty-five years later, "A good man is hard to find" might have been taken as their motto, this was an after-effect of war on a younger generation that "likes to believe the worst of everybody." (A phrase of John Peale Bishop in one of his essays.) It was a delayed reaction, in the jargon of psychology, and one that was rather slow in coming on, for the writers of the twenties still widely shared the faith of the Enlightenment in human perfectibility and good will. The Utopian hope that had few roots in Europe had lingered from colony times in the American mind.

CHAPTER II

THE NEWNESS

I HAD FIRST met Sherwood Anderson in 1917, three years before I moved to Westport, in the rooms of the monthly *The
Seven Arts,* which expressed what the editor called a sense of
"the brighter colour of a new day." James Oppenheim had
written *Songs for the New Age,* Whitmanesque poems that
conveyed this feeling of promise at a time when dozens of
novelists and poets were "discovering" America and a spirit
of rebirth was in the air. "It is our faith and the faith of many
that we are living in the first days of a renascent period . . .
the beginning of greatness," Waldo Frank had written in a
manifesto that appeared in the first number of the magazine.
As I recall it, Waldo Frank was the real creator of *The Seven
Arts,* and, as associate editor, he had procured for this the first
of Sherwood Anderson's *Winesburg* stories. I was invited to
join the staff because my *America's Coming-of-Age* had also
struck the note of the new day.

Ever since I had come home from Europe at the outset of
the war, I had been working in a New York publishing office,
in the Century Company where one saw, drifting in and out,
the gentlemanly old-fashioned authors of the "Howells and
James" age. Howells himself might have been there, the last
of the triumvirate who had survived Mark Twain and Henry
James and whom I had interviewed some years before, the

novelist of a domestic world in which silver weddings and bridal tours, together with the servant problem, filled people's minds. Howells, who had also survived his vogue, stood for an Anglo-American past that seemed now almost as remote as the past of Persia, a day when American writing itself had been taken lightly and every eye but Howells's was turned towards England. But other kindly old men of letters, often wearing beards, dropped in, uniting the Century Company with the Century Club, where with one voice they denounced the new novelists and poets who were equally outlandish in their literary manners and their names. Moreover, they denounced Amy Lowell, who was putting the new poetry on the map with a species of bad manners that belied her name and whom I first saw in the office of *The Century* as, one day, I passed the editor's door. There I observed a bright green expanse, broad as a meadow in springtime,—Amy Lowell's back, —which blocked the door, while her commanding voice rang down the hallway. Like Robert Frost, John Dos Passos and Theodore Dreiser, she too was one of the writers of *The Seven Arts.*

Meanwhile, at the Century Company, I had been busy for many weeks ghost-writing the memoirs of Iliodor, the "mad monk of Russia," who came to the office every day and poured out, through an interpreter, the story that I was to organize into a book. Odorous and fat as a porpoise, this greatest of Russian church orators brought back the mediæval Slavic folk-world, the moujik world of the Slavophiles who wished to preserve the old Russia from what they regarded as the devilish spirit of the West. With fanatical zeal he had defended autocracy and orthodoxy, an idol of the masses and a preacher at the court, where, with his bath ceremonials, Rasputin expounded his highly successful doctrine of "salvation by sin."

Favoured at first by Rasputin, who exiled him at last, he had mingled with the crafty crippled wanderers and the idiot saints in their rags and filth who had crowded the apartments of the Czar. Their mere word destroyed the ministers' plans and reports. Iliodor's story, which took one behind some of Dostoievsky's scenes, suggested a pre-Renaissance Europe surviving in our day, and, along with his disarming smile, his mind struck me as a kind of marsh into which one might sink waist-deep without reaching a bottom. I connected him with Leontyev's saying, "A Russian can be a saint but not an honest man," for one felt that some of his documents must have been forged.

Iliodor had fled to New York, where he became a Baptist and, as I heard, a janitor on the far East Side, disappearing in the vast American human ocean. But could any story have shown more clearly the inevitability of the revolution which occurred in that very year 1917, the year of the short-lived *The Seven Arts* when Russia and America seemed to be equally conscious of a new day? For the war that John Reed saw as the end of the world's youth had not destroyed in these countries hope and faith, and both saw before them what Whitman called "the wide untried domain" which the future, "greater than the past," was preparing for them. They had outgrown their provincialism, and the somewhat vague afflatus of our new magazine expressed an actual spirit in the American air, that sense of a world beginning again which had spread through Europe before the war and which the war had not killed in America or Russia. We were still living with Whitman and Morris, Ibsen, Wells, Romain Rolland, Shaw, all of whom pointed towards the future, feeling in regard to socialism that, as Anatole France remarked, it was "better to be drawn than driven to it." Every writer I came to know called himself a radical, committed to some programme for changing and improving the world. Heywood Broun spoke for them all when he said, "I hit the sawdust trail at each and every lecture" in a class in economics before which his Harvard professor asked radicals to speak; and, moreover, they had, or wished to have, the feeling of a common cause, the sense of a community of writers building a new culture.

This had been more or less Stieglitz's dream in gathering his disciples at "291," which to so many who felt at the time like pioneers in the Indian country seemed a kind of sheltering frontier fort. For the loneliness that Sherwood Anderson had found so disheartening was written all over the faces of the earlier writers, those who, like Edwin Arlington Robinson and even Theodore Dreiser, had been scouts or *avant-couriers* of the new day. I remember, at a public dinner once, sitting beside Robinson, who crouched as it were at the table with his eyes on his plate, looking up once to ask me a question to which I could only reply, "Unfortunately, no." Not another word could he be induced to utter, and he seemed as unfriended and one might say unfriendable as a frost-bitten Arctic explorer astray on an ice-floe. Then there was Theodore Dreiser, whom I first met in Patchen Place and who suggested to me some large creature of the prime wandering on the marshy plains of a human foreworld. A prognathous man with an eye askew and a paleolithic face, he put me in mind of Polyphemus,—*informe, ingens, cui lumen ademptum,*—a Rodinesque figure only half cut from the block; and yet a remark that someone made caused him to blush even up to the roots of his thin grey hair. Dreiser was hyper-sensitive, strangely as one might have thought,—he was a living paradox in more than one way; but a lonelier man there never was or one who seemed more to illustrate the need of the "growing solidarity of American writers." I am quoting a phrase of the time which expressed what its author called "a sense of their common concern, means and object."

It was largely this idea, one of the dreams of *The Seven Arts*, that brought the editors together, and Randolph Bourne, who presently joined us, hoped to form connecting links that would unite the little world of writers. Bourne had himself such a novelist's flair for personal relationships that if anyone could have done this he might have done so, realizing Henry Adams's wish for a "school" of the young that would start new influences in the country. Chekhov, who had had a similar thought, as I discovered later, had planned his "climatic station" to actualize it, appalled as he was by the bitter feuds of the coteries in St. Petersburg and feeling that writers should establish some sort of alliance. They should learn to respect one another's divergent opinions, these men "with hammers in their hands knocking at the conscience of mankind," which might have passed for Bourne's own definition. But whether in Russia or New York, this kind of "enchanted community" was of course a visionary notion, and Chekhov himself had turned against it, while our own Mencken was possibly right in saying that mutual animosity was good for writers. It was at least a sign that they took writing seriously, as Poe had taken it when he laid about him. But when so many writers were lonely and felt like aliens in their own land, the idea of a literary community was natural enough, and it comes back to me now as one of the notes of a time when many ingenuous plans were spreading about. Our decade had much in common with the New England "Newness."

I think it was to Randolph Bourne that I owed my first knowledge of Freud and Jung, to whom *The Ordeal of Mark Twain* was indebted, and *The Seven Arts* owed its existence

to these two thinkers. For the editor and the donor had been
patients of an analyst who had advised them to start it as a
therapeutic measure at a time when, as James Oppenheim
said, a day of birth seemed to be drawing near, for man was
beginning to "awaken to his planetary life." It stood for the
brotherhood of the young, Oppenheim continued, the conquest
of the world by young people of all nations when the new
writers appearing in this country might have been regarded
as the first harvest of the prophecies of Whitman. New books
were "jumping out of the press like a new dollar from a mint-
hopper," to quote David Crockett's homely phrase, books that
were no longer derivative, no longer mimetic. Romain Rolland, whose *Jean-Christophe* spoke for a super-national world
uniting the cultures of Germany, Italy and France, sent us a
message for the first issue of *The Seven Arts* bidding us, in
the name of our "Homer," to rise and act. (For Whitman, who
made one feel at home in every corner of the United States,
was the tutelary genius of the paper.) The Asiatic cultures,
China and Japan, were being born anew, Romain Rolland
said in this pronunciamento, and it was "the work of Americans" who lived at the centre of the life of the world, to
"achieve the fertile union of its great thoughts."

It must have been through Waldo Frank that this message
came to us, for Waldo was a friend already of the French
writer whom he described, in an essay on Romain Rolland, as
"the symbol of our hope . . . A world spirit speaks through
you," Waldo said, addressing him, adding that there was no
break in Rolland between recognition of a fact and whatever
words and deeds were in his power to fulfil it. This was the
case with Waldo too, as we were to see in time when he all but
invited the assaults of Argentine Fascists, and when he was
later attacked by strike-breakers in Kentucky, for he was the

most courageous of men, devoted as he was now, with all his heart and gifts, to *The Seven Arts*. In France a long essay had been written about him, and his book *Our America* had been translated by Jacques Rivière, the director of the *Nouvelle Revue Française*, while he had adopted for some of his work the "unanimism" of Jules Romains,—in fact, he had first begun to write in France. The world there was fashioned for the artist and ruled by his desire, he said, and writing there was regarded as sacramental; but, meeting French writers with a sense that he was a parasite in their world, he had come back to America where he felt he belonged. He had for this country a concern that was almost religious. The American artists whom he met abroad had seldom spoken of it, and had then spoken only to jeer and sneer, but, agreeing with much of what they said, he had felt in their company most of all his own compelling need of going back. Was it not the task of artists and writers to endow the country with what they accused America of lacking?—America, that "fumbling giant child, idealistically hungry but," as he said, "helpless to express its hunger." Anatole France, in his red skull-cap, after inviting Waldo to call, said to him, as they sat by the open fire, "Make no mistake. Europe is a tale that has been told. Our long twilight is before us. But I believe in your American dream."

Waldo, who had returned to America at the beginning of the first world war, just when I returned,—like Randolph Bourne,—felt, as he put it, and as many of us felt, "The European is born on a plateau. America is still at sea-level." For he too had grown up half a European until he discovered Whitman and *Huckleberry Finn* at a time when there were no little theatres, no vivid liberal weeklies, no magazines and few books of the new type. But the more Waldo saw of the country, the more, under its "Duco finish," he felt the "dynamic impulse and the rightness of youth," as he was to observe later in *Chart for Rough Water*, and he began to share Whitman's feeling of the religious destiny that gainsaid whatever was blind and chaotic in it. Living with farmers for a while in the West, working with coal-miners, helping to edit a country newspaper in Kansas, he saw, behind the frenzied surface of the country, the secret spiritual world which the poets knew. This was the world of Jefferson, Thoreau and Ryder, and of Alfred Stieglitz, Sandburg, Robert Frost of which he wrote in *Our America*. At the same time he developed his own planetary feeling as a traveller in Palestine and Egypt, Germany and Poland. *Dawn in Russia*, one of his most spontaneous books, was a lively account of a world that was coming into being, a country of the young that was wholly moved by simple instinctive and intuitive needs in which a great spirit had been born. Waldo was deeply touched by this effort of a backward folk setting out to abolish poverty, ignorance and fear so that men might breathe the fresh air of their emotional natures. He never became a communist, and he well knew that time might twist, that inadequate ideas might destroy this dream of the moment. He was to be disillusioned by the Moscow trials. But he felt strongly the essential health of this new Russia that was so largely the result of an up-surge of youth. John Reed was a symbol there of the real America behind and beneath the "dismal claque of Business," but to Waldo the romantic Reed seemed somewhat unreal; and I remember that he seemed quite unreal to me as I watched him at *The Seven Arts* correcting proofs.

Now, on our new magazine, Waldo "yearned to join the ranks of an army" that, as he said, was "not yet in existence"; and he was looking for a criticism that would draw the battle-

line and release the young "into the joy of consecrated war."
This was the "war of a new consciousness against the forms
and language of a dying culture," and Waldo regretted that
we had no "groups" such as he had known in France, in the
circle of the Vieux Colombier theatre, for example. What a
school that had been, as we ourselves saw when it came to
New York, for the renovating of French dramatic art! Waldo
was looking for something that was alien to our Anglo-Saxon
ways, but his wish, like Randolph Bourne's, sprang from the
feeling of isolation that Waldo expressed in his novel *The
Unwelcome Man*. This was the story of Quincy Burt, who does
not fit into the American scheme, which has no place for
dreamers, for the "superfluous" people in whom lay the promise
of a richer society in the future. Feeling myself as Waldo
felt,—so largely,—about the United States, I saw in this American *Oblomov* one of those novels that were doing what the
Russian novelists had done for Russia, creating a sense of the
vacuity of their life that was sufficiently active to stimulate in
readers the desire to fill it.

Waldo as a novelist was conscientious to the last degree;
and, with his elaborate scenarios, he wrote long biographies in
advance of all the important characters in the book he was
planning. But, greatly liking some of his novels,—and the
humanity in them all,—I was always more at home with his
non-fictional writing. At first, after *The Unwelcome Man*, he
followed the method of unanimism in which the characters
were not individuals but groups,—the regiment, not the soldiers,
the soul of a room instead of the particular persons who occupied it; and, while it was obvious that *City Block* was a brilliant experiment in literary form, the people did not come alive
for me. I could not feel the impact of life in a book of which
the subject was rather the block itself than the persons in it;

and in some of the other ambitious novels I lost the sense of reality in the metaphysical atmosphere that, for me, befogged it. It seemed to me that, with all of Waldo's literary culture and distinguished mind, he was rather an intellectual than a novelist proper, though I had no such feeling in some of the less pretentious books in which he revealed himself as a simple story-teller. How good was *Summer Never Ends,* how good was *The Invaders,* a tale of atomic destruction in the second world war, and good was *Holiday* in its way too, the remarkable story of Negroes in the South that followed in the train of Gertrude Stein's *Three Lives.* Best of all, to me, was the series of tales that Waldo published years later in his book *Not Heaven,* some of which seemed to me altogether masterly and among the finest stories of our time. I mean the stories *Culture of the West, The Cat, The Last Word* and *The Kingdom of Heaven,* a terrible and wonderful tale of the Argentine pampa: stories combining in several cases fantasy and realism with a marked intensity, variety and vibrancy of style.

Waldo used to take others to task for having no philosophy. He attacked Mencken, for instance, for attacking metaphysics; and I was inclined to call this "metafussics," with the greatest of modern art critics, when he rebuked my own indifference to it. (I assume that Berenson was only referring to metaphysics in cases where he thought it out of place.) Waldo was convinced that I had no philosophy because I preferred not to appear to have one, after the fashion of the statesman who said, "My policy is to have no policy," or one might say perhaps in the manner of Sainte-Beuve (who never expressed a theory of criticism). Lincoln knew that "he did what he did because he was what he was," as one of his biographers observed, and I had a philosophy that sprang out of my whole being, but I liked to remember Goethe's remark that he "kept aloof from philosophy," preferring the "standpoint of the natural human understanding." Goethe, who said he was at home with the "common sense point of view," added that philosophical speculation had been most injurious to the Germans, tending to make their style difficult, vague and obscure; and, with the concreteness of my own mind, I could not in any case agree with Waldo's philosophy or metaphysics. It sprang from the Jewish prophetic tradition in its mediæval form, and this allied Waldo to the neo-scholastics, with whom he deplored the descent of man since the old "Catholic synthesis," regarding the modern age as a decline and fall. To Waldo the Enlightenment was shallow because it omitted the divine from its notion of man, whereas nothing could persuade me that in the long run humanism would fail to include every human value. I was convinced that humankind was moving towards a synthesis that would make mediæval Europe seem parochial in contrast.

Literature to Waldo was religious or nothing, and most of the good writers of the time were therefore, from his point of view, creators of "gilded" fiction or decorators merely. He felt they had scarcely more sense that life has a purpose and direction than the "impotent intellectuals of the Café du Dôme." They went along with a civilization that was "top-heavy with machines" and run by machine-minded and machine-exhausted men, and he was drawn to Latin America because, whatever were its defects, "well-being" was not considered the highest good there. It seemed to him obvious that certain values survived in the Hispanic scene that our country had forgotten almost since the days of Roger Williams, for the mystical tradition, the "great tradition" had largely vanished from our general mind, where it had been replaced by the practical tradition. Waldo never lost faith in this country, which he described as "capturable," saying, "There is a bloom within our land which Europe lacks, a generosity and the faith and will which flower from it"; but, feeling that the mystical values flourished still in the Hispanic world, he hoped for a cultural union between the North and the South. Believing that this would restore the traditional wholeness of man, he set out to interpret these worlds to one another, an undertaking of twenty years that produced what seemed to me Waldo's most significant series of books.

He first encountered in the closing year of *The Seven Arts* a poor and exiled fragment of the world of the Spaniards when, in our own Southwest, he had sensed at once that it had something for him and for our people. It was something the absence of which made our proud industrial world, with all its triumphant successes, a danger and delusion, as Waldo wrote later in *South American Journey,* and his intuition soon sent him to Spain, and later to Mexico and Argentina, to find the source of strength this world possessed. It was then he wrote *Virgin Spain,* so full of poetic perception, with its real understanding of the mystical tradition that our practical business world had so wholly lost sight of,—the first, after *Our America,* of the "New World" series that even included his *Bolivar* of years to come. For, seeing in Spain the source of the civilization of Latin America, he saw in this what Bolivar envisaged, one half of the Atlantic world, an organic body, whole and free, an America stretching from the Arctic down to the Horn. This was the world of which Juarez and Lincoln were equally creators, foretold by the New England prophets as by Sarmiento, a world more propitious for the family of man than the old world had ever been, embodying a new sensibility and a new culture.

As a literary ambassador to Latin America Waldo was unique, for there could scarcely ever have been another North

American who was able to enter that world by his deep inner line. No one could have differed more from the usual type of American who represented the threat of the big business of the North; and, knowing Spain first, he was at home with Spaniard, mestizo and Indian alike, loving their dances, their religion, the form of their minds. Along with them he hated their own corrupt governments, in league with sinister elements in this country, and with his ardour of spirit and concern for justice, he entered sympathetically all their minds. He knew the great cultural regions of the Caribbean, the Amazon, the Andes and the pampa, which he presented in his most moving prose, together with the secret Indian life that lay behind them all with its memories of great cultures of the past. He brought before his readers the Venezuelan forest, the mountains and the jungle of the Orinoco, and he who had known so well the writers and writing of modern Spain knew better the writers of Peru, Argentina, Chile. He brought his own countrymen their first news of the vivid intellectual life of the South, while he was the Balzac, I have been told by one who was in a position to know, of a whole school of novelists in Argentina. On his triumphal tours he went far to convince each world that it needed the other to complete it,—the cultures of "bread-and-power" and "art-and-religion,"—while he brought the South Americans the picture of a life in the United States that was remote indeed from the world of the dollar. This was the life of the Puritan mystics, as of Emerson, Thoreau, Whitman and their successors in our time.

I would be looking too far ahead if, in the days of *The Seven Arts*, all this had not been latent in Waldo's writing and if he had not discovered for the magazine so many "seeds beneath the snow." Meanwhile, John Dewey wrote for us, "The war has shown that we are a new body and a new spirit in the world," and it was the hope of developing this that brought us all together, Waldo, Randolph Bourne and the rest of the circle. Especially Louis Untermeyer, Amy Lowell's rival as the spokesman of the "poetry Renaissance," whose great point was that American poetry had ceased to be an escape from life and had become a "spirited encounter with it." To the advancement of this cause Louis brought, first, a catholic taste and, secondly, a peculiar sagacity and wit. As for Randolph Bourne, I had known him for two or three years before we were connected with *The Seven Arts*. He had been writing articles of a personal philosophy, with others about what he called the "school of tomorrow," and we talked and corresponded on the question of bringing writers together, all the more vital in the engulfing blackness of the war. Randolph was obsessed with a sense that we were all "aliens."

Here, as I remember it, he expressed a feeling that most of the writers and artists shared at the moment: what did they have in common with the world as they knew it? Few felt at home in what Tawney called the "acquisitive society," the world of Matthew Josephson's "Robber Barons," and, ever since Edwin Arlington Robinson had said in his boyhood "Business be damned," writers had been repeating this over and over. Had not Henry Adams pointed out how the "bankers" had betrayed the republic? Had not Brooks Adams observed that the "principle of evil" was embodied in the "greed and avarice" of competition? Ezra Pound was on the point of saying that the "usurers" betrayed everything that writers and artists cared for,—those heroes of the big-business world whom the muckrakers had abused and exposed and whom Waldo Frank attacked with O'Neill and Dos Passos? All these writers were in revolt against what Waldo called the "cold lethal simplicities of American business culture," the monstrous disproportion be-

tween business and the other concerns of life in E. E. Cummings's "land of the Cluett shirt." What, in Edmund Wilson's
jingle, had this made of the American man?—

> With his seven motor-cars,
> His twenty kinds of peanut bars,
> His fifty different sorts of hose
> And eighty makes of underclothes.

No imaginative mind could think very much of that. Meanwhile, Veblen had convinced the young that business itself
was perverse, and that its ways were inexpedient also, in contrast to the ways of industry, properly managed; and Sherwood
Anderson's famous flight, when he "walked out" of his office,
had become the symbol of an epoch. Waldo Frank used this
theme in *The Death and Birth of David Markand* as well as in
Summer Never Ends, the heroes of which in both cases abandoned their careers to find their souls in a world remote from
"success." If most of the writers were socialists, was this not,
precisely, what Henry Adams said he "should have been"? In
spite of what Walt Whitman called the "caterwauling" of the
radicals and their "unceasing complaints against everything,"
Whitman had remained a radical with socialist leanings; and
so had Randolph Bourne, and so had I.

Bourne himself was the perfect type of the "clerc" of Julien
Benda, the dedicated "enlightened man," the true-blue intellectual, a word that had only recently come into use. It had
with us a colour of the Russian intelligentsia, the word for
those who, in Russia, formed public opinion and one that
practically meant there the heirs of the Enlightenment who
believed in perfectibility and human evolution. They were
opposed, by definition, to the ideas of orthodoxy, authority,
censorship, reaction, repression and so on,—everything that
Iliodor represented,—believers in progress that they were, in

the natural goodness of men and the heritage of the age of
revolution. In France, Julien Benda used the word "clerc" in
the same sense, and the *trahison des clercs* of which he was
presently to write was largely treason against this mental outlook.
It was the "effort to discourage hope" of the new "romantics of pessimism" with their doctrine of the incurable wickedness of man, those who enjoyed their own "contempt for
others," a feeling that always appealed to the "elegant herd."
Their treason consisted in the pleasure they found in laughing
at the naive souls who thought that some day humanity might
"become better." When at last Benda's book came out, virtually
all the serious writers accepted this definition of the *clerc*,
which embodied their own conception of literary ethics, as anyone, looking back, could see in old numbers of *The New Republic, The Seven Arts, The Nation* or *The Dial.* Bourne
could never have dreamed of the change in the literary climate
of the country that was to take place in decades to come when,
following T. E. Hulme and T. S. Eliot especially, the bright
young people reversed this point of view. What Benda had
called treason they regarded as the true faith: the denial of
progress, pessimism, the incurable wickedness of man and all
the other notions of the neo-scholastics. They followed the
"dignified landlady," Eliot,—in Miss Kathleen Nott's phrase,—
who "retrieved the tribal ornaments from the cupboard where
the guest had hidden them" and quietly "put them back on
the mantelpiece."

These clercs-in-reverse of the future might have had a more
difficult victory if Bourne had lived long enough to counter-
attack them, feeling perhaps that what Benda described as a
certain "barbarity of heart" lay at the root of what he called
their treason. He might even have made short work of those
who found it so pleasing to picture mankind as walled in by an

eternal and inevitable woe; for he was a formidable adversary, of the type of the Encyclopædists, tough-minded and both humane and ironical also. He was even rather like Voltaire in his vivid appeal to the other sex. Numbers of women shrank from Bourne, but others, beautiful and young, were fascinated by the "tiny, twisted, unscared" creature in "his black cloak hopping alone," as John Dos Passos remembered him in *U.S.A.*, the "frightening dwarf" from whom Theodore Dreiser recoiled, one shadowy winter night, on a corner in Greenwich Village in the snow. A chill passed over Dreiser at his first glimpse of Bourne's long arms, his crooked head sunk deep between bony shoulders, with the large ears flattened against the skull, but, meeting this cripple by daylight and talking with him, he could see only Bourne's large clear intelligent eyes. After that he never saw the dwarf in Bourne at all: he saw a powerful body that matched the mind whose literary power with its clarity of thinking impressed Willa Cather too, as it came up fresh and green like marsh-grass under water.

Bourne was even a romantic figure, especially when he was playing Brahms with the "nineteenth-century affection for the piano" that his great friend Paul Rosenfeld ascribed to himself; and for a walking tour he was the perfect companion, as I found when we walked out to Provincetown together. His steps were as quick as a robin's, his spirits never flagged, and he explored every by-way, eagerly scenting the honeysuckle, the bay-leaves and the salt air of the Cape. With him, at Provincetown, I spent an hour with Eugene O'Neill, my first and only meeting with this wonder of the stage who had written for *The Seven Arts* a story that might have been the first sketch of a number of his plays. Before we set out for the Cape we had spent a day in Boston, and, strolling through the old squares and streets roundabout Beacon Hill, I realized for the first time the charm of the town. It seems to me, as I look back, that I had passed through Harvard without in the least perceiving its unity and grace, unique in American cities and to me enchanting; and I feel that I owe to Randolph Bourne my first real discovery of a town that was to mean much to me twenty years later. To style in any form he was acutely responsive.

That was in August, 1917, four months after this country had entered the war, and Bourne, as a dogged pacifist who actively opposed the war, was under the surveillance of the police. It was his writing largely that killed *The Seven Arts,* for the donor could not accept this anti-war position, nor could I, for it seemed to me that to oppose the war was scarcely less futile than opposing an earthquake. Besides, was not Pan-Germanism a terrible menace? I felt rather as John Sloan felt when he left *The Masses* at about this time because that paper also went in for propaganda, attacking the war in a dogmatic fashion; and, like him, I could not see why a magazine that served the arts should throw away its life for any such reason. But Randolph was impelled to oppose the war,—he shrank from violence and force all the more because of his physical weakness; and he recalled at this time Thoreau who had similarly opposed the Mexican war, remarking that his thoughts were "murder to the state."

Bourne said the war outlawed anyone who followed a non-conformist line and refused to act as a symbol of society's folk-ways, and, with his own animus against what he called the war-mind, he had taken more and more to political writing. War, for him, was the "health of the state" and dissent was like sand in the bearings of the great herd-machine that was on the rampage, and he grieved because the universities were driving into limbo those who tried to exercise their minds.

Veblen's was the only intelligent effort in the country that was
not running to war-propaganda, while in England, in spite of
all repression, speculative thought continued to thrive and
even, during the war, with increasing boldness. For Bourne
the war meant the end of American promise; it was driving
everything he valued into the sea; and he was regarded as a
sinister person, dangerous perhaps, who was shadowed by
government detectives. During a submarine scare, on a head-
land that overlooked Buzzard's Bay, they suddenly rose out of
the ground and questioned him, and he was asked on another
occasion to explain the French word *perfide* which one of his
friends used in a telegram. Did not some dark secret lurk behind it? A real blow followed when a trunk that was filled with
his manuscripts vanished between New York and the beach
near by where he spent the last summer of his life with my
wife and me. This trunk was never recovered, and the general
understanding was that it could not have disappeared unless
it had been confiscated by governmental agents.

About this time Hendrik van Loon was also shadowed by
the police, as I became aware when I was with him, because
what he rightly called his plain old-fashioned liberalism had
been taken for the pro-Germanism that was treason at the
moment. This, he was convinced, was because he clicked his
heels together when he was bowing over a lady's hand, for he
had spent five years in Germany and Austria and taken a
doctor's degree at the University of Munich. Then he was suspected of "Bolshevism" because a Russian dictionary was
found in his rooms, the result of an early ambition to become
a famous linguist that had also led him into Arabic and Japanese. This was supposed to be highly irregular and his lodgings
were broken into, his trunks were opened by detectives and his
mail was stolen. Hendrik too I had first met in the office of

The Seven Arts, where he sat on a big table swinging his legs, describing his night in a lifeboat in the English Channel when his ship had been torpedoed. He had been the only correspondent in Antwerp during the siege. Hendrik had not yet written the books that were to make him widely known, but I vividly remember this first glimpse of a man I was to know well when he came to live in Westport later.

CHAPTER III

A FAMILY STORY

To speak for a moment of personal affairs, my wife, whose name was Eleanor Stimson, was the only daughter of two artists. Her father was John Ward Stimson, who had founded in the eighteen-eighties the art school of the Metropolitan Museum in New York, and he had met her mother at the Art Students' League where for a while he taught and she was a pupil. At that time story pictures were the vogue, with period costumes and "ideal" nudes, anecdotes and Barbizon pastoral scenes, and the two shared for a dozen years a more or less idyllic life before they decided to follow separate ways. My wife was accustomed early to a wandering existence. Her father had spent seven years in Paris and her mother had studied in Europe too, living for a year, as a girl, in Turin with Louis Kossuth's sister, Madame Ruttkay, the ancient friend of Miss Kenyon, her aunt. From the patriarch himself she had learned the games of solitaire that she so constantly played as she roamed about the world, games that, as a younger man, Kossuth had invented in order to while away his time in prison. My mother-in-law whiled away her time in painting,—fields of wild flowers, mountain slopes and what not,—wherever she happened to be, seated in a camp-chair, under an umbrella, swathed in veils, with a big straw hat, as if she were posing for a Sargent water-colour.

I had entered this picture early in life, for my mother-in-law and my mother had been school friends at the Seminary of my *Scenes and Portraits*, and we had all gone abroad together when my wife was a little girl and when I was to see my burning bush in Dresden. The little girl had lived, for several years, at Saranac before the débâcle of her family when her father was ill,—in Robert Louis Stevenson's cottage for a part of a year,—and there she had acquired a love of the woods, of tents and camping out, that she was to share later with her children. We were always to have tents stowed away, one glorified tent in particular that might have suited Saladin on campaign,— a canvas house with extensions for platforms and tables,—ready for a fortnight on Big Moose Lake or in the high Sierras or, if such things were possible, in the Swiss mountains. For Lausanne, where my wife went to school, was only a prelusive taste of other later Alpine years or summers, in châlets and hotels at Wengen or Mürren, on the Lac de Champex once or twice or in the valley of the Rhone. She had loved to build fires in the open and clamber over snow-fields in days when there was time for everything and one could spend hours in sunny clearings reading or watching the insects or listening, by some wild stream, to the summer sounds. Or feeling the earth move under her, with a furious secret rush through space, for she shared Whitman's "cosmic" intuition. She could have drawn from memory later almost every peak in certain parts, at least, of Switzerland, and she could have told you just how low the shadows fell in the afternoon and when the Alpenglow was at its height.

After our marriage at Carmel, we were to spend our honeymoon tenting in the Yosemite valley, on the bank of the river,—where I learned how to boil an egg and she to poach one,—and this was a reminiscence of the Adirondack years

when my wife had not yet gone with her mother to Europe.
Before and after she came home to go through Wellesley College, she had lived in hotels and pensions in three or four
countries,—with paint-boxes, spirit-lamps and travelling clocks,
—learning Italian in Capri and spending three years in Paris,
where her brother was studying architecture. I was in England
then and we were often together on both sides of the channel.
I remember days in Epping Forest under the great beech trees
and others at Versailles in the autumn woods, old dull gold in
colour, wonderful at twilight. There one found little marble
pools with marble fauns beside them, half covered with the
red leaves that carpeted the ground. We were both in love with
Europe and always had been. But it comes back to me now that
my wife's deep pride of country had thriven all the more in
her wandering existence. This pride, which had no element of
chauvinism in it, produced in the end a profound effect on
me, and so did her mystical faith in mankind and its future.

Every August, for many years, we spent a few days at East
Hampton, where the Stimsons had immemorially passed their
summers, living with patriarchal simplicity and old-fashioned
elegance in their ample unpretentious Gothic villa. Henry L.
Stimson, the statesman, a cousin of my wife and the head of
the clan after the last uncle's death at ninety-six, often appeared from High Hold, far up Long Island, also drawn there
by the surviving aunts. It was from them we heard the family
stories that aunts, and aunts alone, seem to remember, tales
of the Boudinot brothers and the Peartree Smiths, one of
whom had been painted by Sir Godfrey Kneller. This forbear
had been governor of Jamaica in the days of Queen Anne.
Then there were stories of the Audubon cousins, for another
aunt, more than a century back, had married the romantic
French woodsman, the Columbus of the birds, and my mother·

in-law remembered calling on his children at Minnie's Land, their old place on the Hudson. We heard much more of the Boudinots, one of whom had been offered a dukedom, during the Revolution, by agents of the British, if he could persuade the rebels to make peace with the king, for he had been president of the Continental Congress. Nothing, he wrote to his wife, could have interested him less. But the tragedy of the Stimsons, one of them remarked, was that they were descended from the wrong Boudinot brother. It was Elias who was offered the dukedom, and it was at Elias's house that the father of his country spent the night before his inauguration. However, Elisha made a good showing in Congress, and his daughter, aged five, was the one whom George Washington tossed in his arms as he called her "My little yellow bird." For the child wore at the moment a yellow frock. Later, Alexander Hamilton was the best man at her wedding when this grandmother of my children's great-grandmother finally grew up,—one of a score of similar tales that seemed to carry us very far from the foreground of our Westport life among the artists.

But East Hampton, too, had been an artists' colony like the Norman fishing villages of Étretat and Deauville before they were taken over by the world of fashion, and there still lived Thomas Moran, my father-in-law's ancient friend, the painter of Turneresque sunsets and Western mountains. In the garden of this brisk old man,—short and slight, with a prophet's beard,—lay Robert Browning's gondola, brought over from Venice long after Saint-Gaudens and Alden Weir, E. A. Abbey and William M. Chase had all foregathered near the village duck-pond. They had found touches of Europe there, for they could see America only when they saw it as European, and the lanes brought back England to some of them, while the dunes and windmills suggested Holland and the meadows recalled to others Pont-Aven. At the time my father and mother-in-law had carried on summer sketch classes, mainly for young ladies who had also come down from New York, and they had their studio in the old Clinton Academy where the father of John Howard Payne had once been a teacher. On the bare oaken floor stood the Windsor chairs, the spinning-wheels and the schoolmaster's desk they had found in the loft, and they hung on the walls, among sketches and studies, the costumes, poke-bonnets and fishing-tackle, the reels, nets and anchors they liked to paint. These were the seaside equivalents of the tambourines and round brass plaques, the satin banners painted with chrysanthemums and roses, the decorated earthen pots and the bits of old copper and silver that were dear to so many artists at the moment in the city. Long years were to pass before any of these innocents found themselves obliged to reckon with Matisse and Picasso.

Meanwhile, my own old friend the poet John Hall Wheel-ock had roamed from his earliest childhood the great island beaches, the scene of so many of his poems, early and late, where I often went for a swim with him and once with his uncle Bolton Hall, who had known all the old East Hampton artists. This great Tolstoyan was eighty at the time, but, un-willing to yield to the unwelcome fact, he disported himself in the surf while Jack hovered in the waves around and beside him. He was keeping a protective eye on the adventurous elder. Said Bolton Hall to me, as he cavorted on the top of a wave, "I can teach anyone to swim in a single lesson" . . . "Why, Mr. Hall," said I, "how can you do that?" . . . "By giving him confidence," the ancient replied, taking a header into a wave, from which he emerged defiantly half a minute later. Still the vigilant nephew swam beside him, like an anxious parent duck with one of the chicks.

But, to return to my father-in-law, whatever had become of him, that figure of mystery whom I had never met?

One day, in Westport, as I passed the house of Guy Pène du Bois, I noticed on the adjoining lawn twenty or thirty canvasses that were spread out as if to catch the sun. The owner, a minor official of one of the academies in New York who had known Blakelock before he was sent to the asylum, remembering that he had stowed in his attic all these pictures by his old friend, had brought them down to look them over. And perhaps even to sell them, in the flurry of Blakelock's sudden fame, if the sunlight would brighten them a little; for the painter had used so much bitumen to give them an amber look of age that many of them had turned black altogether. One caught in them here and there the yellow brown and russet notes that characterized George Fuller and Ryder also, with whom the rare good Blakelocks had much in common, but one realized *how* rare these had been and how often the artist had gone astray in the aesthetic twilight of his generation. The pictures, moreover, reminded me of the work of my father-in-law, which I had known well though I had not known him,—pictures that might have been Blakelock's or his old friend D. L. Tryon's, for they were all of the same school and the same epoch. They were all productions of a day when the Goncourts wrote in their journal, *"Le paysage est la victoire de l'art moderne"*; but my father-in-law's pictures too had been banished, they had lived an unsunned attic life, except for the few one saw in obscure museums. He himself seemed to me a symbol of the American artist's fate in the shadowy unrequiting generation when so many who had studied in Paris under the spell of the Barbizon school had struggled to survive in their age of innocence at home.

I sometimes had letters from my father-in-law, for he still

lived in the far West, having broken with his early connections and drifted away there. A graduate of Yale, he had been a rebel in his patrician family's house, and, returning from a long stay in France, he had painted round about New York before he set up as a teacher and aesthetic prophet. Leaving the Metropolitan school, he had established a school of his own, the Artist-Artisan Institute in West Twenty-third Street, where for five years Henry McBride, the champion later of "modern" art, who followed him to Trenton, had been his assistant. Then he had gone West to the "psychic belt" of southern California, the final abode of many another prophet. At times he believed that his great work was universally recognized and he basked in a half-fanciful sense of his own glory, while at other times, like Gauguin, whom he resembled in photographs, he saw himself as a martyr, crucified. With his beak of a nose, wild eyes and flowing moustaches, he combined the brown velveteen jacket of the romantic artist, and the Eastern painters he had left behind were automatons from his point of view, poseurs, little prigs, geese or blockheads. Reading his letters and papers later, I found myself sharing in scenes of which I had caught only glimpses elsewhere.

He had gone to Paris in 1872 when Meissonier was one of the reigning talents, with Bouguereau and Cabanel, the painter of "conscientious" nudes, who was to become presently his own teacher. Living, as he wrote, "with Turgot-like prudence and Walpole-like economy," at least regarding his lodgings in the Hotel de Sparte, he kept in touch with the world at home by reading *The Nation* every week, the journal of the intelligentsia in Boston and New York. With a friend from Yale and a Glasgow boy, a Scottish fellow-student with whom he exchanged national poets, Longfellow for Burns, he formed one of a trio like Trilby's admirers and wore side-whiskers some of the time before he acquired the imperial he brought back from France. The ruins of the Franco-Prussian war were still to be found on all sides, with the great black crater of the Tuileries which he passed every day and the bullet-riddled front of his hotel, while in the Luxembourg gardens one saw the marks of the bullets on the wall against which the Communist leaders had been shot. There was a cyclorama in the Champs-Elysées within which, standing on what seemed to be a bastion of Fort Issy, one found oneself in the midst of the siege of Paris. It was not easy for him to explain why, after the Germans had won the war, President Grant had congratulated Bismarck, considering the old friendship of France and the United States, and my father-in-law was constantly struck by the patient good humour of the French, their courtesy, self-reliance, pertinacity and thrift. For the rest, he delighted in the tumbledown alleys in Paris and the picturesque types he saw on the streets, the beetle-winged bonnets from Alsace, the broad brims from Brittany, the soldiers in jack-boots, the priests in slippers. On Sundays, he wrote to his grandmother, he took John Woolman's Journal and walked out to the Bois de Boulogne to read it. I wondered, reading his letters, if he had met my father, who spent five years in Paris at the same time, a time when Henry James had found it the best of meeting-places in which to observe his countrymen abroad.

Under and behind everything there, my father-in-law felt the smouldering terror that was buried in the communistic hordes. "We live on the slopes of Vesuvius," he wrote, "in Paris." When he was out of town his friends narrated in letters to him the jokes and scandals in the studios and the rivalries between them, the news of the atelier of Jean Paul Laurens together with the protracted rows between the Atelier Cabanel and the Atelier Gérôme. Both the latter were obliged to close.

The Gérômites broke down the door to get their painting-boxes, and the sculptor Saint-Gaudens, reappearing in Paris, went in to see his brother and had his own coat torn in the mêlée that followed. My father-in-law, toiling away under the meticulous Cabanel,—that "mud-god of art," as Huneker called him,—soon won a medal at the Beaux-Arts for his academic drawing. Being "well-grounded in 'light and shadow,'" learning to "express solid form before giving much time to colour,"—it was obvious to him,—was "the key of all future successful work . . . Colour comes naturally and easily after the groundwork has been safely laid, while the jumping forward with too much impatience into a subsequent field has been the ruin of many a promising young talent." But, gladly accepting this discipline, my father-in-law broke away from the Beaux-Arts ideality and classical manner, immensely taken as he was with a great show-piece by Rosa Bonheur of reapers bringing home the hay in the summer twilight. He could not say enough in praise of the huge lumbering wain, the farmers walking beside it with their scythes and rakes, the soft glow of the evening sky and the oxen so painted to the life that one could almost feel their fragrant breath.

My father-in-law had fallen in with a current vogue in Paris, a taste that was universal in the art-world of the moment, and the feeling for this subject, better expressed by Millet on his farm at Fontainebleau, appeared in my father-in-law's own later painting. He was drawn, like so many in the seventies, to the poetry of the common life, in hamlets, on farms, among simple people, especially after a magical summer he spent at Vézelay, the ancient feudal village in the department of Yonne. It was far from any railroad, no tourists came there, and the big kitchen of the inn swarmed with farmers at the end of the day rubbing their elbows on the table and pounding with their glasses. They were gossipy strapping Burgundian duffers with whips and massive sabots or huge boots steaming from the cow-yard, and their guffaws rang down the road as their bellies pressed against the board and they drained their tumblers of the red Bourgogne. My father-in-law and his fellow-students had the inn all to themselves, only disturbed when the widow and children of the famous Montalembert arrived in the middle of the summer for a short visit,—they were obliged to sacrifice their sofa for one of the young marquises to sleep on. What suggestive and interesting subjects the broken landscape offered them, especially the peasants in the fields or during the vintage when the leaves turned to a thousand hues and tossed in the frosty autumn wind. Then groups of the peasants bent over the vines or loaded the baskets they bore on their backs with full clusters of grapes to be trampled in the cellars. My father-in-law delighted in these open-hearted kindly men, stout as Old King Cole in the story-book, as he watched the red blood of the grapes spurting under their sinewy legs and pouring into the big oaken receivers. It was a fine sight in the gloom of the vast stone cellars under the massive arches built by monks; and these men understood an artist's interest in their work and were always ready for a visit from Monsieur Jean.

There he studied sunlight and its wonderful effects on form, rejoicing in the full panorama of a clear day from the first grey flashes of sunrise to the final evening glow, followed by the cool moon and the silhouettes of shadows. Meanwhile, he loved to pass an hour with old Mère Catherine, the mother of the village shoemaker, in her one-room cottage, with baskets and old pots hanging from the rafters while she sewed or sat at the spinning-wheel. He enjoyed her droll homely sayings and Burgundian wit, and he joined her and her son at the feast

of St. Crépin, the shoemaker's patron, when they sat round
a rickety candle at the well-scrubbed board. They had cabbage
soup followed by the rabbit which the son had killed in the
back yard, with a loaf of brown bread and some old wine
stamped out by mother and son and kept in the cellar, and
they drank the health of all honest people everywhere, especially if they were good republicans. For the election was coming on and in this department, a Bonapartist stronghold, the
republic was fighting for its life. My father-in-law took part in
the speech-making. He was more impressed than ever by the
calm self-control of the French when their national life seemed
to be at stake.

It was in 1879 that he returned to New York, finding himself disturbed, as he wrote, by the bumptious ignorance, sharp-
ness and cheek and the monetary standard of merit that seemed
to prevail there. For the rest, he found what Gauguin found in
Copenhagen, the circumscribed, starched, self-righteous life of
conventional people everywhere that Americans sometimes
thought peculiar to themselves. He had spent eight months in
Naples and in Venice, surrounded by Tintoretto's "dreams of a
giant," painting himself in the grand style that he had also
acquired in France, with biblical, architectural and animal
subjects. He had crossed the battlefield of Sédan where the
ruins of villages lay untouched and torn shreds of blue coats
and old army boots still lay about, and, painting landscapes
here and there, he had tramped in Switzerland with rhododen-
dron blossoms stuck in his hat. He had walked across Belgium
and Holland, full of impressions, enough, he wrote, to "burst
like a Dutch dyke," and settling at home, for a while at East
Hampton, near his family's summer house, he began to look
for the scenes he had loved in Europe. "You do not affiliate
with the 'poor rustics,' " he wrote to his mother from New York,

"though they have lots of interest in them, good hearts, experience, mother wit and character for him who is willing to 'see' ''; and he saw, or wished to see, Burgundian peasants and Mère Catherines in the farming and fishing folk gathering their sea-moss. He wrote, "It is our mission as artists today to see the poetry of simple things," and he looked for this in the clover-fields environing the village, oases in the sandy Long Island waste. He painted farm-yards at Montauk, green meadows with grazing cows, ducks leading their broods over the common, scythes hanging from the branches of willow-trees and picturesque old cottages, especially Payne's original "Home Sweet Home." Like Ludlow, the painter, in Howells's novel *The Coast of Bohemia*, who had also just returned from Paris, he was "eager to report the native world on canvas and draw as much pathos out of the farm-folk as Millet had ever drawn from the Barbizon peasants."

When I happened on this novel, it seemed to me that Howells must surely have had in mind my father-in-law, for the fictional artist so greatly resembled the real one who had also painted in the *plein air* of France. Under the American sky again, both were bent on "proving that our life is full of poetry and picturesqueness,"—I am quoting Ludlow's remark in Howells's novel,—and both were full of the great problem "of the relation of our art to our life," while they were equally obliged to contend with "blockheads." For both found themselves at odds with the teaching of the Art Students' League,—the Synthesis, so called, in Howells's novel,—the wooden mechanical system that my father-in-law contrasted with "plastic vitality and truth to organic form." They were both exasperated by the vague shallow talk about art that had been going on for a decade or more and they were determined to celebrate the native world that others saw in terms of Brittany, Nor-

mandy, Holland or England. Delighting in the old houses,
with their brick ovens, kettles and cranes, "so full of artistic
suggestions," as one of them remarked, they persisted in their
search for what my father-in-law described as "sincere American beauty and inspiration."

Sketching and painting himself, meanwhile,—haycocks and
weather-beaten barns, farm-kitchens, scenes of autumn thresh-
ing,—my father-in-law was greatly concerned with what he
called vital art education and the writing and teaching that
expressed his interest in it. Returning from Europe, he had
missed the *esprit de corps* that he had found or felt among
artists in Paris, while he set out to fight the apathetic patriots
who hoped for nothing good in their Nazareth at home. He
began to agitate for a national art society to benefit the genius
of the country and its tastes and outlook, his great point being
that the gap should be closed between the fine and the industrial arts, that artists and artisan should work together. Moreover, whatever a man's life was, he should love his work with
artistic pride, for its own sake and not for the profit of it. He
had to contend, he wrote, with cliques and self-interested snobs
and self-righteous committees, but he never doubted that his
was the wave of the future. "We are, I take it, just now in the
trough of the sea of progress, but the young men are already
born who will ride on the crest of the coming wave." Meanwhile, publishing his essays and poems in *The Studio* and other
magazines, he examined American Indian pottery and painting,
implements, fabrics, artifacts of the Stone and the Bronze age,
which he used in the illustrations of his huge book on the
principles of art, tracing to natural forms the elements of design. For, as a mystic, he was convinced that every design mankind has evolved has been based on some aspect of the
universe, a snow-crystal or a leaf, or perhaps even a constella-

tion, that there exists a harmony between the universe itself and everything men have devised in colour and line.

Far away and long ago seemed this great age of the isms that my father-in-law's letters and papers opened to me, the days when I had been a child and when Utopia seemed close at hand and benevolent motives governed every thinker. For that was the time not only of Tolstoy in Russia but of Edward Bellamy and Henry George at home. As director of the art school of the Metropolitan Museum, my father-in-law had had a resounding success,—the number of pupils rose from forty to four hundred,—while he taught drawing and composition with Olin Warner, Elihu Vedder and William Hamilton Gibson among his assistants. There were classes in decorative design, glass-making, wood-carving and work in brass as well as in painting, sculpture and architecture, and these had been continued at the Artist-Artisan Institute, my father-in-law's own special and personal school. "There is a great movement going on in the United States," Edward Carpenter wrote to him from England, "an immensely rapid uprise in educational, social and transcendental planes of thought, which will not fail, I think, to produce a wonderful people before long; and I congratulate you on your share in the great work." Walter Crane also wrote to tell him about the similar work which the Arts and Crafts movement was doing in England, and letters of friendship and gratitude came from Frederick J. Church and Saint-Gaudens, "Jenny June" Croly and many another. Charles Dudley Warner was full of praise for his "effort to make art a part of our national life," and Hamlin Garland wrote to him and Edwin Markham thanked him for "sowing seed for a future civilization." His philosophy appealed to a few minds in all corners of the world. My father-in-law had written his book when he was ill and in exile, in bleak and dreary days of driving snow, sure that it consisted of sacred revelations which he had spread abroad to help mankind. When Sun Yat Sen wrote to him from China and the poet Tagore from India, he recalled the prophecy that had moved him when he was at work, "Go forth, weeping, bearing precious seed, and thou shalt surely return rejoicing, bringing thy sheathes with thee."

Many years after the twenties and the heyday of *The Dial*, of which Henry McBride had been the art critic, I asked this great discoverer of so many talents of our own day how he regarded the old artist who had been his teacher. My father-in-law's painting, so good at first, in Blakelock's or George Fuller's way, had lost its depth and glow before he vanished, like Lao-tsze, into the West, and his career as a painter recalled to me the classic case, so often repeated in America, of Washington Allston. It exemplified all the old warnings of so many critics about the fate of the artist in our undeveloped country, and it was in my mind no doubt in all my speculations regarding the "problem," as we saw it, of the American writer. At the same time, my father-in-law had anticipated many of our own thoughts, those of my friends and myself, in the early twenties, concerning the relation of American art to American life, for example, and the question of evolving a national from a colonial outlook. But how did Henry McBride regard this wild and fiery aristocrat as a man and a teacher?—this lover of Blake who detested the fashionable Sargent and who wished to upset the academies and all they stood for. He was "a genius, —*manqué* but unmistakable," Henry McBride said, looking back. For the rest, I saw in my father-in-law a mind that was born too soon and that might have fared better in our own twenties, when, as Henry McBride remarked in another connection, "Everything was coming up. You felt it."

CHAPTER IV

THE FREEMAN

R ANDOLPH BOURNE had been dead two years when I went to
live in Westport, and just at that moment, in 1920, appeared a new weekly, *The Freeman,* of which I was the literary
editor for most of a lustrum. This was the creation of two ill-
assorted but remarkable men, a recessive American, Albert Jay
Nock, who was stoical, dry and laconic, and a romantic Englishman, Francis Neilson. I was busy every week two or three
days in the office in New York, but I wrote my reviews and
articles at home.

It was Albert Nock, the actual editor, with whom I dealt
day by day, while Francis Neilson, who was living in Chicago,
appeared at the office only from time to time. A member of
Parliament in England once and the stage-director at Covent
Garden, he had been as a young man an actor in both London
and New York, where he knew the Broadway of Huneker's
time; and he had been as much at home in the old Bohemia
of Union Square as he was now, on visits, in his rooms at the
Ritz. For he had married a daughter of Gustavus Swift, who
financed *The Freeman* as a sort of plaything for him. A friend
of Anton Seidl, who had been Wagner's right-hand man, he
had scoured Munich and Salzburg, Berlin, Vienna and Budapest in search of new talent for his own opera in London. A
prolific librettist and playwright, he had written *The Butterfly*

on the Wheel with various other plays, some of them in
French, among them *Le Baiser de Sang* at the Grand Guignol.
The actors, at lunch with him, had said they needed a good
play, and he replied, "Come to lunch tomorrow and I will have
one for you." His play had had the longest run of any ever
produced at this theatre in Paris. But he struck a true English
note when he said there was nothing so wonderful as a blackbird in full song in a garden in the country.

A florid expansive Wiltshire man, Neilson had studied
Henry George, a favourite of many old actors in the eighties
and nineties, and he had fallen in with Nock because this
American journalist was also devoted to "fundamental economics." Choosing Nock for an editor, he had also met with
the publisher of my *Letters and Leadership* and *America's
Coming-of-Age,* one of those publishers by vocation of whom
four or five appeared as another note of this time of awakening
in letters. With so much experimentation among novelists and
poets, with little theatres opening all over the country and
with competitions for stories and for painting and music, it
was quite natural that these publishers should have sprung up
too, representing a new type and outlook. For, with small hope
of profit, they brought out books for the fun of it, out of sheer
love for literature and beautiful designing, or, in advance of the
older publishers, they foresaw the profit that was sure to accrue
from the new great audience and the many new authors.
B. W. Huebsch, later of the Viking Press but now with a
publishing house of his own, was a cultivated lover of music
who could also, on occasion, turn out an admirable essay on a
literary subject. Like Neilson, the *bon viveur,* and the severe
and disciplined Nock, he had an air of the great world that
one felt in the paper.

As for Albert Nock himself, who was not known at the time

as the highly original essayist he became later, he was a man of mystery who lived behind a mask or, rather, an iron curtain of his own devising. Only a few dim facts emerged out of his heavily shrouded past: he had been an Episcopalian clergyman, a well-known baseball player and a European emissary of the State Department. No one knew even where he lived, and a pleasantry in the office was that one could reach him by placing a letter under a certain rock in Central Park. He seemed pathologically reticent, and I remember in one of his essays a denunciation of obituaries,—he said that "to post a man's death before the idle newspaper reader" could only be described as "gratuitously filthy." For he hated the notion of what he called an "unhidden, naked life, without savour or depth, always on duty to the public." Publicity in any form was abhorrent to him, and this had quixotic results that were sometimes absurd but that one had to admire, at the same time, also. If he had, for instance, an article to publish by someone whose name was in the news, like Maxim Gorky or Constance Markiewicz,—one whom an ordinary editor would have made the most of,—Nock would cause the article to be printed in extra-small type with the signature "C. Markiewicz" or "M. Gorky." He altered the signature of an article by Bernard Shaw so that "George B. Shaw" appeared as the author. In his peculiar reaction against the usual methods of editors, Nock resembled Stieglitz as a picture-dealer; for Stieglitz said he was not a dealer, his gallery was not a gallery and the pictures at his not-exhibitions were not for sale. In the same way Nock might have said that *The Freeman* was not a magazine, he was not an editor himself and his writers were not writers.

In short, with his testy and obstinate look of a Tintoretto doge, he might have taken for his motto "Hide thy life," and he was full of surprises in consequence of this,—one never knew what might turn up in his thought or speech. A Stoic and a crank at once, as well as an Epicurean, he was a formidable scholar and an amateur of music who remembered all the great singers of his day and could trace them through this part or that from Naples to St. Petersburg, London, Brussels and Vienna. He had known all the great orchestras from Turin to Chicago, "as much a participant," he wrote, "as the first violin"; and he had visited half the universities of Europe from Bonn to Bordeaux, Montpellier, Liége and Ghent. He could pick up at random, with a casual air, almost any point and trace it from Plato through Scaliger to Montaigne or Erasmus, and I can cite chapter and verse for saying that whether in Latin or Greek he could quote any author in reply to any question. I believe he knew as well the Old Testament in Hebrew, with many another residuum of his training for orders, for, along with Mr. Dooley, he liked to quote Jeremy Taylor and other old Anglican churchmen like Wilson and Whichcote. A diligently forgotten learning is the mother of culture, he once remarked, but he seemed to have remembered everything, and, besides reading Russian and Spanish with the more usual languages, he had studied Walloon when he was living in Belgium. For the rest, he entered the room at editorial meetings with "the high step and arched back of feline circumspection," his phrase for Jefferson in the salon of Madame de Staël,—Jefferson in whom he saw himself as "the most approachable of men" who was also "the most impenetrable." Idolizing Jefferson, he rather conducted these meetings in the fashion of Lincoln, who had also been a lover of Artemus Ward. As Lincoln transacted the nation's affairs with anecdotes of bears and hogs, tales of frontier circuits and the wisdom of the border, so Nock made his points at meetings of *The Free-*

man with references to Rabelais or with homely old American country saws.

It was Nock's wish that *The Freeman* should be an Abbey of Thelema, and his motto for us all was "Do what you like," for he hoped to realize the old humanists' dream of a human association existing in a state of absolute freedom. He was convinced that freedom was the only principle that had never been tried; he saw it as the basis of Henry George's doctrine; and saying, "I am not what Sam Weller called one of the 'adwice-gratis' order," he encouraged all the editors to ride their hobbies. For two years, in the last page of the paper, I spoke up for socialism with never a word from Nock that this doctrine was abhorrent to the species of anarchist that he was himself, opposed to all state control and even politics of any kind, as a reader could see at once in the front pages of the paper. But really, concerned for education and the quality of the national mind, Nock had no practical regard for economic matters, and he actually despised Henry George's party. The theory was one thing, but he would never have stirred a finger to put this theory into operation, and he felt that the prophet himself was a fool for thinking political action could ever be an instrument for social improvement. For when "people are incapable of managing even the bad economic system they have, would it not be utter lunacy to entrust them with a good one?" Nock was to remark in *A Journal of These Days,* a question that showed clearly enough how perverse he was or, perhaps one should say, how inconsistent. For how can anyone advocate the measure of freedom that Nock desired unless he believes that people can be trusted with it? Obviously, Nock wished to have it both ways. He revered Jefferson and Henry George, whose doctrines were based on a belief that men are generally born good and educable, while he was more and more convinced that men were generally knaves or fools, ineducable "psychical anthropoids," as Mencken might have put it. For with his good friend Mencken he was largely in agreement.

Of course Nock was quite aware of the shift in his own philosophical base,—which manifested itself in his writings later,—but he was rather puzzling in the days of *The Freeman*, when it seemed to me that he was facing both ways. He was evidently ceasing to believe in the doctrines of the Enlightenment while he clung to his faith in the prophet of San Francisco, and he had as much contempt as Mencken for reformers, uplifters and "settlement sharks," saying that "the state of our society is beyond hope of improvement." He was to observe in his *Memoirs of a Superfluous Man* that he had "gone over to the opposition with head unbowed and withers still unwrung," parting company with Jefferson, Rousseau and Condorcet, while he still disliked "anti-republican nostrums" because "at least provisionally" he thought people sufficiently improvable to sustain republics. But enough! Perverse as he may have been, Nock was somehow tonic, and his repose and distinction of style pervaded, from end to end, a paper that was generally known as the best written in the country. What he called, moreover, his "horror of every attempt to change anybody," or even to "wish to change anybody," meant that he relished the element of character in others just as it was; and, whether the mass of men are or are not educable, his notions of education were good for the few. One could not have called him a lover of his fellow men, but he was undoubtedly humane in his fatalistic fashion, for he felt that poor blundering humankind was really doing the best it could, so why despond or censure anybody? He was actually concerned himself only for the remnant.

I think now of Albert Nock as like one of those Persians or
Chinese whom the eighteenth-century Goldsmith and Mon-
tesquieu imagined,—Usbek, for example, of the *Lettres Per-
sanes,*—visitors to their own native lands from some Asiatic
Utopia where everything was quite different and a great deal
better. Nock's virtual Utopia was Belgium, "the country where
I make my home," as he called it in his *Journal of Forgotten
Days,* and for which, when he was away from it, he felt "the
nostalgia that one is supposed to feel for one's native land."
Why Belgium or, for a city, Brussels?—except that he found
there "the most intelligently presented opera" he knew, and
he never forgot that all Europe had once been indebted to the
Low Countries for the gift of music. I think he had emerged
from Brussels for the four years of *The Freeman* and that he
went back to Brussels when *The Freeman* perished. But he
had other haunts abroad, Luxembourg and Portugal, where
he was to write at least one of his books, and another was
Touraine, the province he described in his engaging *Journey
into Rabelais's Country.* A professional exile, a homeless man,
Nock was a scholar-gypsy, resembling the two friends of his
own youth who had given him "the curious impression of
somehow not belonging where they were." He had always
felt in America like a displaced person,—"like a man who had
landed in Greenland with a cargo of straw hats" and who
found no market for his line of goods there, for it seemed to
him that happiness there was built up of purchasable things
so that he could only feel alone in spirit. He was fond of one
county in Rhode Island where character survived in a stand-
ardized world and where cookery remained an honoured art.
But the characteristic American note was a preference for *doing,* not for the *being* or *becoming* that meant everything to

him, and the humanist was distinctly out of the picture. Nock could only retire within himself.

In much of this he might have been thought another Henry Adams, a No-sayer driven into silence by a chorus of Yeas, and I recalled Adams when I read Nock's wish to be buried on the island of Port Cros, off the French coast, "alone with my recollections." He too disliked what he called the brag, bounce and quackery of our civilization, while he knew as little as Henry Adams of the younger writers of his time unless they happened to be his own personal friends. He was scarcely aware at all of the so-called literary renaissance of which *The Freeman* was obviously one of the symbols; and with a certain disgruntled self-consequence he ignored "on principle" contemporary authors and their work. I would even say that he wrote his *Mont-Saint-Michel and Chartres* in the book, *Francis Rabelais: the Man and His Work,* for in this he too defined his best-beloved human type and the epoch in which he would have felt at home. If, regarding his actual time, he quoted Jefferson's casual guess that the other planets used this one as a lunatic asylum, he loved to think of a day when humanists flourished and among them Rabelais, one of the greatest of all. Rabelais for him was the natural affinity of those who in any time resist or elude all pressure to conform, to accept what they believe to be inhumane, and he felt that the reader developed a like superiority by keeping in touch with a writer who was so joyous and so wise. This was Nock's best work, unless one excepts a few essays and his *Theory of Education in the United States,* defining the humane life and, in its interest, contrasting instrumental and formative education. He meant by the latter education for character and intellect, for what a person can *become* or *be,* while instrumental education meant training for proficiency and bore upon what a person can *do* or *get*. Nock distinguished the kind of man produced by universities such as the plain modest Poitiers and our own, which for him were merely training schools, and, feeling that educable people were as rare as their value to society was great, he would have been happy to see the real thing here.

Nothing in a country mattered to Nock except the quality of its life,—for him banks, telephones and railroads only counted in so far as they contributed to this; and it was his insistence on the question of improving our quality of life that made *The Freeman* so exciting. He was always repeating that this is not Murdstone's world, that it is not fundamentally a place to work in but what Murdstone called a place to mope in,—in other words, a world to be enjoyed; and, meanwhile, as Neilson said, he was a master-craftsman and an exacting lover of good prose. Partly for these reasons Arthur Symons, who sent us many essays, wrote to me that the paper interested him "vastly," while the new writer Malcolm Cowley relished the "agreeably acrid taste" that he found in many of our reviews. Beside them, in its reviews, he felt, *The Nation* tended to be "pompous," *The New Republic* "economic" and *The Dial* "arty." As I was in charge of these reviews, I found it all too easy to send a good many books to English reviewers, for they were so competent, as a rule, in contrast to our own that one could dispatch their copy straight off to the printer. But I soon saw that this would never do. We had to build up a staff of American reviewers, though this meant virtually double work for me. When I had spent afternoons ironing out the gaucheries of eminent fellow-countrymen who were often professors, I began to see how right Nock was in preferring "formative" education to our own generally American "instrumental." It was obvious that formative teaching taught one to write.

As it had been on *The Seven Arts*, so I first met on *The Freeman* a number of good writers who became my friends, among them Malcolm Cowley when he returned from France after spending two years among the Dadaists. I had first heard his name when John Brooks Wheelwright, who had known him there, spoke to me somewhat mysteriously of "Burke and Cowley," not Edmund Burke and Abraham Cowley, as it slowly dawned on me, but the two white hopes of his own generation. One was Malcolm Cowley, one was Kenneth Burke, and they were among the scores of Americans who had printed their essays or poems, or, in several cases, magazines in Europe. Malcolm had printed there, in a blue-covered pamphlet, a fine long essay on Racine that we reprinted. Then there was Matthew Josephson, who had returned with *Secession*, which he carried on in Greenwich Village, and my older friends Walter Pach and Daniel Gregory Mason, who kept us constantly in touch with painting and music. Jack Wheelwright had begun to write a history of American architecture. Veblen and Charles Beard wrote for us, and for a while John Macy, of *The Spirit of American Literature*, was a member of our staff; nor should one forget John Gould Fletcher and Newton Arvin, who was soon to produce fine studies of Melville and Hawthorne. John Dos Passos gave us *Rosinante to the Road Again*. Dos Passos had returned from a postwar visit to Spain, and one gathered that he had been glad enough to escape from the tumult of Europe and the feverish world he had to face at home. For, like Waldo Frank, he saw Spain as somehow outside Europe, a land where life was still a kind of dream, and no doubt it intensified greatly by contrast his impressions of the scene with which he was to deal in *The Big Money*. In Spain he discovered Pio Baroja, whose acute sense of reality must have contributed to the making of *Man-*

hattan Transfer. Dos Passos felt that the United States needed acrid writing in order to affect a national mind in which a run-down puritanism was mingled with the ideals of the man in a swivel-chair.

Well I remember Dos Passos in the office of *The Freeman*. His tonsured head,—as it appeared,—was always bent forward, so that, with a sort of Jesuit air of elegant supplication, he suggested a Portuguese saint in a stained glass window. Then I remember too a certain afternoon when Edmund Wilson on the telephone shook my nerves, scolding me for altering the title of his review of some poems of Yeats, an enormity for which I personally was scarcely to blame. There had been a misunderstanding and the change had been made in my absence, though I have no doubt that Wilson was rightly indignant. But in thirty years I have not forgotten the demoralizing onset of that nervously furious presence at the end of the wire. It was a wintry afternoon and I felt like a traveller lost in the snow, beset by a frantic pack of Russian wolves. Yet I admired Wilson as a writer immensely, if only because he ignored that bugaboo of a later time, mass-culture as a deterrent of good writing. He seemed to be always in rapport with a cultivated public, and he found this all the more readily by assuming its existence, a general characteristic of writers for *The Freeman*. The tone of the paper was that of the rigorous amateur, the unspecialized non-professional man of letters; and all our reviews seemed to be written for the interest and pleasure of writing them, not for the mere satisfaction of getting them done.

It was in our office that I met Vernon Parrington, who told me about his *Main Currents of American Thought* and showed me at least some of the earlier chapters. I was perhaps the first person in New York to see them, and later, when I spent a

year in the office of Harcourt, Brace and Co., he sent me the
first two volumes, which Harcourt published. It was a work
that seems typical now of an aspect of the twenties when, as
Hendrik van Loon said, economics was in the air and one
could not get away from it. Parrington was one of the Nekton
who came to *The Freeman,*—to borrow an ichthyological term
for fishes possessing a will of their own that takes them across
tides and currents. These were of course outnumbered by the
literary Plankton, the aimless, directionless drifters, and, along
with them, there were the Jellies of whom William Beebe also
writes. The Jellies came floating down the tide, as this author
puts it, like an endless procession of pale moons.

As for the Nekton, two of these were Henry B. Fuller, the
novelist, and Edwin Muir, who wrote to me from London, a
writer whom I never met, in spite of our long correspondence,
and although we published scores of his essays and reviews.
He was A. R. Orage's assistant on *The New Age,* and it was
Mencken who brought us together after introducing Muir's
first book, in which this writer appeared as a Scottish Zarathustra. An aphorist in the Nietzschean line, with a dry style
and a nimble wit, a philosophic farmer's son from the northern islands, Muir, a psychologist who thought in flashes and
who believed in the plasticity of man, was bent on giving the
race a new direction. As against the complacent and amiable,
he was eager for the world to regain the clean, fresh, hardy,
innocent spirit of the Greeks, and he saw it as the task of poets
and artists not to idealize the origin of man, as writers had
done in the past, but to idealize his goal. He pointed out that
the great literary myths of the last hundred years,—Faust,
Brand, Peer Gynt, Zarathustra,—had all been forecasts of the
future, and his touchstone was the elevation of the type man.
All this brings back the still hopeful note of a time when the

future existed, before the anti-Utopias began to appear. Muir's epigrams had no meretricious glitter but were luminous with the sober light of truth.

Muir, who delighted both Nock and myself, wrote to us presently from Prague, which he found far more stimulating than post-war London, for everything seemed alive to him in the new Czech republic, where there was none of the "heavy English feeling." His own country had seemed to him "terribly dead," while in Prague he found enthusiasm and a light dry air that was almost intoxicating, an atmosphere that was ideal for intellectual work. It had been all but unheard of for an English writer to live in Prague, and it was there, delightfully welcomed by the Czech writers of the twenties, that he began to translate Kafka. Many years later I wondered if Muir's impressions of Czechoslovakia, varied as they were, ample and fresh, would not always be remembered as pictures of that lost republic.

An actual presence at *The Freeman* was Henry B. Fuller, the "father of American realism," as Dreiser called him, who had survived the limbo of the eighteen-eighties. Mencken was astonished to hear that he was still living, and Fuller told me that he was distressed to find himself talked about again as a result of the articles he wrote for our paper. "I have left novel-writing quite behind," he said. "It would be so agreeable to be let alone!" Yet he had only recently published two brief novels, and Randolph Bourne, always alert for anything that was both good and new, had been struck by his *On the Stairs* and *Not on the Screen*. Every book that Fuller produced was an original undertaking, for he broke all his moulds when he had once used them, and these were remarkable experiments in fiction, one showing the value of brevity and one exploring for the novel the technique of the movies. For us he appeared as a man of letters with essays, both scholarly and full of grace, on Beaumarchais and Molière, Dante and Erasmus. The printer might have worked directly from his fine clear script. Fuller was always in my mind when I thought of the prodigal fashion in which mother-ant America forgets its offspring.

CHAPTER V

FROM IRELAND

A FEW DOORS from *The Freeman*, on West Thirteenth Street, another old red-brick building housed *The Dial*, the "freely experimental" magazine, a transfiguration of the fortnightly that had been brought from Chicago some years before. Devoted now wholly to literature and art, it stood for everything modern and new at a time when these words still had a mystical meaning, when it might have been said of the literary world that, like the economic world, it had left the gold standard high and dry. For custom and tradition were in process of being turned inside out, they were being pulled apart and torn to pieces, and only good taste unified the contents of *The Dial*, a miscellany of the new writers and graphic artists. I remember once dining there with A. R. Orage, who had published one of my papers in *The New Age*, that model of high thinking and plain living on salaries of, at most, three pounds a week. The apostle of Gurdjieff to the Americans was an odd combination of an eighteenth-century Johnsonian and a mystic of our day.

Between *The Dial* and *The Freeman* there was no great love lost, for Nock was something more than anti-aesthetic and the editors of *The Dial* were aesthetic or nothing; but some of my friends went back and forth as contributors to both, among them Lewis Mumford and Llewelyn Powys. These two writers for *The Freeman* found wives on *The Dial*, for Llewelyn Powys presently married Alyse Gregory, the editor-in-chief, and Lewis married Sophy, who was her assistant. I thought of Lewis and Sophy Mumford as a new Adam and Eve, with whom the human race might well have started, for one could scarcely have imagined a handsomer pair. I always felt as if they had just stepped out of Utopia and were looking for some of their countrymen, astray on this planet, who were also waiting to get back home again. Paul Rosenfeld was the music critic of *The Dial*, and one met in his rooms in Irving Place virtually all the contributors from Zorach to Alfred Kreymborg and William Carlos Williams. There one saw E. E. Cummings, the last of the Yankee come-outers, who came out all the way in his poetry and drawings, and I remember Marianne Moore, on the long sofa by the fire, reading aloud some of her early poems. The mantel and the walls were covered with Marins, Doves, Hartleys and O'Keeffes. One evening Leo Ornstein removed the lid of the piano and smote the keys so violently that he shook these pictures, expressing for Paul, at least, the convulsive activity of the age of steel and the sharp griefs and sharper joys of youth. Paul, who disliked jazz, greatly admired this East Side boy, this mirror held up to the world of the modern city. But, like Huneker, he felt that he had to "get off somewhere," and I think he never liked at all the abstract painting of Mondriaan or the later Schönberg's frigid wastes.

While I cannot recall Llewelyn Powys at any of Paul's evenings, these two were inevitably friends, unlike as they were, the genial urban music-lover and the hardy wiry Dorset man, so redolent of the grass-grown lanes of his native England. During the first years of what he called "starving myself into success" when, fresh from an African sheep-ranch, he was writing for *The Freeman*, he slept on a roof in Patchen Place, ignoring the rain, indifferent to snow, carrying up his blankets through a trap-door. Always living dangerously, setting at nought the tuberculosis that was to kill him so early, he slept in England, when he went home, in a shelter in the fog of the downs, while, as he wrote to me, "the cold wind 'huffled' through the gorse, crying, 'Woe, woe, woe!'" I thought Llewelyn was half in love with death, as only a man can be who loves life fiercely. He was at home in the open, in town or country, sitting, in Switzerland, towards the last, on fallen logs and water-troughs or perhaps in the stables of the peasants. He loved the smell of the cattle-dung as much as the odour of baking bread, while at night he listened to the lonely sound of a trotting horse on the Alpine road outside. I had seen much of him earlier, before he left America, when he said he could live on bread and water-cress. He loved streams, old stone walls and country roads, like the Wolf Pit road in Westport where he and Alyse often appeared on one of their Connecticut excursions. They would pass the pond near our house where "old Paul," as Llewelyn wrote, "lolled like a woodchuck in the sun," and he himself sometimes wore over his shoulders the all but historic plaid shawl that had once belonged to "Omar Khayyám" FitzGerald. Then the two turned in at our garden gate. There was always some sprig of a flowering bush in Llewelyn's shaggy jacket and a knot of wild flowers in his hand.

Never was the style so much the man, for his old-country looks and ways were all of a piece with his naturally antique prose, as full of rural images as the poetry of Herrick, with some of the verbal magic of earlier writers. For, as he liked to think of shepherds and people who measure the passing of the months by the growth of animals and plants, so he was drawn to literary worthies who had been countrymen also, herbalists, gardeners, lovers of meadows and rivers. They too had lived in the senses out of which, for him, had sprung the Dionysian exultation that he was to celebrate in many of his books, the "state of wonder and gratitude" that he called religion and that he was able to match with a splendour of words.

A very different sort of man was the Anglo-Irish Ernest Boyd, although this acidulous Orangeman with the well-combed silky red-brown beard was also an editor's delight. For, as a literary journeyman, by no means an artist or poet in prose, he was always lucid, learned and thoroughly equipped. A linguist, ferociously accurate, a terror to bungling translators and to pseudo-scholars and other half-baked minds, he constantly recalled to me the literary gladiators of the Grub Street of the age of Pope and Swift. Boyd's cold eye was death to all pretenders. An impenitent rationalist,—his own phrase,—somewhat emotionless and dry, he was more or less versed in the ten literatures of which he wrote studies, and his mind was a copious arsenal of well-digested facts. A biographer of Maupassant, whom he translated, and a lover of Anatole France, Boyd had been rather over-impressed by Mencken, and he liked to lay about him with a literary big stick, debunking and hero-baiting in the mood of the moment. It pleased him to make short work of the idols of others, whether Milton or "Aesthete —Model 1924." As the British consul in Copenhagen he had seen much of Georg Brandes, who had deprovincialized Denmark by introducing the great foreign devils of his time, and he had found Brandes reading Mencken with whom he himself fell in when the consular service took him to Baltimore. Delighting in Mencken's Rabelaisian armoury of epithets,— smut-hounds, literary pallbearers, boy-snouts and so on,—he had straightway followed this other and lesser man-at-arms of letters who was deprovincializing America in a similar fashion. But the best of Boyd came out when he wrote of his own countrymen as a critic and historian of the Irish literary movement. His *Appreciations and Depreciations,* published in Dublin in 1918, a collection of sensitive essays on the writers of this movement, had been for me a treasure of the time.

I had had some correspondence with Boyd before he came to the United States, and at first sight he suggested at once another brown-bearded Orangeman whom I had known in New York some years before. This was at Petitpas', in the company of John Butler Yeats, and the learned man I mean was the Sanskritist Charles Johnston, who had been an early friend of Yeats the poet. With his vaguely Presbyterian look and a chilliness like Boyd's, austere and even majestic, as I recall him, Charles Johnston had founded in Dublin the Hermetic Society, one of the principal springs of the Irish revival. It had been a great part of the "Celtic wave" that had not yet been discredited by Joyce with his contemptuous reference to the "cultic twalette," a movement that had fascinated me ever since my college days and led me to sit at the feet of the grand old Yeats. In the hundreds of hours I spent with him at Petitpas', out in the country, at my own house, in the houses of some of our friends, I felt that I had lived at least within sight of AE, George Moore, John Eglinton, W. B. Yeats and Lady Gregory. For "J.B." had witnessed the whole movement, and of this, as Boyd remarked, one had a complete iconography in his pencil drawings and larger portraits. At any moment, as he talked, he would sketch for me George Moore or Synge to illustrate some point of character that amused him, and I can see now that I was greatly influenced by this, conscious as I was of our own parallel movement.

Two other figures of the Irish revival who were living in

New York and of whom I saw much in years to come were
Padraic Colum, who breathed and spread an atmosphere of
poetry, and his wife Mary,—Mollie,—who wrote for *The Freeman*. Of the young authors of the Irish theatre Padraic was
the first to be produced, and he had inaugurated with Synge,
a few weeks later, the drama of Irish peasant life. Then, writing mainly dramatic lyrics, he was drawn to the heroic age of
Greece, as later the legends of Hawaii attracted him also. In
The Golden Fleece and *The Adventures of Ulysses* he retold,
in lovely prose, tales of great warriors and chiefs who had
something in common with the semi-mythical heroes of his own
country, while Mollie, brought up in the west of Ireland, was
born to love poetry too in a world of strolling musicians and
ballad-singers. She had heard rumours there as a girl of the
poets and playwrights in Dublin whose characters were the
people she knew well,—fiddlers, beggar women on the roads,
—and she presently found herself, at the National University,
"stepping right into the Irish revival." She was to recall in *Life
and the Dream* the days when the names of Yeats and Synge,
magical names, appeared on the Dublin billboards and these
great men had begun to replace with writings about their own
land the English themes of Tennyson, Meredith and Swinburne. As she saw, the language movement and the literary
movement gave the Irish good heart for other matters, awakening in everyone the longing for a national literature and life,
dispelling the defeatist spirit of the provincial past.

In Dublin, as a student, she had idolized the poet Yeats,
who excited all the susceptible young men and women, so that
they followed him through the streets and watched him, sunk
in dream, while his lips moved rhythmically as if he were composing. They liked to think that he was weaving magic spells
in what seemed to be a walking trance, and at their various

clubs he talked about poetry and criticism, as I heard him talk on his first visit to this country. Well I remember him in his black jacket and flowing tie, with his hair over his eyes, as in Sargent's drawing, and I could guess how moving all this must have been to students after long days in Dublin classrooms. Mollie Colum brought back too the tenseness in the air when *The Playboy of the Western World* was first produced and a riot broke out in the theatre, and she had been present at George Moore's lecture on the French impressionists and regularly at AE's famous evenings. There all the talk was of literature and art and the ways in which novels and plays were written, with good practitioners eager to expose their methods and with the great-hearted AE leading the talk. Constantly present in the Dublin scene was the romantic Maud Gonne, the heroine of the revolutionary movement whom I was to see later.

One could imagine Mollie herself, with her slender figure and wild red hair,—she had "come from the country of Isolde," as Richard Strauss remarked,—in the Dublin of a time when everyone seemed to be young and all things seemed to be beginning. The young ran everything, especially the schools of Padraic Pearse in one of which Mollie was a teacher, and imagination and devotion were the notes of the moment, a general dedication to one cause or another. Yeats, impressed by her reviews and saying she had talent as a critic, advised her to become an authority in some literary field, perhaps the French literature that interested her deeply, just as it interested the American writers who had turned away from England to France and Russia. For the sake of their independence they had been obliged to escape from the overwhelming influence of the old mother-country. As a critic Mollie had rare qualifications, for, trained severely as she was in literary scholarship, she was an active participant in a movement of the present, in a small capital city in ferment, as Boston had been once, so that practice and theory were equally vivid to her. Yeats himself had made a cult of discipline, and Mollie had undergone the strict harsh mediæval drill that Joyce described in the "portrait" of his own upbringing. She had taken the same courses and the same degree as Joyce, and, understanding intuitively the writers whom she met, she was well versed in the art of literary living.

I was to profit by this myself in the days of *The Freeman* and afterwards, for, while no one hated more than Mollie anything woolly in thought or style, few were as practically wise in literary matters. She was aware that unsuitable people could wreck a writer's talent, as one saw every day in promiscuous New York, in the atmosphere of Greenwich Village parties, and she had a fine feeling for the enchantment of words and a fierce and rigorous truthfulness, together with the gifts of intensity and accurate perception. No one knew better the difference between real writers and dilettanti or the "highly intelligent commonplace" creators for the market, those who supported the powerful fiction-producing industry whom she described later in *From These Roots*. She detested the decadent realism, the concentration on the exterior life that discredited the interior life in contemporary writing, the flat impoverished materialist philosophy that tended to destroy every expression in words of the life of dream. In her reviews in *The Freeman* she defended from all assaults the writers who were devoted to a true vocation, and, struck by the prestige of English opinion in our still colonial New York, she understood our "nationalist" feeling here. She realized that our problems were somewhat like those she had known at home, and she saw why the Irish revival had so interested me.

For, at a period when I felt so strongly that American literature was coming of age, I could scarcely not have been struck by this earlier movement, when another literary dependency of England was finding its own character and asserting its own national culture, in the phrase of the moment. When later I saw myself accused of cultural flag-waving and chauvinism,—and even of a narrow nationalism,—I realized how remote nowadays had become a point of view that was generally current in the days of which I am writing. I mean it was current in many minds of the "new" literary countries in which an indigenous literature was fairly recent, even in Ibsen's Norway and Dostoievsky's Russia whose literary history was, in a way, still nascent. It might never have occurred to a Frenchman to say what Ibsen said, "Culture is unthinkable apart from national life," and no Englishman need ever have been afraid of losing his Englishness as Dostoievsky was afraid of becoming "less Russian." But when nations are establishing their own cultural autonomy, escaping from outside influences that have annulled this in the past, they are obliged to reject these influences that have overborne them,—how otherwise can they assert their collective selfness? Ireland required the "De-Anglicization" that Douglas Hyde called for precisely at the moment when Yeats was affirming, "There is no fine literature without nationality. You can no more have the greater poetry without a nation than religion without symbols." Whether in writing to Katharine Tynan or in his *Letters to the New Island,* Yeats repeated this over and over, aware as he was necessarily that this idea might be used not to expand but to narrow the horizon of the mind. It was a matter of both time and degree, and at the time he was also aware that the Irish writers had taken too much from English traditions and literature at the expense of their own. It was just when

George Moore's dæmon said to him, "Go to Ireland" that Yeats summoned Synge back from Paris, begging him to steep himself in Irish folklore. He said, "We peer over the wall at our neighbour's garden instead of making our own garden green and beautiful. And yet it is a good garden and there have been great transactions within it."

That we too required "De-Anglicization" Mencken, for one, had clearly seen, although he had never put it in quite this fashion,—he was rather moved by a German racial bias; and was it not evident that, for the moment at least, we had to believe in cultural nationalism also? As for this, English writers especially had always looked down on our literature because it was colonial and imitative, because it lacked raciness, a native autochthonous quality, because our writers were too much like their own. They had always asked us to be ourselves, regretting that we were not, for all our declarations of independence, and this general complaint of the English from the time of Bryant and Irving down had been expressly repeated by Emerson and Whitman. It interested me that in the world of painting the French critics praised John Sloan because he was so different from their own painters, ignoring others, technically abler, who reflected Paris, precisely because Sloan was steeped in his American scene. So I could not understand why I was accused of chauvinism when political nationalism meant to me so little, when I would have been glad to surrender sovereignty, with all the other nations, for the sake of world unity and understanding. I was not preaching America *über alles* or any such nonsense. Cultural identity was all that ever interested me, while the actual America of my belief was the nation of its promise, a nation that too often broke its word. For the rest, in those earlier days, I was stirred by Mazzini and his idea of the function of nations as the workshops of humanity, each with a peculiar gift to contribute to the whole. Mazzini saw humanity as a great army marching to the conquest of unknown lands, and he thought of the peoples as its corps, each with a special duty to perform and a special operation to carry out. Each nation therefore must needs be seen as a living homogeneous entity with its own faith and consciousness of self,—or so, at least, I understood this great man who possessed my mind, with Whitman, Ibsen, Nietzsche and half a dozen others.

Of these one was AE, whose book *The National Being* I somehow connected with Mazzini, for it invoked a national purpose and a literature expressing this along the lines of its own racial genius. For my own effort to put into words a similar thought I must have been indebted to AE, as I was certainly indebted to him for coming to feel that Emerson was the "fountain-head" or "germ-cell" of our culture. I am quoting from the letters I received from that man, "passionately good,"—in the phrase of Unamuno,—to whom even the incredulous Boyd was whole-heartedly devoted. First or last, in *The Irish Homestead* or *The Irish Statesman*, AE reviewed five of my books; and, although I never saw him, I took him for an oracle as, for years, I had taken J. B. Yeats. He was not the only Irishman who loved our great writers. It had not escaped me that Standish O'Grady, whose bardic history of Ireland was the first cause perhaps of the Irish revival, had sung in early days the praises of Whitman; and there was John Eglinton,—Magee,—the "lonely thorn-tree" that "breaks into flower," as, in *Hail and Farewell*, George Moore called him. I could never forget the excitement with which, in the New York Public Library, I read *Two Essays on the Remnant* and *Pebbles from a Brook*, discovering the beautiful essayist for whom, in his own youth, Emerson and Thoreau had meant

more than any other writers. ("With the possible exception
of Wordsworth," he wrote to me later. "At one time I almost
seemed to live their lives. You saw where I came from, mentally and spiritually.") This so-called "Irish Emerson" also affected my point of view as, more and more, I came to feel that
Emerson, Thoreau and Whitman were creators of our one
indigenous tradition of the spirit. But AE especially led me to
see what I had not seen in America at the time when I wrote
America's Coming-of-Age, and, although I was never satisfied
with the *Life of Emerson* that followed this, I owed to him
largely the wish to write it.

I had wonderful letters from AE, usually opening with a
pastel sketch of trees, supernatural figures, the rim of a lake,
sometimes written from Donegal and the whitewashed cottage
he had there in which his happiest days, he said, were spent.
The cottage was set amid mountains, miles from anywhere in
the world, overlooking rocky islets and silvery beaches, and
there on one of his visits he had brought nothing to read but
a twelve-volume translation of the Mahabarata. He encountered there by chance a man who read Indian philosophy and
talked with him one morning for an hour, an instance of what
he called Emerson's law of spiritual gravitation, which brings
together those who are intended to meet. He had first met
Yeats, he said, seemingly by accident, he had talked with
Shaw two hours without knowing who he was, and he had
chanced to fall in with Charles Johnston, the translator of the
Sacred Books of the East, just after he had first found these
books himself. Always knowing that he could not miss the
people who rightly belonged to him, he had never tried to
meet anyone or sought anyone out; for he felt that forestall-
ing the law was like plucking apples before they are ripe and
the relations that followed were never satisfying.

In one letter he took me to task for overrating Swinburne, one of our literary heroes when I was in college, saying he could never have rivalled Blake's gift of making lines that were "like flowers of sound carved out of the air." Nature, he added, had given Swinburne "an interminably long family of words to bring up and an insufficient income of ideas to support them on." Then he dwelt on the subject of poverty and its importance to literary men, a theme that interested many in my generation. For, in reaction as we were against the idea of success and the whole character of a business civilization, we were attracted to failure, so called, to the misfits of E. A. Robinson's world and to poverty as one of the marks of this. "Talent doesn't starve any more," said one of Scott Fitzgerald's men, anticipating the remark of a later writer that "the attic is no place to evolve ideas," but William James felt otherwise when he agreed with Thoreau that poverty and spiritual freedom are not unconnected. When I thought of the "attic" ideas of Paine, of Whitman and of Robinson, in Veblen's world of "pecuniary emulation," I felt that AE must surely be right in his constant recommendation that writers should take the vow of poverty. "All my literary friends are poor," he wrote once, "except Lord Dunsany who was born with an income, and the needs of life are much fewer than people suppose. The two great needs are good talk and plenty of solitude to brood and dig deep. I live now very economically, as my fixed income is about £100 a year, but am I unhappy? Good God, no. Yeats had long years of poverty and never sold his talent. Stephens was living on one pound a week when he wrote *The Crock of Gold*." AE went on, "Writers should stand ready to desert prosperity if it conflicts with the spirit." After his wife's death, when the lights of home were far behind him, he got rid of all his impedimenta, and, keeping only a few shirts and books, as he wrote to me, he felt free to wander like an antique sage.

AE,—George Russell,—was one of those men, like the author of *The Tragic Sense of Life,* who think not only with their brains but with flesh and bone, with their lungs, their hearts and blood, with their whole bodies. No doubt in some ways Gertrude Stein, the oracle of younger men, possessed this rare integrality that makes the seer,—or, in her case, equally, the sibyl,—and she found in Emerson a quality she missed in Hemingway and Faulkner,—in fact, in "all" the new American writers. "Good craftsmen and honest men," they had "passions merely," she remarked in a published conversation, while, as for "passion," they did not have it, though they knew all about it and could sometimes write about it very surely. But, she continued, Emerson, who did not know about it and could not have written about it, really had passion,—words that brought back to me something that AE said apropos of Emerson and our new writers. I doubt if AE knew much about these new writers specifically, or about novelists in general, or the novelist's mind, but he was well up in the America of the past and the present; and he said that the present generation of Americans had "gone from central depths to surfaces" while Emerson himself "went into occult depths."

AE might have said the same thing of *Moby-Dick,* as he actually said it of *Leaves of Grass* and *Walden,* a group of books that in South America and, as I knew, in India were universally regarded as the Scriptures of this country. They expressed the "soul of America," as *The Aryan Path* constantly said, and for me they came to be the standard to which to appeal when I saw the limitations of our actual country. To AE they were the work of planetary minds, and these books had led him to "look to America for the literature and art of the future." My own new serious reading of them completely changed the feeling that I had acquired in college about our old writers. In regard to them I was preparing to write in the twenties what I actually wrote in *Makers and Finders* later.

CHAPTER VI

UA TANE

THE NINETEEN-TWENTIES were "an age of islands," Malcolm Cowley wrote once, when "almost everyone seemed to be looking for an island," when thousands of Americans fled to Majorca, Capri, the West Indies and scores sailed away for the South Seas. They wished to secede from society, they believed in "Secession,"—the name of Matthew Josephson's magazine,—generally in revolt as they were against the bourgeois world they knew and the values of a business civilization. Like Melville, three generations before, like Henry Adams in the eighties, like Charles Warren Stoddard and Lafcadio Hearn, many were drawn to the primitive life in their wish to break away from everything that characterized modern living. They disliked the "duplicity of civilized man" and the "frigid manners of the Christians," as one of the earlier exiles to Polynesia put it, and one and all were inclined to say "Blessed be savagery!"—for them the condition of grace and the true joy of living.

I had known well this point of view some years before the twenties because of my brother-in-law John Francis Stimson, —so named in honour of Jean-François Millet, his artist-father's idol,—who had gone out to Tahiti in 1912. He had been attracted to the South Seas after reading *Typee* and *Omoo* in my house at Palo Alto, when I was teaching there at Stanford

University and Frank was an architect in San Francisco. Formerly a draughtsman of Stanford White, he had studied in Paris at the Beaux-Arts and had shown extraordinary promise in architecture; but, unwilling to be second at Rome or in California, he preferred to be a Caesar somewhere else. He had grown up in the Wall Street suburb of my childhood where, with his sister,—my wife,—and Maxwell Perkins, I had known him from kindergarten days; while, packing a world of chequered adventure into his first thirty years, he had concluded that America was simply a "nightmare." With what he called a "powerful bias toward liberty of action and conscience,"— inherited, as he said, from his father, the painter,—he established himself near the spot where his most intimate friends were to live,—the writers Charles Nordhoff and James Norman Hall. During the next forty years, he was to realize, largely at least, his "dream of becoming the world authority on Polynesia," the "genius" of Charles Nordhoff's phrase with a wider knowledge of the islands and their speech than any Polynesian had ever possessed.

Until the first world war broke out, he had a vanilla plantation on the shore of Cook's Bay on the island of Moorea, where he hung up fragments of the chintz curtains from Captain Cook's own cabin that were sent to him from England by the voyager's descendants. Early up and breakfasting on coffee and bananas, he paddled his outrigger canoe to the reef, spearing fish to supplement his usual diet of fruits and swimming in the blue waters of the lagoon there. For the sharks never came inside the arc of foam that indicated the presence of the reef, while fishes of light indigo and emerald green darted about him as he swam over the white sand and among the coral boulders. He was, like all the Tahitians, athletic and brown, though he was exposed to elephantiasis on this "fee-

fee" island, as well as to various fevers and tuberculosis. He
found he was eating bread from a bakery where the baker
was rotten with leprosy, while he was served for a time by a
syphilitic waitress, and the little polyps of the live yellow coral
on which he scraped his knee one day got into the flesh of the
cut and caused serious trouble. From this came a dreadful sore
which he only cured by soaking it for weeks in carbolic acid.
The soil of the island was so full of germs that he was obliged
to touch every mosquito bite with acid and peroxide. Centi-
pedes, moreover, abounded there and he had neighbours with
elephantiasis whose arms occasionally swelled to the size of
beer-kegs. But, guided as he felt he was by fate, he threw off
all infections, convinced that "something is coming," as he
wrote to his mother, "that will be its own explanation and
justification." He knew he was there "for a purpose," and,
spending several hours a day learning the language of the natives, he began to work for the Mormon missionaries. At first
he corrected their sermons, and presently he compiled for them
a Tahitian-English dictionary and a Tahitian grammar. His
house on the shore looked up to the crest of Mount Rotui with
misty peaks rising from the forest, where the rainbows were
of pale opalescent hues, ethereal as the vanishing shades in the
antique delicate older Japanese prints. He dreamed of a Japanese garden there with little pools and shaded nooks under
the great waterfall tumbling over the cliffs; and he drew up
plans for a houseboat inside the great reef where he could
enjoy a Paul and Virginia existence.

He was full at this time of Lafcadio Hearn, whom he had
discovered at Yale, and he saw in Polynesia a vast field like
Hearn's Japan waiting for someone properly to treat it. With
him it was only a question of the best approach, and his own
aesthetic and literary interest was already yielding to scien-

tific interests, linguistic and ethnic. His second great hope was
to see no more of the "hell" that America was creating for itself. He seemed to prefer "nature men" to the company of
what he called clean-cut Americans on vacation, though he
had civilized cronies in the Cercle Bougainville and especially
his beloved Nordhoff and Hall. Meanwhile, owing to the first
world war and the failure of the vanilla trade, he joined a
ship-outfitter's concern in Papeete, a connection he was to retain for several years until he became an associate of the Bishop
Museum. His mathematical training helped him with the cost-
book, the price-book, the stock-book, the day-book, the journal
and the ledger, and he began to feel that he possessed the qualities which made a good South Sea trader. He even indulged in
day-dreams of making a fortune that reminded me of Mark
Twain's Colonel Sellers, no longer as a vanilla king but by selling concrete tables and chairs to replace the wooden furniture
that was devoured by insects. Then he planned to raise hens
hygienically, something unheard of on the islands, for the natives let their hens run loose with the result that most of them
died from eating mangoes rotting on the ground. But these
were mere fantasies beside the vision that filled his mind and
that he was beginning to realize almost at the outset. He was
already studying a dozen Polynesian dialects six years after his
first arrival on the islands.

He had married a French-Tahitian girl whose four brothers
had all been drowned in Nordhoff and Hall's "Hurricane" of
Hikueru, and he himself was to become, as we saw from time
to time, both more and more French and more and more Tahitian. His native name was Ua Tane, pronounced over him
by Prince Pomare, the corpulent nephew of the former king
whom one saw fishing at the end of the wharf or driving in
his frail buggy about the island. Meanwhile, the Gauguin-

esque quality that was marked in his father's appearance came
out very soon in Frank as well. In the little house in which
Gauguin had lived only ten years before he arrived, he found
a glass door which the artist had painted, and he shared Gauguin's taste for the purple of the Tahitian earth, for the jagged
peaks and the orange and scarlet vegetation. He liked the tropical flowers that were ranker and sharper than the American
flowers with their pastel shades. Frank's letters, which came
every month on the boat that sailed up from New Zealand,
abounded in these objects and scenes, with the bougainvilleas
that riotously grew and blossomed all the year round and the
twenty luscious fruits to be had for plucking them off the
trees, together with the climbing vine that bore musk-melons.

There was much talk in his letters too of the squatters on
his Moorea land and some of the rascally colonial pettifogging
lawyers, along with the psychic adventures and the spirit-con-
versations in which, with all his nihilism, he had great faith.
A fascinated reader of Sir Oliver Lodge and Conan Doyle, he
found a competent medium in Papeete, and, sharing Lafcadio
Hearn's "scientific mysticism," he often heard and communed
with spirit voices. By this means, in fact, he solved the supposedly insoluble problem in chess that was called the "Eight
Self-Block Task." Frank found the key, he said, within three
hours after the request was given to the "operators" to mate-
rialize it; and his triumph was presently celebrated in the chess
magazines. But to one who had always known him this was
not surprising. I remembered that when we were boys he defeated the turbaned automaton that played chess at the entrance of the Eden Musée in New York, a famous player
behind his disguise who was supposed never to have been
beaten; and Frank set other world records in special "task"
fields. He had, as he said once, "the kind of mind that sees

order in complex situations." For the rest, in his letters he sometimes described fishing by lantern light on the reef, or he wrote about the home-grown coffee that one gathered in the morning, roasted in the afternoon and brewed for supper, a supper of sea-centipedes, perhaps, or shrimps. Or he would talk about Nordhoff and Hall, or the Swedish planter whom he liked or Jack London's friend who lived, stark naked, on the mountain. Or one of the broken souls who had arrived in Tahiti.

Then Frank had long talks with the old Queen Marau, the daughter of Arii-taimai whose memoirs had been written by Henry Adams and whose own mind brimmed over with the legends of her childhood. She was the one person in whom was concentrated all the ancient lore of Tahiti. Some time earlier she had sent a servant with a message to the nurse that she wished Frank to call upon her, but, having got up, as he put it, on the wrong side of the bed that day, he was annoyed by the manner of this invitation. He sent back word that in his family,—the formidable family he defied at home,—invitations were sent in a different fashion; and, hearing nothing more from her, he supposed the old lady had taken offence at his hoity-toity response to her suggestion. Then her daughter, the Princess Takau, who had heard of his work, intervened, and the queen sent him a courteous invitation. "She spoke," he wrote, "the most beautiful and elevated English and French, and of course her Tahitian is the most perfect now spoken by any living man or woman. It was a delight and pleasure that I cannot express to you. She greatly admired some of my own translations of the old Tahitian poetry." When, later, he read aloud to her, she said to him, "You read these chants as my ancestors would have spoken them." He took the old queen copies of two of his books, and he sent back to America for a flat reading-glass to enable her to read again with pleasure. Meanwhile, he found in Tahiti one youngish man who had memorized some of the legends when he was a boy and was able to recite them still in the stately old language. Frank took them down at his dictation. One of them recounted the story of a Tahitian cannibal king who had learned cannibalism from his foster-parents, proving, as it seemed to Frank, that, for all the belief to the contrary, this had been a practice in Tahiti.

However, from Frank's point of view, Tahiti was too civilized, and it was too much written about as well. He was eager to visit and study the more distant and interesting islands that were scarcely accessible to Europeans, even at present, where he could learn at first hand, from the old men who remembered them, the ways of this disappearing people. He wished to record its traditions, its folk-tales and genealogies, its cosmogonic formulas, chants and prayers, for he was deeply interested in questions of religion as long as they were exotic and picturesque. As the architect of an East Indian bungalow-palace, he had made a study of Buddhism in San Francisco, along with the hermetic philosophy of ancient Egypt; and he wished now to investigate the old Polynesian religion, hoping to find traces of it on some of the islands. His earliest voyages were mere trips on small trading schooners to represent his company in Papeete, visits to the less distant islands to encourage the planting of cocoa and rubber or anything that would make them more productive. He knew the dialect of the Marquesas, distinct from Tahitian, though similar in structure, and he soon made friends with the native chiefs on these high mountainous islands with their well-watered valleys between the ridges. The islands were bold and wild, with great cliffs abutting on the sea, broken off sheer and scooped out with caverns, for there were no barrier reefs to protect them from the waves, and Frank visited Taipi-vai, the great valley that Melville called Typee, and saw old Marquesan dances still performed there. Later, on sloops and copra schooners, or Chinese trading-vessels, with cargoes of arrowroot, coffee and pandanus mats, he was to range far and wide through the South Seas, recalling to my imagination the voyage among the isles of Melville's hero Taji and Jarl the Skyeman. In Frank's letters I overheard the conversation in the Ti as well, and I seemed to be present at the Feast of Calabashes.

From time to time, at Westport, Frank's friends sought us out, one a French pearl-trader and one a German-American artist who had also spent six years in Tahiti. Thence this young man of romantic descent had sailed to Bora-Bora and later, with Frank also, to the Tuamotus, where civilization had reached the point of introducing beds, not to be slept upon but only under. There Ua,—Frank,—at that time working on his Tuomotuan dictionary and regarded as a chief himself, conversed with the sages, along with the local Mohis and Babbalanjas from whom he gathered in fragments the legends of the islands. To his friends there he had brought gifts of banana plants. In the story of his own island life, this German-American artist related how fluent and soft was Frank's Tuamotuan and how canny he was never to sail without aspirin and rum or without inspecting the vessel on which they were sailing. For now and then the owners poured cement inside along the keel, and this so strained the ribs that in a storm the bottom of the schooner sometimes dropped out. South Sea cruising to Frank was already an old story. He knew all the captains and all the schooners, the rotten and the sound, and always slept on a mat on the quarter-deck. At Bora-Bora the two had seen Frank's old friend Matahi,—the hero of *Tabu*, which had been photographed there,—with his great bronze chest, his frangipani garland, his grass skirt and flowers in his hair. Matahi and his troupe danced for them under the palms.

To Westport, too, for several visits, came James Norman Hall, Frank's "best friend in all the world," who turned back to Tahiti once, after setting out to see China and Japan, so homesick he was for his thatched roof on the island. There time, he said, was a serpent with its tail in its mouth, gliding so smoothly in a circle that one was scarcely aware it moved at all. By nature the hermit of a South Sea Walden, Hall shared Thoreau's hatred of cities and banks, but he was the most humane of men, like Robert Flaherty, Frank's other friend, who was for some time our neighbour in New Canaan. I was to see more in later years of this "father of the documentary film" who produced his *Moana of the South Seas* on one of the islands, while he sold out his interest in *Tabu* when he was not permitted to carry out his full intention in it. He had wished to show beyond peradventure how the impact of civilization destroyed the moral fibre of primitive cultures. "Bob" Flaherty had always been looking on the fringes of the world for traces of the heroic life of earlier ages, remnants of the Homeric scene that had long since vanished with what he accepted sadly as the decline of the West. He who might still have been at home in the world of Audubon and Fenimore Cooper loved the Eskimo country and the Aran islands, and he hoped to find in the South Seas the rustic Greece of the golden age that Henry Adams had said was still alive there. He grieved over the decadence, as he called it, of modern writing, the total absence in it of the nobility of Melville, and he had only contempt for a time that could see nothing but Apeneck Sweeneys and Hemingway's killers, bull-fighters and racketeers. Above all other qualities he loved elevation, and, from his point of view, humanity had sunk, in our world war epoch, to a lower level.

At intervals of about ten years, Frank himself reappeared with his ever-increasing look of a Polynesian idol or one of those chieftains, born to command, authoritative and massive, whom Henry Adams pictured in his South Sea letters. For he had the stout "royal body" of the Ariki, the high chiefs and kings, always well nourished and for that reason all the more respected. Once he came up with Nordhoff and Hall, who said that on the steamer he had lectured to the passengers on the wonders of the islands, enthralling them as, in our house, he enthralled young and old, as Melville had enthralled the Hawthornes when they were at Lenox. He had met on some faraway island a native who remembered cannibalism and the joy of munching an enemy's thigh or arm-bone,—or the plump palm of a hand, a special tidbit,—and who murmured wistfully, "O how good it was!" recalling these delights of human flesh. Frank too had practised the ancient art of fire-walking when, with a dozen initiates, on bare feet, he had traversed a trench full of red-hot stones, immune against any burns, because, like the faithful of whom he was one, he never doubted for a moment that he could do so. At the same time he related how quickly those who lost faith and heart leaped from the coals in agony at the first step. Or he would describe the great fish-drive in the Leeward islands when the circling line of canoes approached the white beach, driving the fish before them as the paddlers with great stones attached to long lines brought these down upon the sea with resounding splashes. The frightened fish moved swiftly into the shallows, and there they were speared and caught by long drags of cocoanut fronds to the sound of the speeches and songs of the watching chieftains.

Sometimes he spoke of the travellers who visited Tahiti,—

for one, Lloyd Osbourne, the stepson of Stevenson, who asked
him for copies of his Polynesian chants. He was sure that
Delius, the composer, would set them to music. One day
Vilhjalmur Stefansson arrived on his way up from New Zealand with wonderful tales of his own Arctic adventures in the
land of the blond Eskimos where with his last bullet he had
shot two caribous at once and saved his party. For they had
all been threatened with starvation. Then Henri Matisse
stopped for a week on his journey round the world and Frank
spent days with him driving about the island road, for this
artist wished to avoid all engagements with officials. Matisse
did not share Gauguin's interest in the people of the island
but he seemed to be fascinated by the tropical colours, the
contrast of brown, green and yellow; and, as Robert Flaherty
was there, Frank brought the two together, apparently to the
great delight of both. Matisse could not hear enough about
Flaherty's own work and the way in which he arrived at his
conceptions. Frank had a special feeling for the few great
skippers who were left and who had what he called wide
horizons and what they called untainted winds to breathe,
Andy Thomson of the "Tagua" and Vigo Rasmussen, the
Dane, with both of whom he had sailed on more than one
occasion. Andy, who had brought him a hat from Manihiki,
was a master-navigator in a cyclone, and Vigo Rasmussen of
Raratonga, a recluse with a deep inner life, was the captain of
the most beautiful schooner in all the South Seas. His cabin
in the "Tiare Taporo" was lined with books. Frank had less
respect for some of the native captains who were unable to
find their position in the ocean. Struck by the danger of this
in cruising, he bought a chronometer and sextant and took
lessons in navigation from the Captain of the Port, so that, as

long as he had a sight of the sun, he could find any position anywhere.

Often I urged Frank to write out the story of his adventures, for they seemed to me as unusual as Sir Richard Burton's, but he had no interest in the picturesqueness of his own life and he said he was not a good observer. He was not detached enough for this, he was too close to the Polynesians; and so, as he put it, he missed the bright colours of the surface of their life, while he sought for the warp and woof of its inner texture. He could not in writing revive the local details that came out so fully in his talk. Intensely drawn to the Polynesians, entirely at home with them, he thought, as it seemed to him, actually as they did, and he remembered moonlight nights when, sitting with them on a beach, he felt they were telling stories of his own forbears. Many of them were convinced that he was literally an incarnation of one of their own high priests or ancient nobles, and he rather encouraged this notion, for it made them feel it was useless to withhold any of their secrets from such a man. They concealed nothing from him and related events of their psychic life which they would never have told their Christian pastors. Remembering the previous travellers, from Captain Cook down to the present, he could think of no one who had had his advantages, for the natives never opened their minds entirely to the missionaries and most of the others were commoners from the native point of view. They had usually been sailors or castaways, and these men did not know how the Ariki acted and spoke in the inviolability of their inner circles.

Once Frank brought back with him two cases bulging at the sides with notebooks and other records of Raivavai, many of them written by Hapai, the venerable son of the last high chief of Mahanatoa. Frank had sailed down on a schooner to

this Austral island, spending many months there but finding
that Hapai had left Raivavai for Tahiti. He had wished to put
his grandchildren in school there, while his wife pined for the
movies, and the couple had settled near Frank's own house
where they lived by making copra, at the same time preparing
candied bananas. Hapai, now the deacon of the Protestant
chapel, was a not uncommon case of fallen grandeur; for some
of the descendants of the heroes of old songs of conquest and
love,—masters of their fate,—lived by selling postcards. With
the aid of his friend Admiral Byrd, Frank employed Hapai for
several years to write out in his own hand the secret teachings
of the island with detailed descriptions of the traditional social
life, canoe-building, house-building, plaiting, weaving and so
on. The old man related how the islanders had built their
ovens and fire-pits, manœuvred their fish-sweeps and chipped
their stone, and he made plans and drawings of the archery
platforms and temple enclosures that were scattered along the
beaches or hidden in the valleys. Earlier explorers had known
only twenty of these stone-walled temples, while Frank's associate Alan Seabrook found two score and ten with massive
upright slabs leaning or fallen. The beautifully tesselated floors
had been displaced or broken by the up-thrusting shrubbery
or the trunks of trees, and the stone images had been shattered
or carried off to fill in the foundation walls of churches. Frank
had explored these temples in the silence of the valleys, a pre-
European forest world such as John Lloyd Stephens had
known a century before in Guatemala.

Raivavai was the scene of some of Frank's most important
work. It was a small island where others had found nothing, so
that no one supposed any of the old lore was left there. On
this great mountain mass the oranges fell to the ground in
showers, like a yellow carpet glimmering through the green of

the trees,—the lagoon teemed with vari-coloured fishes,—and there one of the sages, who became a friend of Frank's, recorded for him old stories of the island. Frank gave him several notebooks in which he could write his accounts of the ancient Polynesian skippers and their exploits and voyages, and every few days, after filling one of these, Tauira'i walked the length of the island to see him. From others Frank collected songs and genealogies going back to the gods who created the world from a void of black water, with recitations of the royal bards that celebrated demigods and heroes at the great feasts remembered from the past. He examined the scenes of the tournaments or emulative battles in which the youthful warriors had exhibited their prowess. From a throng of canoes in the lagoon the people had watched them. These were the young men who had sailed to Hawaii and New Zealand carrying all before them wherever they went, vikings and sea-rovers like Tapu-ehu who had landed with seventy companions at Raiatea. He had greeted with these words the reigning chief, "I have come to fling your warriors, like so much refuse of the beach, into the sea." The divers in those days plunged ninety feet down into the ocean to seize with their bare hands and a noosed rope a great turtle as large as a dining-room table and bring it up at midnight through the black waters. Other tales were gentler, like some of the chants. The subject of one of these was the great ship of Kihotumu, the ship that sailed the Milky Way and swept across the heavens to anchor in the land of one of the god's eight temples. Another related the return of the ship Marama from a certain long voyage among the isles. The steersman, donning his formal robe of office, watched the clouds on the horizon for the headlands of home, and, as the boat sailed in, the voyagers recognized faces on the shore and danced with joy after the years of separation. When they were assured of a friendly welcome, the leader unwrapped the figures of the gods they had carried with them as safeguards against shipwreck and storms, and then he pretended to dry the crimson plumes, his insignia of rank, that were supposed to have been wet by the spray. Not till then did the company venture to land.

Like the great Anaa series of archaic legends, these chants revealed fleeting glimpses of a prehistoric past, a high civilization that had utterly vanished; and Frank could only feel that, if he had not been there, this would have left behind no intelligible ripple. Meanwhile, the tale of his own voyages, extending over thirty years, suggested to me a *Mardi* in a dozen volumes. He sailed to Takaroa, Amanu, Hikueru and to Rapa, the top of an immense submerged volcano only the crater of which, a splendid harbour, rose about the water. (I supposed this had been the scene of Fenimore Cooper's sea-novel that was called *The Crater.*) At Katiu he was all but drowned in a fearful mill-race near the shore with sharp coral rocks on either side. Of the "dangerous isles," the Tuamotus, he visited sixty or seventy, sometimes staying as long as half a year, listening to legends that seemed to refer to some misty Asiatic homeland and chants and songs that were surely a thousand years old. He found on one island a sage, Te Uira a Maro, the most learned bard of all the Tuamotus who knew more than seven hundred chants, some of which seemed to preserve the memory of a great cataclysm in which the ancient homeland sank into the sea. Frank gathered the ancestral herb-lore of these small coral islands, sometimes inhabited by only two hundred people; then he spent two months on the Mangarevan expedition with Sir Peter Buck, who later became the director of the Bishop Museum. He gathered more legends at Mangareva, a beautiful group, at Pinaki and especially at Vahitahi, the treasure island, for songs and folk-tales, of the whole Pacific, where he obtained a jealously guarded pedigree that carried one back to the gods at the beginning of the world. Sometimes he had been just in time to meet the only surviving bards who knew these old records of the past, for he had arrived in Fagatau shortly before Kamake died, and something similar happened at Vahitahi. He had only a few weeks to see Tuhiragi. The people of the island crowded round his thatched hut at night, singing and telling their stories, and he recorded these roughly on the spot, copying them on his typewriter the following morning. Then he asked the story-tellers to correct his errors.

He was especially eager to recover traces of the old religion, the pagan faith that was banned by the missionaries, while the Mormons, the Catholics and the Protestants alike, believing he meant to revive it,—instead of the mere knowledge of it,—bitterly opposed him. The missionaries tabooed all mention of the god of the underworld, Kiho, together with the phallus-worship of the old Polynesians, on pain, for those who had been baptised, of losing a Christian burial and having no children in the meantime. The cult of Kiho, above all, aroused their ill will when Frank brought forward proofs of its former existence, while others in authority blocked his work because of the erotic element in the old religion. He was haunted by the thought that much of his work might be destroyed, like some of Burton's Arabian collection, on the ground that it was too erotic to be published, and Burton's work might have been replaced while he himself was the only source for these records of the world of the old Polynesians. He had gathered them from sages and chiefs who were no longer living,—some of them went back thousands of years; and he was convinced that if anything happened to these notes of his the Polynesian religion would be lost forever. He had cleared up obscurities and conflicting statements for the whole Pacific about the gods, who appeared now in a consistent light, and he had recovered the lost meanings of esoteric words by finding that the words survived on other islands. For the rest, the magnificent chants and prayers seemed to prove that the Polynesians had not come "up" from savagery but were descended from some great civilization in the Asiatic past; and the erotic was bound up with the noble and the tender. For this reason, Frank refused the offer of a great English press to publish the erotic songs in a splendid edition, unwilling as he was to create the impression that Polynesian literature was erotic to the exclusion of other feelings.

I remember one summer when Frank came home in order to study at Yale again and see Edward Sapir and Roland Dixon, who were to become his ardent supporters at a later day when he also had the approval of Malinowski. After many years he had pieced together what he called the Palae-Polynesian, the root language that was common to the South Sea peoples, Samoans, Hawaiians, Tahitians, Maoris and so on, and, believing that Sanskrit was closely related, he was determined to investigate this,—I think he almost learned it during that summer. As always, he brought with him a battery of fountain pens, black, red and green, for his etymological markings, and the typewriter, built for him, with six kinds of type, rank on rank, and a keyboard like the keyboard of an organ. This *matini pata pata,* as the islanders called it, clattered away in his room from dawn till midnight, when he was not at New Haven, and I could see how it was that, in the land of the beachcomber, Frank in his own way had gone so far. I recalled what Margaret Mead said of the casual South Sea world where no one played for high stakes or paid heavy prices or fought to the death for special ends, so that greatness in art or personality was virtually unknown there. Frank was as much the exception as the "white monk of Timbuctoo" who had also been drawn to the dark peoples, in the African desert,—that other great linguist and scholar who had entered so deeply into the secret places of the native life.

Frank had the intensity and energy of Seabrook's Yacouba and he too, moreover, was a dedicated man. Well he knew the fearful dangers of the weak of will who sank into a beguiling lethargy in the Polynesian world, and he had remarked in one of his letters that the only antidote was "a driving purpose and a burning goal." Fortunately able to toil in heat, he had thriven on a diet of breadfruit and fish, varied with cocoanut and taro, while, as he rode breakers in little boats and often landed on jagged reefs, neither peril, discomfort nor pain ever deterred him. He had gladly put up with the fleas and the lice in the tiny cabins in which he sailed, packed in with pigs and chickens and sacks of coffee, suffering in many ways and threatened with gangrene, to the far eastern Tuamotus and Takapoto. All this misery meant nothing to him if he could find one old island man who had been taught as a child the ancient customs, fortunate as he was himself to be able to work, as he wrote, "with joy at something one loves with wholehearted devotion."

CHAPTER VII

NEW YORK

E SPECIALLY DURING the *Freeman* years, when we were all on the alert seeking new talents for the paper, I began to take in the vast resources of New York, which was always entertaining angels unawares. It was, at times, the literary capital of half a dozen countries, with poets and prophets in exile from the Ukraine or Siam, Bulgaria, Brazil and Argentina. A few were great writers who lived in the city unrecognized, while trumpery native geniuses triumphed on Broadway,—spokesmen of humanity or national poets who were sometimes under a cloud at home and lived in the deepest obscurity in the Bronx or Brooklyn. This was true in many a case with writers of Latin America whom only Waldo Frank could properly acclaim, victims of revolutions in their own countries. Kahlil Gibran, the Syrian poet, had a large following in New York and his works were published there in a sumptuous edition, for he was well supported by the Syrian merchants; but who was less esteemed or known than the "Goethe of Hungary," as he was called, who lived over an up-town tailor's shop? That, to be sure, was in Hitler's time, when the prodigal city overflowed with many of the great spirits of central Europe. But when did it not abound with similar exiles?

I never lost the feeling of excitement with which I encoun-

tered these extraordinary men, whose lives in so many cases
were romantic or tragic and whom one sometimes saw at the
New School for Social Research in its first little group of red
brick buildings. The watchword there was always "Humanity,"
as distinguished from "Prosperity,"—the rights of man as opposed to the rights of wealth; and there one met Veblen, now
wizened and old, with his look of an invalid troll, together
with James Harvey Robinson and Charles A. Beard. The age
of reason still flourished there and man had not yet "fallen"
in the minds of these intelligent humanists who were building
the future, or at least felt they were building a future for man
who, far from falling, had risen out of slime and protoplasm.
They scouted the notion that man was naturally disorderly
and had to be held in check by the far-seeing Tory, for it was
obvious that men were conservative by nature and all too ready
to invent obstacles to change. As against Trotter's herd-minded-
ness, they preached an ardent faith in what Robinson called
"salvation through knowledge and laughter," upholding the
"creative" as opposed to the "acquisitive," the note of the business world which they abhorred. It was Bertrand Russell who
developed this antithesis, and it may have been at the New
School that I first heard the sage who suggested the Mad
Hatter of Tenniel's drawing. His voice was like a bagpipe,
a low continuous ah-ah-ah out of which, with a louder hum,
the words arose.

One voluntary exile, the one whom I myself knew best and
with whom I lived for a while at Petitpas', the old artist-
philosopher John Butler Yeats, who died in 1922, had also
been a child of the age of reason. He scouted the notion that
man had fallen and that human nature was essentially bad,
an idea he connected with the "dull" Belfast people who were
puritans and found it good for business; for he had grown up

regarding it as a "gentlemanly trait to think well," as he said, "of our fellow creatures." This was a part of the liberal faith to which I clung instinctively, and so was his belief in the idea of happiness, which he by no means connected with the notion of success. Happiness, from his point of view, was an outward sign of harmony, a concord of all the notes of the man within; but as for the bitch-goddess, whom he had to pretend that he pursued, he naturally cared for this lady nothing at all. Seventy years old when he came to New York, he remained because he saw ahead what he called a "hopeful penury instead of a hopeless." But penury itself had no terrors for him, and he never seemed wiser than when he said,—what Thoreau might have said,—that the "angel of impecuniosity" had not betrayed him. I rode with John Sloan in the first coach at J. B. Yeats's funeral before he was taken away to be buried, under a stone with a Celtic cross, and with W. B. Yeats's inscription, in northern New York state. I almost felt, with Sloan, that I had lost a father; for this "best talker I ever knew," as G. K. Chesterton called him, had been a reassuring presence also in my house. My wife delighted in him, loving the humorous tenderness with which he surveyed our family doings. Once when my older boy ran into a tree and cut his head he recollected how "Willie" as a child had done this, and he said it augured well for my inattentive son, who was plainly also moving in a dream.

What Yeats had been for me, I know that Alfred Stieglitz was for many of my friends, but I never felt at home in the *petite chapelle* either at "291" or the "American Place." It was Stieglitz's line that he who is not with us is against us, somewhat in the manner of Whitman fifty years before, obviously as a result of the feeling, which he shared with the great Walt, that he was involved in a losing battle. Whitman had talked about "our crowd" as if not to be in it meant that you were not merely outside but hostile, and so it was with Stieglitz also. If you could not be his disciple and would not be his enemy, you had to maintain in his presence a certain aloofness. There was, besides, an element of the mystagogue in him, and it irritated people when he pretended that his pictures could not be bought but only "acquired under certain circumstances." This innocent *réclame* was merely a reaction against our shameful cult of advertising, while by holding his light under the bushel he made the light still brighter for those who were under the bushel with him. Stieglitz could have been rich if he had wished to be so, but, scarcely able to maintain his gallery, he said the landlord had supplanted the Lord in the general downfall of art and rejection of the artist. I once heard him say that he would be glad to pile up all his photographs and make a bonfire of them in the middle of the floor, for the world did not deserve to have them in it. But his paranoia made other artists feel that he was one of them, while, standing his ground, he was always there, at all hours of the day or night, like a rock in the sea or a spring in a dry land.

Stieglitz was the sort of man whose life is attended by signs and wonders, coincidences and other notes of the necromancer. Along with the mystagogue, there was an element of the psychic in him, and, once when I was talking with him, thinking, as I talked, "You are, after all, a bit of a Svengali," he said, out loud, pronouncing the word just as I was thinking it, "Someone said the other day that I was a Svengali." But he was more like the Ancient Mariner, with his glittering eye and skinny hand, and the wild tufts of hair that grew out of his ears, who had his will with everyone, for who could choose but hear and listen, when he talked, like a three years' child? The last time I saw him was two weeks before his death. I

was walking down Madison Avenue, and, suddenly realizing
that I had forgotten just where to find the "American Place,"
I exclaimed to the listening air, "What *is* Stieglitz's number?"
And a voice replied "509." It seemed to come from heaven,
but actually it came from a passer-by who had heard me ask
the question, apparently one of the millions of ordinary men
who roam New York and who walked on with no further remark or interest. Once upstairs, I told Stieglitz about this, but
he seemed to take for granted these manifestations. He spoke of
a similar occult intervention that had attended his meeting with
Frieda Lawrence. Then he said he had been thinking about
me because he was reading my son's and my translation of
Amiel's Journal, which he was holding in his hand. Stieglitz
was seated on a couch, with his disciples about him, like
Socrates in the prison in David's picture, as if he too were about
to drink the hemlock; and in fact a few days later he was dead.
No one could have been serener or sweeter than he was that
day; one felt that he had at last spent all his passion.

There were many for whom Stieglitz discovered America in
his photographs of the New York streets, of the ferry-boats and
the waters surrounding Manhattan, the incoming shiploads
of immigrants and the skyline of the city. Meanwhile, the
folk-past of the country, so little known heretofore, began to
arouse attention in the nineteen-twenties when, at the Whitney Museum, the painter Henry Schnakenberg exhibited his
American primitives and related objects. Among these were
ship's figureheads and cigar-store Indians, shown for the first
time as works of art, an interest in which had begun at Ogun-
quit with the painters there, Charles Sheeler, Kuniyoshi and
certain others. This interest Constance Rourke, whom I saw
often during these years, extended to include music, architecture and the work of the Shaker colonies and frontier artists,

for she was already investigating a native American aesthetic past that had been scarcely known except in fragments. Constance Rourke, who had taught at Vassar and studied at the Sorbonne, and who wrote often for *The Freeman*, disclosed to me a West of which I had known little, as a reader of *The Ordeal of Mark Twain* could readily see. In part from reading Emerson, I was already prepared to take a more sympathetic view of our old writers and the country, but in certain respects my horizon was indefinitely broadened by Constance Rourke's eager and eloquent studies. She was already preparing for the general history of American culture of which she finished parts before her death; and she wrote, from time to time, to tell me of the proofs she found that America had its own definite aesthetic tradition.

Constance Rourke had been impressed by Herder's theory that, in every country, the fine arts are an outgrowth of the folk arts and that one finds in these the source of a culture. For the texture of the communal experience determined the character of the folk arts, and she was convinced that our culture, derived from Europe, had diverged from Europe in accordance with our own experience and needs. Just as American Calvinism differed from European Calvinism, so all our original patterns of thought and feeling had been "pulled," as she said, "into new dimensional forms"; and, finding that all our derived ideas had been shaped to new distinctive ends, she was bent on creating,—as I was,—a "usable past." (To speak for a moment of the thirties rather than the twenties.) For would not the knowledge and sense of an indigenous tradition nourish the American artists and writers of the future? Obviously, these artists and writers would be more confident and mature if they could feel they were working "in a natural sequence."

Thus, at a time when American writers were deeply concerned with the country and were beginning to explore its spiritual resources, Constance Rourke brought together a thousand concrete evidences of the widespread folk-culture of the national past. She wrote to tell me of some of these, a painting, for instance, in Michigan, "a Matisse-like fruit piece with unusual variations, amazing in transparency of colour and fine design," or the magnificent chimneys and iron doors she had happened upon in ruins of eighteenth-century furnaces and forges. Or she had discovered wall-paintings in New England, quite unknown hitherto, a curious painter whose name was Voltaire Combe, a mass of unknown early music and much, connected with the old frontier, that she brought out in her studies of Audubon and Crockett. I thought of her when I read Waldo Frank's story about the "artist-painter of Illuria, Ohio," for this J. B. Bonabath was the kind of gifted oddity whom she discovered in many a Western town. The personal pleasure in stripped forms and finished plain surfaces that drew her to the Shaker craftsmen as well as to Sheeler,—regarding whom she wrote an elaborate study,—bore witness to her taste for "the good, the life-giving elements in literature," for *bonae literae* as distinguished from *belles lettres*. She regretted that the former phrase should have dropped out of use in favour of the latter, which stressed only beauty, as she regretted the flight from communal expression in the cosmopolitan literature that was coming to the fore.

In this there were many who agreed with her, in the West especially, and it was certainly true that something went out of our literature when the expatriates of the twenties set the new fashion. There was a war henceforth between the writers of the hinterland and those whom they called the "New York critics,"—the urban intelligentsia who stood for the incoming mode,—and whom, for one, Mary Austin resented, like Vachel

Lindsay, who also felt that literature and art are primarily expressions of the people. This was Carl Sandburg's position, too, with all the American counterparts of the Slavophiles of Russia in their struggle with the cosmopolitan worshippers of Western Europe. But for a long time to come the expatriates were to have their way, with tragic results for certain of the hinterlanders not only in writing but in painting. There were the cases of Grant Wood and John Stuart Curry, for instance, both of whom died "broken-hearted,"—or so said their friend Thomas Hart Benton,—convinced as they were that their enemies were right in saying that they had been wholly on the wrong track. So powerful was the new cosmopolitan fashion.

It was in the twenties that I saw most of the rude forefather of us all, then at the height of his influence, Henry L. Mencken, a full-blooded, warm-hearted man who came up from Baltimore every week and joined us now and then at *Freeman* lunches. Nock, especially, delighted in him, but no one could resist him, for he was the personification of a shrewd good nature, or so he always seemed except on one occasion when I saw how unforgiving he could be. It was at a luncheon at the Brevoort that B. W. Huebsch gave in honour of Sherwood Anderson, whom he was publishing, and all the literary world was there, including Stuart P. Sherman, who had attacked Mencken in several essays. But for Sherman much water had gone under the bridge since he had defended "Puritanism" against the modern literary sansculottes,—and had consequently been the darling of the old guard,—and, following Emerson's belief that where there is power there is virtue, he had gone over to the moderns, lock, stock and barrel. The rising star of the reaction had lost his earlier notion that the twentieth century was wholly the work of the devil, and he was already almost at home in the literary circles that he had once regarded

with suspicion and fear. Wishing to bury the hatchet with
Mencken, he asked to be introduced to him and eagerly
crossed the room to shake his hand. But Mencken would have
none of this friendly gesture. He refused even to look at the
eleventh-hour champion with whom he had exchanged blows
not long before.

Thirty years later few remembered Stuart Sherman's extraordinary vogue, and even the real vogue of Mencken was
almost as brief, although it could never have been forgotten
that he was a literary statesman whose strategy and decisions
affected us all. Whether or not one agreed with anything he
wrote, and much as one may have disliked his tone and temper,
he was one of those men who create the climate in which
writers have to live and the currents of thought and feeling that
carry them along. Who could deny that in very large measure
his essay *The Sahara of the Bozart* was the first cause of the
rebirth of writing in the South?—and Mencken opened the
public mind to the writing of the new racial groups in a literature that was exclusively Anglo-Saxon. With him came in the
realism that had been almost smothered under the evasive idealism of the recent past, and all these were major acts in what
this German-American called the new Aufklärung in the republic. He had cleared away the provincialism in our literary
atmosphere, he had "defaced the coinage" in the manner of
Diogenes, obliterating the mint-marks of false conventions.
Who, moreover, aroused more interest in the American scene
than this new humorous Gulliver in his home-bound travels
who saw his fellow-countrymen as Brobdingnagians and
Houyhnhnms, monstrous, to be laughed at certainly, but never
ignored?

It was a pity, for the rest, that, with his great influence, he
should have known nothing of the past of the country, to

which he was even hostile by temperament and training; and it was also unfortunate that he stopped dead as a critic at the age when the critical mind begins to mature. As for Mencken's "American language," as a literary medium I could not believe in this at all, for it seemed to me that serious writers would always be far more concerned to explore the wonderful resources of traditional English. Where did one find the American language in Mencken's own books, I mean in his own best expository writing, and where did one find it in Willa Cather or Katherine Anne Porter or Thornton Wilder or Edmund Wilson or even Hemingway or Faulkner? It was a pity, finally, that Mencken should have become the dupe of his own stage-personality as a Hitlerite or Hun, an extreme case of the tough-guy pose of those who, for nothing in the world, would ever be taken, in American eyes, for sissies. Having assumed a persona or mask that was at variance with his real self, he felt he had to be consistent with it, and he became a Hitlerite out of bravado. The man who wrote the essay *The Poetry of Christianity,* undoubtedly an expression of his real feelings, had nothing in common with the man who said the ignorant should be encouraged to spawn in order to keep up a steady supply of slaves.

There was no touch of the American language in the tales of Scott Fitzgerald, the typical writer of the twenties, as he seemed later, whom I saw now and then with the friend of my childhood Maxwell Perkins, the publisher who regarded him almost as a son. Scott Fitzgerald wrote to me in praise of my book on Henry James and he said he knew *The Ordeal of Mark Twain* also; then he sent me a copy of *The Great Gatsby* from Capri, where he was staying in 1925. He had found in a bookshop there *America's Coming-of-Age,* which he had bought and read "with enormous pleasure,"—the book that

Huneker reviewed and Carl van Doren read, standing, beside a shelf of new accessions. It was "virtually the first book to voice the new age," Carl van Doren wrote to me at a time when I was scarcely aware that anyone had read it.

I remember a dinner at Ernest Boyd's at which Scott Fitzgerald and Zelda, his wife, arriving an hour late when the others had finished, sitting at table fell asleep over the soup that was brought in, for they had spent the two previous nights at parties. So Scott Fitzgerald said as he awoke for a moment, while someone gathered Zelda up, with her bright cropped hair and diaphanous gown, and dropped her on a bed in a room near by. There she lay curled and asleep like a silky kitten. Scott slumbered in the living-room, waking up suddenly again to telephone an order for two cases of champagne, together with a fleet of taxis to take us to a night-club. That moment and scene bring back now a curious note of the twenties that one did not connect with insanity or tragedy then, while I was drawn to the Scott Fitzgeralds, whom I never really knew but who seemed to me, so obviously, romantic lovers.

CHAPTER VIII

WESTPORT

Mᴏʀᴇ ᴀɴᴅ more, as the twenties advanced, the "exurban-ites" settled in Westport,—those displaced New York-ers, brightly so called, who lived beyond the suburbs but who remained urbanites at heart. As the inventor of the phrase ob-served, they "set the styles and moulded the fashions and peo-pled the dreams of the country," for they were artists, writers and fashion-designers. A few were young men who had sat on terraces outside the Dôme and the Rotonde; and presently, when the summer theatre was well established, I saw Piran-dello on the main street one day. He was peering into a peram-bulator and playing with a baby's toes, no doubt on his way to a rehearsal. But whom and what did one not see in this little town that stood for the resurgence of the moment in the life of the country? A dealer soon opened a gallery there with a show of Rouault and another of Canaletto, Tiepolo and Guardi. Then Cardinal Pacelli, later the Pope, appeared in a Westport garden at a play on a biblical theme that was written by a neighbour. Said he to the author, "There should be more plays like that."

Westport, with the towns roundabout, was the "archetype of exurbs . . . the richest in exurban manifestations,"—to quote the ingenious Spectorsky once again,—one of which was "Cactus" Moore, who was often seen fishing from the bridge when he

was not sitting for a cartoon in *The New Yorker*. It was supposed that this cowboy from Texas concocted half the new
smart words, together with the topical phrases that spread
through the country, passed on by him to the illustrators whom
he served as a model and popularized soon after on the stage in
New York. Then there was Rose O'Neill, who lived in a
pseudo-Italian villa, a fairy-tale house with a fairy-tale name,
in a clearing in the woods beside the river, overlooking a
sunken garden with a pool surrounded by her handiwork,
drooping nude sculptured figures of uncertain sex. In her flowing pink draperies, Rose O'Neill, with bright blonde hair about
her neck, embraced a crowd of followers who lived on her
bounty, for this creator of the Kewpie doll could not quickly
enough divest herself of the fortune that she had made from it.
She endowed at the Hotel Brevoort a circular table, and there
anyone who called himself a poet or a painter could charge to
her account whatever he wished. She herself and the famous
doll figured in the frescoes that John Stuart Curry painted in
the hall of the high school,—for Curry also lived in a grove
by the river,—and in these frescoes he painted as well Theodore
Dreiser and Eugene O'Neill with Sherwood Anderson and
James Earle Fraser, the sculptor. Of me he made a red-chalk
portrait drawing that gave me the look of a Mexican border
bandit. I asked him, whilst he was working on this, what
type in his boyhood in Kansas the boys he had known had
most admired,—was it the big bear hunter or the millionaire
farmer? No, said Curry, the minister was the hero of the boys.
The minister was the type they all looked up to, as they had
looked up to the pilot in Mark Twain's Missouri.

Once Rose O'Neill appeared in our garden, in her pink
satin with the golden slippers in which she had walked two
miles from Carabas. It was a May afternoon and the leaves had

just unfolded,—one had almost heard them unfolding in the last week of April, when the squirrel with the bitten ear frisked in the great oak over the roof and everything growing or flying seemed aquiver with excitement. The tulips and the hyacinths blossomed on the rocky slope, and one caught the secret flight of the robin darting from its nest with wings close to the body so as not to be noticed. The bittersweet vine that Mrs. La Farge had sent us from Saunderstown spread new shoots over the lattice by the door of the study, and tendrils with clusters of lettuce-green leaves straggled out from the dark green patch that covered most of the slope with English ivy. This had all grown from a slip that was brought by an artist who had owned our house from Sir Walter Scott's Ab-botsford in Scotland. It occurred to me that cuttings from this might please someone in the South, so I sent a boxful to Miss Mary Johnston, the old Virginia novelist who had written *To Have and to Hold* and *Prisoners of Hope.* She planted the ivy outside her study windows beside our friend Edward Shel-don's rose-tree, and she said it brought her visions of Melrose and Thomas the Rhymer, while she heard the pibroch about the house at night.

For a good part of a year we had Henry Stuart living with us,—Henry Longan Stuart, who reviewed for the *Times* and who wrote the fine novel *Weeping Cross,*—a romantic English-man of Irish descent and a Catholic of an old English type like some of the cavaliers who fought in the Low Countries. He might have been, in fact, one of the Templars of the first crusades, for, well-born, poor and exempt from worldly ties, he really had all the traits that characterized them. Henry turned his Irish wit against the "Celtic twilight" from which "at any moment a brickbat might emerge," for he was much concerned about the treachery that had caused such havoc in the history of the Irish. A captain in the British army in Italy, he had been wounded and thrown from his horse, then, remaining in Florence for several years, he had lived on a Colorado ranch before he came East as a literary soldier of fortune. Translating many Italian books, he wrote poems in a seventeenth-century mode that could only be found later in old magazines,—for the typewritten book of his poetry was lost after his death,—while *Weeping Cross* recalled the seventeenth century too, alike in tone, style, setting, characters and story. It related the adventures of a cavalier much like himself in the New England of Hawthorne's *The Scarlet Letter,* a soldier half gallant, half monk, and his desperate love affair with a volatile and still more beautiful Hester Prynne. The more or less archaic style, so often a cumbersome device, admirably completed here the illusion of the story.

Extremely attractive to women, Henry was equally drawn to them, while he recoiled from the sexual promiscuity that was so general after the first world war. I remember how he once repulsed a proposal over the telephone. "Madam," his answer was, "you should apply to your husband in matters of that kind." To this the lady replied, "What, you say that! You with a face like yours!" But Henry's face had tragic memories in it, and he knew why the Stoics so carefully controlled their sexual life if only in the interest of their peace of mind. It was a question with him of all or nothing, and he vaguely planned a book in praise of chastity that would have been unique in the twenties I remember. For chastity had come to be defined as merely a convention based on fear that had lost all meaning in a day of contraceptives. Henry remembered William James's characterization of chastity as the principle of all human social elevation,—the subjecting of every present incitement of sense to suggestions of aesthetic or moral fitness;

and he agreed with Albert Nock about the barbaric regression which the "sex" novels of the moment represented. In many of these novels the relations of the sexes were physical merely and therefore undiversified and exactly alike, and what could art do with this characterless subject-matter, sensationally exciting as perhaps it might be? Nock, in his *Memoirs,* wondered why novelists no longer attempted to show how interesting the relations of the sexes could be when they had no physical element in them, as, for example, in the well-known case of d'Alembert and Mlle. de Lespinasse. Henry himself was involved in relations of this kind, and these were almost as complex as the relations between Freud and his wife in the story of this great man's courtship and marriage. Ironical it seemed to me, when I read Ernest Jones's biography, that Freud should have been the father of so many "sex" novels, for this monogamist's own love story contained all the elements which these novels of our time wholly omitted. "With him the word 'puritanical' would not be out of place," Ernest Jones remarked in this connection; and everything in his story was "character," nothing was "sex."

At Westport Henry fell in again with his old friend Hugh Lofting, for he had known well as a boy in England this somewhat dandified lover of snuff who was writing there the "Dr. Dolittle" stories. Hugh Lofting had a study in the woods not far from our house. Then Henry knew Brooks Atkinson, the theatre critic of the *New York Times,* a paradox, a naturalist whose model was Thoreau and who lived in a state of tension between two vocations. No doubt this invigorated both. At least, I know that his country essays were among the liveliest of their kind and time, delightful to one who scarcely followed his theatrical reviews because, in the country, I could not follow the theatre. In Westport I never missed a chance to see him. Once he came out to find again a Wilson's thrush that lived in a shadowy glen on the road to Redding. As we were driving there, he described the tree where the bird should be found; and, sure enough, there he was, almost on the expected branch, as if he were keeping a rendezvous with this great bird-lover. It seemed to me a case of ornithological second sight, worthy of the bird's namesake, Alexander Wilson.

One creator of the New York stage who often came to visit us was my old Harvard friend Lee Simonson, the stage-designer of the Theatre Guild whose first wish had been to paint, in Paris, in the circle of the Steins, Leo and Gertrude. Lee was ill at ease with what he called the anæmia of the American eye, the sallowness and greyness of the typical American palette, tints of oatmeal and sand, as he described them; and he had once noticed, approaching Naples, that the Americans on board the ship had marvelled at the prospect through smoked glasses. With his marked Oriental air,—he said that in a mosque once he was asked why he did not speak Arabic,—Lee had a special taste for brilliant colours, for startling tints in shirts and ties that were usually kept for the Negro trade, as a dealer told him on one occasion. Lee had been drawn to Gauguin because he restored these pure colours that were so alien to the coldness and dullness of New York, and, enchanted in Paris with Cézanne and Picasso, he was especially taken with Matisse's violent colour oppositions. He felt it was his mission to introduce this colour into the neutral background of contemporary living; but, hoping at first to do mural decoration, he soon became convinced that he had set out to learn his craft too late. For his critical faculty was so over-developed that he felt, when he was painting, tormented and strained. Then, seeing his first modern décor in the Ballet Russe of Diaghilev, he realized that the Art Theatre was his true sphere, and he had come home to find playwrights, producers and actors who were bent on revolutionizing the stage in New York.

Lee's personal hero was Bernard Shaw, for whom he did some of his best work, while we all belonged to the generation whose earliest recollection of the stage had been Joseph Jefferson in *Rip van Winkle*. Lee, in our Westport house,—a manic-depressive,—was usually aglow, counselling my wife on the raising of lilies or my boys on the making of beer or planting his choicest dahlia bulbs in the garden. Once, I remember, when we had imprudently rented the house, these bulbs, stored in the cellar, vanished in our absence, and, as they looked exactly like sweet potatoes, we supposed our tenants must have eaten them. Lee had long telephone conversations with Alfred Lunt in the far West,—I think about *Amphitryon 38*,—and, if it rained, he would telephone his children to be sure to wear their proper coats and rubbers. For he was a most meticulous model parent. Meanwhile, between plays, he wrote the essays that appeared in *Minor Prophecies* or in later issues of *The New Republic*, essays in which he shunned the note of the typical critique of the time,—"usually a dress rehearsal for the Last Judgment." He said to me once, "The other fellow's grass is always greener," meaning that writing always seemed more attractive when he was deep in theatre work, but he found writing painful and reading his proofs, he remarked, was like walking in leaden shoes through hot wet sand. Lee, sometimes regarded as blustering and rude, was certainly not modest,—when he was in high spirits he seemed to me like a brass band playing in the house,—but he was the most winning and generous of men and, far from being vain, he had the profound humility of the true-blue artist. With this went, moreover, a copious flow of ideas and the learning that later marked *The Stage is Set*.

Lee said his ideas were corks in a current; but I believe that in *Minor Prophecies* he was the first to suggest a number that were developed presently by others. He had applied to the American museum some of the notions of design that he had worked out also on the stage, recommending early the arranging of objects in period rooms or grouping them to show their relation to the whole structure of their epoch. The rooms in the old museums had been so crammed with objects that the mere process of attention was an agony of effort, and crowding five great works into a space where not one could truly live seemed to him as criminal as the crowding of tenement bed-rooms. This accumulation displayed everything and revealed nothing, and Lee as a painter had been depressed by these vast dreary asylums where shelter was accorded to the waifs and strays of art. He was all for a new museum in which apses were built into walls, perhaps with altars under stained-glass windows, and with reliquaries, bishops' crooks, tapestries and lamps. Then Lee suggested the renting of new pictures for brief periods at a low price, a sort of "trial marriage" between the renter and the picture that might well result in an ultimate purchase, a notion that seemed suited to an experimental time, an age of small apartments and constant moving. Lee himself liked to try things out. He designed ballets for Mordkin; and he once bought and produced a play, well knowing, as he wrote to me, that "only masochists become theatrical producers and only sadists congratulate them."

When I thought ill of Santayana, I had to remember how many of my friends owed everything to his *Reason in Art* and *The Sense of Beauty*. "Let us live in the mind," Santayana's saying, had made a deep impression on the sensitive Lee, and "If it weren't for him," Lee said to me later, "I shouldn't be engaged on my present opus." He was referring to *The Stage is Set,* the great study of stage-design to which he returned whenever engagements were lagging and in which he spoke for the community theatres that played so large a part in our friend Lewis Mumford's regional planning. For scenic design, from Lee's point of view, was an interpretative art that served the needs of society, social and moral, and he believed that all artists should be socially minded and must make their work necessary to society if they were to survive. So he was to write in *Part of a Lifetime,* and he might have been thinking of the great Mexican painters who were so deeply involved in the revolution in their country. "We are all preachers," Lee said to me once; and he said again, "We are all prophets, Puritans like you and Hebrews like Waldo and myself. But," he added, "the practice of letters is a cause, and it will have to be kept one. Or made one again."

What he had in mind here was my notion of the artist and writer as a leader or pathfinder,—a sort of guru,—or what Paul Rosenfeld meant when he spoke of the poet as "the man who can give the race the direction in which it has to go." All our generation had some such belief as this, and nothing marked it off more clearly from the age that followed, the age of John Crowe Ransom and the "new" critics. Literature, for these men, had no public function; they had entirely relinquished, as Ransom said, the notion of the poet as a prophet or a priest; whereas the great writers who had formed our minds had felt it was part of their task "to improve the prevailing order of the world."

I am quoting Ibsen, who also said that literature should be not only "revelative" but "redemptive," a notion that was soon to vanish from the literary mind and that came to seem contemptible and even absurd. But, certain as I felt myself that it was unassailable and destined sooner or later to rearise, I re-

membered through all the coming time the great men who had
stood for it, Ruskin, Emerson, Tolstoy, Romain Rolland; and,
running through earlier centuries, how many could one count?
One and all would have agreed with Chekhov that the "good"
writers convey "a sense of what life ought to be" and that
they are "summoning you towards it," while they have "an
object, immediate or remote, the abolition of serfdom, the happiness of humanity and so on." Had not Strindberg observed
of the artist that he was a "lay preacher," a name in which
Anthony Trollope and Mark·Twain rejoiced, as Bernard Shaw
said that the "man of letters, when he is more than a mere
confectioner, is a prophet or nothing." Even Kipling said he
had a "mission to preach." As it seemed to me, the sole condition was that one should not professedly preach or make direct
appeals to the conscious will, and I was not greatly disturbed
when I was called a preacher. I remembered that Isadora Duncan had been convinced that her dancing might, as a new form
of religion, regenerate the world, while I was aware of the comic
aspects of the "uplift" tendencies of our national life that were
also, in their reformism, connected with preaching. Convinced as I was that writing was truly a vocation, I was convinced also that literature and art existed for the sake of what
Berenson called "life-enhancement,"—making this planet "fit
for human habitation,"—as I shared Walt Whitman's belief
that "first-class works are to be tried by their eligibility to free,
arouse, dilate." I sympathized with Whitman's praise of the
novelists Cooper and Scott because, as he said, they "take life
forward," believing that this would always stand for the major strain in literature, however one admired the various minor
strains.

Some years later, Ford Madox Ford, in *This Was the Nightingale,* expressed the opposing views of these two generations.

"The business of art," he said, "is not to elevate but to render," adding, "Those are the two schools of thought that have eternally divided humanity, and no one in the end will ever know which will win out." *To render* was the aim of the coming generation, just as *to elevate* was the aim of ours; and I never doubted that our "school" would come into its own again when writers tired of "rendering" as their ultimate object. How limited their notion was of literature and art as a game or a "superior amusement"! Our school stood for the old humanist dream of "building a garden in the cosmic wilderness,"—to quote the grandfather of the Huxleys of our time; and it was obvious that humankind could not dispense forever with writers who were devoted to a cause like that. Lee shared my point of view, sceptical as he sometimes was regarding the general influence of great writers, saying, for instance, in a letter to me, "Each age goes about its business like freighters in a harbour. A little of the force that drives it leaks out as a surplus, like oil on harbour waters. For a moment it is iridescent, and beautiful in the right light. But the business of shipping the cargoes of any epoch goes its own way." He wrote again, "I dislike admitting it but I have begun to despair about the relation of literature to life. What are its central images and ideas but occasional solace and occasionally a pastime to the vast majority who live to possess—women, gold, power, political or industrial? It seems to me we make the mistake of persons employed at a mint who like the bas-reliefs stamped on a surface so much that they end by imagining the coins are made for coin collectors. Perhaps they are, ultimately, but they are spent by people to whom it makes no difference whether they are handling the *livre tournois,* or, when that becomes obsolete, the *louis d'or,* or, when that has to be hoarded,—a remnant of another golden age,—get on just as well

with handsomely engraved pieces of paper." But, having said
this, Lee wrote again, "Though I can admit this in general, I
can't as yet admit it in regard to the particular field in which
I am a tenant. I end my book [*The Stage is Set*] with a noble
howl to the philosopher-poets to arise and save the theatre.
And now that it is written I'm quite certain that they won't."

So much for what Lee somewhere called the "irrepressible
evangelism" that marked the American character,—and touched
our own,—a trait we still shared in a way with the novelists of
the muckraking time and the surviving college-settlement writers. Among these were the novelist Robert Herrick, Edgar Lee
Masters and Vachel Lindsay, all of whom had lived at Hull
House in Chicago, where our friend Francis Hackett had
found what he called an "American faith" in place of the usual
patter of success and smartness. All these men felt they were
somehow involved in the great human adventure that James
Harvey Robinson described in his books, pursuing the good of
humanity as their chief interest in the face of tribal society
and its sanctified blindness. Our Westport neighbour Lillian
Wald symbolized this pursuit, along with certain women I
met at her house, among them Grace Abbott of the Children's
Bureau, Alice Hamilton, the Harvard professor, and Jane
Addams, who spent summers on the Connecticut river. I remember Jane Addams's remark that the river was "so friendly,"
with the oil-barges drifting up and down. These "exemplary
women," in the old phrase, resembled the devoted souls who
tried so soon to establish the Spanish republic,—"do-gooders,"
one and all, the wisecrack of the smaller souls who wished to
pull them down to their own level. For how many strangers,
with her courage and glow, had not Lillian Wald, at the port
of New York, vindicated America as the land of promise?—
while, with her copious peacefulness, her deep simplicity and

her repose, Jane Addams suggested Demeter, the earth-mother. A few persons whom I have met have instantly called up for me images of the ancient goddesses and gods,—for one, Alexander Calder in his Hephæstic workshop, my neighbour, the iron-worker deity of the mobiles. Then there was Boardman Robinson, the shapely painter. "Mike" Robinson, naked on a beach, turning hand-springs on the sand, might have given birth to the myth of Bacchus, and I thought of Paul Robeson, years ago, as a kind of Negro Jupiter, thanks to his incomparably spacious voice and presence. Jane Addams had this air of indubitable greatness.

Once, at Lillian Wald's house, I took part in a conversation between Jane Addams and Charles Beard, whom we often went to see in his big slate-coloured house overlooking the Housatonic valley at New Milford. Jane Addams asked him why he had resigned from Columbia and why John Dewey had not done so,—to recall an academic incident of the previous decade,—and the question arose whether Dewey's acceptance of the *status quo* there was not the logical result of his pragmatism. Dewey's integrity was never in doubt, and Jane Addams, for the rest, defended pragmatism with a shake of her head, saying, "I have seen so many people who thought they were right,"—for every crank in Chicago had haunted Hull House. She turned the subject off, as wise old people are apt to do, partly because they have heard too many discussions, but it struck me as odd that she should remember the people who thought they were right and were *not*, forgetting those who thought they were right and *were* so. I remembered her old adoration of Tolstoy, for instance. While the feeling of moral certitude had surely caused much of the evil of the world, had it not initiated more that was good? Charles Beard had not pragmatized when he destroyed his own teaching career by standing up for two colleagues with whom he disagreed, glad to accept, in his contempt for inquisitions and alien control, the insults of certain vulgarians among the trustees. He told me that one of them said to him, "Why do you resign? Don't you know that it's easier for us to find a good professor than a good butler?"

Charles Beard, at his dairy-farm on the ridge over the Housatonic,—in his immense straw hat, haying with his men,—had, more than anyone else I knew, except perhaps Albert Nock, the air and port of one of the founding fathers. He brought back the atmosphere of the early republic, when men were creating a nation and knew they could do so, one of the great pamphleteers of 1776,—he put me in mind of Thomas Paine. He had the same eye for humbugs and shams and the faith in perfectibility, together with a hearty bonhomie and simplicity of nature, and, occasionally wrong-headed as he certainly was, and limited on the poetic side, he was an irreplaceable antiseptic. How valuable was his exposure of the "historical necromancers," along with the assumptions of historical "science."

At New Canaan, closer by, our old friend Maxwell Perkins lived, and Padraic and Mollie Colum spent a number of years in the town, in their accustomed setting of poetry and poets. For one, they knew Bliss Carman, who had taken up quarters at an inn where I spent a winter in New Canaan and who, with his long cloak and his picturesque hair, personified the romantic poet that no one in the new time wished to be. But nothing could have suggested less the glamour of a poet's life than the poor bare little room in which he existed, with nothing visible in it but a bed and a chair, and it was good to know that in his native Canada he was by no means without honour. For who spoke of this poet any longer in New York? He recalled to me the atrocious indifference of our literary world, which tossed away yesterday's talents when they were still active, a fate one could never have foreseen at the time for Edna Millay's rival, the only other reigning woman poet. Elinor Wylie was also living in New Canaan, and there, and at our Westport house, I met this author of *Black Armour*, a phrase that evoked for me an image of herself; for there was something metallic about her and, if not reptilian, glittering and hard, as of some creature living in an iridescent shell. She entered a room with clanking scales, full panoplied for war, like Bonduca or an elegantly slim Valkyrie. This poet was armed at all points, unlike Vachel Lindsay, at the height of his career, the inventor of a new kind of poetry, related to ragtime, who was all too easily made a fool of. Gamaliel Bradford told me later how, in his Wellesley drawing-room, the college girls egged Vachel Lindsay on, baiting this hobbledehoy of genius who was driven at last to suicide, aware of the self-conscious awkwardness of his theatrical declaiming. But I was transported at the Colums' house by the beauty of *The Chinese Nightingale* when, as if in a trance, he recited this poem, repeating the lines that were magical to me, swaying back and forth before the fire.

It was in the twenties that I first met Thomas Wolfe, then still unknown, I think, at the house of Max Perkins,—the giant from the Southern hills, with his puzzled earnest air, who was so soon to begin a momentous career. He was almost as bitter about Jefferson Davis as Sherwood Anderson had been, at Westport,—with far less reason,—about Robert E. Lee, in revolt as he was, and as one saw in *The Hills Beyond*, against the unreality of the legend of the old South. Scarcely knowing who Wolfe was, I was astonished by the animus with which he attacked the new Southern agrarian movement, the

school of the "Fugitive" poets and critics who were bent on
reviving, as he feared, the old regime and all that was fraudu-
lent in it. They pretended that the old regime had favoured
art and literature, dreaming of an aristocratic South that, as
everybody knew, had actually despised the artist and the writer.
Thomas Wolfe recalled to me the diatribes of Mark Twain,
who expressed for these delusions a similar contempt.

I was only then becoming aware of the new movement in
criticism that was emerging in the South with the "formalist"
critics, paralleling the movement in Russia in the opening
years of the first world war whose motto was "Art is always
independent of life." These Russians had cared for form alone,
saying, in the words of one of them, that literature was "a
phenomenon solely of language" and that Gogol's heroes
merely happened to be Russian officials and squires, a fact that
had no more importance than their surroundings. But, whereas
the formalist school in Russia disappeared within two or three
years, the American school was to flourish for decades to come,
devoted to "structural analysis," to the study of "balance and
shifts of tone" and to "functional ambiguities of reference and
syntax." (I am quoting certain of its phrases.) It was almost
to realize Anatole France's prophecy in *La Vie Littéraire* that
"criticism, the youngest of all the literary forms," would "perhaps end by absorbing all the others." As I observed what
seemed to me the blight these "close" critics spread abroad, I
felt they envisaged a literature

> No belly and no bowels,
> Only consonants and vowels,

in the phrase, oddly enough, of John Crowe Ransom. Could
any influence be more sterilizing? And would not this analyti-
cal thinking destroy in readers, in the end, their power of

fantasy and their poetic feeling? I thought of Darwin who said he became conditioned by science to such a degree that he could no longer read a novel. It was Joel Spingarn who first used the phrase "the new criticism," and how would he have felt about grammarians of this kind with their categorical tone and esoteric language? As for me, these "young men rushing into criticism,"—in Ransom's phrase,—caused me to withdraw, slowly, in the other direction; for I scarcely wished any longer to be called a critic when the word assumed these connotations.

CHAPTER IX

A HUMANIST

I THINK IT was in 1922 that my friend Hendrik van Loon
became, for a number of years, a Westport neighbour,—
"the last of the old-fashioned liberals" whom the Smithso-
nian wanted to buy, as he said once, for its collection. This
so-called prince of popularizers was treated with contempt by
certain professional historians and many critics, and in fact
his personality was more significant than his work, for he
usually wrote without tension, *en pantoufles*. But Hendrik
was in no sense a literary hack. Hasty as he may have been,
his writings were all of a piece, consistent unfoldings of his
own special nature, so that he was unique as one of the characters of his time as well as a public figure of importance.
Among what George Orwell called the "smelly little ortho-
doxies" that were already winning so many minds, he was regarded often as a formidable person, and Maxim Gorky said
that Hendrik was one of two historians who could be regarded
as dangerous to Soviet Russia. Gorky's other historian was Os-
wald Spengler. For Hendrik fought every kind of tyranny
over the mind of man, and, once aroused, he fought with great
effect. Moreover, he returned the contempt of the specialists
and pedants. Hendrik lived in the large air of the *homo uni-
versalis*, a true belated man of the Renaissance, a Dutchman

who recalled his beloved Erasmus and who had his own wide learning and zest for life.

He was already an institution and soon became still more so as the author of *Van Loon's Geography* and *Van Loon's Lives*,—in which he appeared as a rather too talkative Plutarch,—the kind of showman who was least respected in an age of cerebration and who seemed to lounge in his books, too much at his ease. Even his plenitude was regarded with suspicion, for Hemingway's "Not too damned much" was a motto of the time. But of Hendrik one could say that, unlike ordinary popularizers, he was inside whatever he wrote about, whether music, his first passion, or the painting in which he might have excelled, or cooking, navigation, ships or maps. From his early childhood these matters were all in his blood. In the Dutch stone cottage he built at Westport, frescoing the walls himself,—he had been asked to do murals for the Waldorf-Astoria in New York,—the study was also a music room, for he had learned to fiddle at ten when he had played Mozart and Haydn with his music-master. Crossing the ocean later, he made friends with Einstein, and the two played in the ship's orchestra together, as Hendrik had played at Munich, with the Schrammelspieler, in his student days, musical orgies that lasted till all hours of the morning. He might have been one of the Dutchmen of old who carried their lutes to the tavern, amusing the tosspots all night with their songs, producing at the same time a copy of Horace and translating some of the odes into a semblance of Dutch.

In the Westport study, his writing-table was littered, like the chairs, with sketches, old maps, atlases, manuals of cooking, and with books in six or seven tongues, one of them Russian, which he had learned in St. Petersburg as a young man. Old atlases had been a part of the household furniture when he was a boy, "both theatre and movie to me in Rotterdam," he said, with maps of the golden age of the Dutch explorers and navigators when some of the cartographers were admirable artists. To them he owed largely his feeling for history and the adventure connected with it, which the modern specialized historians had ceased to feel, and he found that old maps were more apt to give him ideas than pictures or even letters of the past. As a boy in a Dutch port, he had learned to spell, moreover, in the advertisements of ships that were sailing for the Indies. For the rest, he delighted in culinary books, with recipes of the seventeenth century, when Richelieu invented mayonnaise, a characteristic taste of his that figured in the drawings, imaginative, witty and gay, which appeared in his books.

Sketching often with coloured inks, Hendrik captured in a few lines all manner of historic atmospheres, persons and places, Rome in the eighteenth century, Mohammed's Medina or his favourite Thomas Jefferson at Monticello. As in this case, he liked to picture a land overflowing with honey and a table with savoury fowls and bottles of wine, bright bouquets of flowers and bowls of fruit, symbols of liberality and abundance; and he was especially drawn to Jefferson because this great man had won his wife with the violin that he always carried with him. It even went far with Hendrik that Frederick the Great played the flute; and, regarding Emerson, his only complaint was that this humanist had been brought up in the doctrine that you must not notice what you eat. Hendrik liked to think of the times when music and all the other arts were interwoven with the general business of living, from which they were never separated in feeling or thought, and for this he almost condoned the Middle Ages that had, for him, so little common sense. He liked to remember that emperors considered it an honour to be associated with the minnesingers, especially as the troubadour, the minstrel, had been his first ideal of the good life. Hendrik felt that he belonged to a race whose roots were deeply struck into the Rabelaisian earth of the mediæval time, as one saw in the simple folk of both Zealand and Flanders, and he was at home in the whimsicalities, the drolleries, jocosities, quiddities and quips that pleased people four hundred years ago. It struck me that, somehow, his unpretentious drawings recalled the illuminations of the old Netherlandish monks.

Two themes that recurred in these drawings were the Dutch galleon in full sail and the steeple-hatted Dutchman in leather breeches, who appeared as the type figure in many of them, indicating, as it seemed to me, that his imagination was deeply involved in the great age of Holland. It was noticeable that when he was pleased, or otherwise moved or distracted, he always fell back into his native tongue, or at least uttered a few words of it; and nothing could have been more Dutch than his appearance and mode of life in what might have passed for a courtlier Frans Hals's household. (Especially when the baby-chair that had been Emerson's chair as a child was occupied by one of Hendrik's grandsons; for Hendrik had married a great-granddaughter of the "practical navigator" Bowditch and this chair was a gift of the Emersons to a family friend. Well I remember the little red walnut cane-bottomed chair that was fitted for a child of eighteen months.) Hendrik said rightly that if he were dressed in black velvet and frills he would have looked like one of Van der Helst's portraits, gigantic as in fact he was, so that not only his suits and his shirts but also his boots and his hats were made for him. (Until he gave up hats and went about in snowstorms wrapped in his huge ulster but bare-headed.) He said that in berths in sleeping-cars he had to

fold up like a jack-knife; and once when, later, he came for a
visit after he had left Westport, we were obliged to rebuild a
bed for him. The sides had to be extended about four inches.
Coming back from Finland once, he told me how Sibelius had
met him with the words, "Willkommen! Willkommen! How
good it is to see another man who can fold his arms round his
belly and laugh!"

Sibelius, who had read him and asked him for a visit, agreed
that only laughter could save the world, a notion suggesting
not only Frans Hals but many another Hollander of the days
when Holland was the centre of the civilized world. Hendrik
dwelt lovingly on those six decades when the "pancake of
mud" on the North Sea ruled millions of people, red, yellow
and black, when it supplied all Europe with grain, fish, whalebones, linen and hides and its storehouses burst with bales of
nutmeg and pepper. Then Descartes lived in Amsterdam and
thither all roads led that were travelled by artists and writers,
scientists and statesmen, and learned geographers made the
charts by which all the world sailed, with atlases printed on
presses named after the muses. Then lived Van Dieman of
Van Dieman's Land and Tasman of Tasmania, and from Spitz-
bergen to Staten Island, New Zealand and Mauritius, the
Dutch were pioneers of navigation. Formerly the music-masters
of all the other races, they had become supremely a nation of
painters, and every Dutch village had its painter as, later, every
New England village had its mechanical genius and inventor
of gadgets. Then Holland, the greatest of international count-
ing-houses, harboured Spinoza, Grotius, Vondel and Rembrandt.

Half a dozen of Hendrik's books grew out of his pride in
these great days when one small country could not hold the
people who were driven wild with excitement by the sight of

maps, when the Dutch ports were crowded with ships that
bulged with whale-oil, spices, silks, and the streets suggested
a continual county fair. There were splendid paintings on
every hand, and Swedes, Turks, Blackamoors, East Indians,
Germans and Frenchmen brought the whole world to every
Dutchman's door, a memory that made Hendrik feel as if he
had been born with the twentieth-century planetary outlook.
As a child in Rotterdam he had spent days in the Museum of
the Knowledge of This Earth where he first made acquaintance with the world and its wonders and where the figure of
a Laplander hitching a reindeer to a sleigh gave him his first
longing to explore it. Other days he spent on an old training-
vessel, for he had an uncle in the Dutch navy, and there was
nothing he did not know about the rigging of the ships that
were to appear in so many of his drawings. He read books on
polar exploration,—Nansen was his hero,—and especially on
the Dutch explorers who aroused his interest in geography and
history and the age in which they themselves were paramount.
Learning English in *Henry Esmond,* he had found Motley as
captivating as American boys found *Huckleberry Finn,* and he
evoked the Dutch republic in his *Peter Stuyvesant* and in his
book about Rembrandt, *R.v.R.* His wish here was to excavate
seventeenth-century Holland as Schliemann had excavated the
city of Troy, and this was the one book he hoped to be remembered for, a book that, with all its *longueurs,* may well survive.
Hendrik's chief reward, I think, was that it won for him a
letter of high praise from Willa Cather.

The book was a sort of *Kulturroman,* like *The Cloister and
the Hearth,* in which appeared Hendrik's idol Erasmus, the
winning humanist and scholar whom he sketched as often as
he sketched musical instruments, fruit and ships. At the age
of five, on his way to school, in the care of the old family

servant Hein, he had passed every day the birthplace and
statue of Erasmus, whom he had followed a few years later by
going to school at Gouda, where he too had learned his Greek
and Latin. This reasonable, witty, tolerant man was Hendrik's
lifelong model in all respects, good manners, temper, learning,
the first "guest" in *Van Loon's Lives,* in which he was constantly present, an affinity of the author of the book. Hendrik
liked to recall that Erasmus was also an amateur musician, and
he poured out his affection for him in the long introduction he
wrote in time for Erasmus's *In Praise of Folly.* In this book he
found a world in which man was free from the violence, prejudice and greed that still beset him, one step removed as man
actually was from the aboriginal dweller in caves and, even
to this day, the victim of ignorance and fear. In contrast to
this neolithic man with cigarettes and automobiles, a cliff-
dweller reaching his home in an elevator, Erasmus suggested
an intelligent race, well-mannered and forbearing, aware that
many ways of thinking can be equally right. Hendrik was convinced himself that when men were exempt from fear they
were decidedly inclined to be righteous and just, and this had
been the belief of Grotius, another fellow-Dutchman, when he
devised the science of international law. Hendrik had been
brought up, he said, by sound Voltairians, and they had kept
the tolerant spirit that had once made Holland an asylum for
European thinkers of every sort. His own favourite, after Erasmus, was always Montaigne.

But the little Holland of his youth was full of small jealous-
ies and petit-bourgeois cruelties, he wrote later, and, having
means, he had come to this country to study at Harvard and
Cornell with a desire to teach history before he wrote it. Then,
wishing to see what he called the world of great events, he had
witnessed the Russian revolution of 1906, moving from Mos-

cow and Warsaw to Munich, where he had taken his doctor's degree in the spirit of the *Vagantes* of the Middle Ages. After he had served as a correspondent in the first world war, he could say that he had had many adventures, passing through shipwrecks and battles, fire and flood, escaping from his two *bêtes noires,* parochialism and pedantry, and ready to write the history that he knew and felt. He said it was more important to "feel" history than to know it, a statement that certain great writers would have accepted but that opened him to the taunts of smaller minds. Disliking the dull German method that alternated with propaganda,—with nationalistic flag-waving,—in this country, he realized, especially after the war, how gravely Americans needed a comprehensive view of the world's past. For he was appalled by the ignorance both of history and of Europe that led them to make such capital political blunders. But every country was turning itself into a voluntary ghetto with idiotic restrictions about crossing frontiers, and, just at the moment when people were taking to airplanes, their governments, he complained, had become oxcart-minded. Feeling that he was a hopeless realist in a world of green cheese, he attacked the "incurable vice of nationalism," and he was to write his history of this country as an episode in the development of the story of mankind. He saw himself as a pioneer of the new planetary point of view, like Nehru of the *Glimpses of World History* and H. G. Wells, who was obliged to hack down trees and blow up the stumps and lay out the land for the future. He attacked especially the cocksureness and arrogance that caused as much suffering in the present as they had caused in the past, saying that the only heresy was that which proclaimed as heretical all other modes of thinking than its own.

Hendrik's two blind spots were the Spanish and the Irish,—

he was "too terribly Dutch" to be drawn to them; and he might have said that, in any case, they were, of all peoples, the last to comprehend the Erasmian outlook. For the rest, if the upshot was that he wrote largely for children, he was none the less for all that a power over minds and even a creator of the climate of opinion that was preparing the way for a world state. Never again, thanks partly to him, could people say of India that Alexander the Great "discovered" it, as if the Indians had never discovered themselves; and he knew that the great age of exploitation had definitely come to an end, that humanity now had a collective conscience. And who could deny that he had a touch of the true historical afflatus of the writers of pre-scientific times? He carried out the idea of Bagehot that history should be like a Rembrandt etching, casting a vivid light on important causes and leaving all the rest, unseen, in shadow; and, moreover, he had the gift of storytelling that few historians any longer wish to have. He had, above all, an unshakable faith in the rise of mankind from the Protozoa, in spite of all the regressions of the world-war epoch, the mire of crime and brutal deeds into which millions of people sank as, more and more, gangsters ruled the world. He felt it was a duty of civilized man to forward the evolutionary process, believing that, through periods of growth and decline, the race was moving forward and that man was endowed with still unrealized powers. Liberal that he was, however, he did not like Rousseau, the "all-round blackguard, the contemptible bounder," nor did he like the Rousseauian schools in which he taught from time to time, regarding himself as rather a teacher than a writer. It did not please him to see boys and girls learning to "express" themselves by "hammering away at a piano with one hand and with the other eating a piece of cake."

As he grew older, Hendrik's mind turned back to Holland more and more. He recalled what Lessing said, that when the world was coming to an end he himself was going to move to Holland, for there they were always a hundred years behind the times and that would give him a new span of life. Thinking of the old Netherlands, which he said were gone for good, after the Nazi invasion, but which he remembered, he dreamed of writing a historical trilogy of the rise, the short-lived golden age and the slow decline of the country he had known as a boy. He felt that he only could do it in our language, for Pierre van Paassen was too much of a mystic for the sort of work he had in mind, and, troubled about the sub-literary style into which he sometimes fell, he hoped to be able to do it in "acceptable English." He longed, as he wrote to me, to be "the architect of a literary monument to my late native land. It seems a dignified Sir Walter Scottish way of writing the last chapter of one's own life." Meanwhile, he had bought an old Dutch house at Veere where he was to spend a number of winters and summers. He was attracted to Veere perhaps because Erasmus had known it well, and the house had fine oaken ceilings and softly purring stoves, although its walls, he added, were a little wobbly. He bought an etching-press and taught himself to etch there, and he gave Christmas parties for the children of the town. Close by he had written *R.v.R.*, while he wrote his *Lives* at Veere, summoning as "guests" the characters in what he described as "that hall of fame which everyone erects in some secret corner of his brain." His last guest was Jefferson, whom he admired in all ways and who, when his own guests had threatened to leave, sent down for another bottle of a very special port. Hendrik invited Cervantes, too, Emerson, Confucius, St. Francis, Hans Christian Andersen and dozens of others, statesmen, musicians, painters and sages, quiet workers for a decent world, one of whom was the faithful William of Orange. He ransacked old cookbooks for dishes that would please them.

It was after this small Dutch town that he named Nieuw Veere, his last Connecticut house overlooking the Sound. There he was to die in 1943, after crossing the Atlantic many times not only to old Veere but to less familiar spots that especially drew him. He had always liked small countries and felt they favoured freedom of mind, whether Switzerland or Sweden, along with Holland,—he had once lived for a while in Nietzsche's Basel; and he had a special affection for the little countries of northern Europe where he had always felt at home. It pleased him to find that in Finland all the children knew his books, and he hoped for a winter in Norway, a spring in Denmark and one more summer, at least, in Stockholm. He could sketch many parts of this loveliest of all cities, as he called it once, and in time he learned Swedish there in order to translate Bellmann's songs for a children's picture-book of this "Swedish Mozart." One summer he went to Lapland for a second visit. He wrote, "I had to have a second helping," and he found in the wilderness landscape a "suggestion of infinity," for, as he said, "a few Lapps do not count." They were so small, the Lapps, living like birds, building themselves nests wherever they went, sleeping, talking little, following their reindeer in a land that did not seem to be inhabited at all. So one felt alone there with nothing between one and the North Pole, a feeling that did queer things to the brain and set it working along unexpected lines. He had been struggling with a book which he meant to call *The Average Man*, and somehow Lapland brought it into focus. He wrote to me, "The average man is our ruler. So let me try to train him for the job, as Machiavelli tried to educate the Prince." Hendrik's idea of democracy recalled to me the critic Brownell, who had put into words my own conception of it,—"the spread in widest commonalty of aristocratic virtues." Hendrik, who cherished the notion of equality, had no taste whatever for the promiscuous equality of an undeveloped level, and, regarding himself, he once remarked, "The lower metals, like lead, melt easily, but I am not a lower metal."

Hendrik said this at a time when his vast popularity suggested Mark Twain's and his mind was almost as prodigal, impulsive and chaotic. For his abortive plans tumbled over one another. He had a dozen ideas a day, but the mortality among them was like that of our domestic shrimps, he said,—ninety-nine and a half percent of them died at birth. He planned a life of Beethoven, following his *Bach* on a larger scale, together with *The Rise and Fall of the Age of Reason*, a *Candide* in modern dress and *In Praise of Joy*. Meanwhile, he poured out other books, one of them written in a single day, with three days more for the illustrations,—he was always happier, I think, drawing than writing,—some of them Gargantuan books that were best-sellers before they appeared and that were usually translated into twenty other tongues. He sometimes even corrected his proofs by cable, while his correspondence ran to fifteen thousand letters a year and he was beset with photographers and interviewers. In order to "go on a holiday and not on a tabloid trip," he was obliged to keep his movements dark, for he was hounded by "movie people," by "serial people," by "syndicate people" and could not escape *pourparlers* with Hollywood and Hearst. (Though, regarding Hollywood, he spoke the truth when he said, "I understand more about what goes on in Lhasa.") Knighted by the Dutch queen and a guest at the White House, he was always deep in public causes, while he continually reminded himself of the old Buddhist law,

"The holy man does not leave his shrine." To me he wrote, "Farewell to the multitude and back to the wooden tower of Old Greenwich." No use! He could not retire from the battle with Hitler, and with many other victims of the jazz age he was to die early of over-excitement.

Like Mark Twain in certain ways, Hendrik had been all the more so in the triumphal progress of his cruise around the world when, as a guest of the steamship company, he addressed the travellers as he lectured in Hawaii and New Zealand, Zanzibar and Capetown. He found that almost every man, woman and child he encountered had, at one time or another, read one of his books, while he discovered that everywhere the world was dominated by what he described as "the old master magicians." Whether in Polynesia or the Buddhist, the Moslem or the Christian lands, he saw misery caused by a "lack of rational thinking," by "magic" in the hands of the old who were supposedly wise and who kept the young in their places. Meanwhile, "the young men, grown to manhood, find that their comfort and ease depend upon the continued belief in magic,—and so it goes on, world without end and without end of misery." Hendrik continued, "I want for heroes reasonable Erasmian men who understand that this world, while it may never be perfect, could easily be made more agreeable."

As one who loved what Lytton Strachey called "clean brevity," I could not think of Hendrik as an important writer, but he was a bright symbol of a still expansive time that seemed already remote before his death. What he called magic had won the day and there was no room for Erasmian men among writers who abhorred liberal humanism, who felt, with Kierkegaard, that earthly happiness is a sin and that the idea of progress is an infantile illusion. In the new day Comte's belief that the true aim of art is to "charm and ameliorate humanity" had utterly vanished, along with all the notions of the age of reason. But the question was still to be entertained whether the ideas that Hendrik held were nineteenth-century deceits and contemptible fables or whether in the long run they would not prove to be necessary if the human race was to survive and grow. Hendrik, all-curious, compassionate, humane, was one of the lieutenants in the pilgrimage of humanity up from the cavemen, and, for the rest, there were few in our time who so enabled one to share what Burckhardt called the "banquet" of the art of the past.

CHAPTER X

A HAMLET OF TEN HOUSES

N EAR THE up-state road towards Albany, two or three hours
from New York, Joel Spingarn lived in a sheltered valley, or, rather, he summered at Troutbeck in a picturesque,
spreading, ample house surrounded with lawns, old oaks, rivu-
lets and gardens. His domain was a private park that was
planted with rare shrubs and trees, many of them brought from
the Arnold Arboretum, where Joel had been a friend of the
great Charles Sargent, with a rose garden, a sunken garden,
terraces, greenhouses, trellises to support the multiform cle-
matis that was Joel's delight. His collection of more than two
hundred varieties of this flowering climber was renowned in
the world of horticulture.

Troutbeck had long been connected with writers and writing. In two old dwellings on the place the literary farmers, the
Bentons, had lived, correspondents of Thoreau, hosts of Greeley, and the Brotherhood of the New Life of Thomas Lake
Harris had also flourished in Amenia sixty years before. By
Joel's spring John Burroughs had first read *Leaves of Grass*,—
the old farm was redolent of Whitman and Emerson also,
about whom one of the Bentons had written a book; while
Joel himself contributed a note to the "Newness" of our time
that in some ways recalled to me the old one. For as one who
introduced the contemporary thinking of Italy, he too was a

light-bringer of new learning. Troutbeck, moreover, suggested the kind of English country-house that had once brought together philosophers and poets and fostered the literary life and the development of thought; and there was a time, in fact, when Joel hoped to make the valley a home for the muses. He owned what Lewis Mumford called a "hamlet of ten houses,"—the hamlet of the Chinese poets,—adjoining Troutbeck; and, renovating these, he turned them over to literary friends who also came to spend the summer there.

Among the friends who occupied these cottages from time to time were Walter and Magda Pach, the Lewis Mumfords and Geroid Tanqueray Robinson, one of our *Freeman* editors and a great student of Russian rural life. It was easy for me to drive over from Westport to this umbrageous valley where in the summer months good talk abounded, where Ernest Boyd too was a visitor and Lewis and Sophy Mumford presently bought the house where they lived henceforward. Somewhat older than the rest of us, Joel Spingarn might have been called the guardian or incarnation of the *genius loci*, proud, shy, cordial and winning as he was, with a distinctly Italianate air as of some Ferrarese courtier of the days of Tasso. There was a kind of inevitability in the name "De Fiori" that Lewis, in a fictional dialogue, bestowed upon him, for he had more than a touch of the style and manner of certain Italian coteries of the later Renaissance. I wondered if this was not partly the fruit of his early study of the *Galateo*, the *Cortigiano* and other old courtesy books, for in his youth he had steeped himself in the history of chivalric ideals and their evolution from the Romans and the Middle Ages. But there was no suggestion of the exotic in him. For all its aesthetic overtones, his manner was quite natural, and he was really charming like some of his poems, unpretentious poems that were sometimes courtly too in their gallantry and nobility of feeling.

What seemed to me the Italianate note in Joel's personality was definitely marked in his thinking, in the form of his mind, for long before he had written his history of criticism in the Renaissance he had gone to school to the modern Italians also. That book introduced him to Croce, of whom he became an apostle, and, forwarding Croce's ideas at home, with those of Francesco De Sanctis, he hoped to win Americans over to their mode of thought. He would have liked to put an end to the current American jargon that was drawn from psychology, sociology, biology, economics, replacing it with the ideality of the Italian nomenclature, faith, freedom, the spirituality of culture and so on. As early as 1910 he had written *The New Criticism,* a name that was later revived by the school of critics who carried on, substantially, though without credit to him, a critical vein that he had opened up. For the task of the critic, in his view, was to state the intention of the poet and ascertain how far he had fulfilled it, ignoring all questions of value in the study of expression, and the work of the later "new critics," devoted to formal analysis, excluding all other interests, exemplified this. It seemed to be only as an afterthought that he asked the further question, Is what the poet expresses worth expressing?—a question he no more dwelt upon than the "close" critics who followed him in taking for granted everything but expression itself.

All this had its piquancy at a time when American critics were obsessed with what Joel described as "practical wisdom,"—concerns that were psychological, historical and social,—scarcely ever brooding over the meaning of art with the sort of discreet reverence that it properly merits. As for the rest, there was much to be said for the work of Joel's followers, in spite of all one had to say against it, for it tightened the bolts and screws of American writing; and in any case, in his general essays, Joel himself went far beyond the narrow textual interests of many of them. While his specific critical theory seemed to me sterile and thin,—"as brittle as spun glass," Lewis Mumford called it,—he was in other ways a moving spirit, aware as he was that the new literature rising all about us called as well for social criticism. He had been excited by the Armory Show, of which our friend Walter Pach had been to a certain extent the originating spirit, and at that time he had hoped that American writers would follow the painters in their "divine release from custom and convention." For in 1913, measured by their courage, our poetry and fiction had seemed pusillanimous and timid,—anæmic, as Joel felt, academic and faded,— and he held up to ridicule the dry rot of the time with its decayed traditions of Victorian England. He never tired of saying that in art all depends on what Keats called a "fine excess." Attacking in the same breath the specialization of scholarship that copied the vices of the Germans instead of their virtues, he spoke for pluck and freedom in this realm also, and he had lost his professorate as a result of protesting against the removal and ruin of a fellow-scholar. Everyone knew and quoted his lines about the "slayer in scarlet" and the faint-hearted faculty that huddled round him; and, defending his dishonoured friend in *The Fate of a Scholar,* he appealed for the high heart in the teacher's world. Joel's keyword was "creative," a word that savoured of the time and one he applied also to connoisseurship, noting how negative and colourless our Medicis were in the field of taste when they were so dynamic in the field of action.

Eager as Joel was, however, to forward an American renaissance, he was by no means sure of its ultimate triumph, and he could see no reason to suppose that our national energy would flower in the great literature that many of us hoped for. In his heart I think he felt that the United States would end as a still more infertile replica of Rome, a semi-barbarian empire, culturally weak, tutored by the English as the Romans had been tutored by the Greeks. But he enjoyed the stir of the expanding moment, using his own reviews in *The Freeman* to clear up critical problems that had been misunderstood, as he thought, by others. As a kind of partner in a publishing house, in his "European Library," he brought out books by Croce and his friend Gentile, by Remy de Gourmont and G. A. Borgese, with Goethe's literary essays and new Italian, German and Spanish novels. I spent many hours with him in his greenhouses and gardens or in the splendid library, with its casement windows and walls of books, that witnessed a sort of symposium now and then. I remember one of these on the pros and cons of censorship, though who the speakers were I cannot remember; but in *Aesthetics: a Dialogue* Lewis Mumford recorded another that took place in 1921. This was printed as a "Troutbeck Leaflet," one of a series of little brochures that Joel brought out from time to time with essays of E. A. Robinson, Sinclair Lewis, the poet G. E. Woodberry and two or three others. On this occasion Ernest Boyd, Joel, Lewis and I myself discussed our various ideas of criticism.

I do not connect Walter Pach with these conversazioni,— he spent few summers in the valley,—but I already knew him well and often went for walks with him at Troutbeck as in Greenwich Village and Westport later. Walter did not love the country as Joel and Lewis loved it,—he could never have written a book like *Green Memories,* for instance, in which Lewis poured out his affection for the rural scene; for he was a born metropolitan, a lover of city streets and sights who only put up with the country for the sake of the landscape. I think the greenness of the trees meant more to him than the trees themselves,—he had a special relish, as a painter, for green; and he built his little stone cottage at Brewster mainly to please Magda, who loved to paint the flowers she cultivated there. Magda, who had grown up in Dresden, a German of the heroic type, might have been a model for Dürer painting the Madonna, and Walter, a child of the Pach photographers who had invented the dry plate, had certain German characteristics also. He looked, with his drooping hussar's moustache, like a milder contemplative Nietzsche, and his astonishing saturation in the history of art and in art itself reminded one of a German professor of aesthetics. But his humour was American and at any moment he would drop into a broad Yankee manner of speech that savoured of the brothers Prendergast. He was full of anecdotes of his Western lecturing tours at the girls' college, for instance, where the students in a body petitioned the president to remove from their parlour a cast of the Venus de Milo because it aroused impure thoughts in the visiting boys. I wondered if some of the visiting boys had not become the novelists of whom we knew so many in our time and whose thoughts might have been obsessively impure because so many of the girls had been so prudish.

It was through Walter that I had met the Prendergasts when they were still living in New York, on the south side of Washington Square, a remnant of the old Knickerbocker town where Walter himself was to live in coming years. He and Magda told many tales about these childlike brothers, exquisite artists both and most lovable men, whom one day Magda promised a bowl of pea-soup and was then delayed in carrying it round to them. When she opened their door at last, she found them sitting at the board, each with a spoon upraised in a hopeful hand, like a pair of fledgling robins waiting in the nest, a scene that evoked for me the nature of these brothers, as idyllically unworldly as painting monks might be. All the stories that Charles told me after his elder brother's death recalled the fathomless innocence of this happy painter whom I always thought of, because of this trait and his beautiful feeling for colour, as a sort of Yankee Fra Angelico. Walter had recognized at once the quality of Maurice Prendergast, the first American artist to be aware of Cézanne, "old Paul," as Prendergast called him, regarding whom Walter himself had been one of the first Americans to write an essay.

In our time of discovery at home, Walter was one of the first, moreover, to appreciate the "grand provincial," Thomas Eakins, and he had persuaded the Louvre to buy one of the pictures that filled the painter's dark old Philadelphia house. He had known Eakins and, more intimately, Ryder, whom he had visited often in the cave in the slums where this visionary lived in his own dream-world, slowly emerging in the general mind, oblivious as he was to this, at the moment when Herman Melville was also emerging. In college I had never heard Melville mentioned, and although I had read him in California two or three years later many of my friends were unaware of him. He was not generally known, I think, before the South Seas became a vogue or before Raymond Weaver wrote his life. I remember that even quite late in the twenties, when Lewis Mumford undertook to write his biography of Melville, one of the granddaughters of the great man, who was later so helpful to students, was surprised that people were showing an interest in him. She had been aware of him only as a strange old soul whom no one had ever regarded as a person of importance,—"grim as a chimney when the house is gone," as Lewis wrote in one of his own poems; while now all the young looked at each other with a wild surmise as this new planet swam into their ken.

In the fiercely competitive world of the twenties, Walter never received his due as a missionary, so to put it, of the modern painting that was disjoined, as many thought, from the main body of art, which in its length and breadth he knew so fully. He was at home in all epochs and schools from the high days of Egypt, the Chinese, the Greeks, the Aztecs and the Mayans, and he saw no dichotomy between the work of any of them and that of the sculptors and painters he had encountered in Paris. In short, his deep sense of tradition involved an unwavering faith that his "masters of modern art" continued it, and it was with this belief that he played so large a role in choosing for the Armory Show the French sculptures and pictures. If, in the history of American art, this show was the great divide, he, more than anyone else, was responsible for it; for what could Arthur B. Davies have chosen to represent the new age in France if Walter had not for years been living there? He had known, really known, when they were still the wild beasts, Rouault, Braque, Derain, Brancusi, Picasso, and earlier still he had had long talks with Renoir and visited Claude Monet at Giverny. When only a handful of people at home were aware of the post-impressionists, he had steeped himself already in their work, and he had written about all these men, while Matisse had made a portrait etching of him. He, more than anyone else, contributed to select this work, which caused such a revolution in the New York art world at a time when American museums were filled with the pictures that Walter himself denounced in *Ananias, or the False Artist.*

Others, of course, wrote admirably about the modern art of which he knew so well the arterial structure, the nerves, the bones and the flesh as well as the soul; but what distinguished

Walter was the sense of continuity with which he understood
its heredity also. He was enchanted equally by the present and
the past, a feeling that he shared with some of the great art-
critics he knew, especially Roger Fry and Meier-Graefe, and
this enabled him to organize so finely the exhibition for the
World's Fair later. Meanwhile, he and Magda conducted the
annual Independents' show, and he responded early,—in 1922,
—to the intellectual ferment in Mexico City. There, for the first
time, he felt what Waldo Frank had felt, that the New World
was no longer an aspiration but an actual, spiritual and even
a visible fact, for New York seemed a mere prolongation of
London and Paris beside Mexico City in revolution. In Mexico,
as Walter felt and as he wrote to me, there was more new life
apparently than there was in Russia, and he sent me the
superb magazines that were symbols of the Mexican renaissance
in writing, painting, education, music and dancing. The Mexicans were restoring the old pyramids and temples of the pre-
Spanish autochthonous culture also. Walter made friends not
only with Alfonso Reyes and Juan Larrea, whom I was to meet
presently in New York, but with the great painters Orozco
and Diego Rivera whose work was something new under the
sun. Orozco, whose large pictures were still to come and who
was known at the time simply as the cartoonist of the revolution, regularly came to Walter's university classes, while, with
Siqueiros and Rivera, he was evolving a powerful, original,
indigenous Mexican style. No influence from the outside
seemed greatly to affect these painters, although Giotto and
obviously Cézanne had interested Rivera, whom one of Walter's letters had sent to Paris. Rivera had gone as a young man
to Madrid and a letter of Walter's to one of his friends begged
him not to waste time there since the whole contemporary
movement was across the French border. Fifteen years later, in

Mexico, Rivera told Walter how much he owed, he and his friend, to the phrases of an unknown man.

Both then and twenty years afterwards Walter delighted in Mexico, in the stir of the moment there, in the Aztec artifacts he brought back and in a certain monastery where he found sixteenth-century frescoes by a painter who had studied Michelangelo. "The old Mexicans, always intelligent, went to headquarters," he wrote to me, but their new school went nowhere, or virtually nowhere, and owed little to Italy, Spain or France. When, in the early thirties, Diego Rivera was in New York, painting for a down-town school a series of frescoes, I had a feeling, as I watched him working there, that was entirely new in my experience of painters. Walter's and my old friend John Sloan thought he was the greatest American painter and the only one who belonged with the old masters; but, while the scene took one back to some atelier of the Renaissance, there was something that had no precedent in the scene and the man. Crouching on the platform, smiling as he painted, he suggested a burlier Giotto at work on a fresco, but there was an element in him as far removed from the European as if he had been a Hindu or a Chinese; and this was the Mexican Indian note at a pitch that had never been known before and that seemed somehow profoundly American also. I was at that time planning my New England books, and I was struck by his masterly heads of Thoreau and Emerson of which he gave me photographs with cordial inscriptions. He seemed to know these characters by intuition. But he had also read them, for he was a great reader. Walter quoted to him a phrase from Milton's *Areopagitica* and Rivera took up the quotation and completed it in English.

It was to Walter that I owed my meeting with Rivera, and how many other occasions I had to be grateful to this friend who was always at leisure for walks, for talks, for letters. He had time for anyone who shared his own feeling for art, whether new work or the pictures that, as he once said to me, "We have known all our lives and never know." He liked to quote Renoir's remark to him when he had asked the great old man how best to become an artist,—"In the Museum!"—and I could scarcely count the times I was to visit museums with him, whether in New York or in Paris, first or last. It was in the Metropolitan, near which he had grown up and while he was copying there and still in the art school, that he had overheard William M. Chase describe Manet's "Boy with the Sword" as the only picture in the room that could be hung with the old masters. That was in the day when Bouguereau reigned still, before Duveen waved his wand over American collectors, and Walter, awakened, had gone to Spain in charge of Chase's pupils, painting himself and remaining in Europe to study. Jo Davidson, who was in Spain at the time, told me that one could pick up there even a large El Greco for fifty dollars. Jo himself had settled in France in the lovely old house on the river Indre from which he had come to London, where I first met him; and Walter too, living in Paris, had acquired, like Jo, an almost religious feeling for the art of the French. Jo never again could feel at home in the wooden New England villages that came to possess for me a special charm, while I always felt that, in his heart of hearts, Walter could not quite believe that a modern picture *not* French could be the real right thing. I mean it could not be "one of the supreme things," —Walter's own phrase,—and no doubt he was right for the hundred years since Delacroix and Ingres, true as it was that, in our own small world, he recognized so lovingly Copley and Eakins, Prendergast and Ryder. If one could single out any painters who were passions with him, they would be Ingres,

whose life he wrote, Delacroix, whom he translated, and Géri-
cault, of whom he owned two or three examples. He had two
Delacroix water-colours, and I remember a day when he stood
beside one for half an hour, never uttering twice a phrase or
a thought. With every word he revealed some new scrap of
meaning or fresh nuance, and I might have been a child hearing his first fairy-story. For such gifts of demonstration were
altogether new to me. Walter freely took his way through the
underground caverns that no one ever penetrates in the usual
art books.

I always supposed that Winckelmann was rather like Walter,
who might so easily have been himself the learned curator of
pictures and books at some eighteenth-century German grand-
ducal court. What made him so engaging was a constant sense
of the enchantment of art, a discriminating quiet excitement
that never lost its bloom, a feeling that if all men could share
his pleasure in these wonderfully beautiful things the world
would find itself redeemed from evil. He wrote me once to ask
if I knew Copley's letters, really surprising letters that he had
just found; then he wrote to say that I must see the pictures
of John Quidor, a forgotten New York painter who had come
to light. Did I know, moreover, the fine passage in *Don
Quixote* in which the Canon of Toledo discusses books? He
took me to see Joseph Brummer, the clairvoyant dealer, who
could touch in the dark any fragment of sculpture in basalt or
in marble and instantly tell you its provenance in Egypt or
Greece. Or in Burma, Roman Spain or Guatemala. Once
Walter repeated a remark of the daughter of his friend Elie
Faure, whose five-volume *History of Art* he translated, one
that pleased me because I had spent a good part of a week
trying to put into English one of Faure's essays. It was a long
paper for *The Freeman* about Charlie Chaplin, and there

were murky passages in both instalments that I could make neither head nor tail of. So I understood what Faure's daughter meant when she said, "O Papa, I've read such good news in the paper. Elie Faure's books are going to be translated into French."

But, to go back to Troutbeck and the hamlet of ten houses that sheltered in the twenties so many of our friends, I was to know it well for many years to come, sometimes visiting the Spingarns, sometimes the Mumfords. Lewis would come out early for the spring planting, for, with his broccoli, lettuce and beets, he was never more himself there than when he was delving in the earth. He was a lover of lilacs too and the Mackintosh apples in his orchard on a warm September afternoon; and he was a great walker in the woods looking for the first hepatica, the first ripe wild strawberries and the first bloodroot. With Sophy and Geddes, the little boy who was named for the Scottish philosopher, Lewis's own master before the twenties, he noted the first mild night when the frogs burst forth in spring and the day when the red-winged blackbird first rose from the swamp. All three paid daily visits to the buckeye tree to watch its great candles unfolding, and they were to know the year-round span of country life when they spent winters also in the valley. Lewis's deep feeling for the rural scene explained his defence of regionalism against the encroachments of the city,—against the megalopolitan view of life,—as it also explained his understanding of the world of Emerson and Thoreau which, in *The Golden Day,* he presented so finely. Never sharing my negative views of certain of our old writers, he had seen three or four as true world figures, anticipating D. H. Lawrence's notion of them as going in some ways further than any Europeans.

Of all my writing contemporaries, Lewis Mumford was

always the one with whom I felt most sympathetic and closely allied, and from the moment I fell in with him he took for me the place that Randolph Bourne's death had left vacant. I had a fraternal feeling for him that steadily grew with the years, and I connected this with a remark of William James in a letter to his friend Josiah Royce: "In converse with you I have always felt that my life was being lived importantly." It was not that he flattered my vanity,—quite the reverse,—but that in certain respects he enhanced my life, for, sharing some of my beliefs, he so expressed them in his own way that they came back to me with redoubled value. There was nothing of my own thought in his, and his interests were different from mine,—he lived in many worlds I scarcely entered; but there was much in his feeling for life that raised my own to a higher power and the consciousness that he existed nourished me. His monolithic integrity excited and touched me, his gift of keeping life essentially simple, his savage indignation, so rare in our fatalistic time, even his ability to loaf and invite the soul. For, unhasting and unresting, he had this in common with the sages of Diogenes Laertius and our own Walden. Then he had the qualities that Burckhardt called the outstanding traits of all great men,—plenitude and single-mindedness,—with the Palagian optimism that was our one great tradition, summed up in the maxim, "If I ought, I can." In a time that was more and more oppressed with a sense of the vanity of the human will, he was constantly aware of our still untapped resources; his key-word was always "renewal"; and, with all his feeling for the past, he cared less for what *has been* than for what *may be.* Lewis was one of the few men who have not *ideas* but *an idea,* and he was to spend his life working this out.

When I first met him in 1920, he had just returned from

London in the spirit of so many others of my generation who
had been, as it were, converted to the idea of a life at home
after living, or wishing to live, in England or Europe. Lewis
himself often said that by natural sympathy and education
he somehow felt closer to the men of my time than to his own
contemporaries who were ten years younger, the leaders of the
lost generation, disillusioned romantics like Wilson, Fitzgerald,
Dos Passos, Hemingway and Cummings. Actually of the age
of these, he had matured in the confident years, the so-called
innocent years of the pre-war epoch when soldiers were only
tin soldiers, as he said in a letter,—with a liking for brass buttons, music and drums,—and it was his distinction never to lose
their confidence and hope while fully sharing the later consciousness of evil. He had caught in England the last rays of
the morning glow of William Morris's poetic socialism, and he
was to remain a vitalist in a world of mechanists, behaviourists,
determinists, Marxians and so on. In London, still virtually
a boy, he had been managing editor of the *Sociological Review*, and Patrick Geddes, the Scots town planner, urged
Lewis to go to Palestine and plan the new Jerusalem with him
there. Lewis, convinced that "old stocks may rove" while "pioneers must settle down," thanked Geddes for a thousand
thoughts to be tended and developed, but said he must set
them out in an American garden, and, returning to America,
he began walking through the streets and planning with a
new purpose excursions beyond them. Geddes, of whom I myself had a glimpse later in New York,—in a restaurant near the
New School, at a table in a corner,—had shown Lewis how to
interpret cities, their place in civilization, their origins, their
growth, their import for human living. Looking into the past,
examining the present and sketching a future for the general
scene that would best serve the interests of human renewal,

Lewis, whose first book had been *The Story of Utopias,* studied city planning and architecture. He had been interested in housing and he had made friends with community planners, architects, geographers, engineers. Lewis had begun with the human setting before he went on to explore education, aesthetics, ethics and the conduct of life, but, starting with the body of civilization, he was concerned with this only as the outward and visible garment of its heart and soul.

Like Randolph Bourne before him, Lewis was a capital letter-writer, one of the few in a period when novelists and poets were sometimes known never to write letters at all. Like Bourne again, he fought against the cultural humility that had led us to ignore the American past, beginning with what he once described as the pathless waste of our architecture before he wrote *Sticks and Stones* in 1924. In this he revived much that was unknown or forgotten, and he taught thousands to look at banks and at business buildings and railroad stations who had never given these a glance before. It had not occurred to them that such things could be architecture, and Lewis opened a large field here when others were discovering American antiques, American primitives, American folk art and so on. It was he who made household words of the names of Roebling of the Brooklyn Bridge, Richardson, Louis Sullivan and Frank Lloyd Wright, of whom he wrote so admirably in *The South in Architecture, From the Ground Up* and other books. Only when he had written of them did we fully realize that America had native master-builders, and one read these books with some of the excitement that people had found in Audubon's birds or Asa Gray's discovery of the American flora.

In *The Brown Decades,* moreover, Lewis discovered the generation just before our own, a period so close to ourselves that we had never seen it, as he discovered much of the present

in the yearbook that he edited with Paul Rosenfeld, Alfred
Kreymborg and, briefly, myself. I mean the present of the
twenties and thirties that appeared in *The American Caravan,*
a publication which first brought out many writers, at the
time unknown, solitary, stranded and what not, who were
famous later. For Lewis, like William James, whom he admired,
was always in touch with the young and followed them sympathetically through decade after decade, understanding their
spiritual plight after two world wars that virtually destroyed
their faith in the future of man. Born as he said he had been
himself into the cocky pre-war world, he fully realized nevertheless why the young became so grave while only the old, in
the later time, were giddy. He knew that the optimists of the
machine had forgotten that there was madness and night and
that mankind had mystery to contend with, coëxisting with
universal literacy, science and daylight, and why, because they
ignored the darker side of the nature of man, they had been
unprepared for the catastrophe that followed. He could see
why it was that a grimly senescent youth confronted the still
youthful senescents of the older generation, and having, along
with Emerson and Whitman, read Pascal and Saint Augustine,
he was fully able to enter their state of mind. Writers like
Melville and Dostoievsky, with their sense of the presence
of evil, had fitted him to grasp the post-war scene, the disintegrated world in which humankind, convinced of its inade-
quacy, ceased to believe in its own powers of self-renewal.

No one else whom I knew was more aware than Lewis of
all that was dark and tragic in the post-war time, and what
made him unique was that, understanding this, he retained the
energy and faith of the time before it. He kept, in a broken
world, the sense of wholeness, and he had none of the fatalism
of so many younger minds under the mounting threat of atomic

destruction. The notion of destruction involved for him the notion of renewal, disintegration implied reintegration, and what concerned him chiefly was to "create soil again" in a civilization "denuded to the bare rock." For him the resources of humankind were still inexhaustible, requiring only the sense of a new purpose and direction; and, with his feeling for the inner life, he was convinced that the problem of our time was to restore the lost respect for this. For Western man had forgotten it in his concentration on the improvement of the machine. In a world obsessed with determinism, the human person must come back to the centre of the stage, he said, as actor and hero, summoning the forces of life to take part in a new drama; and he saw signs of the approach of spring and a deeper faith for living in the dark winter of the present.

I am speaking here of the forties and fifties, but all this might have been seen already in the Lewis I had known twenty years before.

CHAPTER XI

THIRTY AGAINST AMERICA

IT WAS during the early nineteen-twenties that the word "expatriate" came into play,—although there was nothing new in expatriation,—a word that suggested in later times the flight of young writers from the country of which they felt that they were the *avant-garde*. (Another word that savoured of the moment.) Anywhere, anywhere out of the world, out of the dull American world, was a general cry among those who had returned from the war and who wished never to go back to the Tilbury Towns of their childhood, the Winesburgs, the Spoon Rivers or the Gopher Prairies. In one publishing house or another I had read a manuscript every day by some young person born in some such town who felt that he was too sensitive for these crude surroundings and who said good-bye to Wisconsin, Ohio or Kansas. One and all were obsessed with the problem of the artist in America,—"ever an outcast, a pariah," Henry Miller said,—and with what they considered the sterility of the American scene; and they usually agreed with Samuel Butler that America was "the last place" in which life was "endurable at all for an inspired writer."

There were those who were drawn to the primitive, to the islands that attracted my brother-in-law, especially at this moment when the fame of Melville had just begun to rise in the general mind. For others, like Carl van Vechten, the

Harlem of the Negroes had a similar charm; and there was William Seabrook, who said he had always been running away to deserts and to voodoo temples and to jungles. A few set out for Mexico, John Reed, for instance, for a while, and Katharine Anne Porter, who was writing stories, at a time when Mexican furniture and glass were spreading across the Rio Grande and Mexican art was rising with Rivera and Orozco. Like many another, John Sloan pitched a new tent in Santa Fe. "What a marvellous place the Southwest is for the New Yorker to fall upon," Waldo Frank had written in one of his letters, "with its double layer of Indian and Hispanic cultures, lying there, rotting and rich under the low sun." Waldo had found in the sacred Kiva to which he was admitted "a great incentive to new vision and stronger wisdom"; and in the Indian ceremonials many discovered something real they had never felt in the rituals and ceremonials of home. Near by, at Taos, Mabel Dodge, rejecting "the false new America in the East," traced the "true" America in "the Indian blood stream," while D. H. Lawrence, escaping from a Europe to which so many were eager to go, exclaimed, "To your tents, O America. Listen to your own." He too meant by "your own" the dusky red men.

It was to Europe, and mainly to Paris, that most were determined to find their way, oddly enough in the spirit of Montaigne when he said he had also gone abroad "from a lack of relation to the present conditions of our country." An English visitor in New York remarked to a friend of mine that he could not understand this general hegira: the young Americans whom he saw seemed to be always asking him if he knew of any job they could get in Europe. Why were so many young men swarming to France? A vigorous nation sending its best to a dying civilization, youth rushing to live with senility, —how did this happen? Albert Nock, who had lived in Europe quietly for many years, explained the stampede as part of the "desperation" that characterized young writers during these years, a strange spirit that seemed to rest on a whole generation of young men who were apparently bent on self-destruction. They all reminded him of Turgenev's Misha, generous and truthful, not depraved but wretchedly dissatisfied and giving themselves up, unhappy as they were, for "lost." Regarding this generation, Nock used the same word as Gertrude Stein, of whom he knew nothing at the moment; nor was he aware that this desperation was to give rise to the religion of art that was to thrive in the twenties, especially in Paris. For when so much had been swept away that had made life worth living,— the faith in human goodness, security, tradition,—art, form, colour, craftsmanship was something to cling to, something solid and real in a world of ruin. So it was no wonder, in this feverish decade, that good writing flourished like a prairie fire in a high wind. Meanwhile, as one of the young men said, "There is something the matter with a culture whose youth is eager to desert it . . . Rebellious youth is not wanted here, the imaginative and adventurous and artistically creative"; and he asked, in *The Freeman*, "What can a young man do?"

As Ezra Pound said later, most of these young men left "in disgust," not in the mood of the earlier seekers of culture; and the most talked about of the exiles of 1921 was the writer of this manifesto, Harold Stearns. Only a few months before, I had worked with him and a group of our friends, in Jones Street in Greenwich Village, on the symposium, *Civilization in the United States*, discussing various aspects of American culture. Nock must have had Harold Stearns in mind when he spoke of François Villon as one of the prototypes of the lost generation, for there was an element in Harold Stearns of the mediæval vagabond student who is known, in contemporary parlance, as the literary bum. As everyone knew, he figured soon in *The Sun Also Rises* as the "small, heavy, slow" Harvey Stone who seemed to be always sitting outside the Dôme or the Rotonde with a pile of saucers in front of him, needing a shave. Then, having had "nothing to eat for five days," he would reappear and "go off like a cat . . . pretty sad," a tale he told in his autobiography in which he said the wind always "blew coldest down the street I know." Hemingway bought clothes for him and the ever-to-be-blessed Jo Davidson found a job for him on the Paris *Herald,* while, longing to write about Rabelais the book that Nock actually wrote, he turned out racing stories for sporting papers. For he shared Sherwood Anderson's feeling for horses and the race-track. He wrote to me, "I do not expect ever to come back. I'm leaving Paris when they carry me out"; and he also wrote, "You know for some reason I gather myths about myself as easily as a snowball gathers snow rolling down a hill." In fact, he lived almost to become a myth, "broke and bitter, poor and alone," as he said in *The Street I Know,* "without a friend or a woman to keep me," sleeping on benches on the boulevards in a Paris that became for him, like his New York, a city of dreadful night. At the moment, George Orwell too was down and out there.

Thirteen years were to pass before Harold Stearns came home again, like Melville's Israel Potter, a stranger in a strange land, without clothes or a trunk or a dime, without so much as a packet of cigarettes. Meanwhile, others with happier fortunes turned Montparnasse into a sort of transplanted Greenwich Village, sometimes discovering a talent in themselves with which to return to a native scene that was little to their taste but that usually obsessed them. For, expatriates as they might be, they almost invariably wrote about the "half savage country, out of date," to which Ezra Pound referred in his finest

poem, and they were "always attempting to formulate an attitude toward life in the United States," like the hero of
Edmund Wilson's *I Thought of Daisy*. "Discovering" or "rediscovering" America might have been called their métier at this
time when even an essay on Alfred Stieglitz began with a
psychological history of the country and when the discussion of
any theme seemed to involve first or last a new theory of America, the American character or what not. They were as full of
their country as the Spaniards were of Spain or as the Poles
were of the "Polish question," while their great aim was to
escape from the "moral obligation to be optimistic" and from
"Protestant morality" and "success" in American terms. "What
do you think of Mencken?" was a universal question; and,
knowing little of the past of American writing, they were not
interested in the past of Europe either. They had seldom read
any American books but *Moby-Dick* and *Huckleberry Finn*.
Rejecting English writers almost by instinct, as a matter of
course,—the English who had overawed their predecessors,—
they read the Russian novelists and especially the French, and,
among these, particularly, Flaubert. For Flaubert shared their
contempt for the philistines and the business men of whom
they had seen too much at home.

Well I had known, a few years before, in Paris but mainly
in London, that old excitement, for Americans, of the European scene which all but suggested the sensation of life as
somehow multiplied tenfold that epileptics experience before
their attacks. It was easy to understand the mood of the new-
comers in Paris "where everybody felt at home," as one of
them said, a *patrie* of the imagination that preëxisted in the
memory as it were and as even Jefferson and Franklin might
have felt. Vincent Sheean, who said this, remarked that his
voyage thither had been like the voyage of the "Santa Maria" in

reverse,—the correspondent whose distinction was that he could feel as history the events he was living and observing. Like others from the Middle West who made literary history in Paris, Sheean seemed to have been born a man of the world, and this was a note that characterized the new men who were so unlike the consciously provincial men of old. The exiles of the twenties were prepared to believe the asseveration of Gertrude Stein that Americans were "creating" the new century which the English were "refusing,"—because the twentieth century was "too many" for the English,—a statement that Ezra Pound confirmed when he claimed for Americans virtually all the twentieth-century developments in English verse.

Meanwhile, for American writers, there had never been a time and place so favourable to literary growth,—that is to say, to their technical growth, to the rise of the artist in them,—at a time when artists were looked upon as heroes. For in that nihilistic air the reverence that religion had once absorbed was redirected towards artists, who were regarded as saints, the craftsmen who had maintained their integrity, who had remained inviolate in a world that seemed to be generally tumbling to pieces. There had never been anything quite like the feeling that came to invest for a long generation the literary heroes Mallarmé, Flaubert, Proust, Joyce, Henry James and a few others,—the literary martyrology of the post-war epoch,—a reverence that aroused in the young a spirit of emulation such as real saints have aroused in ages of faith. In a Paris, moreover, where art itself was actively present in the general mind and where every café table and hotel bedroom brought back the name of some great writer, they found exciting teachers in the art of writing who were devoted to the problems of literary form. Beyond even Pound and Gertrude Stein, there was Ford Madox Ford, an Englishman who had found for himself that "to be in touch with youth" was a necessity if he was to write. Ford, temperamentally drawn to the literary army from the Middle West and fully conscious of the stirring of aesthetic life there, felt that the next great literary movement had been predestined to come from there because it had been scarcely touched by the world war. It was the one great tract in the Western world that was still virgin soil for the literary spirit.

Together with the problems of literary art, the art of living was paramount in most of these disaffected American minds, and, constantly comparing the scenes they remembered with all they found in Paris, they could not contain their scorn of the world at home. They were generally convinced that Mencken was right in picturing the United States as a fool's country of boobery and buncombe, and they censured virtually everything in the land they had come from, while, as a rule, they continued to write about it. They "disposed of California scenery," as Sinclair Lewis's Dodsworth said, after he had listened to their talk at café tables, of "the institution of marriage" as well, "Whistler, corn fritters and President Wilson," along with "the use of catsup" and "cement roads." They denounced the tradesmen at home who made soap and motor-cars "instead of collecting old lace," as Dodsworth put it, while they checked up their own profitable holdings in soap and motor-cars, the holdings that enabled them to be "so disposive." There was in fact another way of looking at many American things, and European things also, as others were to feel, when many of the complaints of the twenties came to seem foolish. But it was still more foolish later to condemn the rebels of that day, considering how much of their folly proved to be tonic.

What, later, called for an explanation was the strange unanimity with which a whole generation turned against the country, or at least a large part of the generation that had experi-

enced the first world war, with a few who had begun to write
before it. For in this fruit of the *zeitgeist*, in this general dispraise of the "American way," there was nothing conspiratorial,
there was no collusion, or even, aside from the group who
wrote *Civilization in the United States*, no round-up for the
purpose of talking it over. Yet novelists and poets, playwrights
and critics from every corner of the country seemed to see
mainly the negative in the "jungle," in the "maelstrom," in
the complacent, the uniquely dull, the money-ridden land they
knew, the only land, they felt, in which artists were flouted.
They were like the Russian nihilists of old who, in their time
of negation, found scarcely anything worth saving in their
country and who said, "What can be broken, we shall break.
Smash right and left,"—the final word in the Russian camp
of the young. All this coincided with certain special influences
that played on the literary mind towards the close of the war,
Mark Twain's *The Mysterious Stranger*, for instance, published in 1916, and Adams's *Education*, two years later. Mark
Twain had seen life as meaningless and Adams predisposed
the young to feel that democracy in America was a failure,
while the return of the expatriates from Paris, drifting back
one by one, bred still more furious outcries of comparison and
censure. Those who had lived in the most beautiful of cities,
with so much that pleased the sensual man, together with so
much exposed surface of the human, were convinced that the
ugly town was an American invention, and they saw everywhere spiritual poverty, intellectual anæmia, universities that
looked like shoe factories and a cowardly press.

Repatriated, in other words, the expatriates on the whole
agreed with the "Thirty Against America" who had remained
at home,—a phrase of the old novelist Henry B. Fuller for the
short-lived assemblage of minds from which had sprung *Civili-*

zation in the United States. For, while these were by no means condemnatory merely, or of one mood or point of view, they were inclined to accept the belief of Robert Herrick, Fuller's friend, that ours was the "least lovely" of civilizations. Just before what Harold Stearns later described as his "flight from reality," he had proposed to me, then to Lewis Mumford and finally to Spingarn, Mencken, Ring Lardner and others, a critical survey of American life in virtually every aspect, sport, science, philosophy, poetry, painting and so on. Stearns, who had been living in Greenwich Village since he had left Harvard, where his chosen teacher had been Santayana, was a quintessential Villager who had edited the old fortnightly *Dial* and haunted the Liberal Club and Boni's bookshop. First or last, he had fallen in with most of the writers he drew into this group, Walter Pach, Conrad Aiken, Robert Morss Lovett, —along with those whom I have already mentioned,—Hendrik van Loon, who was living in the Village, Frank Moore Colby, the essayist, Deems Taylor, Elsie Clews Parsons and George Jean Nathan. Another was John Macy, who had married the teacher of Helen Keller and with whom I worked for some months on *The Freeman,* one of the precursors of the critical movement of the twenties. Among the others were Ernest Boyd, who wrote *As an Irishman Sees It,* and Henry Longan Stuart, our Westport friend.

There were few actual meetings of these rebel intellectuals, so called, who were at the same time both bitter and hopeful and who felt that things American were almost always wrong but that there were usually cures for the unlovely and the evil. They were against a social life that seemed emotionally and aesthetically starved as well as against "reaction," the common foe,—the quality and spirit of a business civilization,—against "efficiency," "pecuniary standards" and those who, as Sinclair

Lewis said, made Patrick Henry orations about windshield-wipers. They disliked "Americanitis," the disease of high tension, and they were inclined on the whole to feel with Theodore Dreiser that America was the land of Bottom the Weaver. No doubt they were rather more aware of what they were against than of what they were for; and they were sometimes inaccurate and ignorant, as Bernard De Voto remarked when the climate of opinion changed a few years later. Then it seemed scarcely credible that, as Harold Stearns said, it was next to impossible to get anyone to write about religion. No one could be induced to grapple with a subject that was to become in time almost an obsession.

Perhaps the general negativism of which these essays were a type had certain harmful effects on the coming generation, destroying all confidence in a country that was, after all, the writers' own but that came to be regarded, so often, with scorn. Separated as most of the essayists were from any strong sense of the popular life, they seemed to have little affection for the world they lived in, and some of them showed the Dadaistic influence and the spirit of contempt and futility to which this gave birth. They criticized America by comparing it with Europe, which it never occurred to them to criticize at all, differing in this from Emerson who, having Asia always in mind, surveyed from a great height all the Western cultures. Perhaps it was childish not to see many of the faults of America as a natural result of the feverish growth of the country, along with the immigration that Waldo Frank described as a "chaos of dissolved ethnic cultures." But this undertaking was part of the movement of national self-examination that was involved in our general coming-of-age, while the constant discussion of literary problems made American literature, for the first time, seem really important. In earlier days both Whitman and

Howells had vainly tried to make it so, but too many influences in the country had pointed back to Europe.

Always a symbol, Harold Stearns was more than ever one when he "re-affirmed" America in still another book, reappearing as "a ghost of a generation that has gone" who had found that "after all, a real world exists here." That was at a time when, as Albert Nock said, the trouble in Europe turned one's thoughts "with something almost like tolerance" to this country. With the rise of the Nazi-Fascists, this reversal of feeling was characteristic of many a censorious mind of earlier days, for, with all its abuses, our prosaic republic seemed curiously inculpable beside Mussolini's Italy or Germany or Spain. When had it ever seen anything like the venomous tribal race-hatreds of Europe or the governmental hooliganism or the wholesale bestialities that marked these great civilized nations we admired so much? But that was in the thirties when George Grosz, the painter, coming to New York, found there a "healthier, freer, happier" world than anything he had known in the boiling caldron, the Europe, with its heavy air of oncoming events, he described in *A Little Yes and a Big No*. In the twenties there were few young Americans, few, at least, whom I knew, who felt as many were to feel a decade later.

CHAPTER XII

MY BOOKS

D URING THESE years I was possessed by the notion that
American writers were, for whatever reasons, foredoomed
to fail, a notion that others shared no doubt and that was
taken up later by the novelists Ernest Hemingway and Scott
Fitzgerald. For when Fitzgerald said, "There are no second
acts in American lives," he was repeating in other words Hemingway's remark, "Something happens to our good writers at
a certain age. We destroy them in many ways." What was this
"something" that happened and how could one explain the
obvious miscarriage of many American talents, so that our
literature seemed to me, in the phrase of D. H. Lawrence, "a
disarray of falling stars coming to naught"? Since the high days
of New England only a handful of writers had fully coined the
metal in themselves, as Hawthorne and Emerson had done,
Thoreau and Parkman, while countless others had failed to
grow for want of self-knowledge, perhaps, or was it some lack
in the native soil and air? Our literary world was a kind of
limbo, as it seemed to me, where the wraiths of writers were
blown hither and thither, abortive or, like Henry Adams and
so many others, neglected, and often developing in strange
and monstrous ways.

I had long been full of this idea when I wrote *The Ordeal*

of Mark Twain at Carmel in 1918 and 1919; and the theme was discussed for several years by others who saw that our writers were constantly breaking down or cracking up. They "sold out" or they fizzled out "after looking gigantic at first," as John Hyde Preston was to put it, when they reached early middle age and the light seemed to go out in them and they fell into ruts and formulas or ceased to write. As Mrs. Lightfoot Lee had said in Adams's *Democracy*, they grew six inches high and then they stopped, and even in our more vital time when literary talent abounded we were to see this happen often enough. Was not *The Crack-Up* soon to show how Scott Fitzgerald lost his way, aware that he had not fulfilled his promise?—and there was Sherwood Anderson, who missed the target so many times, producing, after all, so few successes. He knew he had entered too many blind alleys, neglecting his proper gift, following false leads, distracted from his main purpose, knowing himself so little as to think that he could write plays while he was haunted by thoughts of artistic failure. Something like this, it seemed to me, was, with American writers, rather more the rule than the exception,—as one looked back from about 1920,—and I wondered how far one could blame for this the famous provincial conditions that Henry James had bewailed in the story of his youth. How far had they been "visibly killed by the lack of air to breathe," as Santayana said of the young poets who had been his friends? In point of self-knowledge, in any case, and the power of self-development, our writers could seldom compare with the writers of England, who knew so well what they were fitted to do and how to go about it and were able to make so much more of themselves and their gifts. Because of this difference we had few indeed to set beside Shaw, Wells, W. H. Hudson, Kipling, Bennett, Chesterton, George Moore or Yeats.

I was all the more concerned with this because the writer seemed to me so vitally important to society as well as to the reader, full as I was of the ideas not only of Emerson and Whitman but of many of the great modern European writers. For ever since I had turned away from the history of art to literature I had been a voracious reader of the "lives of the poets,"—to use the word in its Crocean sense. I read them as eagerly as a monk reads the lives of the saints,—"to become used to good models," as Nietzsche put it,—and Tolstoy, Chekhov, Dostoievsky, Flaubert and many another confirmed my serious notion of the writer's role. Like Ibsen, for whom literature had its redemptive aspect, Leopardi said that "in literature alone the regeneration of our country can have a substantial beginning," and I had conceived a sort of composite mental picture of the great writer as he might and should be. I thought of him as one who made the fullest use of his own powers and added a new dimension to the world about him; for to me the great writer was not only the voice of his people and his time but one who, in Berenson's phrase, enhanced their life. This implied an organic relation between the writer and his world, and it also implied that if he was to "regenerate" or "redeem" this world he must impose upon it his own values. To accept the values of his world, to adapt himself to his environment, would be to fall short of the model in a fatal fashion, and one would fall short equally if one lost touch with one's natural world, for, that being so, how could one work upon it?

Of course, I am rationalizing here the inner logic of a case that I saw only emotionally during these years, and I do not remember at what point I saw it in these terms, although for a good part of a decade it really obsessed me. It was the case that embodied itself in a biographical trilogy,—two "cautionary" studies and one "exemplary" study,—after my "thesis" in *Mark Twain,* and my "antithesis" in *Henry James,* led, in a *Life of Emerson,* to the "synthesis" of Hegel. In this last I hoped to produce the image of a literary model, a whole and central figure, in American terms, an aim in which I was predestined to fail if only because Emerson's world was too remote from the modern American scene. In this threefold portrait, as it were, of the writer in America I meant to touch all the main aspects of our literary life, its characteristic problems and the typical ways in which it failed, together with the true nature of the writer's success. The work throughout was intended to be emblematic, but I was obliged to feel in the end how partial had been my own success in attempting to canvass in this way so multiform a subject. Regarding the problems of our literary life, Emerson had been resourceful and wise beyond any other American of the present or the past, for no other had thrown so much light on the natural history of the writer and the art of conserving, developing and expending his powers. This was a subject about which I never ceased to think, and as, year after year, I saw our writers stumbling about in the dark, failing in the same old ways or giving up the fight, I wondered why American critics remained so incurious about it, indifferent as they seemed to everything but technical questions.

My *Life of Emerson* was a sort of imputed autobiography, written to a large extent in Emerson's own words, while the other two were psychoanalytic, more or less, and consequently bound to result in distortion. For this method reduces a person to a type, a congeries of inhibitions, complexes and what not, in place of the individual in his concrete fullness, and, in *The Ordeal of Mark Twain,* my over-concern with psychology left no room for literary appreciation. Or, for that matter, human appreciation either. Sherwood Anderson, who was bent on "selling" me "Twain," as he put it, feeling that I did not properly understand him, showed me, when the book was published, where I had fallen short,—I should have sung the praises of *Huckleberry Finn*. Many years later, in New York, when we were dining together under a portrait of Mark Twain in a semi-public room, Sherwood, glancing up at this, said, "There was a lovely man,"—and that was indeed one way of looking at him. He was perhaps more centrally the champion of justice, the hater of shams and the generous lovable genius than the man I had pictured, as Mark Twain's humour had a positive value that I had all but entirely failed to suggest. Then, if he was money-mad, so was Balzac; and how could one speak of failure in connection with a writer who was the most successful of his time, if only because he had written one great book? Later, when I studied Mark Twain again for my literary history, I was to see all these objections clearly, yet I still felt he had made the great refusal and that *The Ordeal of Mark Twain* was substantially just. I remembered how I had put it together as one puts together a picture-puzzle in which every fragment has its inevitable place, and I had not consciously invented the picture,—it sprang for me out of the evidence with almost the natural force of a revelation. I did not see how one could shake the logic of the book.

What was I presenting? Perhaps only half of the real Mark Twain but certainly much, if not the whole, of a well-known abstract character, the typical American author as we knew him at the moment. Sinclair Lewis suggested that I should write another book applying to living authors the verdict of this one. Mentioning names we all knew, he wished me to show how certain talents, apparent at the outset, turned into "dreary machines," whether because of some magazine policy, money or good-fellow friends, or "general Americanitis,"—what was the reason? All American writers knew the pressures of a business civilization, almost all had been urged to go into business, and I had stated the obvious fact that they could not conform to such a world if they were to open new horizons for it. Yet they seemed eager to conform, they did not wish to be "different," and, as if to make amends for the difference they could not escape, they often pretended that they were in business. Or, ashamed of being writers, they gave themselves out in Jack London's way as proprietors of hygienic pigsties or prosperous farmers. Jack London himself had written to Waldo Frank at *The Seven Arts*, saying that if such a magazine had existed twenty years before he would not have turned out his "pap of pretty lies." At authors' dinners I had watched the heavy-jowled nabobs of our magazine world gazing at some visiting writer from across the ocean, some spare, withdrawn soul who had lived perhaps on bread and cheese while he had kept the zest for spiritual adventure. How humble one could see they felt before that image of contemptuous pride, that emblem of literary power. No doubt the chief reason for their failure to grow was that, in this country, the literary tradition was not clear or strong, so that they were never properly aware of the vocation in which the writer finds his real rewards.

So much for the question of "adaptation." The main alternative had always been flight, and this fact had given birth to "the classic debate of American culture, Should an American artist stay at home?" (I am quoting Waldo Frank's *In the American Jungle*.) This I had set out to study in the case of Henry James, the greatest of all the American expatriates or exiles. It seemed to me obvious that "something went wrong with his development," as one of his English admirers, F. R. Leavis, was to observe in time in *The Great Tradition*. Following somewhat the same line that I had taken years before, this critic rejected as "bad" or "not successful" the three long later novels of Henry James, *The Ambassadors, The Golden Bowl* and *The Wings of the Dove*, adding that the famous Prefaces were "not merely difficult but unrewarding," while he took one back to this writer's "happiest" phase. He described *The Bostonians* and *The Portrait of a Lady* as "the two most brilliant novels in the language," saying that, with them and with *Washington Square* and other novels of their time, James's genius functioned at its "freest and fullest." Then what Dr. Leavis called the "hypertrophy of technique" set in and we had the indirections and subtleties of James's decline.

This was precisely what I had said in *The Pilgrimage of Henry James,* although, as it happened, Dr. Leavis, agreeing with my verdict, disagreed with my explanation of it. Yet it seemed to me equally obvious that James, as his brother William said, had lost touch with the "vital facts of human character," and this was because he had lost touch with the people whom he understood, his fellow-Americans either at home or in Europe. In short, he had "forfeited" the "precious advantage in ceasing to tread his native soil" that James imputed to Hawthorne just at the moment when he also said of Turgenev, regarding this matter of the "native soil," that "all great novelists savour strongly of it." He had also said it was dangerous for a novelist "to project himself into an atmosphere in which he has not a transmitted and inherited property"; and was it not evident that he himself failed to assimilate, as a novelist should, the English world that he had set out to conquer? Why, otherwise, after a few attempts to write as an English novelist, did he revert to the abandoned American themes, to the "international subject" that had long since "faded" from his mind, as he had said so emphatically years before?

Of course, all this was to mean little to the critics of a later time for whom indirectness and "difficulty" were positive values, who cared nothing for "character," the "air of reality" or the "solidity of specification" that James himself had called the "supreme virtues" of fiction. They loved his "crooked corridors" in the face of Tolstoy, who wished to get "at once down to business" when he began the greatest of the world's novels, and they were not dissatisfied with James's ghost-like presences floating in a void, shadow-like passionless women and fish-blooded men. It meant little to them that his later fictions were like cobwebs, as Somerset Maugham remarked, "which at any moment the housemaid's broom with brutal common sense may sweep away," for the formalist critics, unconcerned with literature in its relation to life, cared for problems of texture and structure only. But as, more and more, with the passing of time, they dominated the critical world, I questioned, as Whitman had done, these "professional elects," feeling that people of ripe heart and mind who know the world as they know life are always the ultimate judges of the value of novels. (In that sense, Sir Desmond MacCarthy was undoubtedly right when he said, "The public is the critic.") As I knew these people, they usually agreed with William James, who wrote to his brother that "the *core* of literature is solid," and who remarked to another correspondent, "I for one am no longer able to read a word that he [Henry] writes." Yet who was more interested than William James in every phase of real life and in every novel that gave one a feeling for it? He was not a Philistine, as the lovers of Henry James implied when they were obliged to face this condemnation.

So I might have felt sure that I was right in the general estimate of James's work that Dr. Leavis confirmed a few years later, and it struck me as an interesting fact that five novelists wrote to me to say that they agreed with my conclusions. They were all writers of integrity of the older generation who had attempted themselves to novelize the country and who might have been supposed to wish that Henry James had failed when he himself gave up the attempt to do so. But I do not think this was the motive that turned them against his later work, as John Jay Chapman rejected James altogether, saying, "I am so out of sympathy with his temperament that I have never read him, but I read your book . . . muttering all the time that the vaporous subject was not worth" the treatment, "yet feeling it was all true." What Chapman called James's vaporousness was the general objection, and to Ellen Glasgow, who had met him in London several times, James, so unlike Hardy, "seemed to ring hollow." It shocked Robert Herrick, for the rest, that James denatured his early work when he rewrote the conversations in it, when his Christopher Newmans and Longmores ceased to be their American selves and generally spoke in the later Jamesian manner. Aside from this, Herrick was repelled by the "pathetic provincialism" of Henry James's relation to the world he had adopted. He had corrected this young man for addressing him as "Mr. James," saying, "Only butlers do that, my dear Herrick."

With so much corroboration, my mind should have been at rest, I should have felt that for me the case was settled, especially when so many others felt as I did, when, for one, AE, challenging James's false air of profundity, said that he "made intricacies in the shallows." Then there was Paul Elmer More, who, praising Anthony Trollope, spoke of the "endless chatter" of the later Henry James, together with his "tangled sleave of oblique suggestions,"—all of which justified my regret that James had been taken as a model by many beginning novelists in this country. For was he not inevitably sterilizing as an in-

fluence on others? He warned them away from more congru-
ous models like Tolstoy or Dostoievsky, whom he called "baggy
monsters" or "mere fluid puddings," and, imposing upon them
his own "right" form, he kept them from finding their own
form, which ought to have sprung out of their subject-matter.
Moreover, he induced in them a kind of literary opiumism in
which the realities of character ceased to matter and life and
love were felt to be somehow vulgar.

So I was convinced most of the time, but,—to continue with
my doubts,—was this all really due to expatriation, evident as
it so often was that the American emigré seemed to lose in
Europe his natural bearings? There was Edith Wharton whose
work deteriorated more and more after she had "cut her roots,"
in the phrase of Percy Lubbock, as if to prove that the American mind could not maintain its integrity abroad, that it was
all but inevitably compromised in Europe. Why else did Henry
James himself say so often to American friends that he should
not have lost touch with his countrypeople, and was it not
the moral of his life of Story that American artists might better
stay at home? Both James and Edith Wharton were perpetually troubled by a sense that their literary lives might have
been built on a mistake, that perhaps Dostoievsky was right
for them when he said, "A writer should not leave his country
for too long a time. He should live one life with her. Otherwise he is lost." But I had set out to make a case and I could
not be sure of it, for there were other possible explanations of
James's anomalous development or failure to develop, and I
was "harried with doubts," as Arnold Bennett said he was
when he too attacked James's later novels. For him *The Golden
Bowl* was an "arid desert." Was I insensitive, was I blind to
an obvious greatness? I felt that for nothing in the world
would I ever open again any of Henry James's later novels and

that his appearance of depth was wholly an illusion; and yet regarding all this I fell into a state of irresolution that actually became for me a virulent illness. Along with one or two other circumstances, it carried me into a formidable nervous breakdown.

Nor was I encouraged later to feel that I was right when James became one of the idols of a long generation, when the new critics defended his last phase as the major phase and no university was complete without a "Henry James expert." The new climate of opinion in literature, largely created in Paris, had been created wholly by expatriated persons, Pound, Eliot, Gertrude Stein, Joyce, Ford and Lawrence, exiles from their respective countries who could not feel that literature had any vital connection with "native lands." The writer for them was above localities and countries, and, moreover, they were not greatly interested in character as such or the "old-fashioned human element," as D. H. Lawrence called it. People were apt to seem to them as they seemed to Wyndham Lewis, "rather walking notions than 'real' entities," and so there was nothing amiss for them in the later Henry James with his "No. 1" and "No. 2" young men. Meanwhile, when questions of technique filled the minds of critics, he had much of technical interest for them, at a time, moreover, when the religion of art had become virtually the only religion. With the "divine principle" of his work, the "sacred years" that he had known and his "celestial, soothing, sanctifying process," James surrounded himself with an aura of priesthood.

For the rest, with the new generation, the old question of colonialism had gone by the board, and so had the other old question of expatriation. They had ceased to have any meaning for the younger writers, while I myself had been involved in both; and I was to realize, looking back, that I had been quarrelling with myself when I appeared to be quarrelling with Henry James. For, like many of my friends, I too had been enchanted with Europe, and I had vaguely hoped to continue to live there. It struck me that if I was always "straining to read the face of America,"—Paul Rosenfeld's phrase for my obsession,—it was because of an over-determination, and perhaps the question of expatriation had so possessed my mind because this mind itself had been divided. Only my reason had told me what I later came to feel, that the French aphorist Doudon was right when he said, "One must live, struggle and die among one's own." I mean he was right for those who were organized as I was.

In the end the question of Henry James resolved itself for me in a certain general notion of literary values,—that there is a gulf in judgment and feeling between those who see literature in terms of itself and those who see it in terms of a wider connection. In this respect and regarding James, I stood in the second category with AE, Maugham, More, Bennett and an army of others, minds as diverse as they well could be yet all agreeing that substance and depth are indispensable elements of a great novel. They might have agreed that James was a fine literary artist without ceasing to feel that his later work was poor indeed in qualities that are still more important than literary art. Was it not irrelevant to ask, as James asked of Tolstoy and Dostoievsky, "What do they artistically mean?"— for, baggy monsters that they were, along with Dickens, in James's mind, they were no less than supreme as both novelists and writers. And as so many novelists of our own twenties lost their substance and grasp of life, it struck me that the case of James was really a symbol,—I mean those novelists who had grown up in the so-called expatriate religion of art with a feeling that native lands are not important. Judging by these later cases, it seemed to me disastrous for the novelist to lose his natural connection with an inherited world that is deeply his own, when, ceasing to be "in the pedigree" of his own country, he is no longer an expression of the communal life.

CHAPTER XIII

A SEASON IN HELL

"TIMES HAVE always been like these. We were born in an off period, 1880-1914, and we can fool ourselves into believing that that was a 'normal era.' It was not. It was a short and pleasant breathing space. Now we are experiencing normal times." So, in 1938, Hendrik van Loon wrote to me, long after the decade I have been recollecting, when there had been a total change in the climate of opinion and feeling that sways the minds of writers and colours their books. In 1920, in the United States, Utopia had still seemed at hand, as it seemed also in Russia after 1917, although it was a lost cause in the rest of Europe, while the ideas of the Enlightenment were active still in American minds and in the minds especially of American writers. But the time had come when these ideas, as a younger writer was to say, "evoke our doubt or mistrust" and "cause us anguish." I am sure that in these words Jacques Barzun was expressing a widespread point of view of the new generation.

Many have attempted to define the change from the "infra-red" epoch of the past to the "ultra-violet" epoch of the thirties and after,—to follow Arthur Koestler's diagnosis,—when humanity seemed to pass into a dark night of the soul. Nothing could have been more marked than the transformation of the literary world from the state of mind of a dozen years before when, as Waldo Frank had said, at the time of *The Seven Arts,* "There is a murmur of suppressed excitement in the air." It was, he added, "like that which hovers over a silent crowd before the appearance of a great procession." Had this procession come and gone? Certainly no one in 1930 looked for any such thing to appear in the future, for "a dreadful apathy, unsureness and discouragement is felt to have fallen upon us," Edmund Wilson wrote in the following year. Gertrude Stein said, in fact, that there was no future,—there was "no future any more"; while Paul Rosenfeld, editing *The American Caravan,* noted that after 1930 every contribution to this yearbook was tragic. In the great number of papers that were submitted to it, he said, there was not one cheerful composition. Paul was dismayed by this uniform note, so different from that of the time when he, like all our contemporaries, had begun to write and when he had half expected to see "ideas at every street corner and rivers of living water in the street." Over the gate of the thirties one seemed to see the words, "Abandon hope, all ye who enter here."

The writers were generally prepared at least to abandon all interest in the future of the world unless they were Marxists who did not believe in the will and who thought that Utopia was coming by an automatic process; while a series of anti-Utopias in the years to come were to present the future as inevitably dismal. Feeling that they could do nothing whatever to change this unpromising picture, the writers quite naturally looked in the other direction and many began to idealize the Middle Ages that fixed the mind on another world and life. Nor were they more disposed to contemplate the future when the menace of atomic destruction rose over the world and when, like old men who fear that tomorrow they are going to develop some fatal disease, they buried all thoughts of the future in thoughts of the past. Constantly more insecure, they were obsessed with security and the orthodoxy that gave them a feeling of this, and, in their dream of authority and unity, they seemed to wish to avoid the paths that had led to so many developments of the livelier twenties. Adventurousness, curiosity and independence had lost their charm in a world that was full of snares and pitfalls, and they were inclined to share Cardinal Newman's "fierce thoughts against the Liberals" whose gullibility, they felt, had deceived and betrayed them. Nor could they continue to trust themselves when all humanity, as it seemed to them, had revealed such fathomless depths of depravity and evil.

For, with the new generation, the moral effects of the first world war spread to the remotest corner of the realm of writers, and this reproduced the symptoms of the Hellenistic age, as we have been taught by eminent scholars to see it. The sense of failure in that age, the loss of hope in the present world and in organized effort and human calculation, together with the lapse of self-confidence that accompanied this, had developed in the Greeks too a pessimistic mysticism that was focussed on a dream-world far away. Humanism, as the thirties advanced, became more and more a byword, and art, as Ortega said, was dehumanized also, while the mind of the present ransacked the past for earlier minds, both small and great, that confirmed its own disillusion and despair.

*

*   *

Meanwhile, I experienced my own season in hell.

One day during these later years of which I have been writing I happened to visit a certain refugee author, an Austrian, known the world over, with only a few months to live, who had settled in a college town not far away. I found him in a cluttered shabby room in a dreary students' lodging-house, looking out on a back yard full of mud and rubbish, where a closet door stood open revealing his wardrobe, a battered old hat and a threadbare coat or two. In one corner was a kerosene stove on which he evidently cooked the meals that he drew from bottles and cans piled beside it, and various noxious smells and sounds drifted, as the talk went on, through the dingy golden-oak woodwork of the windows and the walls. He remarked that he was sixty-five and it struck me how easy it would be to take all this for granted if one were twenty,—when anything will pass for picturesqueness,—while many another at his age, obliged to exist in a similar way, would have hanged themselves forthwith from the door of the closet. But he was obviously living in quite another world. Apropos of nothing, he suddenly exclaimed, "The Engadine is beautiful. It is really beautiful! I know because I have just been rereading the novel I wrote about it fifteen years ago."

This great man was living in a dream of his own imagination, and all writers, in fact, exist under a sort of spell or, one might say, within a magic circle. They live under a dome of many-coloured glass, and they see the world, including themselves, as this many-coloured glass iridescently stains it. If the dome is broken, if the bubble bursts, as one might otherwise put it, and they see life in its nakedness, or see themselves so,—as mere old men in sordid lodging-houses,—they are apt to fall into the melancholy leading to despair which the monks called acedia in the Middle Ages. Most of the recorded instances of mediæval suicide were occasioned by acedia in the monasteries, I have been told, and something similar surely accounts for the catastrophic endings that have so often marked the lives of writers.

There came a time in the middle twenties when my own bubble burst, when the dome under which I had lived crumbled into ruin, when I was consumed with a sense of failure, a feeling that my work had all gone wrong and that I was mistaken in all I had said or thought. What had I been doing? I had only ploughed the sea, as a certain great man once remarked, and I thought of my writing "with rage and shame," E. M. Forster's phrase for his own feeling about his early work. I was pursued especially with nightmares in which Henry James turned great luminous menacing eyes upon me. I was half aware, in connection with him, of the division within myself, and with all the bad conscience of a criminal I felt I had viewed him with something of Plato's "hard little eye of detraction." In short, in this middle of my life, I was thoroughly bedevilled. I saw myself as a capsized ship at night with the passengers drowned underneath and the keel in the air. I could no longer sleep, I scarcely sat down for a year, I lived in a Plutonian psychical twilight. Even the sun was off-colour to me, I was a prey to vertigo, at moments my brain seemed to be deranged, and when I napped for an hour or so I dreamed that I was about to be hanged or that something had occurred in my blood-stream that was evidently fatal. All my affections and interests fell into abeyance, and it seemed to me that, where normal depressions occasionally sank to zero, mine sank from zero indefinitely down. The nadir of common depressions was the peak of mine. Nine-tenths of all my energy was involved in a neurosis and barely one-tenth was left for living.

I had always been possessed by this idea or that, usually the notion of the book I happened to be writing, which I pursued like a beagle with his nose to the ground; and I was possessed now with a fantasy of suicide that filled my mind as the full moon fills the sky. It was a fixed idea. I could not expel this fantasy that shimmered in my brain, and I saw every knife as something with which to cut one's throat and every high building as something to jump from. A belt was a garotte for me, a rope existed to hang oneself with, the top of a door was merely a bracket for the rope, every rusty musket had its predestined use for me and every tomb in a graveyard was a place to starve in. I could see an axe only as lethal and every bottle meant for me something to be swallowed in splinters or to slash one's wrists with, while even the winter snow fell in order to give one pneumonia if one spent a night lying on the ground. Meanwhile, every morning, when I began to sleep again, I awoke with my arms folded over my breast. I had been dreaming that I was dead at last and unconsciously arranged my limbs in the posture of a mummy.

In my *crise à quarante ans* I shrank from all human relations, and this explained the image Paul Rosenfeld happened upon in the fine essay he wrote about me. He spoke of a house with the shades drawn and a man sitting within, a man who could not hear the knock when life drove up to the door with her merry summons. How could Paul ever have guessed what was happening in that house? Nor did Sherwood Anderson know why it was that we drifted apart when he wrote, "I did not put Brooks aside. He put me aside." But, calling me a New Englander, though he knew well I was not one, he pictured in a striking phrase my mental condition. Observing that I had the "beauty" of the New England mind, he said I suffered from its "cold inner fright."

One of the doctors whom I saw and who had read *The Ordeal of Mark Twain* asked me if I considered that "reason" or "emotion" had been the determining element in my mind and work. The question had never occurred to me, but, recalling my struggles to make this book logical and clear, I replied, "Reason, I suppose," and the doctor smiled. He shook his head and walked away, and I saw at once that he was right. I had always worked by following my nose, I had never been able to think anything out but rather *felt* things out in a cumbersome fashion, and, writing always intuitively, I was emotionally paralyzed now or, as Dr. Brill said, "too disturbed for treatment." My wife had written to Dr. Jung, whom Joel Spingarn knew well and who replied sympathetically and kindly from Zurich. The psychology of my illness, he wrote, was transparent enough: what I had was "chronic melancholia" and "a terribly hard case for treatment, if possible at all." He added, "Things seem to have gone very far," saying that even to attempt a cure would be hazardous under the circumstances. He then suggested the old expedient of a year on a Western ranch, for, in primitive surroundings, complicated situations often dissolved, as he put it, or were eased at least.

The upshot was that, like Peer Gynt, I went back to the button-moulder. I was to spend four years in houses of the dead, or, as one might say, the wounded, or the about-to-be-reborn, at Stockbridge, at Katonah, at White Plains and in England. It struck me at once that my fellow-inmates all had queer eyes, which I took for a sign of the clan I now belonged to, the clan of those to whom they said, "What *were* you?" as if you had actually arrived in the land of shades. All I remember of Stockbridge now was a drive one day to Pittsfield and Herman Melville's farm on a lonely road, where one still saw the name "Arrowhead" boldly carved on the carriage-block and a house all in sagging disrepair. It was a dirtyish yellow and some windows were broken. But there was the big chimney of which Melville had written and the famous piazza he had built, to remind himself in the country of the deck of a ship, with its straw-coloured planks rotting away. Peeping through the boards that covered the windows, I saw some of his old folios within, together with a big ship's model on a bracket on the wall, which took me seventy years back to the day when this *exalté* had also undergone a season in hell.

I was to find myself presently in an English sanitarium where I spent eight months at Harrow-on-the-Hill in a long low Queen Anne manor-house that was later to become the infirmary of the neighbouring Harrow school. There I conceived the delusion that I was about to be buried alive, not in the earth but walled in a small chamber; and I believed that "they" were coming for me. For many mornings, waking early from an artificial sleep, I heard them putting together a large box for me below, a box that, in my fantasy, had arrived in sections to be hammered together in the house with nails or pegs. To me this accounted for the resonant clatter of the housemaids who were merely pulling up the Venetian blinds. If I was not to be buried alive why should people have talked to me about the crypt of St. Paul's or the wax funeral figures,— the Effigies,—in their glass cases in Westminster Abbey? I was persuaded that the doctor had induced Parliament to pass a bill enabling him to bury me alive, a notion that later suggested to me how large was the ego in my cosmos (in the phrase of the elderly German in Kipling's tale). There was even a day when I stood by the table in my circular room in the tower,— it was a sunny spring day, the curtains were flapping, and the daffodils were all out in the grass below,—when I had a sudden vision of the end of the world, a catastrophe caused solely by my fate. For this had occasioned a breakdown of all who were attached to me and who were also, in consequence, buried

alive, while those who were attached to them came to the same
end, and so on, and on, *ad infinitum*. As in some monstrous
cosmic general strike, all mankind was engulfed, all movement
ceased. I could see the steamships stopping in the middle of the
ocean, while invisible waves of horror encircled the world.

There were other trances, like opium dreams, illusions of in-
finite time and space, into which I fell abruptly during these
four years. I remember, at home again, looking up at windows
that had meant much to me not long before, and wondering
how it was possible for me, in 1929, to have bridged the vast
chasm of years since 1906. That year seemed more remote than
the great days of Egypt. Meanwhile, I found myself in the
rose-embosomed hospital that William Seabrook described in
his book *Asylum* where the ornamental iron-work over the
windows disguised the actuality of bars. The long corridor was
hung with steel-engravings of William Tell, the Parthenon,
King Lear and his daughters, and the guards, patrolling the
red carpet, kept under constant surveillance the doorless rooms
in which anything might happen. A rattling of the main door,
at nine o'clock sharp in the morning, proclaimed the official entrance of the froglike doctor, the bearded panjandrum with the
long chain of keys and his retinue of assistants, orderlies and
nurses. Passing from patient to patient, scattering insults and
ironies,—a sort of cold-shock treatment that was then in
vogue,—he would order the hydropathic hose for the man who
had jumped off Brooklyn Bridge and the pack for the young
man who presently drowned himself (when he was permitted
to go home for a Sunday). Then, with carpentry, basketry,
weaving, one went back to the kindergarten, with the hope,
supposedly, that a new man would grow from the little child
one had become again.

Out of the purgatorial mist that now envelops the scene for

me more than one tragic and shadowy character emerges. There was the famous doctor who had become a destructive child and who tried to smash his bedstead in the middle of the night. Then there was the old gentleman whom I saw standing on a chair in his room attaching his suspenders to the chandelier, in a patient methodical effort to encircle his neck, and there was the florist whose name was emblazoned on many a New York street, a religious maniac who was also homicidal. He fell to his knees and prayed one day when four of us were playing bridge, then suddenly sprang up and tried to strangle my partner. There was the newspaper publisher who said he must see the doctor at once about an affair involving ten million dollars, whose aeroplane was ticking outside waiting to take him to Africa where he was going for a spell of big-game hunting. He hadn't a minute to spare, he said, then, seizing a large flower-pot, he threw it through the window and sat down on the floor with a wild laugh. There was a charming old man, besides, whom one saw strolling about the grounds in white flannel trousers and a parti-coloured blazer,—General A., I was told he was, and I knew this could not be true because I had read his obituary ten years before. I had read this because he was the uncle of one of my friends and I had met him when I was a boy; but, dead as he was supposed to be, this really was General A., whose family had announced that he was dead when they shut him up. He had even escaped once and appeared at his club in New York, where the attendants who had known him took him for a ghost and whence he had been spirited back to the hospital again. There, I was told, whenever he could, this beautifully groomed old gentleman rubbed in his hair the poached eggs from his breakfast tray. Dreadful to me was the daily exit of the inmates of the so-called violent ward who appeared, in a long queue, for exercise just before noon, marching in single file, with white-coated orderlies flanking them, and winding through the grounds to the cracking of invisible whips. It was a Doré picture, in real life, from the Inferno. The queue was led by a grey-haired giant, an ex-Presbyterian clergyman, who shouted obscenities and oaths as he capered on the path.

Such are my memories of those years when my existence seemed to me a "lost traveller's dream under the hill"; and even after I came back to life and sailed out clear and free I remained conscious at moments of an abyss beside me. I seemed to catch out of the tail of my eye a cold black draughty void, with a feeling that I stood on the brink of it in peril of my reason; but it was only rarely now that I had this glimpse of the *néant*, and in the end my crisis was invaluable for me. I felt as one of my friends felt after he too struck bottom and had "come up more and more ever since," finding his own grave breakdown a "complete purgation." To me he wrote, "I predict you'll find new springs of energy that you had never suspected"; and so, in fact, it proved to be when I returned to love and work with a feeling that my best years still lay before me. Hawthorne had spoken of the dark caverns into which all men must descend if they are to know anything beneath the surface, or what he called the illusive pleasures of existence. It seemed to me now that I understood him, and I wondered if this did not justify the later phase of the world's mind too and the literary mind that reflected its darkness.

From the Shadow of the Mountain

MY POST-MERIDIAN YEARS

NOTE

THIS IS THE THIRD AND FINAL VOLUME of a series that relates the story of my life. It follows *Scenes and Portraits: Memories of Childhood and Youth* and *Days of the Phoenix: The Nineteen-Twenties I Remember*.

CHAPTER I

AT WESTPORT

W HEN I emerged, in 1931, from the shadow of the mountain,—to use an old expression of the Hudson river,—
I felt, after four years passed in mental hospitals, decidedly
young again but rather dazed. I did not quite feel like the
Prisoner of Chillon who "regained his freedom with a sigh,"
but there remained in my stomach as it were a hard ball of
panic that was never entirely to disappear. It was a glorious
May afternoon and I remember the sunlight falling on rugs
and pictures through the western windows of our little white
cottage in the village of Westport, but this light was somehow
strange and, even when I had recovered my balance, this
strangeness was to linger in the air. I knew that every decade
now was supposed to bring in a different world, that the thirties
were to differ from the twenties as, in time, the forties were to
differ from the thirties and so on; but a kind of murky mental
weather had set in with the thirties that was unlike the clarity
of the decade before. The new world seemed to be all a Magic
Mountain like the International Sanitorium Berghof of Thomas
Mann's novel. There Joaquin said to Hans Castorf, "The climate isn't the only queer thing about us. You're going to see
some things you've never dreamed of. Just wait."

The sibyl Gertrude Stein spoke of this change of atmosphere. One could no longer, she said, be realistic when things had ceased to be real and become strange; and H. G. Wells also referred to the "frightful queerness" that had come into modern life. In fact, in the ocean of relativity that was all about us now, fixed points on the shore had largely vanished. Everybody spoke of the uncertainty of values in this "age of anxiety," as it came to be called, or this "sexual era," as others described a time that was marked by Lee Simonson's "visas over the sexual border." The familiar notions of time, space and natural law, and even of human personality, had faded out. Artists and writers were impelled to express a social consciousness, it is true, that stood for a surviving reality, the idea of justice; and this was the time of the League of American Writers when Hemingway spoke at a congress in Carnegie Hall. I cannot forget the excitement when he appeared on the platform before he went off to Cuba and became a legend. These, moreover, were the years when John Dos Passos produced his bitter trilogy U.S.A. But, in the "proletarian thirties," among the young men who surrounded us, who had often sat on the terrace outside the Dome, or who had been sitting in the Ritz bar in Paris when the stock market at home suddenly crashed, among these young men ideas that were strange in the light of all that had gone before, spoke of the new dehumanization of art. As if the problems of life and the world had become too difficult to face, an art was gradually appearing that was really a game, based on a "loathing for the human," as Ortega put it; and at the same time one heard of the "power of blackness," in Melville's phrase, that was utterly routing the traditional power of light. These notes became more pronounced as time went on.

One suddenly heard, on every side, the solemn word "security," expressing the one felt want of the new generation, security at almost any price for young men who, in the first world war, had suffered as many risks as they could take. The old desire of youth for adventure, in the outward sense at least, seemed to have been snuffed out in this greatest of adventures, and, where everything appeared unreal and strange, one could understand the general wish for a life in which one took no chances. There were misgivings everywhere in this time of troubles, and one found offered for sale even on drugstore counters Kierkegaard's *Fear and Trembling* and *Sickness unto Death*. It was the time when Willa Cather rose to fame because of the calm, the repose that marked her stories, because of her love for the reassuring solidity and depth of old adobe walls and granite dwellings. Meanwhile, to return to the Magic Mountain, its cosmopolitan population, with Russians, Danes and Italians gathered together, Bulgarians, Poles, Mexicans and what not, also marked our little Westport where a new feeling for the planet as a whole had spread as another result of the first world war. This was different indeed from the world-mindedness of the nineteenth century that seemed in the twentieth so provincial, the state of mind of Saint-Simon, for instance, in whose ideal society there were to be four governmental divisions. The whole of Asia and Africa were to be under the jurisdiction of England, Italy, Germany and France, and what Occidental did not think this entirely just? But John Gunther had settled in Westport where Vincent Sheean came for a while to live in an old house across the street, types of the new correspondent who had been behind the scenes in Europe, in Russia, in Asia, everywhere. These men seemed almost to have been born with a pluralistic view of mankind. Nothing less provincial could have been imagined.

Vincent Sheean symbolized, for me, the Middle West, the provenance then of so much of our art and letters, where Frank

Lloyd Wright and Hemingway had grown up near Chicago and where so many, like Sandburg, were now living. Sheean was a product of what Sherwood Anderson called the "Robin's egg Renaissance" before the robin's egg dropped out of the nest. Virtually a man of the world from birth, he had plunged, almost as a boy, into the turmoil of Europe in the early twenties, easily picking up languages and prepared, as he wrote, to "deal with the largest doings of the great." He was thrown with all the statesmen whose measure he took in his *Personal History,* and what Robinson Jeffers called the "dull welter of Asia" was, for Sheean, putting forth new shoots of life. He was to write before long his book on Gandhi, and, having known Primo de Rivera in Spain, he could not believe that H. G. Wells had said a good word for the autocratic Franco. This must have been later in the thirties, during the Spanish civil war, and I had met, in New York, at dinner, this novelist who had once called Franco the "murderous little Christian gentleman." Yet, as opposed to the Loyalists, Wells supported Franco now, saying that he was going to establish a liberal monarchy and the English knew how to deal with men like that. He grew even more emphatic when Franz Werfel, who was present, expostulated, "But Mr. Wells! But Mr. Wells!" Vincent Sheean, who had played tennis with Wells on the Riviera, could not believe anything so un-characteristic.

But Sheean, with his world-consciousness, would have liked the plan that Wells expounded for a world-encyclopædia. Wells had found Harvard congenial, saying of President Conant, "He's a great fellow, he agreed with every word I said"; but he was much concerned that evening with the decline of his own vogue to which he referred vaguely two or three times. He said, "American criticism has always floated on a magic island," which seemed to me, with the "new" critics, truer than ever;

and he remarked at dinner, "At that time I was seeing much of a great American novelist, the man who started all modern writing. Now I wonder who knows the man I mean?" He looked around blankly and nobody answered until I said, "Stephen Crane," whereupon he gave me a hearty handshake. At ten o'clock, taking out his watch, he said he had to go home; then, instantly, he sat down and talked till midnight about the encyclopædia he had in mind. He said a new dark age was coming and the only hope was to assemble all knowledge in the manner of Diderot and his circle. This could be kept underground till the next renaissance.

Although he was seventy-two years old, Wells had not yet reached the final despair in which he wrote *Mind at the End of Its Tether,* saying, "The end of everything we call life is close at hand" and our world of self-delusion is destined to perish. He seemed to have reversed the point of view with which, as a novelist, he had been preëminently a story-teller; and in fact the story was fading away from the novel now,—the story was turned over to the writers of whodunits. The new novelists generally agreed with Sartre about "the foolish business of mere story-telling." Nor was this the only respect in which the fiction of the future was to differ from the fiction of the twenties and earlier years. Theodore Dreiser, like Sinclair Lewis or Ellen Glasgow or Willa Cather, reflected to a large extent the communal life; they presented a broad picture of the society of their time while they created characters that stood for it. Their novels were the products of "saturation," the word that Henry James used for an intimate understanding of the social scene, obtained either by birth or study, but in any case essential and the real *terra firma* of a novelist's art. I wondered how far the world-consciousness that I saw all about me was destined to preclude this saturation, this giving of oneself to a definite locale to the close knowledge of which novelists had once devoted so much attention. The young men I knew were more often familiar with Munich or Paris or Mexico City than with their own Denver or Omaha or Trenton, and this left them with no deep attachment to the country of their origin, still less to any more restricted region. There could be no saturation with any human society in a world that "annihilated distance," as Toynbee put it; and the result was to be what Malcolm Cowley presently described in his book *The Literary Situation*. Every novel came to be dismissed as "naturalistic" that gave a broad picture of a social scene, and "the only novel recognized as worthy" was "one that presents at most a crisis in the lives of a few individuals." Moreover, the study of form without regard to content left some of the novelists high and dry, with no society behind them to write about and with only exotic characters and marginal themes.

In Westport we were surrounded with world-conscious minds like Hendrik van Loon, the historical story-teller, the lover of wit and music, good food, good wine, tolerance and all the other Erasmian virtues. In Hendrik's alphabet, B for Boroba-dour followed A for Athens, and he included Oahu with London and Rome. His *Story of Mankind* created for children the kind of expanded point of view they derived from Nehru's *Glimpses of World History,* in which Siam and Belgium, Sweden and Afghanistan appeared side by side in all their phases. Hendrik was more and more obsessed with the second world war that was coming and that was to destroy in time his beloved Middelburg, the old abbey and all his childhood rec-ollections. Meanwhile, the old-fashioned well-trained English novelist, William McFee, still lived in Westport, though he had "no roots anywhere," he said, "save in the fenceless mead-ows of the sea . . . No background, only a series of backdrops." He had been born on a ship with sea-faring parents who had moved from Canada to London; and, spending his life among Arabs and Greeks, Russians and Chinese, he had remained indefeasibly English. Yet after 1908 he had never lived in England, where he had written his first novel. As a sea-going engineer, writing on watches or in port, he had roamed from Smyrna to Constantinople, from Port Said to Salonica, from the Danube to the Amazon, spending his nights ashore in the wineshops of the world. To the steady drum of the engines, he had listened to the passengers, like his own Mr. Spenlove, the engineer, and his astonishment never ceased at the ways of the Americans and their effect on English men and women. He moved up to Brookfield, eventually, where the country recalled the Malvern Hills,—"These hills will always be my love," he wrote; and then again he moved to a lonely road in Roxbury where he stowed himself away in a tiny cottage. With a ship's bell outside, it was as snug as the captain's cabin in a well-built tramp on the Indian ocean; and there, while he freely aired his prejudices, he read almost every novel that came out. He remarked that American fiction was in the same stage as the drama in Elizabethan times when it was all melodrama; and, calling himself a troglodite, he said he was one of the last of the story-tellers.

In fact, modern writing, as it was called from this time on, was largely the creation of displaced persons, T. S. Eliot and Ezra Pound, James Joyce and Gertrude Stein, all of whom had left behind the countries of their origin and for whom human beings were more or less abstractions. Seceding from what was called mass-culture, they had lost touch with the common humanity that had moved the novelists of the twenties; and yet there was no returning to the concrete world they had left behind or any escape from the planetary feeling of the present.

"Isn't the end of literature somehow already in sight?" a sensitive Austrian émigré wrote to me, and others were writing essays on the "death of poetry" or on the "death of the novel." One of my friends wrote to me, "Since last I saw you the turn of events has more and more convinced me that literature, *per se*, belongs to a time and a cultural atmosphere that no longer exists. So I turn to politics," he continued; but even if it meant the possible death of literature, one could scarcely regret a tendency that brought the world together. Actually, in the atomic age, a world-wide social unity was necessary for everyone's existence, and how could one oppose the kind of world-brotherhood which the mixture of races in America was bringing about? Many of my friends shared this planetary feeling, whether George Biddle or Jo Davidson or Thornton Wilder or Glenway Wescott, who had said *Good-bye to Wisconsin* and had never found another world that he was able to reconstruct in fiction, although in *The Pilgrim Hawk* and *Apartment in Athens* he had written fine isolated studies of foreign settings. Novels, sporadic novels, might continue to be written; but, without saturation, with no immersion in a social scene, could there be novelists of the old massive kind?

There was Sherwood Anderson, never by nature a novelist, although he had experienced the saturation that marked him as a man of the pre-war time; and it was this that gave his best short stories the note of authenticity of one who has "been there." As for literary influences, the odd characters of George Borrow had reminded him of his own small-town people and helped him in a way to shape them in his work; and, just as Willa Cather had been drawn to the composure of Puvis de Chavannes, so Sherwood had been drawn to Van Gogh at the Armory Show. Van Gogh's chairs, towels and pictures on the walls brought back the Mid-Western household scenes and led

him to realize these in his short stories, and Van Gogh corroborated the love of vivid colours that one saw in Sherwood's
dress and appearance. Sherwood was often in Westport, visiting
his brother Karl, the painter who awoke one day feeling that his
painting was good for nothing and who then set to work writing a novel. He asked me to revise this novel and I spent a
month doing so, rewriting almost every sentence; for Karl, in
his effort to avoid the obvious, had used Roget's *Thesaurus,*
assuming that synonyms were identical with the words he
should have used. As a result the style was blurred, as in a
defective colour-print in which the colours do not coincide
with the lines; and when I put it in plain English I was astonished to find that Karl had written a Sherwood Anderson story.
One afternoon Sherwood himself brought Anita Loos to see us
with her husband John Emerson, his old friend. The sprightly
author of *Gentlemen Prefer Blondes* seemed very light-hearted
that day, little and busy, with her red cap, as a ruby-crowned
kinglet.

On another day Robert Frost came to spend the night with
us, talking from the moment I met him at two in the afternoon
until three o'clock in the morning and then again until five in
the afternoon. We had two long walks together and he spoke
of his life and adventures, especially his early life in San Francisco. There he had known Henry George, a friend of his
father's, and his mother had given him Bellamy's *Looking Backward,* which as a boy he had learned by heart. He had thought
of New England then as clam-like and occluded while California was generous and big-hearted. Nobody out there had
regarded pennies, and he remembered holding up a nickel and
a penny to point out the difference between the regions; the
nickel in his mind stood for California and the mean little copper for New England. When he began to write, he felt it was

quite noble of him to have discovered that New England was interesting too. But his best time of life was the six years or more when he and his wife had farmed at Derry in New Hampshire, and he had bought another farm near the top of Vermont where he could go for the hay-fever season. He said he had always been too poor to have pictures in the house and he regretted that he had learned little about art now that his daughter had become a sculptor. But he had gone to Ireland to spend a week with AE, who had given him one of his large paintings, a picture that now hung in his house at Amherst. Frost had won the Pulitzer Prize three times; he had a "season ticket," said Hendrik van Loon.

I had first met Robert Frost far up-town in New York and had walked with him six miles down to my hotel. We had then talked until five in the morning, and this was Robert's regular way of making friends, one meeting that lasted all night. His feeling about New England had changed altogether, and when I wrote *The Flowering of New England* he said it was an "emotional experience for me of the highest,—there's a poem out of it, which you must read one day." He had been tempted lately to leave all, he said, and "constitute myself defender of Puritan New England . . . What do you assume it is that makes people like George Santayana, James Truslow Adams and Henry Wallace hate New England,—her having given herself so generously away to the whole country?" But he said he would consign New England to me "while I turn to fight the battles of the Supreme Court of the United States." He had by that time become a reactionary who had no use for Henry George or Bellamy and who was attacking Franklin Roosevelt and his New Deal by way of making amends to his wife. "I dragged her over the stones," he said to me again and again after the death of his wife; she had hated Roosevelt, taking their hard-earned pennies and throwing them away on the riff-raff of the cities; and to turn against Roosevelt was his only way of atoning for the hardships he had caused her. But in that earlier time this companionable man had talked mainly about the country people, the mail-clerk he had known in Vermont and the real-estate man at Amherst; and, with his endless zest for the play of personality, he recalled Sherwood Anderson talking about his neighbours in the South. He said he wished he could have three lives, one to be a failure and see how he behaved through this, one to be an early success and see how he behaved as a later failure, one to be an early failure and see how he behaved as a later success. He had a good-natured scorn for the New York critics and laughed at them for wishing to be "first among the seconds, as we say about the apple barrels"; and he laughed at a certain novelist who was always accusing him of not being on the firing-line. "I fight with a spear," he said. "They fight with dirks. The dirk is the city weapon. I fight from a long way back."

It seemed to me that Frost's strength was that he shared the popular feelings while he made no concessions to the popular mind; and he gave one the fixed impression that America was sound in essence. He was, like Carl Sandburg, a public poet, and again, like Sandburg, Frost wandered all over the country, familiar with Key West and San Antonio, Colorado and Santa Fe, Montana, where one of his daughters lived, Kansas and Texas. Later, when I lunched with him before he set out for Oxford and Dublin, he said the attacks on materialism were all nonsense. Was it not supposed that God materialized himself in Christ? He was all for the material guided by the spiritual, and he said the Oriental mind had withered away because it considered the spiritual alone. Then he laughed at a writer who said that the important thing was, quite simply, to represent the age. In a dull age the greatest man would therefore be the dullest man and in a confused age the greatest mind was the most confused. Frost might have agreed with Pablo Casals who spoke, in his *Conversations,* of atonal music. This music was supposed to be a reflection of the uncertainty of our chaotic period, and Casals said, "Why should an artist be obsessed with the uncertainties of our time instead of reacting against them by showing his faith in those human values which have survived so many collective catastrophes? However dark our times may seem, art should bring a message of hope."

"What an aura that man has about him!" one of my West-port neighbours said about Robert Frost. As a boy in Indiana he had heard Frost, Masters, Sandburg and Lindsay give public readings, and these poets had started him off on his own literary life. Edgar Lee Masters also came out to see us on a mellow October day when we sat under our apple tree and discussed the state of man and his chance of reaching paradise one way or another. Like most of my Mid-Western friends, he thought of me as a New Englander, not troubling to differentiate between the various species of men who had grown up on the Eastern seaboard. This square-faced bespectacled lawyer-poet had a great interest in his forbears in Vermont, and, as for Emerson, his poems and essays delighted Masters. There was scarcely a word of Emerson's with which he did not agree, and he said that an essay could be written on Emerson's saving wisdom to the youth of America for fifty years past. He defended his erratic book on Abraham Lincoln, though he said he could not guess how it would affect his best friends. It had practically alienated Vachel Lindsay.

Robert Frost had known Gamaliel Bradford whose diary and letters I edited in 1932. At the Bradford house in Wellesley Hills, I had met Merrill Moore, the poet who had once been one of the "Fugitives" of Tennessee and who was now a psychiatrist practising in Boston. Merrill Moore asked Mrs. Bradford for the programme of a symphony concert because he saw a sonnet in it, and he wrote another sonnet on a little bronze statue of Shakespeare in the drawing-room where the Wellesley girls had once teased Vachel Lindsay. On his way home Merrill Moore dictated the sonnets to his wife and she wrote them down while he was driving. There was a kind of waffle-iron in Merrill Moore's brain that turned into the shape of a sonnet every thought that entered it, and he was supposed to have written twenty thousand sonnets. Meanwhile, to the neighbourhood of Boston soon came Rudolph Ruzicka whom I had first known during a summer he had spent at Fairfield, near Westport. After this town he had named the lovely Fairfield type that I have since used in all my books, a type that virtually reproduced Rudolph's own handwriting and that he used himself in his little book on Bewick. He greatly admired this old wood-engraver whom Audubon had known and visited in England. Rudolph was cut off from the country of his birth, Bohemia, and he told me that the translation of *Walden,* printed in Prague with his illustrations, had been withheld from distribution pending an investigation of the "ideological merit" of the book. Rudolph liked to quote the Italian proverb, "In conversation it is easy to draw a cheque of erudition on insufficient funds," but there was never a more erudite man than this book-designer who was almost universally cultivated. Living in Dobbs Ferry and then in New York, he felt the lack of a traditional attachment to some place where he could finally belong, and, settling first in Concord, he went to live in Boston.

Of the Westport painters, I knew best Charles Prendergast, a true primitive old master to whom only Vasari could have done justice. He was a reincarnation of the down-east Yankees who carved figureheads for ships, Hawthorne's Drowne, for instance, of the "wooden image"; and his art of gilded figures grew out of his craft as a carver of picture-frames. His mind was like a brook flowing in the woods with leaves floating on it and flowers on the bank. He always reminded me of the Chinese painter Kakki who said that an artist must nourish in his bosom mildness and magnanimity and that only dwelling in a quiet house, in a retired room with the windows open, could he have good feeling for painting and create the Yu. One met at Prendergast's house some of the older painters. Alfred Maurer came there and W. J. Glackens died there, one morning after breakfast while he was smoking a cigar, but one never saw Everett Shinn there, another of the "Eight" who lived in the village behind a high brick wall. Shinn had lost much of his impulse as a painter, though he made occasional illustrations and worked off his energy writing plays. Then, leaving his wife, he lived for a while in a cottage near the cemetery where his telephone, light and water were soon cut off. Shinn, who had made and lost fortunes decorating theatres, would lie on the beach all day in summer, and he read me letters from Poultney Bigelow sent in envelopes franked by the Kaiser, Bigelow's old school-friend in Germany, turned inside out.

Meanwhile, a legacy that came to my wife and me removed one of the causes of my breakdown and enabled me, in this time of depression, to do the work I chose and that alone. For me there was to be no more writing *invita Minerva*. I was able to refuse the positions that were offered me, the literary editorship of *The Sun* and the managing editorship of *The Saturday Review* and *The New Masses*. I was asked to be managing editor of *The Dial*, which had given me its award, and one day, when William Allen White died, I was asked to be one of the judges of the Book-of-the-Month Club. It seemed to me that, in this position, I would be urged to make the most popular book of the month appear to be the best one. Time, not money, Schopenhauer said, is the true treasure of life, and because money bought them time he argued that thinking people should have means ample enough to allow them leisure. How I agreed with Agassiz's saying, "I have no time to waste in making money!" When I thought what financial security was to mean to me,—and this was confirmed after my mother's death, —I could understand how many talents were destroyed without it and how many lives were marred or seriously injured. Paul Rosenfeld's life was crippled by the comparative poverty to which he was reduced during the depression, the generous Paul who was no longer able to help other people as he had once offered to help me. What became of so many of the hopeful and promising young writers whom I had known in the last twenty years? They were frustrated, bitter, forgotten, disappointed, often enough for lack of money, and only occasionally reconciled to an average existence.

I remember a dinner at Paul's later at which E. E. Cummings went off like a geyser of Yankee humour. He told us about the American soldiers in Africa forcing the Africans to be "free," compelling them to be free against their will. Years after this I saw Cummings in Rome and in New York, but I never forgot how that evening he piled one absurdity on another until they reached a towering comic height. Then, in 1936, Dhan Ghopal Mukurji came to spend in Westport a week with me. He wished me to collaborate with him in a book on Yoga, for he felt that he was unequal to presenting the subject in such a way that Americans could understand it. He said that I should relax and permit literature to flow out of my life "like a milk-coloured stream from a rock," and when he gave me lessons in Yoga I sat cross-legged on the floor, trying to evoke the lotus-blossom at the lower end of my spinal column. But one day he said he had been told by his guru that one should not attempt to combine these efforts with intellectual labour. A few weeks after he had stayed with me, Mukurji took his own life, lost as he was between the East and the West.

There was a little indifferent house of which I saw much in the thirties, a house in New Haven, inconspicuous in the street, where lived George Dudley Seymour, an old lawyer. Nothing marked this house but the polished brass knocker and railings by the door; it extended actually, however, a long way at the rear and within were many treasures. There were a dozen portraits of eighteenth-century Connecticut worthies with certain splendid pictures and other works of art, and George Dudley Seymour, whom Sargent had painted, was a Connecticut worthy himself, a genial benefactor of artists and art. He was the chairman of the art commission of the state, and I had first gone to see him about a historical fresco that one of my Westport friends wished to paint. After that he wrote to me, "I am always at home to you at any hour, day or night," and, quoting Governor Winthrop, he called himself "an obscure person content to lie hid among the retired philosophers." Then, "fabulously" old, but "permanently" mine, he was paralysed so that he could not speak, yet, smiling as ever, he promoted the fame of Nathan Hale whose birthplace he bought and put in order.

How many houses I had seen elsewhere, unimportant outside, but full of wonders within, the house of Denman Ross, for instance, the Harvard worthy whom Berenson called "far more subtle, penetrating and serious" than Roger Fry. This little dwelling on a Cambridge "delta" was, as I remember it, one of the finest museums of Oriental art, surprising to me as a certain small house in Westport where an old magazine editor asked me to call upon him. How did they ever get there, the Bronzino portrait and the Tintoretto that covered, with other treasures, the walls of this cottage? I only know that they were acquired, a year or two later, by the Metropolitan Museum in New York. But what struck me in all these houses was something I took for a symbol of an America that travellers seldom see, something remaining amid the "strangeness," the "queerness" of the time, that seemed to me singularly reassuring. They were as private as the lives of Emily Dickinson and Albert Ryder whose motto might have been "Hide thy life," and I could not forget, in an age of space-ships, world wars and publicity, that the real things of the country were hidden and inward.

CHAPTER II

TRAVELS NORTH AND SOUTH

IN THE migrating season of early summer, all the world visited Westport. The intelligentsia fled in a body from New York, and one of our friends said that living in the village then was rather like living in a revolving door. One had to go away to escape from cocktail parties with "sounds that are not voices," as Ellen Glasgow wrote to me from her summer house on the coast of Maine where she looked down on blue water and across blue water to still bluer hills. The country was so fresh there, she said, that it might have been created at dawn and she felt a closer kinship with its clear outlines and green ponds than she felt with her tropical Virginian splendour of bloom. We often drove at that time to Maine where there were no insects to mar the perfect foliage of the oaks and the maples, where there was scarcely a murmur even from the hemlocks and where the ticking of the old wooden clock in the farmhouse that we rented brought back the odours and the flavours of a hundred years ago. It gave one the feeling of space and time, of clarity, simplicity and amplitude that vanished in the feverish summer time at home.

No one conveyed this feeling of an immemorial American scene as well as Henry Beston at Nobleboro on the northern farm he described in a beautiful book that rebuked the impoverished language of everyday writers. A prose Robert Frost, an artist in words, Henry Beston continued to live in a world of country handicrafts and bright colours, plaid shirts and heavy caps of red, green and blue, where the people caned chairs, hooked rugs and whittled playthings as in the time of Thoreau or of Currier and Ives. He had a great herb garden; he even had a mandrake that had been brought from the Valley of Armageddon; and he read agricultural magazines in which he said sound English continues in our abstract civilization. I could understand, reading him, the vogue of Gertrude Stein, in a world of journalistic clichés and academic jargon, for she seemed to make words new by destroying their context. Henry Beston, with his country lore, rehumanized the American scene in which human beings had become vagrants in space. Moreover, his book seemed to be alive with the creatures of the forest and the sea, gulls, curlews, hawks, deer, the wildcat and the moose. In *The Outermost House,* about Cape Cod, he evoked the great elemental sounds, the sound of rain, the sound of wind in a primeval wood and the sound of the outer ocean on a beach; and, half French himself, in his book on the Saint Lawrence, he recalled the habitants whom he had known upon this river. They did not merely use but cherished the land. Remembering the virtues of the native roots and leaves, Henry Beston loved the old wisdom of the American forest.

Henry Beston fully expressed the savour that Maine had for me, just as he expressed Quebec where a professor whom we knew collected the folk stories of the habitants and their songs. This man, the son of a country doctor who had driven all over the province, played for us on his gramophone some of the ancient ballads and tales that had survived on the

Gaspé from the Middle Ages, tales that were often grim and ballads, once gay in France, that had become sinister and heavy in these far-away forests. But Henry Beston, above all, suggested the feeling of Cape Cod, where I lived for many weeks at one time or another, and Martha's Vineyard especially, that wilder Isle of Wight where I had spent a summer once in England. Martha's Vineyard had the same shape and the same dimensions as the Isle of Wight, with little towns set about in corresponding corners, and with moors, cliffs and a "gay head" at the end. It was a world of beaches, wild roses and bay, where at the opening of our sandy road Thomas Hart Benton lived and Francis Hackett came for frequent visits. There also came a friend of my Tahitian brother-in-law, Vilhjalmur Stefansson, who had found the Arctic friendly and who told me that Ole Rölvaag was all wrong in his account of the monotony of the prairie country. It was supposed that the asylums there were full of people who had lost their minds because of the monotony of the prairie landscape, but Stefansson said this was not true at all. He had grown up on the prairie and loved it, though he said it was easier to love mountains and forests because novels and poems had been mostly written in rolling or rugged country and people had been conditioned to prefer it. But the great man of Martha's Vineyard, for me, was Roger Baldwin, an American of the pre-war type who had a special connection with New England, a defender of the under-dog who had thriven before fatalism and cynicism destroyed the general interest in human causes. Along with the Civil Liberties Union, which he had fathered and led, he shared the old rural concern with plants and birds, and every year, in the loft of his barn, he banded the newly-hatched offspring of a great owl that spent the summer there. I know that there still exists a great army of "bird lovers," as numerous as the Mormons or any other sect, and I remember one occasion on Martha's Vineyard when a pair of purple gallinules suddenly appeared there. The telephone wires burned with the news, just as they burned when the word went about that a Carolina warbler had been seen in the woods. Later, in a Connecticut village where an English robin appeared one day, a delegation went out from Hartford to report it.

I have long believed that the best writers are now the writers of natural history who are ignored commonly in critical circles because they are concerned with permanent things outside the changing human world that interests the novelists and most of the poets. From the point of view of the critics they are off-centre, as they were not in the rural past when farmers, ministers and statesmen knew their forest world and wrote about it. Jonathan Edwards at twelve years old produced a long description of the "wondrous way of the working of the forest spider." But intellectual city-dwellers determine the climate of literature now, and beautiful writing scarcely counts in critical circles any longer when it deals with the facts and shows of nature. Otherwise there would be no writers more critically esteemed than Henry Beston or Rachel Carson or Loren Eiseley, who has related, in *The Immense Journey*, the ascent of man from his dark stairwell. Why are these writers of natural history now called popularizers of science as if all their style went for nothing, as if theirs were the bottom rung of the ladder of science instead of an upper rung of the ladder of art? Wondering about this, I remembered a remark that Matisse made to Walter Pach, "There are times when even very great artists are unacceptable to us because we are pursuing some line of development in which they have no place." How much truer this is of not-so-great artists and writers who deal, in an urban world, with immutable themes.

In the winter we sometimes went south, and one seemed to enter history the moment one crossed the Potomac; for there were old ladies in Alexandria or in Charleston or St. Augustine who opened abysses in the dark backward of time. They told stories about the Civil War that never appeared in the history books, and one old lady at Warrenton remembered the battle of Bull Run and how Generals Pope and McClellan had advanced on the town. Pope had sent word that he would make his headquarters in her family's house, but, knowing his ferocious reputation, they had sent word to General McClellan, asking him to stay with them. When he came,—they had known him in Washington,—he treated them with great consideration, and General Pope was obliged to take a house down the hill. On the battlefield itself, eighty years after the battle, a ragged old man hurried out to guide us. He had been a boy of nine, he had watched the fighting from the Henry house, and "My goodness," he exclaimed, "I wish I could remember things that happened yesterday as well as I remember that day." He had been a helper in the little stone hospital, and he saw the surgeons cutting off hundreds of arms and legs and piling them under a big tree he pointed out.

In these old Southern towns life seemed to have stood still, and I could understand the Southern renaissance of the moment when so many folk legends and myths were still alive there. In the South much of the past survived in the present. I shaved in the morning in Alexandria in the same small mirror that George Washington was supposed to have used for shaving, bought, with the dinner-plates we also used, at the auction in Mount Vernon where the last Washington had lived, a bankrupt. Then, on a rainy night in Kentucky, I watched an old blind ballad-singer, a humble reincarnation of Beowulf and Homer, sitting on a bench with his guitar waiting for a bus while he improvised a ballad on a recent murder.

I remember a lady in Charleston saying, "Lafayette sat *right here*," as she pointed to the left-hand corner of a sofa; and I remember two old ladies who lived in a large house with a sign "Rooms to Let" affixed to the wall. Over the entrance was a massive wrought-iron grille,—a battered marble capital surmounted each of the lofty gate-posts,—and when I rang the bell at the gate an old Negro appeared in a white coat and held out a Sheffield card-tray as he opened the gate. Then over the long flagstones of the garden he bowed us to the front door where two old sisters stood, desperately eager, obviously, to rent their bedrooms. One of them had learned the correct sales-patter, which she delivered in a halting voice, while the other stood by, with Medusa-like hair, silently consumed with shame and rage, having to open their door to these vandals from the North. We were obliged to enter the dilapidated mansion with Chippendale chairs covered with dust, portraits black with dirt, great pieces of silver dim with mould and fine old rugs stained and tattered; but I had a feeling that there was murder in this house and that we might not have survived a night upstairs.

One of my mother's cousins had married the minister of the Huguenot church, a French Episcopalian clergyman, and he had given us letters to one or two old families, with whom the word "cousin" had a magical effect. You had only to remark in a drawing-room that you were somebody's cousin for a pleasant murmur to go round the room, as if to say, How nice! "Will you have a little Gentleman's Relish?" one of these ladies asked, as she poured a cup of tea for me. Another lady showed us, among the early tombstones, where an angel or a death's-head would commonly be, a medallion of an eighteenth-century belle, carved in the stone in her evening gown, as if she were going out to dinner. "Of course," this lady said to me, "We do feel we're a little different." They had had, for a few years, in South Carolina, a provincial house of peers, with four orders of nobility, landgraves, margraves, barons and one other, which had been recognized by the British House of Lords. Eighteenth-century Charleston was a far-away outpost of London, and I saw, in the Goose Creek church-yard, the tombstone of a lawyer who had "set the table on a roar." One could see, in DuBose Heyward's *Mamba's Daughters,* the efforts the Charlestonians made to maintain, in a fluid world, their position in society, as if, like King Canute holding back the ocean, to stop the fluidity that was washing them out.

Charleston struck me as a school of manners, not least among the Negroes, the "quality coloured folks" who were "raised with *ways*"; and they told me on Folly Island about George Gershwin's cousin, the painter, who had written home that he could hardly work there. He was too disturbed by the "bellowing of the alligators and the shouts and cries of the wild blacks," the Uncle Toms and Dinahs who inhabited the island. I remember an old postman with a goatee and an air of General Beauregard who took off his hat to me with a ceremonious bow, and a policeman who was so polite when I parked my car in the wrong place and who quietly hastened after me. He refrained from saying, "Hey, Jack, what's the idea?" Instead of this greeting of the North, he remarked to me in a gentle voice, "Excuse me, sir, I think," etc., etc. But some of the Negroes had to choose between light and heat in their cabins. They had no glass windows but only wooden shutters, and so when they started a fire for cooking they had to close the shutters and live and cook in the dark to keep the heat in. When they opened the shutters to get light, they were obliged to let the fire go out.

In Richmond, coming or going, we saw Ellen Glasgow now and then in the big square grey brick house, with magnolia and holly around it, where she had written all her novels. I had wondered at Sinclair Lewis's remark one day to me, "Can you read Ellen Glasgow? I can't and Willa Cather says she can't either." At that time Sinclair Lewis was living on Central Park West. He saw much of Willa Cather who lived across the park and, as I gathered, saw almost no one else. Was Ellen Glasgow possibly too tame for Sinclair Lewis and too domesticated for Willa Cather, in whom might well have lingered unhappy associations with the Virginia of Ellen Glasgow's novels? I could not understand their distaste for this fine work any more than the statement of a "formalist" critic, who was himself a Southerner, that Ellen Glasgow's novels were "journalistic." She had "style" but no "form," this writer contended, and she could no longer be read when critics "had come to expect a novel to be what good novels had always been, as formally perfect as a poem." *What* novels? I said to myself. Was *Wuthering Heights* formally perfect, or anything of Dickens, Balzac or Dostoievsky? In any case, was it not more important that the author of *The Sheltered Life* was the turning-point in the literary history of the South? She told me in Richmond about a picnic when she was six or seven at which she had eaten a ham sandwich; picking out the fat, she had thrown it away, saying "I never could abide fat!" She had always felt that way, as any reader of her novels could see, and it was Ellen Glasgow who had destroyed the taste for fat in the Southern literary mind.

But no doubt the distaste for Ellen Glasgow of the later Southern writers, or at least of the formalist critics who were mostly Southern, was that she had seen the old South as it really was instead of the idealized South of *I'll Take My Stand*. The Southern revival had begun with minds like hers or like the mind of the philosopher of North Carolina, Thomas Wolfe's "last of the heroes," Horace Williams, who had said, "The Saviour was not a Methodist." Horace Williams had broken the grip of the Southern fundamentalists, just as Ellen Glasgow hated and exposed the "inherent falseness" in much of the Southern tradition; and the agrarians had revived the old fundamentalist orthodoxy along with a romantic view of the antebellum South. No wonder the "new" critics ignored or patronized her, and all the more because she was interested in the creation of character and because she wrote social history or the history of manners, irrelevant interests from their point of view. Ellen Glasgow called herself "a Southerner, though a recalcitrant one," but there was no doubt that she loved Virginia, as we could see when she drove us all over the country of *Barren Ground*. She took us to lunch at the president's house in Williamsburg and to Westover, Claremont Manor and Upper Brandon.

"Oh, Ellen's too full of herself!" Mrs. Charles Dana Gibson said to me when I first met this typical Southern belle, one of the belles and beauties whom Ellen Glasgow knew so well and whom in one book or another she so admirably pictured. Mrs. Gibson had given me one side of her cocktail glass, by way of a loving-cup, in the fashion of a belle. Ellen Glasgow *was* too full of herself, but in that bland Richmond world how could she have carried on if she had *not* been, if she had not barricaded herself and defended her great interest by nursing an anti-social rebellious ego? She once spoke of James Branch

Cabell as having survived "the blighting frustration of every artist in the South," in Richmond where everyone looked with suspicion on what they called "people who write" and no one had any sympathy with her inclinations. She told me that when she was young she had filled an Indian basket with the letters of her first publisher, Walter H. Page,—my own first chief in a far-off day in New York,—and that when she was away from home her sister had burned these cherished letters and used the basket for her own Red Cross knitting. I remembered the complaint of Thomas Nelson Page about the destruction of old family papers that made it so difficult to write the history of the South. He said in one of his essays, "The very proofs of our identity and position have been disregarded and destroyed"; and Ellen told me that as a child, on rainy days at Reveille, she and her friends had burned the old papers in the attic. They had carried down armfuls of her family's love-letters of the eighteenth and even the seventeenth century and laughed over them before they put them in the grate, a way people had, she said, in old Southern houses. The interest of history and literature was the last thing to be thought of in a world that knew only gossip and oratory, and no one saw in it the touch of Greek tragedy, Ellen Glasgow said, when the story of the incest of the Randolphs came to light. The only comment of the Richmond people was, "Why rake up that old scandal?"

When later I told Stark Young that I hoped to write about the South, he replied that "Southern history and the general Southern quality have a curiously illusive essence, almost impossible to define . . . Some critics in New York took *So Red the Rose* as a romance, when it laboriously expresses,— in terms of images and creation, I hope,—a great many Southern traits." I had no doubt that Stark Young was right and that the "illusive essence" was partly a result of the absence of documents and facts, while it was related to the kind of poetry one found in Savannah, for instance, in the Bonaventure cemetery and its overgrown tombs. The long cypress alleys and the camellias blossoming under the Spanish moss, so redolent of *Ulalume* and *Annabel Lee,* brought back an old South that was more poetic than anything else in America, even than Gothic Salem or the Hudson river. I could understand Henry Miller's rhapsody over Louisiana and the colour and warmth bequeathed by the great old plantations to the brief and bleak pattern of our historical life, and I could see why New Orleans had supplanted Boston as a focus of literary interest. Especially when the "bad girl," who was supposed to have abounded there, became a favourite theme of American fiction, but more when the genius of Faulkner evoked a school of followers all over that region of the South.

CHAPTER III

IN THE WEST

YEARS LATER, at Big Sur, I fell in with Henry Miller in his camp-life nest on a ridge overlooking the Pacific. Deep at that time in my literary history, I was eager to see the country, and I had returned for two or three winters to Carmel where I had been married in 1911. Thirty miles south of the village, one could almost have tossed a stone from Henry Miller's cabin into the ocean. There was a glass door at the rear that Miller had painted with symbolic designs expressing his great care for the esoteric, and on a rock outside stood a porcelain bathtub equipped for ablutions in the wind and sun. An anarchist still, he seemed to have outlived the mood of *The Tropic of Cancer,* that "kick in the pants to God, man, destiny, time, love, beauty"; and he wore about his neck a Yemenite amulet, a small silver disk, that his Jewish brother-in-law had given him. He had the air of an aging Buddhist monk, and this lover of romantic mystery and all things arcane to whom America *in toto* was an air-conditioned nightmare had found on the California coast some of the feeling that in Greece had made *The Colossus of Maroussi* the best of his books. He had become a Zen Buddhist, like some of the Beatniks who had found their way already to his high ridge.

I had driven out through the Middle West, and through the Southwest, where there were still people who spoke the old Spanish of Cervantes. I had seen a village of the Stone Age across the Rio Grande, from a twentieth century highway in El Paso, and then one came to the Casa Grande, a huge ceremonial building erected at the same time as the cathedral of Chartres. There were the living pueblos, Acoma and Taos, and there was the tomb of Percival Lowell with its visible sarcophagus under the great dome of bluish glass. I had seen nothing so romantic and dramatic since I had spent a week near the lonely tomb of Chateaubriand on the coast of Brittany. There had been, a few years before, a literary movement at Santa Fe, and there was much weaving at handlooms now while adobe houses were still going up and local poets went in for Indian song-poems. The Southwest and California might have been another country; they were like a northern Chile or Peru; but, as a part of the United States, they extended almost indefinitely its memory and tradition of literature and art. The first wagon had entered this territory in the very year in which Shakespeare wrote *The Merchant of Venice,* and I was shown a madonna that was painted in Mexico, near by, when Michelangelo was still living. All the European epochs were jostled together in the United States, the Middle Ages in the Kentucky blood-feuds, the eighteenth century in Charleston and in Taos prehistoric time.

It struck me on the road that my fellow-countrymen were perhaps the strangest people in the world. I mean the common run who think they are the only normal folk and that all the rest are wops or chinks or dagoes. I watched them in their cars from New Jersey to Missouri, and they seemed to be unable to eat except to the accompaniment of the raucous strains of a radio singing about LUV. They ate at any hour that appealed

to their fancy, with the odour of cheap fried fat heavy on the
air, shakes and burgers, French fries, hot dogs and Seven-Up
mixed, in any sequence, all together. They grabbed their grub
and took it out to devour in their mobile caves to the sound
of "Busy Body Boogie," "That Crazy Mambo Thing" and
"Teach Me Tonight," and it seemed to me that we were the
most uncivilized people on earth, though no doubt also the most
solicitous and kind; for when, at a roadside café, they said,
"How are you this evening, folks?" one sometimes felt that this
greeting came from the heart. The phrase "a real American"
meant, in the West, as I found, simply a liberal, honest and
unprejudiced man: it had none of the sinister overtones with
which the intellectuals whom I had known at home invested it.
But was the word "Easterner" still a magic word there? A friend
in Chicago had written to me, an Easterner himself, "I assure
you that an Easterner is always suspect here. They think that
we think we are superior and dare us to patronize them." He
said the Middle West still seemed unsure of itself and always
"feared its slip might be showing," unlike the self-confident
Far West where I remembered, nevertheless, the prestige the
word "Easterner" had when I had first gone there. The mere
fact that I was a Harvard man, although I had no advanced
degree, procured for me at once a post in one of the universities.
But that day had long passed in Los Angeles, at Stanford and
in Berkeley.

Now, twenty or thirty years later, I saw, in Los Angeles,
streets named after men I had known in that earlier time,
Gayley Avenue, Hilgard Street and especially Wilshire Boulevard named after Gaylord Wilshire, who had lived in London.
Professor Gayley, the charming Irishman who kept open house
in Berkeley and whom I had seen so often in 1911, had introduced me one afternoon to the great Professor Hilgard, who

stopped for a moment to speak on Channing Way. Remembering, along with the author of Gayley's *Classic Myths*, this fine
old man's face and bearing, I realized, seeing these two names
on street signs in Los Angeles, what a long generation had gone
by. When I went to England to teach in 1913, I had seen a good
deal of Gaylord Wilshire in his old house on Hampstead Heath
where, on Sunday afternoons, lions, lionesses and cubs of all
degrees assembled. One day Mrs. Wilshire said to me, "Our
afternoons are always distinctive. We never know what the
symposium will be. Today, you see, it is spooks." One man
there had written a story about a woman who was pestered by
Frank R. Stockton's ghost, and one of the spooks was a "miracle
girl" supposed to have been dying of three diseases when an
angel appeared and told her to arise and walk. This young lady
rebuked me for killing a spider on the hearthstone.

In Los Angeles I met Lion Feuchtwanger, who had lived for
eleven years in his walled garden, although every day his wife
sent him out for a walk up the steep hill outside. Meeting few
Americans, and having escaped from the Nazis, he was convinced that he was surrounded with wolves, that America was
run by an Ogpu while the Russians were free. In his dream of
the Middle Ages, about which he was writing historical novels,
he had scarcely caught a whiff of the real air about him; and he
was so used to being a best-seller that not to be taken by the
Book-of-the-Month Club was, he felt, not to be published at
all. Besides history, his reading consisted mainly of bookseller's
catalogues from all quarters of the world; he put his money
into first editions, and there were in his house hundreds of
shelves with complete original sets of Goethe, Rousseau, Field-
ing, Milton and others. He had a Shakespeare folio and an
edition of Spinoza with the philosopher's own annotations. The
garden from which had been gathered that year eleven thousand

bananas, he said, overlooked a Hindu shrine, a few hundred yards below, in which were buried some of Gandhi's ashes.

I spent an afternoon near Los Angeles, where he lived, with that good and most lovable man, Upton Sinclair, who, in a time of great talents with small hearts, had, it seemed to me, a particularly large one. He stood at the gate of his big Spanish house with the sun beating down,—there were no trees, there was nothing to shade it,—and, on this bright spring day, he received me in a darkened room with all the window-shades closely drawn. Deeply shrouded electric lamps, with bowls of pink camellias, stood in every corner of the room, while his wife, who was scarcely able to move, so frail her heart was, sat in the semi-darkness like a heroine of Poe. He told me that he had prepared for her six hundred pots of rice that year, no new thing for this old believer in experimental diets. At the rear, out in the sun, he showed me two storehouses of corrugated iron, filled with translations of his books in forty-seven languages. Years before, I had written an article saying that I did not like these books and could not believe in them from any point of view, but this statement never satisfied me, especially in recent years when I had a deep feeling of kinship with Sinclair. I was drawn to him all the more when the literary tide turned away from everything we had in common.

I had been judging him by the ordinary scale of novelists, whose material, he said, they collected with a microscope whereas he collected his with a telescope. There was no use in observing that novels are about individuals when he said that institutions were "higher products of evolution," and, when he wrote that he was "impatient of every form of stupidity," why reply that this was not the attitude of a novelist? Upton Sinclair's characters lived only as political minds, they existed only in political views and relations, in what they thought and said, not in what they were. Sinclair had always used fiction for ulterior purposes, and this was the cause of the quarrel between him and the critics. But, although he did not fit into any of the usual categories, he was obviously something on a large scale; and this explained why, in spite of the critics, he interested Einstein and Bernard Shaw, Gandhi, Georg Brandes and Bertrand Russell. He had a passion for improving life and the world.

With Will Durant I also spent an afternoon, the gentle philosopher-scholar in whose study I saw the account-books that contained the two draughts he had written of all his historical volumes. Like Sinclair, he was a lovable man, with his quiet wisdom, and I reflected on comments I had heard that this rare student was a popularizer of other men's discoveries and thoughts. What's in a name? I asked myself. In our servile world of scholarship, a man who is called "Will" instead of "William" cannot get the respect he surely deserves; for this writer was a formidable savant without any question. I was struck by his explanation of the idea of original sin, and the firm grip it had acquired over the human intellect. He thought it was a survival of the prehistoric day when men killed one another in order to survive, an act that became murder in a changed civilization when men had become aware of good and evil. An aberration of the days of innocence, before men had achieved the moral sense, it had suffused with a permanent sense of guilt the collective unconscious.

In old times, at Carmel, where she was already legendary, I had seen much of Mary Austin, who had written *The Flock, Lost Borders* and *The Land of Little Rain,* beautiful evocations of the life of the desert. Having lived among the Indians in the Southwest, she thought of herself as a medicine-woman, a priestess, an inspired leader of the tribe, and she felt the fury of the woman scorned because she was not recognized by the

Americans who were her own tribe. Among these were the "New York critics," as she called them, who could not accept her theories of the American rhythm, the American experience, the American literary form, derived, as she supposed, from the "first Americans, the Indians," with whom she felt our culture was organically connected. In New York, she was always looking for slights, always on the defensive, she became a *femme incomprise,* the "lonely disappointed woman with an empress complex"; for, after writing these fine books, she never found a subject she was at home with. But at Carmel, among her old friends, the chip disappeared from her shoulder, and she was sometimes like an old gypsy fortune-teller, reading the cards and distributing good-luck emblems. She gave me a talisman, covered with Indian signs, a pair of horns and a pine-tree in water-colour, and she sent me some "glyphs," or Amerind poems, in which an object, suddenly seen, fires a train of associations. But she had as many delusions as her people in *Lost Borders* whose minds melted away in the mirages of the desert. She had gone to Rome in 1907 to study Catholic mysticism, in preparation for her book *The Man Jesus,* and she had applied at the Vatican for someone to give her instruction in Catholic doctrine. Cardinal Merry del Val himself had volunteered, she told me, to give her his personal instruction, and she was convinced that, after four or five hours they had spent together, he had fallen in love with her. At that point she had hurried away from Rome.

One evening on the beach, we had a picnic party for Mary Austin. We knew nothing of the Carmel feuds, the quarrels that divided the artists and writers, numbers of whom for years had refused to speak to one another. We asked indiscriminately all whom we knew and wondered at the embarrassments and hesitations that were evident when the people began to appear.

But many feuds, I think, were composed that night, for Mary Austin brought them all together. She was in her element sitting by a camp-fire, which called out all her gifts of story-telling. She told her story of Vasquez and the white horse, regarding which she had no doubts whatever. Vasquez was a Mexican bandit who had lived at Carmel in a little cabin in the San José canyon. We often walked up the canyon to this ruined cabin, round which wild Easter lilies grew, strays, I suppose, from some old garden. Vasquez had had a white horse, which was famous all over the country, for he used to ride this horse up and down the highway that ran between Los Angeles and San Francisco. His specialty was robbing the mail-coach. Finally Vasquez was captured and hanged and his white horse was shot, but the ghost of the horse still haunted the highway, and it always happened that whenever the horse appeared the driver of the mail-coach was killed shortly afterward. Mary Austin had seen this ghost of the white horse. She was riding all night on the mail-coach, sitting beside the driver, and just before dawn, in the darkness, the white horse suddenly appeared trotting along beside the others. Mary Austin had been collecting peach pits, which were used for making munitions in the war, and she had in her lap a bag of these peach pits, which she threw, one by one, on the back of the horse. As long as she could see them bounce off its back, she knew that the horse was there and not an illusion. Then, suddenly, as day broke, the white horse vanished. There was no bush, wall or tree behind which it could have disappeared, for they were driving across an open plain. The horse simply dissolved in the air. On its return journey northward, the stage met with an accident and the driver was killed.

In Westport, one day in the late thirties, I had heard a knock at the front door, and there, when the door opened, stood a man dressed all in black with a shabby little suitcase on the floor beside him. He said he had walked from California, working in the hay-fields, and he asked me for socks and underclothes and, more than that, he wondered if I would give him a shack on my place to live in. He told me that John Steinbeck had put him up on his Western ranch while he wrote two chapters of a novel he had brought with him. I had no such shack on my village half-acre or anything to be compared with John Steinbeck's supposedly great open spaces, but I gladly gave the wanderer the underclothes and socks and offered to read the two chapters of his novel. They seemed to me extremely good, in the style of Hemingway, and I wrote at once to a friend in New York at one of the publishing houses, asking him to give this blackshirt a weekly allowance. He would probably finish in a few months the novel he called *The Middle Way*. My friend arranged to do so, impressed as much as I was by the literary character of these two chapters; but after about six weeks the wanderer disappeared and nothing more was heard of him in New York or elsewhere. He had not added a line to the two chapters, and I wondered if he had really written them.

In Carmel, or rather in Monterey, Steinbeck said he had known this man, and, having read the two chapters, he agreed that they were as remarkable as I had thought them; but the writer had suddenly vanished, and Steinbeck himself supposed that he had copied them out of some published novel. Steinbeck was living in an old adobe house which he had hoped to own when he was a boy; he had just bought this Casa de Soto and planned to spend all the year there, though he worked in the directors' room at the Monterey bank. There was a large living-room, white, with a stove of coloured tiles made for him by Henry Varnum Poor, a big Mexican painting by Sequiros, a wall of books, a bedroom and a primitive kitchen at the rear.

Behind the house was a small garden with rich black earth where Steinbeck had just planted spinach, onions and carrots. Then there was a huge cactus plant with a four-foot trunk that clambered all over the little enclosure. Steinbeck cut off two cactus pears, one yellow and one red, opened them and gave us the hearts.

Steinbeck struck me as big, lively, genial and shrewd. He had a large red face with an upturned nose, and, somehow, the air of a German longshoreman. He said that Monterey was the only small town that was not like a small town: you could do anything there and nobody cared if you did not interfere with other people. It was, on a tiny scale, a cosmopolitan city, but he had been refused a working room in the so-called Professional Building because he could not convince the manager that he was a serious working-man. It seemed to please him that the manager did not know who he was, there in little Monterey. I thought he was established for life there, but a year later, passing the house, I saw at the door a moving-van, and I knew that Steinbeck was on the wing once more.

Sinclair Lewis asked me once what sort of man Steinbeck was, for Lewis had never seen him and knew little about him, and it struck me then that we had no community of literature, such as we had had in the nineteenth century and even later. The writers at that time had all known one another, but now they were as solitary as the rhinoceros roaming the veldt or as lone wolves drifting about a wilderness, and I remembered Sherwood Anderson's proposal that they should write to one another and form in that way some sort of relation. Steinbeck said that he knew Robinson Jeffers very slightly, although he regarded him as a great writer, and he thought that Jeffers had stopped writing because he had entered the real world for which his mind was unprepared. He had known the region of the Big

Sur even longer than Jeffers, for his mother had once been a school-teacher there; but the two had little in common in their points of view. Una Jeffers, asking me if I had met Steinbeck, said she did not really like his books,—he had written a novel that was full of sympathy for the lettuce-pickers, but with no feeling for the owners, and that was not life as she and her husband knew it. For the rest, she said she loved the fog of the Shetland Islands, which made her feel that she was alive. Both she and Jeffers hated the sunlight they lived in, and Jeffers said it was poisonous for him.

There was a flock of white pigeons perching all over Tor House on the day when I met Frieda Lawrence there. She had brought her well-known lover, Captain Angelo Ravagli, who had once been a bersagliere; and, with her big friendly voice and shapeless cotton dress, she looked like the grandmother of all the valkyries. I could believe what she said to one of my friends, "Where I am, there is life!" She remarked that her Taos neighbour Brett had just gone to England, wearing a sombrero, high boots, corduroy trousers and a long stiletto tucked in her right stocking, and that Brett's brother, Viscount Esher, said, "For my part, whenever I see her coming, I dive into the nearest shop." At the rear of the house, Jeffers had planted a pine and eucalyptus grove, and, when Frieda Lawrence arrived, I saw down the alley the well-known love-dance of the pheasants. A very gorgeous wild cock pheasant was circling round the tree-trunks, with three hens performing in regular rhythm, and another visitor exclaimed, "What a coincidence when Frieda and her lover have just come here!"

CHAPTER IV

THE OLDER GENERATION

Though I never sought out older writers, or introduced myself to them, I fell in, early or late, with many of them, sometimes at the end of their lives when they had outlived their vogue and were even more or less broken by the pressures of life. Years before, I had interviewed Howells, I had seen Mark Twain lying in state and I had observed Henry James lecturing at Harvard and later listening to Georg Brandes at a lecture in London. Then I had seen Mary E. Wilkins, a withered brown little old woman in a garish dress and hat, receiving a medal at the Academy of Arts and Letters, and Edmund Clarence Stedman, the poet, the translator of Theocritus, at a performance of the *Ajax* of Sophocles. With his fan-shaped beard and dapper little figure, he was leaning over the balcony in a hall where some Greeks were acting on the lower East Side. At Sanders Theatre in Cambridge, when Henry James lectured on Balzac, I had seen the old Western poet Joaquin Miller pushing his way into the front row of seats, and one day, at the Academy, Edwin Markham suddenly appeared, supposedly out of his mind, in charge of an attendant. Eighty-eight years old, he had a wild look, and, catching sight of Hamlin Garland, he called out over the heads of the crowd, "What are you doing here with all these dressed-up people?"

No doubt many of these older writers, whether great or small, felt like "flattened balloons, once gayly buoyant," as Robert Grant, the Boston novelist, said to me that he felt, adding, "No man can hope to bridge two generations." Alert as he was at eighty-seven,—he took three steps at a time bounding up an old belvedere when I saw him at Nahant,—he was still young in his feelings and tastes and responded very heartily when I sent him *The Enormous Room* of E. E. Cummings. He said the portraits were "hideously graphic" and that in some ways the book had "Dante's Hell beaten by a mile"; but who remembered at that time his own *The Chippendales* and *Unleavened Bread* that were almost equal to Cummings in their power of satire? Howells, who died in 1920, remarked somewhere that "history is an unwilling guest in our unmemoried land." The author of a hundred books who had been writing for fifty years, he had received one day an invitation from a "home correspondence school" to take lessons in story-writing.

I had been obsessed with the chaos of our American world and the stories of remarkable men who had been forgotten, and I was so conscious of our own shortcomings that I did not realize then how often great artists were misprized in other countries. In seventeenth-century Holland, as Hendrik van Loon reminded me, Franz Hals was forced into bankruptcy while Rembrandt was starving; the greatest genius in the language, Vondel, was a broken-down clerk, and the painters Ruysdael and Hobbema were poor and driven. Even in England, important writers were neglected and lost almost as they were in our indifferent country. Who remembered Ralph Hodgson, effaced on a farm in Minerva, Ohio, where he was running a dog-kennel? One day I received a letter from Dame Katherine Furse, who hoped to write something about her father, John Addington Symonds. I had written a juvenile book on Symonds, and Dame Katherine Furse asked me if I knew in America any friends of her father's: could I put her on the track of any material about him? "After he died," she said, "it was as though the sea had closed over him": in all England only Havelock Ellis remembered her father and could tell her anything about him. I was able to give her the names of three American friends of Symonds who had letters of his and memories of him.

One of these friends was Thomas Sergeant Perry,—"the poor dear consistently pessimistic Tom Perry," as Henry James called him in a letter to Howells. A friend of James also from boyhood and the first translator of Turgenev, whom he had introduced to both James and Howells, he had written to me to praise my life of Symonds and continued to write for many years thereafter. "I never have a chance to talk on these subjects with anyone here," for Boston, he said, "is not a literary centre. Until very recently I would pursue Howells with talk, but now I am innocuous for lack of victims"; and he was pessimistic indeed about the state of American letters,—"how scanty and voiceless and self-conscious that literature is," he said, writing at the beginning of the twenties. "In a country not yet formed, only forming itself, there is no soil for literature. No one in this country has any roots anywhere; we don't live in America, we board here, we are like spiders that run over the surface of the water." He enjoyed my old paper *The Freeman*, detesting the political part of it, saying, "Almost all the writers have a revolution in their pockets"; but he remarked, "You have, I think, the best literary journal in the country," if only we would stop chanting about the desirability of an American literature. "I am almost as sick of the two words as I am of 'old glory,' which makes me shudder and feel unclean . . . You can't get a literature by whistling for it any more than you can get a crop of asparagus by laying down the bed six months before the spring when you want it . . . A mould is slowly forming in which time may bring something up, but remember how long it was before Rome got to work and really how small the crop. I think of the long time it took Germany to get to work, and the vastness of Russia and the little produced so far." In a similar vein George Santayana wrote to me about our cultural ferment of the nineteen-twenties, "It is veneer, rouge, aestheticism, art-museums, new theatres, etc., that make America impotent. The good things are football, kindness and jazz bands." Every day Perry went to the Boston Public Library, where later a bronze memorial tablet was erected to his memory; and he wrote that he sat where all the new books were displayed and could see how few of them were worth looking at. He had lived through the dry decades of the post-Civil War time, and perhaps he would not have liked the new books of the twenties when it seemed to the young that everything was beginning again just as it had seemed in the time of Emerson and Hawthorne.

To this grandson of Commodore Perry the world was "going straight to Hell," but he was full of alert curiosity about the Russians and the French and he was a lover especially of Chekhov. He had seen *The Cherry Orchard* in Petrograd in 1908, and as an old translator he was shocked by the version of a Yale instructor "whose English was that of a Chicago street barbarian. . . . If you are in or near New York, sell your last shirt," he wrote to me, "and see the Moscow Art Company in one of Chekhov's plays. . . . Never again will you see such acting, of that you may be certain." (In fact, I never saw an actor to compare with Moskvin, who, sitting before the curtain, acted the part of a switchman on a railroad. Although he spoke in Russian and I did not know a word of Russian, I seemed to understand every word he said.) Perry had turned up some early letters that Henry James had written to him from Bonn and Geneva in 1859 and 1860: they were in a very delicate and fragile state, something like that of the manuscripts at Herculaneum that had been so tenderly uncovered. Perry had been spending the winter on a sugar plantation in Louisiana, but he had known James when they were boys at Newport, and he remembered when *Le Comte Kostia* came out,—"We put the number of the *Revue* into a sailboat and set off on an all-day trip. . . . All of H.J.'s previous life was tinctured with the Gallic juices, Balzac, Georges Sand, Cherbuliez, Musset, they were all at work on the James family." When I was translating Gauguin's hand-written journal, and no doubt complaining about it, he said many painters wrote abominably, but Monet's writing was very clear and Pissarro's was like copperplate,— "his manuscript lay in the middle of a page like one egg in a nest." Perry, who had lived in France, had known both Pissarro and Monet, and he said that Monet and Emerson were the most memorable men he had ever met: they had deeply impressed him with their power. Over the Sage of Concord he had "gently giggled" in 1862 with Henry James and his brother William, but he said that Emerson had "the divine spark and it flashed at times through the scoriae." In France he had met Zola and gone to a Magny dinner with Edmond de Goncourt. "I got the impression of having dined in a pirate's cave," he said, almost in the words of Henry James.

Then, one day, Mrs. Perry wrote to me. Eager to defend old Cambridge and Boston, she wished to explain to me why Henry James had found them "deadly,"—it was not the places themselves "but that his own home was uncongenial to him." Mrs. Perry had been a Miss Cabot, born and brought up in Boston, but she had stayed a great deal at James Russell Lowell's who had called her his youngest child. Lowell's oldest brother, she said, "was my uncle and I was quite able to distinguish the difference between the warm magical bookish atmosphere

of Mr. Lowell's and the cold vacuous intellectuality of Mr.
Norton's at Shady Hill where I sometimes had to go to a dull
dinner with the Lowell family when I was staying with the
Lowells or the poky banality of the James house ruled by Mrs.
James where H.J.'s father used to limp in and out and never
seemed really to 'belong' to his wife or Miss Walsh, large florid
stupid seeming ladies, or to his clever but coldly self-absorbed
daughter who was his youngest child." Mrs. Perry said that
"Tom of course saw more of the sons than of the women folk
and though I know he knew much of what Harry's mother was
like he would be too well-bred to tell you! . . . James's mother
(even to my own perception as a child) was the very incarnation of *banality* and his aunt Miss Walsh who lived with them
not much better. His father always seemed to me genial and
delightful (perhaps partly because he had kissed the Blarney
stone and always called me 'little sunshine' and talked to me as
if I were a grown-up person) but he seemed to me out of place
in that stiff stupid house in Cambridge." Boston and Cambridge,
on which Henry James had turned his back, were "warm and
active and inspiring in those days."

But, to return to Perry himself, he wrote, "Don't be frightened by this sudden rush of letters. I am not a German army
and you are not a cathedral. But my note of yesterday was bitten
off before I had said some of the things I had on the tip of my
pen. . . . I had begun to indulge in Americanisms and that is
a habit as bad as talking about one's immortal soul." Speaking
of my book on Mark Twain, he could not agree with me about
Howells's influence on the author of *Huckleberry Finn,* and
later, with more evidence before me, I came around to his
opinion. Perry had appeared as "Mr. Arbuton" in Howells's
early *A Chance Acquaintance,* and he knew that Howells was
not "an authoritative person. . . . He would gently suggest or

496 FROM THE SHADOW OF THE MOUNTAIN

amiably persuade in minor matters, and often did, but he was never masterful. Nor was Mark Twain an easy victim to the authority of others. No, the trimming, the modifications sprang from his immense love of popularity which was in him from the beginning." Once Perry wrote about the way knowledge creeps into one through the finger-ends while cutting a book: "I have often noticed it. I have cut a book for my wife, she would read me something, always I had seen it. Now, on the rare occasions when I have in my hands a book really worth reading, I take the precaution of holding the book upside down lest I should absorb all the cream from its pages. How the stuff gets to the brain is obscure. It must be something like the process that a Frenchman employs to teach the blind to see with their noses." Perry regretted some of the things he had missed: "When I think that I might have seen Herman Melville, that I refused to go to Buda-Pesth to see Franz Josef crowned King of Hungary, that I never went to Berlioz's concerts, I know that I have accumulated satisfactory grounds for an eternity of anguish." But, although he regretted not having seen Melville, he never read *Moby Dick:* he was always intending to read it but somehow passed it by, like virtually everyone else in his generation. As for Santayana, he wrote to me in 1927, "Wasn't this Melville (I have never read him) the most terrible ranter?" Alone of the older time, the novelist Howells seems to have been fully aware of this great writer.

Perry's letters were collected and edited by Edwin Arlington Robinson, his neighbour in the summer in New Hampshire, where Perry had a farm from which he wrote to me, "I am here in the country bemoaning a bad hay-crop. . . . The farmer is always in trouble, but so is everyone else and will be till we are all become socialists and communists. . . . Then happiness will rule. *Vide* the weekly press" (meaning myself and *The*

Freeman), "excuse my sass." As for the poet Robinson, I met
him at about this time at dinner. He broke silence at one
moment only. Looking up from his plate, on which his eyes
had been steadily fixed, he said to me, "Have you read *Ricey-
man Steps?*" This was a novel by Arnold Bennett which I had
not read, and all I could do was to say so. Then he bowed again
over his plate and spoke no more. He recalled the elder Henry
James's description of Hawthorne at a dinner in Boston, like
"an owl brought blinking into the brilliant daylight and expected to wink and be lively like any Tommy Titmouse or
Jenny Wren." Hawthorne too had kept his eyes "buried in his
plate."

Actually, Robinson and Hawthorne had much in common,
and both were the sort of writers in whom one finds an arcane
connection between themselves and the stories that attach to
their lives. The real Delia Bacon, about whom Hawthorne
wrote in *Our Old Home,* was precisely the sort of person he
was always inventing, and how characteristic it was that he
should have bought in Concord the house of a man who believed he was never going to die. Real life and fiction seemed
to merge in the case of Hawthorne, and this was the case with
Robinson also. One day, during a summer, after he died, when
I was in Maine, my landlady said to me, "Would you like to
see Robinson's birthplace?" She knew the family that had
rented it and we drove over to Head Tide. The house was full
of coats-of-arms and D.A.R. emblems, which the new tenants
had brought in, and on the very spot where Robinson was born,
—"just there," the lady of the house remarked,—began a lively
talk on the subject of forbears. "Were you one of the Portland
Stickneys?" etc. I was distinctly out of it until the lady said to
me, "I have a daughter upstairs who would like to meet you."
She called up the stairwell, "Patience, come down. There's an

author here," whereupon a girl in green pyjamas, obviously dying of consumption, came creeping down the stairs. There was so little left of her that she looked like a painted ghost, and, breathless with excitement, she whispered, for her voice was gone, "Do you know any other authors?" Then it appeared that, lying in bed, she was supporting the family writing articles about old furniture for a Boston paper, while her mother was dreaming of the D.A.R. In the cold fogs from the river, she had scarcely three months to live, and I thought that if ever there was a Robinson story it was this story that was taking place on the very spot where he had been born.

Robinson was a lifelong enemy of the American creed of success, and he had a cult of poverty that appealed to me as a real and vital element of the literary life. AE preached it, and even William James; and I had been much taken in England with the free life of one of my friends who was making a splendid translation of Vasari. He did about a page a day in the English of Vasari's time, and I can remember his beautiful script with the letters interlaced as in some manuscript of the Middle Ages. Walking one summer to Venice, he slept at the Lido, swimming at dawn, and, subsisting on snails and fish which he caught himself, he lived, like Thoreau, on a few pennies a day. Robert Herrick, the novelist, shared, if not this cult, at least a contempt for the American cult of comfort: he broke all the laws of Tawney's "acquisitive society," driven by greed and the lust for power and money. His heroes, whether doctors or scholars, were like Veblen's engineers in their scorn of any but professional aims; and he disliked the business world as much as John Jay Chapman, for whom it was hostile to truth, love and religion. It seemed to Chapman that the Americans had been mentally enfeebled by success, that ours was an unfeeling civilization and that if a man took a stand against

any business interest that interest would strike at him on the
following day. One could hardly expect a picturesque, pleasing
or harmonious social life at a time when trade was dominant as
it was at present, and for him the most interesting periods of
history were those that had been lighted by spiritual bonfires.
He was happy to think of the "martyr age" in which every New
England village produced its Bowditch, Emerson, Sumner or
Phillips, but he was repelled by the Yankee trader faces, keen-
eyed, practical and hard, that looked down in Venice on the
shuddering American tourist; for the old Venetian merchants'
portraits were so much like them. For the rest, he had often
lain awake at night wondering what was the matter with Boston.
As much as Robert Herrick, he felt "the bleakness of American
life as contrasted with European life," but, touched by its irresistible charm, he also felt, like Herrick, that "Europe is not
our way out of the labyrinth." Both these men had first written
to me to praise my book on Henry James, a novelist whom
Chapman regarded as not worth reading. Savage in his indignation and like Herrick in his point of view, he was a pre-
cursor of the critics of the twenties.

I never met John Jay Chapman, though I had fine letters
from him, and he wrote to me at the time of my *crise à quarante
ans*, "I had the worst sort of breakdown in middle life, fierce
and long and baffling, and I feel as if I may know something
about the inside of it." When he said he would like to run over
to see me, I was obliged to say that I was in a mental hospital
and could see no one, and when later I wrote to Barrytown
asking if I could see him, I was told that he was on his death-
bed. But with Robert Herrick I spent a week at York Harbor
in Maine, where he lived during many summers away from his
detested Chicago. As an old Cambridge boy, he had been condemned to pass his life in this centre of "conspicuous consump-

tion" and "conspicuous waste," and, reticent, lonely and somewhat embittered in "our least lovely" of civilizations, he had a
shrewd eye for human foibles. He told me how, visiting Henry
James, he had inadvertently put him to torture on the station
platform at Rye, bidding him farewell: he had compelled James
to reveal himself in a friend's company beside a shabby third-
class compartment. I wondered what Herrick's feeling was
about the great lady upon whom he took me to call on a visit
to Portsmouth. We had gone first to see the house of Thomas
Bailey Aldrich, which had just been fitted up as a period
museum, and the great lady remarked how sensible Mrs. Aldrich
had been not to pretend that the Aldriches were anybody, or
anything more than the family of the captain of a ship. Then
she drew up for us a list of the various strata of Portsmouth society, the supreme shipowners, the lesser shipowners, the
masters and captains of ships and all the other grades of the
local social hierarchy. She might have been the Empress
Theodora describing for two travellers the seven concentric
circles of Constantinople.

In those days visiting was possible still with servants and
roomy old houses like Hamlin Garland's house at Onteora, to
which he also invited me, though I could not go there. I think
he was mainly interested in me for my books about New England, the old home that his family had left for the West about
1848. He had a feeling of homesickness for New England. This
hearty old "son of the Middle Border," about which he had
written his best books, said he had not read my *Mark Twain*,
but he had been told it was "a brief for the suppressed obscen-
ity" that was "a negligible side of Clemens's genius." Garland
hated what he called "this age of nudity and jazz" and he found
even in Thomas Hardy's novels "a growing dependence upon
fornication," but, vigorous, cheerful and busy himself, he had

lost interest in fiction and was more concerned now with the
fourth dimension. He was living in Hollywood, writing about
our continuing memory after death and about the strange crosses
of which a clairvoyant had revealed the burial places in the
desert. "I have gone beyond any illusions about my career," he
wrote. "Few are interested in me now and no one will be interested in me tomorrow." But he was happy in Hollywood whither
he had followed many of his old neighbours of the Middle Border, and he wrote, "I wish you could see our desert flowers this
week—miles and miles of lupin, sand-verbena, poppies and the
like. Seas of purple and gold! When California sets out to do a
thing she does it on a grand scale."

While I saw Hamlin Garland only in New York, I visited
Owen Wister twice, once in Rhode Island and once in Philadelphia. When I arrived at the Long House in Bryn Mawr, he
was playing on the piano, and I remembered how he had been
introduced to Liszt who said he had a remarkable talent for
music. Liszt had known Fanny Kemble, Owen Wister's grandmother, of whom there were four or five portraits, one by Sir
Thomas Lawrence, in the house, with other portraits of other
Kembles and one of Mrs. Siddons, his great-grandfather's sister,
over the library mantel. This was the white-haired masculine
profile surmounting a dark red velvet dress that Sir Joshua
Reynolds had once painted. The house and everything in it
seemed a long way from *The Virginian*, the first book, after
Bret Harte, of a kind that was frequent later, foreshadowing
the generally debased Westerns of the movies. Owen Wister
told me that, calling on Henry Adams who was railing at the
country, he had broken out, "Oh, I can't see it so grimly,"
whereupon Adams rose, walked across the room and, laying his
hand on Wister's shoulder, said, "Keep the faith!" Again, writing to Mrs. Winthrop Chanler, Wister had said that Edith

Wharton must have a "small cold heart." Mrs. Chanler showed the letter to Mrs. Wharton, then, later, speaking to him, she said, "I've expiated it. I've told you!"

Owen Wister took me to an old-fashioned Sunday dinner at the house of Dr. and Mrs. Middleton Fisher, where two old sisters of Mrs. Fisher were also present that day, a household of octogenarians or even older. They had recently sold their great house and moved into another house that evidently seemed to them a cottage in the slums, although it was a big stone dwelling with gables and verandahs that stood in the middle of several acres of lawn. Great boxes of sculpture, unopened, lay on the grass,—one a recumbent river-god from Rome,—and the walls within were covered with Italian paintings, Claude-like scenes of the Tiber and contadini. They suggested the dream of Arcadia of a hundred years ago. A great family group by Benjamin West ran along the hallway, representing Arthur Middleton, the "signer," with his wife and baby, who lived to become the grandfather of Dr. Fisher, the patriarch of eighty-five or so in a buff worsted waistcoat who carved the roast beef and Yorkshire pudding. The old man's mind was wandering,—he died a week later,—and as he sat in his chair after dinner he picked up old books in Italian and Latin and pushed them over to me, murmuring about them. His wife told me that he read seven languages, and his mind was full of the Middletons and Middleton Place near Charleston: the bookcases and most of the books had been brought from there. He turned over the pages of a book by James Truslow Adams and he said that Adams made mistakes: he spoke of a Richard Middleton,—there was no such name in the family, —he must have been thinking of Russell Middleton, once the president of Charleston College. Their moving had evidently been too much for these frail old souls, who were still living in the world of a far-away past; and I thought of the last scene of *The Cherry Orchard*. One could imagine here too the locked doors, as they faded away, and the old servant left behind, forgotten.

CHAPTER V

"MAKERS AND FINDERS"

I HAD SCARCELY been recalled to life before I remembered a week I had spent, in 1914, at St. Malo. The guns were just going off in the first world war; and, held up on my way home in that little Breton city, I had read Chateaubriand's *Génie du Christianisme.* Surrounded as I was by the purple and gold of the great writer's native town, I was carried away by the sumptuous prose of the book, everywhere concrete and expressive, and I then conceived of writing a semi-historical pageant of my own, "creating a usable past," one of my old phrases. Seventeen years later, at St. Augustine, in a ramshackle plantation house, under a magnolia tree covered with blossoms, and with mocking-birds flitting to and fro, I began to read for *Makers and Finders,* my focus of interest for twenty years to come. I had already set out to see the country I was to write about, and, after hundreds of nights during my illness when I heard the clock strike every hour, I had formed the habit of rising with the sun. That is to say, in summer, for on winter mornings I invariably got up at six or a little before.

My emotional tone had entirely changed from the days before my breakdown, when I had seen life so largely in negative terms, when I had been drawn to failures and misfits like Sherwood Anderson's grotesques and Edwin Arlington Robinson's Captain Craig. I had seen Amiel and John Addington Symonds as maladjusted spirits, as I saw in Mark Twain and Henry James victims of their world instead of victors over circumstances. I had had doubts about my treatment of Henry James, regarding whom Owen Wister sent me a letter of Logan Pearsall Smith that corroborated my *Pilgrimage* in certain respects, "Of course to a friend of Henry James's and another expatriated American, the book cannot but be of poignant interest, with its mastery of its subject and of the whole predicament and situation. Having come myself to England much younger than Henry James, and having gone to Oxford, I formed all sorts of friendships and relations. I used to wonder at Henry James's foreign feeling in England, his sense of not being really at home with English people, and I remember his own saying that he felt he understood Americans better and still saw things with American eyes. I suppose I shall have to pay for my expatriation somehow, but I shan't have to pay for it in Henry James's way." But about Mark Twain I could not feel that I had been mistaken, and I was to repeat substantially in *The Times of Melville and Whitman* the thesis of my original book about him. No attempt was really made to reply to the evidence I had assembled. The frustrated writer,—Melville was a type,—had seemed to me characteristic of our still pioneering country, but I had now read Emerson over and over in order to write a biography of him. Besides this "spiritual germ-cell," as AE called him, "of American culture," I had reread thoroughly Thoreau and Whitman; and I had begun to see the figure in the carpet where I had once seen mainly the seamy side. If I did not "reverse" myself, as certain critics said, it is true that something was reversed in me when, besides the visible civilization, I saw the invisible which these great writers had exhibited to me. Lewis Mumford told me later that my changing point of view had been evident in my letters of 1925 when I had been writing the life of Emerson that seemed to me my least successful book. As a sailor in the navy, Lewis had carried Emerson with him, and in *The Golden Day* he had acclaimed the great writers to whom I had done so little justice. Lewis, in fact, was naturalizing in the minds of American readers many artists who had not been regarded as artists, not only the architect Louis Sullivan but Roebling, Eads and Olmsted, creators of new cultural forms in a world of adapters.

This was a time of discovery, or, as Waldo Frank said, of rediscovery, when the expatriate mind was turning homeward, when Parrington was writing his *Main Currents of American Thought* and Carl Sandburg his biography of Lincoln. A hundred years earlier Audubon had discovered the birds of America, George Catlin the American Indians, Asa Gray the plants and John Lloyd Stephens the old Central American peoples, while many minds now were bent on following Stephen Benét's "Westward Star," uncovering the roots of the native American culture. Constance Rourke had undertaken an ample historical account of this, and John Brooks Wheelwright was at work on a history of American architecture for which the notes were "mounting like a sea." So he wrote to me in 1932; but he and Miss Rourke were to die before their work was finished. Harold Stearns came home, after thirteen years in France, to write *America, a Reappraisal,* and Edmund Wilson's *Europe Without Baedeker* expressed a disillusion with the old world that would have been inconceivable twenty years before. Europe was no longer a sanctuary, and John Gould Fletcher wrote to me on his return from England, "To call a thing 'European' now fails to ring a bell in American breasts." He continued, "The list of great European writers seems steadily to grow less," while the growth of American biography and history made America everywhere interesting, so that it seemed possible to live in the remotest corners. "I think Europe is tired out and one cannot expect more from England, France and Italy than they have done. Nobody here sounds new deeps. Of course Europe is a great continent and it will go on emitting sparks of genius like Wells's book in his romance of the 'World Set Free,' but with dimming lustre." So AE said in one of his letters. It was noticeable that the old expatriates Bernard Berenson and Gertrude Stein who had spoken of themselves as "We Europeans" were to call themselves "We Americans" in days to come; and Gertrude Stein said on her return, "So much has happened since I left. Americans are really beginning to use their minds, more now than at any time since the Civil War."

One could scarcely maintain any longer the negative view of the twenties,—of *Civilization in the United States,* for instance,—as one listened to the émigrés who had come from the boiling caldron of Europe, the phrase of George Grosz in his memoirs. One found "universal hatred" there, George Grosz wrote, although it was true that, coming to America, the caricaturist was destroyed in him, for so little here lent itself, he said, to distortion. He could no longer express despair or disillusionment, and the lover of Raphael and Ingres came to the front in him but with far less of the old authority and force. Among other cultural insiders, however, Gaetano Salvemini and G. A. Borgese, who fought with great effect the Fascist Goliath, found themselves productive in a civilization where they had full freedom of expression and action, even if they had to forge for themselves a "new English-speaking subconscious," as another émigré acquaintance said to me. This was a Russian theologian who had been driven to Germany, after the Soviet revolution, and, driven from Germany, after the rise of Hitler, had come to the United States to learn a third language. He had written books in both Russian and German and was attempting to write in English, on the subject of freedom of speech, when he suddenly died.

But the effort to forge for himself a new English-speaking subconscious was a little too much for Borgese, though he wrote his fine book on Fascism in our language. He had hoped to prove that a foreigner could write an idiomatic English poem, and he was obliged to defend with a quotation from Michael Drayton the phrase, in his *Montezuma*, "the jaguars jerked." He meant that the jaguars moved abruptly up and down. But he gave new value to another phrase when he sent me his visiting card inscribed "G. A. Borgese, American Citizen, April 12, 1938." Borgese always called me "Brother," as if I were a fellow-Carbonaro, and he and Salvemini included me, an old lover of Mazzini, in the group that published the manifesto, *The City of Man*. Then there was the tumultuous Ernest Bloch who was living on the coast of Oregon "in silence, with the ocean, woods, clouds, the great spirits of the past" and who told me that one of my books convinced him that he was right in his vision when he composed, in 1926, his symphony "America." I had been introduced to Ernest Bloch, on the street in New York, at the time of his arrival in 1917, and, having heard, in Carnegie Hall, his first grand recital, I was ready to agree with Pablo Casals that he was the greatest composer of our epoch. Now,

living, as he wrote, "in a frightful mental solitude, amidst
all the fads and false values of our time," it "required an in-
credible tension to go on," he continued, "and *create*, in
spite of all." These émigrés were the most appreciative readers
of my historical series, and George Grosz said that he was
taking *Makers and Finders* to Germany three or four weeks
before he died there.

Of course there were thousands of exiles from Europe,
among them Maurice Maeterlinck who spent five years in
New York at about this time: often I looked up at the windows of the Hotel Plaza where this great writer of the past
was living. Maeterlinck might perhaps have said what the
daughter of a great Austrian author wrote in 1941 to me,
"Nobody who has not gone through the harrowing experiences of these last years in Europe can appreciate the marvellous sensation of freedom which I found in this country."
But I doubt if Maeterlinck had any interest in the country.
I only know that he had written well of Emerson, and I am
sure that most of the émigrés saw the distinctive American
tradition in Jefferson, Thomas Paine, Emerson, Whitman and
Lincoln. They expressed, these men, the Pelagian optimism
of the doctrine "If I ought, I can," which Pelagius, in the
fifth century, carried to Rome, the doctrine that recurred in
Emerson's "Self-Reliance" and in most of the peculiarly American thinkers and writers. It had seemed to them that the
Augustinian doctrine of total depravity, allowing no scope
for the will, destroyed the whole point of human effort, and
against the plea of human weakness they were bent on exhibiting the power of human nature.

It seemed to me that this doctrine was operative still in
the American mind and that our literature showed it from
first to last, while it had to fight now against the dispiriting

but fashionable neo-Augustinian obscurantism. What Thoreau called "the low spirits and melancholy forebodings of fallen souls" had been more and more prevalent since the first world war, and these desperate or fatigued hearts were soothed by St. Augustine, whose *Confessions* actually became a best-seller of the time. But Jefferson, Paine, Emerson, Whitman and Lincoln were cited from India to Ireland in appeals from America drunk to America sober, and I had letters from India and saw essays in *The Aryan Path,* referring to Americans, that said, "They have forgotten Emerson and Whitman," writers who were close to the Mahabharata and whose America brought the world together. I had watched Diego Rivera painting in New York his marvellously living heads of Jefferson and all these other worthies in whom he saw the heart of the American tradition. As late as 1959, Kalidas Nag in India said to George Biddle, "India has always revered America for Jefferson and Thomas Paine and Lincoln. Now we sometimes wonder if you have changed as a nation." George had replied, "At times some of us have the same misgivings." It was certainly Jefferson who had given America an import of its own, who had made it not merely a meaningless free-for-all. Sir Herbert Read once said that I could not forgive T. S. Eliot for leaving his country and becoming a British subject. But, with apologies to Sir Herbert Read, this is quite untrue. My objection to Eliot was that he made a popular intellectual cause of attacking what gave America its uniqueness and distinction.

A strong belief in this idea had reconciled me to the vast Philistine waste of an actual country in which twenty thousand persons a year visited the house of Billy the Kid and how many, or how few, visited the house of Hawthorne? Scarcely enough to keep the roof repaired. Americanism had come to mean the opposite of what it had meant once, and the American moral outlook was identified now with the gangster stories or, at best, with technical expertness. So at least George Orwell said in one of his essays. The motto of America was assumed to be "My fist in your face"; and what could one think of a country in which people spent $908 a year for motor cars and only nine dollars for books? But the writers, at least, were always speaking of an unfulfilled promise of which they never quite despaired, and meanwhile our literature had become a world literature, perhaps in default of any other. One sign of this was the deference paid by Yeats, the greatest poet in English of his time, to the two Americans, Eliot and Pound. Was it perhaps true that, as one émigré remarked, "The old countries are dead for many generations"? It was certainly true that two German publishers said to me at an exhibition of their own fine work in printing and format, "Yes, but unfortunately we have nothing to publish." The French, who had once spoken for the world, had little to show now but a few prophets of despair. The Scandinavian countries had no more Nexös or Johannes V. Jensens, no more Knut Hamsuns or Sigrid Undsets; they had only the author of *Barabbas*; and nothing came to us from the Netherlands or from Hungary or Russia. It was plainly a time of exhaustion, at least in northern Europe, and the vacuum was filled by American writers.

Meanwhile, self-confidence in practical affairs had been succeeded by "self-confidence in matters of the mind and taste." So Henry B. Fuller, the old novelist, said in 1925, and he continued, "We are actively interested in ourselves and are actively expressing that interest through the arts—and doing it in our own fashion." The day had passed when American ambassadors went to Buckingham Palace "as fast as their hands and knees could carry them," Mr. Dooley's characterization of Walter H. Page; and American writers had been throwing off their dependence on literary England since Howells promoted the novelists of Russia, Italy and Spain. James Joyce, "the enemy," as John Eglinton called him, "of the whole English literary tradition," was read more in America than in any other country. Besides, a generation had grown up to write that had no associations whatever with England. Yet the past of our literature was little known, partly because Mencken despised the Anglo-Saxon element in it and because Eliot virtually ignored it. Had not James Huneker called "our demigods of plaster and plush, Emerson, Poe, Longfellow, Hawthorne, Lowell, Walt Whitman, the biggest group of self-illuded bores that ever existed"? These influential critics were not interested in the past of a literature of which they were critical leaders; and how many Americans knew their own past as well as the Spaniard who wrote *The Tragic Sense of Life?* Unamuno quoted Channing, Oliver Wendell Holmes and his "favourite American author," Phillips Brooks. "I love the sermons of Phillips Brooks," he said to Bernard Berenson. It seemed to me that this literature and art had by no means been explored, although there were teachers of them in all the universities. There were fifty Americans who were interested in the Western sheriff Wyatt Earp to one who had ever heard of Thomas Cole, the founder of the Hudson River School whose diary and letters would surely reveal one of the most adventurous of artistic lives. Only the other day Herman Melville was drawn out of the shadows, and Emily Dickinson only the day before that, and how many others were there of whom people should all know but of whom biographies had never been written?

There was, for instance, no life of Ernest Fenollosa, the great scholar of the Far East whom the Japanese emperor appointed Commissioner of Fine Arts for the empire and to whom he said once, "You have taught my people to know their own art." I had seen this man from Salem, this graduate of Harvard, described as a "European scholar," and meanwhile I was rebuked for writing about Henry Charles Lea, the historian of the Spanish Inquisition. A well-known professor of American literature asked in a review who this Lea was that one should write about him, although Lea was recognized the world over as the first of all authorities on his subject. To be sure, there existed one life of Lea, but no one had ever written about Alexander Wheelock Thayer who spent his life, as consul at Trieste, collecting the materials for his unsurpassed biography of Beethoven. Then there was Henry Harland, the American founder of *The Yellow Book,* and there was Marion Crawford, the once famous author whose papers and letters were still to be found at Sorrento. There was George Perkins Marsh, the founder of the conservation movement, the ambassador to Italy who died at Vallombrosa and who influenced the forming of the Italian constitution. What great and exciting lives all these had been, virtually uncommemorated by American writers! There was James Jackson Jarves, the early collector of Italian art and a fine writer of art criticism, and there was Hiram Powers, no more a great artist than Joseph Severn, yet English writers had produced two lives of Joseph Severn, while no one had ever written a life of Powers. There was James Huneker, who, although he despised the American past, had done so much to deprovincialize the country, and Frederic E. Church, the painter of Latin American scenes, whose journal and letters were still to be found in an old house overlooking the Hudson. All these names seemed to have been written in water, and it was only the other day that John Lloyd Stephens, the great writer of travels, emerged from the darkness, a man who should be as famous as any of the literary travellers, English or French, whom all the world knows well.

These were a few of the names of men on whom nobody had written at the time when I undertook *Makers and Finders* and who remained to be "discovered" as Henry Adams discovered the scarcely known Yale professor, Willard Gibbs. How many others were there of the sort that other countries evoke, for the sake of the present, from their cultural past? For instance, the Confederate general, David Hunter Strother, the charming old artist and writer who was famous before the Civil War and whose notes, diaries and letters had been preserved, recalling a time when gentlemen drew, naturally and unpretentiously, as they had written sonnets in the time of Shakespeare. But the "teacher critics" set their students to writing one more book on Eliot or Faulkner or Melville or Henry James, the handful of canonical authors who were regarded as Scripture by the orthodoxy that prevailed on almost every campus. While unexplored subjects were lying about in every corner like the relics of Roman cities in Asia Minor, hundreds of students were at work elucidating texts they were not mature enough to make anything out of. We needed free men of letters who could write *con amore,* and not for the sake of academic advancement. English writers did so. Why not ours?

There was no doubt, moreover, that sectional interests prevailed over national interests in our literary purview, that the West distrusted New England and that the South disliked it and would not recognize the merit of its literary past. One of the best critics of the South said that the "slow poison" of New England was at work even at the time of the Revolution, and New England had come to seem a small foreign country in the Western mind, which had risen to

literary power,—a country as remote from anything one had
to know or understand as Holland or Switzerland or Denmark.
It rejected the claims of a region that had produced perhaps
two-thirds of the best literary thinking of the country; for
could one say less of a little domain in which Bowditch's *Practical Navigator*, Webster's *Dictionary*, Bartlett's *Familiar Quotations* and Bulfinch's *The Age of Fable* were comparative
trifles in a brief period that witnessed the appearance of Hawthorne, Emerson, Prescott, Thoreau, Emily Dickinson, Motley,
Dana and Parkman, not to speak of Albert Ryder and Winslow Homer? It was part of my purpose to bring the sections
together and create a feeling for the nation as a literary
whole.

I wrote primarily for the authors of my own time, for I
felt sure that a living sense of the tradition behind them
could not fail to interest these authors. I mean the national
tradition that is, in Walt Whitman's phrase, an "evolutionary
outcome" of the world tradition, the part that represents our
own peculiar experience and that is properly seen as a gateway
to the rest. As for the sense of tradition itself, one could say
that in all the arts it "assures the continuity of creation," as
Stravinsky put it; and it seemed to me that we could best
connect ourselves with the great tradition by way of the tradition that we knew. Or that we *should* know, as one had to
say it, for until quite lately we had had no collective memory,
no sense of a continuous development in our literature and
art. "In America no man and no thing endures for more than
a generation," one of our novelists had said a few years before.
The American past that Mencken was bent on "liquidating"
was mainly a nineteenth-century past, and the nineteenth
century was the *bête noire* of the first world-war mind that
was determined to "kill" it, as Gertrude Stein remarked. The

whole past, not our past alone, vanished with the world wars, and culture, in the nineteenth-century meaning of the word, was largely abandoned during those years. Culture became what one of our humorists called "conversational parsley," and a great aim of writers was to "get rid of the baggage of memory . . . Memory must be killed off," as Henry Miller said. The artists of the nineteen-twenties attacked what they called "the cult of the past," the "decadent past" whose cultural fabric Wyndham Lewis set out to "wreck," and the new generation, growing up with no knowledge of the past, knew and read only a dozen contemporary authors. They grew up "with no cultural background," Katherine Anne Porter said; they "came up . . . were educated, you might say, not at schools at all but by five writers, Henry James, James Joyce, W. B. Yeats, T. S. Eliot and Ezra Pound." A teacher at Smith College told me that in forty years the cultural memory of the students had become a blank: when he first taught there all the students had recognized any allusion to *Jane Eyre, Pendennis* or *The Scarlet Letter,* while a generation later they recognized nothing. America had gained immensely in the space-sense, in its consciousness of the planet, but it had lost almost altogether the time-sense, that is to say, its consciousness of the past.

So naturally the younger writers had little feeling for our tradition; and, as for others, countless Americans of the old stock were growing up without any inherited knowledge of the history of their forbears which the earlier Americans seemed to have had from birth. Meanwhile, millions of foreign-born citizens and children of the foreign-born were unaware that America had a past. Many of these were the "cultural tramps" of whom Ole Rölvaag spoke, the new Americans who had lost their old-world cultural heritage and could not find another in their new-world setting, and in many cases they had come from Europe to escape from their own past: they wished for no past of any sort, only a future. I believed it was important to show in all its concrete fullness the largely unexplored range of our cultural tradition; and, if this appeared to me surprisingly complex and rich, it was partly because I had come late to the study of it. I had been repelled by American history because our historians presented it as almost exclusively military and economic, with scarcely any reference to literature, science and art. We had little of the social history that Trevelyan called the "life-blood of civilization," and did this not, partially at least, explain the short-range mentality that prevails so generally in this country, the fact that "we are a nation of sprinters; we almost never win the distances," as one of my correspondents wrote to me? Speaking of the theatre, Lee Simonson once remarked, "We have not learned to buttress the present with the past. In the interims we have nothing to sustain us. Like youth, we seem to live on our hopes, and not, like the more mature publics of European theatres, on our memories, the interest on our emotional and intellectual investments." Certainly the lack of a tradition was not responsible for all our ills, but did it not partly explain the abortive careers of so many of our writers, and I dare say also of many of our artists? "In Europe that's never been the case," James Thurber said one day, speaking of "the curious idea that the writer's inventiveness and ability will end in his fifties." Was it not true, as Lee Simonson said, that Europeans lived on their memories, the interest on their emotional and intellectual investments? Their past projects itself into their future, and this no doubt continues to be true at a time when Europe is relatively sterile.

I could not take for granted any knowledge of most of the writers whom I discussed in my history of the "Tree," the phrase that Debussy used as a general emblem of all his work and that I took for an emblem of tradition. When someone asked Nicholas Murray Butler about the writers of our day, he replied impatiently, "There aren't any," and I, on the contrary, found too many writers in the past, or so several critics pointed out. I was called undiscriminating, too easily pleased, because, without praising them unduly, I spoke of many who showed "the body of the time," its "form and pressure." My critics had not noted the point that Egon Friedell made in his *Cultural History of the Modern Age*: "The standards of cultural history are by no means the same as those of aesthetics. In the latter, a work of art is valued according to its absolute significance; in the former, with regard to its physiognomic character. Seen in this aspect, it may happen that works of eternal significance receive but a casual mention, and those that stand incomparably lower are considered in detail." I could not be said to have ignored the few great American writers, and, if I was accused of mentioning writers whom my critics had never read, I had my own good reasons for doing so. I was obliged to enter the imaginative feeling of a time when Emily Dickinson, visiting Cambridge, felt it was like Westminster Abbey; and, when it seemed to her that a story by Harriet Prescott Spofford was "the only thing I could not have written myself," how could one ignore Harriet Prescott Spofford? Or how could one ignore *The Pearl of Orr's Island* when one realized how it had influenced Sarah Orne Jewett? It is the minor books or writers that body forth a culture, creating the living chain that we call tradition.

In short, I discussed all the writers at a time when critics admitted only a handful as worthy of discussion, my object being, unlike theirs, not, first of all, aesthetic, but, as Egon Friedell calls it, physiognomic. "Not too damned much," Hemingway's phrase, was a motto of a time when nothing was more distrusted than plenitude, the plenitude of the great men of an exuberant past; for instance, the plenitude of Paderewski whom I heard when he was seventy-two and who gave at the end of his recital no less than twelve encores for a handful of admirers gathered about the piano. I broke in this respect an unwritten law of modern critics, as I broke another by dwelling at length, in a planetary atmosphere, on the literary history of a single nation. For, along with the sense of the past, the sense of nationality had also been largely effaced in the expatriate twenties. Nationality was the thing that Ford Madox Ford hated most; and did not the writers who set the tone of our time agree with him in that age of deliberate exiles? No one seemed to distinguish between the two kinds of patriotism, ignoble patriotism and "the noble kind which aims at ends that are worthy of the whole of mankind" (to quote Albert Schweitzer in *The Decay and Restoration of Civilization*). As any hint of the past came to be called "nostalgic," so any hint of nationalism was "chauvinistic"; and, if I was to carry out my plan, I was obliged to incur the hostility of critics.

CHAPTER VI

INFRA-RED INTO ULTRA-VIOLET

O NE EVENING, at the Academy of Arts and Letters, Carl Sandburg was proposed for membership, and an old white-bearded poet rose to say that the heavens would fall if we elected this roughneck from the West. He read aloud a poem of Carl's about a man shaving in a sleeping-car while he looked out over the prairie, and he defied us to elect the writer of this balderdash who had never apparently heard of Poe or Shelley. I have not reread that poem, which was probably far from aesthetically nice, for all the word-magic of which this poet is capable; and I reflected that Carl Sandburg is a bard, like the popular singers who wandered through Greece, singing the deeds of gods and heroes. Or he is like the poets of eastern Europe, as a Polish writer has described them in *The Captive Mind*. It is the function of these men to speak of subjects that are of interest to all the people, and they are not expected to be aesthetically nice. In short, they are public poets, unlike the newspaper poets but equally unlike the cultivated poets who are fugitives from what they call mass-culture. Carl was the opposite number of the very different Robert Frost, one speaking for the East, the other for the West. Both diffused about them a great air of space and time, as if they had survived from an unhurried older epoch.

At the office of Harcourt and Brace, the publishers, where I had spent a year, I had edited and named Carl Sandburg's *The Prairie Years,* the first two volumes of his life of Lincoln; and there, as my only other exploit in this world of publishing, I had brought in the three volumes of Parrington's great work. Carl Sandburg's passion for Lincoln safeguarded in the general mind the will to resist authoritarianism, and he was the only man I knew who could use in good faith the much-abused phrase "the American Dream." Michelet said that almost all literary men lack the sense of the people and its sap, and Carl, who cared little for the public, was close to the people in whom the healthy life-blood continues to run. He had a passionate spirit of devoted love and faith in man, and he never forgot that the first cry of a new-born baby everywhere says, "I have come through! I am." In him, at a time when the world seemed moribund to others, all things seemed to be beginning; and, like some old Swedish scald, he appealed to high and low, as the "household poets" appealed in generations past. He was at home all over America, whether in the woods of Michigan or in the little Connecticut village where he once came to visit me: he borrowed a guitar from the doctor there, and, as the evening flowed on, all the village dropped in to see him and hear him perform. He sang, recited and told stories until four in the morning, as he might have done ten centuries ago in Sweden on one of those long winter evenings in the castle halls of the Middle Ages. He had written a preface for Segovia's book, and Segovia had said, when Carl played for him, "Your feengers need dees-ee-pleene," which was no doubt true. No more than his poetry was his music aesthetically nice, but one might have said this of many of Walt Whitman's poems. Carl was a folk-genius and one of the rarest. He told me that when the "new" critics attacked him as a poet, he fell back on being a biographer, and when they attacked him there he fell back on folk-lore. To me he recalled Goethe's phrase, "Little men pay with what they do, big people with what they are."

He was as canny as Robert Frost, and the politician was strong in him. He had been asked to be Henry Wallace's "running mate." He had fellowship with Henry Wallace,—this was his key-word, "I had fellowship with him." He had fellowship also with Adlai Stevenson, who lives, he said, in the future, adding, "There *can* be hope of great days to come, great days possible to men and women of will and vision." He told me that he went back to Pater and his essay on Charles Lamb for style and would still read him three or four more times. Then one day, in what he called our "steamboat house" in Bridgewater, the village to which we moved in later years,—the house that looked like an old Fall River boat,—he told me that he had a story about two birds in a doughnut cage who had eaten their cage and flown away, whereupon, put in another cage, they ate that one more slowly. He had another story about two squirrels who had not been introduced and whose only thought was to collect nuts; then one finally met the other and said, "Anything special?" He called these stories "trifles that maintain my sanity." One day I took him to my neighbour Alexander Calder's house, that cross between Montmartre and *The Peterkin Papers,* where Louisa Calder was reading Emerson's essays, and everything in Sandy's workshop, so full of childlike whimsy, suggested to Carl some word or phrase. It was "a planetarium, an aquarium, a gymnasium," and he called one object "astronomical moment" and another "the independent universe." He called Sandy himself a "maker of silent music." Of one of the "new" critics he said that this writer seemed to be a nice smooth plank lying on the ground, but, if you lifted it up, there was a scurrying of little black not so nice creatures underneath it. Then, saying he had been offered two thousand dollars for writing an advertisement, he spoke of "the ease that flowed through me when I said No."

I understood what he meant, for a similar offer had been made to me. I had had several letters from a middle-aged man in Milwaukee who said his only wish was to be a playwright, who had thrown commercial opportunities over his shoulder,—so he wrote,—in order to "pursue the dramatic muse." He was broke, his wife had deserted him, he was in despair and suicidal. Would I help him to get one of his plays produced? Knowing nothing myself about the theatre, I turned the play over to Edward Sheldon, and it was produced for a few days in New York. Then I received another letter from this man whom I had pictured as wasted, hollow-eyed, bleak and dreary. He said he wanted to see me for a particular purpose and would take an afternoon train to Westport. A plump, pink-faced exuberant fellow climbed down to the platform and offered at once to give me a thousand dollars if I would write an advertisement for a famous Milwaukee beer. I would not even have to sign the advertisement. This was the playwright, and he had a large salary as advertising manager of the Milwaukee beer. A similar ease flowed through me when I also said No.

Carl told me this story when we were driving down the Connecticut valley from Dartmouth College. It was a narrow winding road, and when we gave Carl the wheel he began to drive like a man who is drunk or crazy. He had never had such a chance before, he said,—at home he was not permitted to drive at all, and, shouting a new poem that was on his mind, he ricocheted along the road and almost ran into every car that passed us. We were happy to deposit him at last at his brother-in-law Edward Steichen's house, with wide windows overlooking a laurel-bordered pond. There, at Ridgefield, was

Brancusi's golden bird, and there were white-blooming lilies from Africa, masses of tuberous begonias and a drawing by Charles Sheeler in black and white.

Carl Sandburg was the perfect type of the "infra-red" mentality that was giving place in the thirties to the "ultra-violet,"—in the phrase of *The Yogi and the Commissar* of Arthur Koestler,—one of those yea-sayers and lovers of life who were suspected and disliked by the smaller, more intense spirits of the coming generation. He spoke for the generous, expansive note of a time of diastole, when the future still seemed full of promise, while a time of systole had come in when there was "no future any more," in the much-quoted phrase of Gertrude Stein. Carl embodied the prophetic tradition of Jefferson, Emerson, Whitman and Lincoln that persisted, I was convinced, in our collective mind, though all the great causes seemed moribund after the Spanish civil war, with all the great ideas they had expressed. The change in the literary climate was indicated in a dream of which one of my correspondents wrote to me and which I relate in the words of his letter: "I had a dream last spring. I dreamed I was walking on a grassy plain when, above me, two or three hundred feet in the sky, appeared a glass platform. Standing on this platform were three men whom I somehow knew to be Thoreau, Whitman and Emerson. Then there was tossed down to me from one of them a large circular loaf of bread. It landed with a thud squarely at my feet. I picked it up and held it for a moment in my hands. But then some lions appeared and I hurriedly broke up the bread and threw it to them."

This was "a pretty exact picture," my correspondent continued, "of what may be a widespread psychological situation. I love Whitman, Thoreau and Emerson, but I am also afraid of the lions, and I am on the ground with them while Emerson,

Thoreau and Whitman are up in the air." Very exact this picture seemed to me, and interesting; for it exemplified the change in the literary climate that was taking place in the nineteen-thirties. These older writers expressed the prophetic tradition from which we Americans had once derived our nourishment, we who had carried on the nineteenth-century dream of Faust, Brand and Zarathustra, myths that had been forecasts of the future; and the lions now on the ground were the new dominant writers who were antipathetic to their predecessors. These new writers, whether Eliot or Pound or D. H. Lawrence, whether Kafka or Valéry or Auden, were opposed to the "infra-red" note of the past generation. The notion of man's perfectibility in a plastic world had given American writers an impetus and drive to "ameliorate humanity," as Comte put it, and even Frank Norris and Dreiser had not despaired of seeing injustice reduced by human effort. For the rest, the general motto of our art and letters had been Nietzsche's "stimulus to life."

But the ultra-violet state of mind that was taking over the literary scene was based on an eschatological despair of the world, and this was a delayed reaction of the first world war and the exhausted mind of contemporary Europe. The "blood-dimmed tide" of Yeats's phrase had engulfed the spirit of the West, creating a total disbelief in humanity or progress, and the mediæval notion of original sin reappeared to picture men as the predestined victims of their weaknesses and vices. Emerson's faith in self-reliance had sprung from a confidence in human nature that seemed no longer tenable to the younger generation, and Thoreau's demand that the individual should start life all over again struck them as impossibly ironical at this moment. Where Whitman's generous imagination had seen in war-torn Virginia a prodigality of orchards, flowers and fruits, an elastic air, a scenery full of breadth, they could see only the waste land, a sterile and desolate country, a rats' alley full of stony rubbish. As Whitman and Emerson had been impressed by the worth and good sense of the people, the writers of the new time were similarly struck by their lusts, cupidity, violence, sinfulness and evil; and no doubt they expressed the mood of world-war soldiers who had found corruption everywhere they went, in China, Japan, the Philippines, enough to destroy in them their inherited belief in human goodness. Flaubert, the great artist, for whom people in general were fools or knaves and who filled one with a loathing for mankind, became for contemporary writers a patron saint. Writers who disliked their fellow-men had taken over the literary world, and where love had been the dominant note of Romain Rolland, for instance, the note of the new writers was contempt and disgust. They seemed to dislike not only the "mutable rank-scented many" but all the other "hollow men." One felt above everything contempt in the minds of Eliot and T. E. Hulme, and of Joyce, Pound and D. H. Lawrence.

Because they lacked the vision of evil, Whitman and Emerson, according to Yeats, had come to seem superficial, though he might have added that they were not more superficial than the modern writers who lacked the vision of good, the goodness of the unspoiled human nature that Hemingway found in Spanish peasants and Schweitzer and Alan Paton in the African black men. Besides, Whitman found evil enough in *Democratic Vistas* and Emerson in the brutal elements at the core of life, the habits in human beings of the snake and the spider. But writers now were bent on seeing evil and blackness in everything, and they delighted in asserting the imperfectibility of human nature and in saying that man was fated to be barbaric. The denunciation of liberalism, as Julien Benda had pointed out, became virtually obligatory for men of letters, and, while hope was the only four-letter word that was impermissible, the temper of the time brought to light authors of the past who chimed in with the mood of the authors of the present. Lord Acton's constant historical sense of the wickedness of men corroborated Spengler's disbelief in progress, and St. Augustine's view that men have a positive wish to do evil was borne out in Joyce's mediævalism. Yeats was a hater of everything modern, of democracy and science,—he believed in "inequality made law,"—and D. H. Lawrence, who also believed in the divine right of kings, disbelieved in popular education. "Without contraries there is no progression," William Blake said, and even for those who still believed in liberalism and humanism there was something to be gained from this turning of the tide. For them, it inevitably produced new definitions and a cutting down to the bone of their beliefs. Moreover, it produced as well a kind of interiorization that a period of outward expansion had largely ignored. But with Aldous Huxley's *Brave New World* and Orwell's *1984*, all thoughts of the future were virtually blotted out, or all that were not reactionary or nugatory. A future that was only menacing was not to be thought about when people had lost all faith in their power to change it.

My old friend Sir Alfred Zimmern, who was now a Connecticut neighbour, felt outraged by the way in which writers of the time were influenced by the events of the world-war epoch. The wars, from his point of view, were the result of blunders by statesmen at whom the writer ought to look down his nose, and "that writers, of all people, should allow themselves to be turned inside out, or upside down, by headline facts seems to me shocking . . . Having seen some of these politicians close at hand, I protest against their being regarded as makers of history . . . Hitler and Mussolini, Lloyd George and Neville Chamberlain are just butterflies on the wheel . . . It seems to me despicable on the part of a self-respecting writer to allow his whole view of life to be darkened by what are mere incidentals." But whatever it was that caused the wars, their effects were catastrophic, and Eliot's *The Waste Land,* as William Carlos Williams said, "wiped out our world as if an atom bomb had been dropped upon it . . . There was heat in us, a core and a drive that was gathering headway . . . But our work staggered to a halt for a moment under the blast of Eliot's genius . . . All our hilarity ended . . . Our brave sallies into the unknown were turned to dust."

In short, the whole music of our civilization had been reset in a different key just as it had been after the great Lisbon earthquake, that earlier catastrophe of two hundred years ago which so profoundly affected the thinkers of the time. The Lisbon earthquake had put an end to the current optimism, the conviction that "all was for the best in the best of all possible worlds," for it seemed to be incompatible with the previously held belief in a benevolent Providence and the kindness of heaven. Now optimism had vanished once again with the world wars and the mood of the literary world had changed completely. It was divided between the state of mind of Marxists and pessimistic Christians for whom the world consisted only of miserable sinners, and the American tradition went out,— or, rather, went underground,—with all the ideas of the Enlightenment that had given it birth. Mencken had ridiculed this tradition, Eliot rejected it altogether, and the great writers of the twentieth century, as Lionel Trilling said, were opposed to our still innermost liberal convictions. They were all anti-liberal and anti-humanistic, and the literary world seemed to be fixed in the resulting frame of mind as if no other mood were possible for it. Harry Levin's *The Power of Blackness* summed up the dark line that Hawthorne and Melville developed, with a vision of evil like Edgar Allan Poe's, and he described this line as "the true voice of America," embodying the dark wisdom of our deeper minds. But it was the other line of Emerson, Thoreau and Whitman that Tolstoy said inspired him; and one might ask, when has the world connected America with "the power of blackness"? This assumption scarcely went with the oft-quoted remark that Beethoven's Ninth Symphony, affirming the ultimate victory of mankind, was the all-round favourite American composition. Was not Harry Levin forcing the note at a time when thoughts of evil had become an obsession?

In other words, a cultural ice-age took the place of the free-spirited twenties, an age of suspended animation, and writers became like somnolent drivers, yielding to the asphyxiation of the fatalistic fumes that were all about them. Seeking security, their minds went back to the childhood of the race, to the study of myths and origins, to the eternal mother, and one remembered what Gilbert Murray said about the warfare, the prolonged warfare that fell on the world of the Greeks: it brought about a decline of culture, together with a revival of primitive beliefs, the result of a despair of the world and the pressure of forces that men could not control or understand. One found scarcely a trace of the feeling that Alfred North Whitehead expressed, an Englishman who had done much of our thinking for us, "I wish I could convey the sense I have of the infinity of the possibilities that confront humanity,—the limitless variations of choice, the possibility of novel and untried combinations, the happy turns of experiment, the endless horizons opening out." There sounded the old Emersonian note we seemed to have forgotten, although Lewis Mumford continued to sound it in his plucky and ingenious plea for the "renewal of life."

In our singularly disenchanted world, how deep was the fatalism that called any wish to improve things a "God-complex" and that called "do-gooders" the people who cherished this wish. It is true that Aristotle said, when the state is in danger, as our state chronically is,—when the national existence cannot be assured,—attempts to organize the good life must go to the wall. The general mind cannot spend time and thought on any such thing, and no doubt it was natural enough in these conditions that literature should go to the wall also. Perhaps this explained the dehumanization that literature exhibited in our time and the sense that something was very wrong with it. An English critic had written a book that he called *The Withered Branch* to explain what was amiss with the contemporary novel, and another wrote a book that was called *The Broken Cistern* to explain what was amiss with poetry. How many contemporary books spoke of the "end" of something, *The End of Pity, An End to Innocence* and so on, as if they were really suggesting the end of the world, while no one seemed to think of beginnings any longer. "Lie Down in Darkness" was one of the notes of our time, and another was "casting a cold eye," as if all the chances were against one's seeing or finding anyone worthy of attention. A third contemporary note was "A good man is hard to find," which justified our casting a cold eye. The tone of thought of our time appeared to be set by loveless people living in a withered world, harking back to a sterile past and propagating a dislike for life and men. Yet it was only the other day that Mahatma Gandhi said, "Humanity is an ocean. If a few drops of the ocean are dirty, the ocean does not become dirty." Was Metternich wiser in the long run than Grotius, who built his philosophy of international law on a trust in human nature? Was Joseph de Maistre wiser than Mazzini? And did Reinhold Niebuhr, for all his nobility, really know more about mankind than Thomas Jefferson, Confucius or Albert Schweitzer? St. Augustine, the great provincial, knew only the story of the Christian world and the Hebrew patriarchs and kings,—he had no knowledge whatever of the story of the Greeks; and even the Bible had said of man that God was "well pleased with him." What Thomas Jefferson remarked seemed to me reasonable: "I cannot act as if all men were unfaithful because some are so. I would rather be the victim of occasional infidelities than relinquish my general confidence in the honesty of men."

It was not irrelevant to say that the French Revolution, a generation after the Lisbon earthquake, brought back the point of view that the earthquake challenged, a faith in perfectibility and a faith in progress, and while optimism might never return in the old forms the world knew once, it was certain that the mood of despair could not last forever. Either we would vanish altogether in a war of missiles or our mood would ultimately change, though Freud was undoubtedly right in saying that the people of our time "will never again see a joyous world." We know that the Lisbon earthquake was a mere surface wound compared with the universal trauma of the world-war epoch: yet it is certain that without joy life cannot go on indefinitely and that no mood continues in one stay. Diastole must follow systole or the heart stops. So expansion must follow contraction in the general system, and every ending must be followed by the new beginning that no one seemed to contemplate today. When would the new beginning appear? Where would it appear?—if not among the people who have the most vitality, the people of whom one can surely say that they are less depressed than the European peoples by "the man-quake through which we have been passing during the last fifty years." I am quoting Bernard Berenson, who understood very well the sense of futility and weariness in post-war Europe but who believed that Liberalism was bound to reawaken, cast as it was, like Brunhild, under a spell of sleep.

CHAPTER VII

DISAGREEMENTS

I HAD SMALL interest in politics, for I felt with Flaubert that literature was an ocean large enough for me; but I had always been a socialist on the understanding that the levelling was to be not down but up. I was not a socialist in what Wells called "the resentful phase," any more than Norman Thomas or Saint-Simon, who might have been called the founder of the socialist movement, and it seemed to me that socialism, in appealing for the common man, was appealing for his chance to become uncommon. I had in mind the classless world that one saw in *News from Nowhere,* freed from the traits of slavery and the petit-bourgeois; but I believed, like the critic Brownell, in the "aristocratic virtues" that should be "spread in widest commonalty." I felt these virtues should be defended, while one fought to place the masses in a position to share them. Why fight for the sharing of privilege if privilege was not privilege, a benefit, and therefore worth being shared? "Advantages" were obviously advantageous.

Meanwhile, disliking Marxism, I was all for British socialism, unable to see that the British had lost any freedom except the one kind of which we had too much. I mean the economic freedom that enabled us to produce more goods when we had

533

too many goods already, and I hoped to see our standard of living reduced until we were on speaking terms with the rest of a world that was virtually bankrupt. When thinking in duplex apartments was taking the place of the attics in which the thinking of the past had so often occurred, and when the great Republican cry was, not a chicken in every pot, but three cars in every garage, plain living and high thinking seemed to me celestial.

In the "red decade," therefore, with the rise of fascism, I took part in the newly born League of American Writers, an outgrowth of the American Writers' Congress of 1935 that was intended to bring intellectuals together. At that time there was a large market for left-wing publications, and there was a widespread feeling that "something must be started somewhere," as one of my correspondents wrote to me. This person was trying to help a man who was "starting a movement in Tennessee," and he himself presently started a movement to march on Washington, assassinate the President and blow up Congress. But this was the lunatic fringe of a hard core of thinking that appealed especially to writers who were lonely, scattered over the country and irresistibly drawn by the idea of a guild that would bring them together. They were all opposed to the fascism that was at enmity with joy and ready to pool their common interests in the common purpose that was clearly expressed in the "popular front" of the League.

Members of all the political parties were supposed to join in this, defending the democratic cause against the fascists, and they were united on the side of the Loyalists in the Spanish civil war, the particular cause of the moment in all circles. But I noticed at the meetings a large proportion of young men and women who were enthusiastic in promoting the League but who were certainly not writers in any substantial sense of this tortured word. I never knew quite who they were, for they never published anything, and it slowly dawned on me that they were political sitters-in who were taking the League over for the communist party. I did not understand at first how any writer could be enthralled by a party that made mental honesty impossible, but I soon realized why so many were drawn to communism,—they were drawn by the hunger for faith in an irreligious time. A kind of irrational fantasy drew them, and they were drawn also by the sacrifices that communism demanded of the convert. It gave them the feeling of beatitude that religious conversion always gives, even if they had to surrender their spiritual freedom; and this explained their devotion to an underground cause.

One by one the writers who were members of the League resigned, and my own turn came when, as chairman of the Connecticut branch, I was speaking at a mass-meeting in New Haven. Wilbur Cross, the governor of Connecticut, sat on the platform behind me, and suddenly, in the middle of my speech, a note was passed up to me saying, "Announce that Governor Cross has consented to be honorary president." I knew that Governor Cross had consented to nothing of the kind, and I realized that this was merely a ruse to take him by surprise and gain his prestige for the League; so I paid no attention to the note. It was a communist manœuvre, a gambit in the game for power that party members were playing in all the liberal organizations; and I soon disconnected myself from the communistic girls and boys who were destroying the League for all candid writers. I did not foresee at the moment that they were destroying the hope of organizing writers for any liberal action, for any organization that was opposed to what Marx called "the furies of personal interest."

With the collapse of the Loyalists in Spain, all the great causes seemed to be dead; and when Stalin made Hitler his ally the last illusion disappeared that socialism and communism had any real connection. Communism, in fact, did its best to kill democratic socialism, but I would have been ashamed to say that I had not known communists or shared the great hopes of the Russian revolution. I would have been all the more ashamed when men were sent to prison because they refused to betray their friends, as if the only patriotism that was worth anything was a kind that involved dishonour. Meanwhile, the study of Freud and Jung diverted the interest of writers away from political questions into personal questions. In *Travels in Two Democracies,* Edmund Wilson pointed out how unconvincing were the murals in Radio City representing the "upward march of mankind," how pale were the decorative colours and how dim the figures; while the whole idea of progress through collective effort disappeared from the general mind of writers. In many cases they had lost even their feeling for justice; and it was soon not unusual to hear artists say that they had never heard of Sacco and Vanzetti. They had become indifferent to human welfare and they thought it was "impure" to know about such matters. In forty years artists and writers had come full circle; for the reactionism that had given place to progressivism had reversed itself in the years of the wars,—progressivism had given place to reaction. A civilization that was ruled by business was no longer criticized, though it made America hated round the world. We were, in short, a Republican island on a socialistic planet, at odds with all mankind, and our literature seemed passively to accept this fate. For, while writers were not opposed to liberalism, they were no longer actively interested in it. They had become too fatalistic.

One of the results of the change in the literary climate was a series of attacks on me as "the leading patriot of American culture" and as "a narrow and embittered old gentleman with a white moustache" who had stolen his best ideas from Randolph Bourne. This was said in connection with *America's Coming-of-Age,* which I wrote two years before I had heard of Bourne. Then I was a "comrade-in-arms of Bernard De Voto" because I "could see no faults in American life," although I had written of the golden world of writers, so different from the brazen world of every day. Bernard De Voto, moreover, refused to meet me because, as he wrote, he had just attacked me again in certain lectures. "I am a weak vessel," he said, "essentially a genial soul with little backbone," and he was afraid that he would begin to find persuasive reasons why he should suppress or modify his convictions: "Oh, Brooks is a nice chap, he's had as hard a life as the rest of us, in the larger sense we're all working toward the same end, and why make such a fuss?" But it was "important," he concluded, "that the edge of difference ought not to be dulled by any discovery that it was pleasant to spend an evening talking and drinking together." That seemed to me frank and manly, but it did not suggest that I saw eye to eye with Bernard De Voto.

Then at a time when James T. Farrell described me as a "Stalinist,"—he being a Trotskyite himself,—I was called in Russia "a direct agent of Wall Street" and one of my books was banned in communist East Germany. It was said that I had "misused my talents," and a British weekly called me a "critic with skids under" who had lost all my earlier sense of literary values. In point of fact, having written in my youth a kind of social criticism, I had certainly written my best literary criticism in the last volume of *Makers and Finders,* in the chapters on Mencken, Dreiser and Edith Wharton. My historical series itself was called a "family party" and a "voluminous record of filio-pietistic indulgence," reeking of "Yankee racism" and "sentimental nationalism" because I had a mere decent pride in what my own people had accomplished. This work was also called "a special case of merchandizing," although Mrs. Jack Gardner's motto "C'est mon plaisir" had always been mine: I had never had any motive but my own pleasure in writing and I had never thought for a moment of numbers. Does any writer, in fact, ever think of the number of his readers? We write what we write because we are what we are; and then I imagine every writer is surprised to discover that numbers of readers find themselves expressed in what he has written. Another critic condemned my work because he had been unhappily married, and this, he wrote, had "induced a bias of which I hope I am now at least in part free." It was said that "Brooks is not really a critic but a lyric poet *manqué*," and my history was called "anecdotal" when there was not an anecdote in it that was not used for the purpose of exhibiting character. So little did the "new" critics expect to find character in a critical work! One professor found twelve errors in one of my books when six of these errors were his own,—he did not know, for instance, that Melville had two uncles and that I was writing about the one of whom he knew nothing. "The professors certainly have it in for you," Edmund Wilson said to me one day.

I was called a "popularizer," a word that properly means one who makes accessible the discoveries of others, when who had there been for me to popularize? I had done all my own spadework, my history was based on "original sources," and I could feel sure that no one else had gone over my field so thoroughly. Then I had "softened" American literature, ignoring the struggles and triumphs of authors, and I had "hedged" and "weaseled" in revising *The Ordeal of Mark Twain* when I had merely removed exaggerations, the result of the ignorance of youth. I was an "ideological policeman" who, having donned the policeman's blue, had taken up clubs and a gun against all modern authors, attempting to handcuff the writer and blind the witnesses to reality,—I was, in short, a common scold; and a college magazine devoted a whole issue to proving that my work was not worth taking into account. The name of Oliver Allston, suggested by Washington Allston, and incidentally the name of one of my sons, was said to have come from my love of the Puritan qualities of Oliver Cromwell, qualities that my critic described as "all-stone." Above all, I was "nostalgic," a word that re-echoed for twenty years in almost every description of *Makers and Finders*, as if I had longed to live in every moment of a past that I saw through a sort of "amber haze." Anyone who read, for instance, one page of *The Confident Years* could see the absurdity of that.

Every morning, as Zola put it, I was obliged to swallow my toad, and I half wished to reply to my critics with the Arab proverb, "The dogs bark, but the caravan moves on." The caravan certainly moved on, but I could not pretend that I was indifferent to the barking, and I remembered the bitter chagrin of my old professor Irving Babbitt when he was attacked on his appearance in New York. The poet Woodberry had been actually crushed by John Macy's review of his writings in *The Freeman*, and Howells had written to a younger fellow-novelist, "You'll find [the critics] can still hurt you long after their power to please you is gone." But I also remembered what Coleridge said about the "petulant sneers" of reviewers and Henry Adams's remark, "You can't kill a critic. Reply is like scratching their match for them." Especially I remembered Turgenev's last word of advice to writers, "Never try to justify yourselves. Carry on your work, and in time everything will come right."

But would it come right? I often wondered. Some of these accusations were true,—I mean some of those about *Oliver*

Allston,—and Lewis Mumford pointed out why I failed to reach the young as I had reached them in my earlier writings. I had not quite understood why the "power of blackness" had taken over the literary world. Then I remembered George Orwell's remark that a writer's tendency, his "purpose," his "message" was always what made him liked or disliked. "The proof of this," Orwell said, "is the extreme difficulty of seeing any literary merit in a book that seriously damages your deepest beliefs." Had not Claudel said of André Gide, who did not share his Catholic philosophy, "I don't see that Gide has any talent at all"? I was disliked because I felt with Crane Brinton that "We Americans are still children of the Enlightenment," a statement with which Herbert J. Muller, Ashley Montagu and Erich Fromm, all good thinkers, agreed. For myself, like most Americans, I still believed in "reason, freedom, human progress, the whole box of tricks belonging to the classistic-humanistic virtue-ideology," as the Jesuit Naptha said in *The Magic Mountain.* I was an infra-red type surviving in an ultra-violet epoch, and those who disliked this tendency ceased to read me.

In short, I was still "middlebrow," retaining the old American faith, at a time when the intellectuals were inveterately highbrow and when I was said by a certain critic to have supported the highbrow once, in *America's Coming-of-Age,* for instance. My critic had forgotten the motto that book bore on its title-page, a quotation from *Timon of Athens,* "The middle of humanity thou never knewest, but the extremity of both ends." I had written for the cultivated, not the "grey-plaster temperaments" with what William James called their "pedantifying ways," and I still believed that Sainte-Beuve was right in saying that "sound criticism has its action only when it is in concert with the public, and almost in collaboration with it." I could not think that the "close" critics who were the highbrow critics, with their class-room studies, were the true guardians of literature, any more than the journalistic followers of Mencken; and it seemed to me that Sainte-Beuve and Hazlitt, Charles Lamb and Macaulay were all, as the highbrows would have put it, middlebrow writers. I agreed with Thornton Wilder, who remarked in *Writers at Work,* "It would be a very wonderful thing if we could see more and more works which close the gulf between highbrows and lowbrows."

As for the time when I wrote *America's Coming-of-Age,* we cast our lines innocently then and caught whatever came out of the great ocean; but that was before the days of the "new" critics and before the days of an avant-garde. Meanwhile, I had a letter from a young writer in the South who said, "To me the most terrifying thing about the mind of the 'new criticism' is its unwillingness to accept any point of view except its own, or any literature except of the elected party liners. It has taken into the universities the very doctrines of exclusiveness and intolerance which have made the world they are attempting to escape." To me it seemed that the highbrow critics had gone up into a stratosphere that left humanity far behind them, and I felt that their only salvation was to descend to the middlebrow level and reëstablish some sort of relation with our common human nature. We needed a Dostoievsky to tell the intellectuals that they must humble themselves, for they were more to blame for the chaos of our literature than the mass-culture they were always deploring. Henry Adams had set the key for the "new" critics when he said that "society contained no hidden qualities that artists could appeal to." But he said also that John La Farge did not agree with him, and John La Farge was an artist as well as a writer. It was the artists and writers who interested me.

Now it was the change in the literary climate, as well as my point of view, that affected the critical fate of my *Makers and Finders,* and Malcolm Cowley explained this very well in a review of one of my later books: "He had spent twenty years in writing *Makers and Finders* and the first two volumes (1936 and 1940) had been received with unqualified, almost universal praise. The last three volumes (1944–52) were praised with reservations or condemned without them, although the volumes were excellent in themselves and completed a useful and impressive project. What had happened was that fashions had changed, that a new group of writers had reached a position of influence and that they did not accept Brooks's project as critical in their own definition of the word; some of them didn't even bother to understand what he was doing. The new critics were not interested in the historical background of a work of art, or in the experiences or character or intentions of the author, or in the social effects of the work, or in the climate of literary opinion at a given period. They called themselves 'ontological,' in the sense that they were interested in the work itself as pure essence or being. They proposed to study its structure and texture, its internal relations, its rhythms and images and symbols, while leaving everything else to the sheer journalists or the mere scholars. Some of their studies proved to be extremely fruitful, as Brooks himself is willing to acknowledge. He quarrels with them partly because they magnify the importance of form at the expense of subject-matter, but chiefly because they refuse to admit that other critical methods are also justified, including his own"; and, Malcolm Cowley continued, " 'How many writers' conferences,' Brooks says, 'how many books and magazines dwell each year, with fanatical concentration, on the "form" of writing, never diverting a moment's thought from the question, How to write well, to the question, How to live well to be a writer.' All his life Brooks has asked that second question, which was central in his biographies of Mark Twain and Henry James. When he did not find the answer there, or found only part of it, the question led him further. He had observed that most American writers failed to develop and mature after a first display of their individual talents. He believed that their failure was largely due to the lack of a continuous literary tradition, something that would support and sustain the individual writer and give his work 'more than an isolated meaning' . . . At the end of his studies he decided 'that, collectively speaking, our writers formed a guild, that they had even worked for a common end—an elevating end and deeply human—and that living writers, aware of this, could never quite feel as they had before, that they were working alone and working in the dark.' "

In *Makers and Finders*, I might add, it was not my view of life that the "grey-plaster temperaments" quarrelled with,—it was rather with my methods and my governing idea; but with *Opinions of Oliver Allston* the case was very different, though the verdict reflected on all my writing. I seemed to have sinned in attacking the writers who controlled the literary mind of the time, and, in fact, I confess my fault in failing to make it clear that I was not attacking their qualities as artists. I had said specifically that in literary capacity and vigour of style, in talent and even in genius, this was "beyond all question one of the brilliant epochs," and what I condemned was what Orwell called the "purpose" and the "message" of the writers, just as the critics united in condemning me. I might say that Archibald MacLeish did the same thing in *The Irresponsibles*, knowing that the writers he attacked were admirable artists. He and I both said what Orwell said in *Inside the Whale*, that many intellectuals allowed themselves "to be swallowed by the whale," remaining passive, not protesting the conditions of a time in which "only anti-humanism, perversity and jeers could thrive," as one of my correspondents wrote to me. Regarding writers, there are always two points to consider,—the first is their calibre, the second is their tendency. It is by their calibre that one ranks them as writers, but critics in general cannot believe that one appreciates this unless one fully accepts their tendency also. Yet how can one fully accept the tendency of certain contemporary writers whom one's aesthetic sense most heartily enjoys? No one doubts Hemingway's calibre, and few can have failed to enjoy his books; but how can one like his point of view of the typical American super-male, the redblooded he-man who despises "sissyness"? Hemingway has taken his point of view from the bar and the ringside and he has raised it to the level of literature. It is for just this that his cult-followers admire him, and it is just this that worries me. As long as this point of view prevailed on the ringside alone, it did no harm to the things I care for. But when it received the sanction of art it went far to destroy the values on which art itself is based. For what does "sissyness" comprise if not the traits of the sensitive man that art has hitherto cherished and nourished? As one of the soft-boiled myself, I cannot like this tendency, and it seems to me deleterious and regressive.

So, regarding several contemporary writers, I was attacking their tendency just as Belinski, the Russian critic, attacked the great Gogol for his newly acquired reactionary views. But to have attacked in any way idols of the avant-garde was to have invited the censure of critics who were interested mainly in their structures and their textures and who so largely ignored their essential content. How much had gone unsaid when, as Eliot put it, "The critic must not make judgments of worse or better. He must simply elucidate," or when, in the phrase of I. A. Richards, a critic required "the detachment, discrimination, patience, persistence and sharp cutting edge of a biologist,—with the underlying assumption that that is all." Did not this

mean dwelling on the mint and cummin to the total neglect
of weightier matters? It was the result of following "the letter,"
as Eliot prescribed, leaving all to the experts and repudiating
the public that had always been the final judge. Criticism became
an end in itself, an art existing in its own right, and, losing its
feeling of responsibility to the public, it expressed all sorts of
irresponsible positions. It said, for instance, that Joyce's blindness and Darwin's attacks of vertigo were "symbolic self-punish-
ments for the 'impiety' of their work." It also said that Whitman
was not an affirmer of life but a death-worshipping neurotic.
These preposterous statements could never have been made if
criticism recognized a public that would have brought it to
book. In this sense I made war on the so-called teacher-critics,
the "professional elects" who denounced what they described
as "message-hunting" and "author's-intention-hunting" or any
emotional participation in the "subject-experience of a literary
work." Through them, to paraphase Whitehead, a good period
in art died down into scholasticism and pedantry.

Was it true that I had not caught up with the age I was
living in? Or, on the contrary, was it true that I looked to the
future, to an age in which life would again have meaning and
purpose? If the great European writers of our time were hostile to
our beliefs, to our innermost liberal convictions,—feeling with
Yeats that "violence and tyranny" were "not necessarily evil" or
believing with Lawrence in the "dark forces" that would destroy
toleration,—then, however one admired these writers, one had
to regard them with a certain scepticism; and I saw that younger
writers did not regard them sceptically but swallowed their
illiberal ideas with their literary genius. The ideas in question
were slowly destroying the resisting power of imaginative minds,
stifling their confidence in life and their confidence in men,
along with their motive for opposing regimentation. This was

the result of not considering subject-matter but passively accepting everything that had a new style; and thus young writers, nominally liberal, were no longer actively so, and they became fatalistic and increasingly sterile. Partly in consequence of this, as a friend in California wrote to me, "The tide of pessimism and cynicism runs so strong that modern life begins to seem a betrayal of humanity." The oxygen for writers had been drawn out of the atmosphere, the result of ignoring the spirit and following the letter. It seemed to me that a new literary epoch was long overdue.

CHAPTER VIII

AT WESTON

W<small>E HAD</small> built a new house at Weston, four miles from Westport, on a high plateau overlooking the Sound. It was a brick house, painted white, with a verandah at each end and in front a broad stone terrace from which on sunny days one saw Long Island twenty miles away. Our clearing of four acres was surrounded by woods, and one day I saw three deer grazing on the apples that lay on the ground under the old orchard. During the first year wild forest birds were all about us, mourning doves, wood thrushes, whippoorwills and hawks that built their nest in a great oak near by; but after the garden was planted the forest birds disappeared and the village birds discovered us. The robins, catbirds and bluebirds had followed us out.

It was 1941. We had disposed of our cottage in Westport and now, disentangled from village affairs, we could live more serenely with our work and with the friends who came to see us. One of these was Victor von Hagen to whom and his wife we lent the house one winter. Victor was writing at the time a life of John Lloyd Stephens, the old explorer and traveller in the Central American jungle, together with a smaller book on the artist Frederick Catherwood, who had gone with him to

Guatemala and Yucatan. Stephens had written his classic "incidents of travel" about these regions a hundred years before, and Catherwood, who had studied Piranesi in London and the great ruins of Egypt and Greece, had drawn the splendid illustrations that accompanied the text. Catherwood, an architect in New York, had been forgotten, like Stephens, and Victor reconstructed their lives as one reconstructs, for a museum, a dinosaur from two or three petrified bones. He had unearthed Stephens's letters in a New Jersey farmhouse and he discovered Stephens's unmarked grave in an old cemetery on the east side of New York, where the great traveller had been hastily buried during a cholera epidemic. Victor had been stirred by my account of him in *Makers and Finders,* for Stephens was one of the lost writers whom Melville had seen in his childhood and whom I was bent on resurrecting.

Victor had led an adventurous life. His *métier* was the American tropics, and he had lived all over Latin America and among the primitive tribes on the Amazon river. Well he knew the sleepless nights, the howling sore-ridden dogs and the biting insects in the villages of the Kofanes and Huitotoes. He had not yet undertaken the great exploit of his later years, the rediscovery of the ancient Inca highway, the route of Pizarro in Peru, but he had climbed to the original El Dorado, the Andean lake of Guatemala, and he had scaled the southern Sierra Nevada with its Tibetan-like people and looked into the emerald mines of Muzo. As a naturalist living for two years at the headwaters of the Amazon, he had collected specimens for Mexican museums, and he had taken to the London zoo a live quetzal, the sacred bird of the old Mayans. In fact, he had raised quetzal birds in his camp in the forest of Ecuador. Moreover, he had spent six months on the Galapagos islands, among the great turtles that Captain Cook had found there, and now and then he would disappear into some small island of the West Indies. Victor's book on John Lloyd Stephens was largely written in my study in the house at Weston.

I had had my name taken out of the telephone book, and this was partly because of a convict who had been discharged from Sing Sing and who called me night after night. He said he was a friend of Heywood Broun who had run a free employment bureau for several months during the depression, but the generous Broun to whom I wrote did not know his name and I somehow conceived the morbid notion that the man in question was prowling round the house. But one day came the voice of a man I had known when he was a boy, and I later remembered that this boy, thirty years before, had struck me as coming to no good. There had been something sinister about him that warned me against him,—I had never felt that way about any other boy,—but when he uttered his name on the telephone I had forgotten this and I was glad to do what he asked of me. He was a captain, he said, in the army, and on the train to New York his purse and all his money had been stolen, and would I lend him twenty-five dollars to be given him at the General Delivery window? Never hearing from him again, I remembered the little boy of whom I had had such doubts when he was ten years old. We lived for a while in a movie melodrama with a German cook and her son who turned out to be Nazis. Finally we got them out of the house, after the boy had run away four times looking for other Nazis, threatening to murder village schoolchildren and bragging that he was to be the next Führer. Then he began to have epileptic fits. We found that a charitable society in New York had a long case-history of the two; and they agreed to see that the tragic pair would not put poison in anybody else's soup.

To the Weston house came once William Allen Neilson, the

president of Smith College who had been one of my old professors and who still called me "Boy" when I was sixty. It reminded me of my other professor, Edward Kennard Rand, of whom I had been so fond when I was at Harvard, the great mediævalist and classical scholar who had asked me to call him "Ken," saying, "Age counts for nothing among those who have learned to know life *sub specie aeternitatis.*" I had always thought of that lovable man as many years older than myself, although he was perhaps only twenty years older, and he confirmed my feeling, along with the feeling of both my sons, that teachers of the classics are invariably endearing. I must have written to say how much I had enjoyed his fine book *The Building of Eternal Rome,* and I found he had not regretted giving me the highest mark in his old course on the later Latin poets, although in my final examination I had ignored the questions and filled the bluebook with a comparison of Propertius and Coleridge. He had written to me about a dinner he had had with the Benedictine monks at St. Anselm's Priory in Washington. There had been reading at table, especially from two books, Pope Gregory the Great's account of St. Scholastica in his *Dialogues* and my own *The World of Washington Irving.* He said, "Some have criticized your book as being neither literary criticism nor history. Of course it was not meant to be. Some have felt that Washington Irving comes out rather slimly, but let them look at the title of the book." He felt as I felt about this best of all my books, that it was "really tops."

Two or three times, C. C. Burlingham came to lunch with us in Weston, that wonderful man who lived to be more than a hundred years old and whose birthplace had been my Wall Street suburb. His reading ranged from Agatha Christie to the Book of Job and he had an insatiable interest in his fellow-creatures, while his letters were full of gossip about new poli-

ticians and old men of letters with whom he had been intimately
thrown six decades before. I could never forget the gaiety with
which, when he was both blind and deaf, he let me lead him
around his rooms to look at some of the pictures; and once when
he came to see us in New York he walked away in a rainstorm,
unwilling to hear of a taxi or even an umbrella, although he
was at the time ninety years old. There were several men of
ninety or more whom I knew first or last, all of whom were still
productive and most of whom knew one another as if they had
naturally come together at the apex of their lives. I never met
John Dewey, whose style was a sort of verbal fog and who had
written asking me to go to Mexico with him when he was investigating the cause of Trotsky; but I liked to think of him
at ninety swimming and working at Key West long after Hemingway had moved to Cuba. At Lee Simonson's house, I had
dined with Edith Hamilton, the nonogenarian rationalist and
the charming scholar who had a great popular success with *The
Greek Way.* Then there was Mark Howe and there was Henry
Dwight Sedgwick, an accomplished man of letters who wrote
in the spirit of Montaigne and produced in the end a formidable
body of work. I saw Sedgwick often before his death at ninety-
five,—he had remarried at the age of ninety,—and he asked me,
when once I returned from Rome, if I knew the Cavallinis in
the church of St. Cecilia in Trastevere. I had to confess that I
had missed these frescoes, recently discovered, that he had
studied in his eighties. Sedgwick had chosen to follow the philosophy of Epicurus whom, with his followers, Dante put in
hell; but he defended the doctrine in *The Art of Happiness,* and
what indeed could be said against the Epicurean virtues, health,
frugality, privacy, culture and friendship? Of Mark Antony
De Wolfe Howe the philosopher Whitehead said the Earth's
first visitors to Mars should be persons likely to make a good

impression, and when he was asked, "Whom would you send?" he replied, "My first choice would be Mark Howe." This friend of many years came once to visit us in the house at Weston. Then I spoke at the ninetieth birthday party of W. E. Burghardt Du Bois, who embarked on a fictional trilogy at eighty-nine and who, with *The Crisis,* had created a Negro intelligentsia that had never existed in America before him. As their interpreter and guide, he had broken with Tuskegee and become a spokesman of the coloured people of the world.

Mr. Burlingham,—"C.C.B."—wrote to me once about an old friend of mine, S. K. Ratcliffe, whom I had first met in London in 1914 and who also came out for a week-end in Weston. "Did you ever know a man with greater zest for information? And his memory, like an elephant's, stored with precise knowledge of men and things and happenings." His wife, Katie, "as gay as a lark and as lively as a gazelle,"—she was then seventy-six,—had "a sense of humour that has been denied S.K., but neither has any aesthetic perceptions. People and books are enough for them." S.K. was visiting C.C.B. and, not waiting for breakfast, he was off to the University Club, where he spent hours writing obituaries of living Americans for the *Manchester Guardian* or the *Glasgow Herald.* Later, rising ninety, he was beset by publishers for the story of his life and miracles, as he put it, but, calling himself the Needy Knife-grinder, he had spent his time writing short articles and long letters and could not get even a small popular book done. Then, all but blind, he said there was nothing in *Back to Methuselah,*—"G.B.S. ought to have known that,"—and "I look at my bookshelves despairingly, knowing that I can have nothing more to do with them." However, at eighty-five, he had still been busy writing articles, reviewing and speaking, and I had never before known an Englishman who had visited and lectured in three quarters of the

United States. Finally, colleges and clubs took the line that
speakers from England were not wanted any longer, even
speakers like S.K., so unlike the novelists and poets who had
patronized the Americans for many years. With their facile
generalizations about the United States, these mediocrities, as
they often were, had been great successes. While S.K. did not
like Dylan Thomas, I liked his poems very much, but I made
the mistake of telling Dylan Thomas so, whereupon he said to
me, "I suppose you think you know all about me." I should
have replied, "I probably know something about the best part
of you." But I only thought of that in the middle of the night.

Many years later I went to see S.K. in England, where he
was living at Whiteleaf, near Aylesbury, and he showed me
beside his cottage there the remains of the road on which Boadi-
cea is supposed to have travelled. He was convinced that George
Orwell's *1984* was nearly all wrong as it applied to England,
which was "driving forward into uncharted waters," with the
danger of a new tyranny ahead. "But however we go, whatever
our doom, it will not take the Orwellian shape." With facts
mainly in his mind, he was often acute in the matter of style,
and he said, "The young who have as yet nothing to say will
try larks with initial letters and broken lines. But put them before a situation which they are forced to depict,"—he was speaking of the Spanish civil war,—"and they have no hesitation; they
merely do their best to make it real for others." Meanwhile, I
was seeing off and on the octogenarian Frank Jewett Mather,
the art critic, the professor at Princeton who remembered Irving
Babbitt when he was teaching French at Williams College.
Babbitt had not yet worked out the doctrine that brought him
disciples from Paris to Peking, but he was already regarded as
another Dr. Johnson and Mather had climbed Mount Monadnock with him and tramped with him in the Apennines later.

Only in the face of nature had Babbitt relaxed his role of the prophet, for he was keenly sensitive to natural beauty, but, as I had seen at Harvard, he never acquired the composure and detachment of the *hônnete homme* he so greatly admired. Mather felt he owed much to Babbitt for taking art out of a vacuum and relating it to the general concerns of living, saving him from what he called the grim and humourless aesthetic of the New York circle of Kenyon Cox.

But Mather had, in the end, reacted against Babbitt and against the cult of discipline that led Babbitt to use art and literature as means, not as ends. He himself enjoyed the "pleasanter by-products of error" and found his humanist master also grim. Mather was a humanist in the older sense, the kind that is spelled with a small "h," a respector of impulse along with discipline, indulgent to his erring kind, with an educated palate for all the good things of life. He had the zest of the man of letters who was commoner before the "seven devils of war, woe, hatred and murder drove forth the gentle arts from the House of Life,"—as James Huneker once put it; and this led him to revolt against the control of art by "the professors," delightful to them but fatal to the wilding, art. He wrote very finely and freshly on El Greco and Goya, and he was perhaps the first to express a belief with which many have since agreed that Thomas Eakins, Ryder and Winslow Homer were more important painters than Sargent and Whistler; but he would not have argued the point, for Mather was the least contentious of men and one of the most reasonable, humane and openminded. He was a discriminating, learned and witty writer, all the more to be cherished at a time when the beautiful art of criticism had been so largely changed into a dismal science. He was an old friend of Mahonri Young who often came to see us and with whom at intervals we dined at Ridgefield when he was working on his great monument for Salt Lake City. Mahonri had managed to get into this not only his grandfather Brigham Young but the whole history of the old plains, and the monument was perhaps more biography and history than sculpture. I liked much better his fifty volumes of sketches of horses, cows, goats, sheep and dogs. Mahonri's father-in-law Alden Weir had once owned the house and farm, and I recognized instantly the truncated willows in the meadows that I had seen in Albert Ryder's pictures. It turned out that Ryder had often visited Weir.

I had written to my classmate Samuel Eliot Morison, whom I had scarcely known in college, to say how much I liked the picture of his countenance in the book that recorded our class twenty-five years later. The book contained two pictures of each member of the class, one taken "now," the other taken "then," and I had been struck by the rarity of the faces that showed a fine development and the commonplace appearance of most of the others. Boys who had been beautiful in college had been coarsened out of all resemblance, while half a dozen, Jack Wheelock, George Biddle, Ned Sheldon and himself, had grown more and more appealing and distinguished. Sam was touched by my letter, and so began for me a friendship with this reincarnation of the fine historians of an earlier Boston. He was a sailor and he took me to task for the "marine solecisms" in my passage on Dana's *Two Years Before the Mast*. I had used the word "cheerily" when, he said, "cheerly" was "the right, the male, the vigorous and the seamanlike word," but it finally appeared that I had followed another edition in which the word was printed as I had spelled it. He later wrote that the sail from Boston to Trinidad was lovelier than he had ever imagined it could be, with effects of light and shade, stars, great golden trade-wind clouds and rainbows arching showers that blotted out whole valleys. He was much taken with a novel of Marion Crawford's that showed a thorough knowledge of the technique of sailing. This was after Sam had written the life of Columbus that had led him to sail the Atlantic to the coast of Spain.

In college, Sam had known George Biddle, whom I saw constantly during these years and after, George with his look of an officer of the Civil War who remained as hardy as a Mohawk. His air was lean and soldierly, he was all decision and command, and he would walk barefoot for miles on burning asphalt, really unaware of any discomfort. He loved to play on his flute eighteenth-century music, a "sort of alcohol rub-down," as he called it. George was always going away to the South Seas, to India, Roumania, Japan, Israel, the West Indies; he spent two or three years in Tahiti, he went skiing in the Dolomites, he lived in southern Italy and southern California, and he was impressed by the Negroes of Martinique, Guadelupe and Haiti, a "slice of Africa in an eighteenth-century world." In Brazil he was sent north by the Ministry of Education, and there he made hundreds of sketches of the Recife carnival and the round-ups of the vaquero country. In India he followed Vinobaji for two days during which he might have been following Mohammed, with old women kissing the dust at his feet, with roses strewn in his path and with camels, buffaloes and paint-smeared holy men. As a craftsman he was always experimenting with mural painting or ironwork, mosaics, ceramics and lithographs, among them the fine bookplate of death on a white horse, the symbol of a mind that was haunted by the sadness of the time.

Meanwhile, I continued to see much of Bruce Rogers, whom I had met many years before when *The Seven Arts* was just appearing. That was during a summer at Peconic, Long Island, where he seemed to spend most of his time carving a ship's model, for no one ever saw him seriously working. He would sometimes sketch with apparent casualness on the back of an envelope an italicized N or a capital R, and one did not perceive that under a mask he was working with intensity and that his appearance of idleness was a sort of pose. Later I thought of him when I happened on Reynolds's praise of Rubens for seeming to make a plaything of his art. It was "the common coquetry of authors and artists," Reynolds said, "to be supposed to do what excites the admiration of others with the greatest ease and indifference, and almost without knowing what they are about. If what surprises you costs them nothing, the wonder is so much increased." To be done well a work must seem to have been done easily: that might have been the motto of this "tramp printer," as he called himself.

After that summer, Bruce Rogers continued to send me at Christmas one of his slender publications, Thoreau's *Night and Moonlight* or *The Centaur* with the errata slip that made this a famous folio in American printing. When I saw one of these advertised later in a rare-book catalogue for something more than three hundred dollars, I recognized Bruce Rogers' style of understatement in describing as Christmas cards these lovely brochures. He had gone to England as a sort of partner of Emery Walker, the former associate of William Morris on the Kelmscott Press, and I wrote to him asking for a few suggestions for improving the format of *The Seven Arts,* which seemed to me generally awkward and ugly. He replied with a long letter saying that the magazine was "nearly all wrong in every typographical detail." We had chosen the worst type possible, the initials were set incorrectly, with too much white space around them, the margins were almost the worst feature and the whole magazine was printed the wrong way of the grain of the paper. When we made a few changes at once he wrote, "You now have the distinction, I believe, of being the only magazine whose initials fit"; but the advice came too late, for *The Seven Arts* died three or four months later. This great typothete, as someone called him, this prematurely old master, was the opposite number to Stieglitz, the old master of photography, and he was the remote successor of Caxton, Aldus and Benjamin Franklin, who had also called himself a printer. He cared above all for readability. "The most beautiful types," he said, "are the easiest to read"; but he was capable of remarkable nuances. He instructed a compositor to insert uneven thin spaces between certain diamond-shaped units in order to avoid a rigidity that seemed geometric, and he made a Q by cutting off an italic capital T and soldering it to the base of an O at the proper angle. He liked the Italian motto, "Trifles make perfection, but perfection is no trifle."

This learned and whimsical man seemed almost infantile at times in his liking for the most bathetic and execrable puns or word-plays on "fine BRinting" and "Scotch and Bodoni." He designed an ampersand and sent all over the country for specimens of sand-paper, so that he could print his ampersand on amper-sand-paper. He belonged to the world of typophiles that almost rivalled heraldry in its complex emblems and devices; and, for the rest, he had a love of water-mills to which he was constantly referring. His attachment to these water-mills might also have explained his love of Cotman and the English water-colour painters. He had made himself fine water-colour scenes of Naushon island, the Bahamas and England, pictures of Hastings, the Cotswolds and Cambridge where he was for a while the chief book-designer of the Cambridge University press. He had been designing title-pages in the eighteen-eighties at the moment when William Morris was planning the Kelmscott Press, and he presently designed the Oxford Lectern Bible. In the meantime he had a great liking for sailing ships and carved for a Danish square-rigger a figurehead of Joseph Conrad. Alan Villiers told me later that this had been bought by an American collector. For a number of years Bruce made summer trips up the Baltic on grain-barges or Finnish windjammers, and he often stayed in Copenhagen, finding the people there even more sympathetic than the English.

Reading *The Seven Pillars of Wisdom* in 1927, it had occurred to Bruce that T. E. Lawrence was the man to translate the Odyssey anew. He had long wished to print the Odyssey in a style fitting its splendour as a story, and he felt that Lawrence, a man of action who could write swift and graphic English, could make Homer live again. Four years later he was sitting with Lawrence, at Southampton, on the recreation pier, discussing the final points of the translation in which Lawrence had tried to avoid "passenger words" and retain "only words," he said, that "worked." Lawrence won his heart by saying, apropos of his Centaur type, "What a splendid Y, the most difficult letter of the alphabet"; and Lawrence had taken up printing himself, set up a small hand-press and printed his book on the air-force that was called *The Mint*. Coming to England, Bruce Rogers would send a message to Lawrence from the ship, and Lawrence would meet the ship in one of his speed-boats and take him for a trial run down Southampton Water. Bruce Rogers, on his way back to New York, would always stop for a day or two to see Lawrence, and they spent their evenings in a public bar with the proofs spread out on one of the tap-room tables. They talked about ships, the "Joseph Conrad" and the speed-boats that Lawrence was building for the Royal Air Force. About this time I made a translation of some essays of André Gide. I admired these essays greatly, and, having worked over the translation, I obtained Gide's permission to publish it. But I had only one copy of it and the fine printer, who was having a nervous breakdown, lost this copy.

I used to go sailing with Bruce Rogers on the catboat which he kept near by on Candlewood Lake, and later, when I had moved closer to New Fairfield, I saw more of him in his October House. It was ever so charming with its pink brick front and brownish grey pilasters, built, I think, during the Revolution; it stood on a high knoll with a view of the lakes at front and rear and with three kinds of grapes in the arbours. He showed me the little attic room, with a plain cot, in which he slept among old clothes and trunks, with a wildcat from Maine on the floor beside him; and he read me letters from T. E. Lawrence whose Odyssey he had promised to print at the Oxford Press where he had been book-designer. He was planning to give to his own university, Purdue in Indiana, a complete collection of his publications; and he showed me also his first edition of Webster's Dictionary, 1828, which he called one of the finest pieces ever done in America. By that time he was a very old man who had just finished his edition of Dante and who was at work on the *Canterbury Tales*; and, fascinated by the early English authors backward from Chaucer to Beowulf, he asked me where he could find the original Robin Hood ballads. Then he showed me the new terrace and the goldfish pool that he had built, the pool into which he fell one November day and died of pneumonia a few days later.

CHAPTER IX

CATASTROPHE

IN THE Weston house, my wife died one August afternoon,— we had just come back from California,—and for six months after that I felt like a man who is drowning and who does not know which way to turn. I lived during those months in a nightmarish dream, and even now I feel about my marriage as Thomas Merton feels about his vocation, I was "happy in a way that does not want to talk." My wife had felt there was a collective life to which she was contributing, and, with her mystical belief in the human race and its upward climb, she had scarcely for a moment relaxed her gaiety and courage. It seemed to me, after thirty-five years with her, that life had been taken out of my hands and that I was cast adrift on a desperate sea. Only my work saved me from foundering in it.

I then discovered that strange separation of faculties of which the novelist Howells had written "by which the mind toils on in a sort of ironical indifference" to the part that suffers; and, having reached the middle of *The Times of Melville and Whitman*, I was carried on by its momentum. I felt as James Thurber says he feels, "if I couldn't write I couldn't live," together with the corollary of this remark, I could live if I could write. I was obliged to write in order to keep up my tone, for when I was not writing I was out of focus and felt not only disintegrated but somehow degraded. I believed, when I was writing a book, that I was on trial for my life, but when I was not writing I was semi-idiotic, my mind wandered, empty and aimless, and I went through all sorts of meaningless motions and ended the day in a state of self-disgust. Absorbed in my world of the imagination, I felt vexed and hapless whenever the intrusion of the real world jolted me out, yet when I had finished a book I had an obsessive conviction that I would never be able to write another. Moreover, it seemed to be impossible to print correctly. I read the proofs of at least one of my books five times and found two more mistakes on the fifth reading. But writing had always been my secret asylum when I felt ill at ease in life, and all had been well with me when I thought of my work. I was rather like the mad woman in the "house of mystery" at San José, who had built eight hundred rooms in that wooden Vatican. She felt she was going to live as long as she continued to build.

For twenty years I had been reading seven or eight hours a day, and I read the whole body of each writer's work, the poor and bad books along with the rest. I was saturated in my literary history with the period I was writing about so that I often felt I was living in it, and my books were intended to be read as if they were novels; for my treatment of a given author was shredded through the chapters to fit the whole figure into the stream of the epoch. I wrote a page a day, beginning each morning by rewriting the work of the day before, and I no more wished for a holiday than Matisse who said, "It has never amused me to amuse myself." Meanwhile, I sold the house, stored away my possessions and moved to an apartment in New York. The house was bought by John Hersey fourteen years later.

Not long before this catastrophe, my old friend Paul Rosen-feld died. Almost his last act had been to come to the hospital with a bouquet of rare flowers for my wife, and he prom-ised to return two days later with *Tom Jones* for her to read, but he had a heart attack in a moving-picture theatre. Paul said that what others called his generosity was merely his inevitable thanks to the artists who had made the world a luminous place for him, and I could believe what a friend told me Paul had said to her at a time when a third person had hurt her, "Go out and do the nicest thing you can think of for someone else. That will restore the balance in the universe." The wisdom of William James had come to Paul naturally, for he had grown up with the expansive feelings of the earlier years of the cen-tury and scarcely felt at home in a time of reaction. He shared the prophetic beliefs of the old circle of *The Seven Arts* and of those whom he called the "great old Europeans with their feeling of a world full of glorious possibilities and of human beings potentially noble"; and after his death he inspired a follower with a devotion like his own to edit a collection of essays about him. Jerome Mellquist could not rest until he knew Paul would be remembered: he wrote seven hundred letters and he travelled for fifteen months all over the country in order to round up contributions to his *Paul Rosenfeld, Voyager in the Arts*. It was a story of devotion quite unrewarded, and it reminded me of the zeal of the little doctor who appeared at my house, at the time of my breakdown, and offered to cure me. He had read my books, and, hearing of my illness, he had come out to Westport to see me; and he wanted to give up his prac-tice, take a room in the village and devote all his time to getting me well.

No one had cared more for Paul than Alyse Gregory and Llewelyn Powys, who had often walked over from Norwalk in the twenties to call upon us, but Llewelyn had died in 1939 and Alyse was living in England, near Dorchester, at Chydyok, on the southern downs. She had written to me from Davos Platz when Llewelyn was too ill to read or talk, and when she had got up in the darkness at five and had seen the little squares of light appearing, one by one, in the cabins of the peasants. The great sad sanitariums were already a blaze of light after those long hours of waiting. Now on the English coast, where Llewelyn was buried under a great stone shaft, she looked out on fields of ripening barley and bare wild downs and sheep dogs racing in the wind and rounding up the sheep. She watched the swallows feeding their young on the branches of a cherry tree and the blackbirds flying away with a bright red cherry in their yellow beaks. Then, where the grocer drove up only once a year, she toiled, with her milk and provisions, up and down the valleys, living in a Jacobean cottage as the Brontës had lived on their Yorkshire moor and running down a steep slope to greet me. For years later I went to see her there.

Alyse had been in charge of *The Dial* when Paul was a contributor. He had written his *Musical Chronicle* month by month at a time when I first met Newton Arvin who came to my office at *The Freeman* and sat and talked with me on the rim of the tub. For we had taken an old apartment that was not yet made over and the bathroom was the only corner for conversation. It seemed to me that Newton Arvin, that quiet man with a violent mind, would gladly have stood against a wall and faced a fusillade for his convictions. At that time his convictions were on the far left, farther even than my own, but later, when he modified them, he did not go back on them; he never became a reactionary, like so many others. "All of us," he wrote to me, "who took that great bumpy detour of Marxism can very justly be accused of making smooth the way for the college of cardinals that came after us," those who rode into power on the authoritarianism that had first appeared as a doctrine of the left. Waldo Frank still remained of that persuasion, more or less, like Charlie Chaplin who spoke at a dinner that was given for Waldo on his return from a long South American journey. The great-hearted Reinhold Niebuhr was the chairman at that dinner. Waldo, who had lectured in Argentina, Uruguay and Chile, had been beaten in Buenos Aires by fascist storm troopers. He had spoken a language that was quite unlike the language spoken by the business promoters who treated us as if we were Indians," a Latin American writer said, "and our language a dialect of Quechuan"; he knew the religion of the Latin Americans, their dances and their art, and he conveyed in *America Hispaña* a feeling of the tropical cultures that John Lloyd Stephens had written about and that Victor von Hagen recalled in many of his books.

At that dinner I had sat beside Charlie Chaplin, who told me about his recent visit to Japan. He had been carried away by the Japanese theatre. After the dinner he gave a party in a private room, and, pretending that he was a pigeon on the eaves of the Plaza Hotel, he ran about the table fluttering and cooing, making love to a lady pigeon and keeping it up till midnight with a nervous energy that never for a moment slackened. It was like Lee Simonson's energy when he was not demagnetized in one of his recurrent attacks of depression. Lee had designed two ballets for Mordkin, a setting for a condensed Swan Lake and a gay Viennese scene for some waltzes of Strauss, the Johann Strauss whom I had seen as a boy in Vienna, in the very year in which he died. That was in the spring of 1899 and Strauss was conducting his own orchestra there.

Lee Simonson had been at Harvard with my old triumvirate of friends, Edward Sheldon, Maxwell Perkins and John Hall

Wheelock, the first of whom died just before my wife and the second about a year later. Ned Sheldon had been immobilized for nearly thirty years; he could not lift a finger from the bed where he lay; moreover, for ten years he had been blind. No doctor had been able to halt his arthritis, and he could not turn his head, resting on a pillow. Yet, gay as he was and apparently serene, his laughter filled the living-room, dispelling all feeling of compassion for him. He never spoke of his illness or referred to it in any way, and he maintained with his nurses a sort of rigid discipline that kept any suggestion of pity from breaking through. His eyes were bandaged with a narrow black silk mask, and, fully dressed, with a coverlet and a canopy towering over him, he had received visitors all day in his big blue room. The room was always full of flowers and a multitude of books that were read to him, often at night. He read many books on the Civil War, and on a table near his bed was a photograph of his hero, Robert E. Lee. The Confederate side in the war appealed to him deeply.

Towards the end he spoke only in a whisper; his vocal cords were giving out, and he had a thrombosis of the heart just in time, one felt, to save him from a total eclipse of the Not-me. He had usually written or telegraphed whenever I had seen him, and, after the news came that he had died in the night, I received a posthumous message from him. He sent his love and wished that we were having a quiet Sunday, for he knew that my wife was very ill. A few weeks earlier he had written, after we had dined with him, at the little table drawn up beside the bed, "I spent far too much time on Russia, but I suppose the subject is on people's minds these days and I had been listening to the UN meeting for six hours." He was breathlessly interested in the war and well-informed about it, yet he kept up the humorous mood that he had maintained for so many

years and sent me a comic letter on his sixtieth birthday. He
pretended to look down on me for being still only fifty-nine,
and he wrote to me about the pigeons that lived on his pent-
house roof and that he called Mr. and Mrs. Homer. They had
"two babies of their own, the first brood this year. All this re-
minds me that life goes on serenely, regardless of wars." He had
been, during all these years, an oracle for Broadway, though
his life in the theatre was long past and it was many years since
his had been the most conspicuous name among American playwrights. Before he became blind there had been a stage near
his bed and many plays were tried out within his range of
vision. There Geraldine Farrar sang for him, Ruth Draper recited to him, Ethel Barrymore acted for him and Heifetz
played for him. "Of course," Heifetz said, "I shall never play in
Carnegie Hall as I have played for you today." Once I had
lunched there with Ethel Barrymore and, a few years later, when
I had made a speech at the Academy and Ethel Barrymore was
in the audience, I met her afterwards in the crowded corridor.
She said to me, "I'll bet you don't know who I am." Her face
was as familiar to me as any face on a postage-stamp, but in the
excitement of the moment I had lost all presence of mind and
I could not attach a name to this presence in the crowd.

There had been several years before Ned was taken ill when
I had seen little of him, for I knew nothing about the stage
where he was the white-headed boy on the most intimate terms
with half the Broadway celebrities. Among these was Mrs.
Fiske who had played in *Salvation Nell*, "the most daring play,"
one critic said, "that New York has ever seen"; and there was
Margaret Anglin who accepted two of his plays, "as yet unwritten," he said to me, "and only in scenario-sketch form."
William Faversham had leased a theatre in New York and
wanted a play for his next season, and so it went with dozens

of people of the stage to a few of whom he introduced me. Then had come the great days when *Romance* had one of the longest runs in the history of the theatre, when it was played in Norway and Sweden, Egypt, India, Australia and Africa and the French Academy took the unheard-of step of inviting Doris Keane to bring it to Paris. A member of the Academy said it was "pure enchantment," and two theatres in Moscow presented it simultaneously with Maxim Gorky's wife in the title-role. At about that time Ned had rented a palace in Venice where John Barrymore lived for a while with him, and he and Doris spent days in New York searching the pet-shops for a monkey that was small and friendly enough to be easily managed. In England he had met J. M. Barrie of whom he wrote to me that he was "such a queer shy little Scotchman with eyes just like Mrs. Fiske's, except that they were a man's eyes." There he became intimate with Somerset Maugham, and he is supposed to have suggested the writing of Maugham's best novel, *Of Human Bondage.* It was based on his early life as a medical student, and Ned thought that in writing it Maugham could overcome the embarrassment that was caused by a defect in speech. Maugham stuttered and this handicap appeared in the novel as a club-foot. Well I remembered the day when, in London, Ned took me to lunch at Somerset Maugham's. That must have been in 1913. Maugham was living in Mayfair, in an elegant little eighteenth-century house, and it comes back to me that there was a bottle of hock on the table and that Maugham was wearing a black velvet jacket. Over the mantel in the dining-room hung a portrait of Billie Burke, who was playing in his *Mrs. Dot,* and, looking up at the portrait, Maugham said, "That is the lady who has made my fortune."

Several years before that, Ned wrote from Cambridge, "Last night we saw *The Great Divide* for the second time. A jammed house, Mr. Copeland was there. We dined first at the Epicure in Boston under a sort of wiry grape-arbour, a dollar table-d'hôte, not a bit bad." Then I remembered him in his apartment in Gramercy Park with brilliantly coloured macaws for decoration, and his delight in the bawdy came back to me, reading an old letter, when he spoke of a Long Island military camp in the first world war. A hackman, asked if the local girls weren't crazy about the soldiers, answered, "Crazy? Gee, the hospitals is full." Later came the letters from the Los Angeles hospital where, walking eight steps in four minutes, with the aid of two nurses, he had felt "as proud as if I had had twins." In his blindness he had developed a sort of second sight and he would guess the height of some new visitor from the position of his voice, so I was startled when he asked "What does he look like?" referring to an English visitor who left as I arrived one evening. He was ruthless in refusing to meet anyone with whom he could not readily communicate. Ellen Glasgow, who admired heroism of any kind, would have been glad to come to his apartment. I was going to arrange this meeting but Ned said No. Ellen Glasgow was very deaf, and Ned felt he could not whisper into the ear-machine that she managed with such triumphant skill.

Ned, who never mentioned Doris Keane or any subject that concerned himself, had once believed that he could stand up to anything, but he came to feel the need of the religion that he never quite accepted. Yet the instinct of religion was very strong and deep in him, and so was the feeling that led him to say to one of his friends, "You must forgive yourself, too. That is the hardest thing of all." It reminded me of Theodore Dreiser who had gone through life bowed down with a sense of guilt for the way he had lived. I dined once with Arthur Davison Ficke at Ridgely Torrence's in Morton Street, and Ficke had been visiting Dreiser at Mount Kisco. Out for a walk in the afternoon, Dreiser was so silent that Ficke said, "Theodore, is there something you want to tell me? You know it's sometimes a good thing to get worries off your mind." Dreiser turned to him and said with a look of bottomless woe, "Everything I have ever done in my life has been wrong," whereupon Ficke said, "Why, Theodore, don't you think there are times when a man should forgive himself for his own sins?" Dreiser ran off a hundred feet as if he had been stung, then, turning round, with tears pouring down his cheek, he said, "Great God, Ficke, that's the most wonderful thing I ever heard;" and every hour or so for the next two days he repeated, "A man should forgive himself for his own sins." Ficke told me this and I was struck by his own great gallantry; for at that moment he was dying of cancer of the throat, yet, entirely ignoring himself and his troubles and his unrecognized work, he insisted on talking about me. However, I knew that inwardly Ficke felt bitterly about the way his writing had been disregarded.

While Ned lay immobile there, the old romantic theatre gave place to the new realistic mood, and it was symbolic of this change that Eugene O'Neill took over Ned's apartment after he died. Ned had read Thomas Wolfe but he could not believe in Wolfe as a novelist. He had written to me, "The complete imprisonment within his own ego, the distorted way in which he sees other people, the lack of any form, architecture or development (which keeps the book perfectly static), all these things bother me," in spite of "some fine pages of rhapsody which suggest the lyric poet." But my ancient friend Maxwell Perkins said that working with Thomas Wolfe had been the foremost interest of his life. Every night, for many months, Max would go back to Scribner's, after a busy day there, and work till eleven with Wolfe revising his writing, cutting out some-

times wonderful scenes in order that the story should be unfolded entirely through the boy's memories and senses. One
night they had walked all round Central Park while Max told
Tom about a novel he had thought of: it was the story of a
young man who goes in search of a father, the very story that
Tom Wolfe had been destined to write. Max became his father
and confessor. Tom turned to Max to escape from his doubts
about himself, and Max would listen for hours while he poured
out the story of his difficulties. I had scarcely known of this till
I dined once at Max's house on the night when his first grand-
child was born. Just before nine o'clock Max got up and left
us. He was going back to the office to work with Wolfe. Not
long before that, a Harvard instructor, a friend of Wolfe, had
been found dead in Westport under a syringa bush. His body
was discovered in the cemetery down the street from us, a few
hundred yards away. Kenneth Raisbeck was a character in one
of Wolfe's novels, and the first selectman of Westport called
on me that morning to ask if I knew anything about him. His
car had stood all night, with the lights on, directly in front of
our house. Was it a case of murder? Raisbeck had been
strangled, as I remember, with a wire cord about his neck.

Max had felt in college a wish to be a novelist, and he had
turned his energy and will into this vicarious task of "trying to
hang onto the fin of a plunging whale." For so Tom Wolfe, writing as usual about himself, referred to Max as an editor and a
reviser of other men's work; and, if I am not mistaken, Max was
the first editor who had ever performed this function. Formerly
there had been copy-readers and editors only of magazines, but
editors of books were, I suppose, unheard of; writers had submitted manuscripts that publishers took or sent back, but I had
never heard of an author who expected a publisher to do a good
part of his work for him. Max was perhaps the first, as by

common consent he was the best, the editor of Scott Fitzgerald, Hemingway and others, always eager to take on some new novelist or some new writer of short stories. I remember how pleased he was when I called him on the telephone to ask if he would like to publish Sherwood Anderson. Liveright had failed and Sherwood was anxious to make another connection. Max broke all records in his effort to get books right, and how many things he did for authors apart, moreover, from their books, dining in their houses in order to work with them later and sending them veterinarians to care for their dogs and cats. Nor could anyone have been more fertile in suggestions. He suggested titles for books or that someone should write reminiscences or "invent twenty-five crimes,"—this to a writer of mystery-stories,—or that a man who had never seen a war should write a tour of the battlefields, taken in company with an old soldier with whom he disputed about them. He wrote to Hemingway wishing he could go, with Fitzgerald and himself, on a tour of the Virginia battlefields. Suggesting a life of Jeb Stuart to one who presently wrote the book, Max was intensely interested in the Civil War himself, and I think that, like Ned Sheldon, he was chiefly interested in the Confederate side. Tolstoy's *War and Peace* was always his favourite novel, the dimensions of which seemed to grow larger every time he read it. He said, "Any book that has in it a journey during which the plot develops has a strong element of interest," and with his delight in river trips he wrote from the White River in Missouri about a week he spent there shooting ducks with Hemingway, "We saw a good many of the river people living in houseboats that were just like those Mark Twain told about. We heard a most terrific racket around a curve, and then there came a regular old-time Mississippi steamboat with two funnels, side by side, pouring out wood smoke. To a Vermont Yankee it was like going back eighty or ninety years and coming into Mark Twain's world." To Edward Bok he said, "Your books run the danger of giving the impression that you overvalue material success." Max even suggested to Winston Churchill, when he came into Scribner's once,—he seemed to be "much more like an American than an Englishman,"—that he should write the history of the English-speaking peoples which Churchill actually wrote a few years later.

If Max was to be remembered many years after he died,—remembered far better than most of the authors he worked for,—it was largely because of his sympathetic understanding and because of the standard he maintained. Perhaps he remembered Goethe's saying about the importance of being always in touch with masterpieces, "so that the creative spirit may be maintained at its height"; for he could only think of revising a book "in terms of some classic that one measured everything of that kind against. If it is a book about a prostitute, it has to be thought of in terms of Moll Flanders." He was always referring to Defoe's *Memoirs of a Cavalier* or Clarendon's *History of the Rebellion* or Boswell's *Life of Johnson* or Spengler's "incredibly interesting" *Decline of the West*. He was certain that the great books stand between the precious and the trashy and speak to the literate and the masses alike. "The great books reach both," he said; and, feeling that few of the great writers had had a formal education, he objected to the way literature and writing were taught in colleges, "It results in one's getting into the habit of seeing everything through a kind of film of past literature, and not seeing things directly with one's own senses." In this he disagreed with the "new" critics. He suggested to one writer a book on the Civil War with the contrast in his mind of Luther and Erasmus, the "man of cool intelligence" and the "impetuous and intense one . . . you should read all their correspondence." He himself stood with Erasmus while he had to deal with "Luthers," if one may so describe Tom Wolfe, Hemingway and Scott Fitzgerald, all impetuous and intense and, as he said of Tom Wolfe, turbulent half-archangels who were half-rascals. Wolfe and Fitzgerald had died some years before, and I believe he thought Hemingway had nothing more to say, so, when his time came, I wondered whether he had really wished to live any longer. Max had been a man in the grand style who was exceedingly attractive to every artist.

As for "that most courteous soul on earth," as Mrs. Patrick Campbell, in a letter to Ned, called our immutable friend John Hall Wheelock, he had written at least two or three poems that were destined to endure when the whole works of many other poets were forgotten. For few had produced any poems that could be compared with *The Lion House, September by the Sea* and *Noon: Amagansett Beach*. I was to walk with Jack, for many years to come, along the great beach at East Hampton with the pedantic little sandpipers, intent on the prey cast up by the waves, and looking out

> On the pale meadows of ocean, on the barren fields and bare,
> That the sea-bird wanders, that the sea-wind wanders.

He wrote to me of the moonlight there raining down over the unearthly country while the dunes resounded to the drowsy music of crickets and cicadas. Jack had found Tom Wolfe tiring and oppressive at Scribner's, although also at times most engaging, but he had appeared in one of Wolfe's novels and in James Jones's *Some Came Running* as a curiously idealized good and learned professor. Then, like George Herbert, who had lost the muse in his youth, he found himself, after so many deaths, living and versing again. Retiring from an active life of publishing, he wrote finer poems than ever, among them

The Gardener, about his father, full of a deep ancestral piety. Then there was the *House in Bonac, Song on Reaching Seventy* and *A Walk With the Wind,—*

> Waters by heaven rimmed,
>   Beaches where as a boy
> I strode, as eager-limbed
>   Today as then—O joy,
> Still with me, still undimmed,—

poems more profound in feeling, and certainly more his own, than anything he had written in earlier days. Seventy years of the great beach and the old house at East Hampton had gone into the making of these moving vestiges of John Hall Wheelock's later life and thought.

CHAPTER X

A NEW LIFE

J ACK WHEELOCK had known my wife when they were young
at East Hampton, and it was in his New York apartment that
I met my second wife, Gladys Rice, the daughter of Mark
Twain's doctor. Growing up in Irving Place, a few yards from
Gramercy Park, which she described enchantingly in a book
about her childhood, she had written her school compositions in
the bay-window of her family's house, with one eye on the rear
of the Players Club next door. Her father had attended Edwin
Booth on his death-bed there, and she could imagine the company of actors who were gathered in the club, talking about the
theatre and the plays of the moment. She had been married first
in Boston, where she had spent fifteen years and where three of
her four children were still living. There Sargent had drawn a
portrait of her and she had played in a string quartette and
practised with Felix Winternitz, her old teacher. She had been
David Mannes's earliest pupil in New York, and she had had
a full social life in Washington and Paris, where Henry Adams,
of whom she was the last adoptive niece, had read to her from
the unpublished *Mont-Saint-Michel and Chartres*. But of her
one might have said what Bernard Berenson's secretary said to
me of his old master, that, wonderful to relate, he could be so
much of the world yet not be worldly in any sense at all.

Universally sympathetic, imaginative, gay, and almost of my own age, she was called "Gladys" virtually at sight by both young and old, even by children. Busy with her Stradivarius, she played with Allen Tate, whom I regarded as an enemy when I first met him,—for I identified him with the "new" critics,—but whom I ended by acclaiming when I read *The Fathers*, his extraordinary novel of the South in the Civil War. Seldom had I been so impressed by any novel and my uneasy friendship with this fine poet and subtle critic was presently established on a solid basis. I liked to hear Allen and Gladys fervently scratching their way through Haydn and Mozart's duets for two violins,—occasionally joined by George Biddle with his flute,—or through Couperin or Purcell's "Golden Sonata," and I remember Allen saying of my "Coterie Literature" in *Oliver Allston*, "If only that chapter had been left out, how much happier we should all have been!" Sometimes we visited the Tates' rooms in Perry Street with the coal grate, the mahogany heirlooms and the ancestral portraits. During that first winter, Gladys and I went the round of concerts in various churches and museums, concerts of religious music from the court of Louis XIV, motets of Lalande, oratorios of Bach and Handel; or we heard Szigeti playing a Bach concerto and Suzanne Bloch with her virginals and lutes played by Pre-Raphaelite ladies in velvet à la Giorgione. Often Gladys practised Bach sonatas for violin alone. Larry Adler performed for us at our first Christmas party, and later we heard him in Carnegie Hall, which he filled all by himself, playing with his harmonica Mozart and jazz.

We went to many picture shows, Picasso at the Modern Museum, and especially the Metropolitan with all its glories, where I liked best the widespread canvases of Titian, Tintoretto, Veronese and Gladys the small delicately perfect Italians and Dutchmen. She was drawn to the pictures of roses and grapes of the early eighteenth century and the miniature mountains and streams in the backgrounds of the primitives, or a profile painted by Cranach. One day James T. Farrell came to lunch at our apartment. He had attacked me the year before, hitting rather below the belt, but he said to me that day, "I believe you are on the side of the artist." Farrell was writing twelve hours a day, but, an Irishman with a prehensile appetite for learning, he was studying at night at Columbia mediæval philosophy and Freud. Of course he had been trained in Roman Catholic logic. With Sinclair Lewis and Lewis Mumford, to whom he was grossly unfair, he was capable of savage indignation, and I admired him rather for his power than for his direction, although he had become a consistent democratic socialist. Unlike so many others, he was not fatalistic, but I felt that too often he "said everything," which Voltaire called the secret of being a bore.

In the summer we returned to Martha's Vineyard, where I had a cabin for writing in, and where we saw much of Lillian Hellman who, during a picnic on a beach, read us two acts of her play, *The Autumn Garden*. The gaunt shy Dashiell Hammett, who had made an art of the mystery-story, was present on that evening and many others, the man of whom André Gide rashly said that his prose was the best written in America today. Gladys, always active, had gone in for "remedial reading," charmingly responsive to the unfortunate boys whose lives were sometimes wrecked by their inability to read. Direct and compassionate, she conjured out of them all sorts of unsuspected powers, for she was passionately interested in the possibilities of growth that every human being carries within him. The only people she could not abide were the spineless people who did not know when they were being pushed around and who never dreamed of pushing back. Meanwhile, she had learned to like the ways of an almost servantless world, and she who had once had nine servants found that the pleasure of doing for oneself outweighed the expenditure of time and effort.

But, much as we enjoyed New York and the resources of the great town,—the glass-engravers, the shops devoted to old china, the museum of Mexican objects that we found on one of the rear lofts of an office building,—we tired of the plethora of things where too much was going on, too many telephone calls, too many invitations; and there were the eternal cocktail glasses and half-smoked cigarettes that spoke of the last unwelcome party. If we were to miss the concerts and the art museums, think of what we missed by not spending our lives in Paris or London! The quiet of a country village looked very good to us, so, turning to Connecticut again, we spent a year in Cornwall and then bought a house in Bridgewater, a few miles south. It was on the village green, facing the two churches, and, with its great copper beech, its magnolias in full bloom, its huge rhododendrons and white birches, it seemed to bring back the peace of fifty years ago. With its big circular verandah and shut-in garden, and with chairs set about under the trees, it suggested many a Sargent water-colour. We introduced ourselves to the postmaster in the store, for we did not know a soul when we settled in the village, but Gladys was soon playing her violin in one of the churches across the way, an obbligato of César Franck or a Vivaldi andante.

It appeared presently that in all the villages roundabout there were old friends living whom we saw often,—in Sherman, Woodbury, Brookfield and New Milford. Peter Blume, the Mantegna of our day, spent two or three years painting a picture, but every one of these, "The Eternal City" or "Tasso's Oak," was an event of the year when it was finally shown. We watched these pictures growing in all their stages. Malcolm

Cowley, whose only rival as a reviewer of novels was our other good friend Maxwell Geismar, knew all the birds that visited the Sherman valley, the acorn woodpecker, the sickle-billed thrasher and the three varieties of towhee he found in California. Malcolm had written in *Exiles' Return* the classic story of the expatriates of the nineteen-twenties. The Francis Hacketts were at Newtown, in their Danish house, so clean that no devils could ever enter in; and there lived Louis Untermeyer and Henry Schnakenberg, with his Americana and his great fern alley. Maxwell Geismar, perceptive and acute, often drove up from Harrison, and William McFee and Matthew Josephson lived near us too. The Alexander Calders, when they were not in France, were at Roxbury, five miles away. We saw Sandy once in Rome where, on Good Friday, in Saint Anastasia's church in the via Babuino, surrounded with pious old women, rapt, on their knees, I felt a bunny-hug and suddenly, behind us, there was our irrepressible Connecticut neighbour. He was exhibiting his work in the Obolisco gallery, and he was pursued in the streets by youthful Italian adorers who were taking coloured photographs of him. In our rooms at the Academy, he came to tea one afternoon when Mario Praz was also there,—the critic whom we had previously seen in the Villa Guilia,—and when Sandy left, after carrying on in his usual way, Mario Praz exclaimed, "I am glad to have met Alexander *Korda!*"

Another of our neighbours was William M. Ivins, retired from the Metropolitan Museum, who lived in his old house at Hotchkissville, a museum in itself of rare books and works of art, among them a unique series of woodcuts by Titian. There Bill fashioned the quill pens and manufactured the black ink with which he composed his witty letters. He raised the finest peonies there, and, a sceptic, in his blue work-shirt, a contemporary Diogenes, he did his best *not* to find an honest man.

Occasionally, a quasi-hermit, he plopped about New York, dropping, he said, hayseed with every step in shops and streets, but usually, letting the dust accumulate about him, he stayed indoors and went on with his reading. He had picked up Bayle's Dictionary, the first edition, in French, and he amused himself with the two big volumes, unearthing meanwhile a long run of eighteenth-century writing and finding that he could still wallow in Voltaire. Bill had written, among other books, *How Prints Look,* and he wrote there in the country his study of Vesalius, with the famous anatomical woodcuts. It was certainly true that Bill Ivins could easily have created a vogue in the realm in which he reigned. As curator of black and white art, he had only to mention a name, and repeat it three or four times at cocktail parties, to establish a cult for this name in a few months; for every print-dealer in New York would at once place examples in his window. Just so, the classic Mrs. Astor, by dropping a new name two or three times, created, I suppose, social reputations.

The Wheelocks came out to see us, and Peyton Rous, their brother-in-law, who gave his name to the Rous sarcoma, spent a week-end with us every year. This heather-green-clad scientist, with his eager curiosity, who seemed to have come out of a novel by H. G. Wells, would scramble through the wet woods, with his vasculum swung over his shoulder, spying among the fallen leaves a pipsissewa or a veronica, a bit of grey moss or a partridge berry. Then, once a year or so, the tough-minded little South African Scotsman, Alan Paton, dropped in between Kent and Yale, the author of *Cry, the Beloved Country,* whom we came to love and who was always within a hair's-breadth of a South African prison. The Zimmerns, Sir Alfred and Lucie, came over from Springfield or Hartford, with their never-failing vision of human progress, their faith in the future and their religion of hope, where Lucie, who was the daughter of a French Calvinist pastor, conducted a class for taxi-drivers. She said that her general theme was "driving through life," and I liked the story about the little French village where her family had spent vacations away from Paris. When the local priest died, the whole village appealed to her Protestant father,—until the bishop opposed it,—to be their new priest.

Twice my brother-in-law, Frank Stimson, came up from Tahiti, where he had been living since 1912, and he worked in our house twelve hours a day with his multi-lingual type-writer on his dictionary of the Tuamotuan language. Our house was always flooded with the shells that his daughter sent us, the mother-of-pearl that was used as a lure for tuna and bonito fish and others that were iridescent, green or rose. From West-port came Hamilton Basso, and his Toto, our dear friends, who lived on the edge of a forest, overlooking a stream,—Ham, shrewd, witty and all-observant, who might have been a natu-ralist, as aware as Uncle Remus of the ways of animals and birds. For him, as a novelist, the story in a novel was like the backbone in a human being. Riding with the cowhands in Arizona, he delighted in his escape from the "genteel wilder-ness" and the smooth people at home. Coming from New Orleans, he had left the South in order to bring up his son where he would never hear the word "nigger"; yet, in revolt against the South, he was bound up with it,—he had never made a clean break with the world of his childhood. How well he understood its past one could see in *The Light Infantry Ball,* in which realism was mingled with the actual romance of the old South, so unlike the mythology of the pre-Civil war time with its "soft dream of vanished glories." Ham shared Thomas Wolfe's dissent from the writers of *I'll Take My Stand* with their fictitious chivalry and ideals of honour. An engaging

writer of travels, too, he had a way of going off to Finland, or
to Denmark, Brazil or Samoa.

It often made me happy to think of the advantages that
were connected with a writer's life, especially the people it
brought one in touch with; and, when our friends died, there
were the younger writers who, in a sense, were contemporaries
also. For, among writers and artists, there are no ages, and
the world of imaginative minds is self-renewing. Once, for
the winter months, we went to Cambridge, near that special
social enclave that is Boston, where Hans Zinsser, my old
friend at the Harvard School of Medicine, had once urged
me to go and live. But I was afraid it would be too pleasant,
in that all-cultivated world, and that I might be killed by so
much kindness. We spent winters in New York, once below
Washington Square, a region of old brick houses reminiscent
of Dublin, and I wrote there by a window overlooking a
garden in a square near the house where my father was born
a hundred years ago. We saw something of Thornton Wilder,
John Dos Passos, E. E. Cummings, Stephen Vincent Benét
and Edward Hopper, who complained that he was given
credit only for painting lighthouses and that people did not
seem to have looked at the rest of his work. Edward Hopper's
banal scenes, observed under a magic light, were, I thought,
pictorial equivalents of Theodore Dreiser, and his wife told
me that he had read my *New England: Indian Summer*
while he was painting his "Route 6 Through East Ham" on
Cape Cod. My book, she said, "went right into that canvas."
One day I fell in with Lin Yutang and asked him if he did
not feel like a ghost after a morning or a day of writing;
for the long abstraction from everyday affairs made me feel
curiously wan, etiolated, ashy. Yes! Lin Yutang said, he himself felt just so until he rejoined his solid Chinese wife. The

courtly Glenway Wescott, who admired Thornton Wilder and whose own life was a work of art, a believer in clarity and brevity, catholic in taste, had an eager and discriminating interest in younger writers. With his finely finished work, he loved literary politics, and he was, he said, much less a writer than a talker. My wife gave E. E. Cummings, in his rooms in Patchen Place, a much desired lesson in callisthenics, lying outstretched on the floor, with Cummings beside her, while she laughingly exercised the muscles of her back.

In a time of "private" poetry, it struck me that Stephen Vincent Benét exemplified, like Frost and Sandburg, "public speech," so that, with his feeling for what he invoked as the American Muse, he became a sort of national poet laureate. But his work was overshadowed by John Crowe Ransom's fashionable doctrine of poetry no longer written by patriots or prophets, a poetry that Ransom said had gladly lost its public support and solicited only a "small company of adept readers." This was an American form of the French Symbolist doctrine that made poetry a private concern of the poets, and it put an end to Benét's vogue with the critics. But, a child of three generations of West Point men, Benét had been rooted in the history of the country, and he had an astonishing talent for capturing local atmospheres with a special feeling for the long afternoons and the slow rivers of the South. He was a voice of the people, like the household poets of old or like the folk-writers Lindsay, Sandburg and Masters whose reputations had had to struggle against the cosmopolitan aestheticism that had been coming in for a generation. He had the art of making a real folk-legend,— *Johnny Pye and the Fool-Killer, The Devil and Daniel Webster,*—in which inconvenient realities were simplified away, so that these tales had the air of coming out of a timeless past. I saw Stephen Benét fairly often, and he told me that his Webster had been drawn from *The Flowering of New England*.

In these later days, "Marse" John Dos Passos was also creating a new sense of the American past,—of the "head and heart" of Jefferson and "the ground we stand on,"—when this half-Marylander had reverted to his mother's plantation world and had left behind the radicalism of his second period. For his *U.S.A.* had succeeded the aestheticism of his first period in the days of *One Man's Initiation* and *Streets of Night*, and it seemed to me that few things were more interesting than the development of this remarkable writer. An interviewer had come to see me in the middle forties who had just been to Provincetown; there he had interviewed John Dos Passos who was surrounded, he said, with the old Tory novels of Sir Walter Scott. I could see there the tendency that in fact soon declared itself, for Scott, the arch-conservative, had been a favourite of the old Southerners, and Dos Passos could not have been drawn to him if he had not had leanings in the conservative direction. I could see in advance there the apparent reversal of his point of view, although, as a matter of fact, Jefferson would have shared his feeling about people who were ruined by "the big money." Jefferson would have agreed with Dos Passos's attitude towards a world in which only social revolutionaries were worthy of respect, with the confusion of the melting-pot, together with the wrongness and baseness of the capitalistic system in its hour of triumph. Meanwhile, this inventor of new technical devices that made him famous around the world had developed a real affection for Portuguese-speaking Brazil, where he had spoken, like his Portuguese grandfather, the language of the new writers. He even described himself as "a relapsed Portuguese."

Dos Passos was a world-traveller, in Russia, Mexico, the Near East, like so many other writers of our time,—Vincent Sheean, Edmund Wilson, Hamilton Basso,—all of whom were unlike the globe-trotters of former times who had been merely sight-seers and lovers of sensation. The new travellers were eager students in a world that was becoming "one," and Thornton Wilder, for instance, had known the globe literally from China to Peru, the setting of his well-known early story. Wilder's feeling for national temperaments was one of the striking results of his really universal culture. He had known James Joyce, he had fraternized with Camus and Sartre, the writers who made "a vigour and almost a gaiety," as he wrote to me, "out of an accepted despair" that was certainly tonic. He had toured, for the government, Colombia and Ecuador, he took part in the Goethe celebration at Aspen, with Schweitzer and Ortega y Gasset, borne up and along by Goethe, "deep without strain, homely without smallness and all as strong and fortifying as our Alpine torrents." There, he said, "scores of students had hitch-hiked thousands of miles, earning their living by dishwashing or building a near-by air-port." Thornton had lived fully in the age of Spengler, then of Proust, then of Kafka, and, reading Kierkegaard and Lope de Vega, he was looking forward to an old age that was going, he was convinced, to be "buoyantly happy. . . . I am so happy in the fifties that I wish to incorporate into them the inestimable benefits of the sixties, the seventies and the eighties—the permissible selfishness of the aged. . . . I am going to defend myself by calling in the names of Li Po, Anacreon, Sophocles and Justice Holmes,"—all this to explain why he would not serve on committees or waste time reading books by the younger generation. Objecting to what he called the "cold cream portrait painters," he said that an academy does not begin to be useful to society until it has passed its first hundred years; but he had a fine feeling for the French Academy and the glorious *éloges* that Marmontel and Condorcet had delivered there. No one in our day had done more beautiful work than the author of *Heaven's My Destination*, with his power of creating new forms in every fresh romance or play. "There is no arrogance like modesty," he said to my wife one day, apropos of her husband's autobiographical writings.

CHAPTER XI

IMPRESSIONS OF IRELAND

IN THE spring of 1951, I went to Ireland with my wife. After I had got there, I thought of all sorts of reasons why I had originally wished to go there,—for one, that I wanted the greatest possible contrast to the United States after twenty-five years of unbroken immersion in my own country. I hoped to see America from the outside again, as I saw it when I wrote *The Wine of the Puritans* in 1908 and *America's Coming-of-Age* six years later, both books written in England. Then I wished to see it from the most dissimilar intellectual climate in which I could breathe and speak the language.

I hoped to see "characters" in Ireland such as we had once had here, the queer old maids and other odd fish I used to know as a boy, so many of them abolished by psychoanalysis or sent to sanitariums in our streamlined civilization. I hoped to find people better "integrated" than with us, because less modern, and voices with a ring of assurance like those of the old American types whom Fenimore Cooper and Washington Irving described, the "frank sound-hearted sailor" and the "honest soldier," people who lived close to the elements and were brought up in religion and the study of the classics. I suspected that Americans had lived so long the business life, with stocks, paper securities and the like, that they could not any longer see it in its concrete realities as people do in the so-called "backward" countries,—like Ireland, mediæval, Catholic, reactionary, small. I remembered what Gertrude Stein said about Americans, "They have no close contact with the earth such as most Europeans have. Their materialism is not the materialism of existence, of possession, it is the materialism of action and abstraction." I felt with Sherwood Anderson that Americans were at second remove from the soil, bread, fields, stones lying in fields, from the lives of the old artisans and farmers who tasted and felt things through their fingers. Only in Charleston could one have called business the "antique furniture department," Douglas Hyde's name for it in Dublin. At home people talked about health, food, sex, radio, television. What a blessing to get away from advertisements of perfumes! If I saw in Dublin the magazine *Life*, I would say, That is a civilization I don't want to belong to.

Finally, I felt with Thomas Mann that, as time moves faster and faster with every year of our life, travelling is the best way to curb it. "We are aware that the intercalation of periods of change and novelty is the only means by which we can refresh our sense of time, strengthen, retard and rejuvenate it, and therewith renew our perception of life itself. This is the secret of the healing power of change and incident." Older people travel to recover the slow pace of youth.

S.S. *Britannic, April 26th*

Left the ship at Cobh, 8 A.M., on a tender. Fair, warmish spring day. Cobh very like a Mediterranean town, French or Italian,—how surprising. A line of multicoloured stucco house-fronts, blue, pink, yellow, green, facing the harbour. A huge granite Pugin-Gothic cathedral rises over house-tops.

Inactive streets, a few housewives out for marketing, a few priests sauntering about, milk-carts with big containers and dray-horses, shops deserted. A general Sunday air on this Thursday morning. No American electricity in the air, scarcely any pulse, no sounds but those of cart-wheels and horses, with chimes from the cathedral (St. Colman's). Civility and even sweetness in voices and manners, but the ordinary Irish people seem curiously without style in contrast to the English with their soldierly bearing, form in manner and feeling for pageantry in their dress.

At 11:15 we take the train for Cork, changing there for the afternoon train for Dublin. Five hours' journey, first-class carriage rather dirty. Lunch in restaurant car, crude crockery, soup like a watery brown gravy, good stewed meat with tasteless peas and carrots and ready-made jelly. Altogether an "institution" lunch. Swift smooth-running little train with frequent long stops. Runs all afternoon through green farming country. Spring ploughing in fields, wild flowers everywhere, primroses, yellow gorse, small English daisies growing among dandelions. In cottages that we pass wallflowers on all sides, an air of neatness in small houses. The country like a garden, as in England. In towns (Thurles, Charleville, Portarlington, etc.) much grey granite, modern Gothic churches. Passed perhaps two dozen ruined mediæval castles, really only for-tified or castellated dwellings with no architectural preten-sions. History in towns largely ecclesiastical, with memories of old local wars. We passed near Limerick and Kilkenny but not through them and just missed seeing the Rock of Cashel. Scores of miles of lovely quiet pastoral landscape, cows not too plump and sheep unshorn, narrow roads lined with cottages, rivers, the Lea and Blackwater, all agricultural, not a factory chimney anywhere, no smoke, noise or dirt. As we approach

Dublin the stations are finer architecturally, like small Tudor manor-houses. Ruined castles continue to crop up in the fields. Signs of racing at Kildare. Landscape suggests the blue-grass region of Kentucky.

Arrive at Dublin 5:30, sunny late afternoon. An improvised taxi with a smiling chauffeur takes us through miles of streets. He points out the sights, pleased by our exclamations of interest in them. Bicycles everywhere. Young men and women cycling home from work. (Later I saw bicycles banked by the hundred in O'Connell Street, checked for the day for two-pence, under guard.) A great quiet old-fashioned provincial town, in some ways like New York when my father was born there, though of course New York was mean, architecturally speaking. It had little to compare with the great scattered Georgian monuments of Dublin.

The Shelbourne Hotel also like a New York hotel of the 1870's,—the Buckingham, for one, as I remember it,—the utmost in old-fashioned luxury and elegance. Well-polished brass railings, mid-Victorian style in architecture, furniture, etc. Bedrooms twelve feet high and twenty-five feet square, overlooking St. Stephen's Green. (I wake up to the sound of birds crying in the green and look down on a mother-duck followed by her young, tranquilly gliding along a little stream.) Dining-room redecorated in Adam style. All around us streets like those of lower New York as it used to be. Great repose in atmosphere, motor-horns muted, busses quiet.

Needing a haircut, I went into the "Gentleman's Haircutting Saloon" opposite the Shelbourne. The barber, a small archaic Irishman, asked me where I had had my hair cut last. "In New York," said I. Said he, "I thought so," implying that there was a great deal amiss with New York.

So it appears when the name of Mayor O'Dwyer comes up in conversation. He is notorious in Ireland, having been born in Drogheda, I think. The Irish are all ashamed of him and ashamed in general of the goings-on of Irish-American politicians. I am told that the Irish government, being so new, is still innocent of all corruption.

The Irish regard the Irish-Americans as of a totally different race, and I think of the "Shamrock Hotel" that one Glenn McCarthy has just built in Houston, Texas. This "multi-millionaire wild-catter" oil-man goes in, I read the other day, for "big-name dinner-entertainers," and a filet mignon costs eleven dollars in his twenty-one million dollar palace hotel. How unlike the genie in the bottle is the genie out of the bottle whom we see on our side of the Atlantic.

Meanwhile, there is no doubt a chip on the general shoulder of Ireland, and the war of independence against England still goes on. I noted on the "Britannic" a scorn of Ireland and the Irish. The purser had no Irish money to give me and no time-table of trains from Cobh to Dublin, although the Cunarders have been stopping for generations at Queenstown. Just so, there seems to be a studied indifference to England in Ireland, while every secret of American life is well-known here.

At the Shelbourne, I see at a neighbouring table a grizzled bespectacled man, with a straggling grey beard and the air of a scholar. I take him at once for a professor at some French provincial university. Now he turns out to be an American, and not only that but a lawyer from Newburgh-on-the-Hudson bearing my name. We are fourth or fifth cousins. He gives me a book of poems he has written and says he has come to Ireland for two reasons, to see a skylark rise in the air singing and to hear "the best English spoken anywhere." He heard this on Sunday in the sermon at the Church of Ireland cathedral of St. Patrick. Is there, in fact, anything more charming than the well-tempered Irish voice?

The Shelbourne begins to fill up with characters from Somerville and Ross, "Ascendancy" families and dispossessed county families who represent the great Irish hunting and horse-breeding interest. But, on the whole, I am less interested in the hunters than in the hunted, man and beast.

I have presented some of the letters that my friend of forty years, Padraic Colum, gave me in New York, the Padraic Colum whom Frank O'Connor described once as "another Goldsmith,—he has the same midland background of gentle fields and the same gift of absolute pitch, of being always able to give out the middle C of literature." One of these letters was to Thomas MacGreevy, director of the National Gallery of Ireland, who was having all the pictures rehung on newly gilded walls. He asked me about the re-hanging of the Metropolitan Museum in New York, and, when I said the walls there were grey, he answered, "Yes, and, begging your pardon, too Protestant for me." He showed me a fine portrait of Oliver Cromwell which he had hung "in the best light," i.e., in almost total darkness, down by the baseboard and behind a door. Easy to understand how the Irish feel about this Puritan who offered in Ireland a bounty of five pounds "for the head of a wolf or a priest." MacGreevy said I had not realized the effect on Henry James of James's Irish papist forbears. (They were actually of the straitest sect of Presbyterians, although one of our exegetical critics has spoken of James as a "crypto-Catholic.") It was the papist forbears who inspired, he said, the chapter on Chartres in *A Little Tour in France* and his account of riding in a sedan chair. MacGreevy showed me two pictures signed "P.V.," convinced that they were Paolo Uccellos, and, among many fine Spanish works, three Goyas. He said he had seen me in London in 1926 in Leonard Woolf's office;—he was going out and saw my card as I went in.

The Puritanism of the Irish, so like and so unlike our own, comes down, according to Sean O'Faolain, from the early cenobites. Among them the ideal of self-mortification and penance ran wild, and they provided inmates for all the monasteries and hermits for the islands off the Irish and Scottish coasts. One of them hung for seven years from hooks under his armpits, another lay the first night in the same grave with every corpse brought to his church. Still another sat for seven years on the backbone of a whale.

In his pretty garden at Dun Leoghaire, Sean O'Faolain says there are two governments in Ireland, the Dail and the Church. Each of these checkmates the other. We can see this now when the Bishop of Galway is killing Dr. Brown's Maternity Bill, which subsidizes maternity and attempts to put an end to the scandalous infant-mortality rate. This bill would interfere with the control of the family by the Church.

Miss Ria Mooney of the Abbey Theatre takes us to the fashion show at the Hotel Gresham, the first show of the kind ever held in Ireland. A troop of pretty girls, smart and well-groomed, products of a new school for mannequins, displayed costumes of the lovely Irish tweeds in a hundred shades and as fine as silk. President O'Kelly was there, applauded when he rose. This is one of the notes of the new

Republic of Ireland, like the industrial exhibition we saw the other day, showing all the new Irish manufactures, plumbing, farm-machinery and I don't know what. Strange, for I have not seen in the country, south of Belfast, the smoke of a single factory-chimney.

To the Pearl Lounge, a rendezvous of the Dublin intellectuals, where I met many of the new writers. It was cold and damp on this May evening, and we all sat about with overcoats on. There was Robert Smylie, the editor of the *Irish Times,* a big bulky man and a Presbyterian. This is all the more paradoxical when the editor of the London *Times* is, in his turn, a Roman Catholic.

I remember what L. A. G. Strong wrote in *The Sacred River,* "Ireland in the twentieth century is no place for an Irish writer to live in. Ireland today persecutes every writer who is not content to make his act of submission and accept a censorship which in this country, England, would be thought excessive for a girls' school." That brings back what my old friend F.H. told me. He had gone to live in Wexford where he tried to start with his friends a conversation club to meet once a week. But for this he was obliged to get the bishop's permission, and the permission was refused.

No wonder Arland Ussher can be called "the only philosopher in Ireland." Yet writers, in this highly articulate country, continue to abound. Everyone, moreover, seems to be self-possessed. There is no self-consciousness, such as we have at home, on the part of any type, class or person. Barring an occasional shyness, everyone is forthright. Complete aplomb prevails on every hand.

But my new friend Monk Gibbon says, "The heroic imagination has gone, which means that at least half our mental life is dead"; and AE once wrote to me, "We in Ireland are reacting against the idealism which led us to war and civil war and I fear we are in for an era of materialism. In Ireland we have a natural apathy about literature. It began to descend on us after we became self-governing. Before that we were imaginative dreamers." In a similar strain, Molly Colum wrote to me from Ireland two years ago, "This country is strange and lovely, but the old life is all gone. The government is shockingly efficient and is possessed of a fury for cleaning, fixing and building. They have cleared away the old bookstalls from the Liffey quays that used to make that part of the town like a bit of Paris. There is hardly a slum left. The government hasn't quite got out to the West yet, but they have made a beginning by cleaning up the very old fishing village of the Claddagh outside of Galway where people used to have their own customs, dress and wedding ceremonies. The whole intellectual life is dimmed beyond recognition."

We lunch at the University College, founded by Cardinal Newman, with Francis MacManus and the President, Dr. Tierney, a great Greek scholar. Dr. Tierney took us round the buildings through lofty graceful rooms with marble mantel-pieces and ceilings decorated in low relief. There were recessed niches everywhere to hold statuettes. A small round table set for five in the beautiful Apollo room, with figures on the walls of muses and graces made by Italian plasterers for one of the bucks of the Regency time.

As we were parting on the porch, a beggar-woman came up and besought us for money: "Poor old granny I am. I'm cold." But this type of the "crazy old Irishwoman," familiar to my childhood in the United States, has almost disappeared from the streets of Dublin. One seldom sees the workhouse paupers who appear in Liam O'Flaherty's *The Tramp*. How Gorky-esque, how Russian, this writer makes them, like many of the people in O'Flaherty's *The Informer*. It seemed to me that Gallagher, the revolutionary leader in this play, was modelled on Turgenev's Bazarov. How well I remember the drizzling rain in front of the pub and the huge brutal clown, the informer, with his little round hat perched on his massive skull.

But many of the old Irish types we used to meet or hear about seem now to have disappeared. There were the Irish vagabond scholars with whom as a young man I worked in New York. They all knew Greek as well as Latin, they were usually besotted, with broken shoes, and one of them had served in the French Foreign Legion. Then there were the hangers-on one met in fashionable circles, pets of the rich, great spongers who paid their way as gossips, wits and drawing-room entertainers; and there were the shabby-genteel poor relations like Colonel Stephens whom I used to see in London. He made a small income as a spy working for the French government watching the Germans in restaurants there, kicked down stairs now and then by some swell whom he had libelled. It is obvious that the new Irish republic has put an end to these types or at least increased their self-respect.

But how much has Ireland really changed? I was reading the other day Henry Osborn Taylor's *The Mediæval Mind*. Taylor says that the old Irish heroic tales are full of truculence, irrationality, hyperbole and *non-arrival*. In certain tales the *unsteadfast* purpose is notable, "the hero quite forgetting the initial motive of his action." There are on every page "the makings of a brawl."

With all their "cleverness, facility, ardour and energy," in disseminating early Christianity, the deficiency of the old Irish was lack of organization, and they had but little capacity for ordered discipline humbly and obediently accepted for others. Therefore they ceased to lead or even keep pace with others after the first period of evangelization in Western Europe, when what was required was "united and persistent effort for order." Thus Henry Osborn Taylor. Does this partially explain what Toynbee calls the "abortive western Celtic civilization"? Irish art, architecture, writing, philosophy all "ran down like a clock and stopped" after the great efflorescence of the sixth and later centuries.

Of course, the Irish are still turbulent and bellicose, but they take it out in a black eye and seldom go in for murder. I remember reading in a newspaper once that, after 1920, they closed twenty-one gaols in Ireland because they had no one to put in them. But in a play I have just seen, an old woman character, with her arms on her hips, trails her shawl with bravado. In all her gestures were "the makings of a brawl."

What wonderful memories I have of the Irish players, the best, or almost, I ever saw, though I don't forget Copeau's Vieux Colombier or the Russian players whom I also saw in New York. Copeau spent $40 on his décor where the Americans spent $40,000, because they couldn't believe in the play or the actors and had to conceal their doubts with a splendour of equipment. As for the Russians, there was never anyone like Olga Knipper, Chekhov's widow, dowdy enough off the stage but on the stage, in a Turgenev comedy, a radiant young countess. She was possessed by her characters and really protean. How different from our "star" system in which the actress must always be her much-advertised self, whether on or off the stage, and attract all the attention even when others at the rear are doing the business.

Now in Ireland, it may be that the great writers are dead; but with what gusto, at the Gate Theatre, they have just played *The School for Scandal,* and how beautifully natural they are at the Abbey. J. B. Yeats used to say that the Irish were natural writers of plays, for they are all lovers of dialogue who enjoy their neighbours as they watch, as it were, the drama of life. Now Bryan MacMahon tells me of his group of players in Listowel, and a young man from Kilkenny says that every Irish town has a similar group made up of the local tradespeople.

Monk Gibbon takes me to lunch at Trinity College with the Greek scholar, Professor Stanford. On the wall of the dining-room was a portrait of Sir J. P. Mahaffy, the Greek scholar of earlier days, the provost of the college, to whom, when I was fifteen, I had the effrontery to write, asking for his autograph. After lunch Professor Stanford shows us in the Library the Book of Kells, taking it out of the case and turning the pages.

Mahaffy and Edward Dowden were the bigwigs of Anglo-Irish culture, and of Dowden I heard much from J. B. Yeats when I too was living at Petitpas' in New York. Dowden was one of the early admirers and correspondents of Whitman,—so was J. B. Yeats, who later turned against the "emotional man" and caricatured him in drawings in letters to me; but Dowden, the pioneer in the cult of Whitman, was totally indifferent to the Irish literary revival and to the recovery of the ancient Irish heritage during the years of preparation for it. He dissuaded Aubrey de Vere from wasting his time on any Irish heroic subject, and, in order to become another student of Wordsworth and Shakespeare, turned away contemptuously from everything Ireland had produced. He belittled the "mere" Irish element and failed to encourage in any way the Irish literary pioneers; and he paid the penalty, as John Eglinton says, in the isolation of his later years and in the oblivion that descended after his death upon his personality and name.

How like our Anglo-American critics of the time when I was growing up and when our modern literature was brewing,—I mean Brownell, Woodberry and Barrett Wendell who described Stephen Crane's work as "sensational trash." We too had a still colonial academic tradition, one that had little or no relation to the springs of our own life and the new American writers who were going their own way. We had, in short, like Ireland, what Thomas MacDonagh called "a full-grown criticism side by side with a baby literature," and Brownell, Wendell and Woodberry saw the movement of their time only as it were across a gulf. These critics were too inelastic to adapt themselves to a polyracial American literary future, and they clung, as conscious colonials, to their mother England. Yet in other respects they were as American as Dowden was Irish at the time when W. B. Yeats, the son of his great friend J. B. Yeats, crossed over the Pale and made Anglo-Irish literature more Irish than the Irish themselves. As my old friend Ernest Boyd said, "Irish" Ireland was known to Dowden "only as a strange country where poverty, moonlighting, rebellion and ignorance survived"; and he was, like our American critics, "a provincial, treading at a respectful distance in the wake of his superiors."

The old guide at the Guinness Brewery, formerly a worker there, contentedly speaks of porter as "the workingman's drink." Then, without any colour of animus, he refers to stout as "the drink of the upper classes."

All this as if the question of classes had been settled when men were living in caves, as if upper and lower were as plain as black and white. Nor was there any suggestion here of the sometimes hypocritical effort, across the Atlantic, to wipe out these distinctions. Social rebellion seems to be unknown in this nation of historic rebels,—but rebels only against the English.

We have called upon Jack B. Yeats at the Portobello Nursing Home (formerly the Portobello Hotel). Sunset light out of his top-story corner window over the Grand Canal. The swans had just been placed in the canal today. Jack Yeats, who had displaced a tendon in his back, seemed to be a great pet in the nursing home. He received us in a large square well-appointed hospital room with a wood fire in the grate. He is shorter than his father, with a big bony nose and jutting chin such as his father may well have had, concealed by the long white beard. He was dressed with a careless old-fashioned elegance in a black-and-white checked shawl-coat, with a pearl scarf-pin in his black tie and well-polished pumps. He offered us sherry and Irish whiskey.

Jack Yeats is seventy-six years old. His wife died four years ago, his last sister Lily a year ago, and he has no children. He talked much about his father, the "governor," who had a Dublin studio in York Street, with a beautiful eighteenth-century mantelpiece. At breakfast he would read passages of poetry, never because of its speculative interest, for he disliked all abstractions. He read out the first speeches of the *Prometheus Unbound* but never the ecstatic lyricisms of the famous fourth act. He thought Keats a greater poet than Shelley because he was more concrete. Once J. B. Yeats had brought home, when they lived in London, in Bedford Park, the poet of the Sierras, Joaquin Miller, whom Jack Yeats remembered as a cross between Walt Whitman and Buffalo Bill. He thought Joaquin was his mother's idea of a real poet. Jack Yeats greatly admired Bret Harte and painted one of his best pictures as a tribute to him. It is now owned in Belfast by a rich Jewish patron who has a whole roomful of Jack Yeats's pictures. He spoke of his sister as a great "remembrancer"; she had done his remembering for him, whereas he was very vague about family affairs. But he remembered hearing how, during the great famine, his grandfather, a clergyman in County Down, in a very poor Roman Catholic district, had conducted a christening in secret, feeling that he could not make a public celebration of it. He said his father's best pictures were in Charlemont House, where I had already seen them, though the family pictures were in the National Gallery of Ireland. This gentle old man with his courtly manner and charming smile seemed sad and much older than his years in appearance.

Jack Yeats is now by far the most famous painter in Ireland. One sees his pictures everywhere. His later phase is decidedly of the French impressionist type, suggesting Monet, the drawing somewhat obscured in a confusion of colours. In his early work one saw national types, men in carts, playing cards in boats, going to the fair or the races, out-door Irish life, barefooted children, mountain landscapes, horses with heads high, proud, and with flowing manes. Like his old broadsides, these pictures were boldly outlined, reflecting his lifelong passion for Daumier and Goya. One felt in them the affinity between Ireland and Spain and also what Padraic Colum calls "the secret that the Irish are a youthful people and that they are outside the great tiresome states that make the Byzantium of the West."

Our kind friend Monk Gibbon takes us to call upon Mrs. Yeats in Rathmines. We are driven there by the young poet John Ryan, the editor of the little magazine "Envoy." Mrs. Yeats is English, broadly built, with white hair, cordial and direct in manner. She remembers me as a friend of her husband's father, and she shows me, hanging near the front door, J. B. Yeats's last portrait of himself, the one I used to see, never finished, in his room at Petitpas'. The house, in which the poet Yeats never lived, contains all of her husband's books in two large rooms, overlooking a well-cared-for garden. Engravings of Blake cover the walls, seven illustrations of Dante and all the engravings for the Book of Job. Mrs. Yeats has Yeats's notebooks and Lily Yeats's diary. In the basement two sad-looking women were making Christmas cards on the old printing press of the Cuala Press that Miss Elizabeth Yeats once directed. Miss Yeats had bought the press for a few pounds in a little Irish town, where it had printed for many years the local weekly newspaper, and she had a good eighteenth-century font of type cast and the paper made from linen rags. Jack Yeats had drawn his broadsides for the press with designs for hand-coloured prints. Elizabeth Yeats herself had known nothing about the press-work. She disliked machinery and said she was afraid even of a sewing-machine. Her first helpers were children who had just left school.

Except as a listener at a lecture, I was never in the presence of the veiled and ambiguous personality of W. B. Yeats, but who could have doubted that he was an ever and ever greater and greater poet? When I wrote to John Eglinton, however, asking him how this wonderful writer happened to fall under the influence of the Americans Eliot and Pound, he replied, "Yeats was never a man of independent culture and so fell under the influence at all times of better-grounded minds like Lionel Johnson, Arthur Symons, etc."

How many family stories J. B. Yeats told me, the sort of stories that seldom get into biographies. As an artist in London, trying to make a living as an illustrator, he would come home in the evening to the house in Bedford Park. There his wife, lonely in her exile from Sligo, tended her flowers in window-boxes and fed the few poor birds that found their way in to a dim city window. One day, coming home, during those London years, he found Jack creeping about slowly on his hands and knees. "What are you doing?" he said; and Jack replied, "Trying not to get up an appetite." In the background was always their old servant Rose, who went with them every-where and who reminded me of my nurse Rosie, whose letters I used to address to her mother at "Sion Mills, County Tyrone."

J. B. would drag out of his pocket and read to me the letters, black from handling, he had received from his children. The only great portrait of J.B.'s I ever saw in America was his head of John O'Leary, haunting in its depth. One could never have guessed in New York, in Yeats's old age, how masterly were the portraits I have now seen in the Dublin galleries, really a history of Irish culture in his time. Shallow beside them were the portraits of Lavery and Orpen.

Mr. "Con" Curran,—C. P. Curran of Rathgar,—drives us over the Wicklow Hills where men in the bogs were cutting peat. He takes us to Glendalough, and there across the lake we saw St. Kevin's cave on the opposite slope. Now Curran writes to me about J. B. Yeats, who left Ireland at seventy and came to New York, where he died at eighty-three: "My wife was al-most the last to see him. She met him in St. Stephen's Green and he challenged her to admire his new suit of clothes. She knew that some nice old ladies, concerned that such an artist had not been to Italy, had put up a little money to permit him to see at least Florence and the Pre-Raphaelites. The old man stretched out his arms with his new plumage and said he was going to

New York in the morning. 'I may make my fortune there,' he said." His gaiety and what he called his "angel of impecuniosity" captivated me in New York. For years I thought impecuniosity was angelic, that poverty was the only fit condition for an artist or a writer.

I am invited to call upon "Seamus O'Sullivan,"—Dr. James Sullivan Starkey, the editor of the *Dublin Magazine,*—an elegant old gentleman still "attuned," as Padraic Colum says, "to Montaigne's astringent mode." He is seventy-one years old, a great collector of Oliver Goldsmith and the husband of the painter Estella Solomons. He showed me her portraits, very good, of Jack Yeats, Padraic Colum, James Stephens, etc. He also showed me his pictures by AE and one or two pictures painted by W. B. Yeats. AE dedicated his last three books to Dr. Starkey, and he has the copies of my books inscribed to AE. He was surprised that I never met AE who had spoken of me, he said, often.

I have scarcely ever had any letters that moved me as much as AE's. In one, written from the lake in Donegal where he had a cottage, he said, "I got my poems there. My friends fished for trout. I fished by the margin of the great deep which is the only fishing I can wait patiently at for months." In another he wrote, "I feel that Henry James had a mission pursued in spite of himself, the mission of Mark Twain, Walt Whitman, Vachel Lindsay, Carl Sandburg and other American writers which I think is to cut the umbilical cord connecting spiritually the new world with the old. Twain did it with irreverence, James through disillusionment, Whitman by new forms and by being a positive creator." I can't help resenting Arland Ussher's description of AE as,—no doubt a sage,—but a "bombinating" talker. He was very close to Thoreau and Emerson, not least in his agreement with the Oriental doctrines that formed the basis of the Hermetic Society (the root of the Irish literary revival). Yeats said this society had done more for Irish literature than Trinity College in three centuries. A great believer in democracy in the economic life, AE was also for the aristocratic intellect, ideals, poetry and the imagination as the qualities to be looked for in leaders. In all this he reversed the practical American point of view, while he reflected the half-mystical views of Thoreau and Emerson.

I believe the best modern readers of our greatest writers have been Irish. Everyone knows how J. B. Yeats read *Walden* to his son, the poet, who, in consequence of this, wrote *Innisfree*. Then AE and John Eglinton were closely connected in feeling and thought with Emerson, Thoreau and Whitman. John Eglinton,—W. K. Magee,—an old Unionist, has been living in England since the treaty of 1921. It was this Irishman who said, "Mankind may weary of the whole scheme of things at present," and who suggested that we might well expect a new crusade of some new Peter the Hermit.

The mystical note is still strong in Ireland,—a note of many types,—among the Protestants as among the Catholics, who keep up their pilgrimages to Loch Derg (mentioned by Dante). After a vigil in the Basilica they spend three days there on the rocks of the island lashed with rain, stumbling on bleeding knees up steep and slippery places, meditating on the Passion.

Again the kind Monk Gibbon takes us to Roebuck House to call, in Dundrum, upon Maude Gonne, Madam MacBride. She lives there with her son, the present minister of Foreign Affairs. The gate lets us into a big unkempt meadow with the vast old stables at the rear,—the weathervane is a figure of Mercury. The house stands to the right, a large early nineteenth century brick dwelling of Ascendancy grandeur. The paint has been scratched off the front door by the dogs. A grandson lets us into the dark entry,—it is twilight outside,— apologizing for leaving us alone with his grandmother: the maid and all the family have had to be out. He takes us into a large room at the rear, and then he goes off for an evening of electioneering.

The grand old lady is stretched out on a chaise longue, facing the coal fire. She is smoking a cigarette and reading a French yellowback novel. She seems to be glad to see us. "How kind you are," she exclaims, "to come and see a deaf old woman!" She has bold features and deep-set eyes, with a high-bred manner and charming gestures, her voice very distinguished and she herself full of humour. She had been trained to be an actress and one could see how beautiful she had been. She spoke at once of Yeats,—"Willie,"—whom she had known at twenty, he being at that time twenty-one: they had been con- stantly together but, as she said, "like brother and sister,"— there had evidently been no shred of romantic feeling on her side. Willie was then a student in a school of art and John O'Leary's most hopeful recruit.

Then she spoke of the peasant evictions as having set her off on the career that had been for her inevitable. Her mother had died when she was four, and she was brought up by a nurse at Howth. She played with the poor little neighbour children and learned to love them; and when the evictions came in the eighteen-eighties she saw these same people with their houses burned over their heads, left to starve by the tens of thousands. She saw a woman with a day-old baby left by the roadside and little children trying to kindle a fire in the rain. The landlords were destroying the homesteads be- cause they could make more money by cattle-raising, and she knew then that Ireland must "leave the empire." Besides, she had been brought up in France and had become a republican there. No doubt she dramatized herself as a kind of Irish Joan of Arc who had set out to save her country. She told us how she stopped the famine in County Mayo, demanding for each person a shilling a day as well as seed-potatoes to plant in their cottage gardens. She had assembled ten thousand peasants and confronted the Governor with them and her demands. He had only ten policemen to hold them in check, and she was able to say there would be bloodshed unless the government agreed to her terms. She said she had really done very little but had no choice not to do it, and she had "never been afraid of anything." When her mother died, her father had taken her into the room before the coffin was closed, and she had heard him say, more to himself than to her, "Never be afraid of anything, even of death." After that, whenever she began to feel fear, she had thrown back her head. Her father had tried to stop her work in Ireland and cut off her allowance when she protested against the evictions; but later her father had joined her, moved as she had been, resigned from the British army and entered Irish politics. Three weeks after that he died.

Her memory was still perfect. If she had not had trouble with her heart, she would still be, at eighty-seven, as active as ever. She was evidently proud of her son who is doing just what she would like to be doing herself. She feels that the success of the republic is "wonderful" and says that in Ireland now no one needs to "starve."

A day at Bective, in County Meath, with Mary Lavin and her husband in their new white house, the "Abbey Farm." The ruins of the old abbey are in a ploughed field a few yards away. What an exceedingly pretty young woman and what a beautiful writer, actually born near Boston and an emigrant in reverse. She regrets the passing of the Ascendancy, with its fine manners, and the absence in England of her neighbour Lord Dunsany, the inventor of a theogony, a whole mythology, like Melville in *Mardi* and James Branch Cabell.

The long avenue of Bective House was lined with myriads of daffodils. It was like the beginning of a Turgenev story, "In the springtime, in a beechen grove"; and there, in the driveway before the house, raking the gravel, was old Kevin, the gardener, who remembered our friend James Stern,—born in this house,—when he was a boy. "Ah, Master Jimmie," said the old man; "he was a wild little boy. They had to send him away to live on a farm." That was at least thirty-five years ago, and Kevin had been raking the gravel long before that. Below the terrace lay the river Boyne, filled with rushes, and beyond rose the hill of Tara where the harp hung in the *Irish Melodies*. Only earthworks remain there; nothing is left of the "walls."

The harp is still a magic symbol. My wife has an old Egan harp, made about 1800, rather warped and with most of the strings gone. However, it occurred to us to take it to New York and ask at the Metropolitan Museum where it could be restrung. We drove up Madison Avenue through ever-thickening crowds and then set out to walk over to Fifth Avenue. I carried the harp over my shoulder. But we could not cross the streets,— a parade was coming. What a coincidence! We had not known it was St. Patrick's day. Then an Irish policeman caught sight of the harp and beckoned us forward; the crowd opened before us like the Red Sea before the Israelites, and people on all sides exclaimed at the sight of the old Irish harper,—namely, myself. A little boy asked me where the harp came from, and when I said Dublin he murmured in awe, "Dublin city! My father was born in Dublin city!"

We have been visiting in County Down, where my stepsister lives and where "the mountains of Mourne sweep down to the sea." Another world entirely, an Anglo-Irish military world. We are taken to a castle near by with sixty-three bedrooms and a library as large as the rotunda of the Library of Congress, filled with thousands of splendid morocco-bound books. But what a dwelling to fall heir to in the nineteen-fifties! Our hostess has cut in two the vast dining-room with a line of china-closets. On one side hang the family portraits of Kneller, Lely and Sir Thomas Lawrence, on the other she has installed her cooking-range and washing-machine. The family live in screened-off compartments in one of the former drawing-rooms, each one as large as an ordinary house.

A few days in the west of Ireland, and we drive up into Connemara, all one big green farm, as Ireland seems to be everywhere, with donkeys, pigs and chickens astray on the roads and tinkers and gypsies in caravans camping by the roadsides. One could imagine there all the tramps of Synge's plays, the itinerant pedlars and blind beggars on the highway and the black Spanish types that often remind one of Goya and the early broadsides of Jack B. Yeats.

In Galway, Lord and Lady Killanin took us for an all-day drive, with a picnic lunch, in County Clare. We spread out the baskets near the graveyard in the ruins of the Seven Churches. At one moment we stopped in the grounds of Lady Gregory's house, which has been torn down since her death, and we found the great beech-tree with the initials carved in the bark of all the writers,—G. B. S., W. B. Y., G. M., and I don't know how many others,—who had stayed there in Lady Gregory's time. Then on a small country road we drew up suddenly two yards away from Yeats's tower, with the dedication to his wife on a tablet in the wall. The tower was going back to the ruin the tablet prophesied for it, with the door half open and swinging in the wind. We climbed up through the three stories and looked down from the top. The walls were painted within a rather lurid blue that had some astrological or mystical significance.

How strange were the vast expanses of rock through which we drove in County Clare, with tombs of the Bronze Age scattered all about. They were dolmens of the sort one sees at Stonehenge and in some cases had never been disturbed. We saw castles in all stages of development, beginning with the pre-castle stage, a simple enclosure with a wall of stones. There were no modern buildings anywhere in sight to mark the changing centuries or suggest the passing of time. It was as if nothing had happened in twelve hundred years or four thousand years, as if pre-history and the Dark Ages still continued there and the people of those times had simply withdrawn for a day.

CHAPTER XII

IN FRANCE AND ITALY

Jo Davidson wrote to Dublin to welcome us to Europe,—"for I presume," he said, "that Dublin still considers itself part of Europe or at least the world." So, after a month in England, we went to France to stay with Jo and Florence, fourteen miles from Tours, in their Manoir de Becheron at Saché. It was three miles from the loveliest of the châteaux, Azay-le-Rideau. Jo had returned to France after seven years in America, caught and exiled there by the second world war, and he found that the French government had packed away all his sculpture in sixty-five cases in order to safeguard it from the German invaders. It was as if he had died and come home again and fallen heir to his own past, the whole work of his lifetime, where nothing had changed and where the old gardener, the old cook and Gino, his assistant, had watched over the pictures, the books and the grounds. We had the rooms in which Jo's friend Lincoln Steffens had written his autobiography a few years before.

It was in America, at the beginning of the forties, that Jo had knocked on my door at Weston. He was eager to love and to be loved, and we resumed in a moment the intimacy of the far-off time when I had been teaching in 1914 near London.

Spending his affection on Russia too, he was taken for a Communist, for he was possessed by that nostalgia for "the home that had never been a home" which Emma Goldman attributed to all Russian Jews. Even his friend Henry Wallace was also called a Communist, the man who had never read a line of Marx's writings and who made long speeches out of quotations from the Bible,—Henry Wallace of whom AE had written to me, "I found behind all his economics and agricultural science a lovely flower of mysticism." With his prodigious energy, Jo had gone into politics, getting up a gigantic organization to reëlect Franklin Roosevelt. I had gone with him to the White House where the President received us, with others including Joe Cotton and Dorothy Gish. There was also in this delegation a Polish opera-singer who said to Dorothy Gish on the station platform, "Why have you never married? You know everybody has a chance!" which struck me as a rather egregious remark to make to a charming woman of the stage. I had never heard of Joe Cotton, but we had no sooner got out of the taxi, on an apparently empty street, than a swarm of "bobby-soxers" gathered about him. Clamouring for his autograph, they had materialized from nowhere.

Meanwhile, Jo Davidson had made a bust of Helen Keller, with her hands eagerly raised, and he introduced me to this legendary character who had recently come to live in Westport. Helen and Polly, as we always called them,— for Polly Thomson, the Scottish companion, was Helen Keller's indispensable *alter ego*,—had also stayed at Becheron a year before we went there and Jo had painted a portrait of them talking. When they were not occupied with this conversation piece, they wandered together in the garden or strolled in the fields, blue with corn flowers and red with poppies, and in the evening they read together, Polly reading Wells's autobiography and Helen, in braille, *Candide* and Anatole France. They dabbled a little in Rabelais, who was born near by, at Chinon, near the ruined castle that Jo took us to see, and Jo had been at his best with Helen, delighting in the spring of joyousness that bubbled, at the slightest pressure, up to the surface. For Helen radiated happiness, as we had seen in Westport. There, with Jo and Gaetano Salvemini, the old anti-fascist professor at Harvard, we had all met again and again. Salvemini was publishing his "News from Italy" in which we still seemed to hear Mazzini anathematizing another Italian despot; and, of Helen, Polly said, "In all these forty years there hasn't been a day when I have not been amazed by something she has said or done." Now Salvemini, who had returned to Florence, arranged to have Helen "see" the Michelangelo tombs in the Medici chapel. Jo drove down with her, stopping on the way at Genoa to rescue Helen from a *soi-disant* cousin. This lady, eager to claim relationship with such a famous person, had invited Helen to come for a visit. She had married an Italian count, but her original name was Keller, and, like Helen's remote forbears, she had come from Switzerland, the rest being all guess-work and pretension. The lady was not even present when Helen, ready for any adventure, arrived at the palace where Jo found her, and she turned out to be an active fascist who had been a friend of Mussolini. After Helen and Polly left, she sent them a bill for the note-paper they had used there! As for the Medici tombs, Jo said he had never seen them so intimately as when he watched Helen's hands wandering over the forms. A moving scaffold was set up for her to stand on. She had, Salvemini said, ten eyes for sculpture, an art she had always loved and even practised.

Jo had come to visit us in a house we rented in northern Connecticut but, having lived so long in France, he did not

like villages built of wood, even the pretty Palladian village of
Cornwall. Nor had I, once upon a time, before I lived through
in imagination the life that lay behind this wooden village.
Only then did I understand why Walter Gropius came to feel
that wood was the right material for American building. Jo had
made, first or last, wonderful speaking likenesses of many of the
great persons of his time, from Winston Churchill and Anatole
France to Gandhi and Madame Chiang Kai-shek, a "Chinese
cross between Madame Récamier and Claire Booth Luce." Jo
did not admire this lady who had spent a year in New York
and had never once visited Chinatown,—inhabited, she said,
only by coolies,—but she had made the Chinese people "respectable" for the man in the street who had thought of them
as merely laundrymen and chinks. Jo, having sculptured busts
of the statesmen at Versailles, had flown to South America to
make busts of the Presidents, and he had gone to Jugoslavia for
a portrait head of Tito and found himself there surrounded
with sculptors. He said that some of his sitters were short
stories, while others were novels, and that it took two to make
a bust, the important thing being the rapport of the artist and
the sitter; and Jo remarked that the reason why he was not
going to be a writer was that when he wrote he could not sing.
Arnold Bennett had told him he talked so well he could never
write, and yet he was at work on his autobiography,—*Between
Sittings* it was called. He had been getting to feel that he was
Atlas carrying the world,—"like that old gink in the picture
with his feet in the clouds,"—so he bent down, stepped out
from under, stood back and watched, and the world did not
budge a fraction of an inch.

After we left Saché, Jo flew to Israel to spend seven weeks
making busts there, enthusiastic over a country so full of youth
and courage, with so many new types for him to sculpture.

The extremes met there, Jews from the darkest holes of Asia and the most cultivated Jews from America and Europe. He worked in Beersheba on one of the frontiers and spent a week at a coöperative farm near the Sea of Galilee, and he visited several outpost settlements in the vast and rather terrifying desert and dashed up to Jerusalem to make a bust of Weizmann. There were also towns where they were building three houses a day blown up with cement out of a gun. He drove about the country, sometimes in a police jeep, sometimes in a luxurious car with a tub of clay in the baggage compartment, and whenever he saw a new type, a shepherd on the plain, a Yemenite, a Persian or an Indian Jew, Jo jumped out of the car and asked him to pose. He said that in Israel they couldn't believe he was a Jew, for never for a moment in his life had he felt an in-feriority-complex. He did busts of the President, the cabinet, and even one of the Arab sheiks. "You can't stop him," Florence wrote about this mad escapade. In fact, he worked furiously, like a man out of his head, and he himself wrote, "We are exhausted, but it was worth it,"—or would have been if it had not killed him. He had received his book at Tel Aviv and found it was full of changes,—paragraphs had been added,—it was no longer his book; and, terribly agitated, he slashed away at it while his bronchitis turned into pneumonia. He had come home to Saché and had been taken to the hospital at Tours. There, quite suddenly, he died.

Jo was one of the great talkers, sometimes tumultuous, usually keen, all gusto, mimicry and humour, now and then recalling the great talkers of the past for whom conversation was one of the fine arts. But where he was spontaneous, they had been deliberate, preparing themselves for the breakfasts and dinners in which they were to take part and planning the conversation well in advance. They sometimes kept commonplace-books with notes of the remarks of distinguished men, volumes of whose table-talk were subsequently published, and it was largely because of the Boswells who abounded in those days that the lives of the great writers of the time were so clearly remembered. I have often wondered if our age would be known in the future at all, with so few talkers, diarists or letter-writers, with most communications uttered through the telephone or on postcards saying, "Wish you were here." Even in fiction there was less and less realism, recording any kind of significant life. I doubt if fine conversation is held in any esteem at all, for I remember Oliver Gogarty, the Irish poet, for whom there was apparently no place at New York dinner-tables. He was a classical table-talker of a sort that was well-known in the days of Dr. Holmes and Oscar Wilde, but who on Park Avenue cared for this? I gathered that Oliver Gogarty was lost in New York. Until he was picked up dying in the street, he went every night to a West Side saloon, a resort of Irish footmen, grooms and butlers with whom he talked till four or five in the morning. They knew good conversation if their employers did not.

Robert Flaherty took me to lunch once with Oliver Gogarty, who had a sharp word for everybody. He said that he and Joyce were walking in Dublin one day when they saw J. B. Yeats ahead of them,—Yeats whom Gogarty regarded as a bore, with his obsession of the "solitary man." Joyce said to Gogarty, "Let's touch him for a shilling." They did so and Yeats replied, "Certainly not, for, in the first place, I haven't got it, and in the second place, if I gave it to you, you and your friend would spend it for drink." Said Joyce in response to this, "It is not competent for us to discuss the future of a non-existing object." Then, always the scholastic, he added to Gogarty, "I gave him the Razor of Occam." I might have writ-

ten down more of Gogarty's remarks had I not supposed that
they would all appear in one of his books; but I remember his
account of the burial of George Moore's ashes on an island in
one of the Irish lakes. Gogarty rowed the boat over and George
Moore's spinster sister, sitting in the stern, held the urn with
the ashes in her lap. The day was warm and Gogarty, who had
not rowed for forty years, took off first his tall hat, then his
coat, then his waistcoat. At that point the spinster sister said,
"I hope, Dr. Gogarty, you will not remove any further habili-
ments."

It was true that Gogarty talked only of Ireland and the
literary revival there, and this might have been tiresome at
dinner-tables. I asked him if he knew anything about a painter
named H. Phelan Gibb, of whom I owned two or three pictures
and who was one of the two painters of the time who "would
be discovered after they were dead, they being predestined to a
life of tragedy." So Gertrude Stein said in her autobiography,
the other painter being Juan Gris, and she also said that Harry
Gibb was her "first and best English friend" and that Gogarty
was his great friend and patron. Gogarty professed not even to
know his name, and he said, "There were so many of these
fellows sitting on my doorstep." Neither then nor at any other
time, though I wrote in all directions, could I find any trace of
H. Phelan Gibb. In fact, what became of so many of the talents
who abounded in Paris at that time? They disappeared utterly
or ended now and then as attendants at Texas filling-stations.

A few years after visiting Jo Davidson at Saché, we spent a
winter in Rome, where as a boy of thirteen, enthralled by
Italian art, I had stayed in an English pension in the Piazza
Poli. A priest from Australia who was there came back every
night to report the proceedings of the canonization of Pio Nono,
and he told us that the process failed when it was announced

that the pope in question had taken snuff. After that winter
I pored over Bernard Berenson's handbooks in their first burnt-
sienna bindings, and during several years to come I read Ruskin, John Addington Symonds and Vernon Lee about whom
I began to write. Then, when I went to Harvard, Berenson
was already a legend partly because he had selected most of the
pictures in Mrs. Jack Gardner's Fenway Court. There I had
seen the lady whom he called Boston's pre-cinema star, seated
on her throne, observing the observers. Fifty years later still
I read Berenson again, at a time when he felt "out-moded in the
Angry-Saxon world." He had retained his old belief in liberalism and humanism, and he corroborated my own feeling that
these were permanent realities instead of what others regarded
as Victorian illusions. I was all for his faith in "life-enhancement" as the final aim of art, the task of trying to humanize
mankind, and there was something spacious, something Goethean, unique in our time, a marvellous breadth and freshness in his note. What vitality there also was in this man approaching ninety who was to be active still at ninety-three.
Everyone who knew him told anecdotes about him, as, for example, when a guard found him asleep in the Yale Museum,
where he had gone to see the Jarves collection. The guard woke
him up and reprimanded him. "I am Mr. Berenson," the old
man said, "and I'm privileged to sleep in any museum in the
world." In the circle of my friends there were four of his
regular correspondents, and he began to write to me after I had
sent him a book with a few pages devoted to his own writing.
He sent me four books of his, inscribing one with the Virgin
Mary's words to Saint Bernard in a vision, *Bene scripsisti de me.*

Now, during this winter in Rome,—at the American Academy, where we knew Ralph Ellison and Theodore Roethke,
that fine poet from the Far West,—Berenson wrote inviting us

to spend four days at his villa I Tatti in Settignano. We stopped on the way at Lerici to see Percy Lubbock, who had also invited us for a three-day visit, but we suggested rather a lunch on Sunday with this delightfully hospitable table-talker. With his great prelatical belly, partially deaf, he lived in a pleasant villa half-hidden in woods and hanging over the Mediterranean sea, not far from the house where Shelley had spent several months and much like the Californian coast at Carmel. But when I spoke of this, Lubbock shuddered. Three young Englishmen, readers and amanuenses, sat at table with us; and we regretted that we had to be on our way so soon, as we waved good-bye in the rain to the solitary figure in the doorway. Berenson's villa stood on a hill where Mark Twain had also lived, like Leigh Hunt and John Addington Symonds before him and where had supposedly also stood the villa in which the tales of Boccaccio were told. We were given a beautiful set of rooms hung with works of art,—among them a Nattier and a Longhi,—like all the rooms and corridors, for the house was a sort of museum especially of early Florentine and Siennese masters. The frail and tiny little man, scarcely more than five feet tall, moved swiftly, with bird-like steps and the silence of a shadow, and at table he sat bolt upright and as if carved in ivory, speaking with a clear and finished enunciation. Later, with a plaid rug over his knees, concealing a hot-water bottle in his lap, he received, like another Voltaire, the pilgrims from all the world who filled the house at lunch, tea and dinner. One was Arturo Loria, the Florentine professor, who translated him into Italian and who died soon after; and there was Harold Acton, who came to dinner one day, and whom we presently went to see in his great villa on the via Bolognese. The kind Harold Acton, with his Chinese mannerisms and his anachronistic gargoyle smile, walking with fluttering hands and feet turned out, had lived for a number of years in China. He was at work on a history of the Bourbons of Naples with whom I fear he sympathized.

Berenson's talk was all concrete,—he disliked what he called "metafussics,"—and, with his incessant activity of mind, he discussed all manner of subjects, science fiction, the history of trade, the Risorgimento. I did not understand his distrust of Mazzini and Garibaldi,—he seemed to feel that the Italian people had been better off before they were united,—and I could hardly believe that B.B. would have liked a time when Mazzini was imprisoned simply for being "a thinker." But there was great sweetness and liberality in almost all he said, and I could see why my friends George Biddle and Walter Pach always spoke of Berenson as "the dear old man." He quoted Ovid freely, with Platen and German poetry, and, deeply read in the history of the Fuggers and the Medici, he remarked that a knowledge of the history of trade was indispensable for one who wished to know art-history. I remembered what he had written somewhere, "I was born for conversation and not for writing books." In fact, he had written to me, "Comparing small with great, I should have had, like Saint Augustine, four or five amanuenses to take down talk. I am really a born talker, not a born writer."

He worked every morning on his three-volume catalogue of Italian paintings, hoping to complete it in three or four years. After that he expected to go back to writing. In addition, he kept a daily journal, one page each morning when he woke up, for he still lived wholly in the present and the future. Every day at 12:30 we met him at the front door and climbed into the old Ford station-wagon, driven by the stout Welsh chauffeur Parry, who had been in his employ for forty years. At a certain point we all dismounted for a walk, though, small as an atom and almost as light, he had expressed a fear that a wind might rise and blow him away. Standing on a ridge, he pointed to the city of Florence below, creeping out like a tide to swallow him up, and he was afraid it might engulf I Tatti if Harvard, to which he had left it, sold his land. One day the station-wagon stopped in a farm-yard,—one of those shabby half-de-serted farm-yards that had once delighted Henry James,—and Berenson, drawing a great key out of his pocket, unlocked a green wooden gate in a high stone wall. He threw open the gate and there within stood the castle of Vincigliata, an old feudal stronghold, long a ruin, that had been restored by an eccentric Englishman a hundred years ago. This John Temple Leader had also built a romantic grey turret on the edge of a large dark rocky pool, the old quarry, no less, from which Donatello had got the *pietra serena* he used in his sculpture.

Berenson had been "in hiding" in the second world war, when he said he was a carbuncle on Mussolini's neck, and he showed in *Rumour and Reflection,* written at that time, how far outside of art he was accustomed to ranging. That book, he told me, had been refused by all the English and American pub-lishers when another man came to see him, read it, accepted it and sold about twenty thousand copies: it had become the most popular of all his books. He was indignant with a young critic who had also come to see him and had betrayed his con-fidence about Santayana. The young critic had sworn not to mention Berenson's relations with Santayana, with whom he had never had a quarrel, but it was obvious that he disliked this other old savant of the time who had once been, like him, an "awe-stricken pilgrim" in Europe. Both of these men had crossed all the frontiers, but, while Salvemini was Berenson's dear friend,—that other great liberal and humanist,—he re-membered William James's saying, "George keeps his heart on ice." Berenson remarked, "I would go further and say he had no heart,—he was all *pen* . . . There is a French saying, *Il gagne à être connu.* Of Santayana I would say, *Il gagne à ne pas être connu.*" I do not know whether there was anything personal in this adverse feeling, or in his memory of the illiberal Irving Babbitt as a "dull heavy sulker," or in his remark that T. S. Eliot was his "mortal enemy." No one in Berenson's time at Harvard, alert and zestful as he might have been, felt that in youth there was anything to be envied. Youth was looked upon as a causeway between boyhood and manhood, not as a state that anyone wished to prolong, and no one whom Berenson remembered shared the cult of youth of Scott Fitzgerald, Hemingway and Edna Millay. I recalled Joel Spingarn's essay on the fashionable theory of the twenties that all art and wisdom are the products of physical youth and that nothing can be really good unless men still young have done it or liked it.

Many scraps of Berenson's talk later came back to me, observations that he made while I sat beside him or, now and then, in his letters. He said that as a boy in Boston he had gloated over *Cudjo's Cave* in a long forgotten monthly called *Our Young Folks.* He spoke of the well-known affinity between the English and the Arabs, from Sir Richard Burton to T. E. Lawrence, connecting this with the homosexuality that is supposed to flourish in English public schools. He was much taken with Mary MacCarthy, who had recently visited him,— "What a fascinating talker, and what a writer!" She had just published her book on Venice where he was presently going to revisit the glimpses of the moon and revise his own early handbooks. He was planning to spend the following summer rediscovering Florence, almost forgotten in years of travelling elsewhere. He said that, by way of "courting" him, Mabel

Dodge had remarked to him, "You are the greatest American since Abraham Lincoln." At the moment he was excited by a Chinese novel: "Never was I so admitted to the intimacy of the Chinese mind and heart." But Italy was never long out of his mind. When I sent him *The Dream of Arcadia,* he said that sixty years before he had urged his brother-in-law Logan Pearsall Smith to write about Americans in Italy. He continued, "On a lawn in front of the cemetery church at Ferrara there is (I hope still) a beautiful Canovaesque sarcophagus containing the body of a young Bostonian who died there in the twenties of the nineteenth century. As a Protestant he could not be buried in holy ground, in the cemetery itself. I have often itched to write a Pateresque imaginary portrait of this young pilgrim to the land of his spiritual ancestors." Berenson asked, "How early did continental Europe distinguish between an Englishman from Great Britain and one from America? Stendhal was perfectly aware of the difference." Again he wrote, "Why not make a study of the attitudes, I mean the conscious attitudes toward visual art in America during the last 150 years? How well prepared you are for doing it." The subject would have appealed to me in the days when I wrote the life of Symonds and hoped to write a study of Vernon Lee and when I opened *The Wine of the Puritans* with a note about Baja on an Italian midsummer afternoon. Berenson and his lovable companion, Nicky Mariano, wrote letters as kings and queens are supposed to do, as if *you* were the only person living.

Sometimes Berenson wrote to me from his woodsy retreat at Vallombrosa. There, surrounded by the forest, his only neighbours were the parish priest and the men who were in charge of the forest nursery garden. In his summer cottage, W. W. Story had died, and he said, "It was Story's book *Fiammetta* which ranked high among those that gave me a longing for

Italy." Already deaf, he feared that blindness was also coming
on, and in that case he "would be as good as cut off from the
Not-me . . . rather a dreary prospect for one who is still so
passionately interested in the world at large as I am." Again
he wrote from Tripoli, from the marvellous ruins of Leptis
Magna, and I remembered what his wife said in *Across the
Mediterranean* about an earlier journey to Tunisia and Algiers:
"My husband was like a war-horse scenting the battle . . .
His remorseless energy and curiosity invest every step of art-
history with fascination . . . With his insatiable curiosity
about the genesis, the affiliations, the inter-influence of all
forms of art, [in museums] he is so full of excitement that he
stays on and on, and is capable, even, of persuading the care-
takers of out-of-the-way little collections to let him go on
by the light of a candle when all the others are exhausted."
Yet it was part of his great strength that, ranging over all the
arts, he clung on the whole so closely to his own parish, Italian
painting after and before Giotto. There was much in his career
that was ambiguous, no doubt, but his interests were unques-
tionably universal, and I could well believe what Edith Wharton is supposed to have said, "My other friends are ponds.
Berenson is an ocean."

On that earlier visit to France, Gaetano Salvemini, Berenson's
friend, had been a constant subject of talk at Saché. Jo Davidson, who had loved Salvemini too, gave me a pencil sketch he
had made of the great old man in Florence. He had put this in
my hand when he came to see us off in Paris at the boat-train
for Cherbourg, and the first person I saw on the ship, climbing the companionway, was Salvemini, no other. I held the
drawing in front of him; he saw his own head with astonishment, and for the next five or six days, until we reached New
York, we were all generally together. Tired of wandering,

Salvemini had lost the habit of staying in one place; he was on his way back to Harvard to arrange for the publication of his *Mazzini;* and the last I saw of him he was walking off the pier, with one small bag in his hand. This reincarnation of an antique sage, whom kings were eager to consult and who lived as far as one could without money or possessions, appropriately bore the name that in Apulia, where he had grown up, was the last word uttered when the fishing boats went out.

CHAPTER XIII

IN ENGLAND AND AFTER

TWICE WE visited England, once by way of Holland, where we spent a few days at the Hague and Amsterdam. Our ship followed the coast line from Le Havre, and, looking out of the porthole in the early morning, I saw a windmill and a cow and I knew we were approaching Rotterdam. At Haarlem, in the Groote Kerk, we heard a recital of the great church organ to which Mozart had listened,—it was played by the Dutch organist, Piet Kee,—and I remembered how my mother had taken me to hear it, and the great Swiss organ at Fribourg, when I was twelve. At Amsterdam we met Lewis Mumford's opposite number, Wijdeveld, the architect and city-planner, who had designed the interior of the "Nieuw Amsterdam," the ship on which we had crossed the ocean. Concerned with the town of the future, in which sunless houses and narrow airless streets would have ceased to exist, he was looking forward to a new renaissance transcending the scientific phase through which we were passing. He foresaw man's ultimate triumph over the machine and a day when ripeness and serenity of spirit would prevail, a new era, a new world order; and meanwhile he was building for a society of motor-cars, aeroplanes, films and sea-going liners. With Wijdeveld we went to see the exhibition of

Alexander Calder's immense "Black Spider" and other "stabiles."

In England, where the vengeance bombs were falling in history and memory only,—a country I had not seen for twenty-five years,—I was again struck by the richness of a culture with which in the United States we had nothing to compare. In Salisbury, where we spent ten days, there were four bookshops, with the best second-hand bookshop I had ever seen, and, besides the Salzburg marionettes, there were three plays running at the time, a play of Aristophanes, a play about George Herbert and *A Winter's Tale* in a private garden. Exquisitely acted this, and all by amateurs, with music by Purcell and Telemann, issuing from a hidden gramophone in a thicket by the river; moreover, with the loveliest English voices,—and all in a town of twenty thousand persons. At the same time, the spire of the cathedral was in danger of falling, as the walls of the abbey church at Bath seemed to be on the point of collapse, and I wondered how, with the burdens of the present, the English could preserve all these grand remnants of the Middle Ages. At Dorchester there were statues of Thomas Hardy and William Barnes; tablets were generally affixed to the houses of authors, and the Penguins reprinted, ten or twenty books at a time, a million copies of Shaw and Wells and Lawrence. One saw, at Hampton Court, the perpetual keeper of the vine, and the stately English language was still maintained in ordinary use, as in the sign one saw in St. Andrew's Square at Edinburgh, "The amenity of our streets is recommended to your care." I could have agreed with Lewis Mumford in his praise of England: "If I take England at her worst, in her rule over India, and if I add to it every crime, misery and brutality she has committed, I still see in the English, taken as a whole, the unmistakable signs of a civilized people that is capable of self-correction and self-improvement, and that even in India has created by her own example, her own ideas, the very power that is equal to challenging her own regime." The British never fail to respond to tales of solitary courage. They have made almost a popular classic of *Sailing Alone Around the World,* so long all but forgotten in its own country.

But it seemed to me that, in literature at least, England and America were drifting further and further apart, when one thought of the days of Shaw, Wells and Arnold Bennett who seemed to include in their writings the United States also. With little formal education,—and this was true of Kipling, George Moore and W. B. Yeats,—these English authors, with their broad human interests, seemed somehow close to America where the mass of readers shared common assumptions and a common intellectual language. Shaw and Wells had the American faith in improvability, whereas the later writers had lost their feeling for the widely human and were more and more public school boys with the old school tie. They were not universal enough on their own ground to meet the Americans on theirs. With socialism achieved in England, they did not have to defend it; and, with the loss of the empire, they were driven to ride again their aristocratic and reactionary hobbies. They discussed such trivialities as "U" and "Non-U." They abounded in memories of Eton, and their sympathies were of the upper class, occasionally tempered, it is true, by communism; as the English government had turned to the left, the authors had turned to the right, and, amusing as they might be, they spoke to the American mind as the voices merely of a small European country. The American mind was still Cromwellian, the English was cavalier again; and, with the new polyglot American types, the ancestral bond had vanished in the younger generation. To be sure, the superior culture of the English was still evident enough. There were the novels of Aldous Huxley, so full of allusions and references to the history of painting and music, anthropology, zoology, of interest to all cultivated people; and I remembered my first sight of the poet Auden in the Whitney Museum in New York. He had come to an exhibition of William Rimmer's drawings, and I recollect the absorbed curiosity with which he examined each and all. I wondered how many intellectual young Americans would have taken the trouble to examine the work of this little-known artist.

We lunched with Sir Desmond MacCarthy, who had been recently knighted and who did not encourage the use of his title, and this companionable man introduced us to his son-in-law, Lord David Cecil at Oxford and his friend Joyce Cary. Cecil had written biographies that interested me extremely, and it struck me that English biographies were usually better than American because the interest in character in England was not frittered away by Freudianism. I had not, in 1951, read Joyce Cary, though I was soon to make the acquaintance of *The Horse's Mouth*. MacCarthy said to me, "Have you noticed that the good writers are often bad men, and that the good men are often bad writers?"—a variation of the French phrase *Bel esprit mauvais caractère* that I had indeed noticed but rather late in life. For I was so incurably romantic about writers that I wished to think of them as good in all respects,—like the pearl-oysters, the rare creatures in whom the precious deposit exists,—and Robert Frost had said to me once, "You want to believe that great writers are good men. It's an illusion that dies hard." Had I derived the illusion from Ruskin, who thought that artists had to be good until he discovered that they had to be "a little wicked?" Or was it a survival in me of the classic notion of Longinus that "great writing is the echo of a great soul?" I am sure that Paul Rosenfeld had felt as I did, and I have known several artists who seemed to me angelic,—while Maxwell Perkins, who had an extensive knowledge of contemporary writers, said, "They are all sons of bitches." I had found in time that writers were, as often as not, jealous and mean, egotistical, petty and even bad-hearted, "lovers of humanity, by the book," as Dostoievsky put it, although I had also noticed that those who associate with the poor think better of human nature than those who associate with the rich. For me, Dr. Jung had said, in *Modern Man in Search of a Soul*, the last word on this subject: "The artist's life cannot be otherwise than full of conflicts, for two forces are at war within him—on the one hand, the common human longing for happiness, satisfaction and security in life, and on the other a ruthless passion for creation which may go so far as to override every personal desire. The creative forces can drain the human impulses to such a degree that the personal ego must develop all sorts of bad qualities—ruthlessness, selfishness and vanity—and even every kind of vice, in order to maintain the spark of life and to keep itself from being wholly bereft."

While in England, we met Chiang Yee, who had lived there for many years and who was to become in the future a very dear friend, the "Silent Traveller" for whose book on New York I had written a brief admiring preface. Chiang Yee, the painter and writer, born in Kiu-Kiang on the Yangtse river, had been the district governor and a magistrate there, but, unsympathetic with the Chinese political world, he had settled in the West in 1933. In *A Chinese Childhood*, he had related the story of the family house in which fifty persons had lived, including a few servants; and he had followed in the footsteps of his father, a painter of birds, butterflies and flowers, to which the Chinese as a race were devoted. He and his friends on walking trips had sketched and improvised poems at picturesque and legendary spots in the mountains, especially Lu mountain near Kiu-Kiang where the poet Li Po had sung and painted. The "Silent Traveller," the title he adopted, was a translation of his Chinese pen-name, which might have been literally rendered as Dumb Walking Man. His work as a civil servant had kept him talking day and night, and, glad enough to escape from this, he had chosen a name that was not unlike the common phrase for a roaming Buddhist monk.

Living in England, Chiang Yee had come to know the quiet things in the countryside, birds, flowers, trees and streams, and he wrote to me, "It is my strong belief that every creature under heaven desires a kind of simple peaceful life." The English lake district, the subject of one of his books, was a happy field for a Chinese artist, and, while he wrote about this region with a singular freshness and lightness of touch, he interpreted it also in idiograms and pictures. Unaccustomed, as he said, to occidental media and technique, he used his Chinese brushes, inks and colours, following his own native method in painting, and in this and his subsequent travel-books, dealing with English and Scottish themes, he produced effects that were equally novel and charming. He was especially fortunate perhaps because England is a land of mists and fogs, like those one saw in so many of the great Chinese paintings, and the fickle English weather pleased him by constantly changing the aspects of scenes while it stirred him to record the changes in his own feelings. With a veil of rain familiar objects passed through enchanting variations, and even his affection for sunshine increased because it arrived unexpectedly and because, like the objects themselves, it was elusive. He delighted in the soft fresh English green that had, as he remarked, both life in itself and the power of blending other colours, and at every turn the simple things of this countryside that was foreign to him carried his imagination back to China. A group of oaks with twisted trunks or a waterfall on a rugged cliff recalled to his mind's eye some old Sung painting, so that sometimes he followed the Sung style in a picture of his own, and, remembering the poets, hermits and scholars who had meditated on scenes like these, he was prompted to repeat their sayings and anecdotes about them. He was charmed by a cluster of horses in a meadow, by a heathery hillock, green and blue, fading into grey, melting into the dove-coloured sky, by dragonflies clinging to the tops of reeds, a knot of water-lily leaves and buds, a robin or a rose-tree in full bloom. Composing a poem now and then, he interspersed his observations with delightful examples of Chinese calligraphy also, with notes on characters whom he had met, wayfaring folk in city streets, old buildings and the customs of the country. Chiang Yee shared Wordsworth's pleasure in the meanest flower that blows. With none of the clichés of travel-writing, his books possessed the companionable charm of a mind of great natural distinction that was willing to be pleased.

In Oxford, Chiang Yee took us to call on Professor Gilbert Murray, who kept open house on Sunday afternoons, at the villa on Boar's Hill where I was touched by a sign at the gate, "Please come in and look at the flowers." An Italian boy, a student from Rome, a nephew of Lauro de Bosis, and a German girl were there that day, and I liked the remark of Lady Mary Murray, "If you don't believe in progress, out of the house you go!" To the grand old scholar, Gilbert Murray, stoicism was a good system of conduct for those who do not accept revelation but still keep some faith in the purpose of things, and, ninety or more at this time, he was broadcasting still in London, a fine Australian Irishman who was a champion of the under-dog. For he knew as well as Aristotle that a man cannot live a complete life when he is miserably poor or deprived of freedom. Sixty-seven years before, he had been married at Castle Howard, to which we had also been taken by my Roman Catholic connections. They lived near Carlisle, and there, at Great Corby, my stepsister's nephew, Monsignor Christopher Lamb, took us to see the ancient Roman wall.

When we returned to America, we found Chiang Yee again, and, in fact, he soon came to live there. I had wondered if he would find New York congenial. With his fondness for grey rainy days and the misty-moisty English scene, would he like the hard dry light of our stone and steel? In New York he would have for mountain peaks only metallic skyscrapers, and instead of the soft English rain he would have our thoroughly business-like rain that comes down as if it were also made of steel. But he soon found cherry-trees in blossom, in the parks and botanical gardens, and willows with branches tossing in the wind that stirred him to write poems as he painted and drew them, and even the natural rock-formations, the water-falls, thickets and gorges that were immemorial subjects of Chinese painters. There were squirrels with sparkling eyes that were also cherished in Chinese art, and almost every one of his pictures contained a pigeon, a swan, a crane, or wild geese, ducks or sea-gulls flying aloft. He found ponds with white lotus in full bloom, and tall buildings that looked like bamboo shoots as they emerged from the tops of low-hung clouds. In the Yosemite, with a Chinese friend, he wandered around Mirror Lake, Chen playing the Chinese bamboo flute and Yee reading aloud some Chinese poems, while the frogs sang with them in the moonlight. The surrounding peaks and cliffs in mist and rain reminded him of his beloved Lu mountain. Chiang Yee repeated the saying of Mencius that a man should retain his childlike mind, a rebuke to our tiresome ideal of "sophistication," and he said that, in securing the freedoms from ignorance and want, we should also plan for a "freedom from too many desires." That was his reply to our foolish cult of advertising, which exists for the breeding of desires, the more the better.

We found our neighbour Lewis Mumford living in monastic simplicity still, planting his onions and beans in spring and alternating his bouts of work with equally quiescent relaxations. Immensely productive, he took time off gardening, reading and sleeping, without a serious thought in his head, keeping this up until he was bored when he supposed that he was cured as well. Loving Tolstoy's sanity and health, he found that Dostoievsky wore now better than Tolstoy because what had once seemed wicked fantasy had become part of our normal and daily existence. For the morals of the rattlesnake were everywhere, and he had a persistent sense that everything was going wrong, that the captain was drunk and the mates were mad and the crew was affected with sleeping sickness. I am quoting from Lewis's letters to me: he said, for instance, that the young had a deep nostalgia for the twenties whose sense of disillusionment, as compared with their own, was one vast iridescent soap-bubble of hope. I wondered why Lewis, who was so well known in England, Sweden, Holland and Poland, was still not properly known in his own country, perhaps because he was a "generalist," not fabricating the pieces but putting them together in a significant picture. Or was it due to the feeling of boredom the older generation produces when people feel they have been around too long? He stood for the restoration and renewal of man, that poor bewildered creature who had become an impoverished exile from the native land he had left and from a world of mechanism that refused to recognize his existence.

Of Helen Keller, whose mind was always focussed on the great impersonal things and who never thought of personal inconsequences, we had seen more and more, and we knew, and could say, that she was exactly what the general public believed she was. Before she went, with Polly, to Japan, she dined with us and the John Sloans, and Helen, who placed her hand on John Sloan's head, exclaimed that it was a "noble head and strong." While she was on her way to Japan, her house at Westport was burned down, with all her manuscripts and letters, her furniture and books, but presently a carload of presents arrived from her friends in Japan, and the new house became a Japanese museum. There were tables, vases, rugs, pictures, carvings, hangings and porcelain, some ancient and the rest made in Hiroshima, a few years after its destruction. Then she wrote from Latin America, "I caught tantalizing glimpses of the mighty Andes, pre-Christian civilizations and varied strains in the populations. Amazing how they have survived after innumerable civil wars,—Aztecs, Incas and other Indian peoples, Portuguese and Spaniards,—with the land problems and the long droughts that aggravate them and the manifold difficulties of farming." She wrote to me from New Zealand, "the beautiful great little country-island." At eighty, she was still writing appeals for the blind, without any touch of vanity herself, rather like an eager child, and always conscious of "America's exasperating faults." We were just emerging, she said, "from a pygmy chauvinism." I gave her Nehru's *Glimpses of World History* to be put into braille for her voracious fingers.

I am sure that Helen Keller would have said with Edmund Wilson, "I believe in human evolution. I don't see how it is possible to reject the evidence that contemporary humanity, with all its faults, has developed from beings much lower, or to fail to draw the conclusion that we are to develop into something higher still. I believe in progress as the eighteenth century people did." She would not have repudiated the French Revolution that made citizens out of serfs and peasants not long after Prince Charolais shot tilers on the roofs in Paris for the fun of seeing them tumble into the street. That was the value of ordinary men before the age of revolutions, as it had been when Peter the Great, discovering a new kind of gallows, ordered one of his servants to be hanged at once so that he could see how it worked. There had been a time when wars were started over a cardinal's lapdog and illegitimate babies in Venice were thrown into the canals before "conservatories" were invented to save them, a time when prisoners of war were roasted in baker's ovens and workers were forbidden to establish a pension fund for their aged members. This was the kind of fact that various historians refrained from mentioning, those who were anxious to undo the revolutions, facts that show how "we have become," as Bertrand Russell says, "in certain respects progressively less like animals." Inhumanities of this kind were taken for granted, unlike Dachau and Buchenwald, which every human being knows were wrong; and, improvements in these matters were the result, as Julien Benda said, of the teaching of the eighteenth century, "against which the 'masters of modern thought' are in complete revolt . . . those who would blush to be able to say, like Voltaire, 'I have done a little good, 'tis my best work.'" Even the reactionary Chateaubriand came to accept the idea of progress, saying that, if society seems sometimes to move backward, it is always really moving forward. Yet Baudelaire could say, "Belief in progress is a lazy man's creed, a creed for Belgians."

Once we visited Edmund Wilson, whom I had known for three or four decades, in his old family house at Talcottville, where he underwent, in the phrase of Howells, "the lapse from the personal to the ancestral which we all undergo in the process of the years." It was a charming stone house of the early

nineteenth century to which he retreated from Wellfleet when
he felt too crowded in summer there; and on the first evening
we all went for a picnic on the Independence river in a gully
bordered by evergreen trees and damp lichen-covered rocks.
This was one of those "up-state" rivers that Rita was homesick
for, in Wilson's novel, *I Thought of Daisy*, about which indeed she had written a poem with an image of a "lovely flock of
stones" that "tumbled and crashed into splinters the black-silver
mirror" of the water below. Evidently, Wilson, like Rita, enjoyed thinking of "the beauty of stony rivers." The Wilsons
took us to lunch at the Oneida Community where old Mr.
Pierrepont Noyes was still living, the son of the founder in the
eugenic free-love days. Wilson had warned us that at first the
region would seem rather empty, but that everything filled in
around him so that it became more real than Wellfleet; and, in
fact, he had been surprised to find that he was surrounded
there by the Iroquois national movement of which he was to
write. This movement was not unlike Scottish nationalism or
Zionism, with a revival of the old religion and claims for the
property that had been lost because of the encroaching St.
Lawrence seaway. Wilson had been interested earlier in the
Zuni Indians of New Mexico, one of the multifarious concerns
of a critic who could be called, almost uniquely, a writer. He
was, for the rest, an eager player of anagrams and other games,
along with Chinese chequers.

A highly unreasonable rationalist, abounding in violent prejudices, Wilson had no use for Somerset Maugham, and Aldous
Huxley, for him, was not an artist. I could scarcely understand
why he disliked the English, with their "British impudence,"
for example, and this became no clearer to me when he told me
that one of his forbears had been shut up in the Revolution in
a British prison-ship. Nor could he abide the "dreadful" New

England novels of Howells that Christian Gauss, his Princeton professor, had disliked before him. I had no doubt that Christian Gauss shared with Francis Parkman a misconception of the "rise" of Silas Lapham. But I always thought, nevertheless, of Wilson as the most intelligent writer in the country, one who, in a day of grammarians, led the uncloistered life of a many-sided free-ranging man of letters and the world; for his fount of ideas and images seemed never to falter, his range of interests was so wide and his talents so diverse, he was so universally curious and so generally responsive. An artist in several forms, he had touched as a critic on politics, economics, the theatre and music, on actors, magicians and the so-called lively arts, while he was as much at home with Sophocles and Persius as he was with E. E. Cummings and Thornton Wilder. In *Axel's Castle* he had introduced to a whole generation of readers the masters of the post-war literary epoch, and he was perhaps the most lastingly interesting of the prose celebrants of Greenwich Village in the decade he recalled in plays and essays. He produced in *To the Finland Station* a memorable history of modern revolutionary thought, and he created in *The Little Blue Light* a play that would be classical if our theatre were comparable to the theatre of Strindberg or Ibsen. In the day of Whitman's "orbic" mind, he had studied conversational Greek in Greece, Russian in Russia,—he translated Pushkin,—and later, attracted to Israel, he set to work at Hebrew for a fresh understanding of the Bible and the new republic. He had an incomparable feeling for the literary climate in which he lived, for the changes in the time-spirit from decade to decade, an exciting sensitivity that struck me at almost every point in his panoramic portrait of twentieth-century letters.

With his flexible independent mind, detached from all factions and groups, Wilson seemed to collaborate with a cultivated public; and what could do more to maintain this, to create it and sustain it? Besides, he saw literature in terms not of itself alone but of the life of humanity and its chief interests; and he combined the aesthetic with the psychological, social and historical sense, knowing that one must "see the writer as a man in order to appreciate him as an artist." Personally resembling Sainte-Beuve, learned without being bookish, he possessed supremely the gift of wonder, and his sympathies, like Sainte-Beuve's, were largely with the humanitarians, although he too was a sceptic towards every form of faith. It is true that also, like Sainte-Beuve, his intelligence seemed to look down on his heart, which lay there "like a cold moon"; nor did he seem to have a centre. He was afloat, his ship had no anchor. But what a pleasure it was to read his *causeries,* so nimble in style, with the tone of conversation, and to hear him say, "It is up to American writers to try to make some sense of their American world, for their world is now everybody's world"; and "The thing that's upsetting now in politics and literature both is that from the moment we lose the idea that we are concentrating on this country,—and that idea seems completely to have gone by the board,—we don't know where we are any more." I liked this, as I liked the saying of Katherine Anne Porter in one of the essays of *The Days Before:* "Americans are not going anywhere, and I am glad of it . . . In the present [of the second world war] they must live here or nowhere, and they must share the responsibility of helping to make this a place where men can live as men and not as victims, pawns, a lower order of animals driven out to die beside the road or to survive in stealth and cunning."

CHAPTER XIV

AT SEVENTY-FIVE

I AM WRITING this in Bridgewater, the cross-roads Connecticut
village where we have been living for the last twelve years.
In my study at the front of the house, facing the usually silent
street, are gathered relics of my past, the bronze dog that used
to stand on my grandmother's onyx clock and a cluster of oddly
designed clay pipes from various towns in Europe. My brother
and I as little boys collected these when we were abroad to
bring them to our father who had remained at home. On the
mantelpiece is the red sandstone copy of Hadrian's column
found by my father in Rome once, and, beside that, a re-
production of the death-mask of Randolph Bourne that was
given me by the sculptor long ago. There is the glass bell with
a picture in coloured sand that my other grandmother brought
back from the Isle of Wight and a lithograph portrait of John
Quincy Adams from my great-grandfather's Plattsburg house
that I used to have with me in college. All these trifles that
would never fit into a modern house, and that will be scattered
after my death, seem to me to hold my identity together in the
various chances and changes of life.

As I had grown older, I had felt more and more the truth of
one of Sainte-Beuve's observations. Referring to the river of

literature, which flowed on, wide and deep, he spoke of his own relation to it. "When we are young," he said, "we can run beside it and even get in advance of its course; in middle age we are unable to run ahead of it but can only follow panting beside; and in the end it flows past us and to our astonishment we observe that its surface is black with strange little boats which, even as we look, sail beyond the range of our vision." How many generations of critics had felt as Sainte-Beuve felt! —and I thought of Edmund Wilson, ten years younger than myself, who said he had given up trying to read the books of the new writers. He could not follow the strange little boats that swarmed in the river of literature, although he was full of interest in the world about him. I myself turned away to the past uneasily, keeping an always baffled eye on the writers of the present whom, very often, I could scarcely understand. Or, rather, on the books rather than the writers. Although good novels still appeared, there had ceased to be novelists in the sense of the writers of the nineteen-twenties, and I was struck by the remark of a physician that all the doctors were good now but that the great doctors had ceased to exist. The novels, good and bad, seemed to be sporadic; they did not announce new personalities. Or at least they did not seem to me to do so.

I had preferred to be called an essayist rather than a critic, but I had written criticism, and it seemed to me that all American criticism was impermanent, that none of our generalizations lasted more than a few years. I remembered the famous remark of Stieglitz that every five years we had in this country a new generation. Everything changed from decade to decade and all one wrote became, in a short time, irrelevant and obsolete. An architect whom I once met who had done fine building in New York told me that of the hundred and fifty houses he had put up a hundred and forty-eight had been torn down.

He had not the heart to go on and retired at sixty. It seemed to me that my chief hope for some kind of relative permanence was in my historical series *Makers and Finders,* already out of fashion, from the critical point of view of the present, but, as I felt, certain to come back. Reading for this, and writing it, I had spent a ten or twelve-hour day, virtually every day, for nineteen years. I had read about five thousand books in connection with it. For all the attacks of the critics, I was encouraged by letters that I received from often unknown writers. One of them said, "I feel less a nomad whenever I finish one of your books. Even at my loneliest, I feel sustained by the record of men before me who struggled toward consciousness." Another said that, although it was not orthodox literary history, my series "gave our creative writers for the first time a feeling that there is an American literary tradition to which they belong"; a young novelist wrote to me, "My work grows out of what went before. I feel I'm in the line," and still another said, "One gains a real feeling of participation . . . Our struggles of today fall into a new perspective." That had been my hope and intention, my object being emotional, to awaken feeling and imagination, somewhat in the manner of Standish O'Grady's history of Ireland's heroic age that had such an effect on the Irish revival. But although my history was fully translated into Japanese, and many other languages as well, I was referred to at home with a vague respect in critical circles only as the author of *America's-Coming-of-Age.* Everything I had written since, except *The Ordeal of Mark Twain,* was, as I gathered, best not mentioned. Even in Japan, *America's-Coming-of-Age* was printed, with Japanese notes, as a school textbook.

I remembered the saying of my old editor, Albert Jay Nock, "A nation is a spiritual principle evoked by the common possession of a rich legacy of remembrances," but he added, "A spiritual heritage is about the last thing that our enlightened age could be induced to take stock in." He further said that one's attitude towards one's illustrious dead "marks the difference between a nation and an agglomeration." Knowing that our nation was scarcely formed as yet, I had hoped to contribute towards the forming of it, and seeing that my historical series required an explanation, I then turned to *The Writer in America.* I found I had to defend a philosophy that was implicit in my theme and would have been so taken a few years before, but it was now attacked by the reigning school of critics, a school avowedly intolerant and increasingly dictatorial. Under professions of the Christian religion, this school felt it was entitled, as Lionel Trilling put it, to say "Thou fool" to those who still dared to be independent of it, by no means the first time in history in which religion had proved to be useful in a quest for power. In a period of conformity, with no place for the otherwise-minded,—a period of group-thinkers and hidden persuaders, in which only the adjustable and adaptable were admired,—these critics denied the first principle of all creative endeavour; for, as Darwin said, in *The Origin of Species,* isolation was the chief cause of the appearance of new forms and original creation. And who was to be apart and alone, who was to be isolated, if one accepted the orthodoxy of the fashionable critics?

I composed three biographies, the first one of John Sloan, my old friend of the days of Petitpas, when I dined in his studio with J. B. Yeats and with Rockwell Kent and Robert Henri. In the decades between, I had seen Sloan, off and on, though he went for half the year to Santa Fe, preferring the rocky and sandy landscape there to the summer green world of the East. Then, coming one day to Bridgewater, when we had first settled there, he said he had never seen before the rolling hills of

Connecticut and the great civilized trees in the village streets. He felt like a desert scorpion dropped into a green salad, and, reconciled that day to summers in New England, he presently went to stay in Hanover, New Hampshire. He died a few months later there and his wife Helen turned over to me a mass of John Sloan's papers, carefully arranged, his picturesque diary and assorted letters, so that I was soon able to write the story of this modern Hogarth of New York. Berenson, to whom I sent it, as I sent all my later books, said it was "the most interesting and most delightful story of a modern painter and his achievement that has reached my eyes." But Berenson was not convinced that Sloan had found his way to the calling he was made for, writing about art: "I for instance have scarcely ever encountered in print utterances about painting in particular and art in general so closely parallel to my own, and generally better expressed. Your quotations for his classes enthralled me."

From that time on, Berenson read all my books and sent me the most appreciative remarks about them, one, in particular, *Scenes and Portraits,* about which he said, "How much of it could enter into my own autobiography!" For half the names were of people he had known or known about, "as, e.g., in the cases of Sheldon and Perkins." He read *Days of the Phoenix* "with excitement, zest and the keenest interest," he said of *From a Writer's Notebook* that it had "intellectual breadth and depth always," and in *The Dream of Arcadia* he observed that he was "deeply happy" over the chapter about himself. That book was a return to the feeling of enchantment I had experienced in Italy as a boy. Berenson seemed to like my hagiology of Helen Keller, which I had gone to Los Angeles to write, and he asked me to send him some pictures of the architecture I had found so fresh and engaging there. But to him the houses on Sunset Boulevard looked more like "bird-cages for anthropomorphic bipeds than human habitations." He did not live long enough to read the life of Howells that I had intended to write many years before, a novelist, seldom read any longer, although he was soon to be revived, a symbol of a rejected American past. The critics could see nothing good in Howells's few fine novels that were undoubtedly the best of their time and they continued to parrot his phrase about "the more smiling aspects of life" that was so fully contradicted by his later books. Howells had been far less prudish than Mark Twain, as Bernard De Voto showed after reading manuscripts that most of us had never seen. He was rejected as Sinclair Lewis had been also, the novelist who, in his turn, had rejected Howells. Lewis had called Howells, in his Nobel Prize speech, "a pious old maid whose greatest delight is to have tea at the vicarage," an absurd statement that led me to wonder if Lewis had read the novelist he so made light of. This doubt was confirmed when I lunched with Lewis in New York one day and he asked me to go to a second-hand book-store with him. It was in Fifty-ninth Street, and Lewis asked the bookseller for all the Howells novels he had and carried away at least a dozen volumes. This was years after he had received the Nobel Prize and Lewis said he had never read any of them. I hope they included *The Shadow of a Dream* and *The Son of Royal Langbrith,* which would have put an end to all prejudgements.

Sinclair Lewis, a most lovable man, too impetuous, swift to forgive, and capable of a generous indignation, had given Bernard De Voto the literary trouncing of his life and nominated him for the Institute ten minutes later; and when Hemingway foully attacked him, in *Across the River and Into the Trees,* ridiculing this "pock-marked jerk" for his "craters of the moon face,"—referring to Lewis's facial cancer,—I remembered how, in his speech at Stockholm, Lewis had praised Hemingway and the other novelists of Hemingway's generation. He had worked over his documentation as Hemingway worked over his style, and when he died the critics, ignoring Lewis's vision of life, his broad panorama of America and his passion for justice, condemned him as Hemingway condemned him. Admitting only his earliest novels, they overlooked his development, his hatred of the intolerant, the ignorant, the smug, though he seemed to me more mature than those who discarded him as one discards an old pair of shoes. In *Arrowsmith*, the doctor had won happiness by the exercise of his "will power," unlike the characters of Hemingway who had no will whatever, or who could do nothing against circumstances, and yet, as John Peale Bishop said, "dictated the emotions to contemporary youth."

When Lewis asked in a preface whether "this American optimism, this hope and courage, so submerged now in 1935, are not authentic parts of American life," I remembered how little I had once agreed with Lewis that they are in fact "good things to have." This optimism was nothing to boast of, it sprang from a natural buoyancy, the buoyancy for which Bertrand Russell had once admired America, but it indicated a cult of life as marked as the cult of death that had been so commended in the Spaniards. I remembered again how Gandhi's refusal to concentrate on the bad in people "sometimes added inches or cubits to the height of his associates and even the casual visitor felt its potential benefits." So Louis Fischer commented on Gandhi's "creative optimism." With us, it had certainly survived

> The collapsed structure of moral Europe,
> Of whatever was fought for on either side
> After the Sarajevo pistol shot.

It seemed more than ever to me that the fatalism of our literary circles,—the belief in total depravity, the obsession of evil, and all the old fixed ideas of Calvinism, which had paralyzed the mind of New England before Emerson appeared,—had sprung from the general failure of Europe as a result of the world wars and that our literary mind was too weak to resist it. That is to say, it was still not yet mature enough to withstand the mood of discouragement that prevailed in literary Europe, the "fatigued disillusionment of the fifties," as Spender called it.

For it was certain that our literary mind did not express the country, which still believed, on the whole, in human decency and, as Crane Brinton said, "in some kind of progress . . . we are still heirs of the Enlightenment," he said further; and Paul Tillich, in *The Courage To Be,* spoke of the present-day American courage as "one of the great types of courage to be as a part." For "its self-affirmation is the affirmation of oneself as a participant in the creative development of mankind. . . . There is something astonishing in the American courage for an observer who comes from Europe" and who finds it still present in the large majority of people. For the rest, I could not understand Reinhold Niebuhr's argument that the pursuit of happiness is based on an illusion, happiness being a by-product of harmony and the only reality of life being an endless contest between joy and grief. For what better thing than harmony could one pursue, as the Greeks with such great consequences pursued it? It seemed to me that the thought of Confucius, whom Thomas Jefferson so admired and who believed in the goodness of the natural man, was more tenable than the grim Niebuhrian view of life. Moreover, it explained why American culture, in the phrase of Auden, was still "committed to the future." Americans could never accept the belief of Kierkegaard that "earthly happiness is a sin." They were closer to the Chinese who, as Chiang Yee said, looked upon happiness as the greatest good.

Was not the idea of original sin, so totally unscientific, a parochial European mediæval doctrine, as little shared by the Chinese or the Hindus or the Jews as it had been by our own Emerson and Whitman? Seeing sin and evil everywhere seemed to create more evil and sin, wishing evil on humankind, impelling it towards evil. And how Whitman would have rejoiced in the thought of contemporary Africa and Asia, in the nations that had escaped from the hollow of the wave, in the displacement of planetary forces that wrecked the European empires and placed these colonial countries in their own possession. The despair of Europe was surely the result of its exhaustion and shrinkage, and generations would have to pass before, in Robert Frost's phrase, it could learn "what to make of a diminished thing." But Europe's extremity had been the opportunity of Asia and Africa, and a limitless horizon opened out before the peoples there, the hope of peaceful activity in free countries. How could Americans feel that the "decline of the West," certainly true for Europe, was true for them? And yet our literary life was still under the European spell and reflected its apprehension of the end of all things. It disregarded the real feeling of the country, which Faulkner expressed in his speech at Stockholm, "I decline to accept the end of man"; and it took no account of Melville's remark that the time had come for America to "set," not "follow," precedents.

It seemed to me that the time for this had really come. I felt that Americans should set precedents in alliance with Asiatic minds that shared the American buoyancy and vitality; and I agreed with William Carlos Williams, who said about his countrymen, "The Orient, which they fear, is their opportunity to embrace the 'new.'" Helen Keller, journeying round the world, fully understood the aspirations of the Arabs, the Jews, the Japanese, and she carried with her the planetary visions of Emerson and Whitman whom so many Asians took for the American prophets. Then one day Henry Wallace came to see me, glad to be out of politics and certain for another thing that men were never made for travel in space. We spoke of AE, who had told me once that he had come to America mainly to see Wallace, and, talking about Jo Davidson, I put into his hand Jo's old ivory-handled walking-stick, which his wife had brought to me from France. In a speech that Wallace made in our village, he spoke of the need of somehow meeting the mind of the Russians, sure as he also was that Russian communism was bound to fail because it thought only of things and not of life. He took as his motto Walt Whitman's line, "Urge, urge, urge, the procreant urge of the earth." Walt Whitman was always uppermost in the minds of Jo Davidson, of Helen Keller and of Henry Wallace. How did it happen that our writers lagged behind, failing to give us a literature "fit to cope with our occasions," that in their private world they were generally cut off from the great public interests of the time?

Henry Wallace believed that the balance of terror would prevent a third world war. But the thought of the bomb, like the gorgon's eye, turned many minds I knew to stone. Because of it they could not contemplate the future, and it was true that the future lay under the shadow of swords, that everything hopeful in the world at present was a gamble. For this reason the breath of the Western world seemed to have stopped, as if it were in a state of suspended animation, and a young man in San Francisco expressed in a letter to me the spiritual desolation of the sensitive young. "There aren't many of us," he wrote, "who care a particular damn, a few congenital misfits, inveterate malcontents brooding in the public libraries. There are a few of us, serious and sceptical, rather wary, I think, but intensely curious, who wonder what have all the anguished and indignant voices descried and why are they silent. We ask and no one answers. It is as though angry, bold, intemperate words had never been spoken or if, indeed, they had been, they had best be disremembered." In the silence, one could almost have heard a feather drop, as if everyone was waiting for the bomb to fall. We were living in a season closely resembling the decades that preceded the year 1000 when Christians really expected the end of the world.

Then another letter came from a friend in Chicago, "One's only uneasiness is that this is one of those splendid summers, like '14 and '39, when something awful can happen before it ends. But we mustn't think along these lines." Or one had to think with two minds, one of them doing its best to meet the appalling question of missile warfare, and the other harbouring the words *as if*, as if the question of the bomb had been provisionally settled. Emerson quoted Hafiz who described the phrase on the gate of Heaven, "Woe unto him who suffers himself to be betrayed by Fate," and he said, "Men have the power to look not at Fate but the other way. The practical view is the other." In every acre of a quiet lawn, on the loveliest June afternoon, unstylized bull-fights on a miniature scale take place every second. If one's eye were a magnifying-glass one would faint with horror over the stealthy carnage of the worms and insects. The hawk that skims gracefully over the marsh has only murder in its mind and an owl's family requires, for its diet, seven hundred creatures every day, and among these one hundred and fifty mice. Nature is red in tooth and claw, and of course it has to be, but we should lose our wits if we thought about it. Hamilton Basso, who had visited Finland, told me of a case of the practical view. Within a mile from the Russian border he watched a man building a barn, slowly hammering the walls and the beams together, in full sight of the barbed wire and the Russian guns, as if another war were not to be thought of. This man was confiding in the future as if nothing had happened in two world wars to abate the nonchalance with which he regarded it, and why should we not trust the future in the spirit of the Enlightenment the principles of which are not played out, as so many think nowadays? I agreed with Albert Schweitzer that "all real progress in the world is in the last analysis produced by rationalism," and "It will soon become evident that we shall be obliged to take up the same position which the eighteenth century defended so stoutly." Moreover, I agreed with Breasted, the Egyptologist, that what we need more than anything else is confidence in man, and that the story of his rise is a basis for full confidence. The liberal experiment, barely two hundred years old, is of course still immature, but can it be abandoned so lightly?

As for this country, it seemed to me that Alfonso Reyes, the Mexican sage, was right in his essay, *The Position of America:* "Our America should live as though it were always making ready to realize the dream to which its discovery gave rise among the thinkers of Europe, the dream of Utopia, of the happy republic, which lent particular warmth to the pages of Montaigne as he reflected on the surprises and marvels of the New World." We should certainly work for Utopia even if, when we get there, we are bored by its insipidity. It will be time then to imagine something else. Perhaps, long before that, another Buddha may appear and say, "Here are trees,—let us think the matter out"; and mankind will turn its back on offices, factories and motor-cars and set forth on some new kind of adventure.

INDEX

Abbott, Grace, 373

Adams, Henry, 10, 32, 110, 111, 113, 114, 239, 333, 338, 341, 342; *The Education of Henry Adams*, 30, 273, 282, 283; considered democracy a failure, 418; *Mont-Saint-Michel and Chartres*, 311; discovered Willard Gibbs, 514

Addams, Jane, 373, 374

AE, 141, 174, 176, 177, 183, 206, 322, 324, 329; closely connected in thought with Emerson, Thoreau, and Whitman, 606; *The National Being*, 328

Aesthetics: A Dialogue, 397

Aiken, Conrad, 120, 134, 154, 240

American Caravan, The, 436

American Renaissance, 259

American Risorgimento; *see* American Renaissance

Anderson, Karl, 263, 265, 459

Anderson, Sherwood, 259, 263 ff., 267, 272, 358, 363; *Winesburg, Ohio*, 269; drawn to Van Gogh, 458

Anglin, Margaret, 567

Angulo, Jaime de, 195, 199

Armory Show, marked new trend in painting, 258, 396

Arvin, Newton, 313; studies of Melville and Hawthorne, 313; quiet man with violent

mind, 564; convictions far on left, 564

"Ash-can" school, 128, 129

Atkinson, Brooks, 366

Austin, Mary, 200, 357; *The Flock*, 484; *The Land of Little Rain*, 484; *Lost Borders*, 484; studied Catholic mysticism to write *The Man Jesus*, 485

Babbitt, Irving, 110, 111, 121, 124, 125, 138, 222; VWB influenced by, 126

Baker, George Pierce, 109, 121

Baldwin, Roger, and American Civil Liberties Union, 470

Barrymore, Ethel, 567

Basso, Hamilton, 582; *The Light Infantry Ball*, 582

Beard, Charles, 313, 352, 374, 375

Beebe, William, 315

Bell, Eric, 165, 166, 175, 214

Bell, George, 165

Bell, Harold, 105, 133

Bellows, George, 175

Benda, Julien, 283, 637; *trahison des clercs*, 284; denunciation of liberalism, 526

Benét, Stephen Vincent, 584; *Johnny Pye and the Fool-Killer*, 584; *The Devil and Daniel Webster*, 584

Berenson, Bernard, 117, 118, 120, 132, 138, 532, 623;

praised VWB's writing, 619; *Rumour and Reflection,* 622

Beston, Henry, 468, 469; rehumanized the American scene, 469; *The Outermost House,* 469-70

Biddle, George, 555-56

Bishop, John Peale, 268

Björkman, Edwin, 159, 160, 233

Blake, Harrison Gray Otis, 44-45, 47-48, 50, 53, 58

Bourne, Randolph, 6, 223, 238, 273, 275, 282-85, 316, 406

Boyd, Ernest, 321, 322, 328, 361, 394, 397; *Appreciations and Depreciations,* 322; *As an Irishman Sees It,* 419

Bradford, Gamaliel, 376; diary and letters of, edited by VWB, 462

Brandes, Georg, 227, 228, 321; *Main Currents,* 227

Breck, Joe, 160, 162

Briggs, Le Baron Russell, 109, 121

Brooks, Charles (Charlie), VWB's son, 22

Brooks, Charles Edward, VWB's father, 67, 74

Brooks, Eleanor Kenyon Stimson, VWB's first wife: marriage, 40; forebears of, 63-80; family of, 289 ff.; pride of country, 291; death of, 561

Brooks, Gladys Rice, VWB's second wife: background and forebears, 576-77; as violinist, 577; work as teacher of remedial reading, 578

Brooks, Van Wyck: birth in Plainfield, N. J., 5, 6; grandfather Ames, 6; father, Charles Edward Brooks, 6, 11, 12, 67, 69, 71, 72, 74, 75; mother, Sarah Ames Brooks, 6, 10, 12, 14, 15, 67, 94, 130; religion of, 13; automatic Republicanism of family, 14; grandmother, 15, 16, 65, 75, 78; cousins, 17, 18, 66; son, Charles (Charlie), 22; beginnings of interest in art, 23-25, 87, 90; N. Y. *vs.* N. E., 26-27; alien in N. E., 27; scholarly family forebears of, 28; marriages, to Eleanor Kenyon Stimson, 40; great-grandmother, 63; paternal grandparents, 67-68; VWB as socialist, 70, 205-206; European background of, 72, 85-100; influence of art on 87 ff.; nurse of, 92; Harvard education, 101-26; teaching in Leland Stanford, 114; *America's Coming-of-Age,* 115, 237, 244, 264, 305, 537; influence of J. B. Yeats on, 121; of Babbitt, 125; in England, 127-28; closest friends, 133; first book published in London, 135-37; life in N. Y., 153-72, 351-61, 562; work on *The World's Work,* 157; work for the *Chicago Evening Post,* 157-58; leaves Doubleday, 167; hack work on the *Standard Dictionary,* 167; miscellaneous drudgeries, 172; teaching,

Dove, Arthur, 262
Draper, Ruth, 567
Dreiser, Theodore, 10, 156, 270, 272, 285, 316, 363, 570
du Bois, Guy Pène, 294
Du Bois, W. E. B., *The Crisis*, 552
Durant, Will, explanation of origin of sin, 484

Eastman, Max, 206
Eglinton, John, 322, 328; closely connected in thought and emotion with Emerson, Thoreau, and Whitman, 606; *Pebbles from a Brook*, 328; *Two Essays on the Remnant*, 328
"Eight, the," artists, 258
Eiseley, Loren, *The Immense Journey*, 471
Eliot, T. S., 112, 118, 134, 230, 240, 284, 510, 514, 544-45; as the quintessence of Harvard, 112; despised Anglo-Saxon element in American tradition, 512; *The Waste Land*, 528
Ellis, Havelock, 141
Ellison, Ralph, 619
Emerson, Ralph Waldo, 112, 328, 358, 371, 381, 393, 420, 422; "spiritual germ-cell of American culture," 505; "Self-Reliance," 509; found evil in brutal elements at core of life, 526
European exiles in U.S.A.:

Feuchtwanger, 482; Salvemini, 507; Borgese, 507; Grosz, 507; Maeterlinck, 509 "expatriates as avant-garde," 411, 412; oppressed by sterility of the American scene, 411; obsessed with the problem of the artist in America, 411; termed the "lost" generation by Nock and Gertrude Stein, 412; desperation of, gives rise to religion of art, 413; Stearns most talked of, 413; William Seabrook, 412; literary heroes of, 416; found teachers of literary from, 416; dispraise of the "American way" by, 418; felt at home in Paris as *a patrie* of the imagination, 415; new climate of opinion in literature largely created by, 432; religion of art virtually the only religion, 432; return of, 506; reassessment of America by, 506 ff.; Berenson and Gertrude Stein now say "We Americans," 507; negative view of the twenties no longer held by, 508; ignorance of America's past, 512-13; "exurbanites," 362

Fabian Society, 41
Farrar, Geraldine, 567
Faulkner, William, 333, 360, 514; evoked school of followers all over that region of the South, 478

Robinson, Edwin Arlington, 109, 155, 272, 282, 330, 397, 498; and Hawthorne, 497

Robinson, James Harvey, 352, 373

Roethke, Theodore, 619

Rogers, Bruce, 106, 556-60

Rolland, Romain, 274; *Jean-Christophe*, 274

Romains, Jules, 275

Rosenfeld, Paul, 259-63, 285, 370; *Musical Portraits*, 263; *The American Caravan*, ed., 409, 436; on VWB's mental illness, 440; life crippled by poverty, 465; death, 563; wrote *Musical Chronicle* for *The Dial*, 564

Rourke, Constance, 355-57, 506

Royce, Josiah, 108, 121

Ruskin, John, 25, 89, 90, 102, 162, 371; *Modern Painters*, 243

Russell, Bertrand, 352, 637

Russell, George William; *see under* AE

Ruttkay, Louisa (Martha Washington of Hungary), 49, 50, 51, 53, 54, 56-60, 62, 289

Ruzicka, Rudolph, book designer, 463

Ryder, Albert Pinkham, 276, 294, 467

Ryder, Arthur, 93-95, 194

Sainte-Beuve, Charles Augustin, influence of, on VWB, 126, 641

Salvemini, Gaetano, 106; arranged for publication of *Mazzini*, 626

Sandburg, Carl, 259-61, 276, 358, 461, 532; and biography of Lincoln, 506; proposed for membership at Academy of Arts and Letters, 520; attacked by "new" critics, 521

Santayana, George, 106, 107, 110, 369; feline aestheticism of, 107; *Reason in Art*, 369; *The Sense of Beauty*, 369; on cultural ferment in the twenties, 493

Schnakenberg, Henry, 580

Schweitzer, Albert, 652

Secession, 313

Sedgwick, Henry Dwight, *The Art of Happiness*, 551

Seeger, Alan, 175, 176

Seminary, the, 38-62

Seven Arts, The, 258, 269, 270, 271, 273; writers for, 270; exemplifying solidarity of American writers, 273-76, 280, 281, 284, 285, 288, 313; and Bruce Rogers, 557-58; death of, 558

Shaw, George Bernard, 204, 219, 224, 306, 368, 371

Sheean, Vincent, 415; born man of the world, 416; and John Gunther, 453; *Personal History*, 454

Sheldon, Edward, 105, 107, 109, 133, 156, 163, 167, 173, 364, 523, 555, 569; *Romance*, 163

Sherman, Stuart P., 358, 359; as creator of the writers' liter-